The Christian
Bed & Breakfast
Directory

1995-1996 Edition

The Christian
Bed & Breakfast
Directory

1995-1996 Edition

Edited by
Rebecca Germany

A BARBOUR BOOK

ISBN 1-55748-596-8

Published by Barbour and Company, Inc.
P.O. Box 719
Uhrichsville, Ohio 44683

Front cover: Photograph of Dunleith House and Gardens, Natchez, Mississippi.

Backcover: Photograph of The James A. Mulvey Inn, Stillwater, Minnesota.

Table of Contents

How To Use This Book

Have you ever dreamed of spending a few days in a rustic cabin in Alaska? Would you like to stay in an urban town house while taking care of some business in the city? Would your family like to spend a weekend on a midwestern farm feeding the pigs and gathering eggs? Maybe a romantic Victorian mansion in San Francisco or an antebellum plantation in Mississippi is what you've been looking for. No matter what your needs may be, whether you are traveling for business or pleasure, you will find a variety of choices in the 1995-1996 edition of *The Christian Bed and Breakfast Directory*.

In the pages of this guide you will find over 1,200 bed and breakfasts, small inns, and homestays. All of the information has been updated from last year's edition, and many entries are listed for the first time. Although not every establishment is owned or operated by Christians, each host has expressed a desire to welcome Christian travelers.

The directory is designed for easy reference. At a glance, you can determine the number of rooms available at each establishment and how many rooms have private (PB) and shared (SB) baths. You will find the name of the host or hosts, the price range for two people sharing one room, the kind of breakfast that is served, and what credit cards are accepted. There is a "Notes" section to let you know important information that may not be included in the description. These notes correspond to the list at the bottom of each page. The descriptions have been written by the hosts. The publisher has not visited these bed and breakfasts and is not responsible for inaccuracies.

It is recommended that you make reservations in advance. Many bed and breakfasts have small staffs or are run single-handedly and cannot easily accommodate surprises. Also, ask about taxes, as city and state taxes vary. Remember to ask for directions, and if your special dietary needs can be met, and confirm check-in and check-out times.

Whether you're planning a honeymoon (first or second!), family vacation, or business trip, *The Christian Bed & Breakfast Directory* will make any outing out of the ordinary.

REBECCA GERMANY, EDITOR

Alabama

EUTAW

A Humble Bed and Breakfast

401 Main Street, 35462
(205) 372-0104

Just 30 minutes south of Tuscaloosa on
I-59/20, this stately 1840s home is one of
24 Eutaw houses on the National Register
of Historic Places and has been owned by
only two families. We offer elegantly
appointed rooms in period antiques, delightful breakfasts, bicycles for balmy afternoons, and roaring fires for crisp nights.
Won't you join us on one of several restful
porches?

Hosts: August and Elizabeth Humble
Rooms: 2 (1PB; 1SB) $50-75
Either Full or Continental Breakfast
Credit Cards: None
Notes: 2, 5, 7, 8, 10, 12

A Humble Bed and Breakfast

GREENVILLE/FOREST HOME

Pine Flat Plantation Bed & Breakfast

c/o 1555 Dauphin St., Mobile 36604
(205) 471-8024; (205) 346-2739

Pine Flat Plantation Bed and Breakfast
was built in 1825 by an ancestor of the
present owner. This country comfortable
home has recently been lovingly restored
and warmly decorated with cheerful fabrics and interesting antiques. Located just
minutes off I-65 between Greenville and
Pine Apple, Alabama, this plantation home
provides a relaxed, romantic country setting for weary travelers, hunters who want
more than just a hunt, or city folks looking
for a peaceful place to unwind.

Hosts: Jane and George Inge
Rooms: 4 (4PB) $70-90
Full Country Breakfast
Credit Cards: A, B
Notes: 2, 4, 5, 7, 10, 12

MONTGOMERY

The Lattice Inn

1414 South Hull Street, 36104
(205) 832-9931; (205) 264-0075 (FAX)

The Lattice Inn Bed and Breakfast is
Montgomery, Alabama's quiet way to

relax in southern comfort. Located one mile south of downtown, a short distance from the ASF (Alabama Shakespeare Festival), and nestled in the Historic Garden District, this turn-of-the-century home has been lovingly restored to provide a comfortable retreat for today's traveler. Some of the beautiful guest rooms have private baths and fireplaces and are furnished with high postered beds and family antiques. Bountiful breakfasts are served, and the guests are urged to enjoy the pool and decks. We promise to pamper you!

Red Bluff Cottage

Host: Michael Pierce
Rooms: 5(PB) $50-70
Full Breakfast
Credit Cards: A, B, C, D
Notes: 2, 5, 7(in the cottage), 9, 12

Red Bluff Cottage

551 Clay St., P.O. Box 1026, 36101
(205) 264-0556; (205) 262-1872 (FAX)

This raised cottage, furnished with family antiques, is high above the Alabama River in Montgomery's Cottage Hill district near the state capitol, Dextor Avenue, King Memorial Baptist Church, the first White House of the Confederacy, the Civil Rights Memorial, and Old Alabama Town. It is convenient to the Alabama Shakespeare Festival Theater, the Museum of Fine Arts, and the expanded zoo.

The Lattice Inn

Hosts: Mark and Anne Waldo
Rooms: 4 (PB) $65
Full Breakfast
Credit Cards: A, B
Notes: 2, 5, 7,12

NATCHEZ TRACE—SEE MISSISSIPPI

Alaska

ANCHORAGE

Arctic Loon Bed and Breakfast

P.O. Box 110333, 99511
(907) 345-4935 (voice or FAX)

Elegant accommodations await guests in this 6,500 square foot Scandinavian home in the hillside area of South Anchorage. Breathtaking, spectacular views of Mount McKinley, the Alaskan Range, and the Anchorage Bowl are presented from every room. An eight-person Jacuzzi hot tub, sauna, rosewood grand piano, and pool table provide relaxation after a full gourmet breakfast served on English bone china. Fully licensed, quiet mountian setting, near golf course, Chugack State Park, hiking trails, and zoo.

Hosts: Janie and Lee Johnson
Rooms: 3 (1PB; 2SB) $75-90
Full Breakfast
Credit Cards: A, B
Notes: 2, 5, 7, 8, 9, 10, 11, 12

Crossroads Inn

1406 W. 13th Ave., 99501
(907) 258-7378; (907) 258-7007 (FAX)

Ours is a family home, split-level, down-town near Coastal trail. Two rooms have cable TV, all three rooms have access to business machines. Business travelers welcome. Healthy foods. Owners are Mary, a musician/teacher, and Dick, a management consultant/facilitator. Quiet neighborhood. Your comfort is important to us, and you'll enjoy Alaskan hospitality!

Hosts: Mary and Dick La Fever
Rooms: 3 (SB) $80 (plus $15 for child) -$95
Full Breakfast
Credit Cards: A, B, C, E (only for over 4 night stay)
Notes: 2, 5, 7, 8

Hillcrest Haven B&B

1449 Hillcrest Drive, 99503
(907) 274-3086; (907) 276-8411 (FAX)

The recipient of several awards for exceptional service from Anchorage's visitor bureau, this European-style guest house is blessed with the finest views of Anchorage, Denali Cook Inlet, and spectacular sunsets. Located in a secluded wilderness setting, it is convenient to downtown, buses, restaurants, shopping, and airport.

Hostess: Linda M. Smith·
Rooms: 5(2PB; 3SB) $48-85
Continental Breakfast
Credit Cards: A, B, C, D, E, F
Notes: 2, 5, 7, 8, 9, 10, 11, 12

---

welcome; 7 Children welcome; 8 Tennis nearby; 9 Swimming nearby; 10 Golf nearby; 11 Skiing nearby; 12 May be booked through travel agent

Hospitality Plus

7722 Anne Circle, 99504-4601
(907) 333-8504

A comfortable home, delightful and thematically decorated rooms, caring and knowledgeable hosts, sumptuous breakfasts elegantly served, a mountain range within reach, a profusion of wildflowers and moose in the yard. Add to that years of various Alaskan adventures, a Hungarian refugee's escape story, exceptional tour and guiding experience, an avid fisherman, storytelling experts and artistic achievements, and then sum it all up in one word: HOSPITALITY. It doesn't get better than this!

Hosts: Charlie and Joan Budai
Rooms: 3 (1PB; 2SB) $50-75
Full Breakfast
Credit Cards: None
Notes: 2, 5, 7, 8, 10, 11, 12

DENALI NATIONAL PARK

McKinley Wilderness Lodge

P.O. Box 89, 99755
(907) 683-2277; (907) 683-1558

Large, private sleeping cabins, up to four people per cabin, located on Carlo Creek, thirteen miles south of entrance to Denali National Park, Alaska. Barbecue area, picnic area, assistance with wildlife tours, rafting, flightseeing. Transportation for people arriving by train or bus. Restaurants located nearby. Snacks available. Gift shop, friendly personal service. Family-run business.

Hosts: Mike and Deb Planty
Rooms: 11 cabins (5PB; 6SB) $82
Continental Breakfast
Credit Cards: A, B
Notes: 2, 3, 7, 12

DOUGLAS

Windsock Inn Bed and Breakfast

P. O. Box 240223, 99824-0223
(907) 364-2431

Only three families have owned and occupied this historic home built in 1912 in the heart of Douglas, five minutes from downtown Juneau. Pioneer hosts are now retired and spend a portion of the winters south but return each spring to share their Alaskan experience and hospitality with bed and breakfast clientele from all over the world.

Hosts: Julie and Bob Isaac
Rooms: 2 (SB) $50-55
Full Breakfast
Credit Cards: None
Notes: 2, 7, 8, 9, 10, 11, 12

FAIRBANKS

Alaska's 7 Gables Bed and Breakfast

P. O. Box 80890, 99708
(907) 479-0751; (907) 479-2229 (FAX)

Historically, Alaska's 7 Gables was a fraternity house. It is within walking distance of the University of Alaska, Fairbanks campus, yet near the river and airport. The spacious 10,000 square-foot Tudor-style home features a floral solarium, a foyer with antique stained-glass and an indoor waterfall, cathedral ceilings, wedding chapel, conference room and dormers. A gourmet breakfast is served daily. Other amenities include cable TV and phones, library, laundry facilities, jacuzzis, bikes, canoes and skis. Suites are available.

Hosts: Paul and Leicha Welton
Rooms: 11 (9PB; 2SB) $45-160
Full Breakfast
Credit Cards: A, B, C, D, E
Notes: 2, 5, 7, 9, 10, 11, 12

Glacier Bay Country Inn

GUSTAVUS

Glacier Bay Country Inn

P.O. Box 5, 99826
(907) 697-2288; (907) 697-2289 (FAX)

Set in a clearing by lush, green rainforest and a majestic mountain backdrop, the Glacier Bay Country Inn will capture your heart at first sight. Its unique architecture includes multi-angled roofs, dormer windows, log-beamed ceilings, and large porches. Meals feature freshly baked breads and desserts, garden-fresh produce and local seafood—crab, halibut and salmon. Some of the best whalewatching in the world (humpbacks and orcas), kayaking, hiking—and time to just relax!

Hosts: Al and Annie Unrein
Rooms: 9 (8PB; 1SB) $228
Full Breakfast (lunch and dinner included)
Credit Cards: None
Notes: 2, 3, 4, 7, 12

JUNEAU

Alaska Wolf House

P.O. Box 21321, 1900 Wickersham, 99802
(907) 586-2422 (voice and FAX)

Alaska Wolf House is a 4,000 sq. ft. western, red cedar log home located one mile from downtown Juneau. Built on the side of Mt. Juneau, it features a southern exposure enabling the viewing of sunrises and sunsets over busy Gastineau Channel and the moon rising over the statuesque mountians of Douglas Island. Hosts Philip and Clovis Dennis serve an excellent breakfast in The Glassroom overlooking the channel and mountains. Within a short walk is the Glacier hiking-jogging-biking trail and public transportation. Smoke-ree rooms are available with private or shared bathrooms. Suites have kitchens. Plan to enjoy all the amenities of home while experiencing Our Great Land of Foreverness.

Hosts: Philip and Clovis Dennis
Rooms: 5 (2PB; 3SB) $75-95
Full Breakfast
Credit Cards: None
Notes: 2, 5, 7, 11

Pearson's Pond Luxury Inn

4541 Sawa Circle-CD, 99801
(907) 789-3772; (907) 789-6722 (FAX)

Private studio/suites on scenic pond. Hot tub under the stars, rowboat, bicycles, BBQ, guest kitchenette. Complimentary cappuccino, fresh breads, gourmet coffee, popcorn. Near glacier, fishing, rafting, skiing, ferry, airport and Glacier Bay departures. Smoke-free. Quiet, scenic, and lots of privacy in fully equipped studio with private entrance and deck. In-room dining and TV, VCR and stereo—tapes provided. Hosts will make all travel, tours, excursion arrangements. Guests say it's a definite "10"...where expectations are quietly met. Winner of AAA three-diamond award and ABBA three-crown award.

Hosts: Steve and Diane Pearson
Rooms: 3 (1PB; 2SB) $69-148
Full (self-serve) Breakfast
Credit Cards: A, B, E
Notes: 2, 5, 8, 9, 10, 11, 12

SEWARD

The White House Bed and Breakfast

P.O. Box 1157, 99664-1157
(907) 224-3614

This 5,000-square-foot home is surrounded by a panoramic mountain view. One-half of the home is for guest use. Country charm abounds with quilts and hand crafts. Guest TV room and fully equipped kitchen is in common area. Breakfast is self-serve buffet in guest dining area. The Historical Iditarod Trail close by. Also the famed Kenai Fjords National Park is accessed by road or boat.

Hosts: Tom and Annette Reese
Rooms: 5 (3PB; 2SB) $40-55 (winter) $55-75 (summer)
Expanded Continental Breakfast
Credit Cards: A, B
Notes: 2, 5, 7, 11, 12

SITKA

Alaska Ocean View Bed and Breakfast

1101 Edgecumbe Drive, 99835
(907) 747-8310 (voice and FAX)

You will enjoy casual elegance and affordable rates at this superior quality B&B where guests experience a high degree of personal comfort, privacy, and friendly, knowledgeable hosts. Open your day with the tantalizing aroma of bread baking and a generous gourmet breakfast. Close your day with a refreshing soak in the bubbling patio spa (bring swimsuit). Smoke-free. On Airporter & Ferry Shuttle Bus Route. Business travelers and vacationers rate this lodging a definite 12+!

Hosts: Bill and Carole Denkinger
Rooms: 3 (PB) $79-115 (suite); cash discount rate
Full Breakfast
Credit Cards: A, B, C
Notes: 2 , 5, 6 (outdoors only!), 7, 8, 9, 12

Karras Bed and Breakfast "Killer Whale House"

230 Kegwanton Street, 99835
(907) 747-3985

A warm welcome will be yours at our bed

NOTES: Credit cards accepted: A Master Card; B Visa; C American Express; D Discover Card; E Diners Club; F Other; 2 Personal checks accepted; 3 Lunch available; 4 Dinner available; 5 Open all year; 6 Pets

and breakfast overlooking Sitka Sound, the picturesque fishing fleet, and the Pacific Ocean. Located a three minute walk from town, eating, shopping, and most places of interest. The top floor of the B&B has a view of the ocean and marine traffic, volcano, and other mountains. We have a room for lounging, reading, visiting, and watching the endless marine traffic. There is a refrigerator, small kitchen, dining room and small living area on the top floor with another guest room on the ground floor. A full bath is shared by one other bedroom. Bus service is available from the airport or ferry to our home.

Hosts: Pete and Bertha Karras
Rooms: 4 (SB) $30 plus tax
Full Breakfast
Credit Cards: A, B
Notes: 2 (with drivers license), 5, 7, 9

TOK

Cleft of the Rock B&B

Sundog Trail, Box 122, 99780
(907) 883-4219; (907) 883-4219 (FAX; call first)

Cleft of the Rock Bed & Breakfast offers you sparkling, well-maintained accommodations and warm, friendly, Christian hospitality. Nestled in tall black spruce just three miles west of Tok. You can find an inviting, homelike atmosphere in one of our guest rooms, cabins or apartment. An Alaskan hearty breakfast. Children 12 and under stay free.

Hosts: John and Jill Rusyniak
Rooms: 5 (3PB; 2SB) $60-90
Full Breakfast
Credit Cards: A, B
Notes: 2, 5, 6 (with approval), 7, 9, 11, 12

WASILLA

Yukon Don's

1830 E. Parks Hwy, Suite 386, 99654
(907) 478-7472; (800) 478-7472; (907) 376-6515 (FAX)

When you're traveling in Alaska, you don't want to miss staying at Yukon Don's Bed & Breakfast Inn in Wasilla. All of our rooms are decorated with authentic Alaskana. Stay in the Iditarod, Fishing, Denali, or Hunting rooms or choose our suite. Our guests are pampered while relaxing in the Alaska room, complete with Alaskan historic library, video library, pool table, cable television, and gift bar. The all glass "View Room" on our second floor offers the grandest view in the Matanuska Valley. Judge William Hungate, St. Louis, MO said, "It's like seeing Alaska without leaving the house." We also offer phones in each room, Yukon Don's own expanded continental breakfast bar, a sauna, excercise room, and according to Commissioner Glenn Olds (world traveler) "the grandest view he has ever seen from a home." Call Yukon Don's and stay at Alaska's most acclaimed B&B inn.

Hosts: "Yukon" Don and Kristan Tanner
Rooms: 5 (2PB; 3SB) $65-105
Yukon Don's Breakfast Bar
Credit Cards: A, B
Notes: 2, 5, 7, 8, 10, 11, 12

Yukon Don's

Arizona

Mi Casa Su Casa
B&B Reservation Service

P. O. Box 950, Tempe, AZ 85280-0950
(602) 990-0682; (800) 456-0682 reservations;
(602) 990-3390 (FAX)

Our reservation service has over 160 inspected and approved homestays, guest cottages, ranches, and inns in Arizona, Utah, New Mexico, and Nevada. In **Arizona**, listings include Ajo, Apache Junction, Bisbee, Cave Creek, Clarkdale, Dragoon, Flagstaff, Mesa, Page, Patagonia, Payson, Pinetop, Phoenix, Prescott, Scottsdale, Sedona, Sierra Vista, Tempe, Tombstone, Tucson, Yuma, and other cities. In **New Mexico**, we list Albuquerque, Algodones, Chimayo, Los Cruces, Silver City, Sante Fe, and Taos. In **Utah**, listings include Moab, Monroe, Salt Lake City, Springdale, St. George, Tropic. In **Nevada**, we list Las Vegas. Private and shared baths range from $35-150. Full or continental breakfast. Ruth Young, coordinator.

BISBEE

The Greenway House

401 Cole Ave., 85603
(800) 253-3325

The Greenway House, built in 1906, is one of the country's finest historic Craftsman-style mansions. The inn, with the ambience of yesteryear combined with the comforts of today, is ideally suited for romantics, tourists, and business travelers. Eight guest suites are furnished with beautiful antiques. Guest are greeted with complimentary fruit baskets, fresh flowers, and candy. Kitchens are supplied with continental breakfast. Homemade blueberry muffins are delivered each morning. Private baths have clawfoot tubs with showers. Amenities include luxury soaps, bubble bath, robes, and hair dryers. Billiard room. Patios. Private entrances. Off-street parking. Air-conditioned. AAA approved, three-diamond award, and quality rated by Mobile.

Hosts: Dr. George S. Knox and Joy O'Clock
Rooms: 8 (PB) #75-125
Continental Breakfast In-Room
Credit Cards: A, B
Notes: 2, 5, 6 (limited), 7 (limited), 8, 10, 12

FLAGSTAFF

Comfi Cottages
of Flagstaff

1612 N. Aztec, 86001
(602) 774-0731

Near the Grand Canyon, great for families.

NOTES: Credit cards accepted: A Master Card; B Visa; C American Express; D Discover Card; E Diners Club; F Other; 2 Personal checks accepted; 3 Lunch available; 4 Dinner available; 5 Open all

Five individual cottages with antiques and English country motif. Three cottages are two bedroom, one bath; one is a one-bedroom honeymoon cottage; one is a large three bedroom, two baths. Fully equipped with linens, towels and blankets. Kitchens have dishes, pots, pans, coffee-pot, etc. Ready-to-prepare breakfast foods in fridge. Color cable TV and telephone. Bicycles on premises, washer and dryer available, and picnic tables and barbecue grills at each cottage.

Hosts: Ed and Pat Wiebe
Rooms: 7 (PB) $65-185 (for entire cottage)
Guest-Prepared Full Breakfast
Credit Cards: A, B
Notes: 2, 5, 7, 8, 9, 10, 11, 12

The Inn at 410

410 North Leroux St., 86001
(800) 774-2008

The Inn at 410 offers guests four seasons of hospitality in a charming 1907 home, elegantly furnished with antiques, stained glass, and touches of the Southwest. The spacious, sunny living room and lovely garden gazebo provide a peaceful ambience in which to relax. Each guest is pampered with a personal touch that includes oven-fresh cookies, healthy breakfasts, and recommendations for day trips to the Grand Canyon, Indian ruins, hiking, or skiing.

Hosts: Howard and Sally Krueger
Rooms: 9 (7PB; 2SB) $80-110
Full Breakfast
Credit Cards: A, B, C
Notes: 2, 5, 7, 10, 11, 12

Hassayampa Inn

PRESCOTT

Hassayampa Inn

122 East Gurley St., 86301
(520) 778-9434 (voice and FAX); (800) 322-1927

Times have changed, but the Inn, now listed on the National Register of Historic Places, still retains the charm of yesteryear with the amenities of today. The Classic overnight rooms, lace curtains, oak period furniture, and modern bathrooms, along with exceptional service provided by a caring staff, will enhance your visit. Discriminating travelers will find the Inn the ideal destination; just steps from the center of town, Courthouse Square, antique shops, museums, and stately Victorian homes. For the finest in cuisine visit the acclaimed Peacock Room; for a light snack and beverage, relax in the quaint Bar & Grill, or just sit back and enjoy the beauty of the magnificent lobby at the Hassayampa Inn.

Hosts: William M. Teich and Georgia L. Teich
Rooms: 67 (PB) $80-160
Full Breakfast
Credit Cards: A, B, C, D, E
Notes: 2, 3, 4, 5, 7, 8, 9, 10, 12

year; 6 Pets welcome; 7 Children welcome; 8 Tennis nearby; 9 Swimming nearby; 10 Golf nearby; 11 Skiing nearby; 12 May be booked through travel agent

SCOTTSDALE

Valley O' The Sun

P.O. Box 2214, 85252
(602) 941-1281

"Cead Mile Faite" are the words in Gaelic
on the doormat of the Valley O' The Sun
Bed & Breakfast on Papago Drive. It
means "100,000 welcomes." This B&B is
more than just a place to stay. Kathleen
wants to make your visit to the Great
Southwest a memorable one. Ideally located in the college area of Tempe, but still
close enough to Scottsdale to enjoy the
glamour of its shops, restaurants, and theaters. Two guestrooms can comfortably
accommodate four people. One bedroom
has a full-size bed, and the other has twin
beds. Each rooms has its own TV. Within
minutes of golf, horseback riding, picnic
area, swimming, bicycling, shopping, and
tennis, and walking distance from Arizona
State University.

Hostess: Kathleen Curtis
Rooms: 2 (SB) $35
Full Breakfast
Credit Cards: None
Notes: 2 (restricted), 5, 7 (over 10), 8, 9, 10,
11, 12

SEDONA

Briar Patch Inn

H-C 30—Box 1002, 86336
(602) 282-2342; (602) 282-2399 (FAX)

Eight acres of beautiful grounds along Oak
Creek in spectacular Oak Creek Canyon.
Rooms and cottages are all delightfully
furnished with southwestern charm. A

haven for those who appreciate nature
amid the wonders of Sedona's mystical
beauty. Suitable for small workshops.

Hosts: JoAnn and Ike Olson
Rooms: 16 (PB) $135-215
Full Breakfast
Credit Cards: A, B
Notes: 2, 5, 7, 9, 10, 12

Canyon Villa Bed and Breakfast Inn

125 Canyon Circle Dr, 86336
(602) 284-1226; (800) 453-1166; (602) 284-2114
(FAX)

AAA Four-Diamond award bed & breakfast inn, nestled among the red rocks of
Sedona.... Ten luxurious guest rooms
with fantastic views and relaxing whirlpool
tubs. Gourmet breakfast, fireplaces, and a
heated pool.

Hosts: Chuck and Marion Yadon
Rooms: 11 (PB) $95-175
Full Breakfast
Credit Cards: A, B
Notes: 2, 5, 8, 9, 10, 12

The Graham Bed and Breakfast

150 Canyon Circle Drive
(602) 284-1425; (800) 228-1425;
(602) 284-0767 (FAX)

The Graham Inn is an impressive contemporary Southwest inn with huge windows
allowing great views of Sedona's red rock
formations. Each guest room has a private
bath, balcony, and TV/VCR and some
rooms have a jacuzzi and fireplace. All
rooms have many individual features which
make each unique and delightful. Pool and

spa invite guests outdoors. Mobil four-star award 1986-1994. Sedona's Finest.

Hosts: Carol and Roger Redenbaugh
Rooms: 6 (PB) $99-209
Full Breakfast
Credit Cards: A, B, D
Notes: 2, 5, 7, 8, 9, 10, 11, 12 (no fee)

The Graham Bed and Breakfast

Territorial House, An Old West Bed and Breakfast

65 Piki Drive, 86336
(602) 204-2737; (602) 204-2230 (FAX)

Our large stone and cedar house has been tastefully decorated to depict Arizona's territorial era. Each room is decorated to recall different stages of Sedona's early history. Some rooms have private balcony, jacuzzi tub, or fireplace. An enormous stone fireplace graces the living room and a covered veranda welcomes guests at the end of a day of sightseeing around Sedona. A full hearty breakfast is served

at the harvest table each morning. All of this served with western hospitality.

Hosts: John and Linda Steele
Rooms: 4 (PB) $90-130
Full Breakfast
Credit Cards: A, B
Notes: 2, 5, 7, 8, 9, 10, 11, 12

SPRINGVILLE

Paisley Corner

P.O. Box 458, 85938
(602) 333-4665

Step back in time to the Elegance that once was the Wild West! Historic landmark home with Victorian decor. Comfortable, clean rooms each named for a turn-of-the-century lady. Each room includes a private bath and a unique personality all it own. Reservations requested.

Hosts: Cletus and Cheryl Tisdell
Rooms: 4 (PB) $65-75
Full Breakfast
Credit Cards: A, B
Notes: 2, 5, 7, 8, 9, 11, 12

TUCSON

Casa Alegre Bed and Breakfast

316 E. Speedway 85705
(602) 628-1800; (602) 792-1880 (FAX)

Casa Alegre is a distinguished 1915 craftsman-style bungalow, located minutes from the University of Arizona and downtown Tucson. Each of the four guest rooms has been lovingly furnished with unique pieces that reflect the highlights of Tucson's history. Every morning, guests

---

year; 6 Pets welcome; 7 Children welcome; 8 Tennis nearby; 9 Swimming nearby; 10 Golf nearby; 11 Skiing nearby; 12 May be booked through travel agent

awaken to a scrumptious full breakfast and spend their relaxing time in the Inn's serene patio and pool area or by the rock fireplace in the formal living room during the cool winter months.

Hostess: Phyllis Florek
Rooms: 4 (PB) $75-90
Full Breakfast
Credit Cards: None
Notes: 2, 5, 8, 9, 10, 11, 12

El Presidio Bed and Breakfast Inn

297 North Main Avenue, 85701
(602) 623-6151; (501) 297-8764 (at night)

Experience Southwestern charm in a desert oasis with the romance of a country inn. Garden courtyards with Old Mexico ambience of lush, floral displays, fountains, and cobblestone surround richly appointed guest house and suites. Enjoy antique decors, robes, complimentary beverages, fruit, snacks, TVs, and telephones. The 1880's Victorian adobe mansion has been featured in many magazines and the book *The Desert Southwest*. Located in a historic district; walk to fine restaurants, museums, shops, and the Arts District. Close to downtown. Mobil and AAA three-star rated.

Hostess: Patti Toci
Rooms: 3 suites (PB) $85-110
Full Breakfast
Credit Cards: None
Notes: 2, 5, 8, 9, 10, 11, 12

June's Bed and Breakfast

3212 W. Holladay St., 85746
(602) 578-0857

Mountainside home with pool. Majestic towering mountains. Hiking in the desert. Sparkling city lights. Beautiful rear yard and patio. Suitable for receptions.

Hostess: June Henderson
Rooms: 3 (1PB; 1SB) $45-45
Continental Breakfast
Credit Cards: None
Notes: 2, 5, 8, 9, 10, 11

La Posada del Valle

1640 N. Campbell Ave., 85719
(602) 795-3840 (voice and FAX)

Elegant 1920s inn nestled in the heart of Tucson. Five richly appointed rooms. Private bath and entrance. Gourmet breakfast and afternoon tea included. Patios, mountain views, walking distance to the university and hospital. Private parking. We speak German. AAA approved.

Hosts: Tom and Karin Dennen
Rooms: 5 (PB) $90-155 (in-season) $65-85 (out of season)
Gourmet Breakfast
Credit Cards: A, B
Notes: 2, 5, 7, 8, 9, 10, 11, 12

Old Pueblo Homestays Reservation Service

P.O. Box 13603, 85732
(602) 790-0030; (800) 333-9776 reservations;
(602) 790-2399 (FAX)

A B&B reservation service featuring accommodations in individual homes in southeast Arizona and Sedona, ranging from very modest to luxurious, including continental to gourmet breakfast. Brochure free with SASE. William A. Janssen, coordinator.

NOTES: Credit cards accepted: A Master Card; B Visa; C American Express; D Discover Card; E Diners Club; F Other; 2 Personal checks accepted; 3 Lunch available; 4 Dinner available; 5 Open all

Arkansas

EUREKA SPRINGS

Bonnybrooke Farm atop Misty Mountain

Rt. 2, Box 335A, 72632
(501) 253-6903

If your heart's in the country...or longs to be... we invite you to come share in the sweet quiet and serenity that awaits you in your place to come home to.... Five cottages, distinctively different in their pleasure to tempt you: fireplace and jacuzzi for two, full glass fronts and mountaintop views, shower under the stars in your glass shower, wicker porch swing in front of the fireplace and a waterfall jacuzzi ...you're gonna love it!

Hosts: Bonny and Josh Pierson
Rooms: 5 cottages (PB) $85-125
Basket Breakfast
Credit Cards: None
Notes: 2, 5, 9, 12

The Brownstone Inn

75 Hillside Ave., 72632
(501) 253-7505

A present part of Eureka's past. A historical site located on trolley route with luxury Victorian accommodations, private entrances, private baths, gourmet breakfasts, and a personal touch. Featured in *Best Places to Stay in the South.*

Hosts: Marvin and Donna Shepard
Rooms: 4 (PB) $85-95
Full Breakfast
Credit Cards: A, B
Notes: 2, 5, 10, 12 (closed January and February)

Dairy Hollow House: A Country Inn and Restaurant

515 Spring St., 72632
(501) 253-7444; (800) 562-8650

Award winning B&B. Owner-managed country inn and restaurant, the first B&B in Eureka. In two homes, the Farmhouse (a small restored 1880s Ozark farmhouse) and the Main House/The Restaurant at Dairy Hollow (a large 1940s bungalow-style home with additions). The restaurant offers a *prix fixe* dinner menu seven days a week; brunches on holidays and weekends (reservations necessary). Breakfast is delivered right to your door in a split-oak basket. "Home of the *Dairy Hollow House Soup & Bread Cookbook.*"

Hosts: Ned Shank and Crescent Dragonwagon
Rooms: 6 (PB) $125-175
Full Breakfast
Credit Cards: A, B, C, D, E
Closed January
Notes: 2, 4, 7, 9, 10, 12

---

welcome; 7 Children welcome; 8 Tennis nearby; 9 Swimming nearby; 10 Golf nearby; 11 Skiing nearby; 12 May be booked through travel agent

Enchanted Cottages

18 Nut St., 72632
(800) 862-2788

Heart of the Hills Inn

Enchanted Cottages are romantic, private hideaways located in a secluded parklike setting in the historic district just two and one-half blocks to the shops and restaurants. These "storybook" cottages are surrounded by woods and frequently visited by neighborhood families of deer. Each cottage has either an indoor jacuzzi for two or a private outdoor hot tub. You will also find cozy fireplaces, king- or queen-size beds, antique furnishings, cable TV, kitchens, and patios with grills. Special honeymoon and anniversary packages!

Hosts: Barbara Kellogg and David Pettit
Rooms: 3 private cottages (PB) $75-129
Continental Breakfast
Credit Cards: A, B
Notes: 2, 5, 12

Heart of the Hills Inn

5 Summit, 72632
(800) 253-7468

The historic Victorian home is in a quaint town nestled into the Ozark Mountains. Wake up to a scrumptious breakfast, enjoy a gorgeous four-block walk to shops, museums, and galleries, catch a trolley for a spin around the area, or relax in the jacuzzi. Rooms have antiques with a Victorian decor. Come, experience a "touch of true, Southern hospitality."

Hostess: Jan Jacobs Weber
Rooms: 4 (PB) $79-119
Full Breakfast
Credit Cards: A, B
Notes: 2, 5, 7, 9, 10, 12

The Heartstone Inn and Cottages

35 Kings Highway, 72632
(501) 253-8916

An award-winning inn. All private baths, private entrances, cable TV. King and queen beds. Antiques galore. Renowned gourmet breakfasts. In-house massage therapy studio. Golf privileges. Large decks and gazebo under the trees; great for bird-watching. Recommended by: *New York Times, Country Home Magazine, America's Wonderful Little Hotels and Inns, Recommended Inns of the South,* and many more.

Hosts: Iris and Bill Simantel
Rooms: 10 plus 2 cottages (PB) $63-118
Full Breakfast
Credit Cards: A, B, C, D
Notes: 2, 5 (Closed Christmas through January) 9, 10, 12

Red Bud Manor

7 Kings Highway, 72632
(501) 253-9649

This charming Victorian Inn, which offers the nostalgia of yesteryear with the comforts of today, is located in the picturesque Historic District, and on the Victorian-

---

trolley route. The Inn is small and intimate, so that each guest can be pampered. Guest rooms have adjoining private baths, private entrances, queen beds, color TV, refrigerators, and antique furnishings. Jacuzzis are available. Breakfast is gourmet and served outside on the veranda or in the formal dining room.

Hosts: Tandy and Sari Bozeman
Rooms: 3 (PB) $65-109
Full Gourmet Breakfast
Credit Cards: A, B
Notes: 2, 5, 12

Ridgeway House

28 Ridgeway, 72632
(501) 253-6618; (800) 477-6618

Prepare to be pampered! Sumptuous breakfasts elegantly served, luxurious rooms, antiques, flowers, desserts, quiet street within walking distance of eight churches, five-minute walk to historic downtown, trolley one block. Porches, decks, private jacuzzi suite for anniversaries/honeymoons. All my guests are VIPs!! Open all year.

Hostess: Linda Kerkera
Rooms: 5 (3PB; 2SB) $69-109
Full Breakfast
Credit Cards: A, B, C
Notes: 2, 5, 7, 12

Singleton House

11 Singleton, 72632
(501) 253-9111

This old-fashioned Victorian house with a touch of magic is whimsically decorated and has an eclectic collection of treasures and antiques. Breakfast is served on the

balcony overlooking a wildflower garden and fish pond. Walk to the historic district, shops, and cafés. Passion Play and Holy Land tour reservations can be arranged. A guest cottage with a jacuzzi is also available at a separate location. Hands-on apprenticeship program available!

Hostess: Barbara Bavron
Rooms: 5 (PB) $65-95/ Cottage, No Breakfast, $95
Full Breakfast
Credit Cards: A, B, C, D
Notes: 2, 5, 7, 9, 10, 12

Singleton House

Sunnyside Inn

5 Ridgeway, 72632
(800) 554-9499

Lovingly restored, circa 1880 Victorian home in the Historic District. Beautifully appointed. Quiet, restful surroundings are smoke and alcohol-free. Full country breakfasts, private baths, honeymoon suite with jacuzzi, walking distance to downtown, wilderness area from deck.

Hostess: Gladys Rose Foris
Rooms: 6 (PB) $80-95
Full Breakfast
Credit Cards: None
Notes: 2, 5, 7, 12

---

welcome; 7 Children welcome; 8 Tennis nearby; 9 Swimming nearby; 10 Golf nearby; 11 Skiing nearby; 12 May be booked through travel agent

FAYETTEVILLE

Hill Avenue Bed and Breakfast

131 S. Hill, 72701
(501) 444-0865

This century-old home is located in a residential neighborhood near the University of Arkansas, downtown square, and Walton Art Center. This inn is the only licensed Bed and Breakfast in Fayetteville. Comfortable common areas and a large porch are available to guests. Breakfast is served on the porch or in the formal dining room.

Hosts: Cecila and Dale Thompson
Rooms: 2 (SB) $40-50
Full Breakfast
Credit Cards: None
Notes: None

GASSVILLE

Lithia Springs Lodge

R1, Box 77A, HWY 126 North, 72635
(501) 435-6100

A lovingly restored early Ozark health lodge, six miles southwest of Mountain Home in north central Arkansas. Fishing, boating, canoeing in famous lakes and rivers. Scenic hills and valleys, caverns. Silver Dollar City, Branson, Eureka Springs within driving distance. Enjoy the walk in meadow and woods and browse through the adjoining Country Treasures Gift Shop.

Hosts: Paul and Reita Johnson
Rooms: 5 (3PB; 2SB) $40-50
Full Breakfast
Credit Cards: A, B
Notes: 2, 8, 9, 10

HARDY

Olde Stonehouse Bed and Breakfast Inn

511 Main St., 72542
(501) 856-2983; (800) 514-2983; (501) 856-4036 (FAX)

Historic, native Arkansas stone house with large porches lined with jumbo rocking chairs provides the perfect place to relax and watch the world go by. Each room is individually and comfortably furnished with antiques. Central heat and air, ceiling fans, queen beds, private baths. In-town location, block from Spring River and the unique shops of Old Hardy Town. Three country music theaters, golf courses, horseback riding, canoeing and fishing nearby. Attractions: Mammoth Springs State park, Grand Gulf State Park, Evening Shade, AR, Arkansas Traveler Theater. Breakfast is a treat, like Grandma used to make, gourmet but hearty! Evening snacks. Special occasion packages available. Murder mystery dinner parties and packages. Gift certificates. Approved by AAA and ABBA.

Hosts: David and Peggy Johnson
Rooms: 7 and 2 suites (PB) $55-85
Full Breakfast
Credit Cards: A, B, D
Notes: 2, 3, 4, 5, 8, 9, 10, 12

HOT SPRINGS

Vintage Comfort B&B Inn

303 Quapaw, 71901
(501) 623-3258 voice and FAX

Situated on a tree-lined street, a short walk from Hot Springs' historic Bath House

---

NOTES: Credit cards accepted: A Master Card; B Visa; C American Express; D Discover Card; E Diners Club; F Other; 2 Personal checks accepted; 3 Lunch available; 4 Dinner available; 5 Open all year; 6 Pets

Row, art galleries, restaurants, and shopping. Guests enjoy a comfortably restored Queen Anne house built in 1907. Four spacious rooms are available upstairs, each with private bath, ceiling fan, and period furnishings. A delicious full breakfast is served each morning in the Inn's dining room. Vintage Comfort is known for its comfort and gracious Southern hospitality.

Hostess: Helen Bartlett
Rooms: 4 (PB) $60-85
Full Breakfast
Credit Cards: A, B, C, E
Notes: 2, 5, 7 (over 5 years), 8, 9, 10, 12

Vintage Comfort Bed and Breakfast Inn

LITTLE ROCK

The Empress of Little Rock

2120 South Louisiana, 72206
(501) 374-7966

Imagine an evening in the family parlor at The Empress, surrounded by luxurious antiques, the warm fire draining away the tension of a busy day, stretched out in your Victorian dressing jacket and that special book you've been postponing for the "right time." Each of the five rooms at The Empress conveys such a feeling in your own private sitting area and bath, two with clawfoot tubs. Completed in 1888, Hornibrook Mansion is on the national register and was the most opulent residence in the state boasting seven fireplaces, rich walnut wainscoting in formal areas, parquet floors, magnificent double stairwell, eight foot square stained glass skylight, and a three-and-a-half story tower. Now is the "right time." The Empress of Little Rock, the "forgotten" experience. No smoking.

Hosts: Robert H. Blair and Sharon Welch-Blair
Rooms: 5 (PB) $85-125
Both Full and Continental Breakfast
Credit Cards: A, B, C
Notes: 2, 5, 7 (over 10), 8, 9, 10, 12 (10% discount applies)

WINSLOW

Sky-Vue Lodge

22822 N. Hwy. 71, 72959
(501) 634-2003; (800) 782-2003

Located on Scenic 71 near Fayetteville, Sky-Vue Lodge offers a 25-mile view of the Ozark Mountains. Enjoy the spectacular view from the porch of your charming cabin, which has heating and air conditioning for year-round comfort. Hike on our 83 acres, or enjoy a perfect environment for the entire family. Facilities are ideal for retreats, conferences, reunions, and weddings. Three delicious meals available daily.

Hosts: Glenn and Janice Jorgenson
Rooms: 7 cottages (PB) $40-50
Full Breakfast
Credit Cards: A, B
Notes: 2, 4, 5, 7, 8, 9

welcome; 7 Children welcome; 8 Tennis nearby; 9 Swimming nearby; 10 Golf nearby; 11 Skiing nearby; 12 May be booked through travel agent

California

Bed and Breakfast of California—A State-Wide Reservation Service

3924 E. 14th Street, Long Beach, 90804
(310) 498-0552; (310) 597-5220 (FAX); (800) 383-3513

B&B of Los Angeles helps travelers make reservations anywhere in California. Our accommodations include private home-stays in San Diego, Los Angeles, Santa Barbara, Malibu, Cambria, San Francisco and dozens of others throughout the state. We also work with historic inns, guest houses, and ranches. Rates range from $45-95 per night, including a full breakfast.

Our **"Kids Welcome"** program is geared toward family travel. These homes emphasize comfort, hospitality and affordability. Please call for information or to order a directory.

Rent A Room

11531 Varna St., Garden Grove, 92640
(714) 638-1406

This is a referral service that books private homes **between Los Angeles and San Diego**. No inns are on this list; these Bed and Breakfasts are in the British tradition. Most of the offerings are close to Southern California attractions such as Disneyland, Knott's Berry Farm, San Diego Zoo, Sea World, Universal Studios, Anaheim Convention Center, and the beaches. One to three rooms in each home. All rooms have private baths. Full breakfasts served in all bookings. $45-70.

ALAMEDA

Garratt Mansion

900 Union St., 94501
(510) 521-4779; (510) 521-6796 (FAX)

This 1893 Victorian halts time on the tranquil island of Alameda. Only 15 miles to Berkeley or downtown San Francisco. We'll help maximize your vacation plans or leave you alone to regroup. Our rooms are large and comfortable, and our breakfasts are nutritious and filling.

Hosts: Royce and Betty Gladden
Rooms: 7 (5PB; 2SB) $80-130
Full Breakfast
Credit Cards: A, B, C, E
Notes: 2, 5, 7, 8, 9, 10, 12

NOTES: Credit cards accepted: A MasterCard; B Visa; C American Express; D Discover Card; E Diners Club; F Other; 2 Personal checks accepted; 3 Lunch available; 4 Dinner available; 5 Open all year; 6 Pets

ALBION

Fensalden Inn

P.O. Box 99, 95410
(707) 937-4042; (800) 959-3850

Overlooking the Pacific Ocean from twenty
tree-lined pastoral acres, Fensalden Inn
offers a quiet respite for the perfect getaway. A former stagecoach way station,
the inn offers a restful, yet interesting stay
for the traveler. There are eight guest
quarters; some are suites with fireplaces
and kitchens; all have private baths with
showers or tubs; and most have beautiful
ocean views. Come and whale watch, join
the deer on a stroll through our meadow,
or just relax and enjoy!

Hosts: Scott and Frances Brazil
Rooms: 8 (PB) $85-130
Full Gourmet Breakfast
Credit Cards: A, B
Notes: 2, 5, 8, 9, 10, 12

ANGWIN

Forest Manor

415 Cold Springs Road, 94508
(707) 965-3538, (800) 788-0364;
(707) 965-3303 (FAX)

Tucked among the forest and vineyards of
famous Napa wine country is this secluded
20-acre English Tudor estate, described
as "one of the most romantic country inns
... a small exclusive resort." Enjoy the
scenic countryside near hot air ballooning, hot springs, lake, and water
sports. Fireplaces, verandas, a 53-foot
pool, spas, spacious suites (one with
Jacuzzi), refrigerators, coffeemakers,
home-baked breakfasts. Hosts are former

medical missionaries.

Hosts: Harold and Corlene Lambeth
Rooms: 3 (PB) $99-179 off-season;
$119-239 in-season
Full Breakfast
Credit Cards: A, B
Notes: 2, 5, 7 (over 12), 8, 9, 10, 12

AUBURN

Power's Mansion Inn

164 Cleveland Ave., 95603
(916) 885-1166; (916) 885-1386 (FAX)

The magnificent mansion which is now
known as Power's Mansion Inn was built
from a gold fortune, and no expense was
spared to make it an elegant showplace.
This legendary century-old Victorian has
been lovingly restored to the grandeur of
yesteryear—eleven lavishly decorated
rooms are filled with antique furniture from
the Old Country. Poofy satin comforters
atop high brass and porcelain. . .lavish
decor to make you feel pampered. The
innkeeper provides a delicious full breakfast and lots of tender care. The staff is
more than helpful in offering suggestions
and answering questions about the Gold
Country.

Rooms: 11 (PB) $79-149
Full Breakfast
Credit Cards: A, B, C
Notes: 2, 5, 7 (prearranged), 8, 9, 10, 11, 12

AVALON

Gull House

P.O. Box 1381, 90704
(213) 510-2547

Two deluxe suites on the lower level of our

contemporary home, each with a separate entrance, large living room with gas-log fireplace, a morning room with refrigerator and table, bedroom, and bath. Breakfast is served on the patio by the pool, spa, and gas barbecue. Within walking distance of all island activities—beaches, golf, tennis, boating, fishing, biking, horesback riding, and picnic facilities.

Hosts: Bob and Hattie Michalis
Rooms: 2 suites (PB) $135-145
Continental Breakfast
Credit Cards: None
Closed Nov. 1 - April 1
Notes: 1 (in advance), 7, 8, 9

BISHOP

The Chalfant House B&B

213 Academy, 93514
(619) 872-1798

This 1900 semi-Victorian, two-story house includes country antique furnishings and handmade quilts. There are five rooms and two suites. Tea is served in the afternoon; ice cream sudaes are served in the evenings. Enjoy TV/VCR, library, and a fireplace in the parlor. Central air and ceiling fans. No smoking.

Hosts: Fred and Sally Manecke
Rooms: 7 (PB) $60-90
Full Breakfast
Credit Cards: A, B, C
Notes: 2, 5, 7, 8, 9, 10, 11

The Matlick House Bed and Breakfast

1313 Rowan Lane, 93514
(619) 873-3133; (800) 898-3133 (for reservations)

This turn-of-the-century ranch house, originally owned by the ranching Matlick family, is nestled at the base of the valley between the Whites and the Sierra Nevada Mountains. The two-story house with the spacious first and second story is shaded by eighty-year-old elms and offers guests five rooms with private baths, furnished with antiques, handmade quilts, and lace curtains. Some rooms boast views of the Sierras. Full country breakfast of fresh orange juice, meat and egg dishes is served in the dining area. Special dietary requests are happily filled. Wine with hors d'oeuvers is served in the parlor evenings. Hiking and fishing are among the activities available in the area.

Hosts: Ray and Barbara Showalter
Rooms: 5 (PB) $79-89
Full Breakfast
Credit Cards: A, B, C, D
Notes: 2, 3, 4, 5, 7(12 and over), 8, 9, 10, 11, 12

CALISTOGA

Calistoga Wayside Inn

1523 Foothill Blvd., 94515
(800) 845-3632; (707) 942-0645

A warm, inviting Mediterranean-style home, built in the 1920s, situated in a secluded garden setting. Rooms have king or queen beds, private baths. Enjoy the garden and patio, or curl up by the fireplace. Savor a Calistoga country break-

---

NOTES: Credit cards accepted: A Master Card; B Visa; C American Express; D Discover Card; E Diners Club; F Other; 2 Personal checks accepted; 3 Lunch available; 4 Dinner available; 5 Open all year; 6 Pets

fast, afternoon refreshments, herb tea in the evening. Restaurants, shops, and spas nearby. Gift certificates.

Hosts: Pat and Carmine
Rooms: 3 (PB) $95-135
Full Breakfast
Credit Cards: A, B, C
Notes: 2, 5, 7, 8, 9, 10, 12

Foothill House

3037 Foothill Blvd., 94515
(707) 942-6933; (800) 942-6933; (707) 942-5692
(FAX)

"The romantic inn of the Napa Valley," according to a *Chicago Tribune* travel editor. In a country setting, located in the western foothills just north of Calistoga, the Foothill House offers spacious suites individually decorated with antiques. All suites have private baths and entrances, fireplaces, small refrigerators and air conditioning. Some have jacuzzis. A luxurious cottage is also available. A gourmet breakfast is served each morning and appetizers and refreshments each evening.

Hosts: Gus and Doris Beckert
Rooms: 3 (PB) $115-220
Full Breakfast
Credit Cards: A, B, C
Notes: 2, 5, 8, 9, 10, 12

Foothill House

Hillcrest Bed and Breakfast

3225 Lake County Highway, 94515
(707) 942-6334

Hilltop, rambling country home filled with antique silver, china, art work and furniture. Rooms have balconies with breathtaking views of lush Napa Valley. Swimming, hiking, and fishing on forty acres of family owned property since 1870. Guests have use of trampoline, spa, pool, balcony barbecue area, and fireplace in guest parlor.

Hostess: Debbie O'Gorman
Rooms: 6 (4 PB; 2 SB) $45-90
Continental Breakfast
Credit Cards: None
Notes: 2, 5, 6, 8, 9, 10, 11, 12

Quail Mt. Bed and Breakfast

4455 North St. Helena Hwy., 94515
(707) 942-0316

A secluded, luxury, romantic B&B located on 26 heavily wooded acres 300 feet above Napa Valley with vineyard on the estate. All king-size beds, private baths, and decks. Picnic facilities on premises. A full breakfast is served in the solarium, guest, common room; decks that wrap around the house; or in winter, in the formal dining room. Complimentary refreshments in the afternoon. Reservation deposit required.

Hosts: Alma and Don Swiers
Rooms: 3 (PB) $100-125
Full Breakfast
Credit Cards: A, B
Notes: 2, 5, 8, 10, 12

welcome; 7 Children welcome; 8 Tennis nearby; 9 Swimming nearby; 10 Golf nearby; 11 Skiing nearby; 12 May be booked through travel agent

CAMBRIA

The Pickford House Bed and Breakfast

2555 MacLeod Way, 93428
(805) 927-8619

Eight large rooms done in antiques. All private baths with clawfoot tubs and showers. The front three rooms have fireplaces and a view of the mountains and valley. All rooms have a TV and king- or queen-size bed. Wine, fruit, and breads served at 5PM. Located near beaches and wineries and only seven miles from Hearst Castle. Third person only $20. Full breakfast served from 8-9AM in our antique dining room with cozy fireplace. Gift certificates available. Abundance of parking space. Check in after 3pm, check out 11 am.

Hostess: Anna Larsen
Rooms: 8 (PB) $85-125 plus tax
Full Breakfast
Credit Cards: A, B
Notes: 2, 5, 7

CARLSBAD

Pelican Cove Inn

320 Walnut Ave., 92008
(619) 434-5995

This romantic inn is located 200 yards from the beach and features eight rooms all with: private baths (some spas), feather beds, down comforters, fireplaces, and TVs. A full breakfast that can be enjoyed in your room, the gazebo, or the oceanview deck is included. Excellent restaurants and shopping are within walking distance.

Hosts: Kris and Nancy Nayudu
Rooms: 8 (PB) $85-175
Full Breakfast
Credit Cards: A, B, C
Notes: 2, 5, 8, 9, 10, 12

CARMEL-BY-THE-SEA

Sunset House

PO Box 1925, 93921
2 SE Camino Real (Between Ocean and 7th)
(408) 624-4884; (408) 624-4890 (FAX)

Sunset House, a romantic Inn, located on a quiet residential street, captures the essence of Carmel. Experience the sound of the surf, being close to the beach and yet only two blocks from quaint shops, galleries, and restaurants that make Carmel famous. Two rooms have ocean views and all rooms have brick wood-burning fireplaces, and charming sitting areas, and all rooms are furnished with lovely antiques.

Hosts: Camille and Dennis Fike
Rooms: 4 (PB) $130-170
Expanded Continental Breakfast
Credit Cards: A, B, C
Notes: 2, 5, 6, 7, 8, 9, 10, 12

CARMEL VALLEY

The Valley Lodge

Carmel Valley Road at Ford Road, Box 93, 93924
(408) 659-2261; (800) 641-4646;
(408) 659-4558 (FAX)

A warm Carmel Valley welcome awaits the two of you, a few of you, or a small conference. Relax in a garden patio room or a cozy one- or two-bedroom cottage with fireplace and kitchen. Enjoy a sump-

---

NOTES: Credit cards accepted: A Master Card; B Visa; C American Express; D Discover Card; E Diners Club; F Other; 2 Personal checks accepted; 3 Lunch available; 4 Dinner available; 5 Open all year; 6 Pets

tuous continental breakfast, our heated pool, sauna, hot spa, and fitness center. Tennis and golf are nearby. Walk to fine restaurants and quaint shops of Carmel Valley village, or just listen to your beard grow.

Hosts: Peter and Sherry Coakley
Rooms: 31 (PB) $95-135; $155 one-bedroom cottage; $235 two-bedroom cottage
Expanded Continental Breakfast
Credit Cards: A, B, C
Notes: 2, 5, 6 (extra fee), 7, 8, 9 (on-site), 10, 12

CASSEL

Clearwater House on Hat Creek

P.O. Box 90, 96016
(916) 335-5500 (voice and FAX)

Clearwater House is a quiet retreat for fishermen and families. It is a handsome turn-of-the-century farmhouse offering seven bedrooms and baths. The staff is friendly and professional and the meals and service first-class. Clearwater's exceptional guides offer private guiding and fly fishing schools for anglers of all levels on the local spring creeks and freestone waters. Other activities include biking, hiking, and driving tours, visits to Lassen National Park, birding, tennis, and golf. An easy five-hour drive north of San Francisco or one hour from Redding airport.

Hosts: Dick Galland and Lynn Bedell
Rooms: 7 (PB) $210-260
Full Breakfast
Credit Cards: A, B
Open late April - Nov. 15
Notes: 2, 3, 4, 7, 8 (on premises), 9 , 10, 11, 12

CLOVERDALE

Ye Olde' Shelford House

29955 River Road, 95425
(707) 894-5956; (800) 833-6479

This 1885 country Victorian is located in the heart of wine country, with six beautifully decorated rooms with family antiques, fresh flowers, homemade quilts, and porcelain dolls by Ina. A gourmet breakfast is served in our delightful dining room. We will make reservations for you at one of the many good restaurants nearby. Before you retire, you can enjoy the many games in the recreation room, then get into the hot tub to relax after a busy day. Pool and tandem 10-speed bicycles available. Air conditioned.

Hosts: Ina and Allen Sauder
Rooms: 6 (PB) $85-110
Full Breakfast
Closed January
Credit Cards: A, B, D
Notes: 2, 5, 7, 8, 9, 10, 12

Ye Olde' Shelford House

COLOMA

Coloma Country Inn

345 High St., PO Box 502, 95613
(916) 622-6919

Built in 1852, this country Victorian farm-house is surrounded by five acres of private gardens in the middle of a 300-acre state park. Main house has five guest rooms and the carriage house has two suites. All rooms feature country decor, including quilts, stenciling, American antiques, and fresh flowers. Hot-air balloon with your host from the backyard meadow or white-water raft from the South Fork American River one block from the inn.

Hosts: Alan and Cindi Ehrgott
Rooms: 7 (5PB; 2SB) $89-120
Full Breakfast
Credit Cards: None
Open late April - Nov. 15
Notes: 2, 5, 7, 8 , 9 , 10,12

COLOMA/LOTUS

Golden Lotus B&B Inn

1006 Lotus Rd., PO Box 830, Lotus, 95651
(916) 621-4562

1857 Pre-Victorian surrounded by herb-flower gardens. Frontage on the American River (fishing and gold panning). One mile to Coloma Gold Discovery Park. Escape from the ordinary. Discover the special world awaiting you in any one of our special rooms: The Secret Garden (private entrance), Wish-Upon, Pirates Cove, Orient Express, Westward Ho, and Tranquility. Complete library. Restaurant in 1855 brick building. Separate antique

store and Tea Room on site. White water rafting. Reike available.

Hosts: Bruce and Jill Smith
Rooms: 6 (PB) $75-95
Full Breakfast
Credit Cards: A, B
Notes: 2, 3, 4, 5, 6 (prearranged), 7 (6 and over), 11, 12

COLUMBIA

Fallon Hotel

Washington Street, Columbia State Park, 95310
(209) 532-1470; (209) 532-7027 (FAX)

Since 1857 the Fallon Hotel in the historic Columbia State Park has provided hospitality and comfort to travelers from all over the world. It has been authentically restored to its Victorian grandeur, and many of the antiques and furnishings are original to the hotel. We welcome you to come visit our Fallon Hotel, Fallon Theater, and old-fashioned ice cream parlor for a taste of the Old West.

Host: Tom Bender
Rooms: 14 (13PB; 1SB) $50-90
Continental Breakfast
Credit Cards: A, B, C
Notes: 2, 5 (weekends only Jan-March), 7, 8, 9, 10, 11, 12

ELK

Elk Cove Inn

6300 South Highway 1, P.O. Box 367, 95432
(800) 275-2967; (707) 877-3321 (FAX)

This 1883 Victorian is nestled atop a bluff overlooking the ocean. Enjoy wide vista views amid the relaxed and romantic set-

---

NOTES: Credit cards accepted: A Master Card; B Visa; C American Express; D Discover Card; E Diners Club; F Other; 2 Personal checks accepted; 3 Lunch available; 4 Dinner available; 5 Open all year; 6 Pets

ting of a rural village. Behind the main house are four cabins, two with fireplaces and skylights. The main house, where a full breakfast is served in the dining rooms, has three large oceanview rooms, a parlor, and deck. There is access to a driftwood-strewn beach and numerous scenic trails for hiking and biking nearby.

Host: Elaine Bryant
Rooms: 10 (PB) $98-200
Full Gourmet Breakfast
Credit Cards: None
Notes: 2, 5, 8, 10

Elk Cove Inn

EUREKA

Carter Victorians

301 "L" Street, 95501
(707) 444-8062 (voice and FAX)

Carter Victorians encompassed three lovely Victorians: the Carter House Inn, an exact replica of a circa 1884 San Fransico house that was destroyed in the 1906 earthquake; the classic 25-room Hotel Carter, and the newest addition, the three-room, single-level Bell Cottage. Each

offers a distinctly clean and artful blend of classic Victorian architecture with stylish, contemporary interior settings, all in a warm, hospitable environment. A great variety of luxurious rooms, each appointed with original local art, fine antiques, and generous amenities such as fireplaces, whirlpools, bay views, skylights, double-head showers, soaking tubs with marina views, king-size beds, telephones, VCRs and a video tape library, cable TV, CD stereo systems and CD library, honor bars, and minfridges. "The best of the best," according to *California Living Magazine*.

Hosts: Mark and Christi Carter
Rooms: 32 (PB) $115-225
Full Breakfast
Credit Cards: A, B, C, D, E
Notes: 2, 4, 5, 7, 8, 9, 10, 12

An Elegant Victorian Mansion

1406 "C" Street, 95501
(707) 444-3144; (800) EVM-1888

Exclusively for non-smokers: an 1888 National Historic Landmark of opulence, grace and grandeur offering deluxe lodging and world-class service. Authentically restored Victorian interiors, family antiques, flower gardens. Gourmet breakfast. Secured garage parking, laundry service, bicycles, sauna; best mattresses in the world. Near ocean, redwoods. Complimentary bay cruise. AAA and Mobil rated.

Hosts: Doug and Lily Vieyra
Rooms: 4 (2PB; 2SB) $75-125
Full French Gourmet Breakfast
Credit Cards: A, B
Notes: 2, 3, 5, 8, 9, 10, 11, 12

welcome; 7 Children welcome; 8 Tennis nearby; 9 Swimming nearby; 10 Golf nearby; 11 Skiing nearby; 12 May be booked through travel agent

Shannon House B&B

2154 Spring Street, 95501
(707) 443-8130

The Shannon House is an 1891 Victorian that has been lovingly restored by the owners. It features period wallpapers and antiques throughout. The inn is situated on a quiet residential street in Eureka, a town of about 25,000. The town offers a walk through history with its various museums featuring Indian history, logging, working steam engines, and maritime history. Within short distance are miles of trails running through old growth redwood forests and along secluded beaches.

Hosts: David and Barbara Shannon
Rooms: 3 (1PB; 2SB) $55-75 + tax
Full Breakfast
Credit Cards: C, D
Notes: 2, 5, 7, 8, 9, 10, 12

A Weaver's Inn

1440 B Street, 95501
(707) 443-8119

A Weaver's Inn is the home and studio of a fiber artist and her husband. The home is a stately Queen Anne Colonial Revival house built in 1883 and remodeled in 1907. Placed in a spacious fenced garden, it is airy and light, cozy and warm even when veiled by wisps of fog. Arriving early, you might visit the studio, try the spinning wheel before the fire, or weave on the antique loom, before having refreshments. The Victorian parlor offers a piano and elegant relaxing.

Hosts: Bob and Dorothy Swendeman
Rooms: 4 (2PB; 2SB) $60-85
Full Breakfast
Credit Cards: A, B, C, D
Notes: 2, 5, 6, 7, 8, 10, 12

FERNDALE

The Gingerbread Mansion Inn

400 Berding Street, P. O. Box 40, 95536
(707) 786-4000; (800) 952-4136

Exquisitely turreted, carved, and gabled, the Gingerbread Mansion Inn is truly a visual masterpiece. The nine, romantic guest rooms all offer private baths, some with old-fashioned clawfoot tubs and fireplaces (for fireside bubble baths!). Also included is a morning tray service, full breakfast, afternoon tea, turn down service (with bedside chocolates), use of the four antique-filled parlors, and old-fashioned bicycles. All this makes the Gingerbread Mansion Inn the place to stay for pampered relaxation.

Host: Ken Torbert
Rooms: 9 (PB) $125-195
Full Breakfast
Credit Cards: A, B, C
Notes: 2, 5, 10, 12

Grey Whale Inn

FORT BRAGG

Avalon House

561 Stewart St., 95437
(707) 964-5555; (800) 964-5556

A 1905 Craftsman house in a quiet, residential neighborhood, three blocks from the ocean, and two blocks from the Skunk train. Rooms with private baths, fireplaces, whirlpool tubs, down comforters, and ocean views. Enjoy all the romance of the Mendocino Coast, even if you never leave your room. No smoking allowed!

Hostess: Anne Sorrells
Rooms: 6 (PB) $70-135
Full Breakfast
Credit Cards: A, B, C, D
Notes: 2, 5, 7, 8, 10, 12

Glass Beach Bed and Breakfast Inn

726 N. Main St., 95437
(707) 964-6774

We are a gracious guest house offering elegance, relaxation, and the comforts of home. Built in the early 1920s and renovated in 1980. Each room is furnished in its own distinct style. All rooms have private baths with tub/shower combination. We offer our guests one of the best breakfasts in town.

Hosts: Nancy Cardenas and Richard Fowler
Rooms: 9 (PB) $70-125
Full (Prepared to Order) Breakfast
Credit Cards: A, B
Notes: 2, 5, 7, 8, 9, 10, 12

Grey Whale Inn

615 N. Main St., 95437
(707) 964-0640; (800) 382-7244 (Reservations);
(707) 964-4408 (FAX)

Handsome four-story Mendocino Coast Landmark since 1915. Cozy rooms to expansive suites, all have private baths.

Ocean, garden or hill, or town views. Some have fireplaces, TV, one has jacuzzi tub, all have phones. Recreation area: pool table/library, fireside lounge, TV theater. Sixteen-person conference room. Full buffet breakfast features blue-ribbon breads. Friendly, helpful staff. Relaxed seaside charm, situated six blocks to beach. Celebrate your special occasion on the fabled Mendocino Coast!

Hosts: John and Colette Bailey
Rooms: 14 (PB) $85-180
Full Breakfast
Credit Cards: A, B, C, D
Notes: 2, 5, 7, 8, 9, 10, 12

Pudding Creek Inn

700 North Main, 95437
(707) 964-9529; (800) 227-9529; (707) 961-0282 (FAX)

Two lovely 1884 Victorian homes adjoined by a lush garden court offer comfortable and romantic rooms all with private baths. Your stay includes buffet breakfast with fresh fruit, juice, main dish, and tantalizing homemade coffee cakes served hot. Antiques, fireplaces, personalized sightseeing assistance. Near scenic Skunk Train excursion, beaches, dining, shops, galleries, hiking, tennis, and golf. Mention this book for a 15% discount off room rate.

Hosts: Garry and Carole Anloff
Rooms: 10 (PB) $65-125
Full Breakfast
Credit Cards: A, B, C, D
Notes: 2 (by prior arrangement), 5, 7, 8, 9, 10, 12 (10%)

FRESNO

Mary Lou's Bed and Breakfast

5502 W. Escalon Ave., 93722
(209) 277-2650

Mary Lou's B&B in Fresno, CA is just three miles east of Hwy. 99 off the Herndon ramp. Stop on your way to Yosemite or Sequoia National Parks. Twin beds, private bath, guest sitting room, and air-conditioning await your arrival.

Hosts: Mary Lou and Merle Robinson
Rooms; 1 (PB) $50-60
Full Breakfast
Credit Cards: None
Notes: 2, 5, 7, 10

GEORGETOWN

American River Inn

P.O. Box 43, Main at Orleans St., 95634
(916) 333-4499; (800) 245-6566

Innkeepers Will and Maria Collin carry on the century old tradition of graciousness in a setting far removed from the fast pace of modern living. You are invited to cool off in a beautiful mountain pool or relax in the spa. Some may choose a day of bicycling amid the colorful breathtaking daffodils, iris and the brilliant yellow-gold scotch broom. The bicycles are provided. Their historic Queen Anne Inn can provide the ideal setting for your corporate off-site meeting or retreat. All meeting necessities and food catering services are available. The inn can accommodate up to 35/40 participants. Please call for detailed information for your group.

Hosts: Will and Maria Collin
Rooms: 18 (12PB; 6SB) $85-115
Full Breakfast
Credit Cards: A, B, C, D, E, F
Notes: 2, 3, 5, 7, 8, 9, 10, 11, 12

GEYSERVILLE

Campbell Ranch Inn

1475 Canyon Road, 95441
(707) 857-3476; (800) 959-3878

A 35-acre country setting in the heart of the Sonoma wine country offers a spectacular view, beautiful gardens, tennis court, swimming pool, hot tub, and bicycles. We have five spacious rooms with private baths, fresh flowers, fruit, king beds, and balconies. Full breakfast is served on the terrace, and we offer an evening dessert of homemade pie or cake.

Hosts: Mary Jane and Jerry Campbell
Rooms: 5 (PB) $100-165
Full Breakfast
Credit Cards: A, B
Notes: 2, 5, 10, 12

HALF MOON BAY

Old Thyme Inn

779 Main Street, 94019
(415) 726-1616

The Inn has 7 guest rooms, all with private baths. We are a restored 1899 Queen Anne Victorian, located on historic Main Street in the downtown area. Some rooms have fireplaces and double size whirlpool tubs. The theme is our English-style herb garden; all rooms are named after herbs. Atmosphere is friendly and informal. We serve beverages in the evening and a hearty breakfast each morning. Nearby activities

---

NOTES: Credit cards accepted: A Master Card; B Visa; C American Express; D Discover Card; E Diners Club; F Other; 2 Personal checks accepted; 3 Lunch available; 4 Dinner available; 5 Open all year; 6 Pets

include: golf, whale-watching, tidepools, shopping. Many fine restaurants are close-by, some within walking distance.

Hosts: George and Marcia Dempsey
Rooms: 7 (PB) $75-210
Full Breakfast
Credit Cards: A, B
Notes: 2, 5, 7, 8, 9, 10, 12

Old Thyme Inn

HEALDSBURG

Healdsburg Inn on the Plaza

110 Matheson Street, 95448
(707) 433-6991; (800) 431-8663

A quiet place in the center of town where history and hospitality meet. This historic 1900 brick Victorian, once a Wells Fargo Express building, now houses our nine-room bed and breakfast. Rooms done in sunrise/sunset colors feature fireplaces, queen beds, private bathrooms, fluffy towels, and a rubber ducky. Breakfast is served in our sun-filled solarium. Enjoy browsing through our art gallery, antique and gift shops on the first floor.

Host: Genny Jenkins and LeRoy Steck
Rooms: 9 (PB) $115-175 (midweek rates discounted)
Full Breakfast
Credit Cards: A, B
Notes: 2, 5, 8, 9, 10

IDYLLWILD

Wilkum Inn Bed and Breakfast

P.O. Box 1115, 92549
(909) 659-4087; (800) 659-4086

Come home to warm hospitality and personal service in a friendly mountain ambience. The two-story shingle-sided inn is nestled among pines, oaks and cedars. Warm knotty pine interiors and a cozy river rock fireplace are enhanced by the innkeepers' antiques and collectibles. Expanded continental breakfasts of special fruits and breads, such as crepes, Belgian waffles or *abelskivers*, fortify guests for a day of hiking or visiting unique shops and art galleries.

Hosts: Annamae Chambers and Barbara Jones
Rooms: 5 (3PB; 2SB) $65-95
Expanded Continental Breakfast
Credit Cards: None
Notes: 2, 5, 12

IONE

The Heirloom

214 Shakeley Lane, P.O. Box 322, 95640
(209) 274-4468

Travel down a country lane to a spacious, romantic English garden and a petite Colonial mansion built circa 1863. The house features balconies, fireplaces, and heirloom antiques, along with a gourmet breakfast and gracious hospitality. Located in the historic gold country, close to all major northern California cities. The area abounds with an-

welcome; 7 Children welcome; 8 Tennis nearby; 9 Swimming nearby; 10 Golf nearby; 11 Skiing nearby; 12 May be booked through travel agent

tiques, wineries, and historic sites. Within walking distance to a golf course.

Hosts: Melisande Hubbs and Patricia Cross
Rooms: 6 (4PB; 2 SB) $60-92
Full Breakfast
Credit Cards: A, B, C
Closed Thanksgiving and Christmas
Notes: 2, 5, 9, 10, 12

JULIAN

Butterfield Bed and Breakfast

2284 Sunset Drive, Box 1115, 92036
(619) 765-2179; (619) 765-1115 (FAX)

Our cozy five-room inn is located in the historic mountain community of Julian. We pamper our guests with romantic suites and a whimsical Christmas cottage. The garden gazebo provides a beautiful setting for our country gourmet breakfast and afternoon weddings. Terraces with waterfalls and fountains let you relax in the serene setting. Romantic candlelight dinners. Holidays are most special at Butterfield's.

Hosts: Ray and Mary Trimmins
Rooms: 5 (PB) $79-119
Full Breakfast
Credit Cards: A, B
Notes: 2, 4, 5, 7, 8, 10, 12

KLAMATH

Requa Inn

451 Requa Road, 95548
(707) 482-8205; (707) 482-0844 (FAX)

Historical 1914 inn located at the mouth of majestic Klamath River, in the heart of Redwood National Park. Nearby activities include hiking, beaches, birding, whale watching, fishing, and boating. Four rooms with views of the river. Panoramic views from the lobby and dining room. Available for weddings, meetings, and parties. Special rates for large groups or extended stays.

Hosts: Sue Reese and Leo and Melissa Chavez
Rooms: 10 (PB) $70-95
Full Breakfast
Credit Cards: A, B, C, D
Notes: 4, 7

KERNVILLE

Kern River Inn Bed and Breakfast

P.O. Box 1725, 119 Kern River Dr., 93238
(619) 376-6750; (800) 986-4382

A charming, classic country riverfront B&B located on the wild and scenic Kern River in the quaint little town of Kernville within the Sequoia National Forest in the southern Sierra Mountains. We specialize in romantic getaways. All bedrooms have private baths and feature river views; some with whirlpool tubs and fireplaces. Full breakfast. Walk to restaurants, shops, parks, museum. A short drive to giant redwood trees. An all-year vacation area with fishing, skiing, hiking, biking, white-water rafting, Lake Isabella.

Hosts: Jack and Carita Prestwich
Rooms: 6 (PB) $69-89
Full Breakfast
Credit Cards: A, B
Notes: 5, 9, 10, 11

NOTES: Credit cards accepted: A Master Card; B Visa; C American Express; D Discover Card; E Diners Club; F Other; 2 Personal checks accepted; 3 Lunch available; 4 Dinner available; 5 Open all year; 6 Pets

LAGUNA BEACH

Eiler's Inn

741 South Coast Highway, 92651
(714) 494-3004

Twelve rooms with private baths and a courtyard with gurgling fountain and colorful blooming plants are within walking distance of town and most restaurants; half block from the beach.

Hosts: Henk and Annette Wirtz
Rooms: 12 (PB) $100-130
Full Breakfast
Credit Cards: A, B, C
Notes: 2, 5, 8, 9, 10, 12

LAKE ARROWHEAD

Bluebelle House Bed and Breakfast

263 South State Highway 173, P.O. Box 2177, 92352
(714) 336-3292; (800) 429-BLUE-California

The cozy elegance of European decor in an alpine setting welcomes you to Bluebelle House. Guests appreciate immaculate housekeeping, exquisite breakfasts, warm hospitality, and relaxing by the fire or out on the deck. Walk to charming lakeside village, boating, swimming, and restaurants. Private beach club and ice skating are nearby; winter sports 30 minutes away. Ask about discounts!

Hosts: Rick and Lila Peiffer
Rooms: 5 (3PB; 2 SB) $85-120
Full Breakfast
Credit Cards: A, B
Notes: 2, 5, 9, 11

Storybook Inn

28717 Highway 18, P.O. Box 362, Skyforest 92385
(909) 336-1483

An elegant, classic bed and breakfast with nine bedrooms and private baths. All rooms are professionally decorated around the theme of a book with designer linens and abundant pillows. Many have private sitting areas and glass porches; two suites have fireplaces. A separate rustic "Call of the Wild" cabin has a stone fireplace, deck and three bedrooms and two baths. A nightly social hour features an array of hot and cold hors d'oeuvres, refreshments, hot chocolate chip cookies and milk to top off your day. Mornings full breakfast can be served to your room, or eaten on our oval dining table enjoying our spectacular 100-mile alpine view or in fine weather one can breakfast al fresco.

Hosts: Kathleen and John Wooley
Rooms: 9 (PB) $98-185 (cabin is $200)
Full Breakfast
Credit Cards: A, B, C, D
Notes: 2, 3, 5, 7, 8, 9, 10, 11, 12

LODI

Wine and Roses Country Inn

2505 W. Turner Rd., 95242
(209) 334-6988; (209) 334-6570 (FAX)

Nestled in a secluded five-acre setting of towering trees and old-fashioned flower gardens, our inn is a beautiful, charming, and romantic 92-year-old historical estate that has been converted to an elegant country inn with nine guest rooms and a

---

welcome; 7 Children welcome; 8 Tennis nearby; 9 Swimming nearby; 10 Golf nearby; 11 Skiing nearby; 12 May be booked through travel agent

special two-room suite with terrace. Handmade comforters, antiques, collectibles, fresh flowers, library, evening refreshments, delightful breakfasts. Full restaurant featuring "wine country" dining for lunch, dinner, and Sunday brunch. Lake with boating, swimming, fishing, golf, tennis, shopping, museum, zoo within five minutes. Delta Waterways, Old Sacramento Gold Country within 30 minutes.

Hosts: Kris Cromwell, and Del & Sherri Smith
Rooms: 10 (PB) $99-145
Full Gourmet Breakfast
Credit Cards: A, B, C
Notes: 2, 3, 4, 5, 7, 8, 9, 10, 12

LONG BEACH

Lord Mayor's Inn
435 Cedar Avenue, 90802
(310) 436-0324 (voice and FAX)

An award-winning historical landmark, the 1904 home of the first mayor of Long Beach invites you to enjoy the ambience of years gone by. Rooms have 10-foot ceilings and are decorated with period antiques. Each unique bedroom has its private bath and access to a large sundeck. Full breakfast is served in the dining room or deck overlooking the garden. Located near beaches, close by major attractions, within walking distance of convention and civic center and special events held downtown. The right touch for the business and vacation traveler.

Hosts: Laura and Reuben Brasser
Rooms: 5 (PB) $85-105
Full Breakfast
Credit cards: A, B, C
Notes: 2, 5, 7, 9, 10, 12

LOS OSOS

Gerarda's B&B
1056 Bay Oaks Dr., 93402-4006
(805) 534-0834

Gerarda's three-bedroom ranch-style home is comfortably furnished and offers wonderful ocean and mountain views from the elaborate flower gardens in front and back. Gerarda, the hostess, speaks five languages and will welcome you warmly. She cooks a wonderful family-style breakfast. A few miles from state parks, Morro bay, Hearst Castle, San Luis Obispo, universities, and shopping center.

Hostess: Gerarda Ondang
Rooms: 3 (1PB; 2SB) $28-45
Full Breakfast
Credit Cards: None
Notes: 2, 5, 7, 8, 9, 10, 12

MARIPOSA

Finch Haven
4605 Triangle Road, 95338
(209) 966-4738 (voice and FAX)

A quiet country home on nine acres with panoramic mountain views. Birds, deer, and other abundant wildlife. Two rooms, each with private bath and private deck. Queen and twin beds. Nutritious breakfast. In the heart of the California Gold Rush Country near historic attractions. Convenient access to spectacular Yosemite Valley and Yosemite National Park. A restful place to practice Mark 6:31 and to enjoy Christian hospitality.

Hosts: Bruce and Carol Fincham
Rooms: 2 (PB) $75
Continental Plus Breakfast
Credit Cards: None
Notes: 2, 5, 7, 8, 9, 11, 12

Oak Meadows, too Bed and Breakfast

5263 Highway 140 North, P. O. Box 619, 95338
(209) 742-6161; (209) 966-2320 (FAX)

Just a short drive to Yosemite National Park, Oak Meadows, too is located in the historic Gold Rush town of Mariposa. Oak Meadows, too was built with New England architecture and turn-of-the-century charm. A stone fireplace greets you upon arrival in the guest parlor, where a continental-plus breakfast is served each morning. All rooms are furnished with handmade quilts, brass headboards, and charming wallpapers. Central heat and air conditioning.

Hostess: Francie Starchman
Rooms: 6 (PB) $69-89
Expanded Continental Breakfast
Credit Cards: A, B
Notes: 2, 5, 11, 12 (10%)

Winsor Farms Bed and Breakfast

5636 Whitlock Road, 95338
(209) 966-5592

A country home seven miles north of Mari-

posa, just off Highway 140 to Yosemite National Park. This peaceful hilltop retreat among majestic pines and rugged oaks offers two rooms decorated for your comfort and convenience. An extended continental breakfast is served. The town of Mariposa is the Gateway to the Mother Lode Gold Country, with famous Court House, Museums, and History Center. Yosemite National Park, a scenic wonder of the world with waterfalls, granite cliffs, Sequoia Big Trees, birds, and animals.

Hosts: Donald and Janice Haag
Rooms: 2 (SB) $40-50
Extended Continental Breakfast
Credit Cards: None
Notes: 2, 5, 7 (restricted)

MENDOCINO

Antioch Ranch

39451 Comptche Road, 95460
(707) 937-5570; (707) 937-1757 (FAX)

Antioch Ranch—providing a Christian atmosphere of peace; a place for refreshment and renewal. Located just five and a half miles inland from the picturesque town of Mendocino, the Ranch features four guest cottages on twenty acres of rolling hills, redwoods, and apple orchards. Each cottage has its own style and ambiance. Rustic, yet comfortable, they feature woodstoves, complete kitchens with a microwave, two bedrooms, a bath, and open living/dining room.

Hosts: Jerry and Cat Westfall
Rooms: 4 two-bedroom cottages (PB) $55-75
Breakfast on request basis.
Credit Cards: None
Notes: 2, 5, 7, 8, 9 (beach)

welcome; 7 Children welcome; 8 Tennis nearby; 9 Swimming nearby; 10 Golf nearby; 11 Skiing nearby; 12 May be booked through travel agent

Mendocino Village Inn

44860 Main St., Box 626, 95460
(707) 937-0246; (800) 882-7029

An 1882 Queen Anne Victorian with gardens, frog pond, and sun deck. Many rooms with fireplaces and ocean views. Style is eclectic with emphasis on clean, comfortable, and welcoming. We are close to the beach and walking distance to all shops and restaurants.

Hosts: Kathleen and Bill Erwin
Rooms: 13 (11PB; 2SB) $70-175
Full Breakfast
Credit Cards: None
Notes:

MT. SHASTA

Mt. Shasta Ranch B&B

1008 W. A. Barr Road, 96067
(916) 926-3870; (916) 926-6882 (FAX)

The inn is situated in a rural setting with a majestic view of Mt. Shasta and features a main lodge, carriage house, and cottage. Group accommodations are available. Our breakfast room is ideally suited for seminars and retreats with large seating capacity. The game room includes piano, Ping-Pong, pool table, and board games. Guests also enjoy an outdoor jacuzzi. Nearby recreational facilities include alpine and Nordic skiing, fishing, hiking, mountain bike rentals, surrey rides, and museums. Call for pastor's discount.

Hosts: Bill and Mary Larsen
Rooms: 9 (4PB; 5SB) $55-80
Cabin: 1
Full Breakfast
Credit Cards: A, B, C
Notes: 2, 5, 7, 8, 9, 10, 11, 12

NAPA

Arbor Guest House

1436 "G" St., 94559
(707) 252-8144

Antique furnished, gracious 1906 Colonial transition home and carriage house separated by trumpet vine covered arbor. Bask in double in-room spa tubs and before crackling fireplaces in Winter Haven or Autumn Harvest Rooms. Rose's Bower provides an intimate getaway with fireplace. Afternoon refreshments and delicious full breakfast served fireside or in garden by thoughtful hosts/owners. Near wineries, gourmet restaurants, Wine Train, ballooning, golf, and shopping. All private baths and queen beds.

Hosts: Bruce and Rosemary Logan
Rooms: 5 (PB) $85-165
Full Breakfast
Credit Cards: A, B
Notes: 2, 5, 8, 9, 10, 12

Blue Violet Mansion

443 Brown St., 94559
(707) 253-2583; (707) 257-8205 (FAX)

Cross the threshold of this graceful Queen Anne Victorian mansion and return to the elegance of the 1880s. Situated on a quiet street with an acre of private gardens in historic Old Town Napa and walking distance from downtown shops and restaurants. Winner of the prestigious Landmarks Preservation Award of Excellence in 1993, this lovingly restored inn is an intimate and romantic home offering large, cheerful rooms with fireplaces, balconies, and private baths or spas. Guests are encouraged to feel at home in the grand

---

NOTES: Credit cards accepted: A Master Card; B Visa; C American Express; D Discover Card; E Diners Club; F Other; 2 Personal checks accepted; 3 Lunch available; 4 Dinner available; 5 Open all year; 6 Pets

front rooms and enjoy the garden gazebo and grape arbored deck outside. Enjoy an evening of romantic elegance with a private candlelight champagne dinner, in-room massages for two, flowers, and gift service. Picnic lunches. Bicycles for neighborhood riding. Hot air ballooning and golf packages available. Near Wine Train.

Hosts: Bob and Kathy Morris
Rooms: 10 (PB) $115-185 (amenitie extra)
Full Breakfast
Credit Cards: A, B, C
Notes: 2, 4, 5, 7, 8, 9, 10, 12

Hennessey House B&B

1727 Main Street, 94559
(707) 226-3774; (707) 226-2975 (FAX)

Hennessey House, a beautiful Eastlake-style Queen Anne Victorian located in downtown Napa, is listed in the National Register of Historic Places. It features antique furnishings, fireplaces, whirlpools, patios, and a sauna. The dining room, where a sumptuous breakfast is served, features one of the finest examples of a hand-painted stamped tin ceiling in California. Just a short walk to the Wine Train! Golf packages available.

Hostesses: Lauriann and Andrea
Rooms: 10 (PB) $80-155
Full Breakfast
Credit Cards: A, B, C
Notes: 2, 5, 7, 10, 12

La Belle Epoque

1386 Calistoga Avenue, 94559
(707) 257-2161; (800) 238-8070; (707) 226-6314 (FAX)

Elaborate Queen Anne architecture and extensive use of stained glass are comple-

mented by elegant period furnishings. This century-old Victorian boasts six tastefully decorated guest rooms, each with private bath, two with fireplaces. A generous, gourmet breakfast is offered each morning, either by fireside in the formal dining room or in the more relaxed atmosphere of the inn's plant-filled sunroom. Walk to Old Town, Wine Train, Opera House. On-grounds parking and air-conditioned throughout.

Hosts: Merlin and Claudia Wedepohl (owners)
Rooms: 6 (PB) $110-155
Full Gourmet Breakfast
Credit Cards: A, B, C, D
Notes: 2, 5, 8, 9, 10, 12

The Parsonage Bed and Breakfast Inn

NEVADA CITY

The Parsonage Bed and Breakfast Inn

427 Broad St., 95959
(916) 265-9478; (916) 265-8147 (FAX)

History comes alive in this 125-year-old home in Nevada City's Historic District. Cozy guest rooms, parlor, dining and family rooms are all lovingly furnished with the innkeeper's pioneer family antiques. Breakfast is served on the veranda or in the formal dining room.

Hostess: Deborah Dane
Rooms: 6 (PB) $65-115
Extended Continental Breakfast
Credit Cards: A, B
Notes: 2, 5, 7, 9, 11, 12

PACIFIC GROVE

The Martine Inn

155 Oceanview Blvd., 93950
(408) 373-3388; (800) 852-5588 (for reservations)
(408) 373-3896 (FAX)

The Martine Inn is a 13,000 sq. ft. 1890s manor overlooking the rocky coastline at Monterey Bay. Each of our nineteen guest rooms has a private bath, authentic museum quality antiques, fresh fruit, and fresh roses. Watch the waves crash against the rocks. Savor the warmth at your wood-burning fireplace. Delight your tastebuds with breakfast served on old Sheffield, silver, Victorian style china, crystal, and lace.

Host: Don Martine
Rooms: 19 (PB) $125-230
Full Breakfast
Credit Cards: A, B, C
Notes: 2, 5, 8, 9, 10, 12

PALM SPRINGS

Casa Cody Country Inn

175 South Cahuilla Road, 92262
(619) 320-9346; (619) 325-8610 (FAX)

A romantic, historic hideaway is nestled against the spectacular San Jacinto mountains in the heart of Palm Springs Village. Completely redecorated in Santa Fe decor, it has 17 ground-level units consisting of hotel rooms, studio suites, and one- and two-bedroom suites with private patios, fireplaces, and fully equipped, tiled kitchens. Cable TV and private phones; two pools; secluded, tree-shaded whirlpool spa.

Hosts: Therese Hayes and Frank Tysen
Rooms: 17 (PB) $45 summer-$175 (suite) winter
Continental Breakfast
Credit Cards: A, B, C
Notes: 2, 5, 6 (limited), 7 (limited), 8, 9, 10, 11

PALO ALTO

Adella Villa

P.O. Box 4528, 94309-4528
(415) 321-5195; (415) 325-5121 (FAX)

Luxurious 20s Italian villa on one acre of

Adella Villa

NOTES: Credit cards accepted: A Master Card; B Visa; C American Express; D Discover Card; E Diners Club; F Other; 2 Personal checks accepted; 3 Lunch available; 4 Dinner available; 5 Open all year; 6 Pets

lovely manicured gardens with pool, fountains, antiques and music room featuring Steinway grand piano. Four-thousand-square-foot inn with all the amenities! Pamper yourself in one of our jacuzzi tubs. Enjoy a full breakfast. Refreshments available throughout the day. Thirty minutes from San Francisco.

Hostess: Tricia Young
Rooms: 5 (PB) $99-110
Full Breakfast
Credit Cards: A, B, C, E
Notes: 2, 5, 8, 10, 12

PLACERVILLE

Combellack-Blair House

3059 Cedar Ravine, 95667
(916) 622-3764

This gracious Queen Anne Victorian home has stood as a landmark to travelers and Placerville alike for nearly a century. When you enter the front door you will enjoy the magnificent sight of the spiral staircase, which is a work of art. The front parlor is a collection of period furnishings recalling the 1890s. The house is located in quaint and historical Placerville. One block away is Main Street with many interesting antique shops, restaurants, and specialty boutiques.

Hosts: Al and Rosalie McConnell
Rooms: 3 (PB) $89-99
Full Breakfast
Credit Cards: A, B
Notes: 5, 10, 11

River Rock Inn

1756 Georgetown Drive, 95661
(916) 622-7640

Innkeeper Dorothy Irvin welcomes you to the gold country's River Rock Inn. Its comfortable rooms tastefully furnished with antiques. Relax on the spacious deck with uninterrupted view of the river. The large living room encourages you to relax with TV, conversation or listening to the sounds of the river. Gold Mine tours, Marshall State Park, fishing, hiking, whitewater rafting are all available nearby. Hot tub on premises to relax in after activities.

Hostess: Dorothy Irvin
Rooms: 4 (2PB; 2(half baths)) $80-100
Full Breakfast
Credit Cards: None
Notes: 2, 7, 8, 10, 11, 12

POINT REYES STATION

Carriage House Bed and Breakfast

325 Mesa Road, P.O. Box 1239, 94956
(415) 663-8627; (415) 663-8431 (FAX)

Adjacent to the Point Reyes National Seashore, one hour north of San Francisco. Built in the 1920s and recently remodeled into two peaceful spacious suites. Bedrooms have queen beds, living room with fireplaces, queen sleeping couch, single daybed, and antiques. Full baths, complete kitchens, TV, outdoor BBQs. Families welcome, childcare available with advance notice. Over 100 miles of nearby trails for hiking, bicycling, horseback riding, bird watching, beach combing and whale-watching. Suite can accommodate five.

Hostess: Felicity Kirsch
Rooms: 2 (PB) $110-130
Choice of Continental or Full Breakfast
Credit Cards: None
Notes: 2, 5, 7, 9, 10, 12 (10%)

welcome; 7 Children welcome; 8 Tennis nearby; 9 Swimming nearby; 10 Golf nearby; 11 Skiing nearby; 12 May be booked through travel agent

The Tree House Bed and Breakfast

P.O. Box 1075, 94956
(415) 663-8720 (voice and FAX)

Secluded on the Inverness Ridge with a breathtaking view of Point Reyes Station that looks like a postcard picture and changes color with every season. This is a bird watchers paradise all year round, or enjoy whale watching from December through April. Studio with fireplace, wet bar, large deck, and direct access to the National Seashore Park. Explore the park with its endless hiking trails almost at your doorstep, or horseback riding from the stable nearby.

Hostess: Lisa P. Patsel
Rooms: 3 (PB) $90-110
Full Breakfast
Credit Cards: A, B, C
Notes: 2, 5, 6, 7, 8, 12

REDONDO BEACH

Breeze Inn

122 South Juanita Ave., 90277-3435
(310) 316-5123

Located in a quiet modest neighborhood. Large suite with private entrance, private bath with spa, antiques, Oriental carpet, California king bed, and breakfast area with microwave and toaster oven, and stocked refrigerator for continental breakfast. Good ventilation with skylight and ceiling fan. Outside patio. One room also available with twin beds and private bath. A brochure is available with map. Near Los Angeles, Disneyland, Universal City, and approx.

five blocks to pier and beach.

Hosts: Morris and Betty Binding
Rooms: 2 (PB)
Continental Breakfast (extra charge for full)
Credit Cards: None
Notes: 2, 5, 7 (over 5), 8, 9, 10

Ocean Breeze Bed and Breakfast

122 S. Juanita Ave., 90277
(310) 316-5123

Norris and Betty welcome you to a luxurious and comfortable stay. Our amenities include a refrigerator, microwave, breakfast corner, and king or twin beds. Rooms have good sleeping areas that are quiet and well-ventilated. A separate entrance and TV with remote control are available. Ask Norris about his antique collection. We are five blocks from the beach with 21 miles of bike path. Near Los Angeles, Hollywood, and Disneyland. Minimum of two nights stayed and rates vary depending on number of total nights stayed. Weekly rates and senior discounts available.

Hosts: Norris and Betty Binding
Rooms: 2 (PB) $45-65 (two nights minimum)
Continental Breakfast (extra charge for full)
Credit Cards: None
Notes: 2, 5, 7 (over five), 8, 10, 11

ST. HELENA

Bartels Ranch and Country Inn

1200 Conn Valley Road, 94574
(707) 963-4001; (707) 963-5100 (FAX)

"Heaven in the Hills." Situated in the heart

NOTES: Credit cards accepted: A MasterCard; B Visa; C American Express; D Discover Card; E Diners Club; F Other; 2 Personal checks accepted; 3 Lunch available; 4 Dinner available; 5 Open all year; 6 Pets

of the world-famous Napa Valley wine country is this secluded, romantic, elegant country estate overlooking a "100-acre valley with a 10,000-acre view." Honeymoon "Heart of the Valley" suite has sunken jacuzzi, sauna, shower, stone fireplace, and private deck with vineyard view. Romantic, award-winning accommodations, expansive entertainment room, poolside lounging, personalized itineraries, afternoon refreshments, pool table, fireplace, library and terraces overlooking the vineyard. Bicycle to nearby wineries, lake, golf, tennis, fishing, boating, mineral spas, and bird watching. Come dream awhile!

Hostess: Jami Bartels
Rooms: 4 (PB) $99-275
Expanded Continental Breakfast
Credit Cards: A, B, C, D
Notes: 2, 3, 4, 5, 8, 9, 10, 12

Cinnamon Bear Bed and Breakfast

Cinnamon Bear Bed and Breakfast

1407 Kearney Street, 94574
(707) 963-4653

Cinnamon Bear is furnished in the style of the 1920s with many fine antiques. Gleaming hardwood floors and Oriental carpets add to its unique elegance. Relax in front of the fireplace in the living room, or watch the world go by on the spacious front porch. Puzzles, games, and books are available in the parlor for your enjoyment, or peruse a selection of local menus.

Hostess: Genny Jenkins and LeRoy Steck
Rooms: 4 (PB) $135-155 (midweek discount rates)
Full Breakfast
Credit Cards: A, B
Notes: 2, 5, 8, 9, 10

SAN FRANCISCO

Amsterdam Hotel

749 Taylor Street, 94108
(415) 673-3277; (800) 637-3444;
(415) 673-0453 (FAX)

Originally built in 1909, the hotel reflects the charm of a small European hotel. It is situated on Nob Hill, just two blocks from the cable car.

Hostess: Orisa
Rooms: 31 (26PB; 5SB) $49-89
Continental Breakfast
Credit Cards: A, B, C
Notes: 5, 7, 8, 9, 10, 12

Casa Arquello

225 Arguello Blvd., 94118
(415) 752-9482

Comfortable rooms in this cheerful, elegant flat are only 15 minutes from the center of town in a desirable residential neighborhood convenient to Golden Gate Park, the Presidio, Golden Gate Bridge, restaurants, and shops. Public transportation is at the corner.

Hostess: Emma Baires and Marina McKenzie
Rooms: 5 (2PB; 3SB) $55-72
Continental Breakfast
Credit Cards: None
Notes: 2, 5, 7, 8, 9, 10

welcome; 7 Children welcome; 8 Tennis nearby; 9 Swimming nearby; 10 Golf nearby; 11 Skiing nearby; 12 May be booked through travel agent

The Grove Inn

890 Grove St., 94117
(415) 929-0780; (415) 929-1037 (FAX)

The Grove Inn is part of a historic Victorian setting: The Alamo Square. Centrally located, The Grove Inn is within reach of the Golden Gate Park, symphony, opera, and the Museum for Modern Arts. It is reasonably priced and managed by experienced innkeepers. This is the eleventh season for The Grove Inn.

Hosts: Klaus and Rosetta Zimmerman
Rooms: 20 (14PB; 6SB)) $65-85
Continental Breakfast
Credit Cards: A, B, C
Notes: 5, 7, 8, 10, 12

The Grove Inn

The Inn at Union Square

440 Post Street, 94102
(415) 392-3510; (415) 989-0529 (FAX)

An elegant, small European-style hotel in the heart of the financial, theater, and shopping districts. Each floor has an intimate lobby and fireplace where guests wake to enjoy complimentary continental breakfast, relax with afternoon tea, and evening wine and hors d' oeuvres. Rooms are individually decorated with beautiful fabrics, and comfortable Georgian furniture. Terrycloth robes are provided. Pent-

house accommodations include a cozy sauna, whirlpool bath, fireplace, and wet bar. Personalized service and attention to detail.

Host: Mr. Brooks Bayly
Rooms: 30 (PB) $120-300
Expanded Continental Breakfast
Credit Cards: A, B, C, E, F (JCB)
Notes: 2, 5, 7, 12

The Monte Cristo

600 Presidio Avenue, 94115
(415) 931-1875; (415) 931-6005 (FAX)

The Monte Cristo has been a part of San Francisco since 1875, located two blocks from the elegantly restored Victorian shops, restaurants, and antique stores on Sacramento Street. There is convenient transportation to downtown San Francisco and to the financial district. Each room is elegantly furnished with authentic period pieces.

Host: George Yuan
Rooms: 14 (11PB; 3 SB) $63-108
Full Buffet Breakfast
Credit Cards: A, B, C, D, E
Notes: 5, 7, 12

The Washington Square Inn

1660 Stockton St., 94133
(415) 981-4220; (800) 388-0220; (415) 397-7242 (FAX)

The Washington Square Inn offers the charm and hospitality of a country inn, one block from Telegraph Hill, in the heart of San Francisco's historic North Beach area. It is a special hotel for those who care about quiet and comfort with liberal dashes of elegance. Each of our rooms has been decorated and individually furnished with English and French antiques by San Francisco designer, Nan Rosenblatt. For the vacationing visitor, the Washington Square Inn is the essence of San Francisco. For those in the city on business, we offer every convience plus a pleasant change from the ordinary.

Host: Mr. Brooks Bayly-General Manager
Rooms: 15 (10PB; 5SB)) $85-180
Expanded Continental Breakfast
Credit Cards: A, B, C, E
Notes: 2, 5, 7 12 (10%)

SAN GREGORIO

Rancho San Gregorio

Route 1, Box 54, 94074 (Hwy. 84)
(415) 747-0810; (415) 747-0184 (FAX)

Five miles inland from the Pacific Ocean is an idyllic rural valley where Rancho San Gregorio welcomes travelers to share relaxed hospitality. Picnic, hike, or bike in wooded parks or on ocean beaches. Our country breakfast features local specialties. Located 45 minutes from San Francisco, Santa Cruz, and the Bay area.

Hosts: Bud and Lee Raynor
Rooms: 4 (PB) $70-145
Full Breakfast
Credit Cards: A, B, C
Notes: 2, 5, 7, 10

SANTA BARBARA

Long's Sea View B&B

317 Piedmont Road, 93105
(805) 687-2947

This ranch-style home overlooking Santa Barbara has views of the ocean and Chan-nel Islands. The guest room with private entrance is furnished with antiques and king bed. A huge patio and gardens are available. Near all attractions, beach, and Solvang. Your friendly host will be happy to provide you with maps and information about the area.

Host: LaVerne Long
Room: 1 (PB) $75-79
Full Breakfast
Credit Cards: None
Notes: 2, 8, 9, 10

Montecito Bed and Breakfast

167 Olive Mill Rd., 93108
(805) 969-7992

Enjoy a spacious room with private bath, private entrance, TV, phone, desk, and eating area. Patio jacuzzi is available for your use. Includes homemade continental breakfast and coffee. Room has garden atmosphere and looks out on a vista of trees and mountains. Located close to Westmont College and just above coastal village shopping and restaurants. Approx. one-half mile to the beach.

Hostess: Linda Ryan
Rooms: 1 (PB) $50-60
Continentall Breakfast
Credit Cards: None
Notes: 2, 5, 7, 8, 9, 10, 12

The Old Yacht Club Inn

431 Corona Del Mar Drive, 93103
(805) 962-1277; (800) 549-1676 California;
(800) 676-1676 U.S.A. (reservations only);
(805) 962-3989 (FAX)

The inn at the beach! These 1912 California Craftsman and 1925 early California-

welcome; 7 Children welcome; 8 Tennis nearby; 9 Swimming nearby; 10 Golf nearby; 11 Skiing nearby; 12 May be booked through travel agent

style homes house nine individually decorated guest rooms furnished with antiques. Bicycles, beach chairs, and towels are included, and an evening social hour is provided. Gourmet dinner is available on Saturdays.

Hostesses: Nancy, Sandy, and Lu
Rooms: 9 (PB) $90-160
Full Breakfast
Credit Cards: A, B, C, D, E
Notes: 2, 3 (picnic), 4 (Saturdays), 5, 7, 8, 9, 10, 12

The Parsonage

1600 Olive St., 93101
(805) 962-9336

A unique and memorable visit awaits the visitor in the city's most notable Victorian home, built in 1892. Featured in this authentically restored minister's home are spacious rooms, all with private baths and an elegant three-room honeymoon suite, with panoramic ocean and mountain views. Full breakfast. Walking distance to parks, mission, restaurants, and shopping.

Hosts: Hilde Michelmore and Jane Faire
Rooms: 6 (PB) $95-140; suite $185
Full Breakfast
Credit Cards: A, B, C
Notes: 2, 5, 7(over 12), 8, 9, 10, 12

The Parsonage

SAN LUIS O BISPO

Garden Street Inn

1212 Garden Street, 93401
(805) 545-9802

The grace and simplicity of yesteryear prevail at the 1887 Italianate Queen Anne home situated one block from a 1772 mission and the old-fashioned downtown in one of the nation's celebrated California communities. Classic Victorian decor in nine guest rooms and four suites appointed with antiques, fireplaces, jacuzzis, and historical, cultural, and personal memorabilia. Homemade full breakfast, spacious outside decks, and well-stocked library. Close to Hearst Castle, Pismo Beach, Morro Bay, and Cambria.

Hosts: Dan and Kathy Smith
Rooms: 9 and 4 suites (PB) $90-160
Full Breakfast
Credit Cards: A, B, C
Notes: 2, 5, 8, 9, 10, 12

SANTA CRUZ

Babbling Brook Inn

1025 Laurel Street, 95060
(408) 427-2437; (800) 866-1131;
(408) 427-2457 (FAX)

The foundations of the inn date back to the 1790s when padres from the local mission built a grist mill to take advantage of the stream to grind corn. In the 19th century, a water wheel generated power for a tannery. Then a few years later, a rustic log cabin was built, which remains as the heart of the inn. Most of the rooms are chalets in

---

NOTES: Credit cards accepted: A Master Card; B Visa; C American Express; D Discover Card; E Diners Club; F Other; 2 Personal checks accepted; 3 Lunch available; 4 Dinner available; 5 Open all year; 6 Pets

the garden, surrounded by pines and redwoods, cascading waterfalls, and gardens.

Hostess: Helen King
Rooms: 12 (PB) $85-150
Full Breakfast
Credit Cards: A, B, C, D, E
Notes: 2, 5, 8, 9, 10, 12

Chateau Victorian

118 First St., 95060
(408) 458-9458

Chateau Victorian was turned into an elegant B&B with a warm, friendly atmosphere in 1983. Built around 1885, the Inn is only one block from the beach. All seven rooms have a queen-size bed, a private, tiled bathroom, one of which has a clawfoot tub with shower, and a fireplace, with fire logs provided. Each room also has its own heating system, controlled by the guest. Wine and cheese are available for guests in the late afternoon. Chateau Victorian is within walking distance to downtown, the Municpal Wharf, the Boardwalk Amusement Park and fine, as well as casual, dining.

Hostess: Alice June
Rooms: 7 (PB) $110-140 + tax
Expanded Continental Breakfast
Credit Cards: A, B, C
Notes: 2, 5, 8, 9, 10, 12 (no commissions)

SANTA ROSA

Pygmalion House

331 Orange Street, 95407
(707) 526-3407

Pygmalion House, one of Santa Rosa's historical landmarks, is a fine example of Victorian Queen Anne architecture. This charming home was built in the 1880s on land owned by one of the city's leading developers, Mr. Thomas Ludwig. This house withstood the great earthquake and fire of 1906 that devastated much of Santa Rosa's heritage. Pygmalion House is a member of the Bed and Breakfast Innkeepers of Northern California.

Hostess: Lola L. Wright
Rooms: 5 (PB) $60-75
Full Breakfast
Credit Cards: A, B, C
Notes: 2, 5, 8, 9, 10, 12

SEAL BEACH

The Seal Beach Inn and Gardens

212 Fifth Street, 90740
(310) 493-2416; (800) HIDEAWAY;
(310) 779-0483 (FAX)

Just outside Los Angeles and 20 miles from Disneyland, nestled in a charming beachside community is The Seal Beach Inn, French Mediterranean in style. Our Old World inn is surrounded by wrought iron balconies and lush gardens. The rooms vary, but all are furnished with antiques, hand-painted tiles, and lace comforters. Sit by the fireplace in our library, or listen to the fountains. Suites and all the services of a fine hotel are available.

Hosts: Marjorie Bettenhausen and Harty Schmaehl
Rooms: 23 (PB) $118-185
Full Breakfast
Credit Cards: A, B, C, D, E, F
Notes: 3, 4, 5, 8, 9, 10, 12

---

welcome; 7 Children welcome; 8 Tennis nearby; 9 Swimming nearby; 10 Golf nearby; 11 Skiing nearby; 12 May be booked through travel agent

SONOMA

Sparrows' Nest Inn

424 Denmark St., 95476
(707) 996-3750

Sparrow's Nest Inn for a lovely stay away from it all.... A charming private, country cottage with English garden and courtyard in the heart of Sonoma Valley. One mile from the historic town square. Accommodations include fresh flowers, bedroom with Laura Ashley bedding, living room, cable TV/VCR, phone, air-conditioning, bath, and kitchenette. We think all of our guests are special and do our best to make a visit to Sparrows' Nest enjoyable and memorable.

Hosts: Thomas and Kathleen Anderson
Rooms: 1 (single cottage) (PB) $85-105
Both Full and Continental Breakfast available
Credit Cards: A, B, C
Notes: 2, 5, 6 (by special arrangement), 7, 8, 10

SONORA

Lavender Hill Bed and Breakfast Inn

683 S. Barretta, 95370
(209) 532-9024

Come home...to a 1900s Victorian home overlooking the historic gold rush town of Sonora. At sunset you can watch the world form a wraparound porch, and enjoy a country walk through yeararound flower gardens. In the morning, you wake to a home-cooked breakfast and have the opportunity to listen, and share experiences with others, perhaps planning your day to include hiking in Yosemite, fishing,

biking, river rafting, or even a scenic steam train ride. Afternoons and evenings could include a stroll to downtown antiuque shops and boutiques, fine dining, and topped off with your enjoyment of one of the professional repertory theatres. We will be glad to plan a dinner theater package for your stay. Gift certificates also available. One visit will have you longing to return "home"—home to Lavender Hill.

Hosts: Jean and Charlie Marinelli
Rooms: 4 (2PB; 2SB) $70-80
Full Breakfast
Credit Cards: A, B, C
Notes: 2, 5, 7, 8, 9, 10, 11, 12

Blue Spruce Inn

SOQUEL

Blue Spruce Inn

2815 Main St., 95073
(408) 464-1137; (800) 559-1137; (408) 475-0608 (FAX)

Spa tubs, fireplaces, quiet gardens, and original local art foster relaxation for our guests. The Blue Spruce is four miles south of Santa Cruz, one mile inland from Capitola Beach—an ideal location that blends the flavor of yesteryear with the comfort of

---

NOTES: Credit cards accepted: A Master Card; B Visa; C American Express; D Discover Card; E Diners Club; F Other; 2 Personal checks accepted; 3 Lunch available; 4 Dinner available; 5 Open all year; 6 Pets

today. Hike in the redwoods. Bike through country fields. Walk to fine dining. Relax in the outdoor hot tub. Professional, personal attention is our hallmark. Visit us soon!

Hosts: Pat and Tom O'Brien
Rooms: 5 (PB) $80-125
Full Breakfast
Credit Cards: A, B, C
Notes: 2

SUMMERLAND

Inn on Summer Hill

2520 Lillie Ave., 93067
(805) 969-9998 (voice and FAX); (800) 845-5566

America's highest rated B&B awaits you with visually captivating English country decor and world class amenities. Set in the seaside village of Summerland, just five minutes south of Santa Barbara, this California Craftsman-styled award-winning Inn, built in 1989, offers sixteen mini-suites with ocean views, firplaces, jacuzzi tubs, canopy beds, video and cassette players and original art and accessories. Sumptuous full gourmet breakfasts, hor d'oeuvres and desserts add to the uncompromising comfort and charm. Guest rooms provide a directory of local activities along with concierge service and special packages for the discerning traveler in the mood for something out of the ordinary. The Automoblie Club and *Country Inns Magazine* have also rated the Inn one of the "Best in the Country."

Hostess: Verlinda Richardson
Rooms: 16 (PB) $160-275
Full Breakfast
Credit Cards: A, B, C, D
Notes: 3 (picnic only), 5, 8, 9, 10, 12

Inn on Summer Hill

Summerland Inn

2161 Ortega Hill Road, P.O. Box 1209, 93067
(805) 969-5225

Located minutes from beautiful Santa Barbara, this newly built New England-style bed and breakfast is a must for southern California travelers. Enjoy ocean views, fireplace rooms, brass and four-poster beds, country folk art, biblical quotations, and Christian motifs. Christian reading material is available. All rooms include cable TV and free local calls.

Hosts: James Farned and Farah Unwalla
Rooms: 11 (PB) $55-130 (10% discount to
Christian Bed and Breakfast Directory patrons)
Continental Breakfast
Credit Cards: A, B, C, E
Notes: 2, 5, 7, 8, 9, 10

SUTTER CREEK

The Foxes in Sutter Creek

77 Main St., P.O. Box 159, 95685
(209) 267-5882; (209) 267-0712 (FAX)

An award-winning Inn offering seven large, elegant suites with private baths, queen beds, air-conditioning, wood-burning fireplaces, and covered parking. Gourmet breakfast "cooked to order" and brought to your room, or in the garden. Morning newspapers. Downtown location near

welcome; 7 Children welcome; 8 Tennis nearby; 9 Swimming nearby; 10 Golf nearby; 11 Skiing nearby; 12 May be booked through travel agent

antique shops, art galleries, wine tasting, and restaurants. Three-star Mobil rating. Named the "Best" in the Gold Country by authors Don and Betty Martin. Certified members of C.A.B.I.B.B.I.A.C. and C.L.I.A.

Hosts: Pete and Min Fox
Rooms: 7 (PB) $95-135
Full Breakfast (cooked to order)
Credit Cards: A, B, D
Notes: 2, 5 (closed Dec. 24+25), 8, 9, 10, 11(1 1/2 hours), 12

Sutter Creek Inn

75 Main Street, P.O. Box 385, 95685
(209) 267-5606

The inn is known for its fireplaces, hanging beds, and private patios. All rooms have private baths and electric blankets. All guests gather 'round the kitchen fireplace to enjoy a hot breakfast. A large library in the living room invites guests to while away the time before afternoon refreshments.

Hostess: Jane Way
Rooms: 18 (PB) $50-135
Full Breakfast
Credit Cards: None
Notes: 2, 5, 7, 8, 9, 10, 11, 12

TRINIDAD

Trinidad Bay Bed and Breakfast

560 Edwards Street, P. O. Box 849, 95570
(707) 677-0840

Our Cape Cod-style home overlooks beautiful Trinidad Bay and offers spectacular views of the rugged coastline and fishing

harbor below. Two suites, one with fireplace, and two upstairs bedrooms are available. We are surrounded by dozens of beaches, trails, and Redwood National Parks; within walking distance of restaurants and shops. Breakfast delivered to guests staying in suites, while a family-style breakfast is served to guests in rooms.

Hosts: Paul and Carol Kirk
Rooms: 4 (PB) $105-155
Expanded Continental Breakfast
Credit Cards: A, B
Closed December and January for rest and repair
Notes: 2, 8, 10

UKIAH

Vichy Hot Springs Resort and Inn

2605 Vichy Springs Road, 95482
(707) 462-9515

Vichy Springs is a delightful two-hour drive north of San Francisco. Historic cottages and rooms await with delightful vistas from all locations. Vichy Springs features naturally sparkling 90-degree mineral baths, a communal 104-degree pool, and Olympic-size pool, along with 700 private acres with trails and roads for hiking, jogging, picnicking, and mountain bicycling. Vichy's idyllic setting is a quiet, healing environment.

Hosts: Gilbert and Marjorie Ashoff
Rooms: 14 (PB) $125-160
Full Breakfast
Credit Cards: A, B, C, D, E, F
Notes: 2, 5, 7, 8, 9, 10, 12

NOTES: Credit cards accepted: A Master Card; B Visa; C American Express; D Discover Card; E Diners Club; F Other; 2 Personal checks accepted; 3 Lunch available; 4 Dinner available; 5 Open all year; 6 Pets

VENTURA

Bella Maggiore Inn
67 South California St., 93001
(805) 652-0277; (805) 648-2150 (FAX)

An intimate European-style B&B, one
hour north of Los Angeles. Garden courtyard with fountain, lobby with fireplace
and piano. Comfortable rooms and suites
all have fireplaces and spa tubs. Full
breakfast served in our courtyard restaurant, Nona's. Special rates for business
travelers and groups. We are three blocks
from the beach and walking distance to
several fine restaurants.

Host: Thomas J. Wood
Rooms: 24 (PB) $75-150
Full Breakfast
Credit Cards: A, B, C, D, E
Notes: 3, 4, 5, 7, 8, 9, 10, 12

La Mer
411 Poli Street, 93001
(805) 643-3600

Built in 1890, this is a romantic European
getaway in a Victorian Cape Cod home.
A historic landmark nestled on a green
hillside overlooking the spectacular California coastline. The distinctive guest
rooms, all with private entrances, are each
a European adventure, furnished in European antiques to capture the feeling of a
specific country. Bavarian buffet-style
breakfast and complimentary refreshments;
midweek packages; horse carriage rides.
AAA and Mobil approved.

Hostess: Gisela Flender Baida
Rooms: 5 (PB) $80-155
Full Breakfast
Credit Cards: A, B
Notes: 2, 5, 8, 9, 10, 12

DeHaven Valley Farm

WESTPORT

DeHaven Valley Farm
39247 North Highway One, 95488
(707) 961-1660; (707) 961-1677 (FAX)

The 1875 Victorian farmhouse sits amid
twenty acres of meadows and hills, next to
the Pacific Ocean. The cozy parlor offers
a crackling fire, piano, books, games, and
VCR movies. The upstairs deck overlooks the ocean—perfect for reading or
dozing. A hot tub on the hill offers spectacular daytime views and superior evening
stargazing. Entertainment is provided by
the resident goats, donkeys, llamas, sheep,
and cats. Wenesday through Saturday,
the chef prepares delicious four-course
dinners. Mendocino County wines are
featured on the wine list. DeHaven is
convenient to Mendocino village, the Skunk
Train, the Lost Coast, and the giant redwoods of Humboldt County.

Hosts: Jim and Kathleen Tobin
Rooms: 8 (6PB; 2SB) $85-135
Full Breakfast
Credit Cards: A, B, C
Notes: 2, 4, 5, 7

welcome; 7 Children welcome; 8 Tennis nearby; 9 Swimming nearby; 10 Golf nearby; 11 Skiing nearby; 12
May be booked through travel agent

Howard Creek Ranch

P. O. Box 121, 95488
(707) 964-6725 (voice and FAX)

Howard Creek Ranch is a historic 1867 oceanfront farm bordered by miles of beach and mountains in a wilderness area. Flower gardens, antiques, fireplaces, redwoods, a 75-foot swinging foot bridge over Howard Creek, cabins, hot tub, sauna, cold pool, and nearby horseback riding are combined with comfort, hospitality, and good food.

Hosts: Charles and Sally Grigg
Rooms: 10 (8PB; 2SB) $55-145
Full Breakfast
Credit Cards: A, B
Notes: 2, 5, 6 (by arrangement), 7 (by arrangement)

WHITTIER

Coleen's California Casa

P. O. Box 9302, 90608
(310) 699-8427

Come to the top of the hill and find paradise. This home is less than five minutes from the #605 freeway, yet seems rural. The peacefulness is enhanced by the luxuriant patio where you will enjoy a full breakfast prepared by your home economist hostess. Near Disneyland, Knott's Berry Farm, and the beach, you will enjoy a king-size electric adjustable bed or extra long twin beds, private bath, private entrance, off-street parking and a restful stay amid beautiful flowers and plants. The magnificent view of the city will enhance your leisurely enjoyment.

Hostess: Coleen Davis
Rooms: 3 and 2 suites (4PB; 1SB)) $80-95
Full Breakfast
Credit Cards: None
Notes: 2, 3, 4, 5, 7, 8, 9, 10

Howard Creek Ranch

NOTES: Credit cards accepted: A Master Card; B Visa; C American Express; D Discover Card; E Diners Club; F Other; 2 Personal checks accepted; 3 Lunch available; 4 Dinner available; 5 Open all year; 6 Pets

Colorado

B&B Agency of Colorado (located in Vail)

P.O. Box 491, Vail 81658
(303) 949-1212; (800) 748-2666; (303) 949-6870
(FAX—call first)

Come and enjoy the splendor of Colorado summer or winter. We are the only reservation service in Colorado representing over 150 private homestays and inns **statewide**. Each property is personally inspected and approved to ensure the highest quality. From mountain retreats to centrally-located Victorian properties, each one is quite special where warmth and charm abounds. MasterCard and Visa welcomed. Kathy Westerberg, coordinator.

ALLENSPARK

Allenspark Lodge

184 Main, P.O. Box 247, 80510
(303) 747-2552

A classic high mountain bed and breakfast, nestled in a flower-starred village. Comfortable rooms, warm hospitality and magnificent surroundings make our historic, cozy, beautifully remodeled lodge the ideal place for that vacation weekend, recep-

tion, reunion, or retreat. Let the magic begin! Hot tub, continental breakfast, hospitality, and game room, near Rocky Mountain National Park.

Hosts: Mike and Becky Osmun
Rooms: 14 (5PB; 9SB) $45-80
Continental Breakfast
Credit Cards: A, B, D
Notes: 2, 3, 4, 5,8, 9, 10, 11, 12

ASPEN

Little Red Ski Haus

118 East Cooper, 81611
(303) 925-3333; (303) 925-4873 (FAX)

We are a quaint historic lodge that has had only one owner for 32 years. The 104-year-old Victorian house has additional rooms for a total of 21 bedrooms. Christian hosts look forward to welcoming Christian groups to their lodge. Rates vary depending on number of guests and private or shared baths. No smoking.

Hosts: Marge Babcock; Rily and Jeannene Babcock
Rooms: 21 (4PB; 17SB) $52-80
Continental Breakfast in summer-fall
Includes Full Breakfast
Credit Cards: A, B, C
Notes: 7, 8, 9, 10, 11

---

year; 6 Pets welcome; 7 Children welcome; 8 Tennis nearby; 9 Swimming nearby; 10 Golf nearby; 11 Skiing nearby; 12 May be booked through travel agent

BRECKENRIDGE

Allaire Timbers Inn

9511 Hwy. #9, South Main St., P.O. Box 4653, 80424
(303) 453-7530; (800) 624-4904 (out of state);
(303)453-8699 (FAX)

Distinctive Log Inn—named to "Top 10 New Inns of 1993" by Inn Marketing Review. Ten individually decorated guest rooms have private baths and private deck. Romantic suites offer private hot tub and fireplace. The Inn provides gourmet breakfasts, afternoon treats, and spectacular mountain views from on outdoor spa. Close to historic downtown and to ski slopes. Wheelchair accessible.

Hosts: Jack and Kathy Gumph
Rooms: 10 (PB) $115-230
Full Breakfast
Credit Cards: A, B, C, D
Notes: 2, 5, 10, 11, 12

Cotten House B&B

102 S. French St., P.O. Box 387, 80424
(303) 453-5509

Located in the heart of beautiful Breckenridge, the B&B is a restored 1886 Victorian home. Enjoy some of the history of this 130-year-old district photo-essayed on our walls. Three cozy, clean rooms with fresh flowers await you. We serve a full, seven-day menu breakfast, fresh ground coffee, and afternoon refreshments in a friendly atmosphere. Winter activities are available at our front door on the free shuttle bus; nightlife, restaurants, and shopping on Main Street are two blocks away; and the summer sports and special events in our mountain climate are unforgettable. Wildflowers and colorful Aspens fill our spring and fall.

Hosts: Pete and Georgette Contos
Rooms: 3 (1PB; 2SB) $50-90
Continental Breakfast
Credit Cards: None
Notes: 2, 5,7, 8, 9, 10, 11

Cotten House Bed and Breakfast

COLORADO SPRINGS

Holden House—1902 Bed and Breakfast Inn

1102 West Pikes Peak Avenue, 80904
(719) 471-3980

Historic 1902 storybook Victorian and carriage house filled with antiques and family treasures. Guest rooms boast feather pillows, individual decor, period furnishings and queen beds. One disabled access room available. Suites include fireplaces, "tubs for two," and more! Centrally located in residential area near historic Old Colorado City, shopping, restaurants and attractions. "The Romance of the Past with the Comforts of Today." Two friendly resident cats—Muffin and Mingtoy. AAA/Mobil approved. Full gourmet breakfast.

Hosts: Sallie and Welling Clark
Rooms: 6 (PB) $70-105
Full Gourmet Breakfast
Credit Cards: A, B, C, D, E
Notes: 2, 5, 8, 9, 10, 12

NOTES: Credit cards accepted: A Master Card; B Visa; C American Express; D Discover Card; E Diners Club; F Other; 2 Personal checks accepted; 3 Lunch available; 4 Dinner available; 5 Open all

Room at the Inn Bed and Breakfast

618 N. Nevada Ave., 80903
(719) 442-1896

Experience a peek at the past in this recently restored Victorian B&B. Enjoy...the charm of a classic three-story turreted Queen Anne furnished with period antiques...the romance of fireplaces, plush robes, whirlpool tubs for two, and cut flowers...and gracious hospitality featuring full breakfasts, afternoon tea, and turn down service. Conveniently located near downtown, Colorado College, and USOTC. Off street parking, outdoor hot tub, retreat facilities, and much more. Discount for church staff.

Hosts: Jan, Chick, and Kelly McCormick
Rooms: 7 (PB) $80-115
Full Breakfast
Credit Cards: A, B, C, D
Notes: 2, 5, 7(over 12), 8, 12 (Denver)

Room at the Inn Bed and Breakfast

Castle Marne—A Luxury Urban Inn

1572 Race Street, 80206
(303) 331-0621; (303) 331-0723 (FAX)

Chosen by *Country Inns Magazine* as one of the "Top 12 Inns in North America." Come fall under the spell of one of Denver's grandest historic mansions. Your stay at the Castle Marne combines Old World elegance with modern day convenience and comfort. Each guest room is a unique experience in pampered luxury. All rooms have private baths. Afternoon tea and a full gourmet breakfast are served in the cherry-paneled dining room. Castle Marne is a certified Denver Landmark and on the National Register of Historic Structures.

Hosts: The Peiker Family
Rooms: 9 (PB) $85-190
Full Breakfast
Credit Cards: A, B, C, D, E, F
Notes: 2, 3, 4, 5, 8, 9, 10, 11, 12

Queen Anne B&B Inn

2147 Tremont Place, 80205
(303) 296-6666; (800) 432-INNS (except Colorado); (303) 296-2151 (FAX)

Facing quiet Benedict Fountain Park in Downtown Denver are two side-by-side National Register Victorian homes with fourteen guest rooms including four gallery suites. Fresh flowers, chamber music, period antiques, phone, and private baths are in all rooms. Six rooms have special tubs, one a fireplace. The inn is only walking distance to the Capital, 16th St. Pedestrian Mall, Convention Center, and Larimer Square. Among its many awards: Best 12 B&Bs nationally, Ten Most Romantic, Best of Denver, and Best 105 in

year; 6 Pets welcome; 7 Children welcome; 8 Tennis nearby; 9 Swimming nearby; 10 Golf nearby; 11 Skiing nearby; 12 May be booked through travel agent

Great American Cities. Inspected/approved by AAA, Mobil, ABBA, and Distinctive Inns of Colorado.

Host: Tom King
Rooms: 14 (PB) $75-155
Full Breakfast
Credit Cards: A, B, C, D, E
Notes: 2, 5, 8, 9, 10, 11, 12

Queen Anne Bed and Breakfast Inn

DURANGO

Country Sunshine B&B

35130 Highway 550 North, 81301
(303) 247-2853; (800) 383-2853

This spacious ranch home on the Animas River has Ponderosa pines, quilts, and an informal atmosphere. It is a safe place for children and adults. A spacious hot springs spa is available to relax in, and there are plenty of common areas. The friendly hosts are in their sixth season.

Hosts: Jim and Jill Anderson
Rooms: 6 (PB) $65-85
Full Breakfast
Credit Cards: A, B
Notes: 2, 5, 7, 9, 10, 11, 12

Logwood Bed and Breakfast— The Verheyden Inn

35060 U. S. Highway 550, 81301
(303) 259-4396

Built in 1988, this 4800-square-foot red, cedar log home sits on 15 acres amid the beautiful San Juan Mountains and beside the Animas River. Guest rooms are decorated with a southwestern flair. Homemade country quilts adorn the country-made queen-size beds. Private baths in all guest rooms. A large, river rock fireplace warms the elegant living and dining areas in the winter season. Award-winning desserts are served in the evening. Pamper yourselves. Come home to LOGWOOD.

Hosts: Debby and Greg Verheyden
Rooms: 5 (PB) $65-75
Full Breakfast
Credit Cards: A, B
Notes: 2, 5, 7 (over eight), 9, 10, 11, 12

EATON

The Victorian Vernada

515 Cheyenne Avenue, P.O. Box 361, 80615
(303) 454-3890

We want to share with you our beautiful two-story Queen Anne home with a large wraparound porch. It also has a view of the Rocky Mountains which are 45 minutes away. Our guests enjoy the spacious and comfortable rooms, balcony, fireplaces, bicycles-built-for-two, baby grand, player piano, and one room has a private whirl pool bath. We are just 50 minutes from north Denver. A memorable and

---

NOTES: Credit cards accepted: A Master Card; B Visa; C American Express; D Discover Card; E Diners Club; F Other; 2 Personal checks accepted; 3 Lunch available; 4 Dinner available; 5 Open all

elegant stay for a moderate price.

Hostess: Nadine White
Rooms: 3 (1PB; 2SB) $45-60
Full Breakfast
Credit Cards: None
Notes: 2, 5, 7, 8, 9, 10, 11, 12

ESTES PARK

The Quilt House Bed and Breakfast

P.O. Box 399, 80517
(970) 586-0427 (303 area code until April 1995)

We have three bedrooms upstairs for our guests, plus a lounge where guests can read, look at the mountains, and have a cup of coffee or tea. A beautiful mountain view can be enjoyed from every window of this sturdy mountian home, yet it is just a 15-minute walk from downtown Estes Park. We are only four miles from the entrance of Rocky Mountain National Park. The hosts will help with information concerning hiking trails, car drives, wildlife viewing, shopping, etc.

Hosts: Hans and Miriam Graetzer
Rooms: 3 (1PB; 2SB) $50-60
Full Breakfast
Credit Cards: None
Notes: 2, 5, 8, 10

Romantic Riversong

P.O. Box 1910, 80517
(303) 586-4666; (303) 586-6185

Riversong, a nine room mountain inn, is nestled at the end of a winding country lane on 30 wooded acres. There are trout streams and ponds, hiking trials, and porch swings. Many of the rooms have breathtaking views of the snow-capped peaks and the nearby Rocky Mountain National Park; most have fireplaces and spacious whirlpool tubs for two. At Riversong, you'll be lulled to sleep by the melody of our mountain stream.

Hosts: Gary and Sue Mansfield
Rooms: 93 (PB) $95-180
Full Gourmet Breakfast
Credit Cards: A, B
Notes: 2, 4, 5, 11, 12

FAIRPLAY

Hand Hotel B&B

P.O. Box 459, 531 Front St., 80440
(719) 836-3595

The Hand Hotel, built in the 1930s, overlooks the north fork of the South Platte River and Mosquito Range at an elevation of 9,950 feet. The hotel was totally renovated in 1987 to a turn-of-the-century Western/Victorian motif. The South Park area offers excellent hiking, jeeping, fishing, and South Park City Museum in the summer and a Nordic Center in Fairplay or downhill skiing in Breckenridge just 23 miles away. We're on the quiet side of the divide. Come see for yourself and enjoy.

Host: Pat Pocius
Rooms: 11 (PB) $60 (summer) $48 (off-season)
Extended Continental Breakfast
Credit Cards: A, B
Notes: 2, 5, 6 (add $5), 7 (with restrictions), 11

GEORGETOWN

The Hardy House

605 Brownell, P.O. Box 0156, 80444
(303) 569-3388

The Hardy House with its late-19th-century charm invites you to relax in the parlor by the potbellied stove, sleep under feather comforters, and enjoy a candlelight breakfast. Georgetown is only 55 minutes from Denver and the airport. Surrounded by mountains, it boasts unique shopping, wonderful restaurants, and close proximity to seven ski areas.

Hostess: Carla and Mike Wagner
Rooms: 4 (PB) $73-77
Full Breakfast
Credit Cards: A, B
Notes: 2, 5, 7 (over 13), 11, 12

The Hardy House

GREEN MOUNTAIN FALLS

Outlook Lodge Bed and Breakfast

P.O. Box 5, 6975 Howard St., 80819
(719) 684-2303

A quaint lodge nestled at the foot of Pike's Peak. Built in 1889 as the parsonage for the Church of the Wildwood. Features stained-glass windows and hand-carved balustrades. Rooms furnished with brass beds and other antiques. Nearby swimming, hiking, tennis, fishing, horseback riding, restaurants, and shopping. Outlook Lodge provides nostalgia with a relaxing atmosphere.

Hosts: Hayley and Pat Moran
Rooms: 8 (6PB; 2SB) $45-70
Full Breakfast
Credit Cards: A, B
Notes: 2, 5, 8, 9, 10, 12 (October-May)

LEADVILLE

Wood Haven Manor

P.O. Box 1291, 809 Spruce, 80461
(719) 486-0109; (800) 748-2570

Enjoy the taste and style of Victorian Leadville by stepping back 100 years in this beautiful home located on the prestigious "Banker's Row." Each room is distinctively decorated in Victorian style with private bath. One suite with whirlpool tub. Spacious dining room, comfortable living room with fireplace. Historic city with a backdrop of Colorado's highest mountains. Enjoy snowmobiling, biking, hiking and more.

Hostess: Jolene Wood
Rooms: 8 (7PB; 1SB) $60
Full Breakfast
Credit Cards: A, B, C, D
Notes: 2, 5, 7, 8, 9, 10, 11, 12

MANITOU SPRINGS

Historic Ute Pass Motel

1132 Manitou Ave., 80829
(719) 685-5171

Surrounded by Fountain Creek, its location is serene and secluded. Each room is

---

NOTES: Credit cards accepted: A Master Card; B Visa; C American Express; D Discover Card; E Diners Club; F Other; 2 Personal checks accepted; 3 Lunch available; 4 Dinner available; 5 Open all

different and some are connected, making the Ute Pass Motel an ideal location for family reunions. Antique-furnished rooms, color, cable TV, air conditioning, laundry facilities, meeting area, and covered patio/picnic are on Fountain Creek. Many of the units have kitchens, and some offer covered porches, which are great for people-watching. Regardless of how you decide to spend your time, the staff will be more than happy to help you make your plans.

Hostess: Suzie Hawkins
Rooms: 18 (17PB; 2SB)) $44-86
Breakfast not included.
Credit Cards: A, B, C
Notes: 5, 7, 8, 9, 10, 11, 12

NATHROP

Deer Valley Ranch
16825 C.R. 162, 81236
(719) 395-2353; (719) 395-2394 (FAX)

Colorado's Christian family guest ranch welcomes you to the heart of the Rocky Mountains. The hosting ranch family provides the best of western hospitality in a unique Christian atmosphere. In summer, enjoy horseback riding, white water rafting, hiking, tennis, hot springs pools, four-wheel drives, fishing, golf, and evening entertainment. In winter, enjoy snowmobiling and Nordic and alpine skiing. Off-season rates available.

Hosts: Harold L. DeWalt / John P. Woolmington
Rooms: 23 (PB) $95
Full Breakfast
Credit Cards: None
Notes: 2, 3, 4, 5, 7, 8, 9, 10, 11, 12

OURAY

The Damn Yankee Bed and Breakfast
P.O. Box 709, 100 Sixth Avenue, 81427
(303) 325-4219; (800) 845-7512; (303) 325-0502 (FAX)

Relax your body. Ten uniquely appointed rooms await, each with a private bath and entrance. Cabins along the river will be available in 1995. Drift off to the soothing music of a mountain stream from your luxurious queen-size bed. Snuggle under a plush down comforter. Sit back and watch your favorite film on cable television. Drink in the fresh mountain air. Relax in our hot tub. Or, gather around the parlor with friends and sing along to music from a baby grand piano. Feast your senses. You'll receive complimentary fresh fruit upon arrival. Enjoy afternoon snacks in our towering observatory. And savor a hearty, gourmet breakfast, as you watch the sun glint over the mountaintops.

Hosts: Mike Manley and Marj Gibson
Rooms: 10 (PB) $60-145
Full Hearty Gourmet Breakfast
Credit Cards: A, B, C, D
Notes: 2, 5, 8, 9, 10, 11, 12

Ouray 1898 House
322 Main Street, P. O. Box 641, 81427
(303) 325-4871

This 90-year-old house has been completely renovated and combines the elegance of the 19th century with the comfortable amenities of the 20th century. Each room features a TV and a spectacular view of the San Juan Mountains from its deck. Eat a health-conscious, full break-

---

year; 6 Pets welcome; 7 Children welcome; 8 Tennis nearby; 9 Swimming nearby; 10 Golf nearby; 11 Skiing nearby; 12 May be booked through travel agent

fast on antique china. Jeep rides, horse-back riding, and the city's hot spring pool are a few of the local diversions.

Hosts: Lee and Kathy Bates
Rooms: 4 (PB) $58-78
Full Breakfast
Credit Cards: A, B
Notes: 2, 7, 8, 9, 10

PAGOSA SPRINGS

Davidson's Country Inn

P.O. Box 87, 81147
(303) 264-5863

Davidson's Country Inn is a three-story log house located at the foot of the Rocky Mountains on 32 acres. The inn provides a library, a playroom, a game room, and some outdoor activities. A two-bedroom cabin is also available. The inn is tastefully decorated with family heirlooms and antiques, with a warm country touch to make you feel at home. Two miles east of Highway 160.

Host: Silbert Davidson
Rooms: 7 (3PB; 4SB) $48-62
Full Breakfast
Credit Cards: A, B
Notes: 2, 5, 7, 8, 9, 10, 11, 12

Abriendo Inn

PUEBLO

Abriendo Inn

300 West Abriendo Avenue, 81004
(719) 544-2703; (719) 542-6595 (FAX)

Experience the elegance of an estate home as you delight in the pleasure of personal attention and hospitality. Antiques, crocheted bedspreads, and brass and four-poster beds take you to a getaway to yesterday with the conveniences you expect of today. Breakfast is always hearty, home-baked, and served in the oak wainscoted dining room or one of the picturesque porches. Located within walking distance of restaurants, shops, and galleries...all in the heart of Pueblo. The Abriendo Inn is on the National Register of Historic Places.

Hosts: Kerrelyn and Chuck Trent
Rooms: 10 (PB) $54-95
Full Breakfast
Credit Cards: A, B, C, E
Notes: 2, 5, 7 (over 7), 8, 10, 11, 12

SALIDA

Gazebo Country Inn

507 E. 3rd., 81201
(719) 539-7806

A 1901, restored Victorian home with magnificent deck and porch views. Gourmet breakfast and private baths. Located in the heart of the Rockies. White water rafting on the Arkansas River and skiing at the Monarch Mountain Lodge are a few of the amenities. We are committed to your

---

NOTES: Credit cards accepted: A Master Card; B Visa; C American Express; D Discover Card; E Diners Club; F Other; 2 Personal checks accepted; 3 Lunch available; 4 Dinner available; 5 Open all

comfort and relaxation.

Hosts: Don and Bonnie Johannsen
Rooms: 3 (PB) $45-65
Full Breakfast
Credit Cards: A, B
Notes: 2, 5, 8, 9, 10, 11, 12

SILVERTON

Christopher House

P. O. Box 241, 821 Empire Street, 81433
(303) 387-5857 June-September;
(904) 567-7423 October-May

This charming 1894 Victorian home has the original, golden oak woodwork, parlor fireplace, and antiques throughout. All bedrooms offer comfortable mattresses, wall-to-wall carpeting, and a mountain view. Guests are warmly welcomed with mints and fresh wildflowers. A full breakfast is served to Christian and Irish music. Conveniently located only four blocks from the town's narrow-gauge train depot, Old West shops, restaurants, and riding stables. Guest transportation to and from the train depot is available.

Hosts: Howard and Eileen Swonger
Rooms: 4 (1PB; 3SB) $42-52
Full Breakfast
Credit Cards: None
Notes: 2, 7, 8, 10, 12

VAIL

B&B Agency of Colorado

P.O. Box 491, 81658
(303) 949-1212; (800) 748-2666; (303) 949-6870
(FAX—call first)

Come and enjoy the splendor of Colorado

summer or winter. We are the only reservation service in Colorado representing over 150 private homestays and inns statewide. Each property is personally inspected and approved to ensure the highest quality. From mountain retreats to centrally located Victorian properties, each one is quite special where warmth and charm abounds. MasterCard and Visa welcomed. Kathy Westerberg, coordinator.

WESTCLIFFE

Purnell's Rainbow Inn

104 Main Street, 81252
(719) 783-2313

Purnell's Rainbow Inn—comfortable, hospitable western-style inn situated between the magnificent Sangre de Cristos and Wet Mountains in historic Westcliffe. Four bedrooms, uniquely decorated, provide genuine comfort. A great room offers big-screen TV, game table, and books for reading pleasure. Full breakfast features freshly baked muffins, special entrees, and seasonal fruits. Mountain bike rentals, hiking supplies and maps, fishing information, and cross-country skiing opportunities are readily available for a memorable Wet Mountain Valley experience.

Hosts: David and Karen Purnell
Rooms: 4 (2PB; 2SB) $50-60
Full Breakfast
Credit Cards: A, B
Notes: 2, 5, 7, 9, 10, 11, 12

---

year; 6 Pets welcome; 7 Children welcome; 8 Tennis nearby; 9 Swimming nearby; 10 Golf nearby; 11 Skiing nearby; 12 May be booked through travel agent

Connecticut

Bed and Breakfast, Ltd.

P.O. Box 216, New Haven, CT 06513
(203) 469-3260

Bed and Breakfast, Ltd. offers over 125 accommodations throughout **Connecticut, Massachusetts,** and **Rhode Island**—from elegantly simple to simply elegant. We offer incredible variety, both in home styles and in price ranges. A quick call assures accurate descriptions and availability. (Host homes nationwide are invited to join our growing network.)

Director: Jack M. Argenio
Rooms: 125+ (60PB; 65SB) $50-125
Credit Cards: (at some) A, B, C
Notes: 2 (at some), 5, 7 (at some), 8, 9, 10, 11

BRISTOL

Chimney Crest Manor

5 Founders Drive, 06010
(203) 582-4219

Experience quiet elegance in this splendid 32-room Tudor mansion. Chimney Crest is listed on the National Historical Register and located in the Federal Hill historic district. Minutes away from Litchfield Hills, guests will find antiques, wineries, parks, art galleries, museums, and restaurants. Stay in the spacious suites for pleasure or on business. Guest are treated with warm attentive hospitality set in the splendor and style of a bygone era. Mobile Travel Guide three-star rating.

Hosts: Dante and Cynthia Cimadamore
Rooms: 11 and 4 suites (PB) $75-135
Full Breakfast
Credit Cards: A, B, C
Notes: 5, 7, 8, 9, 10, 11, 12

Chimney Crest Manor

CLINTON

Captain Dibbell House

21 Commerce Street, 06413
(203) 669-1646

Our 1886 Victorian, just two blocks from the shore, features a wisteria-covered, century-old footbridge and gazebo on our half-acre of lawn and gardens. Spacious living room and bedrooms are comfortably furnished with antiques and family heirlooms, fresh flowers, fruit baskets, home-baked treats. There are bicycles,

---

NOTES: Credit cards accepted: A Master Card; B Visa; C American Express; D Discover Card; E Diners Club; F Other; 2 Personal checks accepted; 3 Lunch available; 4 Dinner available; 5 Open all

nearby beaches, and marinas to enjoy.

Hosts: Helen and Ellis Adams
Rooms: 4 (PB) $75-95
Full Breakfast
Credit Cards: A, B, C, D
Notes: 2, 8, 9, 10, 12

CORNWALL BRIDGE

Cornwall Inn
Route 7, 06754
(800) 786-6884

The Cornwall Inn is a charming country inn dating back to 1810. Rooms are decorated with antiques and king- or queen-size beds. Enjoy country dining in a home atmosphere. Outdoor pool for summer enjoyment. The Inn is located in the northwest corner of Connecticut with the Housatonic River nearby for fly fishing, canoeing, and tubing. Hiking, biking, antiquing, skiing, auto racing, and foliage bring many travelers.

Rooms: 12 (10PB; 2SB) $50-115
Full Breakfast
Credit Cards: A, B, C, D
Notes: 2, 3, 4, 5, 6, 7, 9, 10, 11, 12

ESSEX

The Griswold Inn
36 Main Street, 06426
(203) 767-1776; (203) 767-0481 (FAX)

More than a country hotel. More than a comfortable bed, an extraordinary meal. . . The "Gris" is what Essex is all about. It embodies a spirit understood perhaps only as one warms up to its potbelly stove or is hypnotized by the magic of a crackling log in one of its many fireplaces. It is a kaleidoscope of nostalgic images: A lovely country place. An historic collection of Antonio Jacobsen marine art. A gentle smile and a helping hand from a waitress. A cuisine unmatched for its genuineness and purity.

Hosts: Vicky and William Winterer
Rooms: 25(PB) $90-175
Continental Breakfast
Credit Cards: A, B, C
Notes: None

GLASTONBURY

Butternut Farm
1654 Main Street, 06033
(203) 633-7197 (voice and FAX)

This 18th-century architectural jewel is furnished in period antiques. Prize-winning dairy goats, pigeons, and chickens roam in an estate setting with trees and herb gardens. The farm is located ten minutes from Hartford by expressway; one and one-half hours to any place in Connecticut.

Host: Don Reid
Rooms: 3 (PB); Suite (PB); Apartment PB) $65-85
Full Breakfast
Credit Cards: C
Notes: 2, 5, 7, 8, 9, 10, 11, 12

MIDDLEBURY

Tucker Hill Inn
96 Tucker Hill Road, 06762
(203) 758-8334; (203) 598-6052 (FAX)

A gracious New England Colonial home, Tucker Hill is situated on lovely grounds and lightly shaded by ancient oaks and maples. The setting suggests rural life, yet the location is convenient to downtown

year; 6 Pets welcome; 7 Children welcome; 8 Tennis nearby; 9 Swimming nearby; 10 Golf nearby; 11 Skiing nearby; 12 May be booked through travel agent

business and shopping. Originally opened as a Tea Room in 1923, the Inn was a busy trolley stop on the line from Waterbury. Sometime later, it became Lift the Latch Inn and was operated as a restaurant and catering business for forty years. This was a favorite place for brides, well over 900 weddings have taken place here.

Hosts: Susan and Richard Cebelenski
Rooms: 4 (2PB; 2SB) $60-90
Full Breakfast
Credit Cards: A, B, C
Notes: 2, 5, 7, 8, 9, 10, 11, 12

MYSTIC

Harbour Inne and Cottage

Edgemont Street, 06355
(203) 572-9253

Harbour Inn and Cottage is located in downtown Mystic, overlooking the Mystic River and only one mile from Seaport and two miles from the Mystic aquarium. The Inne has several rooms each containing a double-size bed, color cable TV, air-conditioning, fireplace, and a private bathroom. The Inne also has a kitchen that is open to all guests, and a common room with a fireplace. The cottage can sleep up to six people. It has a bedroom with two beds, and a fireplace. There is also a sofabed in the kitchen/living room for two more people. The cottage also has a private bath and its own parking. Hot tub spa on deck of cottage. Pets welcome.

Host: Charles Lecouras, Jr.
Rooms: 6 (PB) $45-95; Cottage (PB) $125-200
No meals provided, but guests have kitchen privileges.
Credit Cards: None
Notes: 5, 6, 7, 8, 9, 10

Steamboat Inn

73 Steamboat Wharf, 06355
(203) 536-8300; (800) 364-6100; (203) 572-1250 (FAX)

"Intimate and elegant," all of our rooms are directly on the Mystic River in the heart of downtown Mystic's historic district. Most rooms have fireplaces; all have whirlpool baths, TVs, telephones, and individual AC and heat. Visitors to Mystic usually visit the Seaport Museum, Mystic Aquarium, and Old Mystic Village. There's lots to do.

Hostess: Kitty Saletnik
Rooms: 10 (PB) $95-250
Continental Breakfast
Credit Cards: A, B, C
Notes: 2, 5, 8, 9, 10, 12

The Palmer Inn

MYSTIC/NOANK

The Palmer Inn

25 Church St., Noank, 06340
(203) 572-9000

The Palmer Inn is an elegant seaside mansion in the historic fishing village of Noank, one block from the water and two miles to downtown Mystic. The Inn is within walking distance of tennis, sailing, art galleries, swimming, and a fine lobster house. This 1907 Inn is all decorated in antiques with

BLACKBERRY RIVER INN

original wallcoverings and stained-glass windows. Offering gracious lodging and personalized service year round. No smoking.

Hostess: Patrica Ann White
Rooms: 6 (PB) $115-195
Continental Breakfast
Credit Cards: A, B, C
Notes: 2 (in advance), 5, 8, 9, 10

NEW HAVEN—SEE BED AND BREAKFAST, LTD. (PAGE 66)

NORFOLK

Blackberry River Inn
Route 44, 06058
(203) 542-5100; (203) 542-1818 (FAX)

Three white Williamsburg buildings, situated on 27 scenic, rural acres, nestled in the Berkshires. Built in 1763, this 231-year-old Colonial Inn is on the National Register of Historical Places, and offers twenty charming rooms. Nearby hiking, riding, tennis, fishing, lakes for swimming and boating, rivers for rafting, skiing, Tanglewood and Norfolk music festivals, and sleigh and carriage rides.

Hostess: Jeanette Angel
Rooms: 20 (12-14PB; 8-9SB) $75-150
Generous Continental Breakfast
Credit Cards: A, B, C
Notes: 5, 7, 8, 9, 11, 12

Greenwoods Gate Inn
105 Greenwoods Rd. E., 06058
(203) 542-5439

Warm hospitality greets you in this beautifully restored 1797 Colonial home. Small and elegant with four exquisitely appointed guest suites—each with private bath (one with jacuzzi). Fine antiques, fireplaces, and sumptuous breakfasts to indulge you. Yankee Magazine, calls this "New England's most romantic Bed and Breakfast." Country Inns Bed & Breakfast Magazine: "A Connecticut Jewel." New for 1994! Deanne Raymond's reowned Romantic Cooking Classes. Call for details.

Hosts: George and Marian Schuwaker
Rooms: 4 suites (PB) $150-215
Gourmet Breakfast (afternoon tea and refreshments before going out to dinner)
Credit Cards: None
Notes: 2, 5, 7 (over 12), 8, 9, 10, 11, 12

year; 6 Pets welcome; 7 Children welcome; 8 Tennis nearby; 9 Swimming nearby; 10 Golf nearby; 11 Skiing nearby; 12 May be booked through travel agent

NORTH STONINGTON

Antiques and Accommodations

32 Main Street, 06359
(203) 535-1736; (800) 554-7829

Stroll through our well-tended gardens filled with edible flowers and herbs. Relax on our porches and patios. Our country retreat is located 2.5 miles from I-95, minutes from Mystic Seaport, Aquarium, and superb beaches. Gracious hospitality awaits you at our lovingly restored homes: antiques, canopy beds, fireplace, private baths, air conditioned rooms, cable TV. Greet the day with our acclaimed four-course candlelight breakfast. Always an abundance of fresh flowers. We welcome children who appreciate antiques.

Hosts: Thomas and Ann Gray
Rooms: 3 and 2 cottages (PB) $95-195
Full Breakfast
Credit Cards: A, B
Notes: 2, 5, 7, 8, 9, 10, 12

OLD LYME

Old Lyme Inn

85 Lyme Street, 06371
(203) 434-2600; (203) 434-5352 (FAX)

This 1850s Victorian country inn has 13 guest rooms all with private baths, telephones, TVs, air-conditioning, and a complimentary country, continental breakfast. Located in the historic district of this art colony, The Old Lyme Inn is known nationally and internationally for its romantic setting and outstanding food. Near Mystic, Essex, and the Connecticut shoreline.

Hostess and owner: Diana Field Atwood
Rooms: 13 (PB) $98-144 +tax
Country Continental Breakfast
Credit Cards: A, B, C, D, E
Notes: 2, 3, 4, 5 (closed first two weeks of Jan.), 6, 7, 8, 9, 10, 12

OLD MYSTIC

Red Brook Inn

P. O. Box 237, 2750 Gold Star Hwy., 06372
(203) 572-0349

Nestled on seven acres of old New England wooded countryside, bed and breakfast lodging is provided in two historic buildings: the Haley Tavern, circa 1740, is a restored center-chimney colonial tavern. The Crary Homestead, circa 1770, is a Colonial built by sea captain Nathaniel Crary. Each room is appointed with period furnishings, including canopy beds, and there are many working fireplaces throughout the inn. A hearty breakfast is served family style in the ancient keeping room. Enjoy a quiet, colonial atmosphere near Mystic Seaport Museum, antique shops, and Aquarium. Colonial dinner weekends are also available November and December. No smoking.

Hostess: Ruth Keyes
Rooms: 9 (PB) $119-189
Full Breakfast
Credit Cards: A, B
Notes: 2, 5, 7, 8

NOTES: Credit cards accepted: A Master Card; B Visa; C American Express; D Discover Card; E Diners Club; F Other; 2 Personal checks accepted; 3 Lunch available; 4 Dinner available; 5 Open all

SIMSBURY

Simsbury 1820 House

731 Hopmeadow Street, 06070
(203) 658-7658; (203) 651-0724 (FAX)

Located in the heart of Connecticut's beautiful Farmington River Valley, a graciously restored country manor overlooks the center of historic Simsbury. The inn retains the integrity of its original design while offering accomodations with modern amenities and personal service. Thirty-four unique sleeping rooms are decorated with fabric, wall hangings, and reproductions reminiscent of the 18th and 19th centuries. Local, regional, and national publications consistently award rave reviews to the restaurant at the Simsbury 1820 House. The peaceful location offers country living with easy access to metropolitan museums, concert halls, professional theatre, sports events, and shopping. Excellent facilities for business meetings, banquets, and weddings.

Host: Wayne Bursey
Rooms: 34 (PB) $85-135
Continental Breakfast
Credit Cards: A, B, C, D, E
Notes: 2, 3, 4, 5, 6, 7, 8, 9, 10, 11, 12

THOMPSON

A Taste of Ireland

47 Quaddick Road, 06277
(203) 923-2883

Charming country cottage c. 1780 on National Historic Registry. Fireplaced sitting room. Home library of Irish literature and Celtic music. Hosts well-versed in assisting guests in geneology research and travel planning to "the old sod." Authentic imported foods and beverages complete the full breakfast served in atrium room overlooking gardens and lovely stone walls. Home is located in quiet corner of N.E. Connecticut—a nature lover's retreat area.

Hosts: Elaine Chicoine and husband Jean
Rooms: 3 (PB) $60-70
Full Irish Breakfast
Credit Cards: None
Notes: 2, 5, 6, 7, 8, 9, 10, 11

WETHERSFIELD

Chester Bulkley House Bed and Breakfast

184 Main Street, 06109
(203) 563-4236

Nestled in the historic village of Old Wethersfield, this classic Greek Revival house has been lovingly restored by innkeepers Frank and Sophie Bottaro to provide a warm and gracious New England welcome to the vacationer, traveler, or businessperson. Built in 1830, the house boasts five delightfully airy guest rooms, each with a unique character and decorated with period antiques and vintage design details.

Hosts: Frank and Sophie Bottaro
Rooms: 5 (3PB; 2SB) $65-85
Full Breakfast
Credit Cards: A, B, C
Notes: 2, 5, 7, 8, 9, 10, 11, 12

---

year; 6 Pets welcome; 7 Children welcome; 8 Tennis nearby; 9 Swimming nearby; 10 Golf nearby; 11 Skiing nearby; 12 May be booked through travel agent

Delaware

Bed and Breakfast of Delaware

Box 177, 3650 Siverside Road., Wilmington, 19810-2211
(302) 479-9500

Mostly hosted private residences. Some small inns. In **Pennsylvania**—in Brandywine Valley, Cadds Ford, West Chester, New Hope, Landenberg, Oxford, and Kennett Square. In **Delaware**—Wilmington, New Castle, Newark, Odessa, Dover, Bridgeville, Laurel, Milford, Lewes, Dagsboro, Milton, and Selbyville. Near the University of Delaware in Newark and Del-Tech campuses in Wilmington, Stanton, and Georgetown. Others are on the Eastern Shore of **Maryland** and **Virginia**'s Chesapeake Bay. Many are on the National Register. Near Winterthur, Longwood Gardens, and the Atlantic Ocean. Rates: $55-160. $5 surcharge for one-night stay.

NEW CASTLE

William Penn Guest House

206 Delaware Street, 19720
(302) 328-7736

Visit historic New Castle and stay in a charmingly restored home, circa 1682, close to museums and major highways.

Hosts: Richard and Irma Burwell
Rooms: 4 (1 PB; 2 SB) $45-70
Continental Breakfast
Credit Cards: None
Notes: 2, 7 (over 12), 8

REHOBOTH BEACH

Lord and Hamilton Seaside Inn

20 Brooklyn Avenue, 19971
(302) 227-6960

Founded in 1872 by the Methodists as a campground, Rehoboth has maintained a family emphasis and atmosphere even to the present time. Rehoboth has been known for years as "The Nation's Summer Capital." The Lord and Hamilton Seaside sits on the original plot of land purchased by the Reverend R.W. Todd,

---

NOTES: Credit cards accepted: A Master Card; B Visa; C American Express; D Discover Card; E Diners Club; F Other; 2 Personal checks accepted; 3 Lunch available; 4 Dinner available; 5 Open all

founder of Rehoboth Methodist Campground. Each room in the inn has its own distinctive personality although a rose motif is evident throughout the house. The bedrooms are comfortably furnished, clean, cheerful, and inviting with designer sheets and towels and accented with handcrafted quilts that Marge has been collecting for years. We are looking forward to your stay with us.

Hosts: Marge and Dick Hamilton
Rooms: 7 (3PB; 4SB) $50-100
Expanded Continental Breakfast
Credit Cards: None
Notes: 2, 8, 9, 10

The Royal Rose Inn Bed and Breakfast

41 Baltimore Ave.
(302) 226-2535

A charming and relaxing 1920s beach cottage this bed and breakfast is tastefully furnished with antiques and a romantic rose theme. A scrumptious breakfast of homemade bread, muffins, egg dishes, and much more is served on a large screened-in porch. Air-conditioned bedrooms, guest refrigerator, and off street parking are real pluses for guests. Centrally located one and a half blocks from the ocean and boardwalk. Midweek specials; weekend packages; gift certificates. Open May through October.

Hosts: Kenny and Cindy Vincent
Rooms: 7 (3 PB; 4 SB)
Continental Plus Breakfast
Credit Cards: None
Notes: 2, 7 (over 6), 8, 9, 10

Tembo Bed and Breakfast

100 Laurel St., 19971
(302) 227-3360

Tembo, named after Gerry's elephant collection, is a white frame beach cottage set among old shade trees in a quiet residential area just one block from the beach. Furnished with antique, comfortable furniture, hand-braided rugs, paintings, and carvings by Delaware artists. A cozy ambience pervades the casual, hospitable atmosphere.

Hosts: Don and Gerry Cooper
Rooms: 6 (1PB; 5SB)
Continental Breakfast
Credit Cards: None
Notes: 2, 6 (off-season), 8, 9, 10

SMYRNA

The Main Stay

41 S. Main St., 19977
(302) 653-8960

A home away from home in the heart of the

---

year; 6 Pets welcome; 7 Children welcome; 8 Tennis nearby; 9 Swimming nearby; 10 Golf nearby; 11 Skiing nearby; 12 May be booked through travel agent

historic town of Smyrna, just 40 miles south of Wilmington, six miles from the 15,000-acre Bombay Hook National Wildlife Refuge and fifteen miles from Dover Air Force Base. There are Oriental rugs and antique furniture, as well as needlework and handmade quilts, to accent the traditional character of this Colonial-style house. Relax on the porch, in the sunroom, or in front of the fireplace. Two bedrooms, each with twin beds and full bathroom between. Laundry facilities also available. Social drinking is our custom, but smoking outside only, please.

Hostess: Phyllis Howarth
Rooms: 2 (SB) $45
Hearty Gourmet Breakfast
Open November 1 to April 30
Credit Cards: None
Notes: 6 (restricted), 7, 10

WILMINGTON

The Boulevard Bed and Breakfast
1909 Baynard Blvd., 19802
(302) 656-9700

This beautifully restored city mansion was originally built in 1913. Impressive foyer and magnificent staircase leading to a landing complete with window seat and large leaded-glass windows flanked by 15-foot columns. Full breakfast served on screened porch or formal dining room. Bedrooms furnished with antiques and family heirlooms. Close to business district and area attractions.

Hosts: Charles and Judy Powell
Rooms: 6 (4PB; 2 SB) $60-75
Full Breakfast
Credit Cards: A, B, C
Notes: 2, 5, 7, 8, 10

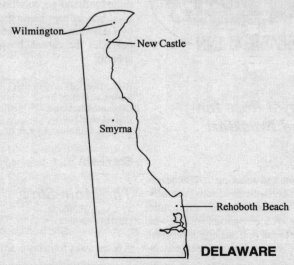

NOTES: Credit cards accepted: A Master Card; B Visa; C American Express; D Discover Card; E Diners Club; F Other; 2 Personal checks accepted; 3 Lunch available; 4 Dinner available; 5 Open all

District of Columbia

Adams Inn

over 40 ethnic restaurants. It has clean, comfortable home-style furnishings. Adams Inn, located north of the White House near the National Zoo, is convenient to transportation (Woodley Park-Zoo Metro), convention sites, government buildings, and tourist attractions.

Hosts: Gene and Nancy Thompson
Rooms: 25 (12 PB; 13 SB) $45-90
Expanded Continental Breakfast
Credit cards: A, B, C, D, E
Notes: 2, 5, 7, 12

Adams Inn

1744 Lanier Place NW, Washington, DC 20009
(202) 745-3600; (800) 578-6807

This turn-of-the-century town house is in the Adams-Morgan neighborhood with

Bed N' Breakfast Ltd.

P.O. Box 12011, Washington, DC, 20005
(202) 328-3510; (202) 332-3885 (FAX)

A reservation service representing over 80 properties in Washington, DC and nearby Maryland and Northern Virginia. Unique accommodations include private home bed and breakfast, guest houses, inns and hotels, and unhosted one- and two-bedroom apartments. Many restored and historic Victorians, some with jacuzzi tubs and fireplaces. Children welcome. Major credit cards accepted. Personal checks accepted if presented two weeks prior to arrival. Jacqueline Reed, coordinator.

---

year; 6 Pets welcome; 7 Children welcome; 8 Tennis nearby; 9 Swimming nearby; 10 Golf nearby; 11 Skiing nearby; 12 May be booked through travel agent

The Reeds

P. O. Box 12011, Washington, DC 20005
(202) 328-3510; (202) 332-3885 (FAX)

Built in the late 1800s, this large Victorian home features original wood panelng, including a unique oak staircase, stained glass, chandeliers, Victorian-style lattice porch, and art nouveau and Victorian antiques and decorations. It is a double lot and it has a garden with fountains and an old-fashioned swing. The house has been featured in the *Washington Post* and the *Philadelphia Inquirer* and as part of "Christmas at the Smithsonian." It is located ten blocks from the White House at historic Logan Circle.

Hosts: Charles and Jackie Reed
Rooms: 6 (1 PB; 5 SB) $55-85
Continental Plus Breakfast
Credit Cards: A, B, C, E
Notes: 2 (two weeks in advance only), 5, 7, 8, 9

Swiss Inn

1204 Massachusetts Ave, Washington, DC 20005
(800) 955-7947

The Swiss Inn is a small, family-owned inn located in downtown Washington, DC. We are just ten minutes walking distance to the White House, National Geographic, Chinatown, the convention center, Ford's Theatre, and many other attractions. We do not serve breakfast but all of our rooms are equipped with full kitchenettes. Many of our guest prepare their own breakfast, lunch, or dinner.

Host: Ralph Nussbaumer
Rooms: 7 (PB) $58-98
Breakfast is not served.
Credit Cards: A, B, C, D, E
Notes: 2, 5, 6, 7

Swiss Inn

NOTES: Credit cards accepted: A Master Card; B Visa; C American Express; D Discover Card; E Diners Club; F Other; 2 Personal checks accepted; 3 Lunch available; 4 Dinner available; 5 Open all

Florida

AMELIA ISLAND

Elizabeth Pointe Lodge

98 South Fletcher Ave., 32034
(904) 277-4851; (904) 277-6500 (FAX)

The main house of the lodge is constructed in an 1890s Nantucket shingle style with a strong maritime theme, broad porches, rockers, sunshine, and lemonade. Located prominently by the Atlantic Ocean, the inn is only steps from often deserted beaches. Suites are available for families. A newspaper is delivered to your room in the morning, and breakfast is served overlooking the ocean.

Hosts: David and Susan Caples
Rooms: 20 (PB) $95-150
Full Breakfast
Credit Cards: A, B, C
Notes: 2, 3, 4, 5, 7, 8, 9, 10, 12

Florida House Inn

22 S. 3rd Street, P.O. Box 688, 32034
(904) 261-3300; (800) 258-3301; (904) 277-3831 (FAX)

Located in the heart of our Victorian seaport village, Florida's oldest hotel dates from 1857. Recently restored, our award-winning inn is the perfect combination of historic charm and modern convenience. Each room is a comfortable blend of antiques and reproductions, vintage quilts, handmade rugs, and polished pine floors. Deluxe rooms offer fireplaces, jacuzzis, or original clawfoot tubs. We serve a full breakfast each morning. A cozy English-style pub, original boarding house restaurant, and brick courtyard with gazebo are all a part of the Florida House experience.

Hosts: Bob and Karen Warner
Rooms: 11 (PB) $70-125
Full Breakfast
Credit Cards: A, B, C, E
Notes: 2, 3, 4, 5, 7, 8, 9, 10, 12

AMELIA ISLAND/FERNANDINA BEACH

Bailey House

28 South Seventh St., 32034
(904) 261-5390

Visit an elegant Queen Anne home furnished in Victorian period decor. The beautiful home, with magnificent stained glass windows, turrets, and a wraparound porch, was built in 1895 and is on the National Register of Historic Places. The recently renovated home offers the comfort of air-conditioning and private baths. The location in Fernandina's historic district is within walking distance of excellent restaurants, antique shopping, and many historic churches. No smoking or pets please.

Hosts: Tom and Jenny Bishop
Rooms: 5 (PB) $75-115
Extended Continental Breakfast
Credit Cards: A, B, C
Notes: 2, 5, 7 (over 9), 8, 9, 10, 12

BRANDON

Behind the Fence

1400 Viola Dr @ Countryside, 33511
(813) 685-8201

Retreat into the simplicity and tranquility of life in a bygone era with all the conveniences of today's world. Come to Florida and choose your accommodations from a cottage by our pool to a private room in our antique-filled New England Salt-Box house. Nearby parks and river canoeing offer lots of opportunities for family activities. Homemade Amish sweet rolls are featured and "relaxing" is the word most guests use to refer to their stay "behind the fence." Country furniture for sale and tours available on request. AAA 3-star.

Hosts: Larry and Carolyn Yoss
Rooms: 5 (3PB; 2SB) $65-75
Expanded Continental Breakfast
Credit Cards: None
Notes: 2, 3, 5, 6 (some), 7, 8, 9, 10

The Son's Shady Brook

COLEMAN

The Son's Shady Brook Bed and Breakfast

P. O. Box 551, 33521
(904)PIT-STOP (748-7867)

Offering a refreshing change. Modern home, beautifully decorated rooms with comfortable beds and private baths. Overlooks springfed creek on 21 secluded, wooded acres. A relaxing retreat for elderly, handicapped, newlyweds, and others. Central air, heat, and sound system. Enjoy piano, library, fireplace, and more. Solitude and tranquility with therapeutic, scenic, picturesque surroundings. Easy to find, rural setting within 50 miles from Central Florida attractions, Orlando, and Tampa.

Hostess: Jean Lake Martin
Rooms: 4 (PB) $50-60
Full Breakfast
Credit Cards: A, B, C
Notes: 2, 3 (by arrangement), 4 (by arrangement), 5, 8, 9, 10

FORT MYERS

Embe's Place and Art Gallery

5570-4 Woodrose Ct., 33907
(813) 936-6378

This town house-type home is designed to be your home away from home. The spacious accommodation includes a bright and cheery suite with a large, private bath and dressing area. Located 15 minutes from the beaches, Sanibel and Captiva

---

NOTES: Credit cards accepted: A Master Card; B Visa; C American Express; D Discover Card; E Diners Club; F Other; 2 Personal checks accepted; 3 Lunch available; 4 Dinner available; 5 Open all

Islands, fine shopping, good restaurants, and the University of Florida. Resident cat.

Hostess: Embe Burdick
Rooms: 1 (PB) $55
Continental Breakfast
Credit Cards: None
Notes: 2, 5, 8, 9, 10

HOLMES BEACH

Harrington House Beachfront Bed and Breakfast
5626 Gulf Drive, 34217
(813) 778-5444; (813) 778-0527 (FAX)

Centrally located on the Anna Maria Island, in the small city of Holmes Beach directly overlooking the Gulf of Mexico, Harrington House awaits your visit. The largest three-story home on the island was constructed in 1925 and was owned by the first mayor of Holmes Beach. Flower gardens, in-ground pool, and beachfront swimming are attractive features you'll find at Harrington House. Our great room lends itself to reading, watching TV, listening to music, or just sitting and talking creating new friends or getting acquainted with old ones. Christmastime is especially festive at Harrington House. Rooms are gorgeously decorated each with its own atmosphere. Breakfast is served on the porch overlooking the sea or in the formal dining room.

Hosts: Jo and Frank Davis
Rooms: 11 (PB) $59-149
Credit Cards: A, B, C
Notes: 2, 5, 8, 9, 10, 12

INVERNESS

Crown Hotel
109 N. Seminole Ave., 34450
(904) 344-5555; (904) 726-4040 (FAX)

Experience the elegance of authentic Victorian decor in one of our 34 individually styled rooms. Your choice of dining in Churchill's Grill or our British Fox and Hound Pub. Centrally located in the secluded hill of Inverness activities. Available activities within the area include canoeing, horseback riding, golfing, and bicycling trails. The perfect place for a quiet, relaxing getaway.

Hosts: Mr. and Mrs. J. Sumner
Rooms: 34 (PB) $55-70
Continental Breakfast
Credit Cards: A, B, C, E
Notes: 2, 3, 4, 5, 6, 7, 8, 9, 10, 12

KEY WEST

Center Court—Historic Inn and Cottage
916 Center St., 33040
(305) 296-9292; (305) 296-7012 (FAX)

Beautifully renovated Key West home from 1873, located one block from Duval and Truman Ave. On quiet, historic lane, yet within walking distance of every Old Town attraction and beaches. This elegantly appointed and handicapped accessible inn has hair dryers, cable TV, telephones, A/C, and fans in each room. Common area has heated pool, jacuzzi, exercise pavillion, fish and lily pond, and lush, tropical gardens. AAA approved,

year; 6 Pets welcome; 7 Children welcome; 8 Tennis nearby; 9 Swimming nearby; 10 Golf nearby; 11 Skiing nearby; 12 May be booked through travel agent

three-diamonds. German and Spanish spoken.

Hostess: Naomi Van Steelandt
Rooms: 6 (PB) $78-128
Full l Breakfast
Credit Cards: A, B, C, D
Notes: 5, 6, 7, 8, 9, 10, 12

Whispers B&B

409 William St., 33040
(305) 294-5969; (800) 856-SHHH

Located in the heart of Old Town, Whispers, a 150-year-old Victorian-style house, offers its guests the luxury of a private resort (free use of a lap pool, private beach, and health spa) yet the quaintness of a B&B. Whispers also offers its guests a full and varied gourmet breakfast. So come down and enjoy Key West—and come home to Whispers.

Host: John Marburg
Rooms: 7 (5PB; 2SB) $69-150
Full Gourmet Breakfast
Credit Cards: A, B, C, D
Notes: 2, 5, 8, 9, 10, 12

KISSIMMEE

Unicorn Inn

8 S. Orlando Ave., 34741
(407) 846-1200; (407) 846-1773 (FAX)

The Unicorn—the only colonial style bed and breakfast inn in Kissimmee—is located in Historic Downtown off the Broadway, opposite the new police station. It is also only 300 yards from the famous bass fishing of Lake Tohopekalegia, close to golf courses, and near to all the main attractions like Disney World, Wet and Wild, and Sea World. Plus approximately

300 yards from Amtrack and 150 yards from Greyhound. Our inn comprises six rooms, plus two adjoining rooms, or two suites all with private baths. British owned and run by Fran and Don Williamson of Yorkshire, England. Our rule is: Make Yourself At Home. Airport pickups; shuttle to and from attractions.

Hosts: Don and Fran Williamson
Rooms: 8 (6PB) $55
Full or Light Breakfast
Credit Cards: None
Notes: 2, 3 , 5, 7, 8, 9, 10

LAKELAND

Sunset Motel & R.V. Park

2301 New Tampa Highway, 33801
(813) 683-6464

This resort motel with pool and clubhouse is central to Cypress Gardens, Disneyworld, Sea World, Universal Studios, Busch Gardens, and more. Walk to banks and shopping. TV, telephone, and refrigerator in all rooms; microwaves and grills available; kitchenettes, apartments, suites. Inquire about progress on doubling of facilities in late 1994 and increasing of amenities and options.

Hosts: Eunice, Clifton, Will, and Bill
Rooms: 14 (PB) $38-89
Continental Breakfast (on request)
Credit Cards: A, B
Notes: 5, 7, 9, 12

Chalet Suzanne

NOTES: Credit cards accepted: A Master Card; B Visa; C American Express; D Discover Card; E Diners Club; F Other; 2 Personal checks accepted; 3 Lunch available; 4 Dinner available; 5 Open all

LAKE WALES

Chalet Suzanne Country Inn and Restaurant

3800 Chalet Suzanne Dr., 33853
(813)676-6011; (800)433-6011; (813)676-1814
(FAX)

Listed on the National Register of Historic Places, Chalet Suzanne has been family owned and operated since 1931. It is on 100 acres in a fairy-tale setting. Thirty guest rooms have all the amenities. Our four-star restaurant serves breakfast, lunch, and dinner. We also have gift shops, a ceramic studio, swimming pool, soup cannery, and lighted airstrip. We are proud to say that our soups accompanied Jim Irwin on Apollo 15 to the moon. Ask about our mini-vacation special.

Hosts: Carl and Vita Hinshaw
Rooms: 30 (PB) $125-185
Full Breakfast
Credit Cards: A, B, C, D, E, F
Notes: 2, 3, 4, 5, 6, 7, 8, 9, 10, 12

MICANOPY

Shady Oak Bed and Breakfast

203 Cholokka Blvd., 32667
(904)466-3476

The Shady Oak stands majestically in the center of historic downtown Micanopy. A marvelous canopy of old, live oaks; quiet, shaded streets; and many antique stores offer visitors a memorable connection to Florida's past. This three-story, 19th century-style mansion features five beautiful, spacious suites, private baths, and porches, jacuzzi, Florida room, and widow's walk. Three lovely, historic churches within walking distance. Local activities include antiquing, bicycling, canoeing, bird watching, and much more. "Playfully elegant accommodations, where stained glass, antiques, and innkeeping go together as kindly as warm hugs with old friends."

Host: Frank James
Rooms: 5 suites (PB) $85-145
Full Breakfast
Credit Cards: A, B, D
Notes: 2, 3, 4, 5, 7, 9, 10, 12

NEW SMYRNA BEACH

Indian River Inn and Conference Center

1210 South Riverside Drive, 32168
(904)428-2491; (904)426-2532 (FAX)

Built in 1916, this inn is the oldest extant hotel in Volusia County. It has been lovingly restored and remodeled to meet all current standard of security, comfort, and convenience without sacrificing its charm and character. A gracious atmosphere of warmth and friendliness, unsurpassed in today's often frantic life-style, can be found here. We are located on the Atlantic Intercoastal Waterway minutes from I-95 and I-4 between Daytona Beach and the Kennedy Space Center. Church groups and buses welcomed.

Hosts: Ed and Donna Ruby
Rooms: 27 + 15 suites (PB) $50-115
Continental Breakfast
Credit Cards: A, B, D
Notes: 2, 3+4 (available Thanksgiving - Easter), 5, 7, 8 (on premises), 9, 10, 12

year; 6 Pets welcome; 7 Children welcome; 8 Tennis nearby; 9 Swimming nearby; 10 Golf nearby; 11 Skiing nearby; 12 May be booked through travel agent

Night Swan Intracoastal Bed and Breakfast

512 South Riverside Drive, 32168
(904) 423-4940; (904) 423-4940 (FAX)

Come watch the pelicans, dolphins, sailboats, and yachts along the Atlantic Intracoastal Waterway from our beautiful front room, our wraparound porch, or your room. Our spacious three-story home has kept its character and charm of 1906 in the Historic District of New Smyrna Beach, with its central fireplace and its intricate, natural wood in every room. We are located between Daytona Beach and Kennedy Space Center, on the Indian River, just two miles from the beach. AAA approved.

Hosts: Chuck and Martha Nighswonger
Rooms: 6 (PB) $59-99
Expanded Continental Breakfast
Credit Cards: A, B, C
Notes: 2, 5, 8, 10, 12

ORLANDO

The Courtyard at Lake Lucerne

211 North Lucerne Circle, 32806
(407) 648-5188; (800) 444-5289; (407) 246-1368 (FAX)

A unique property made up of three historic buildings furnished with antiques and surrounding a tropically landscaped brick courtyard, this establishment is located in the historic district on the southern edge of downtown Orlando, convenient to everything central Florida has to offer. Rooms have phones and cable TV; two suites have double jacuzzis and steam showers. Selected by *Country Inns Magazine* as one of 1992's "Best Inn Buys" and by Herb Hillier for *The Miami Herald* as one of the ten best inns in Florida for 1992.

Hosts: Charles Meiner and Paula S. Bowers
Rooms: 22 (PB) $65-150
Expanded Continental Breakfast
Credit Cards: A, B, C, E
Notes: 2, 5, 7, 12

Perri House B & B

10417 State Road 535, 32836
(407) 876-4830; (800) 780-4830; (407) 876-0241 (FAX)

Perri House is a quiet, private country estate inn secluded on 20 acres of land adjacent to the Walt Disney World Resort complex. Because of its outstanding location, Disney Village and Pleasure Island are only three minutes away; EPCOT center is only five minutes. An upscale continental breakfast awaits you each morning. A refreshing pool and heated spa relax you after a full day of activities. Each guest room has its own private bath, entrance, TV and phone. The Perri House grounds are being developed and landscaped to become a future bird sanctuary.

Hosts: Nick and Angi Perretti
Rooms: 6 (PB) $65-85
Continental Breakfast
Credit Cards: A, B, C, D
Notes: 2, 5, 7, 8, 9, 10, 12

The Rio Pinar House

532 Pinar Drive, 32825
(407) 277-4903

Located in the quiet Rio Pinar golf community 30 minutes from Disney World, Sea World, and Universal Studios, the Rio Pinar House features comfortable rooms. A full breakfast is served in the formal dining room or on the screened-in porch overlooking the yard.

Hosts: Victor and Delores Freudenburg
Rooms: 3 (PB) $45-55
Full Breakfast
Credit Cards: None
Notes: 2, 5, 7, 8, 10

ST. AUGUSTINE

Carriage Way Bed and Breakfast

70 Cuna Street, 32084
(904) 829-2467

Built in 1883, a Victorian home located in the heart of the historic district amid unique and charming shops, museums, and historic sites. The atmosphere is leisurely and casual, in keeping with the general attitude and feeling of Old St. Augustine. All guest rooms have a private bath with a claw foot tub or shower. Rooms are furnished with antiques and reproductions including brass, canopy, or four poster beds. A full home-baked breakfast is served.

Hosts: Bill and Diane Johnson
Rooms: 9 (PB) $49-105
Full Breakfast
Credit Cards: A, B, D
Notes: 2, 3&4 (picnic), 5, 7 (over 8), 8, 9, 10, 12

Castle Garden Bed and Breakfast

Castle Garden Bed and Breakfast

15 Shenandoah Street, 32084
(904) 829-3839

Stay at a Castle and be treated like royalty! Relax and enjoy the peace and quiet of "royal treatment" at our newly restored 100-year-old Castle of Moorish Revival design where the only sound you'll hear is the occasional roar of a cannon shot from the old fort 200 yards to the south, or the creak of solid wood floors. Awaken to the aroma of freshly baked goodies as we prepare a full, mouth-watering, country breakfast just like "Mom used to make." The unusual coquina stone exterior remains virtually untouched while the interior of this former Castle Warden Carriage House boasts two magnificent bridal suites complete with soothing in-room jacuzzi, sunken bedrooms, and all of life's little pleasures! Amenities: complimentary wine, chocolates, bikes, and private parking.

Host: Bruce L. Kloeckner
Rooms: 6 (PB) $49-150
Full Breakfast
Credit Cards: A, B, C, D
Notes: 5, 7, 8, 10, 12

Old Powder House Inn

38 Cordova Street, 32084
(800) 447-4149; (904) 824-4149

Towering pecan and oak trees shade verandas with large rockers to watch the passing horse-drawn buggies. An introduction to a romantic escape in the charming turn-of-the-century Victorian inn. Amenities include high tea, hors d'oeuvres, jacuzzi, cable TV, parking, bicycles, family hospitality, picnics, special honeymoon

year; 6 Pets welcome; 7 Children welcome; 8 Tennis nearby; 9 Swimming nearby; 10 Golf nearby; 11 Skiing nearby; 12 May be booked through travel agent

packages, anniversaries, and birthdays.

Hosts: Al and Eunice Howes
Rooms: 9 (PB) $59-109
Full Breakfast
Credit Cards: A, B
Notes: 2, 5, 7, 8, 9, 10, 12

St. Fancis Inn

St. Fancis Inn
279 St. George St., 32084
(904) 824-6068; (800) 824-6062 (FAX)

Built in 1791, the Inn is a beautiful Spanish
Colonial building. The courtyard garden
provides a peaceful setting for traditional
hospitality. Accommodations range from
double rooms and suites to a five-room
cottage—all have private bath, cable TV,
central AC/heat, and many have fireplaces.
The Inn is centrally located in the historic
district within easy walking to restaurants,
shops, and historic sites.

Hosts: Stan and Regina Reynolds
Rooms: 14 (PB) $52-125
Continental Plus Breakfast
Credit Cards: A, B
Notes: 2, 5, 7 (limited), 8, 9, 10, 12

ST. PETERSBURG

The Heritage Holiday Inn
234 Third Ave. N., 33701
(813) 822-4814; (813) 823-1644 (FAX)

The Heritage Holiday Inn is downtown

St. Petersburg's most charming unique
property, featuring gracious hospitality
and southern charm. The Heritage combines the glamour and exuberance of the
early 1920s architecture and furniture,
with comfortable, up-to-date rooms and
suites. On site is the Heritage Gille, an
award-winning restaurant that features
excellent cuisine and one of Tampa Bay's
finest art galleries.

Host: Stan Ockwig
Rooms: 71 (PB) $58-90
Full Breakfast
Credit Cards: A, B, C, D, E
Notes: 3, 4, 5, 7, 8, 9, 10, 12

Mansion House

Mansion House
105 5th Ave. NE, 33701
(813) 821-9391 (voice and FAX)

Proprietors Alan and Suzanne left Wales
in February of 1991 to embark on a
remodeling venture of a turn-of-the-
century southern home in St. Petersburg.
Alan, interested in water color painting,
woodwork, and design, used his skills to
the full whilst Suzanne cleverly coordinated the interiors to achieve a Floridian-
style B&B with an English flair. Located
within walking distance of marina, pier,
museums, sunken gardens. Excellent shop-

NOTES: Credit cards accepted: A Master Card; B Visa; C American Express; D Discover Card; E
Diners Club; F Other; 2 Personal checks accepted; 3 Lunch available; 4 Dinner available; 5 Open all

ping and superb beaches.

Hosts: Suzanne and Alan Lucas
Rooms: 6 (PB) $60-65
Full English Breakfast
Credit Cards: A, B, D
Notes: 2, 5, 8, 9, 12

SAINT PETERSBURG BEACH

Island's End Resort

1 Pass-A-Grille Way, 33706
(813) 360-5023; (813) 367-7890 (FAX)

The compelling appeal of all that paradise
can offer abounds at Island's End. Deep
blue sky, turquoise waters, exotic sunrise,
and sweets all work in concert to relax and
entertain you. Island's End features six
unique, well-appointed guest homes including a fantastic three-bedroom house
with atrium and private pool. Try your
hand at fishing day or night from one of the
best docks on Florida's west coast.

Hosts: Jone and Millard Gamble
Rooms: 6 (PB) call for prices
Continental Breakfast on Tuesdays, Thursdays,
and Saturdays
Credit Cards: A, B
Notes: 2, 5, 7, 8, 9, 10

TARPON SPRINGS

East Lake Bed and Breakfast

421 Old East Lake Rd., 34689
(813) 937-5487

Private home on two and a half acres,
situated on a quiet road along Lake Tar-

pon, close to the Gulf of Mexico. The
hosts are retired businesspeople who enjoy new friends and are well informed
about the area. The room and adjoining
bath are at the front of the house, away
from the family quarters. The room has
central air, color TV, and telephone.
Breakfast includes fresh fruit, juice, entree,
and homemade breads and jams. Close to
many Florida attractions.

Hosts: Dick and Marie Fiorito
Rooms: 1 (PB) $40
Full Home-cooked Breakfast
Credit Cards: None
Notes: 2, 5, 8, 9, 10

VENICE

The Banyan House

519 South Harbor Drive, 34285
(813) 484-1385; (813) 484-8032 (FAX)

Experience the Old World charm of one of
Venice's historic Mediterranean homes,
circa 1926, on the Gulf coast. Relax in the
peaceful atmosphere of our lovely courtyard dominated by a huge banyan tree.
This provides an unusual setting for the
garden patio, pool, and jacuzzi. Central to
shopping, beaches, restaurants, and golf.
Complimentary bicycles. No smoking.
Minimum two night stay.

Hosts: Chuck and Susan McCormick
Rooms: 9 (PB) $59-99
Deluxe Continental Breakfast
Credit Cards: None
Notes: 2, 5, 7 (over 12), 8, 9, 10

---

year; 6 Pets welcome; 7 Children welcome; 8 Tennis nearby; 9 Swimming nearby; 10 Golf nearby;
11 Skiing nearby; 12 May be booked through travel agent

Georgia

ATLANTA

Beverly Hills Inn

65 Sheridan Drive, 30305
(404) 233-8520 (voice and FAX); (800) 331-8520

A charming European-style hotel with 18
suites uniquely decorated with period furnishings offers fresh flowers, continental
breakfast, and the little things that count.
We're a morning star, not a constellation;
a solitary path, not a highway. Only some
will understand, but then, we don't have
room for everybody!

Hosts: Bonnie and Lyle Klienhans
Rooms: 18 (PB) $80-450
Continental Breakfast
Credit Cards: A, B, C, E
Notes: 2, 5, 6, 7, 8, 9, 10, 12

Oakwood House B&B

951 Edgewood Ave. NE, 30307
(404) 521-9320

Get away—in the city—to our relaxing
small inn. Your hosts live next door.
Located in Atlanta's oldest suburb, just
two miles east of downtown, Oakwood
House is perfect for business and pleasure
travelers. Easy access via car and subway. In the city of Rhett and Scarlett,
Coca Cola, Martin Luther King, Jr., and
the 1996 Olympics, you'll enjoy our rooms

and new whirlpool suite. Discounts to
travel agents. Free theater tickets (seasonal). One child in the room free. No
smoking home.

Hosts: Judy and Robert Hotchkiss
Rooms: 5 (PB) $60-125
Enhanced Continental Breakfast
Credit Cards: A, B
Notes: 2, 5, 7, 12

Shellmont Bed and Breakfast Lodge

Shellmont Bed and Breakfast Lodge

821 Piedmont Avenue, Northeast, 30308
(404) 872-9290

Built in 1891, Shellmont is on the National
Register of Historic Places and is a City of
Atlanta Landmark Building. A true Victorian treasure of carved woodwork, stained
and leaded glass, and unique architecture
located in Midtown—Atlanta's restau-

NOTES: Credit cards accepted: A Master Card; B Visa; C American Express; D Discover Card; E
Diners Club; F Other; 2 Personal checks accepted; 3 Lunch available; 4 Dinner available; 5 Open all

rant, theater, and cultural district, one mile from downtown. It is furnished entirely with antiques.

Hosts: Ed and Debbie McCord
Rooms: 5 (PB) $69-99
Continental Breakfast Plus
Credit Cards: A, B, C, E
Notes: 2, 5, 7 (limited), 8, 10

The Woodruff B&B Inn

223 Ponce de Leon Avenue, 30308
(404) 875-9449; (800) 473-9449; (404) 875-2882 (FAX)

Prepare yourself for Southern charm, hospitality, and a full Southern breakfast. The Woodruff Bed and Breakfast Inn is conveniently located in Midtown Atlanta. It is a 1906 Victorian home built by a prominent Atlanta family and fully restored by the current owners. Each room has been meticulously decorated with antiques. The Woodruff has a very colorful past which lends to the charm and history of the building and the city. Close to everything. Ya'll come!

Hosts: Joan and Douglas Jones
Rooms: 13 (PB) $69-295
Full Breakfast
Credit Cards: A, B, D
Notes: 2, 5, 7, 8, 12

CLEVELAND

Tyson Homestead Inn

3268 Helen Hwy., 30528
(706) 865-6914

A warm welcome awaits you at this pleasant Colonial home situated on a large wooded, landscaped area with lake out front. Located on state highway 75 (not alternate 75) less than five minutes from Cleveland, Gateway to the Mountains and home of Babyland General, and ten minutes to Helen.

Hosts: J. T. and Mary Tyson
Rooms: 5 (2PB; 3SB) $45-65
Continental Plus Breakfast
Credit Cards: None
Notes: 2, 5, 7, 11, 12

Whitworth Inn

FLOWERY BRANCH

Whitworth Inn

6593 McEver Road, 30542
(404) 967-2386

Contemporary country inn on five wooded acres offers relaxing atmosphere. Ten uniquely decorated guest rooms with own baths. Two guest living rooms. Full country breakfast served in large sunlit dining room. Meeting/party space available. Thirty minutes northeast of Atlanta at Lake Lanier. Nearby attractions and activities include boating, golf, beaches and water parks. Close to Road Atlanta and Chateau Elan Winery/Golf Course. Easily accessible from major interstates. Three-diamond AAA rating.

Hosts: Ken and Christine Jonick
Rooms: 10 (PB) $55-65
Full Breakfast
Credit Cards: A, B
Notes: 2, 5, 7, 8, 9, 10, 12

year; 6 Pets welcome; 7 Children welcome; 8 Tennis nearby; 9 Swimming nearby; 10 Golf nearby; 11 Skiing nearby; 12 May be booked through travel agent

HAMILTON

Wedgwood B&B

P. O. Box 115, Highway 27 and Mobley, 31811
(706) 628-5659

Callaway Gardens 5 miles; Roosevelt's Little White House in Warm Springs 18 miles. This 1850 home radiates the warmth, friendliness, and enthusiasm of your hostess. The inside is Wedgwood blue with white stenciling. Spacious rooms are comfortably furnished with period antiques. Personalized service and complimentary refreshments. No smoking.

Hostess: Janice Neuffer
Rooms: 3 (PB) $65-75
Full Breakfast
Credit Cards: None
Notes: 2, 5, 7, 8, 9, 10, 12

HELEN

Chattahoochee Ridge Lodge and Chalets

P.O. Box 175, 30545
(800) 476-8331; (706) 878-3144; (706) 878-4032 (FAX)

Alone on a woodsy mountain above a waterfall the lodge has five new rooms and suites (kitchens and fireplaces) with private entrances, TV, AC, free phones, and jacuzzi; plus double insulation and back-up solar for stewards of the earth. In the lodge and cabins you'll like the quiet seclusion, large windows, and deep-rock water. We'll help you plan great vacation days, including Bob's oom-pah band at a German restaurant. Decor includes wide-board knotty pine, brass beds, full carpeting, and paddle fans.

Hosts: Mary and Bob Swift
Rooms: 5 plus cabins (PB) $45-75
Continental Breakfast
Credit Cards: A, B, C, D
Notes: 2, 5, 7, 8, 9, 10

Dutch Cottage B&B

P.O. Box 757, 114 Ridge Rd., 30545
(706) 878-3135

Located in a beautiful alpine village in the mountains of north Georgia, a tranquil waterfall and ivy-covered hillside lead to this European-style bed and breakfast located in an idyllic wooded setting. Choose from three comfortable rooms, each with private bath, AC, and TV, or a charming hilltop honeymoon chalet. Full breakfast buffet. Walk to town. Open May through October.

Hosts: Bill and Jane Vander Werf
Rooms: 3 (4) (3PB; 1SB) $59-75
Credit Cards: None
Notes: 2, 7, 9, 10

Habersham Hollow Country Inn and Cabins

Route 6, Box 6208, Clarkesville, GA 30523
(706) 754-5147

Nestled in the northeast Georgia mountains, this elegant country B&B features king beds, fireplace, private baths, and TVs in each room. Nearby on the secluded wooded grounds are cozy fireplace cabins with fully equipped kitchens, TV, and deck with BBQ grills where well-mannered pets are welcome.

Hosts: C. J. and Maryann Gibbons
Rooms: 4 (PB) $85-145
Full Breakfast
Credit Cards: A, B
Notes: 2, 5, 6, 7, 8, 9, 10, 11

NOTES: Credit cards accepted: A Master Card; B Visa; C American Express; D Discover Card; E Diners Club; F Other; 2 Personal checks accepted; 3 Lunch available; 4 Dinner available; 5 Open all

MOUNTAIN CITY

Blackberry Patch B&B

P.O. Box 601—Blacks Creek Dr., 30562
(706) 746-5632

To describe the area calls to mind phrases like "breathtaking beauty," "serene atmosphere," "profound tranquility," and "freshly washed mountain air." Bob and Bobbie Havlish have been B&B hosting for ten years and are known worldwide. Fireplace in living room. Air-conditioning. Rocking chairs to enjoy evening sounds. For "I don't intend to move relaxation," we've got a hammock under the trees. Luxury accommodations. Private baths. "You couldn't pick a better place!"

Hosts: Bob and Bobbie Jean Havlish
Rooms: 3 (PB) $50-65
Continental Plus Breakfast
Credit Cards: None
Notes: 2 (and travelers' checks), 5, 7 (well-behaved), 8, 9, 10, 11

York House, Inc.

P. O. Box 126, York House Rd., 30562
(800) 231-YORK (9675)

This lovely 1896 bed and breakfast inn has a country flair and is listed on the National Register of Historic Places. It is nestled among the beautiful north Georgia mountains and is close to recreational activities. Completely renovated, the 13 guest rooms are decorated with period antiques and offer cable color TV. Guests begin their day with a continental breakfast served on a silver tray. The York House is located between Clayton and Dillard, Georgia, a quarter-mile off Hwy 441.

Hosts: Jimmy and Phyllis Smith
Rooms: 13 (PB) $64-79 + tax
Continental Breakfast
Credit Cards: A, B, C, D
Notes: 2, 5, 7, 8, 9, 10, 11, 12

ST. MARYS

Goodbread Inn Bed and Breakfast

209 Osborne Street, 31558
(912) 882-7490

This 1875 Victorian Inn is in the historic district of a quaint fishing village nine miles east of I-95, halfway between Jacksonville, FL, and Brunswick, GA. Each antique-filled room has its own bath, fireplace, ceiling fan, and AC. Restaurants and Cumberland Island ferry within walking distance.

Hosts: Betty and George Krauss
Rooms: 4 (PB) $50-60 + tax
Full (seated) Breakfast
Credit Cards: None
Notes: 2, 5, 10, 12

Goodbread Inn Bedand Breakfast

---

year; 6 Pets welcome; 7 Children welcome; 8 Tennis nearby; 9 Swimming nearby; 10 Golf nearby; 11 Skiing nearby; 12 May be booked through travel agent

SAUTEE

The Stovall House
1526 Hwy. 225 North, 30571
(706)878-3355

Our 1837 Victorian farmhouse, restored in 1983, is listed on the National Register of Historic Places. Located on 26 acres in the historic Sautee Valley, the Inn has views of the mountains in all directions. The recipient of several awards for its attentive restorations, the Inn is furnished with family antiques and decorated with hand-stenciling. The restaurant, open to the public, features regional cuisine prepared with a fresh difference and served in an intimate yet informal setting. It's a country experience!

Host: Ham Schwartz
Rooms: 5 (PB) $63-70
Continental Breakfast
Credit Cards: A, B
Notes: 2, 4, 5, 7, 8, 9, 10

SAVANNAH

17 Hundred 90 Inn and Restaurant
307 E. President Street, 31401
(912)236-7122; (800)487-1790; (912)236-7123 (FAX)

Romance abounds at 17 Hundred 90. The Inn's original brick walls, stone floors, flickering candles, and fireplaces in every room transport guests into the charming world of the eighteenth century. *Sea Breeze Magazine* says of the restaurant and lounge, "17 Hundred 90 is one of the most elegant dining experiences on the

great southern coast."

Hosts: Dick and Darline Lehmkuhl
Rooms: 14 (PB) $89-129
Continental Breakfast
Credit Cards: A, B, C
Notes: 2, 3 (weekdays), 4, 5, 6 (small), 7, 8, 9, 10, 12

Eliza Thompson House
5 W. James St., 31401
(912)236-3620

The Inn is a warm melding of the traditions and charms of the last century coupled with the comforts of today. The blend of old and new is evident in the rich elegance of gleaming heart pine floors and period furnishings combined with the comforts of direct dial phones, color TV, and a private bath. This is the best of both worlds. The main house has twelve stately guest rooms; Miss Eliza's Carriage House contains twelve more rooms. You will be sure to dine in style. Every morning, a complimentary newspaper is provided with breakfast.

Rooms: 25 (PB) $88-108
Delux Continental Breakfast
Credit Cards: A, B, C
Notes: 2, 5, 7, 8, 9, 10, 12

Jesse Mount House
209 West Jones Street, 31401
(912)236-1774

An elegant Georgian town house built in 1854 in the historic district. Some suites have whirlpool baths. One includes a full kitchen. All rooms have phone, VCR, and gas-log fireplace. Bicycles and off street parking are available. Private gar-

NOTES: Credit cards accepted: A Master Card; B Visa; C American Express; D Discover Card; E Diners Club; F Other; 2 Personal checks accepted; 3 Lunch available; 4 Dinner available; 5 Open all

den with fountains. The house is decorated with antiques.

Hostess: Sue Dron
Rooms: 4 (PB) $125-150
Continental Breakfast
Credit Cards: A, B
Notes: 2, 5, 6, 7, 8, 10, 12

Joan's on Jones

17 West Jones Street, 31401
(912) 234-3863; (912) 234-1455 (FAX)

In the heart of the historic district, two charming bed and breakfast suites grace the garden level of this three-story Victorian private home. Each suite has a private entry, off street parking, bedroom, sitting room, kitchen, bath, private phone, and cable TV. Note the original heart pine floors, period furnishings, and Savannah gray brick walls. Innkeepers Joan and Gary Levy, restaurateurs, live upstairs and invite you for a tour of their home if you're staying two nights or more.

Hosts: Joan and Gary Levy
Rooms: 2 suites (PB) $85-95
Continental Breakfast
Credit Cards: None
Notes: 2, 5, 6 (dogs in garden suite only), 7, 8, 9, 10, 12

Lion's Head Inn

120 East Gaston Street, 31401
(912) 232-4580; (800) 355-LION; (912) 232-7422 (FAX)

A stately 19th century mansion situated in a quiet neighborhood just north of picturesque Forsyth Park. This lovely 9,200 sq. ft. home is filled with fine Empire antiques. Each guest room is exquisitely appointed with four-poster beds, private baths, period furnishings, fireplaces, TVs, and tele-

phones. Each morning enjoy a deluxe continental breakfast, and in the evening enjoy wine and cheese on the sweeping veranda overlooking the marbled courtyard.

Hostess: Christy Dell'Orco
Rooms: 6 (PB) $105-120
Deluxe Continental Breakfast
Credit Cards: A, B, C
Notes: 2, 5, 7, 8, 9, 10, 12

Pulaski Square Inn

203 West Charlton Street, 31401
(912) 232-8055; (800) 227-0650

The Pulaski Square Inn is a historic town house built in 1853. It is located in downtown Savannah within walking distance of the river and historical places of interest. It is beautifully restored with the original pine flooring, marble mantles, and chandeliers. It is furnished with Oriental rugs, antiques, and traditional furniture.

Hosts: JB and Hilda Smith
Rooms: 9 (7PB; 2SB) $48-125
Continental Breakfast
Credit Cards: A, B, C
Notes: 2, 5, 7, 8, 9, 10, 11, 12

SENOIA

Culpepper House

35 Broad Street, 30276
(404) 599-8182

Step back 120 years to casual Victorian elegance at the Culpepper House. Enjoy a four-poster, canopy bed next to a fireplace, with sounds of the night coming through the window.... Wake to a gourmet breakfast then take a tandem bike ride through the historic town, visit area shops

year; 6 Pets welcome; 7 Children welcome; 8 Tennis nearby; 9 Swimming nearby; 10 Golf nearby; 11 Skiing nearby; 12 May be booked through travel agent

and picturesque countryside, or just sit on the porch and rock. Only 30 minutes from Atlanta.

Hostesses: Maggie Armstrong and Barb Storm
Rooms: 3 (1PB; 2SB) $75
Full Gourmet Breakfast
Credit Cards: A, B
Notes: 2, 5, 6 (limited), 8, 9, 10, 12

Culpepper House

THOMASVILLE

Deer Creek Bed and Breakfast

1304 Old Monticello Rd., 31792
(912) 226-7294

Visit world renowned 19th century resort, Thomasville, GA, frequently visited by presidents and inhabited by business tycoons. Affordable luxury at Deer Creek nestled among pines and magnolias on beautiful grounds sloping to stream. Suite with full breakfast served elegantly in private dining room. Beamed 16 ft. cathedral ceiling, large fireplace, and ceiling fans in

suite opening to treetop deck. Private bath. Window walls afford scenic view. Next to South's second oldest golf course. Near historic tours, antique shops, and fine restaurants.

Hosts: Bill and Gladys Muggidge
Rooms: 2 (1PB; 1SB) $65-75
Full Breakfast
Credit Cards: None
Notes: 2, 5, 7, 10, 12 (min. two night stay)

WARM SPRINGS

Hotel Warm Springs

P.O. Box 351, 17 Broad Street, 31830
(706) 655-2114; (800) 366-7616

Relive history and the Roosevelt Era in our 1907 hotel, restaurant, ice cream parlor, and gift shops. Authentically restored and beautifully decorated with Roosevelt furniture and family antiques. Featuring our cozy honeymoon suite with king bed, suspended canopy, victorian antiques, red heart tub, god fixtures, breakfast in bed, flowers, champagne, and chocolates. Our large living and dining room with Queen Anne furniture, Oriental rugs, and crystal teardrop chandelier is ideal for group meetings. Nestled in quaint Warm Springs Village—a shopper's paradise, home of FDR's Little White House, 14 miles from Callaway Gardens, and one hour from Atlanta.

Hosts: Lee and Geraldine (Gerrie) Thompson
Rooms: 14 (PB) $60-160
Southern Breakfast Feast
Credit Cards: A, B, C, D
Notes: 2, 3, 4, 5, 7, 8, 9, 10, 11 (water), 12

NOTES: Credit cards accepted: A Master Card; B Visa; C American Express; D Discover Card; E Diners Club; F Other; 2 Personal checks accepted; 3 Lunch available; 4 Dinner available; 5 Open all

Hawaii

HAWAII-KAMUELA

Kamuela Inn
P.O. Box 1994, 96743
(808) 885-4243; (808) 885-8857 (FAX)

Comfortable, cozy rooms and suites with private baths, with or without kitchenettes, all with cable color television. Complimentary continental breakfast served in our coffee lanai every morning. Situated in a quiet, peaceful setting just off Highway 19. Conveniently located near shops, retail outlets, banks, theatres, parks, tennis courts, museums, restaurants, and post office. The big island's famous white sand beaches, golf courses, horseback rides, valley and mountain tours are only minutes away.

Hostess: Carolyn Cascavilla
Rooms: 31 (PB) $54-165
Continental Breakfast
Credit Cards: A, B, C, D, E
Notes: 2, 5, 7, 8, 9, 10, 11, 12

KAILUA

Jeanne's Inn
57 Pilipu Place, 96734
(808) 262-9530; (808) 262-1387 (FAX)

One-bedroom unit with double bed, kitch-enette, private bath, and private entrance. Two-bedroom, cool unit with large deck overlooking pool and hot tub. There's a queen bed and twins and full bath with oversize soaking tub. Full kitchen and play room with queen-size futon sofa and second full bath. Cable TV, VCR, and telephone. 200 yards from beautiful Kailua Beach. Beach chairs, boogie boards, snorkel gear, fruit basket, and Kona coffee.

Hosts: Jeanne and Bill Hailer
Rooms: 3 (PB) $45-95
Fruit Basket Breakfast
Credit Cards: None
Notes: 2, 5, 7 (over 12), 8, 9, 10

KAUAI—KOLOA

Island Home
1707 Kelaukia St., 96756
(707) 742-2839

Enjoy Kauai's Sunny southshore at Island Home in Poipu. Just minutes to walk to great snorkeling and swimming beaches, turtle watching, restaurants, and the beautiful Hyatt Regency. Our units offer private entrances, lanai or deck, TVs, VCRs, compact refrigerators, microwaves, beach and picnic gear with laundry facilities available. Queen- or king-size beds are of-

---

year; 6 Pets welcome; 7 Children welcome; 8 Tennis nearby; 9 Swimming nearby; 10 Golf nearby; 11 Skiing nearby; 12 May be booked through travel agent

Island Home

fered. Inquire about special rates for those in ministry. Three night minimum.

Hosts: Michael and Gail Beeson
Rooms: 2 (PB) $65-75
Continental (large) Breakfast
Credit Cards: None
Notes: 2 (and travelers'), 5, 8, 9, 10, 12

KAILUA-KONA

Hale Maluhia Bed and Breakfast

76-770 Hualalai Road, 96740
(808) 329-5773; (800) 559-6627; (808) 326-5487
(FAX)

Graicious up-country Kona plantation living, off of the beaten path, on a beautiful acre of Holualoa coffee land. Large rambling home with good beds, private baths, and plenty of room to have some time alone. Exceptional Chinese slate and tile spa, massage table, and beach/snorkel equipment. Continental plus breakfast with farm eggs, daily fresh breads, local fruits and juices, 100% pure Kona coffee. Also included is cable TV/VCR, first class video library, and games including Sega. Easy access to Kona airport and close to town. The discovery of Hale Maluhia, in the heart of the Kona recreational paradise, is the fulfillment of many who dream of experiencing a touch of Old Hawaii. Please write or call for a free brochure.

Hosts: Ken and Ann Smith
Rooms: 5 and 3 cottages (6PB; 2SB) $50-110
Continental Breakfast Plus
Credit Cards: A, B, C, D
Notes: 2, 5, 7, 8, 9, 10, 11, 12

KAUAI—PRINCEVILLE

Hale 'Aha "House of Gathering"

P.O. Box 3370, 3875 Kamehameha Drive, 96722
(800) 826-6733; (808) 826-9052 (FAX)

VACATION, HONEYMOON, or RETREAT in this peaceful resort setting on the golf course, overlooking the ocean and majestic mountains of the Garden Isle. On one side, enjoy Hanalei, where "South Pacific" was filmed, with one beach after another leading you to the famous, lush, Napoli Coast hiking trails. Hale 'Aha has been written about in many books and

---

NOTES: Credit cards accepted: A Master Card; B Visa; C American Express; D Discover Card; E Diners Club; F Other; 2 Personal checks accepted; 3 Lunch available; 4 Dinner available; 5 Open all

magazines, but only a brochure can tell it all. Enjoy bananas, papayas, and pineapple from your host's garden.

Hosts: Herb and Ruth Bockelman
Rooms: 2 and 2 suites (PB) $85-210
"More Than" Continental Breakfast
Credit Cards: A, B
Notes: 2, 5, 8, 9, 10, 12

MAUI-KULA

Elaine's Up Country Guest Rooms

2112 Noalae Rd., 96790
(808) 878-6623; (808) 878-2619 (FAX)

Quiet country setting. Splendid ocean and mountain views. All rooms have private baths, full kitchens, and sitting room privileges. Guests are welcome to cook breakfast or whatever meals they like. Next to our main house is a delightful cottage made to order for a family. One bedroom with queen-size bed and twin beds in the loft. Large kitchen. We ask that our guests do not smoke or drink.

Hosts: Elaine and Murray Gildersleeve
Rooms: 3 plus one cottage (PB) $55-110 +tax
No Breakfast Served
Credit Cards: F
Notes: 2, 5, 7, 9, 10, 12

MAUI-LAHAINA

Blue Horizons

P.O. Box 10578, 96761
(808) 669-1965; (800) 669-1948; (808) 661-1896 (FAX)

Want to mingle with the "locals" over breakfast, yet have all the privacy of your own one-bedroom apartment complete with private bath and kitchen? Well, this spacious B&B offers it all! Just minutes north of Lahaina and with great views of Lanai and Molokai, choose one of our two guest rooms with private baths or one of the three kitchen units. Feel right at home at poolside or while viewing spectacular ocean sunsets!

Hosts: Jim and Beverly Spence
Rooms: 5 (PB) $75-95
Continental Breakfast
Credit Cards: A, B, C
Notes: 2, 5, 7 (over 12), 8, 9, 10, 12

The Guesthouse

1620 Ainakea Road, 96761
(808) 661-8085; (800) 621-8942; (808) 661-1896 (FAX)

Conveniently located between the historic whaling town of Lahaina and the beach resort of Kaanapali, The Guesthouse offers four guest rooms, each with a different touch of *Aloha*. All have air-conditioning, color TVs, refrigerators, private patios and their own jacuzzies! Enjoy the conveniences of home with our modern kitchen and laundry facilities. Relax at poolside or take a short stroll to the beach. We know your visit will be special, so whether you are a diver or on your honeymoon, expect outstanding accommodations at a moderate price.

Hosts: Fred and Tanna Branum
Rooms: 4 (PB) $75-95
Full Breakfast
Credit Cards: A, B, C,
Notes: 2, 4, 5, 7 (over 12), 8, 9, 10, 12

Old Lahaina House Bed and Breakfast

P.O. Box 10355, 96761
(800) 847-0761; (808) 667-5615 (FAX)

We have rooms with private or shared bath. All are air-conditioned with TV, phone, and other features. We are two blocks from historic Lahaina town and only a one minute walk to a nice neighborhood beach. We have a 27,000 gallon pool and private tropical courtyard. All rooms are non-smoking. Your "home" in Hawaii.

Hosts: John and Sherry Barbier
Rooms: 5 (2PB;3SB) $60-95
Tropical Continental Breakfast
Credit Cards: A, B, C
Notes: 5, 7, 8, 9, 10, 12

The Walkus

c/o Trinity Tours, 1620 Ainakea Road, 96761
(808) 661-8085; (800) 621-8942; (808) 661-1896 (FAX)

Visit Maui. . .from home to home. . . . Have the privacy of this entirely new four-bedroom, three bath home (the den can be used as a fifth bedroom). Sunbathe at poolside, relax in the jacuzzi, or take a short stroll to "Baby Beach" right in Lahaina. With central air-conditioning, modern laundry facilities, and a kitchen that lacks nothing, you'll be right at home. Great for families or small groups.

Rooms: 4 + den (1PB;4SB) $395
Self-serve Breakfast
Credit Cards: A, B, C
Notes: 2, 5, 7, 8, 9, 10, 12

OAHU-AIEA

Pearl Harbor View Bed and Breakfast

99-442 Kekoa Place, 96701
(808) 487-1228 or (808) 486-8838; (808) 487-1228 or (808) 261-6573 (FAX)

Lush tropical garden. Two bedrooms, bath, living room, complete kitchen. Upstairs apartment in two-story private home. Sleeps up to 5 guests. Antique oriental furniture.

Hostess: Doris Reichert
Rooms: 1 apartment (2 bedrooms) (PB) $65-75
Continental Breakfast
Credit Cards: A, B
Notes: 2, 5, 7, 12

Idaho

COEUR D'ALENE

Cricket on the Hearth

1521 Lakeside Avenue, 83814
(208) 664-6926

Cricket on the Hearth, Coeur d'Alene's first bed and breakfast inn, has a touch of country that gives the inn a "down home" aura. Each of the five guest rooms is furnished in theme, from romantic to unique. After a relaxing weekend around the inn with its two cozy fireplaces and delicious full breakfast, guests are sure to find staying at Cricket on the Hearth habit forming.

Hosts: Al and Karen Hutson
Rooms: 5 (3PB; 2SB) $50-80
Full Breakfast
Credit Cards: None
Notes: 2, 5, 8, 9, 10, 11

Gregory's McFarland House and Bed and Breakfast

601 Foster Avenue, 83814
(208) 664-1232 (voice and FAX)

Surrender to the elegance of this award-winning historical home, circa 1905. The full breakfast is gourmet to the last crumb.

Guests will be delighted by an ideal blending of beauty, comfort, and clean surroundings. Jerry Hulse, travel editor for *The Los Angeles Times* wrote, "Entering Gregory's McFarland House is like stepping back 100 years to an unhurried time when four posters were in fashion and lace curtains fluttered at the windows." Private baths, air-conditioning, non-smoking house. If planning a wedding, our resident minister and professional photographer are available to make your special day beautiful.

Hosts: Winifred, Stephen, and Carol Gregory
Rooms: 5 (PB) $65-120 + tax
Full Gourmet Breakfast
Credit Cards: A, B
Notes: 2, 5, 8, 9, 10, 11, 12

Gregory's McFarland House

---

year; 6 Pets welcome; 7 Children welcome; 8 Tennis nearby; 9 Swimming nearby; 10 Golf nearby; 11 Skiing nearby; 12 May be booked through travel agent

Katie's Wild Rose Inn

5150 Couer d'Alene, 83814
(208) 765-9474

Looking through the pine trees to Lake Coeur d'Alene, Katie's Wild Rose Inn is a haven for the weary traveler. Only 600 feet from the public dock and beach road, the inn has four cozy rooms, one with its own jacuzzi. Guests can relax in the family room beside the fireplace or enjoy a game of pool. A full breakfast is served on the deck or in the dining room where you can admire the view.

Hosts: Joisse and Lee Knowles
Rooms: 4 (2PB; 2SB) $55-95
Full Breakfast
Credit Cards: A, B
Notes: 5, 8, 9, 10, 11, 12

Katie's Wild Rose Inn

LEWISTON

Shiloh Rose Bed and Breakfast

3414 Selway Dr., 83501
(208) 743-2482

The Shiloh Rose, decorated in a warm, country-Victorian style, offers a spacious three-room suite as your home away from home. Lace curtains, fragrant potpourri, and fresh roses in season invite you to linger. Have your morning coffee in the sitting room with a real wood-burning stove. Browse through the overflowing bookshelves, enjoy the TV/VCR...or the grand piano. A complete breakfast is served in the dining room or on the deck overlooking the valley. The views are fantastic. Join us, you'll love it!

Hostess: Dorothy A. Mader
Rooms: 1 (PB) $65-70
Full Breakfast
Credit Cards: A, B
Notes: 2, 5, 7 (over 10), 8, 9, 10, 11

Illinois

ARCOLA

Curly's Corner B&B

R.R. 2, Box 590, 61910
(217) 268-3352

This ranch-style, centrally air-conditioned farmhouse is located in the heart of a prairie farmland quiet Amish community. Your hosts Warren and Maxine are dedicated to cordial hospitality and will gladly share information about the area and provide a suggested tour of Amish businesses. Curly's Corner has four lovely and comfortable bedrooms, queen-size beds, TVs, etc. In the morning enjoy a wonderful breakfast of homemade biscuits, fresh country sausage, bacon, eggs, etc.! Curly's Corner is one-half mile north of beautiful Rockome Gardens; also close to three universities and historical sites.

Hosts: Warren and Maxine Arthur
Rooms: 4 (2PB; 2SB) $50-60
Full Breakfast
Credit Cards: None
Notes: 2, 5, 7 (over 10), 8, 9, 10

Golds Bed and Breakfast

CARLYLE

Country Haus

1191 Franklin, 62231
(618) 594-8313; (800) 279-4486: (618) 594-8415 (FAX)

A turn-of-the-century Eastlake-style home decorated in cordial country comfort. Settle into the library with a good book or snuggle up to watch TV. Relax in the hot tub on the back deck gazebo, or visit Carlyle Lake for fishing, swimming, sailing, or hiking. A museum and golf courses are nearby. Pamper yourself with homey hospitality at Country Haus B&B Inn.

Hosts: Ron and Vickie Cook
Rooms: 5 (PB) $45-55
Full Breakfast
Credit Cards: A, B, C, D, E
Notes: 2, 5, 8, 9, 10, 11

CHAMPAIGN

Golds Bed and Breakfast

2065 County Road 525 E., 61821
(217) 586-4345

Historic farmhouse furnished with antiques. Easy access to I-74 and all area attractions, including University of Illinois, antique shopping, golf, parks, and museums. Delicious continental breakfast served on

---

year; 6 Pets welcome; 7 Children welcome; 8 Tennis nearby; 9 Swimming nearby; 10 Golf nearby; 11 Skiing nearby; 12 May be booked through travel agent

1820 harvest table. Fresh country air and beautiful sunrises and sunsets contribute to your total relaxation.

Hosts: Rita and Bob Gold
Rooms: 3 (1 1/2PB; 2SB) $45
Continental Breakfast
Credit Cards: None
Notes: 2, 5, 7, 10, 12

CHICAGO

Amber Creek's Chicago Connection

1260 N. Dearborn, Chicago (Mail: P.O. Box 5, Galena, 61036)
(815) 777-9320

Charming apartment half block from Ambassador Hotel, on Chicago's Gold Coast in quiet, secure building. Tastefully decorated, spacious living room with nice views, including lake. Full kitchen, full bath. Romantic bedroom with king bed, down quilts, extra pillows. Linens and towels provided. Walk to lake, Water Tower, Michgan Avenue shopping. Half block to airport limousine and public transportation. Parking garage next door. Ideal for one couple. Queen-sized futon provides sleeping for additional guests.

Hostess: Kate Freeman
Rooms: 1 (PB) $75-125
Continental Breakfast
Credit Cards: A, B, C, D
Notes: 2, 3, 4, 5, 7, 9, 12

The Margarita European Inn

COLLINSVILLE

Maggie's B&B

2102 N. Keebler, 62234
(618) 344-8283

Beautiful, quiet, country setting just minutes from downtown St. Louis. Near hospital, restaurants, and shopping. Cooking with natural ingredients. Antiques and art objects collected in worldwide travels. Games, cable TV, and hot tub with terrycloth robes and house slippers.

Hostess: Maggie Leyda
Rooms: 5 (4PB; 1SB) $35-70
Full Breakfast
Credit Cards: A, B
Notes: 2, 5, 6, 7 (by arrangement), 8, 9, 10, 12

EVANSTON

The Margarita European Inn

1566 Oak Avenue, 60201
(708) 869-2273; (708) 869-2353 (FAX)

The romantic at heart will truly enjoy this modest and charming European-style inn in Evanston, the home of Northwestern University. Relax in the grand parlor with the morning paper or in the roof garden at sunset. Explore the numerous antique and specialty shops nearby. On rainy days, curl up with a novel from our wood-paneled English library, or indulge in a culinary creation from our critically acclaimed northern Italian restaurant, Va Pensiero.

Hosts: Barbara and Tim Gorham
Rooms: 49 (15PB; 34SB) $40-90
Continental Breakfast
Credit Cards: A, B, C
Notes: 2, 3, 4, 5, 7, 8, 9, 10, 12

GALENA

Avery Guest House

606 South Prospect Street, 61036
(815) 777-3883

This pre-Civil War home located near Galena's main shopping and historic buildings is a homey refuge after a day of exploring. Enjoy the view from our porch swing, feel free to play the piano, watch TV, or join a table game. Sleep soundly on comfortable queen beds, then enjoy our hearty continental breakfast in the sunny dining room with bay window. Mississippi river boats nearby.

Hosts: Flo and Roger Jensen
Rooms: 4 (2SB) $45-60
Expanded Continental Breakfast
Credit Cards: A, B
Notes: 2, 5, 7, 8, 9, 10, 11, 12

Belle Aire Mansion

11410 Route 20 West, 61036
(815) 777-0893

Belle Aire Mansion guest house is a pre-Civil War Federal home surrounded by 11 well-groomed acres that include extensive lawns, flowers, and a block-long, tree-lined driveway. We do our best to make our guests feel they are special friends.

Hosts: Jan and Lorraine Svec
Rooms: 5 (PB) $65-140
Full Breakfast
Credit Cards: A, B, D
Notes: 2, 7, 8, 10, 11

Brierwreath Manor

Brierwreath Manor Bed and Breakfast

216 North Bench Street, 61036
(815) 777-0608

Brierwreath Manor, circa 1884, is just one block from Galena's Main Street and has a dramatic and inviting wrapround porch that beckons to you after a hard day. The house is furnished in an eclectic blend of antique and early American. You'll not only relax but feel right at home. Two suites offer gas-log fireplaces. Central air-conditioning, ceiling fans, and cable TV add to your enjoyment.

Hosts: Mike and Lyn Cook
Rooms: 3 (PB) $80-90
Full Breakfast
Credit Cards: None
Notes: 2, 5, 8, 9, 10, 11

Park Avenue Guest House

208 Park Avenue, 61036
(815) 777-1075

1893 Queen Anne Painted Lady. Wrap-around screened porch, gardens, and gazebo for summer. Fireplace, opulent Victorian Christmas in winter. One suite

year; 6 Pets welcome; 7 Children welcome; 8 Tennis nearby; 9 Swimming nearby; 10 Golf nearby; 11 Skiing nearby; 12 May be booked through travel agent

sleeps three, and there are three antique-filled guest rooms, all with queen-size beds and fireplaces. Located in quiet residential area, it is only a short walk to Grant Park or across footbridge to Main Street shopping and restaurants.

Rooms: 4 (PB) $65-95
Hearty Continental Breakfast
Credit Cards: A, B, D
Notes: 2, 5, 8, 9, 10, 11

Pine Hollow Inn
4700 N. Council Hill Rd., 61036
(815) 777-2975

Pine Hollow is located on a secluded 110-acre Christmas tree farm just one mile from Main Street Galena. Roam around the grounds and enjoy the wildlife or simply put your feet up, lean back and enjoy the country from our front porch. We provide all the comforts of home in a beautiful country setting. Each of our rooms is decorated in a country style with four-poster queen-size beds, fireplaces, and private bath. Whirlpool bath suites are available.

Hosts: Sally and Larry Priske
Rooms: 5 (PB) $75-100
Continental Breakfast
Credit Cards: A, B, D
Notes: 2, 5, 8, 9, 10, 11, 12

HARRISBURG

House of Nahum
90 Sally Holler Lane
(618) 252-1414

Come discover the warmth and comfort of a country B&B, nestled in the Shawnee National Forest. The House of Nahum provides a charming, personalized atmosphere. Relax on an old-fashioned veranda with complimentary lemonade, iced tea, and goodies. Enjoy a charming antique-furnished room with a private bath and views of the forest. Conveniently located within 30 minutes of famous historic sights and places in southern Illinois.

Hostess: Sona Thomas
Rooms: 4 (PB) $65-85
Full Breakfast
Credit Cards: A, B
Notes: 2, 5, 9, 12

HIGHLAND

Phyllis' Bed and Breakfast
801 9th St., 62249
(618) 654-4619

Highland, known as "Neu-Schweizerland," is located just 30 miles east of St. Louis. The inn was built around the turn of the century and is close to town square, stores, shops, and restaurants. In the square is a gazebo where festivals and music concerts are held in the summer. At Christmas time, the square and gazebo are decorated for the season. Points of interests include Latzer Homestead, Lindendale Park/Fairgrounds, Wicks Organ Company, and other fascinating landmarks. Each room is uniquely decorated. Smoking only on the deck and no alcoholic beverages permitted.

Hostess: Phyllis Bible
Rooms: 5 (3PB; 2SB) $45-55
Hearty Continental Breakfast
Credit Cards: A, B
Notes: 2, 5, 8, 9, 10

NOTES: Credit cards accepted: A Master Card; B Visa; C American Express; D Discover Card; E Diners Club; F Other; 2 Personal checks accepted; 3 Lunch available; 4 Dinner available; 5 Open all

JERSEYVILLE

The Homeridge Bed and Breakfast

1470 North State St., 62052
(618) 498-3442

Beautiful, warm, brick 1867 Italianate Victorian private home on 18 acres in comfortable, country atmosphere. Drive through stately iron gates and pine tree-lined driveway to 14-room historic estate of Senator Theodore Chapman. Expansive pillared front porch; hand-carved, curved stairway to spacious guest rooms and third floor. 20' x 40' swimming pool. Central air-conditioning. Located between Springfield, IL, and St. Louis, MO.

Hosts: Sue and Howard Landon
Rooms: 4 (SB) $65
Full Breakfast
Credit Cards: A, B
Notes: 2, 5, 7 (over 14), 8, 9 (on grounds), 10

METROPOLIS

Park Street House B&B

310 Park Street, 62960
(618) 524-5966

Graced with original oak woodwork, antiques, and private collections, each room has unique character. This circa 1910 home is ideally located in a small river town within walking distance to shops, restaurants, riverfront, and the Superman museum. Minutes away from Fort Massac State Park, the American Quilt Museum, antique shops, and many scenic parks with hiking trails. Enjoy breakfast in dining room or on the balcony overlooking Washington park. Resident bent willow furniture craftsman.

Hosts: Ron and Melodee Thomas
Rooms: 4 (PB) $45-75
Full Breakfast
Credit Cards: A, B
Notes: 2, 5, 7, 12

Park Street House

MOUNT CARMEL

The Poor Farm B&B

Poor Farm Rd., 62863-9803
(800) 646-3276

From 1857 to 1949 the Wabash County Poor Farm served as home for the homeless. Today the Poor Farm B&B is home for the traveler who enjoys a warm friendly atmosphere and a gracious glimpse of yesteryear. Located next to a 25-acre park with a well-stocked lake, within walking distance from perhaps the finest 18-hole municipal golf course in Illinois; and a 15 minute drive lands you in the spectacular 270-acre Beall Woods Conservation Area and Nature Preserve!

Hosts: Liz and John Stelzer
Rooms: 4 (2 suites and 2 doubles) (PB) $45-85
Full Country Breakfast
Credit Cards: A, B, C, D
Notes: 2, 3+4 (for large groups of 10-30), 5, 7, 8, 9, 10, 12

---

year; 6 Pets welcome; 7 Children welcome; 8 Tennis nearby; 9 Swimming nearby; 10 Golf nearby; 11 Skiing nearby; 12 May be booked through travel agent

NAUVOO

Mississippi Memories Bed and Breakfast

Box 291, RR 1, 62354
(217) 453-2771

Located on the banks of the Mississippi, this gracious home offers lodging and elegantly served, all-homemade, full breakfast. Each room features fresh fruit and flowers. In quiet, wooded surroundings, it's just two miles from historic Nauvoo with 30 restored Mormon-era homes and shops. Two decks offer spectacular sunsets, drifting barges, and bald eagle watching; piano; two fireplaces; and library. AAA three-diamond rated. No smoking, alcohol, or pets to interupt your stay.

Hosts: Marge and Dean Starr
Rooms: 5 (2PB; 3SB) $59-79
Full Breakfast
Credit Cards: A, B
Notes: 2, 5, 8, 9, 10

OAKLAND

Johnson's Country Home

109 E. Main Street, 61943
(217) 346-3274

This two-story brick Italianate style home, built in 1874 has had many uses in its years of history. During the Great Depression it was a multifamily dwelling. Later it was used for a VFW post—a restaurant known as the Old House. It was a storage building for farm equipment prior to the Johnson's ownership. Today it is again a lovely home, listed in the Coles County Register of Historic Places.

Hosts: Reece and June Johnson
Rooms: 2 (SB) $40
Continental Breakfast
Credit Cards: None
Notes: 2, 7, 8, 9, 10

PETERSBURG

A Bit of Country

122 W. Sheridan, 62675
(217) 632-3771

Our guests enter strangers and depart friends. This home has the warmth of Victorian living with a lovely collection of period furniture, beautifully decorated rooms with private baths and, most important, hospitality. We are located in the historic district of Petersburg, two miles from Lincoln's New Salem. We are just minutes from Springfield and other Lincoln historic sites.

Hosts: Jay and Mary Lou Jackson
Rooms: 3 (2PB, 1SB) $40
Full Breakfast
Credit Cards: None
Notes: 2, 5, 7, 8, 9, 10, 12

QUINCY

The Kaufmann House

1641 Hampshire, 62301
(217) 223-2502

Heart-warming hospitality, that's what you feel as you are welcomed into the genuine Midwest charm and hospitality of Quincy, the twice-acclaimed "All-American City." Imagine yourself sleeping in an intimate Victorian bedchamber, freshly treated with flowers and light, or slumbering on a painted iron bed among brightly pieced quilts in the simplicity of early American atmosphere. .

NOTES: Credit cards accepted: A Master Card; B Visa; C American Express; D Discover Card; E Diners Club; F Other; 2 Personal checks accepted; 3 Lunch available; 4 Dinner available; 5 Open all

.then waking to the delicious aroma of piping hot, homemade rolls, coffee and tea, complemented by chilled, fresh fruit— served to you on the stone terraced patio or the antique-filled Ancestor Room. Come, indulge and pamper yourself.

Hosts: Emery and Bettie Kaufmann
Rooms: 3 (1PB; 2SB) $45-65
Gourmet Continental Breakfast
Credit Cards: None
Notes: 2, 5, 7, 9, 10, 12

STREATOR

Dicus House B&B

609 E. Broadway St., 61364
(815) 672-6700

Located near Starved Rock State Park, 90 miles southwest of Chicago. 1890 Historic Register Home, carved woodwork, six marble fireplaces, four guest rooms, private baths, air-conditioning. Enjoy the large front porch, antique-filled rooms, and hearty breakfast. Relax and be pampered. IBBA inspected and approved. Private English teas, lunches, and dinners for groups up to 25 people by special arrangement.

Hosts: Felicia and Art Bucholtz
Rooms: 4 (2PB; 2SB) $45-55
Full Breakfast
Credit Cards: A, B, C, D
Notes: 2, 3+4 (by arrangement), 5, 7 (over 10), 10

WINNETKA

Chateau des Fleurs

552 Ridge Road, 60093
(708) 256-7272

This authentic French, country home was built in 1936 on three-fourths acre filled with magnificant trees, expansive lawns, and English gardens. A home filled with antiques as well as comforts. Private baths, jacuzzi, A/C, hardwood floors, telephone in room, TV, fireplaces in common rooms, and lovely views from every window. Only four blocks to Northwestern Train commuting to the Chicago Loop in 30 minutes. Lake Michigan is 10 blocks and O'Hare Airport 30 minutes west.

Hostess: Sally H. Ward
Rooms: 2 (PB) $95
Full Breakfast
Credit Cards: None
Notes: 2, 5, 7 (over 11), 8, 9 (20' by 40', on grounds), 10, 11, 12

Chateau des Fleurs

year; 6 Pets welcome; 7 Children welcome; 8 Tennis nearby; 9 Swimming nearby; 10 Golf nearby; 11 Skiing nearby; 12 May be booked through travel agent

Indiana

AUBURN

Hill Top Country Inn

1733 Co. Rd. 28, 46706
(219) 281-2298

The Hill Top Country Inn offers a quiet and beautiful setting with country porches, walking area, and distinctive bed chambers and sitting room. Our rooms are decorated with a variety of quilts, stenciling, and country antiques. Places to visit in the area include antique shops, museum, lakes, and parks.

Hosts: Chuck and Becky Derrow
Rooms: 4 (1PB; 3SB) $50-70
Full Breakfast
Credit Cards: None
Notes: 2, 5, 7, 12

Hill Top Country Inn

Yawn to Dawn B&B

211 W. Fifth St., 46706
(219) 925-2583

Enjoy the friendly atmosphere of a 1900s home decorated with touches of antiques and collectibles. Within the Auburn area you'll find the Auburn Cord Duesenberg Museum, The National Auto and Trucks Railroad and Art Museums, shopping malls, theaters, Pokagon State Park, fine dining, golf courses, and a beautiful children's zoo, all located 5 to 30 minutes from Yawn to Dawn. Whether traveling I-69 or the IL/IN/OH toll road, Yawn to Dawn is your place to rest.

Hosts: Don and Shirley Quick
Rooms: 3 (SB) $45
Full Breakfast
Credit Cards: None
Notes: 2, 5, 8, 9, 10, 11

BRISTOL

Tyler's Place

19562 St. Rd. 120, 46507
(219) 848-7145

Tyler's Place is located in the heart of Amish country. On a 27-hole golf course, with five rooms available, you can relax on the deck enjoying the outdoor water gar-

---

NOTES: Credit cards accepted: A Master Card; B Visa; C American Express; D Discover Card; E Diners Club; F Other; 2 Personal checks accepted; 3 Lunch available; 4 Dinner available; 5 Open all

den, and the warm Hoosier hospitality. Full breakfast. Enjoy a back-roads tour of Amish country. Three miles from I80-90 toll road.

Hostess: Esther Tyler
Rooms: 4 (2PB; 2SB) $50-75
Full Breakfast
Credit Cards: A, B
Notes: 2, 5, 7, 8, 9, 10, 11

CORYDON

The Kintner House Inn

101 South Capitol Ave., 47112
(812) 738-2020

AAA rated, this completely restored inn, circa 1873, is on the National Register of Historic Places and is furnished with Victorian and country antiques. It features five fireplaces and serves a full breakfast in the dining room. The staff prides itself on personal attention and guests' comfort. Fifteen elegant rooms all with private baths and color TVs; five with fireplaces and seven with VCRs. A hideaway for romantics.

Hostess: Mary Jane Bridgwater
Rooms: 15 (PB) $39-89
Full Breakfast
Credit Cards: A, B, C, D, E
Notes: 2, 5, 8, 9, 10, 11

CRAWFORDSVILLE

Davis House

1010 W. Wabash Ave., 47933
(317) 364-0461

You'll enjoy the unique colonial atmosphere of this 1870 country mansion.

Located in a quiet neighborhood, convenient to Wabash College and several local museums. Renovated in 1940, this historic home combines the original grace with the modern guest conveniences. Common rooms available for group meetings. Limited smoking.

Hosts: Jan and Dave Stearns
Rooms: 5 (PB) $49-65
Full Breakfast
Credit Cards: A, B, C, D
Notes: 2, 5, 7, 12

Sugar Creek Queen Anne Bed and Breakfast

901 W. Market, P. O. Box 726, 47933
(317) 362-4095; (800) 392-6293

Surrounded by beautiful flowers and shrubs, located in the heart of Crawfordsville, Sugar Creek's Queen Anne Bed and Breakfast welcomes all who enjoy a cozy, warm atmosphere. Built in 1900, the home features Victorian decor with statues throughout. Breakfast is served beside lace-curtained windows. Four lovely rooms, each with a private bath, await guests. An added feature is the jacuzzi room for a relaxing atmosphere. Honeymooners are offered a special package rate which includes flowers and non-alcoholic champagne in their room. Each guest's stay includes a limo sightseeing tour of historical Crawfordsville: Lane Place, Lew Wallace Study, and Old Jail Museum. The B&B is also available for weddings, receptions, and groups.

Hostess: Mary Alice and Hal Barbee
Rooms: 4 (PB) $60
Deluxe Continental Breakfast
Credit Cards: A, B
Notes: 2, 5, 7, 8, 9

year; 6 Pets welcome; 7 Children welcome; 8 Tennis nearby; 9 Swimming nearby; 10 Golf nearby; 11 Skiing nearby; 12 May be booked through travel agent

FRANKLIN

Oak Haven Bed and Breakfast

Route #2, Box 57, 46131
(317) 535-9491

Our 1913 home is nestled among large trees that give a feeling of tranquility to our country setting. Enjoy the beautifully decorated rooms, antiques, and oak woodwork and floors throughout our home. Come play our player piano or relax on the porch swing. A full country breakfast is served in our formal dining room. We are conveniently located 25 minutes south of Indianapolis and close to golf courses and shopping centers. Come experience our country hospitality!

Hosts: Alan and Brenda Smith
Rooms: 4 (2PB; 2SB) $45-70
Full Breakfast
Credit Cards: A, B
Notes: 2, 5, 7, 10

GOSHEN

Timberidge Bed and Breakfast

16801 SR 4, 46526
(219) 533-7133

The Austrian chalet, white pine log home is nestled in the beauty of the quiet woods, just two miles from Goshen and near many local points of interest. Our guests enjoy the privacy of a master suite. A path through the woods is frequented by birds, squirrels, deer. Nearby are Amish farms where field work is done by horsedrawn equipment. Timberidge offers the best of city and country—close to town, yet removed to the majestic beauty of the woods that evokes a love of nature and a reverence for God's creation. AC and TV.

Hosts: Edward and Donita Brookmyer
Rooms: 1 master suite (PB) $60
Full and Continental Breakfast Available
Credit Cards: None
Notes: 2

HARTFORD CITY

De'Coys' Bed and Breakfast

1546 W 100 N, 47348
(317) 348-2164

Located just west of Hartford City, Indiana, De'Coys' Bed and Breakfast offers its clients extraordinary, attractive guest rooms with many special "Hoosier" touches. Guests enjoy a relaxed rural atmosphere in an old restored country home enriched with many amenities not customary to the typical hotel or motel setting. Each room demonstrates its own character, featuring antique furnishings and comfortable arrangements. An overnight stay includes a complimentary breakfast consisting of homemade specialties served from the thrasher kitchen.

Hosts: Chris and Tiann Coy
Rooms: 5 (1PB; 4SB) $44-50
Full Breakfast
Credit Cards: None
Notes: 2, 5, 7

NOTES: Credit cards accepted: A Master Card; B Visa; C American Express; D Discover Card; E Diners Club; F Other; 2 Personal checks accepted; 3 Lunch available; 4 Dinner available; 5 Open all

HUNTINGTON

Purviance House
326 South Jefferson, 46750
(219) 356-4218 or (219) 356-9215

Built in 1859, this beautiful home is on the National Register of Historic Places. It features a winding cherry staircase, ornate ceilings, unique fireplaces, and parquet floors and has been lovingly restored and decorated with antiques and period furnishings to create a warm, inviting atmosphere. Amenities include TV in rooms, snacks, beverages, kitchen privileges, and library. Near recreational areas with swimming, boating, hiking, and bicycling. Historic tours available. One-half hour from Fort Wayne; two hours from Indianapolis.

Hosts: Bob and Jean Gernand
Rooms: 4 (2PB; 2SB) $40-65
Full Breakfast
Credit Cards: A, B, C, D
Notes: 2, 5, 7, 8, 9, 10

INDIANAPOLIS

Carriage House Bed and Breakfast
6440 N. Michigan Rd., 46268
(317) 255-5658

Relax and enjoy all the comforts of home in your own private quarters. Located within ten to fifteen minutes of most Indianapolis events. Can accommodate groups of six to eight. Upstairs suite includes large whirlpool bath. Our facilities are smoke free and please, no alcohol on the premises.

Hosts: David and Sue Wilson
Rooms: 2 (2PB) $50-75
Full Breakfast
Credit Cards: None
Notes: 2, 5, 10

KNIGHTSTOWN

Old Hoosier House
7601 S. Greensboro Pike, 46148
(317) 845-2969; (800) 775-5315

Central Indiana's first and favorite country bed and breakfast located at historic Knightstown, midway between Indianapolis and Richmond. Ideally situated for sightseeing and shopping Indianna's "Antique Alley." Golf on the adjoining eighteen hole Royal Hylands golf course. Golf package available. Handicap accessible. Member of Indiana Bed and Breakfast Association and American Historic Inn, Inc.

Hosts: Tom Lewis and Jean Lewis
Rooms: 4 (3PB; 1SB) $57-67 plus tax
Full Breakfast
Credit Cards: None
Notes: 2, 5, 7, 8, 10, 12

LAGRANGE

A Step Back in Time The 1886 Inn
P. O. Box 5, 212 W. Factory St., 46761
(219) 463-4227

The 1886 Inn bed and breakfast is filled with historic charm and elegance. Every room is aglow with old-fashioned beauty. It is the finest lodging in the area, yet affordable. Ten minutes from Shipshewana

year; 6 Pets welcome; 7 Children welcome; 8 Tennis nearby; 9 Swimming nearby; 10 Golf nearby; 11 Skiing nearby; 12 May be booked through travel agent

flea market.

Hosts: Duane and Gloria Billman
Rooms: 4 (PB) $89
Expanded Continental Breakfast
Credit Cards: A, B
Notes: 2, 5, 8, 10

Weaver's Country Oaks

0310 N. US. 20, P.O. Box 632, Shipshewana,
46565
(219) 768-7191

This very comfortable two-level home is
located just three miles from Shipshewana,
amongst Amish farmland. Located on
three and a half acres of well landscaped
property. Tasteful country decor throughout the home with delicious country breakfast. Special rates for full-house reservations. Open all year. Nearby attractions
include reknowned summer flea market,
weekly auctions, golf courses, natural wildlife reserves, museums, many shops and
Amish stores.

Hosts: Catherine and LaMar (Rocky) Weaver
Rooms: 4 (PB) $65-75
Full Breakfast
Credit Cards: A, B
Notes: 2, 5, 8, 10

METAMORA

The Thorpe House Country Inn

P.O. Box 36, Clayborne Street, 47030
(317) 932-2365 or (317) 647-5425

Visit the Thorpe House in historic
Metamora where the steam engine still
brings passenger cars and the grist mill still
grinds cornmeal. Spend a relaxing evening
in this 1840 canal town home. Rooms are

tastefully furnished with antiques and country accessories. Enjoy a hearty breakfast
before visiting more than 100 shops in this
quaint village. Our family-style dining room
is also open to the public.

Hosts: Mike and Jean Owens
Rooms: 4 + two-room suite (PB) $70-125
Full Breakfast
Credit Cards: A, B, D
Notes: 2, 3, 4, 6, 7, 10, 12

MIDDLEBURY

Bee Hive B&B

Box 1191, 46540
(219) 825-5023

Come visit Amish country and enjoy Hoosier hospitality. The Bee Hive is a two-story,
open floor plan with exposed handsawed
red oak beams and a loft. Enjoy our
collection of antique farm machinery and
other collectibles. Snuggle under handmade quilts and wake to the smell of
freshly baked muffins. A guest cottage is
available.

Hosts: Herb and Treva Swarm
Rooms: 4 (1PB; 3SB) $52-70
Full Breakfast
Credit Cards: A, B
Notes: 2, 5, 7, 8, 9, 10, 11

Bee Hive Bed and Breakfast

The Country Victorian

The Country Victorian
435 South Main St., 46540
(219) 825-2568

Come celebrate 100 years of lovely Victorian living. Our home is a fully updated Victorian with lots of charm and original style. Located in the heart of Amish country, relax on the porch and watch buggies drive by. In colder months, sit by the fireplace to chat or curl up with a good book. We offer complimentary gourmet desserts for evening refreshment. Get pampered and experience the loving family atmosphere where children are welcome. Very accessible to Indiana's toll road (I-80/90) and handy to Shipshewana. Other local attractions include Amish-style restaurants and crafters, community festivals, University of Notre Dame and Goshen College.

Hosts: Mark and Becky Potterbaum
Rooms: 4 (2PB; 2SB) $89
Full Breakfast
Credit Cards: A, B
Notes: 5, 7, 10, 11, 12

A Laber of Love—Bed and Breakfast by Lori
11030 CR 10, 46540
(219) 825-7877

New Cape Cod home located in northern Indiana Amish farm country on three acres—two of which are wooded. Screened-in gazebo in woods ideal for quiet time or just relaxing. Queen-size beds and private baths. Air conditioned. (Guests rooms are located upstairs.) Close to large flea market open from May to October on Tuesdays and Wednesdays. Lots of shopping in Middlebury and Shipshewana. Home-baked cinnamon rolls highlight continental breakfast. No smoking or alcohol.

Hostess: Lori Laber
Rooms: 2 (PB) $55
Continental Breakfast
Credit Cards: None
Notes: 2, 5, 10, 12

Look Out B&B
14544 CR 12, 46540
(219) 825-9809

Located in the Amish country of northeast Indiana. Near the Menno-Hof (Amish-Mennonite Information Center); Shipshewana auction and flea market; antique, craft, and gift shops; famous restaurants; and the 1832 Bonneyville mill. Enjoy the spectacular view with a country-style breakfast in the sunroom. Swim in the private pool, or walk the wooded trails.

Hosts: Mary-Lou and Jim Wolfe
Rooms: 5 (3PB; 2SB) $50-70
Full Breakfast
Credit Cards: A, B
Notes: 2, 5, 7, 9, 10, 11

year; 6 Pets welcome; 7 Children welcome; 8 Tennis nearby; 9 Swimming nearby; 10 Golf nearby; 11 Skiing nearby; 12 May be booked through travel agent

Mary's Place

305 Eugene Drive, PO Box 428, 46540
(219) 825-2429

A modern home with three available guest rooms. Amenities include queen-size beds, air-conditioning, private entrance, private family room, and cable TV. Call or write for reservations.

Hosts: Alvin and Mary Kauffman
Rooms: 5 (3PB; 2SB) $45-50
Continental Breakfast
Credit Cards: None
Notes: 2, 5, 7, 10

Patchwork Quilt Country Inn

11748 CR2, 46540
(219) 825-2417; (219) 825-5172 (FAX)

Relax and enjoy the simple grace and charm of our 100-year-old farmhouse. Sample our country cooking with home-made breads and desserts. Tour our back roads, and meet our Amish friends. Buy handmade articles, then return to the inn and rest in our quaint guest rooms.

Hostesses: Maxine Zook and Susan Thomas
Rooms: 9 (SB) $50.95-95
Full Breakfast
Credit Cards: A, B
Closed January, some holidays, and Sundays
Notes: 2, 3, 4, 8, 10, 11, 12

Yoder's Zimmer mit Frühstück Haus

P.O. Box 1396, 504 S. Main, 46540
(219) 825-2378

We enjoy sharing our Amish-Mennonite heritage in our spacious Crystal Valley home. The rooms feature handmade quilts and antiques. Antiques and collectibles can be seen throughout the home. Three of our rooms can accommodate families. There are several common rooms available for relaxing, reading, TV, games, or socializing. Facilities are also available for pastor-elder retreats. Air conditioned, playground, swimming pool.

Hosts: Wilbur E. and Evelyn Yoder
Rooms: 5 (5 rooms to 2.5SB) $52.50
Full Breakfast
Credit Cards: A, B
Notes: 2, 5, 7, 8, 9, 10, 11, 12

MIDDLETOWN

Country Rose B&B

5098 North Mechanicsburg Rd., 47356
(317) 779-4501; (800) 395-6449

A small town garden bed and breakfast looking out on berry patches and flower gardens. Awake early or late to breakfast of fried mush, fried apples, and country Tennessee biscuits. 50 minutes to Indianapolis, 20 minutes to Anderson and Ball State University.

Hosts: Rose and Jack Lewis
Rooms: 2 (1suite; 1SB) $45-65
Full Breakfast
Credit Cards: None
Notes: 2, 5, 7, 8, 10

NAPPANEE

Market St. Guesthouse

253 E. Market Street, 46550
(219) 773-2261; (800) 497-3791

Three-story brick Colonial home completely restored. On National Register of

NOTES: Credit cards accepted: A Master Card; B Visa; C American Express; D Discover Card; E Diners Club; F Other; 2 Personal checks accepted; 3 Lunch available; 4 Dinner available; 5 Open all

Historical Places. Private baths, full breakfast. Near Shipshewana and Notre Dame.

Hostess: Sharon Bontrager
Rooms: 5 (3PB; 2SB) $50-60
Full Breakfast
Credit Cards: A, B
Notes: 2, 4 (reservations one week in advance,
5, 8, 9, 10, 11

Victorian Guest House

302 E. Market Street, 46550
(219) 773-4383

Antiques, stained glass windows and pocket doors highlight this 1887 Historical Register mansion. Nestled amongst the Amish Countryside where antique shops abound. A warm welcome waits as you return to gracious living with all the ambiance of the 1800s. Everything has been designed to make your "Bed & Breakfast" stay a memorable one. Close to Notre Dame and Shipshewana. Two hours from Chicago. Complimentary evening tea and sweets. "Prepare for a memory."

Hosts: Bruce and Vickie Hunsberger
Rooms: 6 (PB) $39-75
Full Breakfast
Credit Cards: A, B, D
Notes: 2, 5, 8, 9, 10

Victorian Guest House

NASHVILLE

Day Star Inn

87 E. Main St., P.O. Box 361, 47448
(812) 988-0430

Day Star Inn is in downtown Nashville in beautiful Brown County. There are over 200 shops and restaurants, art galleries, country music shows, drama theatres, and more. We are two miles from scenic Brown County State Park, and many churches for worship. We require no smoking, alcohol, or pets. All rooms have private baths and cable TV.

Hosts: Ed and Vivian Taggart
Rooms: 5 and parlor (PB) $70-85
Continental Plus Breakfast
Credit Cards: A, B
Notes: 2, 5, 7, 8, 9, 10, 11, 12

Wraylyn Knoll B&B

2008 Greasy Creek. Rd., P.O. Box 481, 47448
(812) 988-0733

Wraylyn Knoll B&B is a family-owned and operated large main house with four guest rooms, small cottage with two guest rooms, and lots of common areas. In-ground swimming pool, fishing pond, hiking trails over 12 acres. On a high hill, great view. Croquet and porch swings. Awesome view of the stars. Help yourself to refreshments in the evening. Cool breezes and warm welcomes! We welcome small groups, too.

Hosts: Marcia and Larry Wray
Rooms: 6 (PB) $65-85
Full Breakfast on Weekends (Continental on Weekdays)
Credit Cards: A, B
Notes: 2, 5, 7, 8, 9, 10, 11, 12

year; 6 Pets welcome; 7 Children welcome; 8 Tennis nearby; 9 Swimming nearby; 10 Golf nearby; 11 Skiing nearby; 12 May be booked through travel agent

PAOLI

Braxtan House Inn Bed and Breakfast

210 North Gospel St., 47454
(812) 723-4677; (800) 6BRAXTAN

The Inn is an 1893 Queen Anne Victorian listed on the National Register of Historic Places. The Braxtan Family converted it into a hotel in the 1920s, and the house has been restored and furnished with antiques. Ski Paoli Peaks, enjoy Patoka Lake, explore the cave, and canoe the country nearby. Close to Louisville, KY, and Bloomington, IN.

Hosts: Duane and Kate Wilhelmi
Rooms: 6 (PB) $55-65
Full Breakfast
Credit Cards: A, B, C, D
Notes: 2, 5, 7, 8, 9, 10, 11, 12

Rosewood Mansion Inn

PERU

Rosewood Mansion Inn

54 N. Hood, 46970
(317) 472-7151; (317) 472-5575 (FAX)

The Rosewood is a lovely Victorian home in downtown Peru, IN. A welcome change from impersonal hotel accommodations, we offer the warmth and friendliness of a private home, with the privacy and elegance of a fine hotel, for a truly unique experience. Consider the Rosewood Mansion for your next romantic getaway, anniversary, party, business meeting, or corporate retreat. Whether business or pleasure brings you to Peru, the Rosewood Mansion rewards you with a wonderful experience at a moderate price.

Hosts: Lynn and Dave Hausner
Rooms: 8 (PB) $65-80
Full Breakfast
Credit Cards: A, B, C, D
Notes: 2, 5, 7, 8, 9, 10, 12

RICHMOND

Norwich Lodge and Conference Center

920 Earlham Dr., 47374
(317) 983-1575 (voice and FAX)

Surrounded by 400 acres of woods and streams, Norwich Lodge is open year-round and provides the ideal getaway for anyone who wants to escape life's daily routine. Outside the Lodge a choice of paths can lead you on a fascinating escapade through one of nature's most scenic and beautiful playgrounds. You can hike along winding creeks, pause to watch the wildlife, or spot a variety of birds that inhabit the surrounding countryside.

Hostesses: Melissa Bickford and Lois Hood
Rooms: 15 (PB) $35-45
Continental Breakfast
Credit Cards: A, B
Notes: 2, 5, 7, 8, 9

NOTES: Credit cards accepted: A Master Card; B Visa; C American Express; D Discover Card; E Diners Club; F Other; 2 Personal checks accepted; 3 Lunch available; 4 Dinner available; 5 Open all

Philip W. Smith Bed and Breakfast

2039 East Main St., 47374
(800) 966-8972

Elegant Queen Anne Victorian family home located in East Main-Glen Miller Park Historic District, right on the IN-OH border off I-70. Built in 1890 by Philip W. Smith, the two-and-a-half story brick has Romanesque details and features stained glass windows and ornate-carved wood. Four distinctive guest rooms: two with full-size beds, two with queen-size beds. Unwind in the evening with homemade snacks, coffee, and tea. Awaken to a breakfast highlighting fresh, regional ingredients. Stroll through four historic districts, listen to outdoor concerts in the park, hike Whitewater River Gorge, relax in the garden at the B&B, and shop unique shops of Richmond and "Antique Alley." AAA. ABBA.

Hosts: Chip and Chartley Bondurant
Rooms: 4 (PB) $65-75
Full Breakfast
Credit Cards: A, B, D
Notes: 2, 5, 7, 10, 11, 12

ROCKPORT—SEE OWENSBORO, KENTUCKY

SHIPSHEWANA

Morton Street Bed and Breakfast

140 Morton Street, P. O. Box 775, 46565
(219) 768-4391; (800) 447-6475; (219) 768-7469 (FAX)

Located in the heart of Amish country in Shipshewana you will find yourself within walking distance of all kinds of shops and the famous Shipshewana flea market. Special winter and weekend rates available.

Hosts: Joel and Kim Mishler and Esther Mishler
Rooms: 10 (PB) (call for rates)
Full Breakfast
Credit Cards: A, B, D
Notes: 2, 5, 7, 10, 11, 12

Philip W. Smith Bed and Breakfast

SOUTH BEND

Queen Anne Inn

420 W. Washington; 46601
(219) 234-5959; (219) 234-4324 (FAX)

This Queen Anne Neo-Classical home built in 1893 was moved in order to preserve the historical structure. Frank Lloyd Wright bookcases, original hand-painted wallpaper, and an ornately carved tiger oak staircase are classics for the house. Guests can relax in the music room, the

year; 6 Pets welcome; 7 Children welcome; 8 Tennis nearby; 9 Swimming nearby; 10 Golf nearby; 11 Skiing nearby; 12 May be booked through travel agent

library, or the wrap around porch. The inn is located near Notre Dame, the Studebaker Museum, and many other historic places. A great place to relax and reflect.

Hosts: Pauline and Bob Medhurst
Rooms: 5 (PB) $65-95
Full Breakfast
Credit Cards: A, B, C
Notes: 2, 5, 7, 8, 9, 10, 11(cross country)

TIPPECANOE

Bessinger's Hillfarm Wildlife Refuge Bed and Breakfast
4588 State Road 110, 46570
(219) 223-3288

This cozy log home overlooks 265 acres of rolling hills, woods, pasture fields, and marsh with 41 islands. It is ideal for geese and deer year-round. This farm features hiking trails with beautiful views, picnic areas, and benches tucked away in a quiet area. Varied seasons make it possible to canoe, swim, fish, bird-watch, hike, and cross-country ski. Start with a country breakfast and be ready for an unforgettable experience.

Hosts: Wayne and Betty Bessinger
Rooms: 3 (PB) $55-65
Full Breakfast
Credit Cards: None
Notes: 2, 5, 9, 10, 11, 12

WARSAW

Candlelight Inn
503 E. Fort Wayne St.
(219) 267-2906; (800) 352-0640; (219) 269-4646 (FAX)

A 1860 Italianate home renovated by Bill and Debi Hambright. The Inn features eleven-foot ceilings, natural woodwork, a grand stairway, marble fireplace, antique-filled rooms, and large porch. Whirlpool tubs available along with queen- and king-size beds, phones, and cable TV in each room. Our Victorian home offers all the old world charm with today's modern comforts.

Hosts: Ron and Lori McSorley
Rooms: 11 (PB) $69-135
Full Home-cooked Breakfast
Credit Cards: A, B, C
Notes: 2, 5, 8, 9, 10, 12 (no commission)

Iowa

AMANA COLONIES

Die Heimat Country Inn

Main Street, Homestead, 52236
(319) 622-3937

Die Heimat Country Inn is located in the historic Amana Colonies. It was built in 1854 and is listed on the National Register of Historic Places. The inn is decorated with locally handcrafted walnut and cherry furniture, with many homemade quilts and antiques throughout. Cash, personal check, or traveler's check is the preferred payment.

Hosts: Warren and Jacki Lock
Rooms: 19 (PB) $36-65
Full Breakfast
Credit Cards: A, B, D
Notes: 2, 5, 6, 7, 9, 10

BURLINGTON

Lakeview B&B

11351 60th Street, 52601
(319) 752-8735; (800) 753-8735; (319) 752-5126
(FAX)

Built from the ruins of the county's third oldest home, the elegant country home stands where stagecoach passengers once slept. Now your retreat to Lakeview is a mix of the old and the new on 30 acres of magnificent country charm. The house features crystal chandeliers, antiques, collectibles, and a circular staircase. Outdoors you can enjoy a swim in our pool; fishing in our three-acre lake stocked with catfish, bass, crappie, and bluegill; or just spend time making friends with our family of miniature horses. Guests can also take advantage of our large video library of noted Christian speakers. A video studio is available for recording and small conferences.

Hosts: Jack and Linda Rowley
Rooms: 4 (PB) $45-60
Expanded Continental Breakfast
Credit Cards: A, B
Notes: 2, 5, 8, 9, 10, 12

The Schramm House Bed and Breakfast

616 Columbia St., 52601
(319) 754-0373 (voice and FAX)

Step into the past when you enter this restored 1870s Victorian in the heart of the Historical District. High ceilings, parquet floors, original oak woodwork, wainscoting, and antique furnishing create the mood of an era past. Experience Burlington hospitality while having lemonade on the porch or tea by the fire with your gracious hosts. Walk to the Mississippi River, antique shops, restaurants, and more. An architectural masterpiece awaits you in the

City of Steeples.

Hosts: Sandy and Bruce Morrison
Rooms: 2 (PB) $65-75
Full Breakfast
Credit Cards: A, B
Notes: 2, 5, 7, 8, 9, 10

CALMAR

Calmar Guesthouse

103 North Street, 52132
(319) 562-3851

Newly remodeled, this century-old Victorian home was built by attorney John B. Kaye and has stained glass, antiques, and upstairs and downstairs sitting rooms with cable TV. It is located close to Bily Clocks in Spillville, the smallest church, Spook Cave, Niagara Cave, Lake Meyer, bike trails, golf courses, a community college, Norwegian museum, and Luther College in Decorah. Breakfast is served in the formal dining room. Bicycle trails are nearby.

Hostess: Lucille Kruse
Rooms: 5 (SB) $35-45
Full Breakfast
Credit Cards: A, B
Notes: 2, 5, 7, 8, 9, 10, 11

CENTERVILLE

One of a Kind

314 West State, 52544
(515) 437-4540 (voice and FAX)

One of a Kind is a stately three-story brick home built in 1867. Situated in one of Iowa's delightful small communities. You will be within walking distance of antique shops, the town square, city park with tennis courts, swimming pool, etc. Twelve-minute drive to Iowa's largest lake.

Hosts: Jack and Joyce Stufflebeem
Rooms: 5 (2PB; 3SB) $35-60
Full Breakfast
Credit Cards: A, B
Notes: 2, 3, 4, 5, 8, 9, 10, 11, 12

ELK HORN

Joy's Morning Glory

4308 Main St., Box 12, 51531-0012
(712) 764-5631

Be special guests in our beautiful refurbished 1912 home. As our guest, you will be greeted by an abundant array of flowers that line our walkways. Inside, your choice of floral decorated bedrooms awaits you as well. Breakfast is prepared on Joy's antique cookstove and served in the dining room, front porch, or flower-filled backyard. Elk Horn community is home to the largest rural Danish settlement in the United States. The town has a working windmill and is home to the National Danish Immigrant Museum and the Tivoli Festival.

Hosts: Joy and Merle Petersen
Rooms: 3 (SB) $45
Full Breakfast
Credit Cards: None
Notes: 2, 7 (over 10), 8, 9, 10
Closed January

FOREST CITY

The 1897 Victorian House

306 South Clark St., 50436
(515) 582-3613

Offering you hospitality in this turn-of-the-

NOTES: Credit cards accepted: A Master Card; B Visa; C American Express; D Discover Card; E Diners Club; F Other; 2 Personal checks accepted; 3 Lunch available; 4 Dinner available; 5 Open all

century Queen Anne Victorian home. As a guest at The 1897 Victorian House, you may choose from four beautifully decorated bedrooms, each with a private bath. Breakfast, included in your room rate, is served every morning in our dining room, and we specialize in homemade food. An antique shop is located on premises, and tours of various local interests are available. Gift certificates are available. Come relax in Forest City, a quiet yet progressive rural community.

Hosts: Richard and Doris Johnson
Rooms: 4 (PB) $50-70
Full Breakfast
Credit Cards: A, B
Notes: 2, 3&4 (by reservation), 5, 7 (by arrangement), 9, 10, 12

The 1897 Victorian House

FORT MADISON

Kingsley Inn

707 Avenue H, 52627
(319) 372-7074; (800) 441-2327; (319) 372-7096 (FAX)

Experience complete relaxation in 1860s Victorian luxury. Fourteen spacious rooms are furnished in period antiques with today's modern comforts. Awaken to the aroma of "Kingsley Blend" coffee and enjoy the specialty breakfast in the elegant morning room. Private baths (some whirlpools),

CATV, AC, and telephone. Stroll to replica of 1808 Fort, museum, parks, shops, and antique malls. Fifteen minutes from historic Nauvoo, Illinois. Treat yourself to a relaxing lunch or dinner at our unique restaurant, Alpha's on the Riverfront.

Hosts: Myrna M. Reinhard
Rooms: 14(PB) $65-105 (off season rates)
Continental Plus Breakfast
Credit Cards: A, B, C, D, E
Notes: 2, 3, 4, 5, 7(limited), 9, 10, 12

GRINNELL

Clayton Farms Bed and Breakfast

621 Newburg Rd., 50112
(515) 236-3011

Extra nice contemporary farm home on 320-acre livestock, grain operation. Swimming, fishing area with screened shelter house in season on three-acre farm pond. Family room with fireplace, TV, VCR, library of movies, kitchenette, and central air. Family-style breakfast, homemade breads, rolls, jams, jellies. Ideal accommodations for pheasant hunters. Packages for groups of hunters. Seven miles from Grinnell College. One hour from Des Moines and Iowa City. No smoking. Member of the Iowa Bed and Breakfast Innkeepers Association and the Iowa Lodging Association. Call or write for a brochure.

Hosts: Ron and Judie Clayton
Rooms: 3 (1PB; 2SB) $47.25-55.50 (special hunters' package)
Full Breakfast
Credit Cards: A, B
Notes: 2 (for deposit only), 6 (hunting dogs), 7 (eight and over), 8, 9, 10, 11

year; 6 Pets welcome; 7 Children welcome; 8 Tennis nearby; 9 Swimming nearby; 10 Golf nearby; 11 Skiing nearby; 12 May be booked through travel agent

IOWA CITY

Bella Vista Place Bed and Breakfast

2 Bella Vista Place, 52245
(319) 338-4129

Daissy has furnished her lovely air-conditioned 1920s home with antiques and artifacts she has acquired on her travels in Europe and Latin America. Conveniently located on Iowa City's historical northside with beautiful view of the Iowa River, within walking distance from downtown and the University of Iowa. The Hoover Library, the Amana Colonies, and the Amish center of Kalona are all nearby. A full breakfast, with Daissy's famous coffee, is served in the dining room's unique antique setting. Daissy is fluent in Spanish and speaks some French. From I-80: take Dubuque St. Exit 244, turn left on Brown St., then first left on Linn St. one block to #2 Bella Vista Place.

Hostess: Daissy P. Owen
Rooms: 4 (2PB; 2SB) $45-75
Full Breakfast
Credit Cards: None
Notes: 2, 5, 7 (over 10), 8, 9, 12

Haverkamp's Linn St. Homestay Bed and Breakfast

619 N. Linn St., 52245-1934
(319) 337-4363

Enjoy the warmth and hospitality in our 1908 Edwardian home filled with heirlooms and collectibles. Only a short walk to downtown Iowa City and the University of Iowa main campus, and a short drive to the Hoover Library in West Branch, to the Amish in Kalona, and to the seven Amana Colonies.

Hosts: Dorothy and Clarence Haverkamp
Rooms: 3 (SB) $35-45
Full Breakfast
Credit Cards: None
Notes: 2, 5, 7, 8, 9, 12

KNOXVILLE

La Grande Victorian Bed and Breakfast

802 E. Montgomery, 50138
(515) 842-4653

If you are looking for a quiet time of relaxing, romance, or leisure—or if you are a businessperson needing a studious atmosphere in a unique, lovely old home with timeless ambiance of yesteryears and many comforts of today—try us! No smoking or alcohol, please.

Hosts: Merlin and Charlotte Nelson
Rooms: 3 (PB) $70-125
Full Breakfast
Credit Cards: A, B
Notes: 2, 5, 9, 10

LECLAIRE

Monarch B&B Inn and McCaffrey House B&B

303 South Second St., 52753
(319) 284-3011; (800) 772-7724 (for reservations)

The Monarch B&B Inn (late 1850s) and the McCaffrey House B&B (1870) are working together to provide you with ideal settings for relaxation, meetings, and re-

NOTES: Credit cards accepted: A Master Card; B Visa; C American Express; D Discover Card; E Diners Club; F Other; 2 Personal checks accepted; 3 Lunch available; 4 Dinner available; 5 Open all

treats. Wooden floors, high ceilings, and antique furniture help the homes retain their original charm while air-conditioning, enclosed porches, open decks, and off street parking provide modern-day comforts. Magnificent Mississippi River views, antique shopping, and Buffalo Bill Museum await you in LeClaire, IA.

Hosts: David and Emilie Oltman and Jean Duncan
Rooms: 7 (4PB; 2SB) $45-65
Full or Continental Breakfast
Credit Cards: None
Notes; 2, 3, 4, 5, 7, 10, 12

MAQUOKETA

Squiers Manor Bed and Breakfast

418 West Pleasant Street, 52060
(319) 652-6961; if no answer please call Banowetz
Antiques at (319) 652-5121

Squiers Manor Bed and Breakfast is located in the West Pleasant Street Historic District. This 1892 Queen Anne mansion features walnut, cherry, and butternut woods throughout. Enjoy period furnishings, queen-size beds, in-room phone and television, private baths, single and double jacuzzis. Come hungry and enjoy delicious, candlelight evening desserts and breakfast (more like brunch) served in the elegant dining room. Virl's and Kathy's goal is to make your stay as pleasant and enjoyable as possible. Give us a call today!

Hosts: Virl and Kathy Banowetz
Rooms: 6 (PB) $65-95
Full Breakfast
Credit Cards: A, B, C
Notes: 2, 5, 7, 8, 9, 10, 11, 12

MARENGO

Loy's Farm Bed and Breakfast

2077 KK Ave, 52301
(319) 642-7787

This beautiful, modern home is on a working grain and hog farm with quiet and pleasant views of rolling countryside. A farm tour is offered with friendly hospitality. Pheasant hunting can be enjoyed. The large recreation room includes a pool table, table tennis, and shuffleboard. Swing set and sand pile are in the large yard. Close to the Amana Colonies, Tanger Mall, Kalona, Iowa City, West Branch, and Cedar Rapids. I-80, Exit 216 north, one mile.

Hosts: Loy and Robert Walker
Rooms: 3 (1PB; 2SB) $50-60
Full Breakfast
Credit Cards: None
Notes: 2, 4 (by reservation), 5, 6 (caged), 7, 8, 9, 10 (four courses), 12

PELLA

Heritage House B & B

1345 Highway 163, Leighton, IA 50143
(48 miles SE of DSM, Iowa)
(515) 626-3092

In business since 1983, this lovely 1918 farm home has TVs and central air conditioning. Rooms were redecorated and newly carpeted in 1993. The Victorian room is filled with antique furniture and an old pump organ. Located near Pella, Iowa, famous for Tulip Time the second week of May. Historical tours are available year-around to experience a touch of Holland. Dutch shops and gourmet restaurants.

Many antique shops are nearby. Near Knoxville, Iowa—the sprint car racing capital. Enjoy a gourmet breakfast served in the formal dining room with crystal and lace. Member IBBIA and ILA.

Hostess: Iola Vander Wilt
Rooms: 2 (PB) $45-50
Full Breakfast
Credit Cards: None
Closed January
Notes: 2, 7(with restrictions), 8, 9, 10, 11, 12

PRINCETON

The Woodlands

PO Box 127, 52768
(800) 257-3177

...a secluded woodland escape that can be as private or social as you wish. The Woodlands Bed & Breakfast is nestled among pines on 26 acres of forest and meadows in a private wildlife refuge. Guests delight in an elegant breakfast by the swimming pool or by a cozy fireplace, while viewing the outdoor wildlife activity.

Hosts: The Wallace Family
Rooms: 2 (PB) $60-115
Full Breakfast
Credit Cards: None
Notes; 2, 3, 4, 5, 6 (limited), 7, 8, 9, 10, 11, 12

Blue Belle Inn

SAINT ANSGAR

Blue Belle Inn

513 W. 4th Street, P.O. Box 205, 50472
(515) 736-2225

Rediscover the romance of the 1890s while enjoying the comfort and convenience of the 1990s in one of six distinctively decorated guest rooms at the Blue Belle Inn. The festive Victorian Painted Lady features air conditioning, fireplaces, and jacuzzis. Lofty tin ceilings, gleaming maple woodwork, stained glass, and crystal chandeliers set in bay and curved window pockets create a shimmering interplay of light and color. Enjoy breakfast on the balcony or gourmet dining by candlelight.

Hostess: Sherrie C. Hansen
Rooms: 6 (5PB; 1SB) $40-120
Full Breakfast
Credit Cards: A, B
Notes: 2, 3, 4, 5, 7, 9, 10, 12

SPENCER

Hannah Marie Country Inn

4070 Hwy. 71, 51301
(712) 262-1286; (712) 262-1244 (FAX)

The romance of country: claw foot tubs and whirlpools, central air, softened water, bubble bath by lantern light in our romantic Lamplighter Room, or in the oasis in the Enchanting Safari Room. Herb gardens, Wedding Garden, croquet on the lawn. "Best B&B in Iowa 1990," *Des Moines Register* Readers. "One of the Top 50 Inns in America," by *Inn Times,*

NOTES: Credit cards accepted: A Master Card; B Visa; C American Express; D Discover Card; E Diners Club; F Other; 2 Personal checks accepted; 3 Lunch available; 4 Dinner available; 5 Open all

1991. Lunch/dinner at our Carl Gustav House Bistro. Iowa Great Lakes area, West Bend, and Grotto nearby.

Innkeeper: Mary Nichols
Rooms: 5 (PB) $55-89
Full Breakfast ending with cappuccinos.
Credit Cards: A, B, C, D
Open April - mid Dec.
Notes: 2, 3, 4, 6 (outside), 7, 8, 9, 10, 12 (10%)

SWEDESBURG

The Carlson House

105 Park St., 52652
(319) 254-2451

Accommodations have an old-world charm in this stylishly decorated home in a Swedish-American country village. Guests enjoy the candlelight breakfast with Swedish treats, historical mementos, and gracious hosts. Guest facilities include a sitting room with TV, extensive reading materials, and wide porches for relaxation. The pleasant grounds of the Carlson House are next to the buildings of the Swedish-American Museum of Swedesburg.

Hosts: Ned and Ruth Ratekin
Rooms: 2 (PB) $45
Full Breakfast
Credit Cards: None
Notes; 2, 3, 5, 7, 12

The Carlson House

WALNUT

Antique City Inn Bed and Breakfast

400 Antique City Dr., P.O. Box 584, 51577
(712) 784-3722

This 1911 Victorian home has been restored and furnished to its original state. Enjoy a nostalgic experience of simplicity of life, craftmanship of yesterday, quiet living and small town hospitality. One block from malls and stores with 250 antique dealers. Home has beautiful woods, dumb waiter icebox, French doors, and wraparound porch.

Hostess: Sylvia Reddie
Rooms: 5 (1PB; 4SB) $42 (includes tax)
Full Breakfast
Credit Cards: A, B, C
Notes: 2, 3, 4, 5

Clark's Country Inn

701 Walnut Street, Box 533, 51577
(712) 784-3010

Iowa's antique capital, one mile south of I-80 between Omaha and Des Moines. Six malls, individual shops, over 200 dealers, open all year. 1912 two-story home, oak interior, antiques. Newly-remodeled guest rooms, private baths, king/queen beds, central air, full breakfast. MC/Visa deposit required. No smoking.

Hosts: Ron and Mary Lou Clark
Rooms: 3 (PB) $52
Full Breakfast
Credit Cards: A, B
Notes: 2, 5, 7(over 12), 8, 9, 10, 12

year; 6 Pets welcome; 7 Children welcome; 8 Tennis nearby; 9 Swimming nearby; 10 Golf nearby; 11 Skiing nearby; 12 May be booked through travel agent

WEBSTER CITY

Centennial Farm B&B

1091-220th Street, 50595-7571
(515) 832-3050

Centennial Farm is a bed and breakfast
homestay located on a farm that has been
in the family since 1869. Tom was born in
the house. Guests may take a ride in a
1929 Model A pickup truck, if desired. In
a quiet location near several good antique
shops. Member of Iowa Bed and Breakfast Innkeepers Association, Inc. Air conditioned. Twenty-two miles west of I-35
at Exit 142 or Exit 144.

Hosts: Tom and Shirley Yungclas
Rooms: 2 (SB) $35
Full Breakfast
Credit Cards: None
Notes: 2, 5, 7, 8, 9, 10

WILLIAMSBURG

Lucille's Bett und Breakfast

R.R. 2 Box 55-2835, 52361
(319) 668-1185

Experience Gemütlichkeit (German hospitality) in our country home. Family-style
country breakfast with homemade breads,
apfel kuchen, kolaches, etc., graciously
served. The peaceful, quiet atmosphere
lends itself to the perfect getaway retreat.
Take I-80 to exit 225, Little Amena.

Hosts: Dale and Lucille Bell
Rooms: 2 (plus queen size sofa sleeper) (SB)
$55-60
Full Breakfast
Credit Cards: None
Notes: 2, 3, 4, 5, 7, 9, 10, 12

Lucille's Bett und Breakfast

NOTES: Credit cards accepted: A Master Card; B Visa; C American Express; D Discover Card; E
Diners Club; F Other; 2 Personal checks accepted; 3 Lunch available; 4 Dinner available; 5 Open all

Kansas

ABILENE

Victorian Reflections Bed and Breakfast Inn

820 NW Third, 67410
(913) 263-7701

Enjoy the Victorian splendor of one of Abilene's finest historic homes. Victorian Reflections is located on beautiful Third Street in the historic Hurd House. Relax in parlors or one of the home's many porches. The city park, pool, and tennis courts are adjacent to the home which is also within walking distance of Abilene's many attractions.

Hosts: Don and Diana McBride
Rooms: 4 (PB) $45-65
Full Breakfast
Credit Cards: A, B
Notes: 2, 5, 7 (over 9), 8, 9, 10, 12

GREAT BEND

Peaceful Acres B&B

Rt. 5, Box 153, 67530
(316) 793-7527

Enjoy a mini-farm, sprawling, tree-shaded, old farmhouse furnished with some antiques. If you like quiet and peace, chickens, goats, guineas, kittens in the spring, and old-fashioned hospitality, you need to come and visit us. Breakfast will be fixed

from homegrown products. We are near historical areas, Sante Fe Trail, Ft. Larned, Cheyenne Bottoms, zoo, and tennis courts. Member of the Kansas Bed and Breakfast Association.

Hosts: Dale and Doris Nitzel
Rooms: 3 (SB) $30
Full Breakfast
Credit Cards: None
Notes: 2, 5, 6, 7, 8, 12

HALSTEAD

Heritage Inn

300 Main, 67056
(316) 835-2118

The Heritage Inn offers you the charm of the 1920s, yet the conveniences of the 90s. Each room is beautifully decorated and includes private bath, cable TV, in-room refrigerators, individual heating, air-conditioning, etc. Each morning you will be "our guest" for breakfast which is served in our cozy hotel cafe. While enjoying a leisurely breakfst, you can swap stories with other guests, or get acquainted with local business men and women, and neighbors of the community.

Hosts: Jim and Geri Hartong
Rooms: 7 (PB) $29; $4 for each additional person
Full Breakfast
Credit Cards: A, B
Notes: 2, 3, 4, 5, 7, 8, 9, 10, 12

---

year; 6 Pets welcome; 7 Children welcome; 8 Tennis nearby; 9 Swimming nearby; 10 Golf nearby; 11 Skiing nearby; 12 May be booked through travel agent

MELVERN

Schoolhouse Inn

Rural Route 2, Box 87, 66088
(913) 549-3473

Two-story limestone building built in 1870
sets on a one-and-a-half-acre lawn. In
1986 it was entered in Kansas Historic
places. This Inn is a place you need to
come and visit. The guests can visit in a
parlor with antique furniture or sit around a
large table in the dining room and enjoy
playing games. Four large bedrooms upstairs furnished with antique and contemporary furnishings where guests can relax
while reading a good book or looking at
magazines. Enjoy this B&B for celebrating
your anniversary or just a quiet getaway to
our small town of Melvern.

Hosts: Rudy and Alice White
Rooms: 4 (2PB; 2SB) $50-55
Full Breakfast
Credit Cards: A, B
Notes: 2, 5, 7, 9

NEWTON

Hawk House Bed
and Breakfast

307 W. Broadway, 67114
(316) 283-2045

This elegant 1914 home has original light
fixtures, wallpaper from Europe, and
stained glass windows waiting your arrival.
Three blocks from downtown, where
quaint shops and antiques can be found.
Close to bike paths, historical sites, and
good restaurants. Guest rooms offer
queen-size beds and antique furniture.
Facility is available for meetings, retreats,

weddings, and receptions. Member Kansas B&B Association.

Hosts: Lon and Carol Buller
Rooms: 4 (1PB; 3SB) $50-60
Full Breakfast
Credit Cards: A, B
Notes: 2, 5, 7, 8, 9, 10

VALLEY FALLS

The Barn B&B Inn

Rural Route 2, Box 87, 66088
(913) 945-3225: (913) 945-3226 (FAX)

In the rolling hills of northeast Kansas, this
101-year-old barn has been converted
into a bed and breakfast. Sitting high on a
hill with a beautiful view, it has a large
indoor heated pool, fitness room, three
living rooms, king or queen beds in all
rooms. We serve you supper, as well as a
full breakfast, and have three large meeting
rooms available.

Hosts: Tom and Marcella Ryan
Rooms: 20 (PB) $67-78
Full Breakfast and Supper
Credit Cards: A, B, C, D
Notes: 2, 3, 4, 5, 7, 8, 9, 10, 12

Schoolhouse Inn

Kentucky

BARDSTOWN

Kenmore Farms

1050 Bloomfield Rd., US 62E, 40004
(502) 348-8023; (800) 831-6159

Our 1860s Victorian-Italianate home on 165 acres features antique furnishings, oriental rugs, poplar floors, and a gleaming cherry stairway. Four gracious rooms are decorated with four-poster or Victorian-style beds and beautiful vintage linens. Private baths. Full country breakfast. Enjoy Southern hospitality, a tranquil farm setting, and the convenience of being near tourist attractions of historical Bardstown. Also within an hour's drive of Louisville, Lexington, Shakertown Village, and Mammouth Cave.

Hosts: Dorothy and Bernie Keene
Rooms: 3 (PB) $70
Full Breakfast
Credit Cards: None
Notes: 2, 5, 7 (over 12), 8, 9, 10

Jailer's Inn

111 W. Stephen Foster Ave.
(502) 348-5551

Beautiful historic building, built in 1819 and used as a jail until 1874, then used as the Jailer's residence until 1987. Completely renovated and decorated with an-

tiques and heirlooms. Deluxe continental breakfast served in lovely courtyard in summertime. All bedrooms have private baths, one with jacuzzi. Rated: AAA, Mobil Oil, ABBA. Located in the center of Historic Bardstown.

Hostess: Fran McCoy
Rooms: 6 (PB) $55-90
Deluxe Continental Breakfast
Credit Cards: A, B, C
Notes: 2, 7, 8, 9, 10, 12

Jailer's Inn

ELIZABETHTOWN

The Olde Bethlehem Academy Inn

7051 St. John Rd., 42701
(502) 862-9003; (800) 662-5670; (502-862-3038 (FAX)

Located on 20 lush acres, this romantic country inn was once the stately home of

---

year; 6 Pets welcome; 7 Children welcome; 8 Tennis nearby; 9 Swimming nearby; 10 Golf nearby; 11 Skiing nearby; 12 May be booked through travel agent

Governor John LaRue Helm and a former girls' academy. Built in 1818 and restored in 1981, this inviting retreat with gardens visible from every room is a true testament of 19th century culture. All rooms feature private bath and full air-conditioning. Gourmet restaurant on premises.

Hosts: Ric and Viviana Delgado
Rooms: 7 (PB) $75-150
Full Breakfast
Credit Cards: A, B
Notes: 2, 3, 4, 5, 6, 7, 8, 10, 12 (10%)

GEORGETOWN

Log Cabin Bed and Breakfast
350 N. Broadway, 40324
(502) 863-3514

This authentic log cabin has two bedrooms, fireplace, kitchen/family room, and air-conditioning. Georgetown is a quiet, historic town five miles north of the Kentucky Horse Park and 12 miles north of Lexington. Facilities are completely private.

Hosts: Clay and Janis McKnight
Rooms: 1 (PB) $64
Expanded Continental Breakfast
Credit Cards: None
Notes: 2, 5, 6, 7, 8, 9, 12

Pineapple Inn
645 S. Broadway, 40324
(502) 868-5453

Located in beautiful Georgetown, Kentucky, our beautiful home, built in 1876, is on the National Register. Country French dining room, large living room. Three bedrooms with private baths upstairs: Grandma's Country Room with full bed, Victorian Room also with full bed, and Americana Room with twin beds. Main Floor Derby Room with queen-size bed with canopy and private bath with hot tub. The home is furnished with antiques and very beautifully decorated. Full breakfast served.

Hosts: Muriel and Les
Rooms: 4 (3PB; 1SB) $60-75 + tax
Full Breakfast
Credit Cards: A, B
Notes: 2, 5, 7, 8, 9, 10, 12

HARRODSBURG

Canaan Land Farm Bed and Breakfast
4355 Lexington Rd., 40330
(606) 734-3984

Step back in time to a house nearly 200 years old. Canaan Land B&B is a historic home, c.1795. Rooms feature antiques, collectibles, and feather beds. Full breakfast and true Southern hospitality. This is a working sheep farm with lambing. Your host is a shepherd/attorney, and your hostess is a handspinner/artist. Farm is secluded and peaceful. Close to Shaker Village. This is a nonsmoking B&B.

Hosts: Fred and Theo Bee
Rooms: 3 (PB) $65-75
Full Breakfast
Credit Cards: None
Notes: 2, 5, 9 (on premises), 10

NOTES: Credit cards accepted: A Master Card; B Visa; C American Express; D Discover Card; E Diners Club; F Other; 2 Personal checks accepted; 3 Lunch available; 4 Dinner available; 5 Open all

LOUISVILLE

Kentucky Homes Bed and Breakfast, Inc.

1219 South Fourth Ave., 40203
(502) 635-7341; (502) 636-3845 (FAX)

A reservation service for a number of different B&Bs in Louisville and throughout the state.

Owner: JoAnn Jenkins
Rooms: Apx. 45; $45-80
Full Breakfast
Credit Cards: A, B
Notes: 2, 5, 7, 8, 9, 10, 12

The Victorian Secret Bed and Breakfast

1132 South First Street, 40203
(502) 581-1914

"Step inside and step back 100 years in time" describes this three-story, Victorian brick mansion in historic Louisville. Recently restored to its former elegance, the 110-year-old structure offers spacious accommodations, high ceilings, and original woodwork. The Louisville area, rich in historic homes, will also tempt railbirds and would-be jockeys to make a pilgrimage to the famous track at Churchill Downs, Home of the Kentucky Derby.

Hosts: Nan and Steve Roosa
Rooms: 6 (2PB; 4SB) $48-78
Continental Breakfast
Credit Cards: None
Notes: 5, 7, 8, 9, 10, 11, 12

MOREHEAD

Appalachian House

910 Willow Dr., 40351
(606) 784-5421

The Appalachian House is our home. We were both teachers, now retired. The house is a museum of sorts with collections of antique glass and ceramic fruit jars; antique tools, mostly woodworking; antique and modern cameras; handmade Appalachian toys; a collection of wood earrings; and a collection of handmade music instruments, including dulcimers, lure, and bowed and picked psalteries.

Hosts: Allen and Betty Lake
Rooms: 2 (SB) $48
Full Breakfast
Credit Cards: None
Notes: 2, 5, 7 (not geared to small children)

NICHOLASVILLE

Sandusky House

1626 Delaney Ferry Road, 40356
(606) 223-4730

A tree-lined drive to the Sandusky House is just a prelude to a wonderful visit to the Bluegrass. A quiet ten-acre country setting amid horse farms yet close to downtown Lexington, Kentucky Horse Park, and Shakertown. The Greek Revival Sandusky House was built circa 1850 from bricks fired on the farm. A 1780 one-thousand-acre land grant from Patrick Henry, Governor of Virginia, given to Revolutionary War soldier,

---

year; 6 Pets welcome; 7 Children welcome; 8 Tennis nearby; 9 Swimming nearby; 10 Golf nearby; 11 Skiing nearby; 12 May be booked through travel agent

Jacob Sandusky.

Hosts: Jim and Linda Humphrey
Rooms: 3 (PB) $69
Full Breakfast
Credit Cards: A, B
Notes: 2, 5, 7 (over 12)

OWENSBORO

Friendly Farms

5931 Hwy. 56, 42301 (**or**) Hwy. 45 & Oak Grove
Rd., Rockport, IN 47635
(502) 771-5590; (502) 771-4723 (FAX)

Friendly Farms offers two comfortable cabins within ten minutes drive of each other across state lines. Red House in Kentucky is adjacent to an indoor tennis club where Ramsey Tennis Schools camps are held in season. It sits next to an apple orchard and has horses in the pasture field behind. It has three bedrooms, one queen and two with two bunk beds. A former tenant house, the quaint country cottage has in addition a sitting room, laundry room, and bath with shower and separate tub. Breakfast is served in the clubhouse. Barn Cottage is named for its location next to the Ramsey Riding Stables in Rockport, IN, which offers trail riding and lessons. The lovely country condo cottage is finely appointed with antiques and furnished patio overlooking the countryside and horse pastures. It has three bedrooms and laundry room with shower and separate tub. Regrigerator is stocked with breakfast "fixins." Only 45 minutes to Holiday World.

Hostess: Joan G. Ramsey
Cottages: 2 (PB) $55-85
Continentall Breakfast
Credit Cards: A, B
Notes: 2, 5, 6, 7, 8, 9 (out door)

PADUCAH

1857's Bed and Breakfast

127 Market House Square, P.O. Box 7771, 42002
(502) 444-3960; (800) 264-5607

The 1857's Bed and Breakfast is in the center of Paducah's historic downtown on Market House Square. The three-story building was built in 1857 and is on the National Register of Historic Places. The first floor is a cafe. The second floor guest rooms have been renovated in Victorian Era style and period furnishings abound. Also available for guest enjoyment on the third floor is a game room with a view of the Ohio River. The game room features an elegant mahogany billiards table. Hot tub also on the third floor. Advance reservations advised.

Hosts: Steve and Deborah Bohnert
Rooms: 2 (SB) $55-65
Continental Plus Breakfast
Credit Cards: A, B
Notes: 2, 5, 12

Ehrhardt's B&B

285 Springwell Lane, 42001
(502) 554-0644

Our brick Colonial ranch home is located just one mile off I-24, which is noted for its lovely scenery. We hope to make you feel at home in antique-filled bedrooms and a cozy den with a fireplace. Nearby are the beautiful Kentucky and Barkley lakes and the famous Land Between the Lakes area.

Hosts: Eileen and Phil Ehrhardt
Rooms: 2 (SB) $35
Full Breakfast
Credit Cards: None
Notes: 2, 7 (over 6), 8, 9, 10

NOTES: Credit cards accepted: A Master Card; B Visa; C American Express; D Discover Card; E Diners Club; F Other; 2 Personal checks accepted; 3 Lunch available; 4 Dinner available; 5 Open all

Rosedale Bed and Breakfast

Paducah Harbor Plaza

201 Broadway, 42001
(502) 442-2698; (800) 719-7799

Paducah Harbor Plaza B&B guests thrive
on the attention and hospitality of their
innkeepers. On the first floor, guests will
find the building's original copper ceilings,
marble columns, ceramic tile floors, and
stained glass windows restored to their
original beauty. Four guest rooms are
located on the second floor. Each is
comfortably furnished with early 20th century antique furniture and warm, handmade quilts. The air-conditioned rooms
feature 10 ft. ceilings, original windows,
ceiling fans, and tongue-and-groove
painted floors. Historic downtown
Paducah offers many attractions, fine restaurants, and cultural events.

Hosts: Beverly and David Harris
Rooms: 4 (SB) $55-125
Continental Plus Breakfast
Credit Cards: A, B, C
Notes: 2, 5, 7, 8, 9, 10, 11, 12

PARIS

Rosedale Bed and Breakfast

1917 Cypress Street, 40361
(606) 987-1845

Tucked into three secluded acres in Paris,
KY, Rosedale invites you to take time for
yourself and to leave the cares of the world
at the end of the driveway. Listed on the
Historic Register, the 14-room Italianate,
brick home is furnished in antiques, was
built in 1862, and was the home of Civil
War General John Croxton. Guests will
enjoy a social parlor complete with games,
television, VCR, and small library. Across
the foyer, the living room provides the
perfect place for quiet reading and reflection. Both rooms feature beautiful, working fireplaces. Voted the 1994 best B&B
in the five-county Bluegrass region.

Hosts: Katie and Jim Haag
Rooms: 4 (2PB; 2SB) $65-85
Full Breakfast
Credit Cards: A, B
Notes: 2, 5, 6 (kennel close), 7 (over 11), 8, 9, 10

SIMPSONVILLE

Old Stone Inn

6905 Shelbyville Rd, US Hwy. 60 W., 40067
(502) 722-8882

Historic Old Stone Inn B&B holds a special place in the hearts of Kentuckians and
travelers worldwide for its fine dining and
beautiful Christian atmosphere. Our lunch
and dinner menus allow for a mouth-watering variety of tastes—then relax and
enjoy. After dinner, browse through the
Inn where you will see items for your family

year; 6 Pets welcome; 7 Children welcome; 8 Tennis nearby; 9 Swimming nearby; 10 Golf nearby;
11 Skiing nearby; 12 May be booked through travel agent

to purchase in our gift shop.

Hostesses: Joyce Hutcherson and Paula Anderson
Rooms: 4 (SB) $75
Full Breakfast
Credit Cards: A, B
Notes: 2, 3, 4, 5, 7, 10

Maple Hill Manor

SPRINGFIELD

Maple Hill Manor

2941 Perryville Road, 40069
(606) 336-3075

Listed on National Register of Historic Places, we are located on 14 tranquil acres in the scenic Bluegrass region. It took three years to build, circa 1851, has ten-foot doors, thirteen-and-a-half-foot ceilings, nine-foot windows, cherry spiral staircase, stenciling in the foyer, three brass and crystal chandeliers, and nine fireplaces. The honeymoon hideaway has canopy bed and jacuzzi. One hour from Louisville and Lexington. No smoking.

Hosts: Bob and Kay Carroll
Rooms: 7 (PB) $60-80
Full Breakfast
Credit Cards: A, B
Notes: 2, 5, 7, 8, 9, 10, 12

WILMORE

Scott Station Inn Bed and Breakfast

305 East Main St., 40390
(606) 858-0121

The Scott Station Inn is located in downtown, historic Wilmore, Kentucky, just three blocks from famous Asbury College, Asbury Seminary, and only minutes from Shakertown, Fort Harrod, and Lexington, Kentucky. Beautifully refurbished in 1990, this 100-year-old farmhouse has kept the charm of an old Kentucky home. Our inn has four rental rooms with private baths. We welcome pastor-staff and Sunday school retreats, family reuions, and wedding parties.

Hosts: Sandy and Mike Jansen
Rooms: 4 (PB) $49.95
Full Breakfast
Credit Cards: A, B
Notes: 2, 5, 7

Scott Station Inn Bed and Breakfast

NOTES: Credit cards accepted: A Master Card; B Visa; C American Express; D Discover Card; E Diners Club; F Other; 2 Personal checks accepted; 3 Lunch available; 4 Dinner available; 5 Open all

Louisiana

JACKSON

Milbank Historic House

P.O. Box 1000-3045 Bank Street, 70748
(504) 634-5901

Located in the beautiful Felicianas of Louisiana, Milbank is a massive romantic antebellum mansion. It has a varied and interesting history. Rooms are furnished with authentic antique furniture of the late 1800s. Persian rugs, ormolu clocks, carved settees, poster beds, armoires, and much more. Upstairs galleries to stand on and enjoy scenic backyard—large backyard. Delicious breakfast, friendly hosts. Owners are Mr. and Mrs. M.L. Harvey.

Hosts: Paul and Margurite Carter
Rooms: 3 (PB) $75
Full Breakfast (Continental available on request)
Credit Cards: A, B
Notes: 5 (except holidays), 7 (12 and up), 10

NEW ORLEANS

623 Ursulines

623 Ursulines Street, 70116
(504) 529-5489

Seven clean and quiet accommodations with modern comforts in the Old World charm of the historic Vieux Carre. Located within a short walking distance of all the famous sights and sounds of Old New Orleans, the world renowned restaurants, Jackson Square with the magnificent St. Louis Cathedral, Cabildo, Presbytere, and sidewalk artists—the French Market for coffee and *beignets*, the busy Mississippi River, the many treasure-filled antique shops along Royal Street, and of course, the night life of Bourbon Street. Just around the corner is the historic home of General Beauregard and the first convent of the Ursuline Nuns built in 1734.

Host: Don Heil
Rooms: 7(PB) $65-80
No Breakfast
Credit Cards: None
Notes: 2, 10

Milbank Historic House

year; 6 Pets welcome; 7 Children welcome; 8 Tennis nearby; 9 Swimming nearby; 10 Golf nearby; 11 Skiing nearby; 12 May be booked through travel agent

Fairchild House

1518 Prytania Street, 70130
(504) 524-0154; (800) 256-8096; (504) 568-0063
(FAX)

Designed circa 1841, this Greek Revival residence is rich with the history of the 19th century. Situated among the picturesque oaks of the Lower Garden District, the house is located seventeen blocks from the French Quarter and eight blocks from the Convention Center. The eight rooms, each with private bath/shower, are decorated in a refined antique setting. In addition, the house features hardwood floors. Complimentary refreshments served upon arrival. Tea is served from 3:30 to 5:00 PM, except on holidays and Sundays.

Hostess: Beatriz O. Aprigliano
Rooms: 8 (PB) $70-100
Continental Breakfast
Credit Cards: A, B, C
Notes: 2, 5, 7, 10, 12

La Maison

608 Kerlerec St., 70116
(504) 271-0228

La Maison was built in 1805 in the Historic Faurbourg Marigny area. It is within walking distance of the French Quarter (3 blocks) and many restaurants. Each mini-suite has queen and double beds, sitting room, phone, color TV, and lovely courtyard. Parking is available across from the cottage. Reservations are required.

Hostess: Alma F. Hulin
Rooms: 7 (PB) $65-125
Continental Breakfast
Credit Cards: None
Notes: 2, 5, 12

New Orleans Bed and Breakfast and Accommodations

P.O. Box 8163, 70182
(504) 838-0071; (504) 838-0140 (FAX)

New Orleans Bed and Breakfast and Accommodations is a reservation service with approximately one hundred units **throughout New Orleans**. We have accommodations in historic sections like The Garden District as well as the new condominiums of the Riverfront in the Warehouse District (these units are very convenient to the Convention Center). NOB&B is celebrating its fifteenth year. Owner Sarah Margaret Brown is always pleased to assist guests. Prices range from $50 to $200.

La Maison

NOTES: Credit cards accepted: A Master Card; B Visa; C American Express; D Discover Card; E Diners Club; F Other; 2 Personal checks accepted; 3 Lunch available; 4 Dinner available; 5 Open all

Whitney Inn

1509 St. Charles Ave., 70130
(504) 521-8000; (504) 525-5532 (FAX)

Newly renovated 19th century town house.
Conveniently located on historic St. Charles
Avenue street car line. Valet parking,
cable TV, and telephones. Private, relaxing sanctuary in the heart of the city. French
Quarter, art district, and music clubs are
only minutes away! Rates increase to $125-
150 during Mardi Gras and the Jazz Fest.

Hosts: Sally Cates and Mitchell Cumbow
Rooms: 10 (PB) $75-125
Continental Breakfast
Credit Cards: A, B, C
Notes: 2, 3, 4, 5, 7, 8, 12

St. Charles Guest House

1748 Prytania Street, 70130
(504) 523-6556

A simple, cozy, and affordable pension in
the Lower Garden District on the streetcar
line is 10 minutes to downtown and the
French Quarter. Continental breakfast is
served overlooking a charming pool and
patio complete with banana trees. Tours
are available from our lobby.

Hosts: Joanne and Dennis Hilton
Rooms: 30 (26 PB; 4 SB) $30-75
Continental Breakfast
Credit Cards: A, B
Notes: 2 (in advance), 5, 7, 8, 9

PONCHATOULA

The Bella Rose Mansion

255 North Eight Street, 70454
(504) 386-3857

"When only the best will do" Bella Rose is
on the National Historical Register in the
heart of America's Antique City and Plantations. Thirty-five minutes from New
Orleans Airport and 45 minutes from Ba-
ton Rouge. Romantic heart-shaped jacuzzi,
suites and unique rooms, exquisite spiral
staircase crowned with a stained glass
dome, the finest in the South. Marble
walls, indoor tennazzo shuffleboard court,
heated pool, solarium with a fountain of
Bacchus and a European-style casino on
premises are only a few of the magnificent
features that await you at the Bella Rose
Mansion Country Club. Now doing weddings and parties.

Hostess: Rose James
Rooms: 2 jacuzzi suites and 4 rooms (PB)
Full Breakfast
Credit Cards: A, B
Notes: 5, 8, 9, 10

The Bella Rose Mansion

year; 6 Pets welcome; 7 Children welcome; 8 Tennis nearby; 9 Swimming nearby; 10 Golf nearby;
11 Skiing nearby; 12 May be booked through travel agent

PORT VINCENT

Tree House in the Park

16520 Airport Road, Prairieville, 70769
(800) Le Cabin (800) 532-2246)

A Cajun cabin in the swamp on "stilts" with two B&B rooms and a bridal suite, all fully air conditioned. Each room has a private entrance, private bath, TV, VCR, queen-size waterbed, each with hot tub on a private deck under the stars, and steps down to the pool and sun deck. Bridal suite has double jacuzzi bath inside also. Boat slip and fishing dock. Four ponds, an island with a gazebo, footbridges, swings, and benches. Two piroques and a double kayak for float trip included. Very private, peaceful, and beautiful five acres of cypress and Spanish moss swaying in the breeze.

Hostess: Fran and Julius Schmieder
Rooms: 2 + bridal suite (PB) $110-150
Full Breakfast and Supper
Credit Cards: A, B
Notes: 2, 5, 9, 12

ST. FRANCISVILLE

Dogwood Plantation

4363 LA Hwy. 966, Box 81, 70775
(800) 635-4790; (800) 767-5831 (FAX)

An 1803 log core building located on five acres with pond. Furnished in period antiques, all rooms have private facilities.

Hosts: Pat and Roland Bahan
Rooms: 2 (PB) $85-95
Continental Breakfast
Credit Cards: A, B, C, D, E
Notes: 5, 9, 10, 12

WHITE CASTLE

Nottoway Plantation Inn and Restaurant

Louisiana Highway 1, P.O. Box 160, 70788
(504) 545-2730; (504) 545-9167; (504) 545-8632 (FAX)

Built in 1859 by John Randolph, a wealthy sugar cane planter, Nottoway is a blend of Italianate and Greek Revival styles. Nottoway is the largest remaining plantation home in the South. Its guest rooms are individually decorated with period furnishings. Wake up with juice, coffee and homemade muffins served to your room.

Hostesses: Cindy Hidalgo and Faye Russell
Rooms: 13 (10 rooms, 3 suites) (PB) $125-250
Full Breakfast
Credit Cards: A, B, C, D
Closed Christmas Day
Notes: 2, 3, 4, 5, 8, 9, 10, 12

Nottoway Plantation Inn and Restaurant

NOTES: Credit cards accepted: A Master Card; B Visa; C American Express; D Discover Card; E Diners Club; F Other; 2 Personal checks accepted; 3 Lunch available; 4 Dinner available; 5 Open all

Maine

ALFRED

Clover Hill Farm B&B

RR 1, Box 2Y1A. 04002
(207) 490-1105

Unwind on our peaceful organic farm. Pet the animals. Gather your own eggs. Enjoy a bountiful breakfast. We are happy to accommodate your special dietary requirements. Hike or ski on 100 acres of rolling hills and woodland or drive a short distance for beaches, fishing, outlet shopping, and a great variety of other activities. We are just one-and-a-half hours from Boston, six hours from New York City, and 30 minutes from ocean beaches and Kennebunkport.

Hostess: Margit Lassen, Ph. D.
Rooms: 3 (SB) $65-85
Full Breakfast
Credit Cards: A, B, D
Notes: 2, 5, 7, 8, 9, 10, 11

BAR HARBOR

The Atlantic Oakes—The Willows

P.O. Box 3, Eden Street, 04609-0003
(207) 288-5801; (800) 33MAINE; (207) 288-5802 (FAX)

We have restored the Sir Harry Oakes mansion/summer cottage on our grounds. This charming home was named *The Willows* after the willow trees on the entrance drive. About 200 summer cottages were built in Bar Harbour from 1880 to 1890. *The Willows* was built in 1913, one of the last estates built. The large wooden hotels (now gone) were built from 1865 to 1885. No matter how large and ostentatious the summer homes were, they were always called "cottages." *The Willows* is located on the grounds of the Atlantic Oakes By-The-Sea. There are four tennis courts and indoor and outdoor pools available for use by B&B guests.

Hosts: The Coughs
Rooms: 9 (PB) $49-196
Customers choice of continental or full breakfast.
Credit Cards: A, B
Notes: 5, 7, 8, 9, 10, 12

Black Friar Inn

10 Summer Street, 04609
(207) 288-5091

Black Friar Inn is a completely rebuilt and restored inn incorporating beautiful woodwork, mantels, windows, and bookcases from old mansions and churches on Mount Desert Island. Gourmet breakfast includes homemade breads, pastry, and muffins, fresh fruit, eggs du jour, waffles, etc. Afternoon refreshments are provided. All rooms

---

year; 6 Pets welcome; 7 Children welcome; 8 Tennis nearby; 9 Swimming nearby; 10 Golf nearby; 11 Skiing nearby; 12 May be booked through travel agent

have queen beds. Within easy walking distance of the waterfront, restaurants, and shops, with ample parking available. Short drive to Acadia National Park.

Hosts: Barbara and Jim Kelly
Rooms: 6 (PB) $85-110
Full Breakfast
Credit Cards: A, B
Closed winter months
Notes: 2, 7 (over 11), 8, 9, 10

Hearthside B&B

7 High Street, 04609
(207) 288-4533

Built in 1907 as a private residence, the inn features a blend of country and Victorian furnishings. All rooms have queen beds, some have a private porch, fireplace, whirlpool bath and/or air-conditioning. We serve a homemade full breakfast, afternoon tea and homemade cookies, and evening refreshments. Located on a quiet side street in town, we are five minutes from Acadia National Park.

Hosts: Susan and Barry Schwartz
Rooms: 9 (PB) $55-75 in winter; $75-115 in season. Special off season packages available.
Full Breakfast
Credit Cards: A, B
Notes: 2, 5, 8, 9, 10, 11

The Inn at Canoe Point

The Inn at Canoe Point

Box 216, 04609
(207) 288-9511

Following the curved drive, you'll pass through two acres of trees leading to the water's edge and the Inn at Canoe Point. Our secluded location is two miles from Bar Harbor. Relax in front of the granite fireplace in the ocean room where you can enjoy a view of Frenchman's Bay and the mountains beyond. From the surrounding deck you can look out over the ocean while listening to the rolling surf. Mt. Desert Island and Acadia National Park have enough diversified activities to keep the visitor busy for days or even weeks at a time.

Hosts: Don Johnson and Esther Cavagnaro
Rooms: 5 (PB) $125-225 (in season) $80-150 (off season)
Full Breakfast
Credit Cards: None
Notes: 2, 5, 8, 9, 10, 11 (x-country)

Long Pond Inn

Box 361, Mt. Desert, ME 04660
(207) 244-5854

Centrally located on the shore of beautiful Long Pond near the quaint village of Somesville, our Inn offers one of the quietest choices of country lodging on Mount Desert Island. The Inn is our year-round home built with vintage materials recovered from dismantled estates, summer cottages, country stores, and hotels. Long Pond Inn's four guest bedrooms are charmingly appointed featuring queen-size beds and private baths; one with a jacuzzi tub. After breakfast, stroll the Inn's lavish vegetable, herb, and flower gardens or enjoy a swim or paddle on the Long Pond in one of our rental canoes. Within 15 minutes of Long Pond Inn in any direction is all that Mount Desert Island has to offer: Bar Harbor, Northeast Harbor, Southwest Harbor, and breathtaking Acadia National Park. Since our family includes two Springer Spaniels, other pets are not permitted. We at Long Pond look forward to hosting you soon and in years to come.

Hosts: Bob and Pam Mensick
Rooms: 4 (PB) $75-95
Full Breakfast
Credit Cards: A, B
Notes: 2, 9, 10

The Maples Inn

16 Roberts Ave., 04609
(207) 288-3443; (207) 288-0356 (FAX)

Built in early 1900, The Maples Inn originally housed the wealthy summer visitors to Mt. Desert Island. It is on a quiet, residential, tree-lined street. Guests will be away from the traffic of Bar Harbor, yet within walking distance of attractive boutiques, intimate restaurants, and the surrounding sea. For the perfect romantic getaway, reserve the White Birch Suite, complete with a blue and white tiled, working fireplace. Your palate will be treated to some of our breakfast recipes that have been featured in *Gourmet* and *Bon Appetit*. Acadia National Park is just minutes away.

Rooms: 6 (PB) $90-140 (in-season) $60-95 (off-season)
Full Breakfast
Credit Cards: A, B, D
Notes: 2, 3 (picnic), 5, 7 (over 7), 8, 9, 10, 11

Wayside Inn

11 Atlantic Ave., 04609
(207) 288-5703 (voice and FAX); (800) 722-6671

A beautiful English Tudor building decorated in early Victorian offering private and semiprivate rooms with fireplaces. Full gourmet breakfast served. Located on a quiet side street in historic district within walking distance to all in-town activities. Open all year. Lower rates off season. A weekly rate is available in our Victorian guesthouse.

Hosts: Steve and Sandi Straubel
Rooms: 8 (6PB; 2SB) 70-140 (seasonal rates available)
Full Breakfast
Credit Cards: A, B
Notes: 2, 5, 7, 8, 9, 10, 11, 12

BATH

Fairhaven Inn

Rural Route 2, Box 85, North Bath Road, 04530
(207) 443-4391

A 1790 Colonial nestled on the hillside overlooking the Kennebec River on 20 acres of country sights and sounds. Beaches, golf, and maritime museum nearby, plus cross-country ski trails, wood fires. Gourmet breakfast is served year-round. Candlelight dinners available in winter.

Hosts: Sallie and George Pollard
Rooms: 8 (7PB; 2SB) $60-80
Full Breakfast
Credit Cards: A, B, C
Notes: 4 (weekend package), 5, 6 (by arrangement!), 7 (by arrangement!), 8, 9, 10, 11 (cross-country)

---

year; 6 Pets welcome; 7 Children welcome; 8 Tennis nearby; 9 Swimming nearby; 10 Golf nearby; 11 Skiing nearby; 12 May be booked through travel agent

BELFAST

The Jeweled Turret Inn

16 Pearl Street, 04915
(207) 338-2304; (800) 696-2304 (in state)

This grand lady of the Victorian era, circa 1898, offers many unique architectural features and is on the National Register of Historic Places. The inn is named for the grand staircase that winds up the turret, lighted by stained and leaded glass panels with jewel-like embellishments. Each guest room is filled with Victoriana and has its own bath. A gourmet breakfast is served. Shops, restaurants, and waterfront are a stroll away.

Hosts: Carl and Cathy Heffentrager
Rooms: 7 (PB) $65-85
Full Breakfast
Credit Cards: None
Notes: 2, 5, 8, 9, 10, 11, 12

Mountain Road House

BETHEL

Sunday River Inn and Cross Country Ski Center

RR 2, Box 1688, 04217-9630
(207) 824-2410; (207) 824-3181 (FAX)

Sunday River Inn is a small country resort built around winter sports. A nationally renowned cross-country ski center is adjacent to the inn, and Sunday River Ski Resort with seven mountains of alpine skiing is one-half mile away. A wood-fired sauna and hot tub, a skating rink, snowshoe trails, and dogsledding are also available. With all this the guests still return for the *food*!

Hosts: Steve and Peggy Wright
Rooms: 17 (2PB; 15SB) $62-75 prepaid
Full Breakfast and Dinner
Credit Cards: A, B, C, D
Notes: 2, 4, 7, 8, 9, 10, 11, 12

BLUE HILL

Mountain Road House

Rural Route 1, Box 2040, 04614
(207) 374-2794

Located on the only road that traverses the face of Blue Hill Mountain, our 1890s farmhouse offers views of the Bay while only one mile from the village. Choose twin, double, or queen size bedrooms, each with private bath. Early bird coffee/tea available at 7 AM, the breakfast with a hot entree, fresh fruit, and coffee cake. Enjoy antiquing, galleries, craft shops, bookstores, musical events, fine dining, hiking, coastal villages, and of course Acadia National Park. No smoking.

Hosts: Carol and John McCulloch
Rooms: 3 (PB) $60-80
Full Breakfast
Credit Cards: A, B
Notes: 2, 5, 7, 12

NOTES: Credit cards accepted: A Master Card; B Visa; C American Express; D Discover Card; E Diners Club; F Other; 2 Personal checks accepted; 3 Lunch available; 4 Dinner available; 5 Open all

BOOTHBAY HARBOR

Anchor Watch B&B

3 Eames Rd., 04538
(207) 633-7565

Our seaside captain's house welcomes you to Boothbay Region. It's a pleasant walk to unique shops, fine dining, and scenic boat trips. A delicious homemade breakfast is served in the sunny breakfast nook looking out to the sea. Quilts, stenciling, and nautical decor make our four bedrooms comfortable and cozy. Enjoy your afternoon tea in the attractive sitting room facing the ocean. Your host captains the Monhegan and Squirrel Island ferries from nearby Pier 8.

Hostess: Diane Campbell
Rooms: 4(PB) $70-95
Full Breakfast
Credit Cards: A, B
Notes: 2, 5, 8, 9, 10, 12

Harbour Towne Inn

71 Townsend Ave., 04538
(207) 633-4300; (800) 722-4240

THE FINEST B&B ON THE WATERFRONT. Our refurbished Victorian Inn retains turn-of-the-century ambience while providing all modern amenities. The colorful gardens and quiet, tree-shaded location slopes right to the edge of the beautiful New England harbor. Choose an Inn room with or without an outside deck for scenic views or a Carriage House room with waterfront decks. Our luxurious penthouse is a modern and spacious home that sleeps six people in absolute luxury and privacy. Come stay with us just once and you will know why our guests return year after year.

Host: G. Thomas (manager)
Rooms: 12 (PB) $49-120; penthouse $125-225
Continental Breakfast
Credit Cards: A, B, C
Notes: 2, 5 (exept manager's vacation), 7 (well behaved), 8, 9, 10, 11, 12

Harbour Towne Inn

BRUNSWICK

Harborgate B&B

Rural Delivery 2, Box 2260, 04011
(207) 725-5894

This contemporary redwood home is 40 feet from the ocean. Flower gardens and wooded landscape provide gracious relaxation. Two ocean-facing, first-floor bedrooms are separated by a guest living room with patio. Dock for swimming and sunbathing. Close to Bowdoin College, L. L. Bean, and sandy beaches. Wide selection of stores, gift shops, and steak and seafood restaurants. Summer theater, college art museum, Perry McMillan Museum, and historical society buildings and events.

Hostess: Carolyn Bolles ·
Rooms: 2 (SB) $60
Continental Breakfast
Credit Cards: None
Closed November - April
Notes: 2, 9

year; 6 Pets welcome; 7 Children welcome; 8 Tennis nearby; 9 Swimming nearby; 10 Golf nearby;
11 Skiing nearby; 12 May be booked through travel agent

BUCKSPORT

Old Parsonage Inn
P.O. Box 1577, 190 Franklin St., 04416
(207) 469-6477

The Clough family invites you to share their historic Federal home, formerly the Methodist parsonage, located one half mile from coastal Route 1. All rooms are tastefully decorated and retain original architectural features. Third floor houses an 1809 Masonic Hall. Private guest entrance, kitchenette in the breakfast/sitting room. Short walk to waterfront and restaurants. Convenient for day trips to Acadia, both sides of Penobscot Bay, and historic Fort Knox.

Hosts: Judith and Brian Clough
Rooms: 3 (1PB; 2SB) $50
Full Breakfast
Credit Cards: A, B
Notes: 2, 7, 8, 9, 10

CLARK ISLAND

Craignair Inn
533 Clark Island Road, 04859
(207) 594-7644; (207) 596-7124 (FAX)

Located on the water, the inn is near great hiking trails along the shore or through the forests. The inn was formerly a boarding house for stonecutters from the nearby quarries that provide great swimming. The annex was once the village chapel. A peaceful and secluded setting located ten miles south of Rockland in St. George.

Hostess: Theresa Smith
Rooms: 22 (8 PB; 14 SB) $72-91
Full Breakfast
Credit Cards: A, B, C
Notes: 2, 4, 6, 7, 8, 9, 10, 11, 12

DAMARISCOTTA

Brannon-Bunker Inn
HCR 64, Box 045, 04543
(207) 563-5941

Brannon-Bunker Inn is an intimate and relaxed country bed and breakfast situated minutes from sandy beach, lighthouse, and historic fort in Maine's mid-coastal region. Located in a 1920s Cape, converted barn, and carriage house, the guest rooms are furnished in themes reflecting the charm of yesterday and the comforts of today. Antique shops, too!

Hosts: Jeanne and Joe Hovance
Rooms: 7 (5PB; 2SB) $55-65
Expanded Continental Breakfast
Credit Cards: A, B, C
Closed Christmas week
Notes: 2, 5, 7, 8, 9, 10, 12

Down Easter Inn
Bristol Road, Routes 129 and 130, 04543
(207) 563-5332; (201) 267-1697 winter

The Down Easter Inn, one mile from downtown Damariscotta, is in the heart of the rocky coast of Maine. On the National Register of Historic Places, it features a two-story porch framed by Corinthian columns. Minutes from golfing, lakes, and the ocean. Nearby are lobster wharfs for local fare and boat trips around Muscongus Bay and to Monhegan Island. The inn features 22 lovely rooms with TVs.

Hosts: Mary and Robert Colquhoun
Rooms: 22 (PB) $70-80
Continental Breakfast
Credit Cards: A, B
Notes: 2, 9, 10

NOTES: Credit cards accepted: A Master Card; B Visa; C American Express; D Discover Card; E Diners Club; F Other; 2 Personal checks accepted; 3 Lunch available; 4 Dinner available; 5 Open all

ELIOT/KITTERY

The Farmstead

379 Goodwin Rd., 03903
(207)748-3145 or (207) 439-5033

Lovely country inn on three acres. Warm friendly atmosphere exemplifies farm life late 1800s. Guest rooms are Victorian in style. Each has mini-refrigerator and microwave for late evening snacks or special diet. Full breakfast may include blueberry pancakes or french toast, homemade syrup, fruit, and juice. Handicap accessible. Minutes from Kittery Factory Outlets, York Beaches, and Portsmouth, NH, historic sites. One hour from Boston.

Hosts: Meb and John Lippincott
Rooms: 6 (PB) $48
Full Breakfast
Credit Cards: A, B, C
Notes: 2, 5, 6, 7, 12

Country at Heart Bed and Breakfast

FREEPORT

Captain Josiah Mitchell House

188 Main Street, 04032
(207) 865-3289

Two blocks from L. L. Bean, this house is

a five-minute walk past centuries-old sea captains' homes and shady trees to all shops in town. After exploring, relax on our beautiful, peaceful veranda with antique wicker furniture and "remember when" porch swing. State inspected and approved. Full breakfast included in room rate. Family owned and operated.

Hosts: Loretta and Alan Bradley
Rooms: 6 (PB) $68-85 (winter rates are reduced)
Full Breakfast
Credit Cards: A, B
Notes: 2, 5, 9, 10, 11, 12

Country at Heart Bed and Breakfast

37 Bow Street, 04032
(207) 865-0512

Our cozy 1870 home is located off Main Street and only two blocks from L. L. Bean. Park your car and walk to the restaurants and many outlet stores. Stay in one of three country-decorated rooms: the Shaker room, Quilt room, or the Teddy bear room. Our rooms have hand-stenciled borders, handmade crafts, and either antique or reproduction furnishings. There is also a gift shop for guests.

Hosts: Roger and Kim Dubay
Rooms: 3 (PB) $65-75
Full Breakfast
Credit Cards: None
Notes: 2, 5, 7, 9, 10, 11, 12

GREENVILLE

Greenville Inn

Norris Street, P.O. Box 1194, 04441
(207) 695-2206 (voice and FAX)

Restored 1895 lumber baron's mansion

on a hillside overlooking Moosehead Lake and the Squaw Mountains. A large leaded-glass window decorated with a painted spruce tree, gas lights, embossed wallcoverings, and carved fireplace mantles grace the inn. A sumptuous continental breakfast buffet is included with the room. In the evening our restaurant is open to the public. Open year-round.

Hosts: Elfi, Susie, and Michael Schnetzer
Rooms: 9 (7PB; 2SB) $55-90
Full Breakfast
Credit Cards: A, B, D
Notes: 2, 4, 7, 8, 9, 10, 11, 12

Greenville Inn

KENNEBUNK

Sundial Inn

P.O. Box 1147, 48 Beach Ave., 04043
(207) 967-3850; (207) 967-4719 (FAX)

Unique oceanfront inn furnished with turn-of-the-century Victorian antiques. Each of the 34 guest rooms has a private bath, phone, color TV, and air conditioning. Several rooms also offer ocean views and whirlpool baths. Visit Kennebunkport's art galleries and studios, museums, and gift shops. Go whalewatching, deep-sea fish-

ing, or hiking at the nearby wildlife refuge and estuary. Golf and tennis are nearby. Continental breakfast features muffins and coffee cakes. Wheelchair accessible.

Hosts: Larry and Pat Kenny
Rooms: 34 (PB) $65-155
Continental Breakfast
Credit Cards: A, B, C, E
Notes: 5, 8, 9, 10, 11

KENNEBUNKPORT

The Captain Lord Mansion

P. O. Box 800, 04046-0800
(207) 967-3141; (207) 967-3172 (FAX)

The Captain Lord Mansion is an intimate and stylish inn situated at the head of a large village green, overlooking the Kennebunk River. Built during the War of 1812 as an elegant, private residence, it is now listed on the National Historic Register. The large, luxurious guest rooms are furnished with rich fabrics, European paintings, and fine period antiques, yet have modern creature comforts such as private baths and working fireplaces. Christians, as well as gracious hosts and innkeepers, Bev Davis, husband, Rick Litchfield, and their friendly, helpful staff are eager to make your visit enjoyable. Family-style breakfasts are served in an atmospheric country kitchen.

Hosts: Bev Davis and Rick Litchfield
Rooms: 16 (PB) $79-149 Jan.-May; $149-199 June to Dec. (conference room available)
Full Breakfast
Credit Cards: A, B, D
Notes: 2, 5, 8, 9, 10, 11 (cross-country)

The Green Heron Inn

P.O. Box 2578, Ocean Avenue, 04046
(207) 967-3315

Comfortable, clean, and cozy ten-room bed and breakfast. Each guest room has private bath, air conditioning, and color TV. A full breakfast from a menu is served. "Best breakfast in town."

Hosts: Charles and Elizabeth Reid
Rooms: 10 (PB) $65-120
Full Breakfast
Credit Cards: None
Notes: 2, 5, 6 (restricted), 7, 8, 9, 10

The Inn at South Street

P.O. Box 478A, 04046
(207) 967-5151

Now approaching its 200th year, this stately Greek Revival house is in Kennebunkport's historic district. Located on a quiet street, the inn is within walking distance of restaurants, shops, and the water. There are three beautifully decorated guest rooms and one luxury apartment/suite. Private baths, queen-size beds, fireplaces, a commons room, afternoon refreshments, and early morning coffee. Breakfast is always special and is served in the large country kitchen with views of the river and ocean. Rated A+ Excellent by ABBA.

Hosts: Jacques and Eva Downs
Rooms: 3 and 1 suite (PB) $85-120;
$155-185 suite
Full Breakfast
Credit Cards: A, B
Notes: 2, 8, 9, 10, 11, 12

The Kennebunkport Inn

One Dock Square, P.O. Box 111, 04046-0111
(207) 967-2621; (800) 248-2621; (207) 967-3705
(FAX)

Classic country inn located in the heart of Kennebunkport near shops and historic district, beaches, boating, and golf. Originally a Sea Captain's home, the Inn maintains its charm with antique furnishings, two elegant dining rooms, Victorian pub, and piano bar. Serving breakfast and dinner, May through October, the inn is recognized for its fine food. Rooms are available year-round.

Hosts: Rick and Martha Griffin
Rooms: 34 (PB) $59.50-179
Full Breakfast and Dinner available in restaurant
Credit Cards: A, B, C
Notes: 4, 5, 8, 9, 10, 12

KENT'S HILL

Home Nest Farm

Box 2350, 04349
(207) 897-4125

Off the beaten track, on a foothill of the Longfellow Mountains of West Central Maine's lake district, Home Nest Farm offers a 60-mile panoramic view to the White Mountains. A place for all seasons, it includes three historic homes, furnished with period antiques: the main house (1784); Lilac Cottage (c. 1800); and the Red Schoolhouse (c. 1830). Local activities include sheep tending, berry picking, Living History Farm Museum, exploring many trails (maintained for snowmobiling and skiing in the winter), swimming, fishing, boating (boats provided). Two day

year; 6 Pets welcome; 7 Children welcome; 8 Tennis nearby; 9 Swimming nearby; 10 Golf nearby; 11 Skiing nearby; 12 May be booked through travel agent

minimum stay.

Hosts: Arn and Leda Sturtevant
Rooms: 4 (PB) $50-95
Closed in March and April
Full Breakfast
Credit Cards: None
Notes: 2, 7, 9, 10, 11

KITTERY

Enchanted Nights B & B

Rt. 103, 29 Wentworth Street, 03904
(207) 439-1489

Affordable luxury 75 minutes north of Boston, Coastal Maine. Fanciful and whimsical for the romantic at heart. French and Victorian furnishings, with CATVs. Three minutes to historic Portsmouth's dining, dancing, concerts in the park, historic homes, theater, harbor cruises, cliff walks, scenic ocean drives, beaches, charming neighboring resorts, water park, and outlet malls. Whirlpool tub for two. Full breakfast or $12 less and enjoy a Portsmouth cafe. Pets welcome. No smoking indoors.

Hosts: Nancy Bogenberger and Peter Lamandia
Rooms: 6 (5PB; 2SB) $47-135
Full Breakfast
Credit Cards: A, B, C, D
Notes: 2, 5, 6, 7, 8, 9, 10, 12

Enchanted Nights

MILLINOCKET

Katahdin Area B&B

94-96 Oxford Street, 04462
(207) 723-5220

We are located 17 miles south of the entrance to Baxter State Park, the gateway to Katahdin, Maine's highest peak. With a population fewer than 7,000, Millinocket has small-town charm. The spectacular "Grand Canyon of the East" on Gulf Hagas is a short distance from here off Route 11 South. Appalachian Trail access; 156 miles of groomed trails; walking distance to Main Street, restaurants, shops, houses of worship. Cross-country skiing and white water rafting opportunities available.

Hosts: Rodney and Mary Lou Corriveau
Rooms: 5 (1PB; 4SB) $40-50
Full Breakfast
Credit Cards: None
Notes: 2, 5, 7, 8, 9, 10, 11

PORTLAND

Inn on Carleton

46 Carleton St., 04102
(207) 775-1910 (voice and FAX); (800) 639-1779

The Inn on Carleton is a graciously restored 1869 Victorian town house located in Portland's historic West End. Situated on a quiet, tree-lined street in a unique residential neighborhood of Victorian architecture, the Inn on Carleton is close to the center of downtown Portland. It is a short walk to the Portland Museum of Art, Maine Medical Center, The Performing Arts Center and the city's business district. Close at hand are Casco Bay's Calendar Islands, the international ferry to Nova

---

NOTES: Credit cards accepted: A Master Card; B Visa; C American Express; D Discover Card; E Diners Club; F Other; 2 Personal checks accepted; 3 Lunch available; 4 Dinner available; 5 Open all

Scotia, and the Old Port area with its cobbled streets, colorful shops, and many fine restaurants. All rooms are air-conditioned.

Hosts: Phil and Sue Cox
Rooms: 7 (4PB; 3SB) $75-90 (seasonal rates available)
Full Breakfast
Credit Cards: A, B, D
Notes: 2, 5, 7, 8, 9, 10, 11, 12

RANGELEY

Northwoods B&B

P. O. 79, Main Street, 04970
(207) 864-2440

An historic 1912 home of rare charm and easy elegance, Northwoods is centrally located in Rangeley Village. With spacious rooms, a lakefront porch, expansive grounds, and private boat dock, Northwoods provides superb accommodations. Golf, tennis, water sports, hiking, and skiing are a few of the many activities offered by the region.

Hosts: Carol and Robert Scofield
Rooms: 4 (3PB; 1SB) $60-75
Full Breakfast
Credit Cards: A, B
Notes: 2, 8, 9, 10, 11, 12

SACO

Crown 'n' Anchor Inn

P.O. Box 228-121 North St., 04072-0228
(207) 282-3829

Located in the Thacher-Goudale House, a National Register Home in the state of Maine, the Crown 'n' Anchor Inn is a fully restored federal house in the Adamesque

style with Greek Revival temple front and furnished throughout with period and country antiques. After a bountiful breakfast or a busy day, socialize in the parlor or curl up with a good book in the library.

Hosts: John Barclay and Martha Forester
Rooms: 6 (PB) $50-95
Full Breakfast
Credit Cards: A, B
Notes: 2, 5, 6, 7(by arrangement), 8, 9, 10, 11, 12

SEARSPORT

Brass Lantern Inn

P.O. Box 407, US Rt. 1, 81 W. Main St., 04974
(207) 548-0150; (800) 691-0150

Nestled at the edge of the woods, this gracious Victorian inn, built in 1850 by a sea captain, overlooks Penobscot Bay. Features include an ornate tin ceiling in the dining room, antiques, an extensive doll collection, and a shop on premises specializing in collectible trains. Each guest room has a private bath and is designed for a comfortable stay. Near Penobscot Marine Museum. Open all year, The Brass Lantern will be lit to welcome you!

Hosts: Pat Gatto, Dan and Lee Anne Lee
Rooms: 4 (PB) $65-75
Full Breakfast
Credit Cards: A, B
Notes: 2, 5, 7, 8, 9, 10, 11, 12

Homeport Inn

E. Main St., Rt. 1, 04974
(207) 548-2259; (800) 742-5814

Enjoy the unusual with a restful stop at this fine example of a New England sea captain's mansion, listed in the Historic Register and appointed with period an-

year; 6 Pets welcome; 7 Children welcome; 8 Tennis nearby; 9 Swimming nearby; 10 Golf nearby; 11 Skiing nearby; 12 May be booked through travel agent

tiques and family heirlooms. Enjoy the many midcoast attractions such as nearby Acadia National Park, sailing, cruises, local museums, and galleries, antique shops, golf, and the Maine coast. Weekly rental, oceanfront, Victorian cottages on estate.

Hosts: Edith and George Johnson
Rooms: 10 (6PB; 4SB) $55-75
Full Breakfast
Credit Cards: A, B, C, D, F (enroute)
Notes: 2, 5, 7, 8, 9, 10, 11, 12

Thurston House B&B Inn

8 Elm Street, P. O. Box 686, 04974
(207) 548-2213; (800) 240-2213

This beautiful Colonial home, circa 1830, with ell and carriage house was built as a parsonage for Stephen Thurston, uncle of Winslow Homer, who visited often. Now you can visit in a casual environment. The quiet village setting is steps away from Penobscot Marine Museum, beach park on Penobscot Bay, restaurants, churches, galleries, antiques, and more. Relax in one of four guest rooms, one with bay view, two great for kids, and enjoy the "forget about lunch" breakfasts.

Hosts: Carl and Beverly Eppig
Rooms: 4 (2PB; 2SB) $45-60
Full Breakfast
Credit Cards: A, B
Notes: 2, 5, 7, 8, 9, 10, 11, 12

SOUTH GOULDSBORO

The Bluff House Inn and Restaurant

Rt. 186, P.O. Box 169, 04607
(207) 963-7805

Resting high above Frenchman Bay, the Bluff House offers everything necessary for a relaxing and enjoyable stay any time of the year. Explore Schoodic Peninsula and all the splendors of the Frenchman Bay area. Kayak or canoe from our shore, hike, bike, cross-country ski, or just relax by the fireside. We provide a million dollar view and a stress free way of life.

Hosts: Joyce and Don Freeborn
Rooms: 8 (PB) $55-75
Full Breakfast
Credit Cards: A, B, C, D, E
Notes: 4, 5

SOUTHWEST HARBOR

The Island House

P. O. Box 1006, Clark Point Rd., 04679
(207) 244-5180

Relax in a gracious, restful seacoast home on the quiet side of Mount Desert Island. We serve such Island House favorites as blueberry scones and fresh fruit crepes. A charming private loft apartment is available. Acadia National Park is only a five-minute drive away. Located across the street from the harbor, near swimming, sailing, biking, and hiking.

Hostess: Ann R. Bradford
Rooms: 4 (SB; PB off season) $50-95
Full Breakfast
Credit Cards: A, B
Notes: 2, 5, 7 (over 11), 9, 1

The Lamb's Ear Inn

P.O. Box 30, Clark Point Road, 04679
(207) 244-9828

Our old Maine house was built in 1857. It is comfortable and scenic, away from the

---

NOTES: Credit cards accepted: A Master Card; B Visa; C American Express; D Discover Card; E Diners Club; F Other; 2 Personal checks accepted; 3 Lunch available; 4 Dinner available; 5 Open all

hustle and bustle. Private baths, comfortable beds with crisp, fresh linens. Sparkling harbor views and a breakfast to remember. Come and be a part of this special village in the heart of Mount Desert Island surrounded by Acadia National Park.

Hosts: Elizabeth and George Hoke
Rooms: 6 (PB) $75-125
Full Breakfast
Credit Cards: A, B
Notes: 2 (restricted), 7 (limited), 8, 9, 10, 12

The Lamb's Ear Inn

SWANS ISLAND

Jeannie's Place
PO Box 1607, 14364 Sedwick Ave., 20688
(410) 326-0454

Featured in *The New York Times*, this charming B&B overlooks Burnt Coat Harbor, a beautiful natural bay filled with picturesque lobster boats and sailing yachts. Three charming bedrooms and one cabin with breathtaking water views. Cots available for larger groups. Swans Island, accessible by ferry from Bass Harbor, should be part of your getaway to Bar Harbor and Southwest Harbor. Come if

you relish peace and quiet!

Hosts: Jeannie and Llewellyn Joyce
Rooms: 3+cabin (1PB (cabin); 3SB) $45
Continental Breakfast
Credit Cards: None
Notes: 2, 3, 4, 5, 7, 9

THOMASTON

Cap'n Frost B&B
241 West Main (U.S. Route 1), 04861
(207) 354-8217

Our 1840 Cape is furnished with country antiques, some of which are for sale. If you are visiting our mid-coastal area, we are a comfortable overnight stay, close to Monhegan Island and a two-hour drive to Acadia National Park. Reservations are helpful.

Hosts: Arlene and Harold Frost
Rooms: 3 (1PB; 2SB) $40-45
Full Breakfast
Credit Cards: None
Notes: 2, 5, 9, 11

WALDOBORO

Broad Bay Inn and Gallery
1014 Main St., P.O. Box 607, 04572
(207) 832-6668; (800) 736-6769

Broad Bay Inn and Gallery is a lovingly restored 1830s inn, handsomely appointed with Victorian furnishings, canopy beds, paintings, piano, art and theatrical library, as well as a selection of foriegn films. Established art gallery and gift shop is in the barn. Walk down to the river, tennis, theatre, and antique shops. A short drive

year; 6 Pets welcome; 7 Children welcome; 8 Tennis nearby; 9 Swimming nearby; 10 Golf nearby; 11 Skiing nearby; 12 May be booked through travel agent

will take you to the lighthouse, Audubon Sanctuary, and fishing villages. Send for a free brochure.

Hostess: E. Libby Hopkins
Rooms: 5 (1PB; 3SB) $45-75
Full Breakfast
Credit Cards: A, B
Notes: 2, 7 (over 10), 8, 9, 10, 12

Broad Bay Inn and Gallery

WATERFORD

Kedarburn Inn
Rt. 35, 04099
(207) 583-6182

Nestled in the foothills of the White Mountains. This beautiful white frame house was built in 1858 and is set beside the flowing Kedar Brook which runs to the shores of Lake Keoka. Whether you come for outdoor activities such as golf, sailing, and swimming, or simply want to enjoy the countryside, let us pamper you in our relaxed atmosphere.

Hosts: Margaret and Derek Gibson
Rooms: 6 (4PB; 2SB) $69-88
Full Breakfast
Credit Cards: A, B
Notes: 2, 5, 6, 7, 9, 10, 11, 12

The Parsonage House Bed and Breakfast
Rice Road, P. O. Box 116, 04088
(207) 583-4115

Built in 1870 for the Waterford Church, this restored historic home overlooks Waterford Village, Keoka Lake, and Mt. Tirem. It is located in a four-season area providing a variety of opportunities for the outdoor enthusiast. The Parsonage is a haven of peace and quiet. Three double guest rooms are tastefully furnished. Weather permitting, we feature a full breakfast on the screened porch. Guests love our large New England farm kitchen and its glowing wood-burning stove.

Hosts: Joseph and Gail St. Hilaire
Rooms: 3 (1PB; 2SB) $45-75
Full Breakfast
Credit Cards: None
Notes: 2, 3, 5, 7, 9, 10, 11

WELD

Kawanhee Inn Lakeside Lodge
Mt. Blue, Webb Lake, Box 119, 04285
(winter: 7 High St., Farmington, ME 04938)
(207) 585-2000; [winter: (207) 778-4306]

Kawanhee Inn is located on Webb Lake ("Webb Beach, one of the top ten beaches of New England"—*US Air Magazine* '94) Early morning excursion by canoe will allow you to see moose feeding by the water's edge and the sun rising over the western mountains. Have breakfast before climbing Tumbledown Mountain or going gold panning in the Swift River. Bring your mountain bike, tennis rackets,

---

or enjoy a game of golf nearby. Before dinner on the screened porches, swim on our private, sandy beach.

Hostess: Martha Strunk
Rooms: 9 (5PB, 4SB) $65-85
Continental Breakfast
Credit Cards: A, B
Notes: 3 (packed), 4, 7, 8, 9, 10, 12

YORK BEACH

Homestead Inn B&B

P.O. Box 15, 03910
(207) 363-8952

Friendly, quiet and homey—four rooms in an old (1905) boarding house; connected to our home in 1969. Panoramic view of ocean and shore hills. Walk to beaches (2), shops, and Nubble Lighthouse. Great for small, adult groups. Fireplace in living room. Breakfast served in barn board dining room and outside on private sun deck.

Hosts: Dan and Danielle Duffy
Rooms: 4 (SB) $59
Continental Breakfast
Credit Cards: None
Notes: 2, 8, 9, 10, 12

YORK HARBOR

Bell Buoy B&B

570 York Street, P.O. Box 445, 03911
(207) 363-7264

At the Bell Buoy, there are no strangers, only friends who have never met. Located minutes from I-95 and U.S. 1, minutes from Kittery outlet malls, and a short walk to the beach, enjoy afternoon tea served either on the large front porch or the living

room. Fireplace and cable TV. Home-made breads or muffins are served with breakfast in the dining room each morning or on the porch.

Hosts: Wes and Kathie Cook
Rooms: 5 (2PB; 3SB) $65-85
Full Breakfast
Credit Cards: None
Notes: 2, 6, 7 (over six), 9, 10

York Harbor Inn

Route 1A, P.O. Box 573, 03911
(800) 343-3869; (207) 362-3545 ext. 295 (FAX)

For more than 100 years, the historic charm and hospitality of York Harbor Inn have welcomed those seeking distinctive lodging and dining experiences. A short walk takes you to a peaceful, protected beach. A stroll along Marginal Way reveals hidden coastal scenes and classic estates. Golf, tennis, biking, deep-sea fishing, and outlet shopping are close by. Air conditioning, antiques, phones, private baths, ocean views, and fireplaces. Full dining room and tavern with entertainment.

Hosts: Joe and Garry Dominguez
Rooms: 35 (29 PB; 6SB) $69-139
Continental "Plus" Breakfast
Credit Cards: A, B, C, E, F
Notes: 2, 3, 4, 5, 7, 8, 9, 10, 11, 12

Kawanhee Inn Lakeside Lodge

---

year; 6 Pets welcome; 7 Children welcome; 8 Tennis nearby; 9 Swimming nearby; 10 Golf nearby;
11 Skiing nearby; 12 May be booked through travel agent

Maryland

ANNAPOLIS

April's Guest House

472 Fawn's Walk, 21401
(410) 626-8391 (voice and FAX)

Stay in a friendly, comfortable place in a quiet wooded community near historic Annapolis. Explore nearby Baltimore, Washington, Virginia, (30 minutes away). Take a walk down our country roads or nature trails to the Chesapeake Bay. Play tennis across the street. Enjoy award-winning restaurants, followed by a relaxing stroll around our city dock. Shop for antiques or tour our many art galleries and restored historic homes.

Hostess: April Holthaus
Rooms: 3 (1PB; 2SB) $60-80
Continental Breakfast
Credit Cards: None
Notes: 2, 5, 7, 8, 10

The Barn on Howard's Cove

500 Wilson Road, 21401
(410) 266-6840

The Barn on Howard's Cove welcomes you with warm hospitality to a restored 1850s horse barn overlooking a beautiful cove off the Severn River. You will be convenient to both Washington, D.C., and Baltimore and very close to historic Annapolis. Begin the day with choice of full breakfast served in dining area overlooking river or in our new solarium or on the deck which is also on the the river. Beautiful gardens, rural setting, antiques, quilts. Two guest rooms await you. One room has a loft and private deck on the river. Docking in deep water provided.

Hosts: Graham and Libbie Gutsche
Rooms: 2 (2P1/2B; shared shower/tub) $70
Full Breakfast (Continental if desired)
Credit Cards: None
Notes: 2, 5, 7, 8, 10, 12 (10%)

Chesapeake Bed and Breakfast

408 Cranes Roost, 21401
(410) 757-7599 (voice and FAX)

Comfortable English country town home nestled in wooded community near Chesapeake Bay and Magothy River. Furnished in antiques, Orientals, and contemporary. Bedroom choices include a king, queen, and single. Perfect for family vacation or couple's getaway. Guest space has private living room. Marked nature trail. Hostess was local restaurant critic and can recommend dining choices. Only 10 minutes from historic Annapolis, the U.S. Naval Academy, St. John's College, boating, and otheR marine adventures. Prefer

---

NOTES: Credit cards accepted: A Master Card; B Visa; C American Express; D Discover Card; E Diners Club; F Other; 2 Personal checks accepted; 3 Lunch available; 4 Dinner available; 5 Open all

a two night minimum.

Hostess: Carolyn Curtis
Rooms: 3 (1PB; 2SB) $60-80
Continental Breakfast
Credit Cards: None
Notes: 2, 5, 7, 8, 10

Chez Amis Bed and Breakfast

85 East Street, 21401
(410) 263-6631; (800) 474-6631

Around 1900 Chez Amis "House of Friends" was a grocery store. Still evident are the original oak display cabinet, tin ceiling, and pine floors. One half block from Capitol, one block from the harbor, minutes by foot to the Naval Academy. "European Country" decor with antiques and quilts. Four guest rooms with two private baths. King and queen brass beds, TVs, central AC, terry robes, coffee service, and down comforters in every room. Don is a retired Army lawyer; Mickie a former D.C. tour guide. They welcome you with true "Southern," Christian hospitality!

Hosts: Don and Mickie Deline
Rooms: 4 (2PB; 2SB) $75-95 + tax
Full Breakfast
Credit Cards: A, B
Notes: 2, 5, 12

Duke and Duchess B&B

151 Duke of Gloucester St., 21401
(410) 268-6323

A beautifully renovated 1850 home located in the Historic District of Annapolis. Just a short walk to the U.S. Naval Academy, City Dock, restaurants, and shopping. Furnished tastefully with antiques and artwork, guests can relax and enjoy an atmosphere of cozy elegance. The B&B offers clean, comfortable accommodations with modern conveniences, including central air-conditioning. A complimentary breakfast is served in the dining room or, weather permitting, in the garden. Advance reservations by phone.

Hostess: Doris Marsh
Rooms: 2 (PB) $95-150
Full Breakfast
Credit Cards: A, B, C
Notes: 2, 5, 6, 7

Pendennis Mount B&B

1905 Thomas Drive, 21401
(410) 757-0127

Pendennis Mount B&B is conveniently located on a quiet street in scenic Annapolis near the beautiful Overlook overlooking the Naval Academy and the Stern River. We are about one mile from the U.S. Naval Academy and three miles from the Annapolis city dock and the historic downtown area. Washington, D.C. and Balitmore are both within an hour's drive.

Hostess: Celia Yu
Rooms: 2 (1PB; 2SB) $ 50-55
Full Breakfast (Continental available)
Credit Cards: None
Notes: 2, 5, 7, 12

Pendennis Mount Bed and Breakfast

BERLIN

Merry Sherwood Plantation

8909 Worcester Highway (Rt. 113), 21811
(410) 641-2112; (800) 660-0358; (410) 641-3605
(FAX)

This 1859, pre-Civil War mansion allows the visitor to experience a glorious step back in time. Recently restored, this elegant and opulent home is furnished throughout with authentic Victorian antiques. Situated on 19 acres of beautiful 19th-century landscaping, upon entering the main gates, you definitely begin your very special getaway. Enjoy formal ballroom, stately dining room, warm fireplaces, and superb breakfast and loving hospitality. Just minutes to Assateague national seashore. Listed on the Register of Historic Places.

Host: Kirk Burbage
Rooms: 8 (6PB; 2SB) $95-150
Full Gourmet Breakfast
Credit Cards: A, B
Notes: 2, 5, 8, 9, 10, 12

CHESTERTOWN

Claddaugh Farm Bed and Breakfast

160 Claddaugh Lane, 21620
(410) 778-4894 (voice and FAX); (800) 328-4894
(for reservations)

Claddaugh Farm B&B is located two miles south of historic Chestertown on Route 213. It is a Victorian-style home with rooms on the second and third floors. We have three-and-a-half acres of ground

with three kennels for your pets. We welcome children of all ages. We serve a delightful, full continental breakfast.

Hosts: Florence and David Bustard
Rooms: 4 and 1 suite (2PB; 4SB) $65-150
Full Continental Breakfast
Credit Cards: A, B
Notes: 2, 5, 6 (kennel), 7, 9, 10

Merry Sherwood Plantation

ELKTON

Garden Cottage at Sinking Springs Herb Farm

234 Blair Shore Road, 21921
(410) 398-5566; (410) 392-2389 (FAX)

With an early plantation house, including a 400-year-old sycamore, the garden cottage nestles at the edge of a meadow flanked by herb gardens and a historic barn with a gift shop. It has a sitting room with fireplace, bedroom, bath, air conditioning, and electric heat. Freshly ground coffee and herbal teas are offered with the country breakfast. Longwood Gardens and Winterthur Museum are 50 minutes away. Historic Chesapeake City is nearby with excellent restaurants. Sleeps three in two rooms. Third person pays only $25.

Hosts: Bill and Ann Stubbs
Room: 1 (PB) $85
Full Breakfast
Credit Cards: A, B
Notes: 2, 5, 7, 8, 10, 12

FREDERICK

Middle Plantation Inn

9549 Liberty Road, 21701-3246
(301) 662-8231

From this rustic inn built of stone and log, drive through horse country to the village of Mount Pleasant. The inn is located several miles east of Frederick on 26 acres. Each room is furnished with antiques and has a private bath, air conditioning, and TV. The keeping room, a common room, has stained glass and a stone fireplace. Nearby are antique shops, museums, and many historic attractions. Located within 40 minutes of Gettysburg, Pennsylvania, Antietam Battlefield, and Harper's Ferry.

Hosts: Shirley and Dwight Mullican
Rooms: 4 (PB) $85-95
Continental Breakfast (optional)
Credit Cards: A, B
Notes: 2, 5, 8, 9, 10, 12

GAITHERSBURG

Gaithersburg Hospitality Bed and Breakfast

18908 Chimney Place, 20879
(301) 977-7377

This luxury host home just off I-270 with all amenities, including private parking, is located in the beautifully planned community of Montgomery Village, near churches, restaurants, and shops, and is ten minutes from D.C. Metro Station or a convenient drive south to Washington, D.C., and north to historic Gettysburg, PA, and Harper's Ferry. This spacious bed and breakfast has two rooms with private baths; one has a queen bed. Also offered are a large, sunny third room with twin beds, and a fourth room with a single bed. Hosts delight in serving full, home-cooked breakfasts with your pleasure and comfort in mind.

Hosts: Suzanne and Joe Danilowiiz
Rooms: 4 (2PB; 2SB) $45-55
Full Breakfast
Credit Cards: None
Notes: 2, 7, 8, 9, 10, 12

HAGERSTOWN

Lewrene Farm Bed and Breakfast

9738 Downsville Pike, 21740
(301) 582-1735

Enjoy our quiet, Colonial country home on 125 acres near I-70 and I-81, a home away from home for tourists, business people, and families. We have room for family celebrations. Sit by the fireplace or enjoy the great outdoors. Antietam Battlefield and Harper's Ferry are nearby; Washington, D. C., and Baltimore are one and one-half hours away. Quilts for sale.

Hosts: Irene and Lewis Lehman
Rooms: 5 (3PB; 2SB) $55-95
Full Breakfast
Credit Cards: A, B
Notes: 2, 5, 7, 8, 9 10, 11

---

year; 6 Pets welcome; 7 Children welcome; 8 Tennis nearby; 9 Swimming nearby; 10 Golf nearby; 11 Skiing nearby; 12 May be booked through travel agent

Sunday's Bed and Breakfast

39 Broadway, 21740
(800) 221-4828

This elegant 1890 Queen Anne Victorian home is situated in the historic north end of Hagerstown. Relax in any of the many public rooms and porches or explore the many historic attractions, antique shops, fishing areas, golf courses, museums, shopping outlets, and ski areas that are nearby. You'll experience special hospitality and many personal touches at Sunday's. A full breakfast, afternoon tea and desserts, evening refreshments, fruit baskets, fresh flowers, special toiletries, and late night cordial and chocolate are just some of the offerings at Sunday's. We are located less than 90 minutes from Baltimore and Washington, DC.

Host: Bob Forrino
Rooms: 3 (1PB; 2SB) $65-95
Full Breakfast
Credit Cards: None
Notes: 2, 4, 5, 6, 7, 8, 9, 10, 11, 12

Sunday's Bed and Breakfast

OAKLAND

The Oak and Apple Bed and Breakfast

208 N. Second Street, 21550
(301) 334-9265

Circa 1915, this restored Colonial Revival sits on a beautiful large lawn with mature trees and includes a large, columned front porch, enclosed sun porch, parlor with fireplace, and a cozy gathering room with television. Awaken to fresh continental breakfast served fireside in the dining room or on the sun porch. The quaint town of Oakland offers a wonderful small-town atmosphere, and Deep Creek Lake, Wisp Ski Resort, and state parks with hiking, fishing, swimming, boating, and skiing are nearby.

Hosts: Ed and Jana Kight
Rooms: 5 (3PB; 2SB) $55-80
Expanded Continental Breakfast
Credit Cards: A, B
Notes: 2, 5, 8, 9, 10, 11, 12

ST. MICHAELS

Parsonage Inn

210 North Talbot Street (Rt. 33), 21663
(800) 394-5519

This late Victorian, circa 1883, was lavishly restored in 1985 with seven guest rooms, private baths, and brass beds with Laura Ashley linens. Three rooms have working fireplaces. The parlor and dining room are in the European tradition. Striking architecture! Two blocks to the maritime museum, shops, and restaurants.

NOTES: Credit cards accepted: A Master Card; B Visa; C American Express; D Discover Card; E Diners Club; F Other; 2 Personal checks accepted; 3 Lunch available; 4 Dinner available; 5 Open all

Mobil three-star rated.

Hostess: France Goupil
Rooms: 8 (PB) $80-130
Full Breakfast
Credit Cards: A, B
Notes: 2, 5, 7, 8, 10, 12

Wades Point Inn on the Bay

P. O. Box 7, 21663
(410) 745-2500

For those seeking the serenity of the country and the splendor of the bay, we invite you to charming Wades Point Inn, just a few miles from St. Michaels. Complemented by the ever-changing view of boats, birds, and water lapping the shoreline, our 120 acres of fields and woodlands, with one mile walking or jogging trail, provide a peaceful setting for relaxation and recreation on Maryland's eastern shore.

Hosts: Betsy and John Feiler
Rooms: 15 winter, 25 summer (15PB; 10SB) $75-175
Continental Breakfast
Credit Cards: A, B
Notes: 2, 5, 7, 8, 10

SILVER SPRING

Varborg

2620 Briggs Chaney Road, 20905
(301) 384-2842

This suburban Colonial home in the countryside is convenient to Washington, D.C., and Baltimore, just off Route 29 and close to Route 95. Three guest rooms with a shared bath are available. Hosts are happy to share their knowledge of good, nearby restaurants.

Hosts: Bob and Pat Johnson
Rooms: 3 (SB) $30-50
Full Breakfast (or continental if desired)
Credit Cards: None
Notes: 5, 7, 8

Webster House

SOLOMON

Webster House

P.O. Box 1607, 14364 Sedwick Ave., 20688
(410) 326-0454

Our B&B is an updated, reproduction of the old Webster House that stood on this property 113 years ago. Two rooms are in the main house. The "Lydia Beekman" is charmingly decorated in tea rose and lace with an oak, queen-size bed. The "Vanderpool" room is a stately green and tapestry with a cherry queen. These rooms share a unique bath. For a private getaway, "The Haven" is available. It is decorated in glen plaid, with a private bath, kitchenette, and deck. We offer a hearty, island breakfast served on the porch. Enjoy the peacefulness and refresh yourselves in our spa. Sailing, boating, and fishing nearby.

Hosts: Peter and Barbara Prentice
Rooms: 3 (1PB; 2SB) $70-85
Full Breakfast
Credit Cards: None
Notes: 2, 9

Massachusetts

Golden Slumber Accommodations B&B Inn Reservation Service

640 Revere Beach Blvd., Revere, 02151
(617) 289-1053; (800) 892-3231; (617) 289-9112 (FAX)

Golden Slumber features an unrivaled array of screened accommodations on the **Seacoast of Massachusetts** including Cape Cod, the North and South Shores, and Greater Boston. From sprawling oceanfront villas to quaint, romantic country road retreats, our gracious historic residences and unique contemporary facilities offer the paramount in Yankee hospitality. Several feature incomparable water views, canopy beds, fireplaces, private entrances, and swimming pools. More than 130 rooms available; 95% with private baths. No reservation fee! Children welcome. Limousine and gift service. Brochure/directory available. Rates: $55-220. Leah A. Schmidt, Owner and Director of Hospitality.

Golden Slumber Accommodations

Beechwood

BARNSTABLE VILLAGE

Beechwood

2839 Main Street, 02630
(508) 362-6618

The Beechwood is a beautiful example of Queen Anne Victorian restoration. It is furnished with unusual period antiques, including a carved queen-size canopy bed, a hand-painted cottage bedroom set, and a fainting couch. A large suite on the second floor accommodates three to four people. Tea is served by the fireplace in the parlor during the winter, and lemonade and iced tea are served on the veranda in the summer. The Beechwood is a romantic retreat to the graciousness of the 19th century and the many pleasures of Cape Cod!

Hosts: Debbie and Ken Traugot
Rooms: 6 (PB) $110-140
Full Breakfast
Credit Cards: A, B, C
Notes: 2, 5, 7 (over 12; only one room to accommodate under 12), 8, 9, 10, 12

NOTES: Credit cards accepted: A Master Card; B Visa; C American Express; D Discover Card; E Diners Club; F Other; 2 Personal checks accepted; 3 Lunch available; 4 Dinner available; 5 Open all

BOSTON

A B&B Agency of Boston (and Boston Harbor Bed & Breakfast)

47 Commercial Wharf, 02110
(617) 720-3540; (800) 248-9262

Downtown Boston's largest selection of guest rooms in historic bed and breakfast homes including Federal and Victorian town houses and beautifully restored 1840s waterfront lofts. Available nightly, weekly, monthly. Or choose from the loveliest selection of fully furnished private studios, one and two bedroom condominiums, corporate suites, and lofts with all the amenities including fully furnished kitchens, private baths (some with jacuzzis), TV, and telephones. Available nightly, weekly, monthly. Exclusive locations include waterfront, Faneuil Hall/Quincy Market, North End, Back Bay, Beacon Hill, Copley Square, and Cambridge.

Host: Ferne Mintz
Rooms: 120 (80PB; 40SB) $65-120
Continental Breakfast
Credit Cards: A, B
Notes: 2, 5, 7, 12

Beacon Hill B&B

27 Brimmer Street, 02108
(617) 523-7376

Be a guest in my historic home...first three floors of six-story, brick, 1869 Victorian row house in Boston's most elegant and convenient, gas-lit, residential neighborhood. Easy walk to tourist attracions: Freedom Trail, Quincy Market, convention center, Boston Common, "Cheers," shops, restaurants, subway, and parking. Spa-

cious rooms with double or queen beds, fireplaces, Oriental rugs, TV, and A/C. Elevator for luggage. Hostess, a caterer, speaks French and enjoys sharing her home of 27 years and her knowledge of Boston.

Hostess: Susan Butterworth
Rooms: 3 (PB) $120-145
Full Breakfast
Credit Cards: None
Notes: 2 (for deposit), 5, 7, 12

BROOKLINE

Beacon Inn

1750 and 1087 Beacon Street, 02146
(617) 566-0088; (617) 397-9267 (FAX)

These turn-of-the-century town houses have been converted into two of Brookline's most charming guest houses. The original woodwork is reminiscent of their 19th-century construction, and the lobby fireplace offers a friendly welcome to travelers. Large, comfortably furnished, sunny rooms provide pleasant accommodations at a reasonable price. The Beacon Inn is minutes away from downtown Boston. The area offers a wide variety of restaurants, shops, museums, theater, and other tourist attractions.

Hosts: Megan Rockett and Dan McMann
Rooms: 24 (14PB; 9SB) $49-86
Continental Breakfast
Credit Cards: A, B, C
Notes: 5, 7, 12

Beacon Plaza

1459 Beacon St., 02146
(617) 232-6550

The Beacon Plaza is family owned and

---

year; 6 Pets welcome; 7 Children welcome; 8 Tennis nearby; 9 Swimming nearby; 10 Golf nearby; 11 Skiing nearby; 12 May be booked through travel agent

operated for approximately forty years. We are conviently located on the Green line which stops across the street from us. We are 15 minutes to downtown Boston and 20 minutes to Logan Airport. Our rooms are clean and neat and we offer the use of our community kitchens to our guests. Some rooms available with TV and/or air-conditioning.

Hosts: The Pappas Family
Rooms: 40 (20PB; 20SB) $45-85
Sorry, no breakfast. (Coffee and pastry available across the street.)
Credit Cards: none
Notes: 5, 7, 9, 12

CHATHAM—CAPE COD

The Cyrus Kent House Inn

63 Cross Street, 02633
(508) 945-9104 (voice and FAX)

A 19th century sea captain's house reborn and now a gracious inn! Built in 1877, the Inn has been completely restored and furnished in period antiques and reproductions. Enjoy the subtle mingling of past and present, found within our quiet, informal Inn. Every room provides a unique experience—our fireplaced suites make a special retreat! Walking distance to beaches, shops, and restaurants.

Hostess: Sharon Mitchell Juan
Rooms: 9 (PB) $125-165
Continental Breakfast
Credit Cards: A, B
Notes: 2, 5, 7 (over 9), 8, 9, 10, 12

The Cyrus Kent House Inn

CHELMSFORD

Westsview Landing

4 Westview Ave, P. O. Box 4141, 01824
(508) 256-0074 (voice or FAX)

This large, contemporary home overlooking Hart's Pond is located three miles from Routes 495 and 3, 30 miles north of Boston, and 15 minutes south of Nashua, New Hampshire. It is close to historic Lexington, Concord, and Lowell. Many recreational activities, including swimming, boating, fishing, and bicyling are nearby; and there is a hot spa on the premises.

Hosts: Robert and Lorraine Pinette
Rooms: 3 (SB) $40-60
Full Breakfast
Credit Cards: None
Notes: 2, 6, 7, 8, 9, 10, 11

CONCORD

Hawthorne Inn

462 Lexington Road, 01742
(508) 369-5610

Fast by the ancient way, that the Minute Men trod to first face the British Regulars, rests this most colorful inn where history and literature gracefully entwine. On earth once claimed by Emerson, Hawthorne, and the Alcotts, the Hawthorne Inn beckons the traveler to refresh the spirit in a winsome atmosphere abounding with antique furnishings and delight the eye exploring rooms festooned with handmade quilts, original artwork and archaic artifacts.

Host: G. Burch
Rooms: 7 (PB) $100-160
Continental Plus Breakfast
Credit Cards: A, B, C, D
Notes: 2, 5, 7, 8, 9, 11

DANVERS

Cordwainer B&B at the Samuel Legro House

78 Center Street, 01923
(508) 774-1860

A circa 1854 home on the National Register of Historic Places, featuring beamed ceilings, canopy queen beds, fireplaces in the kitchen and the living room. The swimming pool is open from June to September for your enjoyment. Danvers is located twenty miles north of Boston and five miles west of Salem.

Hostess: Peggie Blais
Rooms: 4 (1PB; 3SB) $55-75
Expanded Continental Breakfast
Credit Cards: None
Notes: 5, 7, 8, 9, 10

Isaiah Hall Bed and Breakfast Inn

DENNIS

Isaiah Hall Bed and Breakfast Inn

152 Whig St., P.O. Box 1007, 02638
(508) 385-9928; (800) 736-0160; (508) 385-5879 (FAX)

Enjoy country ambience and hospitality in the heart of Cape Cod. Tucked away on a quiet historic side street, this lovely 1857 farmhouse is within walking distance of the beach, restaurants, shops, and playhouse. Delightful gardens surround the Inn with country antiques, Oriental rugs and quilts within. Most rooms have private baths and queen-size beds. Some have balconies or fireplaces. Near biking, golf, and tennis. AAA three-diamond rating and ABBA three crown award.

Hostess: Marie Brophy
Rooms: 11 (10PB; 1SB) $59-107
Expanded Continental Breakfast
Credit Cards: A, B, C
Notes: 2, 7(over 7), 8, 9, 10, 12

DENNISPORT

The Rose Petal B&B

152 Sea St., P.O. Box 974, 02639
(508) 398-8470

A picturesque, traditional New England home, complete with picket fence, invites guests to share this historic 1872 residence in a delightful seaside resort neighborhood. Stroll past century-old home to a sandy beach. Home-baked pastries highlight a full breakfast. A comfortable parlor offers TV, piano, and reading. Enjoy queen-size beds, antiques, hand-stitched quilts, and spacious and bright baths.

Conveniet to all Cape Cod's attactions. Open all year. ABBA approved.

Hosts: Dan and Gayle Kelly
Rooms: 3 (2PB; 1SB) $49-89
Full Breakfast
Credit Cards: A, B
Notes: 5, 7, 8, 9, 10, 12

EAST FALMOUTH

Bayberry Inn
226 Trotting Park, 02536
(508) 540-2962

At Bayberry Inn we specialize in families. We have two rooms that work well for parents, children, and the extended families. We have a quiet location with just a short drive to beaches, island ferries, restaurants, outlet stores, and golf. Special rates for clergy. Come, relax, and be pampered. Christian hospitality is our specialty.

Hosts: Joel and Anne Marie Peterson
Rooms: 2 (PB) $70 (seasonal); $40 Nov. to April
Full Breakfast
Credit Cards: None
Notes: 2, 5, 6, 7 (cribs available), 9, 10, 12

EAST ORLEANS

Ivy Lodge
194 Main St., Box 1195, 02643-1195
(508) 255-0119

A guest house since 1910, this smoke-free 1864 Greek Revival home is graced with family photos and antiques. A morning wake-up breakfast basket is found outside each guest room door, to be enjoyed in your room or under a shade tree on the spacious grounds. Located midway between ocean and bay beaches in beautiful, historic Orleans at the elbow of Cape Cod. Walking distance to shops and restaurants. Other amenities close by.

Hosts: David and Barbara McCormack
Rooms: 3 + apartment (1PB; 2 SB) $55-65; apartment $100
Continental Breakfast
Credit Cards: None
Notes: 2, 5, 7 (in apartment), 8, 9, 10

Ivy Lodge

Nauset House Inn
Box 774, 143 Beach Road, 02643
(508) 255-2195

A real, old-fashioned, country inn farmhouse, circa 1810, is located on three acres with an apple orchard, one-half mile from Nauset Beach. A quiet romantic getaway. Large common room with fireplace and a brick-floored dining room where breakfast is served. Cozily furnished with antiques, eclectic—a true fantasy.

Hosts: Diane and Al Johnson; John and Cindy Vessella
Rooms: 14 (8 PB; 6 SB) $45-95
Full or Continental Breakfast
Credit Cards: A, B
Notes: 2, 8, 9, 10

NOTES: Credit cards accepted: A Master Card; B Visa; C American Express; D Discover Card; E Diners Club; F Other; 2 Personal checks accepted; 3 Lunch available; 4 Dinner available; 5 Open all

Ship's Knees Inn

186 Beach Road, P.O. Box 756, 02643
(508) 255-1312; (508) 240-1351 (FAX)

This 170-year-old restored sea captain's
home is a three-minute walk to beautiful
sand-duned Nauset Beach. Inside the
warm, lantern-lit doorways are 19 rooms
individually appointed with special Colonial color schemes and authentic antiques.
Some rooms feature authentic ship's knees,
hand-painted trunks, old clipper ship mod-
els, braided rugs, and four-poster beds.
Tennis and swimming are available on the
premises. Three miles away overlooking
Orleans Cove, the Cove House property
offers three rooms, a one-bedroom efficiency apartment, and two cottages.

Hosts: Jean and Ken Pitchford
Rooms: 22, 1 efficiency apartment, 2 heated
cottages (11 PB; 14 SB) $50-100
Continental Breakfast
Credit Cards: A, B
Notes: 2, 5, 7 (limited), 8, 9, 10, 12

EDGARTOWN—MARTHA'S VINEYARD

The Arbor

222 Upper Main Street, P.O. Box 1228, 02539
(508) 627-8137

This charming Victorian home was originally built on the Island of Chappaquiddick
and moved by barge to its present location; a short stroll to the village shops, fine
restaurants, and the bustling activity of
Edgartown harbor. The rooms are typi-
cally New England, furnished with antiques and filled with the fragrance of fresh
flowers. Peggy will gladly direct you to
unspoiled beaches, walking trails, fishing,

and all the delights of Martha's Vineyard.

Hostess: Peggy Hall
Rooms: 10 (8PB; 2SB) $85-135 (off season rates
available)
Continental Breakfast
Credit Cards: A, B
Notes: 2, 7 (over 12), 8, 9, 10, 12

Captain Dexter House of Edgartown

35 Pease's Point Way, Box 2798, 02539
(508) 627-7289

Our historic inn offers both charm and
hospitality. Enjoy beautiful gardens. Savor a home-baked continental breakfast
and evening aperitif. Relax in a four-
poster, lace canopied bed in a room with
a working fireplace. Stroll to the harbor,
town, and restaurants. Bicycle or walk to
the beach. Let our innkeepers make your
vacation something special!

Hosts: Rick and Birdie
Rooms: 11 (PB) $65 (off-season)-$190 (in-season)
Continental Plus Breakfast
Credit Cards: A, B, C, E
Notes: 2, 7, 8, 9, 10, 12

Colonial Inn of Martha's Vineyard

38 North Water Street, 02539
(508) 627-4711; (800) 627-4701; (508) 627-5904
(FAX)

The charm of Martha's Vineyard is ech-
oed by the history and style of the Colonial
Inn, overlooking the harbor in the heart of
historic Edgartown. Affordable luxury
awaits you. All rooms have heat,
air-conditioning, color cable TV, and telephones. Continental breakfast is served in

the sunroom with patio seating available.

Hostess: Linda Malcouronne
Rooms: 42 (PB) $60-215
Continental Breakfast
Credit Cards: A, B, C
Closed January-March
Notes: 2, 3, 4, 7, 8, 9, 10, 12

Governor Bradford Inn of Edgartown

128 Main Street, P.O. Box 239, 02539-0239
(508) 627-9510

Built in 1860, the Governor Bradford Inn was moved to its present location by horse-drawn wagons. In 1980 the Victorian Gothic home was expanded to its present size and converted to a bed and breakfast inn. The guest rooms are luxurious and comfortable with modern conveniences. Most have king-size beds! The many common rooms include a homey living room with fireplace and a modern conference room. The full breakfast includes such specialties as Belgian waffles and Eggs Benedict. All types of functions can be held at the inn.

Hosts: Ray and Brenda Raffurty
Rooms: 16 (PB) $60-210
Full Breakfast
Credit Cards: A, B, C
Notes: 2, 5, 7 (over 12), 8, 9, 10, 12

The Shiretown Inn

21 North Water St., P.O. Box 921, 02539
(508) 627-3353; (800) 541-0090; (508) 627-8478 (FAX)

Shiretown Inn on the island of Martha's Vineyard, listed in the National Register of Historic Places. In the center of Edgartown, one block form the Chappaquiddick Ferry and yacht harbor. 1700s whaling captains's

houses, carriage houses, cottage, all with private baths. Some rooms have canopy bed, harbor and garden views, deck, cable color TV, air-conditioning. Lovely Garden Terrace Restaurant and Pub. Call us toll free.

Rooms: 33 (PB) $49-259
Continental Breakfast
Credit Cards: A, B, C, D
Notes: 2, 3, 4, 7, 8, 9, 10, 12

ESSEX

George Fuller House

148 Main Street, 01929
(508) 768-7766

Built in 1830, this handsome Federalist-style home retains much of its 19th-century charm, including Indian shutters and a captain's staircase. Three of the guest rooms have working fireplaces. Decoration includes handmade quilts, braided rugs, and caned Boston rockers. A full breakfast may include such features as Cindy's French toast drizzled with brandy lemon butter. Gordon College and Gordon Conwall Seminary are close by.

Hosts: Cindy and Bob Cameron
Rooms: 7(PB) $70-115
Full Breakfast
Credit Cards: A, B, C, D, E
Notes: 2, 5, 7, 8, 9, 10, 12

FALMOUTH

Captain Tom Lawrence House Inn

75 Locust Street, 02540
(508) 540-1445; (800) 266-8139

1861 whaling captain's residence in his-

NOTES: Credit cards accepted: A Master Card; B Visa; C American Express; D Discover Card; E Diners Club; F Other; 2 Personal checks accepted; 3 Lunch available; 4 Dinner available; 5 Open all

toric village close to beach, bikeway, ferries, bus station, shops, and restaurants. Explore entire Cape, Vineyard, and Plymouth by day trips. Six beautiful guest rooms have private baths, firm beds, some with canopies. Antiques, a Steinway piano, and fireplace in sitting room. Homemade delicious breakfasts include specialties from organic grain. German spoken. All rooms have central air-conditioning. No smoking!

Hostess: Barbara Sabo-Feller
Rooms: 6 (PB) $75-104
Full Breakfast
Credit Cards: A, B
Closed January
Notes: 2, 7 (over 12), 8, 9, 10

Grafton Inn

261 Grand Ave. S., 02540
(508) 540-8688; (800) 642-4069; (508) 540-1861 (FAX)

Oceanfront Victorian. Miles of beach and breathtaking views of Martha's Vineyard. Sumptuous full breakfast served on enclosed porch overlooking Nantucket Sound. Tastefully decorated rooms with period antiques. Thoughtful amenities. Flowers, homemade chocolates. Complimentary bicycles. Late afternoon wine and cheese. Walk to restaurants, shops, and Island ferry. Seven rooms are air-conditioned. Open all year. No smoking! AAA and Mobil rated.

Hosts: Liz and Rudy Cvitan
Rooms: 11(PB) $75-135
Full Breakfast
Credit Cards: A, B, C
Notes: 2, 5, 8, 9, 10

Palmer House Inn

81 Palmer Avenue, 02540
(508) 548-1230; (800) 472-2632 (reservations only); (508) 540-1878 (FAX)

"High Victorian" in style, The Palmer House Inn has rich woodwork and floors, period furniture, stained glass windows, and old photos, books, and memorabilia everywhere. The main inn has eight guest rooms; the guest house features four large corner rooms, two with whirlpool tubs; and the cottage suite has a large bedroom with whirlpool tub, separate parlor, and kitchenette. All accommodations feature romantic laces, plump pillows, fine linens, and firm posturepedic mattresses blending today's comfort with yesterday's elegance.

Hosts: Ken and Joanne Baker
Rooms: 13 (PB) $65-150
Full Gourmet Breakfast
Credit Cards: A, B, C, D, E
Notes: 2, 5, 7, 8, 9, 10, 12

Village Green Inn

40 W. Main Street, 02540
(508) 548-5621

Gracious, old, 1804 Colonial-Victorian is ideally located on Falmouth's historic village green. Walk to fine shops and restaurants, bike to beaches and picturesque Woods Hole along the Shining Ski Bike Path. Enjoy 19th-century charm and warm hospitality amidst elegant surroundings. Four lovely guest rooms and one romantic suite all have private baths and unique fireplaces (two are working). A full gourmet breakfast is served featuring delicious house specialties. Many thoughtful ameni-

year; 6 Pets welcome; 7 Children welcome; 8 Tennis nearby; 9 Swimming nearby; 10 Golf nearby; 11 Skiing nearby; 12 May be booked through travel agent

ties are included.

Hosts: Linda and Don Long
Rooms: 5 (PB) $85-120
Full Breakfast
Credit Cards: A, B, C
Notes: 2, 8, 9, 10

FALMOUTH HEIGHTS

The Moorings Lodge
207 Grand Avenue South, 02540
(508) 540-2370

Captain Frank Spencer built this large, lovely Victorian home in 1905. It's directly across from a sandy beach with lifeguard safety and it is within walking distance of good restaurants and the island ferry. Your homemade, buffet breakfast is served on a glassed-in porch overlooking the island, Martha's Vineyard. Your airy rooms with private baths add to your comfort. Call us home while you tour the Cape!

Hosts: Ernie and Shirley Bernard
Rooms: 8 (6PB; 2SB) $60-90
Full Breakfast
Credit Cards: A, B
Notes: 2, 7 (over 6), 8, 9, 10

FAIRHAVEN

Edgewater B&B
2 Oxford St., 02719
(508) 997-5512

A gracious waterfront mansion on historic Poverty Point, site of original whale ship building in Fairhaven. Five rooms each with private bath, some with spectacular water views. Two suites with working fireplaces. All rooms have cable TV. Quiet location and spacious lawns, yet close to I-95, Historic New Bedford, beaches, Martha's Vineyard/Cuttyhounk ferries, and factory outlets. Off street parking.

Hostess: Kathy Reed and Family
Rooms: 5 (PB) $60-80
Continental Breakfast
Credit Cards: A, B, C
Notes: 2, 5, 8, 9, 10, 12

HARWICH PORT

Harbor Walk
6 Freeman Street, 02646
(508) 432-1675

This Victorian summer guest house was originally built in 1880 and is furnished with eclectic charm. A few steps from the house will bring you into view of Wychmere Harbor and further along to one of the fine beaches of Nantucket Sound. The village of Harwich Port is only one half mile from the Inn and contains interesting shops and some of the finest restaurants on Cape Cod. Harbor Walk offers six comfortable rooms with twin or queen beds. An attractive garden and porch are available for sitting, lounging, and reading. Open May through October.

Hosts: Preston and Marilyn Barry
Rooms: 6 (4PB; 2SB) $45-60
Full Breakfast
Credit Cards: None
Notes: 6 (limited), 7, 8, 9, 10, 12

Sea Breeze Inn

HYANNIS

Sea Breeze Inn
397 Sea Street, 02601
(508) 771-7213

Sea Breeze is a 14-room quaint bed and breakfast. It is just a three-minute walk to the beach and 20 minutes to the island ferries. Restaurants, nightlife, shopping, golf, tennis are within a ten-minute drive. Some rooms have ocean views. An expanded continental breakfast is served between 7:30 and 9:30 each morning. All rooms are air conditioned.

Hosts: Patricia and Martin Battle
Rooms: 14 (PB) $49-95
Expanded Continental Breakfast
Credit Cards: A, B, C
Notes: 2, 5, 7, 8, 9, 10, 12 (10%)

LENOX

Garden Gables Inn
141 Main St., P.O. Box 52, 01240
(413) 637-0193; (413) 637-4554 (FAX)

220-year-old charming and quiet inn located in historic Lenox on five wooded acres dotted with gardens. 72-foot swimming pool. Some rooms have fireplaces, and sitting rooms are furnished with antiques and a Steinway grand piano. All rooms have private baths, and some also have whirlpool tubs and private porches. Breakfast is included. In-room phones are provided and the famous Tanglewood Festival is only one mile away. Restaurants are all within walking distance.

Hosts: Mario and Lynn Mekinda
Rooms: 14 (PB) $65-180
Full Breakfast
Credit Cards: A, B, C, D
Notes: 2, 5, 7 (over 12), 8, 10, 11

LYNN

Diamond District Bed and Breakfast
142 Ocean Street, 01902-2007
(800) 666-3076; (617) 599-4470

This 17-room architect designed clapboard mansion was built in 1911 by a Lynn shoe manufacturer. Features include a gracious foyer and a grand staircase, a spacious fireplaced living room with ocean view, French doors leading to an adjacent veranda that overlooks the gardens and ocean, and a banquet-size dining room. Antiques and Oriental rugs fill the house. Other furnishings include an 1895 rosewood Knabe concert grand piano. Custom Chippendale dining room table and chairs and custom 1870s Victorian bed and twin beds by custom furniture makers of Boston. Each room boasts the elegance of yesteryear. No smoking.

Hosts: Sandra and Jerry Caron
Rooms: 8 (4PB; 4SB) $75-85
Full Breakfast
Credit Cards: A, B, C, D, E
Notes: 2, 5, 6 (small, well behaved), 7 (inn not child proof), 8, 9, 10, 12

MARBLEHEAD

Harborside House
23 Gregory Street, 01945
(617) 631-1032

An 1850 Colonial overlooks picturesque Marblehead Harbor, with water views from the paneled living room with a cozy fireplace, period dining room, sunny breakfast porch, and third-story deck. A generous breakfast includes juice, fresh fruit,

---

year; 6 Pets welcome; 7 Children welcome; 8 Tennis nearby; 9 Swimming nearby; 10 Golf nearby;
11 Skiing nearby; 12 May be booked through travel agent

home-baked goods, and cereals. Antique shops, gourmet restaurants, historic sites, and beaches are a pleasant stroll away. The owner is a professional dressmaker and a nationally-ranked competitive swimmer. No smoking.

Hostess: Susan Livingston
Rooms: 2 (SB) $60-75
Expanded Continental Breakfast
Credit Cards: None
Notes: 2, 5, 7 (over 10), 8, 9

Spray Cliff on the Ocean
25 Spray Avenue, 01945
(508) 744-8924; (800) 626-1530

Panoramic views stretch out in grand proportions from this English Tudor mansion, circa 1910, set high above the Atlantic. The inn provides a spacious and elegant atmosphere inside. The grounds include a brick terrace surrounded by lush flower gardens where eider ducks, black cormorants, and sea gulls abound. Fifteen miles from Boston.

Hosts: Diane and Dick Pabich
Rooms: 7 (PB) $105-200
Continental Breakfast
Credit Cards: A, B, C, D, E
Notes: 5, 8, 9, 12

NANTUCKET

Eighteen Gardner Street Inn
18 Gardner Street, 02554
(508) 228-1155; (800) 435-1450

The Gardner Street Inn was built by Captain Robert Joy during the prosperous whaling era. Today his home has been carefully restored and **voted the Best Bed and Breakfast on Nantucket** for the past two years. Your accommodations will include our wonderful Nantucket breakfast served in the dining room each morning and comfortable air-conditioned guest rooms in the summer. Roaring fireplaces will warm your heart and fresh-baked cookies will fill your senses during the quiet season. For your enjoyment, the Inn provides complimentary bicycles, beach towels, and guest refrigerators. Whatever time of year, you will find our courteous staff happy to assist you with all your holiday planning.

Hosts: Roger and Mary Schmidt
Rooms: 17 (15PB; 2SB)
Continental "Nantucket" Breakfast
Credit Cards: A, B, C, D
Notes: 2, 5, 7, 8, 9, 10, 12

Le Languedoc Inn and 3 Hussey St. Guest House
24 Broad Street, Box 1829, 02554
(508) 228-4298; (508) 228-4682 (FAX)

Le Languedoc Inn and Restaurant is strategically located within the "Old Historic District." Luncheon and dinner are served daily. Continuing a tradition that began in Nantucket's whaling days, the Inn offers fine accommodations. Le Languedoc maintains and manages #3 Hussey Street Guest House which is located nearby on a residential street.

Hosts: Maydene Thompson Mason
Rooms: 10 (3PB; 7SB) $50-150
Continental Breakfast
Credit Cards: A, B, C, D
Notes: 2, 4 (reservations), 6, 7, 12

NOTES: Credit cards accepted: A Master Card; B Visa; C American Express; D Discover Card; E Diners Club; F Other; 2 Personal checks accepted; 3 Lunch available; 4 Dinner available; 5 Open all

House of the Seven Gables

32 Cliff Road, 02554
(508) 228-9446

A 150-year-old Victorian, The House of Seven Gables is a quiet, informal guest house. There is a parlor with a television and a fireplace for your comfort and relaxation. A continental breakfast is served to your room. The rooms are bright and sunny and some have a view of the harbor. Museums, restaurants, tennis, and beaches are all within walking distance.

Hostess: Suzanne Walton
Rooms: 10 (8PB; 2SB) $40-150
Continental Breakfast
Credit Cards: A, B, C
Notes: 2, 5, 8, 9, 10

Martin House Inn

61 Centre St., P.O. Box 743, 02554
(508) 228-0678

In a stately 1803 mariner's home in Nantucket's historic district, a romantic sojourn awaits you—a glowing fire in a spacious, charming living/dining room; large, airy guest rooms with authentic period pieces and four-poster beds; a lovely yard and veranda for peaceful summer afternoons. Our complimentary breakfast includes inn-baked breads and muffins, fresh fruit, and homemade granola.

Hosts: Channing and Ceci Moor
Rooms: 13 (9PB; 4SB) $60-145
Expanded Continental Breakfast
Credit Cards: A, B, C
Notes: 2, 5, 7 (over 5), 8, 9, 10

The Woodbox Inn

29 Fair Street, 02554
(508) 228-0587

The Woodbox is Nantucket's oldest inn, built in 1709. It is one and one-half blocks from the center of town, serves "the best breakfast on the island," and offers gourmet dinners by candlelight. There are nine units, queen-size beds, private baths, including one and two bedroom suites with working fireplaces.

Host: Dexter Tutein
Rooms: 9 (PB) $125-200
Full Breakfast Available
Credit Cards: None
Notes: 2, 4, 7, 8, 9, 10, 12

OAK BLUFFS

The Beach Rose, Martha's Vineyard

Box 2352, Columbian Ave., 02557
(Nov.-May address: 12 Rands Dr., Wayne, NJ 07470)
(508) 693-6135

This charming home, nestled in an oak and pine woodland on the beautiful island of Martha's Vineyard, is uniquely decorated in country antique style. Greet the morning with a continental plus breakfast of fresh fruits, a delicious entrée du jour, homemade muffins and jams, and freshly brewed beverages. Your hosts provide warm hospitality and personal attention. They can direct you to such places as the gingerbread cottages of the 19th century camp meeting grounds, the Gay Head Cliffs and the historic whaling homes of Edgartown. The Vineyard has a myriad of sightseeing and other activities including unspoiled

---

beaches, walking trails, sailing, fishing, biking, and much more. Courtesy transportation to and from ferry. Rates vary with the seasons.

Hosts: Gloria and Russ Everett
Rooms: 3 (SB) (house has two baths) $80-95
Expanded Continental Breakfast
Credit Cards: None
Open May-October
Notes: 2, 7, 8, 9, 10

ONSET

The Onset Pointe Inn

9 Eagleway, P.O. Box 1450, 02558
(508) 295-8442; (800) 35-ONSET

This beachfront mansion with cottage and guest house is right on the water. All accommodations enjoy water views and the private beach is a step away. The casually elegant decor is enhanced by sunlight, bright colors, and spectacular views. Private terraces, spacious verandas, a sun porch, and a beachside gazebo provide room to relax and play. This Queen Anne-style inn was built in 1890 and restored a century later by the owner. The Inn received the National Trust first prize for preservation in its B&B category.

Hostess: Ellie Hoch
Rooms: 14 (PB) $55-140
Continental Breakfast
Credit Cards: A, B, C, D
Notes: 2, 5, 7 (restricted), 8, 9, 10

The Farmhouse at Nauset Beach

ORLEANS

The Farmhouse at Nauset Beach

163 Beach Rd., 02653
(508) 255-6654; (508) 240-1900 (FAX)

Enjoy our unique blend of a delightfully quiet country licensed bed and breakfast in a seashore setting. We're a half mile from the beautiful Nauset Beach. Some rooms have ocean views. Eat breakfast on the outside deck. Wander around the 1.6 acres, sit on lawn chairs and read, or stroll through the cedar trees listening to our Cape birds. Recreational activities and restaurants one mile. Residential section of town. Very friendly atmosphere.

Hostess: Dot Standish
Rooms: 8 (5PB; 2SB) $42-95
Continental Plus Breakfast
Credit Cards: A, B
Notes: 2, 5, 7, 8, 9, 10, 12

REHOBOTH

Gilbert's B&B

30 Spring Street, 02769
(508) 252-6416

Our 150-year-old home is special in all seasons. The in-ground pool refreshes weary travelers, and the quiet walks through our 100 acres give food for the soul. Guests also enjoy the horses. We praise God for being allowed to enjoy the beauty of the earth and want to share this beauty with others. No smoking inside the house.

Hosts: Jeanne and Martin Gilbert
Rooms: 3 (SB) $45-50
Full Breakfast
Credit Cards: None
Notes: 2, 5, 6 (horses only), 7, 8, 9, 10, 12 (10%)

NOTES: Credit cards accepted: A Master Card; B Visa; C American Express; D Discover Card; E Diners Club; F Other; 2 Personal checks accepted; 3 Lunch available; 4 Dinner available; 5 Open all

ROCKPORT

Lantana House

22 Broadway, 01966
(508) 546-3535

An intimate guest house in the heart of historic Rockport, Lantana House is close to Main Street, the T-Wharf, and the beaches. There is a large sun deck reserved for guests, as well as TV, games, magazines and books, a guest refrigerator, and ice service. Nearby you will find a golf course, tennis courts, picnic areas, rocky bays, and inlets. Boston is one hour away by car.

Hostess: Cynthia A. Sewell
Rooms: 7 (5PB; 2SB) $60-75
Continental Breakfast
Credit Cards: None
Notes: 2, 5, 7, 8, 9, 10

SALEM

Amelia Payson Guest House

16 Winter Street, 01970
(508) 744-8304

Built in 1845, 16 Winter Street is one of Salem's finest examples of Greek Revival architecture. Elegantly restored and beautifully decorated, each room is furnished with period antiques and warmed by a personal touch. Located in the heart of Salem's historic district, a five-minute stroll finds downtown shopping, historic houses, museums, and Pickering Wharf's waterfront dining. The seaside towns of Rockport and Gloucester are a short drive up the coast; downtown Boston is only 30 minutes away by car or easily reached by train

or bus. Color brochure available. No smoking.

Hosts: Ada and Donald Roberts
Rooms: 4 (PB) $65-85
Continental Plus Breakfast
Credit Cards: A, B, C
Notes: 5, 9, 10

The Salem Inn

7 Summer Street, 01970
(508) 741-0680; (508) 744-8924 (FAX)

In the midst of the historical and beautifully restored city of Salem is The Salem Inn, originally three town houses built in 1834 by Captain Nathaniel West. The captain would have approved of the spacious, comfortably appointed guest rooms with a blend of period detail and antique furnishings. Some have working fireplaces. Ideal for families are two-room suites complete with equipped kitchen. All rooms have air conditioning, phones, TV. Complimentary continental breakfast served in our two intimate dining rooms, rose garden, and brick terrace. Rail and bus transportation available to Boston, only 18 miles away. Jacuzzis available.

Hosts: Richard and Diane Pabich
Rooms: 21 (PB) $99-150
Continental Breakfast
Credit Cards: A, B, C, D, E
Notes: 2, 4, 5, 6, 7, 9, 10, 12

SANDWICH

Bay Beach B&B

1-3 Bay Beach Lane, Box 151, 02563
(508) 888-8813

Cape Cod is the pristine setting for Bay Beach, an extraordinary contemporary bed and breakfast. Bay Beach has spacious

---

year; 6 Pets welcome; 7 Children welcome; 8 Tennis nearby; 9 Swimming nearby; 10 Golf nearby; 11 Skiing nearby; 12 May be booked through travel agent

suites with private baths, some with jacuzzis, oceanfront decks, cable TV, telephones, refrigerators, air conditioning, compact disc player, and unparalleled amenities. Bicycles, exercise room, plus a full continental breakfast. A non-smoking property for adults only. Visit nearby museums, boardwalk, and fine restaurants within walking distance! Rated four diamonds from AAA.

Hosts: Emily and Reale J. Lemieux
Rooms: 5 (PB) $125-195
Continental Breakfast
Credit Cards: A, B
Notes: 2, 8, 9, 10, 12

Captain Ezra Nye House

152 Main Street, 02563
(800) 388-CAPT; (508) 933-2897 (FAX)

Whether you come to enjoy summer on Cape Cod, a fall foliage trip, or a quiet winter vacation, the Captain Ezra Nye House is the perfect place to start. Located 60 miles from Boston, 20 from Hyannis, and within walking distance of many noteworthy attractions, including Heritage Plantation, Sandwich Glass Museum, and the Cape Cod Canal. Award winning—Readers Choice, Best B&B Upper Cape, *Cape Cod Life* magazine, and named one of Top Fifty Inns in America by *Inn Times*.

Hosts: Elaine and Harry Dickson
Rooms: 7 (5PB; 2SB) $55-90
Full Breakfast
Credit Cards: A, B, C, D
Notes: 2, 5, 7 (over six), 8, 9, 10, 12

The Summer House

158 Main Street, 02563
(508) 888-4991

This exquisite 1835 Greek Revival home

featured in *Country Living* magazine is located in the heart of historic Sandwich village and features antiques, working fireplaces, hand-stitched quilts, flowers, large sunny rooms, and English-style gardens. We are within strolling distance of dining, museums, shops, pond, and the boardwalk to the beach. Bountiful breakfasts and elegant afternoon tea in the garden.

Hosts: David and Karyl Merrell
Rooms: 5 (1PB; 4SB) $55-75
Full Breakfast
Credit Cards: A, B, C, D
Notes: 2, 5, 7 (over 5), 8, 9, 10, 12

SOUTH DARTMOUTH

The Little Red House

631 Elm St., 02748
(508) 996-4554

A charming gambrel Colonial home located in the lovely coastal village of Padanaram. This home is beautifully furnished with country accents, antiques, lovely living room with fireplace, luxuriously comfortable four-poster or brass-and-iron beds. A full homemade breakfast in the romantic, candlelit dining room is a delectable treat. Close to the harbor, beaches, historic sites, and a short distance to New Bedford, Newport, Plymouth, Boston, Cape Cod. Martha Vineyard's ferry is just 10 minutes away.

Host: Meryl Zwirblis
Rooms: 2 (SB) $60-65
Full Breakfast
Credit Cards: None
Notes: 2, 5, 8, 9, 10, 12 (10%)

NOTES: Credit cards accepted: A Master Card; B Visa; C American Express; D Discover Card; E Diners Club; F Other; 2 Personal checks accepted; 3 Lunch available; 4 Dinner available; 5 Open all

SOUTH DENNIS

Captain Nickerson Inn

333 Main Street, 02660
(508) 398-5966; (800) 282-1619

Delightful, Victorian sea captain's home built in 1828 and changed to present Queen Anne style in 1879. There are five guest rooms decorated with period four-poster or white iron queen beds and Oriental or handwoven rugs. The fireplaced living room is comfortable yet lovely and has cable TV, VCR, and stained glass windows. The dining room is also fireplaced and has a stained glass picture window. The Inn, which is situated on a bike path, offers complimentary bicycles to guests. Area attractions include golf, beaches, paddleboats, horseback riding, museums, fishing, craft and antique shops, and a local church which houses the oldest, working pipe organ in this country. Smoking restricted to front porch. ABBA approved.

Hosts: Pat and Dave York
Rooms: 5 (3PB; 2SB) $55-85
Full Breakfast
Credit Cards: A, B, D
Notes: 2, 4 (weekends only), 5, 7, 9, 10, 12

SOUTH LANCASTER

Deershorn Manor B&B and Conference Center

P.O. Box 805, 357 Sterling Rd., 01561
(508) 365-9002; (508) 365-3253 (FAX)

Deershorn Manor, built circa 1886 for the Honorable Herbert Parker, Attorney General of the Commonwealth of Massachusetts, 1901-1905, rests within acres of formal gardens with gazebos and foun-

tains, bordering wildlife sanctuary. Tranquil and historic, its large library with religious books and prayer corner, four-season solarium, and parlor with baby grand piano complement any getaway. Let the Manor's Doric pillars and formal circular staircase usher you into a bygone era of elegance. Non-smoking indoors.

Host: S.P. Lamb
Rooms: 10 (5PB; 5SB) $35-95
Continental Breakfast
Credit Cards: None
Notes: 2, 5, 7, 8, 9, 10, 11, 12

STOCKBRIDGE

Arbor Rose Bed and Breakfast

Box 114, 8 Yale Hill Rd., 01262
(413) 298-4744

Lovely, old, New England mill house with pond, gardens, and mountain view. Walk to Berkshire Theater and Stockbridge Center. Beautiful rooms, comfy, good beds, antiques, paintings, and sunshine. Fireplace and TV in common room. Home-baked mmm... breakfast.

Hosts: Christina M. Alsop and family
Rooms: 4 (2PB; 2SB) $55-150
Home-baked continental breakfast; Full breakfast on weekends
Credit Cards: A, B, C
Notes: 2, 5, 7, 8, 9, 10, 11, 12

The Inn at Stockbridge

P.O. Box 618, Route 7 (north), 01262
(413) 298-3337; (413) 298-3406 (FAX)

This eight room inn is situated on a 12-acre plot one mile north of the village of Stockbridge. This Georgian Colonial, built in the early 20th century as a country estate, has retained its features of elegance and comfort. Located in the heart of the four season Berkshire Hills, it is close to all local attractions including the Norman Rockwell museum, Tanglewood, Berkshire Theater, and several ski areas. A memorable full breakfast and gracious hospitality are the highlights.

Hosts: Lee and Don Weitz
Rooms: 8 (PB) $80-245
Full Breakfast
Credit Cards: A, B, C
Notes: 2, 5, 7 (over 11), 8, 9, 10, 11, 12

Historic Merrell Inn

STOCKBRIDGE—SOUTH LEE

Historic Merrell Inn
1565 Pleasant St., South Lee, 01260
(413) 243-1794

One of New England's most historic old stage coach inns, located in the heart of the Berkshire Mountains in western MA. The rooms are all beautifully decorated with color coordinated linens and luxury amenities like A/C and fireplaces. The Inn is in a tiny New England village on two acres of fenced grounds which extend to the banks of the Housatouie River. A hearty country

breakfast of each guest's choice is served each morning. AAA three-diamond, Mobil three-star, and ABBA three-crowns.

Hosts: Charles and Faith Reynolds
Rooms: 9 (PB) $65-145
Full "Cook-to-Order" Breakfast
Credit Cards: A, B
Notes: 2

STURBRIDGE

The Colonel Ebenezer Crafts Inn
Rt. 131, P.O. Box 187, 01566
(508) 347-3313; (800) PUBLICK

The Colonel Ebenezer Crafts Inn was built in 1786 by David Fiske, Esquire, on one of the highest points of land in Sturbridge, which offered him a commanding view of his cattle and farmland. The house has since been magnificently restored by the management of the Publick House. Accommodations at Crafts Inn are charming. There are two queen-size canopy beds, as well as some four-poster beds. Guests may relax by the pool or in the sun room, take an afternoon tea, or enjoy sweeping views of the countryside. Breakfast includes freshly-baked muffins and sweet rolls, fresh fruit and juices, and coffee and tea. Those seeking a heartier breakfast, lunch, or dinner can stroll down to the Publick House located just over a mile away.

Hostess: Ms. Shirley Washburn
Rooms: 8 (PB) $60-150
Continental Breakfast
Credit Cards: A, B, C, E
Notes: 2, 5, 7, 9, 10

NOTES: Credit cards accepted: A Master Card; B Visa; C American Express; D Discover Card; E Diners Club; F Other; 2 Personal checks accepted; 3 Lunch available; 4 Dinner available; 5 Open all

Sturbridge Country Inn
530 Main Street, 01566
(508) 347-5503; (508) 347-5319 (FAX)

At this historic 1840s inn each room has a fireplace and private whirlpool tub. It is close to Old Sturbridge Village and within walking distance of restaurants, shops, antiques. Breakfast available in room. Repertory theater nightly in barn July 1 through Oct. 25.

Host: Mr. MacConnel
Rooms: 9 (PB) $69-149
Continental Breakfast
Credit Cards: A, B, C, D
Notes: 2, 4, 5, 7, 8, 9, 10, 11, 12

STURBRIDGE—WARE

Antique 1880 Bed and Breakfast
14 Pleasant Street, 01082
(413) 967-7847

Built in 1876, this Colonial style has pumpkin and maple hardwood floors, beamed ceilings, six fireplaces, and antique furnishings. Afternoon tea is served by the fireplace; breakfast is served in the dining room or on the porch, weather permitting. It is a short, pretty country ride to historic Old Sturbridge Village and Old Deerfield Village; hiking and fishing are nearby. Midpoint between Boston and the Berkshires, this is a very comfortable bed and breakfast.

Hostess: Margaret Skutnik
Rooms: 5 (2PB; 3SB) $40-65
Full Breakfast
Credit Cards: None
Notes: 2, 5, 8, 9, 10, 11, 12

TYRINGHAM

The Golden Goose
Main Rd.—Box 336, 01264
(413) 243-3008

Warm, friendly circa 1800 B&B nestled in secluded valley. Near to Tanglewood, Stockbridge, skiing, and hiking. All homemade jams, applesauce, and biscuits, fresh fruit in season, and hot and cold cereals. Open all year.

Hosts: Lilja and Joe Rizzo
Rooms: 7 (5PB; 2SB) $65-125
Semi-Full Breakfast
Credit Cards: A, B, C, D
Notes: 2, 5, 7, 8, 9, 10, 11, 12

Captain Dexter House of Vineyard Haven

VINEYARD HAVEN— MARTHA'S VINEYARD

Captain Dexter House of Vineyard Haven
100 Main St., P. O. Box 2457, 02568
(508) 693-1066

Your perfect country inn! Built in 1840, the house has been meticulously restored and exquisitely furnished to reflect the charm of that period. You will be surrounded by flowers from our garden and pampered by innkeepers who believe in old-fashioned hospitality. The inn's eight romantic guest rooms are distinctively decorated. Several rooms have working fireplaces (as does the parlor) and four-poster canopy beds. Stroll to town and harbor.

Hosts: Rick and Birdie
Rooms: 8 (PB) $55 (off-season)-$160 (in-season)
Continental Breakfast
Credit Cards: A, B, C, E
Notes: 2, 5, 7, 8, 9, 10, 12

The Hanover House

10 Edgartown Rdl, P.O. Box 2107, 02568
(508) 693-1066

Located on the island of Martha's Vineyard, The Hanover House is a large, old inn that has been brought into the 20th century while still retaining the charm and personalized hospitality of the gracious, old inns of yesteryear. Decorated in a classic country style that typifies a New England inn, Hanover House is just a short wald from town and the ferry. Non-Smoking.

Hosts: Ron and Kay Nelson
Rooms: 15 (PB) $68-188
Continental Breakfast
Credit Cards: A, B, C, D
Notes: 2, 5, 8, 9, 10, 12

YARMOUTH PORT

The Colonial House Inn

277 Main St., Rt. 6A, 02675
(508) 362-4348; (800) 999-3416; (508) 362-8034
(FAX)

This registered historical landmark has antique appointed guest rooms, private baths, and air-conditioning. It features gracious hospitality, old world charm, and traditional New England cuisine. Full li-

quor license, fine wines, and an indoor heated swimming pool. Lovely grounds, large deck, reading room, TV room, and Victorian living room. Close to nature trails, golf, tennis, antique shops, beaches, and shopping.

Host: Malcolm J. Perna
Rooms: 21 (PB) $50-85
Continental Breakfast
Credit Cards: A, B, C, D
Notes: 2, 3, 4, 5, 6, 7, 8, 9, 10, 11, 12

One Centre Street Inn

One Centre St. and Old Kings Hwy., 02675
(508) 362-8910

Once a parsonage (circa 1824) One Centre Street is located on the historic north side of Cape Cod. Take a short walk or bike ride to antique shops, nature trails, fine restaurants, and Gray's Beach with its long boardwalk and incomparable sunsets. Rooms are handsomely furnished in Queen Anne decor. A sumptuous breakfast awaits you in the dining room or out on the porch. You may even order a gourmet picnic to take to the beach.

Hostess: Karen Iannello
Rooms: 4 (2PB; 2SB) $75-110
Full Breakfast
Credit Cards: A, B
Notes: 2, 5, 7 (over 12), 8, 9, 10, 12

The Colonial House Inn

NOTES: Credit cards accepted: A Master Card; B Visa; C American Express; D Discover Card; E Diners Club; F Other; 2 Personal checks accepted; 3 Lunch available; 4 Dinner available; 5 Open all

Michigan

BATTLE CREEK

Greencrest Manor

6174 Halbert Road, 49017
(616) 962-8633; (616) 962-8633 (FAX)

To experience Greencrest is to step back in time to a way of life that is rare today. From the moment you enter the iron gates, you will be mesmerized. This French Normandy mansion situated on the highest elevation of St. Mary's Lake is constructed of sandstone, slate, and copper. Three levels of formal gardens include fountains, stone walls, iron rails, and cut sandstone urns. Air conditioned. Featured "Inn of the Month" in *Country Inns* magazine, August 1992 edition, and chosen as one of their top twelve inns in the nation for 1992.

Hosts: Tom and Kathy Van Daff
Rooms: 8 (6PB; 2SB) $75-170
Expanded Continental Breakfast
Credit Cards: A, B, C
Notes: 2, 5, 7, 8, 10, 11

BAY CITY

Clements Inn

1712 Center Ave., 48708-6122
(517) 894-4600; (517) 895-8535 (FAX)

This 1886 Queen Anne-style Victorian home features six fireplaces, magnificent woodwork, an oak staircase, amber-colored glass windows, working gas lamps, organ pipes, two claw foot tubs, and a third-floor ballroom. Each of the six bedrooms includes cable TV, telephone, a private bath, and air-conditioning. Special features include in-room gas fireplaces, an in-room whirlpool tub, and the 1200-square foot, fully furnished (including kitchen) Alfred Lord Tennyson Suite.

Hosts: Brian and Karen Hepp
Rooms: 6 (PB) $74-125
Continetal Breakfast
Credit Cards: A, B, C, D
Notes: 2, 5, 7, 8, 10, 12 (10%)

Stonehedge Inn Bed and Breakfast

924 Center Avenue (M25), 48708
(517) 894-4342

With stained glass windows and nine fireplaces, this 1889 English Tudor home is indeed an elegant journey into the past. The magnificent open foyer and staircase lead to large, beautiful bedrooms on the upper floors. Original features include speaking tubes, a warming oven, chandeliers, and a fireplace picturing Bible stories and passages on Blue Delft tiles. In the historic district, Frankenmuth is 20 miles away. Birch Run Manufacturer's Market-

---

year; 6 Pets welcome; 7 Children welcome; 8 Tennis nearby; 9 Swimming nearby; 10 Golf nearby; 11 Skiing nearby; 12 May be booked through travel agent

place is 35 miles away.

Hostess: Ruth Koerber
Rooms: 7 (7SB) $75-85
Expanded Continental Breakfast
Credit Cards: A, B, C, D
Notes: 2, 5, 7, 8, 9, 10, 11, 12

CHARLEVOIX

Aaron's Windy Hill B&B

202 Michigan, 49720
(616) 547-2804; (616) 547-6100

Victorian-style home with huge riverstone porch where you can enjoy a homemade buffet-style breakfast. Each of the eight spacious rooms are individually decorated and each has its own bath. Three rooms can accommodate up to five guests. One block north of drawbridge, shops, and restaurants, and one block east of Lake Michigan's swimming and sunsets.

Hostess: Nancy DeHollanden
Rooms: 8(PB) $65-95
Continental Plus Breakfast
Credit Cards: None
Open May 15 through October 30.
Notes: 2, 7, 8, 9, 10

CLIO

Chandelier Guest House

1567 Morgan Road, 48420
(810) 687-6061

Relax in our country home. Enjoy bed and breakfast comforts including choice of rooms with twin, full, or queen beds. You may wish to be served full breakfast in bed, or beneath the beautiful crystal chandelier, or on the sun porch with a view of surrounding woods. Located minutes from

Clio Amphitheater, Flint Crossroad Village, Birch Run Manufacturer's Marketplace, Frankenmuth, and Chesaning. Senior citizen discount. Call for directions. Hospitality Award 1993.

Hosts: Alfred and Clara Bielert
Rooms: 2 (1SB) $49.95-54.95
Full Country Breakfast
Credit Cards: None
Notes: 2, 5, 7, 10, 12

Aaron's Windy Hill B&B

COLDWATER

Batavia Inn

1824 West Chicago Road, U.S. 12, 49036
(517) 278-5146

This 1872 Italianate country inn has original massive woodwork, high ceilings, and restful charm. Seasonal decorations are a specialty. Christmas festival of trees. Located near recreation and discount shopping. In-ground pool, cross-country skiing, and fifteen acres of wildlife trails. Guest pampering is the innkeepers' goal with treats, homemade breakfasts. Perfect for small retreats.

Hosts: E. Fred and Alma Marquardt
Rooms: 5(PB) $59-74
Full Breakfast
Credit Cards: A, B
Notes: 2, 5, 8, 9, 10, 11

NOTES: Credit cards accepted: A Master Card; B Visa; C American Express; D Discover Card; E Diners Club; F Other; 2 Personal checks accepted; 3 Lunch available; 4 Dinner available; 5 Open all

ELK RAPIDS

Cairn House Bed and Breakfast

8160 Cairn Hwy., 49629
(616) 264-8994

Built in the style of an 1880s Colonial home and located 15 minutes north of Traverse City, two miles from Grand Traverse Bay and Port of Elk rapids. Rooms furnished to make you feel at home. Full breakfast served in the nook in the all-oak kitchen. Boat trailer parking available.

Hosts: Roger and Mary Vandervort
Rooms: 3 (PB) $65
Full Breakfast
Credit Cards: None
Notes: 2, 7, 8, 9, 10, 11, 12

FENNVILLE

The Kingsley House Bed and Breakfast

626 West Main Street, 49408
(616) 561-6425

This elegant Queen Anne Victorian was built by the prominent Kingsley family in 1886 and selected by *Inn Times* as one of 50 best bed and breakfasts in America. It was featured in *Innsider* magazine. Near Holland, Saugatuck, Allegan State Forest, sandy beaches, cross-country skiing. Bicycles available, three rooms with whirlpool baths and fireplaces, and a getaway honeymoon suite. Enjoy the beautiful surroundings, family antiques. Breakfast is served in the formal dining room.

Hosts: David and Shirley Witt
Rooms: 8 (PB) $75-150
Full Breakfast
Credit Cards: A, B, C, D
Notes: 2, 5, 8, 9, 10, 11, 12

The Kingsley House

FRANKENMUTH

Bavarian Town Bed and Breakfast

206 Beyerlein St., 48734
(517) 652-8057

Beautifully redecorated Cape Cod dwelling with central air-conditioning and private half-baths in a peaceful, residential district of Michigan's most popular tourist town, just three blocks from Main Street. Bilingual hosts are descendants of original German settlers. Will serve as tour guide of area, including historic St. Lorenz Lutheran Church. Color TV with comfortable sitting area in each room. Shared kitchenette. Leisurely served full breakfasts with homemade baked food. Shared recipes. Superb hospitality.

Hosts: Louie and Kathy Weiss
Rooms: 2 (P1/2B, shower is shared) $50-55
Full Breakfast
Credit Cards: None
Notes: 2, 5, 7, 8, 9, 10

---

year; 6 Pets welcome; 7 Children welcome; 8 Tennis nearby; 9 Swimming nearby; 10 Golf nearby; 11 Skiing nearby; 12 May be booked through travel agent

Bed and Breakfast at the Pines

327 Ardussi Street, 48734
(517) 652-9019

Welcome to our friendly; "non-smoking," ranch-style home in a quiet residential neighborhood within walking distance of main tourist areas and famous restaurants. Hosts offer sightseeing ideas and suggestions of the area, along with Michigan travel tips. Bedrooms furnished with heirloom quilts, ceiling fans, and fresh flowers; shared shower with terry robes provided. A family-style breakfast of house specialties served in the dining area. Favorite recipes shared with guests.

Hosts: Richard and Donna Hodge
Rooms: 2(1PB; 1SB) $40-45
Expanded Continental Breakfast
Credit Cards: None
Notes: 2, 5, 6, 7

GRAND HAVEN

Boyden House Inn Bed and Breakfast

301 South 5th, 49417
(616) 846-3538; (616) 847-3645 (FAX)

Built in 1874, our charming Victorian inn is decorated with treasures from faraway places, antiques, and original art. Enjoy the comfort of air-conditioned rooms with private baths and whirlpool baths. Some rooms feature fireplaces or balconies. Relax in our common room and veranda surrounded by a beautiful perennial garden. Full, homemade breakfast served in our lovely dining room. Walking distance to boardwalk beaches, shopping, and restaurants.

Hosts: Carrie and Berend Snoeyer
Rooms: 6 (PB) $65-120
Full Breakfast
Credit Cards: A, B, C
Notes: 2, 5, 7, 8, 9, 10, 11, 12

Seascape Bed and Breakfast

20009 Breton, **Spring Lake**, 49456
(616) 842-8409

On private Lake Michigan beach. Relaxing lakefront rooms. Enjoy the warm hospitality and "Country Living" ambiance of our nautical lakeshore home. Full, homemade breakfast served in gathering room with fieldstone fireplace or on the sun deck. Either offers a panoramic view of Grand Haven Harbor. Stroll or cross-country ski on dune land nature trails. Open all year around, offering a kaleidoscope of scenes with the changing of the seasons. Stay Sunday-Thursday and get one night free!

Hostess: Susan Meyer
Rooms: 3 (PB) $65-95
Full Breakfast
Credit Cards: A, B
Notes: 2, 5, 8, 9, 10, 11, 12 (no commission)

Seascape Bed and Breakfast

HARBOR SPRINGS

Mottls Getaway

1021 Birchcrest Ct., 49740
(616) 526-9682

Perfect for a ski excursion or summer getaway, this B&B apartment includes two bedrooms with twin beds, a kitchenette with stove and refrigerator, large stone fireplace in furnished living room, and a private outside entrance. The nearby ski resorts of Boyne Highlands, Boyne Mountain, and Nubs Nob, along with numerous cross-country ski trails, provide winter sports activities. Beautiful beaches, excellent golf courses, and a variety of hiking and biking trails are summer features.

Hostess: Carol Mottl
Rooms: 2 (PB) $50
Full Self-Serve Breakfast
Credit Cards: None
Notes: 2, 5, 7, 8, 9, 10, 11

HOLLAND

Dutch Colonial Inn

560 Central Avenue, 49423
(616) 396-3664

Relax and enjoy a gracious 1928 Dutch Colonial. Your hosts have elegantly decorated their home with family heirloom antiques and furnishings from the 1930s. Guests enjoy the cheery sun porch, honeymoon suites, fireplaces, or rooms with whirlpool tubs for two. Festive touches are everywhere during the Christmas holiday season. Nearby are Windmill Island, wooden shoe factory, Delftware factory, tulip festival, Hope College, Michigan's finest beaches, bike paths, and cross-country ski trails. Corporate rates are available for business travelers.

Hosts: Bob and Pat Elenbaas, Diana Klungel
Rooms: 5 (PB) $70-125
Full Breakfast
Credit Cards: A, B, C, D
Notes: 2, 5, 8, 9, 10, 11, 12

Reka's Bed and Breakfast

300 N. 152nd Avenue, 49424
(616) 399-0409

"True Dutch atmosphere" is found in this unique new bed and breakfast in Holland, MI. Close to bicycle paths, Lake Michigan beaches, Lake Macatawa, Manufacturers' Outlet Mall, downtown Holland, Hope College, theaters, restaurants, etc. The guest rooms offer king- and queen-size beds, air conditioning, and walkouts to the patio where at times you may spot a deer or other wildlife and where you are able to enjoy amazing sunsets in the most quiet setting. We serve a delicious full breakfast that will satisfy all. The B&B has been professionally designed and decorated with Blue Delft Vases and much more wonderful art for your enjoyment.

Hosts: Kay and Rein Wolfert
Rooms: 3 (PB) $80
Full Breakfast
Credit Cards: A, B, F
Notes: 2, 5, 7, 8, 9, 10, 11, 12

INTERLOCHEN

Sandy Shores B&B

4487 State Park Hwy. 49643
(616) 276-9763

Your "home away from home." Large living room, glassed-in porch, decking. Rooms tastefully furnished. Guests have access to all facilities including yard and private, sandy beach on Duck Lake. Convenient to summer/winter activities, shopping, and dining. Within walking distance to Interlochen Arts Academy. 17 miles SW of Traverse City.

Hostess: Sandra E. Svec
Rooms: 3 (SB) $70-80
Continental Plus Breakfast
Credit Cards: None
Notes: 2, 5, 9, 10, 11, 12

IONIA

Union Hill Inn B&B

306 Union Street, 48846
(616) 527-0955

Enjoy a peaceful and romantic getaway amongst pre-Victorian splendor. Elegant historic 1868 Italianate home noted for its expansive veranda and panoramic view. Only two blocks from downtown. Rooms tastefully decorated with antiques. Each room has a TV and clock radio. Central air. Union Hill Inn—*Where love and peace abide.*

Hosts: Tom and Mary Kay Moular
Rooms: 5 (SB) $50-65
Full Breakfast
Credit Cards: None
Notes: 2, 5, 7, 8, 9, 10, 11, 12

LAKE CITY

Bed and Breakfast in the Pines

1940 S. Schneider St., 49651
(616) 839-4876

A quaint chalet nestled among the pines on shimmering Sapphire Lake. Each bedroom has its own outside door leading to its own deck facing the lake. Enjoy our large fireplace and warm hospitality. Handicap ramp. 13 miles east of Cadillac. No alcohol, smoking, or pets. Enjoy downhill and cross-country skiing, fishing, swimming, hiking, biking, and boating.

Hostess: Reggie Ray
Rooms: 2 (1PB; 1SB) $65
Full Breakfast
Credit Cards: None
Notes: 2, 5, 8, 9, 10, 11

Bed and Breakfast in the Pines

LELAND AREA/MAPLE CITY

Leelanau Country Inn

149 E. Harbor Hwy, Maple City, 49664
(616) 228-5060; (616) 228-5013 (FAX)

For over 100 years, the inn has stood ready to be of service. We feature eight country-appointed guest rooms and a 150-seat award-winning restaurant specializing in fresh seafood flown directly to us from Boston, choice steaks, homemade pasta, and a large array of desserts. All items are made from scratch. Eight miles south of Leland on M-22. Surrounded by churches

---

NOTES: Credit cards accepted: A Master Card; B Visa; C American Express; D Discover Card; E Diners Club; F Other; 2 Personal checks accepted; 3 Lunch available; 4 Dinner available; 5 Open all

of all faiths.

Hosts: John and Linda Sisson
Rooms: 6 (SB) $30-40
Continental Breakfast
Credit Cards: A, B, C
Notes: 2, 4, 5, 6, 7, 8, 9, 10, 11

LUDINGTON

Doll House Inn

709 E. Ludington Avenue, 49431
(616) 843-2286; (800) 275-4616

Gracious 1900 American Foursquare, seven rooms including bridal suite with whirlpool tub for two. Enclosed porch, smoke- and pet-free, adult accommodations. Full heart-smart breakfast. Air conditioning, corporate rates, bicycles, cross-country skiing, walk to beach, town, special weekend and murder/mystery packages—fall and winter. Transportation to and from car ferry-airport.

Hosts: Joe and Barb Gerovac
Rooms: 7(PB) $60-95
Full Breakfast
Credit Cards: A, B
Closed December 20 to January 3.
Notes: 2, 5, 8, 9, 10

The Inn at Ludington

701 E. Ludington Ave., 49431
(616) 845-7055; (800) 845-9170

Comfort and elegance are yours to enjoy in our historic 1889 Queen Anne Victorian. Ludington's only "painted lady" inn is conveniently located "on the avenue," within walking distance of shops, restaurants, beach, and car ferry. Six rooms, all with private baths, are lovingly decorated with treasured antiques and cherished collectibles. Our bountiful breakfast features

locally grown and made in Michigan products. Special event weekends include Murder Mysteries, Dickens Christmas, Harvest Festival, and more!

Hostess: Diane Shields
Rooms: 6 (PB) $65-85
Full, Buffet Breakfast
Credit Cards: A, B, C
Notes: 2, 3 (picnic), 5, 7, 8, 9, 10, 11, 12

MACKINAC ISLAND

Haan's 1830 Inn

Huron Street, P. O. Box 123, 49757
Winter: 3418 Oakwood Dr., Island Lake, IL 60042
(906) 847-6244; winter (708) 526-2662

The earliest Greek Revival home in the Northwest Territory, this inn is on the Michigan Historic Registry and is completely restored. It is in a quiet neighborhood three blocks around Haldiman Bay from bustling 1800s downtown and Old Fort Mackinac. It is also adjacent to historic St. Anne's Church and gardens. Guest rooms are furnished with antiques. Enjoy the island's 19th-century ambience of horsedrawn buggies and wagons.

Hosts: Nicholas and Nancy Haan; Vernon and Joy Haan
Rooms: 7 (5PB; 2SB) $80-120
Deluxe Continental Breakfast
Credit Cards: None
Closed late October to mid-May
Notes: 2, 7, 8, 9, 10. 12

MENDON

Mendon Country Inn

440 W. Main, 49072
(616) 496-8132; (FAX) (616) 496-8403

Overlooking the St. Joseph River, this

romantic country inn has antique guest rooms with private baths. Free canoeing, bicycles built for two, fifteen acres of woods and water, restaurants, and Amish tour guide. Featured in *Country Living* and *Country Home* magazines. Nine jacuzzi suites with fireplaces.

Hosts: Dick and Dolly Buerckle
Rooms: 18 (PB) $50-150
Expanded Continental Breakfast
Credit Cards: A, B, C, D
Notes: 2, 5, 7, 8, 9, 10, 11, 12

ONEKAMA

Lake Breeze House

5089 Main Street, 49675-0301
(616) 889-4969

Our two-story frame house on Portage Lake is yours with a shared bath, living room, and breakfast room. Each room has its own special charm with family antiques. Come relax and enjoy our back porch and the sounds of the babbling creek. By reservation only. Boating and charter service available.

Hosts: Bill and Donna Erickson
Rooms: 3 (1P1/2B; 2SB) $55
Full Breakfast
Credit Cards: None
Notes: 2, 5, 8, 9, 10, 11

OWOSSO

R & R Ranch

308 East Hibbard Road, 48867
(517) 723-3232 day; (517) 723-2553 evening

A newly remodeled farmhouse from the early 1900s, the ranch sits on 130 acres overlooking the Maple River valley. A large concrete circle drive with whiteboard fences leads to stables of horses and cattle. The area's wildlife includes deer, fox, rabbits, pheasant, quail, and songbirds. Observe and explore from the farm lane, river walk, or outside deck. Countrylike accents adorn the interior of the farmhouse, and guests are welcome to use the family parlor, garden, game room, and fireplace. Newly installed central air-conditioning.

Hosts: Carl and Jeanne Rossman
Rooms: 3 (SB) $45
Continental Breakfast
Credit Cards: None
Notes: 2, 5, 6, 7, 10

PENTWATER

Historic Nickerson Inn

P.O. Box 986, 262 Lowell St., 49449
(616) 869-8241; (616) 869-6151 (FAX)

The Historic Nickerson Inn has been serving guests with "special hospitality" since 1914. Our inn was totally renovated in 1991. All our rooms have private baths, with air-conditioning. We have two jacuzzi suites with fireplaces and balconies overlooking Lake Michigan. Two short blocks to Lake Michigan beach, and three blocks to shopping district. New ownership. Open all year. Casual fine dining in our 80-seat restaurant. Excellent for retreats, workshops, year-round recreation.

Hosts: Gretchen and Harry Shiparski
Rooms: 10 rooms, 2 suites - 12 total (PB) $75-95 (rooms), $150-175 (suites)
Full Breakfast
Credit Cards: A, B,
Notes: 2, 4, 5, 7 (over 12), 8, 9, 10, 11 (cross country), 12

NOTES: Credit cards accepted: A Master Card; B Visa; C American Express; D Discover Card; E Diners Club; F Other; 2 Personal checks accepted; 3 Lunch available; 4 Dinner available; 5 Open all

PLAINWELL

The 1882 John Crispe House

404 East Bridge Street, 49080-1802
(616)685-1293

Enjoy museum-quality Victorian elegance on the Kalamazoo River. Situated between Grand Rapids and Kalamazoo just off US 131 on Michigan 89, the John Crispe House is close to some of western Michigan's finest gourmet dining, golf, skiing, and antique shops. Air conditioned. No smoking or alcohol. Gift certificates are available.

Hosts: Ormand and Nancy Lefever
Rooms: 5 (3PB; 2SB) $55-95
Full Breakfast
Credit Cards: A, B
Notes: 2, 5, 7, 8, 10, 11

SAUGATUCK

The Maplewood Hotel

428 Butler St., 49453
(616) 857-1771; (616) 857-1773 (FAX)

The Maplewood Hotel architecture is unmistakably Greek Revival. Some rooms have fireplaces and double jacuzzis. Other areas include a library, dining room, lounge, sun room, screened porch, and lap pool. An elegant brunch is served on Sundays. Situated in downtown Saugatuck, within walking distance to all shops and restaurants.

Hosts: Catherine Simon and Sam Burnell
Rooms: 15 (PB) $65-155
Full Breakfast
Credit Cards: A, B, C
Notes: 2, 3, 5, 7, 8, 9, 10, 11, 12

"The Porches" Bed and Breakfast

2297 Lakeshore Drive, Fennville 49408
(616) 543-4162

Built in 1897, "The Porches" offers five guest rooms each with private bath. Located three miles south of Saugatuck, we have a private beach and hiking trails. The large common room has a TV. We overlook Lake Michigan with beautiful sunsets from the front porch.

Hosts: Bos and Ellen Johnson
Rooms: 5 (PB) $69-79
Continental Plus Breakfast—Full on Sundays
Credit Cards: A, B
Open May 1 to November 1.
Notes: 2, 7 (Sunday-Thursday), 8, 9, 10

Twin Gables Country Inn

P.O. Box 881, 900 Lake Street, 49453
(616) 857-4346

Overlooking Kalamazoo Lake, The State Historic Inn, central air-conditioned throughout, features 14 charming guest rooms with private baths, furnished in antiques and country. Wintertime cross-country skiers relax in indoor hot tub and cozy up to a warm crackling fireplace, whilst summer guests may take a refreshing dip in the outdoor pool and enjoy glorious sunsets on the front veranda overlooking the lake. Three separate two- and one-bedroom cottages are also available. Open all year.

Hosts: Denise and Michael Simcik
Rooms: 14 (PB) $68-98
Expanded Continental Breakfast
Credit Cards: A, B, C, D
Notes: 2, 5, 7 (prior arrangements), 8, 9, 10, 11, 12

year; 6 Pets welcome; 7 Children welcome; 8 Tennis nearby; 9 Swimming nearby; 10 Golf nearby; 11 Skiing nearby; 12 May be booked through travel agent

SHELBY

The Shepherd's Place Bed and Breakast

2200 32nd Avenue, 49455
(616) 861-4298

Enjoy a peaceful retreat in a country atmosphere yet close to Lake Michigan beaches, dunes, fishing, golfing, and horseback riding. Choose between our comfortable and cozy accommodations with queen-size bed or twin beds—both with private baths. Full breakfast is served in our new dining room or porch overlooking bird haven. No smoking allowed.

Hosts: Hans and Diane Oehring
Rooms: 2 (PB) $55-60
Full Breakfast
Open May 15 until October
Credit Cards: None
Notes: 2, 9, 10

WEST BRANCH

The Rose Brick Inn

124 East Houghton Avenue, 48661
(517) 345-3702

A 1906 Queen Anne-style home with a graceful veranda, white picket fence, and cranberry canopy, the Rose Brick Inn is tucked in the center two floors of the Frank Sebastian Smith House listed in Michigan's Register of Historic Sites. It is located on downtown Main Street in Victorian West Branch. Golfing, hiking, biking, cross-country skiing, snowmobiling, hunting, shopping, and special holiday events await you year-round. Jacuzzi and air conditioning.

Host: Leon Swartz
Rooms: 4 (PB) $48-58
Continental Breakfast
Credit Cards: A, B
Notes: 2, 5, 7, 8, 9, 10, 11

The Parish House Inn

YPSILANTI

The Parish House Inn

103 S. Huron St., 48197
(313) 480-4800; (313) 480-7472 (FAX)

AAA approved. Conveniently located in the Ann Arbor/Ypsilanti area. Easy access to the I-94 expressway and 20 minutes from Detroit-Metro Airport. This 100-year-old, restored, Victorian house once belonged to the first Congregational Church, and now offers comfortable lodging for personal and business travelers. Touch tone phones, clocks, and TVs in every room. FAX available. Enjoy patio and two parlors. Walk to dinner.

Hostess: Mrs. Charles Mason
Rooms: 9 (PB) $70-120
Full Breakfast
Credit Cards: A, B, C
Notes: 2, 5, 8, 9, 10, 11, 12

NOTES: Credit cards accepted: A Master Card; B Visa; C American Express; D Discover Card; E Diners Club; F Other; 2 Personal checks accepted; 3 Lunch available; 4 Dinner available; 5 Open all

Minnesota

ALBERT LEA

Victorian Rose Inn
609 W. Fountain, 56007
(507) 373-7602; (800) 252-6558

Queen Anne Victorian home (1898) in
virtually original condition, with fine woodwork, stained glass, gingerbread, and antique light fixtures. Antique furnishings,
down comforters. Spacious rooms, one
with fireplace. Air-conditioned. Full breakfast. Business/extended-stay rates; gift
certificates. Children by arrangement; no
pets; no smoking.

Hosts: Darrel and Linda Roemmich
Rooms: 4 (2PB; 2SB) $50-65
Full Breakfast
Credit Cards: A, B
Notes: 2, 5, 7, 8, 10, 12

Elm Street Inn

CHATFIELD

Lunds' Guest Houses
218 Southeast Winona Street, 55923
(507) 867-4003

These charming 1920s homes are decorated in the 1920s and 1930s style and
located only 20 minutes from Rochester,
at the gateway to beautiful Bluff country.
Personalized service includes kitchens, living and dining rooms, two screened
porches, TV, piano, and organ.

Hosts: Shelby and Marion Lund
Rooms: 8 (6PB; 2S1.5B) $65
Continental Breakfast
Credit Cards: None
Notes: 2, 6 (restricted), 7 (restricted), 8, 9, 10, 11

CROOKSTON

Elm Street Inn
422 Elm Street 56716
(218) 281-2343; (800) 568-4476; (218) 281-1756
(FAX)

Georgian Revival (1910) home with antiques, hardwood floors, stained and beveled glass. Wicker-filled sun porch. Old-
fashioned beds, quilts, terry robes, fresh
flowers. Memorable candlelight full breakfast; intimate dinners available. Bicycles.

year; 6 Pets welcome; 7 Children welcome; 8 Tennis nearby; 9 Swimming nearby; 10 Golf nearby;
11 Skiing nearby; 12 May be booked through travel agent

Limo to casino; community pool next door. Murder mystery and quilting weekends. Special anniversary and honeymoon packages. Children welcome, no pets, no smoking.

Hosts: John and Sheryl Winters
Rooms: 4 (2PB; 2SB) $55-65
Full Breakfast
Credit Cards: A, B, C
Notes: 2, 3, 4, 5, 7, 8, 9, 10, 12

DULUTH

The Mansion
3600 London Rd., 55804
(218) 724-0739

This magnificent home was built in 1928. The seven-acre estate is nestled on 525 feet of Lake Superior beach with manicured lawns, woods, and gardens. Guests are encouraged to make themselves at home on the grounds and inside the mansion. The common rooms include the library, living room, three-season porch, gallery, dining room, and trophy room. Come and let us share our home with you!

Hosts: Sue, Warren, and Andrea Monson
Rooms: 11 (7PB; 4SB) $95-195
Full Breakfast
Credit Cards: A, B
Notes: 2, 5, 10, 11, 12

FERGUS FALLS

Bakketopp Hus
Rural Route 2, Box 187 A, Long Lake, 56537
(218) 739-2915

Quiet, spacious lake home with vaulted ceilings, fireplace, private spa, flower garden patio and lakeside decks. Antique furnishings from family homestead, four-poster, draped, French canopy bed, private baths. Here you can listen as loons call to each other across the lake in the still of dusk, witness the fall foliage splendor, relax by a crackling fire, or sink into the warmth of the hot tub after a day of hiking or skiing. Near antique shops, Maplewood State Park. Ten minutes off I-94. Gift certificates available. Reservation with deposit.

Hosts: Dennis and Judy Nims
Rooms: 3 (PB) $65-95
Full Breakfast
Credit Cards: A, B, D
Notes: 2, 5, 7, 8, 9, 10, 11

HOUSTON

Addie's Attic Bed and Breakfast
P.O. Box 677, 117 S. Jackson St., 55943
(507) 896-3010

Beautiful turn-of-the-century home, circa 1903; cozy front parlor with curved glass window. Games, TV, player piano available. Guest rooms decorated and furnished with "attic finds." Hearty country breakfast served in dining room. Near hiking, biking, and cross-country skiing trails, canoeing, and antique shops. Weekday rates. No credit cards.

Hosts: Fred and Marilyn Huhn
Rooms: 4 (SB) $45-50
Full Breakfast
Credit Cards: None
Notes: 2, 5, 8, 10, 11

NOTES: Credit cards accepted: A Master Card; B Visa; C American Express; D Discover Card; E Diners Club; F Other; 2 Personal checks accepted; 3 Lunch available; 4 Dinner available; 5 Open all

LANESBORO

Historic Scanlan House Bed and Breakfast

708 Parkway Avenue South, 55949
(507)467-2158; (800)944-2158

Visit the Victorian elegance and charm of a wealthy banker's mansion. This ginger-bread-style home was built in 1889 by Michael Scanlan (known as the founder of Lanesboro) and is Lanesboro's largest and oldest operating bed and breakfast. We have fireplaces, whirlpool tubs for two, unique gifts, and, of course, our famous five-course breakfast. The interior is adorned throughout with elegant wood-work, stained glass, and the ornate built-in furnishings typical of a fine and exquisite turn-of-the-century residence. Seen in *Midwest Living Magazine* and *AAA Home and Away*.

Hosts: Kristen, Mary and Gene Mensing
Rooms: 5 (PB) $55-130
Full Breakfast
Credit Cards: A, B, C, D
Notes: 2, 5, 8, 9, 10, 11, 12

LUTSEN

Lindgren's Bed and Breakfast

Country Road 35, P.O. Box 56, 55612-0056
(218)663-7450

1920s log home in Superior National Forest on walkable shoreline of Lake Superior. Knotty cedar interior decorated with wildlife trophies. Massive stone fireplaces, finnish sauna, whirlpool, baby grand piano, and color TV/VCRs. In center of area known for skiing, golf, stream and lake fishing, skyride, mountain biking, snowmobiling, horseback riding, alpine slide, fall colors, superior hiking trails, and mear boundary waters canoe are entry point. Spacious manicured grounds. One-half mile off Highway 61 on the Lake Superior Circle Tour.

Hostess: Shirley Lindren
Rooms: 4 (PB) $80-120
Full Hearty Breakfast
Credit Cards: A, B
Notes: 2, 5, 7 (over 12), 8, 9, 10, 11, 12

The Northrop-Oftedahl House

OWATONNA

The Northrop-Oftedahl House

358 East Main Street, 55060
(507)451-4040

This 1898 Victorian with stained glass is three blocks from downtown. It has pleasant porches, grand piano, six-foot footed bathtub, souvenirs (antiques and collectibles from the estate). Northrop family-owned and operated, it is one of 12 historical homes in the area, rich in local history with an extensive reading library, backgammon, croquet, badminton, bocce, and

---

year; 6 Pets welcome; 7 Children welcome; 8 Tennis nearby; 9 Swimming nearby; 10 Golf nearby; 11 Skiing nearby; 12 May be booked through travel agent

more. Near hiking, biking trails, golf, tennis, parks, snowmobiling, and 35 miles to Mayo Clinic. Special group rates for retreats.

Hosts: Jean and Darrell Stewart
Rooms: 5 (SB) $39-56
Continental Breakfast; Full breakfast on request
Credit Cards: None
Notes: 2, 3 (by arrangement), 4 (by arrangement), 5, 6 (by arrangement), 7, 8, 9, 10, 11

ST. CHARLES

Thoreson's Carriage House Bed and Breakfast

606 Wabasha Avenue, 55972
(507) 932-3479

Located at the edge of beautiful Whitewater State Park with its swimming, trails, and demonstrations by the park naturalist, we are also in Amish territory and minutes from the world-famous Mayo Clinic. Piano and organ are available for added enjoyment. Please write for free brochure.

Hostess: Moneta Thoreson
Rooms: 2 (SB) $35-40
Full Breakfast
Credit Cards: None
Notes: 2, 5, 7, 8, 9, 10

SANBORN

Sod House on the Prairie

Rt. 2, Box 75, 56083
(507) 723-5138

A unique opportunity to step back in time, retreat from life's hustle and bustle, and be a sod house pioneer for the night. The 36' by 21' sod house has two-feet-thick sod walls, and was built in the tradition of the prairie homesteaders. It is surrounded by restored prairie grasses, and is furnished authentically with furnishings of the era. Just like in the 1880s, oil lamps will be your lighting. . .an old-fashioned pitcher and bowl on a washstand will be your sink. There is no running water. The outhouse is also built of sod and sits nearby. The sod house is heated by wood-burning stoves and wool blankets, quilts, and buffalo robes are provided. There is no air-conditioning for summer, but the thick walls keep it cool inside. From May to Labor Day the exhibit is open for touring. A gift shop features handmade items by Native Americans, as well as pioneer crafts by local crafters.

Hosts: McCone Family
Rooms: 1 unit with two double beds (PB)
Reservations only.
Full Breakfast
Credit Cards: None
Notes: 2, 5, 6 (with approval), 7, 9, 10

Sod House on the Prairie

NOTES: Credit cards accepted: A Master Card; B Visa; C American Express; D Discover Card; E Diners Club; F Other; 2 Personal checks accepted; 3 Lunch available; 4 Dinner available; 5 Open all

SPRING LAKE

Anchor Inn
Highway 4, 56680
(218) 798-2718

Lodge in the Chippewa National Forest on the Bigfork Canoe Trail; built in the early 1920s and originally used by duck hunters. Decorated with antique furniture and memorabilia. Shared bath. Delicious breakfast. State parks, historic sites, and restaurants nearby. Boats and motors available. Reservations. Open May through October. No smoking!

Hosts: Charles and Virginia Kitterman
Rooms: 4 (SB) $30-55
Full Breakfast
Credit Cards: A, B
Notes: 2, 7, 8, 9, 10

STILLWATER

James A. Mulvey Residence Inn
622 W. Churchill St., 55082
(612) 430-8008

This is an enchanting place. Built in 1878 by lumberman, James A. Mulvey, the Italianate residence and stone carriage house grace the most visited historic rivertown in the upper Midwest. Exclusively for you are the grand parlor, formal dining room, Victorian sun porch, and five fabulously decorated guest rooms filled with art and antiques. Four-course breakfast, double-whirlpools, fireplaces, mountain bikes, and air-conditioning. Welcome refreshments. Grace-filled service from innkeepers who care.

Hosts: Rev. and Mrs. Truett Lawson
Rooms: 5 (PB) $80-139
Full 4-Course Breakfast
Credit Cards: A, B
Notes: 2, 5, 8, 9, 10, 11

TYLER

Babette's Inn
308 S. Tyler Street, 56178
(800) 466-7067

Privacy, luxury and small town peace await you at Babette's Inn. Located in the Danish-American village of Tyler, Minnesota, the inn features European cuisine, antiques, gift shop, free use of vintage bicycles, books and foreign films. Fireplaces, porches, and bay windows grace this historic brick home. Close to Pipestone National Monument, Laura Ingalls Wilder pageant and America's second largest wind turbine project.

Hosts: Jim and Alicia Johnson
Rooms: 3 (PB) $45-65
Full Breakfast
Credit Cards: A, B
Notes: 2, 5, 7, 8, 9, 10, 11, 12

Anchor Inn

Mississippi

FRENCH CAMP

French Camp Bed and Breakfast Inn

Box 120, One Blue Lane, 39745
(601) 547-6835; (601) 547-6790 (FAX)

The inn is located on the historic Natchez Trace National Parkway halfway between Jackson and Tupelo, Mississippi. It has been constructed from two restored, authentic hand-hewn log cabins, each more than 100 years old. Indulge in Southern cooking at its finest: sorghum-soaked "scratch" muffins, creamy grits, skillet-fried apples, fresh cheese, scrambled eggs, crisp slab bacon, and lean sausage, with two kinds of homemade bread and three homemade jellies. Life doesn't get any better!

Hosts: Ed and Sallie Williford
Rooms: 4 (PB) $60
Full Breakfast
Credit Cards: B
Notes: 2, 3, 4, 5, 6, 7, 8, 9, 12

French Camp

LONG BEACH

Red Creek Colonial Inn

7416 Red Creek Rd., 39560
(601) 452-3080 (voice or FAX)

Raised French cottage built in 1899 by a retired Italian sea captain to entice his young bride away from her parent's home in New Orleans. Red Creek Colonial Inn is situated on eleven acres with ancient live oaks and fragent magnolias, and delights itself in peaceful comforts. With a 64-foot porch, including porch swings, our inn is furnished in antiques for our guests' enjoyment. Ministerial discount of 10%.

Hosts: Sharon and Denis Crowder
Rooms: 5 (3PB; 2SB) $49-69
Continental Plus Breakfast
Credit Cards: None
Notes: 2, 3 (advance request only), 4 (advance request only), 5, 7, 9, 10, 12 (10%)

MERIDIAN

Lincoln, Ltd. Bed and Breakfast Mississippi Reservation Service

P.O. Box 3479, 2303 23rd Avenue, 39303
(601) 482-5483; (800) 633-MISS; (601) 693-7447 (FAX)

Service offers B&B accommodations in

NOTES: Credit cards accepted: A Master Card; B Visa; C American Express; D Discover Card; E Diners Club; F Other; 2 Personal checks accepted; 3 Lunch available; 4 Dinner available; 5 Open all

historic homes and inns in the whole state of **Mississippi**, also southeast **Louisiana**, **Western Tennessee**, and **Alabama**. One phone call convenience for your B&B reservations and trip planning through Mississippi. Experience history; we offer antebellum mansions, historic log houses, and contemporary homes. Also, there is a B&B suite on the premises. Call for details and brochure. Barbara Lincoln Hall, coordinator.

NATCHEZ

Dunleith

84 Homochitto, 39120
(601) 446-8500; (800) 433-2445; (601) 446-6094 (FAX)

Dunleith is listed on the National Register of Historic Places and is a national landmark. It is located on 40 acres near downtown Natchez. Eleven rooms, three in main house and eight in courtyard wing. Full Southern breakfast served in poultry house. All rooms have private baths and working fireplaces. No children. Reservations required.

Hostess: Nancy Gibbs
Rooms: 11 (PB) $85-130
Full Breakfast
Credit Cards: A, B, C, D
Notes: None

NATCHEZ TRACE

Natchez Trace Bed and Breakfast Reservation Service

P.O. Box 193, Hampshire, TN, 38461
(800) 377-2777

This reservation service is unusual in that all the homes listed are close to the Natchez Trace, the delightful National Parkway running from Nashville, Tennessee, to Natchez, Mississippi. Kay can help you plan your trip along the Trace, with homestays in interesting and historic homes along the way. Locations of homes include Nashville, Franklin, Hampshire, **Tennessee**; Florence, **Alabama**; and Corinth, French Camp, Kosciusko, Vicksburg, Lorman, and Natchez, **Mississippi**. Rates from $60-125.

PORT GIBSON

Oak Square Plantation

1207 Church Street, 39150
(601) 437-4350; (800) 729-0240; (601) 437-5768 (FAX)

This restored antebellum mansion of the Old South is in the town General U. S. Grant said was "too beautiful to burn." On the National Register of Historic Places, it has family heirloom antiques and canopied beds and is air conditioned. Your hosts' families have been in Mississippi for 200 years. Christ is the Lord of this house. "But as for me and my house, we will serve the Lord," Joshua 24:15. On U.S. Highway 61, adjacent to the Natchez

---

year; 6 Pets welcome; 7 Children welcome; 8 Tennis nearby; 9 Swimming nearby; 10 Golf nearby; 11 Skiing nearby; 12 May be booked through travel agent

Trace Parkway. Four-diamond rated by AAA.

Hosts: Mr. and Mrs. William Lum
Rooms: 12 (PB) $75-95; special family rates
Full Breakfast
Credit Cards: A, B, C, D
Notes: 2, 5, 7

TUPELO

The Mockingbird Inn Bed and Breakfast

305 N. Gloster, 38801
(601) 841-0286; (601) 840-4158 (FAX)

Discover the romance of a different place and time in an echanting getaway within the convenient confines of the city. Each guest room represents the decor from a different area of the world and a different era in time. Delicious, hearty breakfast and evening refreshment included and two upscale restaurants in lovely old homes across the street. A health club is also nearby; $5 per visit.

Hosts: Jim and Sandy Gilmer
Rooms: 7 (PB) $65-95
Full Breakfast
Credit Cards: A, B, C, D
Notes: 2, 5, 6, 7 (over 13), 10, 12

VICKSBURG

Cedar Grove Mansion Inn

2200 Oak Street, 39180
(800) 862-1300; (601) 634-6126 (FAX)

Vicksburg's largest antebellum mansion on five acres of gardens with swimming pool, tennis court, croquet lawn, exercise room, and a Mississippi River-view from the roof garden. Civil War cannonball still lodged in the parlor wall. Experience "Gone With the Wind" Southern ambiance. Piano bar and gourmet candlelight dining after 6PM. AAA four-diamond.

Hosts: Ted Mackey and Estelle Mackey
Rooms: 30 (PB) $95-160
Full Breakfast
Credit Cards: A, B, C, D, E
Notes: 4, 5, 8, 9, 10, 12

WEST

The Alexander House

210 Green St., PO Box 187
(601) 967-2266

Step inside the front door of the Alexander House Bed and Breakfast and go back in time to a more leisurely and gracious way of life. Victorian decor at its prettiest and country hospitality at its best is guaranteed to please your senses. Captain Alexander, Dr. Joe, Ulrich, Annie, and Miss Bealle are all rooms waiting to cast their spell over those who visit. Day trips to historic or recreational areas may be charted or chartered.

Hosts: Ruth Ray and Woody Dinstel
Rooms: 5 (3PB; 2SB) $65
Full Breakfast
Credit Cards: None
Notes: 2, 4, 5, 12

The Alexander House

Missouri

BOONVILLE

Morgan Street Repose

611 East Morgan, 65233
(816) 882-7195

1869 National Historic Registered Home delightfully restored for a romantic, gracious, hospitable stay. Filled with heirlooms, antiques, books, games, and curiousities to delight you. Our extravagant breakfasts are formally served in one of three dining rooms or Secret Garden. Situated one block to antique/specialty shops, restaurants, and Katy biking/hiking trail. Rental bikes available. Afternoon tea served.

Hostess: Doris Shenk
Rooms: 3 (PB) $58-75
Full Gourmet Breakfast
Credit Cards: None
Notes: 2, 5, 7 (older), 12

BRANSON

Cameron's Crag

P. O. Box 526, Point Lookout, 65726
(417) 335-8134; (800) 933-8529; (417) 335-8134
(FAX)

Located high on a bluff overlooking Lake Taneycomo and the valley, three miles south of Branson, enjoy a spectacular view from a new spacious, detached, private suite with king bed, whirlpool tub, kitchen, living and bedroom area. Two room suites with indoor hot tub, king bed, and private bath. A third room has a private entrance, queen bed, view of the lake, private hot tub on deck.

Hosts: Glen and Kay Cameron
Rooms: 4 (PB) $75-95
Full Breakfast
Credit Cards: A, B, C
Notes: 2, 4, 5, 12

Ozark Mountain Country Bed and Breakfast Service

Box 295, 65615
(417) 334-4720; (800) 695-1546; (417) 335-8134
(FAX)

Ozark Mountain Country has been arranging accommodations for guests in **southwest Missouri** and **northwest Arkansas** since 1982. Our services are free. In the current list of over 100 homes and small inns, some locations offer private entrances and fantastic views, guest sitting areas, swimming pools, jacuzzis, or fireplaces. Most locations are available all year. Personal checks accepted. Some homes welcome children; a few welcome pets (even horses). Write for complimen-

---

year; 6 Pets welcome; 7 Children welcome; 8 Tennis nearby; 9 Swimming nearby; 10 Golf nearby; 11 Skiing nearby; 12 May be booked through travel agent

tary host listing and discount coupon. Coordinator: Kay Cameron. $35-145.

CARTHAGE

Brewer's Maple Lane Farm Bed and Breakfast

Rural Route 1, Box 203, 64836
(417) 358-6312

Listed on the National Register of Historic Places, this Victorian home has 20 rooms furnished mostly with family heirlooms; four guest rooms. Our 240-acre farm is ideal for family vacations and campers. We have a playground, picnic area, hunting, and fishing in our 22-acre lake. Nearby are artist Lowell Davis' farm and Sam Butcher's Precious Moments Chapel.

Hosts: Arch and Renee Brewer
Rooms: 4 (SB) $50
Expanded Continental Breakfast
Credit Cards: None
Notes: 2, 5, 7, 8, 10, 12

CONCORDIA

Fannie Lee Bed and Breakfast

Rural Route 1, Box 203, 64836
(816) 463-7395

An elegant restored three-story Victorian house furnished with antiques and European paintings. Beautiful grounds with a large rose garden enclosed by a Victorian iron fence. The grounds consist of one three-story hosue, a two-story carriage house and another two-story house, all completely restored. Four luxury rooms, one suite, and a reading room. Cocktail and hors d'oeuvres on arrival.

Host: John W. Campbell
Rooms: 4 (2PB; 2SB) $50
Full Breakfast
Credit Cards: A, B, C
Notes: 2, 5, 6, 8, 9, 10, 12

DEFIANCE

The Parsons House

211 Lee Street, P.O. Box 38, 63341
(314) 798-2222; (314) 798-2220 (FAX)

This restored 1842 Federal-style home overlooks the wide Missouri River valley. Listed on the Historic Registry, it features fireplaces, a walnut staircase, and many antiques. For your enjoyment, an organ, piano, books, and games of bygone times. Closeby are the Katy Bicycle Trail, the Daniel Boone Home, and Missouri wineries, yet downtown St. Louis is only 35 miles away. Breakfast in the parlor, garden, or on one of the porches. Resident dog, cat, computer consultant, and artist.

Hosts: Al and Carol Keyes
Rooms: 2 (SB) $50-60
Full Breakfast
Credit Cards: A, B
Notes: 2, 5 (except Christmas), 7 (limited), 10

The Parsons House

Fifth Street Mansion

HANNIBAL

Fifth Street Mansion Bed and Breakfast Inn

213 South Fifth Street, 63401
(314) 221-0445; for reservations only call
(800) 874-5661

Built in 1858 in Italianate style by friends of Mark Twain, antique furnishings complement the stained glass, ceramic fireplaces, and original gaslight fixtures of the house. Two parlors, dining room, and library with hand-grained walnut paneling, plus wraparound porches provide space for conversation, reading, TV, games. Walk to Mark Twain historic district, shops, restaurants, riverfront. The mansion blends Victorian charm with plenty of old-fashioned hospitality. The whole house is available for reunions and weddings.

Hosts: Mike and Donalene Andreotti
Rooms: 7 (PB) $65-90
Full Breakfast
Credit Cards: A, B, C, D
Notes: 2, 5, 7, 8, 9, 10, 12

HERMANN

Die Gillig Heimat

HCR 62, Box 30, 65041
(314) 943-6942

Capture the beauty of country living on this farm located on beautiful rolling hills. The original Gillig home was built as a log cabin in 1842 and has been enlarged several times. Awake in the morning to beautiful views in every direction, and enjoy a hearty breakfast in the large, country kitchen. Stroll the pastures and hills of the working cattle farm while watching nature at its best. Historic Hermann is nearby.

Hosts: Ann and Armin Gillig
Rooms: 2 (PB) $55-65
Full Breakfast
Credit Cards: None
Notes: 2, 5, 7 (by arrangement)

The Mary Elizabeth House

220 W. Sixth Street, 65041
(314) 486-3281

Experience the charm of Hermann while staying at The Mary Elizabeth House, a gracious 1895 Victorian "gingerbread" house. Enjoy the privacy of your own "home" knowing that your hosts, next door, are ready to serve you. The spacious accommodations include a large queen, canopy, bedroom; full bath; sitting, living (with sofa bed), and dining rooms; porches; and patio. Theorum paintings and portraits complement the antique decor. A sumptuous breakfast, including homemade yeast breads, awaits

year; 6 Pets welcome; 7 Children welcome; 8 Tennis nearby; 9 Swimming nearby; 10 Golf nearby;
11 Skiing nearby; 12 May be booked through travel agent

you in the morning.

Hosts: John and Linda Maloney
Rooms: 1 (PB) $90
Full Breakfast
Credit Cards: None
Notes: 2, 4 (weekends), 5, 8, 9, 10, 12

Trisha's Bed and Breakfast

JACKSON

Trisha's B&B
203 Bellevue, 63755
(314) 243-7437; (800) 651-0408

Innkeepers, Gus and Trisha welcome guests to their 1905 Victorian home in Jackson, Cape Girardeau's county seat. The Wischmann home is located only 3 blocks from an excursion steam train. Smiles abound as vintage lingerie collections are discovered in the lovely guest rooms. Four bedrooms are available, three with private baths, with the fourth having a private half bath and shared shower. Breakfast is a gourmet delight as visitors feast on home-baked goodies, homegrown and hand-picked fresh fruit, and delicious entrees.

Hosts: Gus and Trisha Wischmann
Rooms: 4 (3PB; 1SB) $65-75
Full Breakfast
Credit Cards: A, B, C
Notes: 2, 4, 5, 7 , 8, 9, 10, 12

KANSAS CITY

Bed and Breakfast Kansas City
P. O. Box 14781, Lenexa, KS 66285
(913) 888-3636

This reservation service can arrange your accommodations in **Kansas City or the St. Louis, Missouri**, area. From an 1857 plantation mansion on the river to a geodesic dome in the woods with hot tub, there is a price and style for everyone. Victorian, turn-of-the-century, English Tudor, and contemporary are available. Double, queen, or king beds, most with private baths. The service represents 35 inns and homes. $40-125.

Southmoreland on The Plaza
116 E. 46th St., 64112
(816) 531-7979; (816) 531-2407 (FAX)

Classic New England Colonial mansion located between renowned Country Club Plaza (shopping/entertaining district) and Nelson-Atkins and Kemper Museums of Art. Elegant B&B ambience with small hotel amenities. Rooms with private decks, fireplaces, or jacuzzi baths. Special services for business travelers. Sport/dining privileges at nearby Historic Private Club. Only 1993 and 1994 Mobil Travel Guide four-star inn award in twenty states.

NOTES: Credit cards accepted: A Master Card; B Visa; C American Express; D Discover Card; E Diners Club; F Other; 2 Personal checks accepted; 3 Lunch available; 4 Dinner available; 5 Open all

Only B&B to receive Midwest Travel Writers' "Gem of the Midwest" Award.

Hostesses: Penni Johnson, Susan Moehl
Rooms: 12 (PB) $100-145
Full Breakfast
Credit Cards: A, B, C
Notes: 2, 5, 8, 9, 10, 12

MINERAL POINT

Green Acres Farm Family Bed and Breakfast

Rt. 1, Box 575, 63660
(314) 749-3435

A small active family farm on Big River, 65 miles south of St. Louis. We have a Noah's Ark where part of our 100+ farm pets live. There is everything from Abraham the donkey to Zachariah the goose. Accommodations in four second-story rooms with private baths and balconies. Rooms sleep 2 to 8 people. Homemade goodies await you when you arrive, a healthy evening snack, and a full, country breakfast included.

Hostess: Virginia Dickinson
Rooms: 3 + 1 family suite (PB) $39-59
Full Breakfast
Credit Cards: A, B
Notes: 5, 7

NEVADA

Red Horse Inn

217 S. Main, 64772
(800) 245-3685

Experience the friendly hospitality of the Red Horse Inn, a turn-of-the-century home furnished in antiques. Guests can walk to the town square or relax on the front porch, deck, or shaded backyard. We are located in historic Nevada, MO, between Kansas City and Joplin. Come stay with us on your visit to Cottey College, or on your way to Branson. Come as a guest and leave as a friend.

Hosts: Victor and Sharon McCullough
Rooms: 5 (4PB; 4SB) $40-45
Full Breakfast
Credit Cards: A, B
Notes: 2, 5, 7, 8, 9, 10

PARKVILLE (KANSAS CITY)

Down to Earth Lifestyles Bed and Breakfast

12500 NW Crooked Rd., 64152
(816) 891-1018

Unique getaway haven offering the best of midwestern country and city living. Indoor heated pool, plus 86 acres with farm animals, fishing ponds, wildlife, walking, and jogging areas. Full special-order breakfast served at place and time of guest's choice.

Hosts: Lola and Bill Coons
Rooms: 4 (PB) $75
Full Breakfast
Credit Cards: None
Notes: 2, 5, 7, 8, 9, 10, 11

year; 6 Pets welcome; 7 Children welcome; 8 Tennis nearby; 9 Swimming nearby; 10 Golf nearby; 11 Skiing nearby; 12 May be booked through travel agent

PLATTE CITY

Basswood Country Inn Resort

15880 Interurban Road, 64079-9185
(816) 858-5556 (voice and FAX)

Come stay where the rich and famous relaxed and played in the 1940s and 1950s! These are the most beautiful, secluded, wooded, lakefront accommodations in the entire Kansas City area. Choose from two-bedroom, full kitchen suites, 1935 cottage, or king suites. Five miles from Kansas City International Airport.

Hosts: Don and Betty Soper
Rooms: 7 (PB) $66-125
Cottage: 1 (PB) $93
Continental Breakfast
Credit Cards: A, B, D
Notes: 2, 5, 7, 9, 10, 11, 12

ST. GENEVIEVE

Inn St. Gemme Beauvais

78 North Main St., 63670
(800) 818-5744

Jacuzzis, hord' oeurves, and private suites filled with antiques only begin your pampering stay in Missouri's oldest, continually operating bed and breakfast. The romantic dining room, complete with working fireplace, is the perfect setting for an intimate breakfast. The Inn has been recently redecorated and is walking distance to many shops and historical sites. Packages available for that special occasion, as well as picnics to take on hiking trails.

Hostess: Janet Joggerst
Rooms: 7 (PB) $69-125
Full Breakfast
Credit Cards: A, B
Notes: 2, 3, 5, 7, 8, 9, 10

ST. JOSEPH

Harding House Bed and Breakfast

219 N 20th St., 64501
(816) 232-7020

Gracious turn-of-the-century home. Elegant oak woodwork and pocket doors. Antiques and beveled leaded glass windows. Historic area near museums, churches, and antique shops. Five unique guest rooms. Eastlake has romantic woodburning fireplace and queen-size bed; Blue Room has antique baby crib. Children welcome. Full breakfast with homemade pastry. Harding House Restaurant, downtown, serves dinner Wednesday thru Saturday from 5-9PM, buffet on Sunday 11:30AM until 2:30PM.

Hosts: Glen and Mary Harding
Rooms: 4 (1PB; 3SB) $45-55
Full Breakfast
Credit Cards: A, B, C, D
Notes: 2, 4 (Wed-Sat), 5, 7, 12

ST. LOUIS

Geandaugh House Bed and Breakfast

3835-37 South Broadway, 63118
(314) 771-5447

Built circa 1790, the limestone "Prairie House" section of the Geandaugh House, located in South St. Louis, is one of the

NOTES: Credit cards accepted: A Master Card; B Visa; C American Express; D Discover Card; E Diners Club; F Other; 2 Personal checks accepted; 3 Lunch available; 4 Dinner available; 5 Open all

oldest structures in the state. A Federal-style brick addition was added in the 1800s. Antiques and collections fill the inn revealing Gea and Wayne's love for history. Irish lace curtains, handmade quilts, and old pharmacy cupboard in the dining room are some of the unique furnishings. As a pastor and retired music teacher, Wayne and Gea are eager to share their home with travelers seeking lodging in a Christian atmosphere. They have two cats and one dog, a Great Pyrenees.

Hosts: Gea and Wayne Popp
Rooms: 4 (PB) $60
Full Breakfast
Credit Cards: A, B, E
Notes: 2, 5 (except Christmas), 12

Lafayette House Bed and Breakfast

2156 Lafayette Avenue, 63104-2543
(314) 772-4429

This 1876 Victorian mansion with modern amenities is in the center of things to do in St. Louis and on a direct bus line to downtown. It is air conditioned and furnished with antiques and traditional furniture. Many collectibles and large, varied library to enjoy. Families welcome. Resident cats and dog.

Hosts: Sarah and Jack Milligan
Rooms: 4 + 1 suite (2PB; 3SB) $50-75
Full Breakfast
Credit Cards: A, B
Notes: 2, 5, 7, 8, 9, 10, 12

SPRINGFIELD

The Mansion at Elfindale Bed and Breakfast

1701 S. Fort, 65807
(417) 831-5400; (417) 831-2965 (FAX)

Welcome to the elegance of the magnificent gray stone structure. Built in the 1800s, The Mansion features ornate fireplaces, stained glass windows, and unique architecturally designed rooms. We invite you to choose from 13 private suites. Each is a color essay designed with maximum comfort in mind, and each luxuriate in all the splendor of the Victorian era. A hearty breakfast is served in our dining room.

Host: Jef Wells
Rooms: 13 (PB) $60-95
Full Breakfast
Credit Cards: A, B, C, D, E
Notes: 2, 5, 10, 12

Lafayette House Bed and Breakfast

---

year; 6 Pets welcome; 7 Children welcome; 8 Tennis nearby; 9 Swimming nearby; 10 Golf nearby; 11 Skiing nearby; 12 May be booked through travel agent

Montana

BOZEMAN

Lindley House

202 Lindley Place, 59715
(406) 587-8403

A unique and elegant Victorian Inn featuring antiques, artwork, and period wall coverings to make your stay warm and comfortable. Private baths and honeymoon suite available. University town has much to offer. Within walking distance to theatres, galleries, fine restaurants, and specialty shopping. In the heart of fly-fishing country, close to Bridger Bowl ski area, and numerous outdoor recreational attractions. Personal attention, good food, and privacy are our specialties. No smoking.

Hostess: Stephanie Volz
Rooms: 4 with 2 suites (PB) $75-250
Full Breakfast
Credit Cards: A, B
Notes: 2, 3, 5, 8, 9, 10, 11

COLUMBIA FALLS

Park View Inn Bed and Breakfast

904 4th Ave. W., P.O. Box 567, 59912
(406) 892-PARK (7275)

Park View Inn is located in a small town

setting with views of Glacier National Park and our own city park across the street, which is complete with swimming pool, basketball court, and children's play area, as well as beautiful trees and picnic areas. We know you'll enjoy our two-story Victorian home with two suites and two luxury rooms or one of our three cabins, especially our honeymoon cottage featuring jacuzzi and canopy bed.

Hosts: Gary and Jayne Hall and Family
Rooms: 7 (3PB; 2SB) $45-95
Both Full and Continental Breakfast available
Credit Cards: A, B
Notes: 2, 5, 6 (prearranged), 7, 8, 9, 10, 11

Lindley House

EMIGRANT (YELLOWSTONE NATIONAL PARK)

Paradise Gateway Bed and Breakfast

P.O. Box 84, 59027
(North entrance to Yellowstone National Park.)
(406) 333-4063; (800) 541-4113

Paradise Gateway B&B, just minutes from Yellowstone National Park, offers quiet, charming, comfortable guest rooms in the shadow of the majestic Rocky Mountains. As day breaks, enjoy a country gourmet breakfast by the banks of the Yellowstone River, a noted blue ribbon trout stream. A "cowboy treat tray" is served in the afternoon. Enjoy summer and winter sports. Only entrance open to Yellowstone year 'round. Call for reservations.

Hosts: Pete and Carol Reed
Rooms: 3 (PB) $85-95
Full Country Gourmet Breakfast
Credit Cards: A, B
Notes: 2, 5, 8, 9, 10, 11, 12

EUREKA

Huckleberry Hannah's Montana Bed & Breakfast

3100 Sophie Lake Road, 59917
(406) 889-3381

Nearly 6,000-square-feet of old-fashioned, country-sweet charm, the answer to vacationing in Montana. Sitting on 50 wooded acres, and bordering a fabulous trout-filled lake with glorious views of the Rockies. This bed and breakfast depicts a quieter time in our history when the true pleasures of life represented a walk in the woods or a moonlight swim. Or maybe just a little early morning relaxation in a porch swing, sipping a fresh cup of coffee, and watching a colorful sunrise. The surrounding area is 91% public lands, perfect for hiking, biking, hunting, fishing, and swimming. It's a cross-country skier's dream in winter, also easy driving distance to downhill skiing in Whitefish. And don't forget those comfortable sunny rooms and all that wonderful home-cooked food. The B&B is owned and operated by the author of one of the Northwest's Best-Selling Cookbooks "Huckleberry Hannah's Country Cooking Sampler." Questions cheerfully answered. Ask about kids and pets and Senior Discounts! Local airport nearby. Free brochure.

Hosts: Jack and Deanna Doying
Rooms: 5 + Lake Cottage (PB) $50-75
Full Breakfast (Continental available upon request)
Credit Cards: A, B, D
Notes: 2, 3, 4, 5, 6 (some), 7, 8, 9, 11, 12

GLENDIVE

The Hostetler House Bed and Breakfast

113 North Douglas Street, 59330
(406) 365-4505; (406) 365-8456 (FAX; call first)

Located two blocks from downtown shopping and restaurants, The Hostetler House is a charming 1912 historic home with two comfortable guest rooms, sitting room, sun porch, deck, gazebo, and hot tub. Full gourmet breakfast is served on Grandma's china. On I-94 and the Yellowstone River, we are close to parks, swimming pool, tennis courts, golf course, antique shops,

---

year; 6 Pets welcome; 7 Children welcome; 8 Tennis nearby; 9 Swimming nearby; 10 Golf nearby; 11 Skiing nearby; 12 May be booked through travel agent

and churches. Craig and Dea invite you to, "Arrive as a guest and leave as a friend."

Hosts: Craig and Dea Hostetler
Rooms: 2 (SB) $45
Full Gourmet Breakfast
Credit Cards: None
Notes: 2, 5, 8, 9, 10, 11 (x-country), 12

The Hostetler House

KALISPELL

Stillwater Inn

206-4th Avenue East, 59901
(406) 755-7080; (800) 398-7024

Relax in this lovely historic home built in 1900, decorated to fit the period, and furnished with turn-of-the-century antiques. Four guest bedrooms, two with private baths. Full gourmet breakfast. Walking distance to churches, shopping, dining, art galleries, antique shops, Woodland Park, and the Conrad Mansion. Short drive to Glacier National Park, Big Mountain skiing, six golf courses, excellent fishing and hunting. Please, no smoking in the house.

Hosts: Pat and Jane Morison
Rooms: 4 (2PB; 2SB) $70-85
Full Breakfast
Credit Cards: A, B
Notes: 2, 5, 7, 8, 9, 10, 11, 12

LAUREL

Riverside Bed and Breakfast

2231 Theil Rd., 59044
(800) 768-1580; (406) 646-8306 (FAX)

Just off I-90, fifteen minutes from Billings, on a main route to skiing and Yellowstone National Park. Fly fish the Yellowstone from our backyard; soak away stress in the hot tub; llinger and llook at the lloveable llamas; take a spin on our bicycle built for two; enjoy a peaceful sleep, a friendly visit, and a fantastic breakfast.

Hosts: Lynn and Nancy Perey
Rooms: 2 (PB) $60
Full Breakfast
Credit Cards: A, B
Notes: 2, 5, 7 (over 10), 10, 11, 12

RED LODGE

Willows Inn

224 S. Platt Ave., PO Box 886, 59068
(406) 446-3913

Nestled beneath the majestic Beartooth Mountains in a quaint historic town, this delightful turn-of-the-century Victorian, complete with picket fence and porch swing, awaits you. A light and airy atmosphere with warm, cheerful decor greets the happy wanderer. Five charming guest rooms, each unique, are in the main inn. Two delightfully nostalgic cottages with kitchen and laundry are also available. Home-baked pastries are a specialty. Videos, books, games, afternoon refresh-

---

NOTES: Credit cards accepted: A Master Card; B Visa; C American Express; D Discover Card; E Diners Club; F Other; 2 Personal checks accepted; 3 Lunch available; 4 Dinner available; 5 Open all

ments, and sun deck.

Hosts: Kerry, Carolyn, and Elven Boggio
Rooms: 5 + 2 cottages (3PB; 2SB) $50-75
Continental Plus Breakfast
Credit Cards: A, B, D
Notes: 2, 5, 7 (restricted), 8, 9, 10, 11, 12

VALIER

Pine Terrace Bed and Breakfast

Rt. 3, Box 909, 59486
(406) 279-3801; (800) 446-6924

Pine Terrace B&B is a country home decorated with antique furnishings. Two upstairs bedrooms are available with a shared bath. These are non-smoking, no alcohol rooms. You may be awakened by pheasants, turkeys, and peacock that live in the park-like backyard. Located nine miles west off I-15 on highway 44 or five miles east of Valier. Call toll free for reservations. Open June to November.

Hosts: Dick and Carole DeBoo
Rooms: 2 (SB) $32.50
Continental Breakfast
Credit Cards: A, B
Notes: None

VIRGINIA CITY

Stonehouse Inn Bed and Breakfast

Box 202, 306 East Idaho, 59755
(406) 843-5504

Located on a quiet street only blocks away from the historic section of Virginia City, this Victorian stone home is listed on the National Register of Historic Places. Brass beds and antiques in every room give the inn a romantic touch. Five bedrooms share two baths. Full breakfasts are served each morning, and smoking is allowed on our porches. Skiing, snowmobiling, golfing, hunting, and fly fishing nearby.

Hosts: John and Linda Hamilton
Rooms: 5 (SB) $50 + tax
Full Breakfast
Credit Cards: A, B
Notes: 2, 4, 5, 7, 8, 10, 12

Nebraska

BERWYN

1909 Heritage House at Berwyn

P.O. Box 196, 101 Curran, 68819
(308) 935-1136

A warm welcome awaits you in this lovely three-story Victorian/country home with air conditioned rooms. Heritage House is located in central Nebraska on Highway 2, which is one of the most scenic highways in America. Enjoy a country breakfast served in an elegant dining room, country kitchen, or sun room.

Hosts: Meriam and Dale Thomas
Rooms: 5 (1PB; 4SB) $40-75
Full Breakfast
Credit Cards: None
Notes: 2, 5, 7, 8, 9, 10, 12

FREMONT

Bed & Breakfast of Fremont

1624 East 25th Street, 68025
(402) 727-9534

The B&B of Fremont is a two-story colonial home, situated on 4-1/2 acres. Guest facilities include four private bedrooms, sitting room, upper balcony, and lower-level Garden Room. Great for small retreats and family reunions! Group rates and senior citizen discounts.

Hosts: Paul and Linda VonBehren
Rooms: 4 (1SB) $40-55
Full Breakfast
Credit Cards: None
Notes: 2, 5, 7, 8, 9, 10, 12

Bed & Breakfast of Fremont

NOTES: Credit cards accepted: A Master Card; B Visa; C American Express; D Discover Card; E Diners Club; F Other; 2 Personal checks accepted; 3 Lunch available; 4 Dinner available; 5 Open all

MURDOCK

Farm House Bed and Breakfast

32617 Church Rd., 68407
(402) 867-2062

Hotel Wilber

Originally built in 1896, The Farm House provides a glimpse back to country life past, complete with expansive 10-foot ceilings, wood floors, an oak spindle staircase, antiques, and even a front porch swing. Room decor and furnishings throughout provide a feeling of comfortable country elegance. Air-conditioned. Half hour from Lincoln and Omaha.

Hosts: Mike and Pat Meierhenry
Rooms: 2 (SB) $35
Full Breakfast
Credit Cards: None
Notes: 2, 5, 6, 7, 8, 10

OMAHA

The Jones'

1617 South 90th Street, 68124
(402) 397-0721

Large, private residence with large deck and gazebo in the back. Fresh cinnamon rolls are served for breakfast. Your hosts' interests include golf, travel, needlework, and meeting other people. Located five minutes from I-80.

Hosts: Theo and Don Jones
Rooms: 3 (1PB: 2SB) $25
Continental Breakfast
Credit Cards: None
Notes: 2, 5, 6, 7, 8, 10

WILBER

Hotel Wilber

W. Second and S. Wilson Streets, P.O. Box 641, 68465
(402) 821-2020

Whether you are in pursuit of business or pleasure, need a room for an intimate social gathering or business meeting, or just desire a romantic, peaceful weekend away, Hotel Wilber is an ideal retreat. Upon entering our lobby, you will begin your step back to the old country. Experience Old World charm in the dining room, bar, garden, or one of our ten antique-filled bedrooms. Just thirty minutes southwest of Lincoln. From I-80 exit 388, head south on Nebraska Hwy 103 to Junction of Hwy 103 and 41, then one block west and one block north. Group retreat rates available.

Hostess: Frances L. Erb
Rooms: 10 (SB) $42.95-69.95
Full Breakfast
Credit Cards: A, B
Notes: 2, 3, 4, 5, 7, 9

year; 6 Pets welcome; 7 Children welcome; 8 Tennis nearby; 9 Swimming nearby; 10 Golf nearby; 11 Skiing nearby; 12 May be booked through travel agent

Nevada

INCLINE VILLAGE

Haus Bavaria

593 North Dyer Circle, P. O. Box 3308, 89450
(702) 831-6122; (800) 731-6222

This European-style residence in the heart of the Sierra Nevadas, is within walking distance of Lake Tahoe. Each of the five guest rooms opens onto a balcony, offering lovely views of the mountains. Breakfast, prepared by your host Bick Hewitt, includes a selection of home-baked goods, fresh fruit, juices, freshly ground coffee, and teas. A private beach and swimming pool are available to guests. Ski at Diamond Peak, Mt. Rose, Heavenly Valley, and other nearby areas.

Host: Bick Hewitt
Rooms: 5 (PB) $110
Full Breakfast
Credit Cards: A, B, C, D
Notes: 2, 5, 8, 9, 10, 11, 12

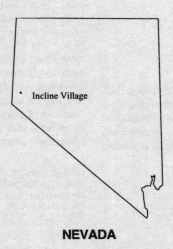

· Incline Village

NEVADA

NOTES: Credit cards accepted: A Master Card; B Visa; C American Express; D Discover Card; E Diners Club; F Other; 2 Personal checks accepted; 3 Lunch available; 4 Dinner available; 5 Open all

New Hampshire

ALBANY

Kancamagus Swift River Inn

P.O. Box 1650, Rt. 112 Kancamagus Hwy.,
03818
(603) 447-2332

This is a quality inn with that Old World flavor in a stress-free environment. Located in the White Mountains of New Hampshire in the Mt. Washington Valley on the most beautiful highway in the state, the Kancamagus Highway, one and one-half miles off route 16. We are only minutes from all factory outlets, attractions, and fine restaurants.

Hosts: Joseph and Janet Beckenbach
Rooms: 10 (PB) $40-90
Continental Breakfast
Credit Cards: None
Notes: 5, 7, 8, 9, 10, 11, 12

ASHLAND

Glynn House Victorian Inn

43 Highland Street, 03217
(603) 968-3775; (800) 637-9599;
(603) 968-9338 (FAX)

A picture-perfect example of the Victorian era, guests marvel at the inn's cupola towers and gingerbread, wraparound porch. Upon arrival, guests are greeted by a magnificent foyer accented with carved oak woodwork and pocket doors. The inn is beautifully furnished with Queen Anne furniture offering guests the warmth and hospitality of being "home" in the 1890s! Each bedroom has its own mood, distinguished by unique interior decor, period furnishings, and amenities.

Hosts: Karol and Betsy Paterman
Rooms: 6 (PB) $75-125
Full Breakfast
Credit Cards: A, B
Notes: 2, 5, 7 (limited with restrictions), 8, 9, 10, 11, 12

BRADFORD

The Bradford Inn

Rural Route 1, Main Street, Box 40, 03221
(603) 938-5309; (800) 669-5309

The Bradford Inn was built as a small hotel in the 1890s. It has two parlors for guest use, one with a fireplace, one with a TV. J. Albert's Restaurant features Colonial-style cuisine specializing in German, Austrian, and Polish dishes. "Well worth the trip," says M. DePauld. The area abounds in outdoor activities in all seasons and offers craft and antique shops, auctions, summer

---

year; 6 Pets welcome; 7 Children welcome; 8 Tennis nearby; 9 Swimming nearby; 10 Golf nearby; 11 Skiing nearby; 12 May be booked through travel agent

theater, local fairs, and festivals. We can accommodate small groups (28-34) for retreats, family parties, or church outings.

Hosts: Tom and Connie Mazol
Rooms: 12 (PB) $59-79
Full Breakfast
Credit Cards: A, B, C, D, E, F
Notes: 2, 4, 5, 6, 7, 8, 9, 10, 11, 12

Candlelite Inn Bed and Breakfast

RR 1, Box 408, Old Center Road, 03221
(603) 938-5571

An 1897 country Victorian Inn nestled on three acres in the Lake Sunapee Region. All of our guest rooms are tastefully decorated and have queen beds, private baths, and mountain views. A gazebo porch is there for your enjoyment on a lazy summer day. And in the parlor is a corner fireplace for those chilly evenings. A full breakfast is served in our lovely dining room or in the sun room overlooking a babbling brook and pond. Within minutes to skiing, hiking, antiquing, and restaurants. We are a non-smoking inn.

Hosts: Les and Marilyn Gordon
Rooms: 6 (PB) $65-75
Full Breakfast
Credit Cards: A, B, D
Notes: 2, 5, 7, 8, 9, 10, 11

Candlelite Inn Bed and Breakfast

Mountain Lake Inn

Route 114, PO Box 443, 03221
(603) 938-2136

Mountain Lake Inn, built in 1764, is on 165 acres of lawns, meadows, and wooded mountainside. A meandering mountain trail leads up the hill alongside a rushing stream that has waterfalls. Across the road is Lake Massasecum, where there is a private beach and a canoe for exploring the shoreline. In winter there are cross-country and downhill ski areas nearby and snowshoeing on the grounds of the Inn.

Hostess: Pat Hendry Lubrano
Rooms: 9 (PB) $85
Full Breakfast
Credit Cards: A, B, D
Notes: 2, 4, 5, 7, 9, 10, 11, 12

CAMPTON

Mountain-Fare Inn

Mad River Rd., P.O. Box 553, 03223
(603) 726-4283

In New Hampshire's White Mountains. Lovely 1840s village home with the antiques, fabrics, and feel of country cottage living. Gardens in summer; foliage in fall; a true skiier's lodge in winter. Accessible, peaceful, warm, friendly, affordable. Hearty breakfasts. Unspoiled beauty from Franconia Notch to Squam Lake. Four-season sports, soccer field, music, and theatre. Wonderful family vacationing.

Hosts: Susan and Nick Preston
Rooms: 10 (7PB; 3SB) $50-90
Full Breakfast
Credit Cards: A, B, D, E
Notes: 2, 5, 7, 8, 9, 10, 11, 12

NOTES: Credit cards accepted: A Master Card; B Visa; C American Express; D Discover Card; E Diners Club; F Other; 2 Personal checks accepted; 3 Lunch available; 4 Dinner available; 5 Open all

MapleHedge Bed and Breakfast Inn

CHARLESTOWN

MapleHedge B&B Inn

Main St., P.O. Box 638, 03603
(603) 826-5237

Rather than just touring homes two-and-a-half centuries old, make one your "home away from home" while visiting western New Hampshire or eastern Vermont. MapleHedge offers five distinctly different bedrooms with private baths and antiques chosen to complement the individual decor. It has very tastefully added all modern day amentities such as central air-conditioning, fire sprinkler system, and queen beds. Enjoy a gourmet breakfast in the grand dining room of this magnificent home on the National Register and situated among 200-year-old maples and lovely gardens.

Hosts: Joan and Dick DeBrine
Rooms: 5 (PB) $80-90
Full 3-course Breakfast
Credit Cards: A, B
Notes: 2, 5, 7 (over 12), 8, 9, 10, 11, 12

COLEBROOK

Monadnock B&B

One Monadnock Street, 03576
(603) 237-8216; (800) 698-8216 (in NH only)

Located one block off Main Street, with easy access to shops and restaurants, in a quiet, picturesque, country community of 2,500 people, this 1916 house has a natural fieldstone porch, chimney, and foundation. Inside it has gorgeous, natural woodwork. Three guest bedrooms upstairs include two with double beds sharing facilities and one with a double and single bed with private half-bath. Common areas are available for relaxing or playing games and watching a large-screen TV. A roomy balcony is good for relaxing and soaking up the sun's rays.

Hosts: Barbara and Wendell Woodard
Rooms: 3 (SB) $43-54
Full Breakfast
Credit Cards: A, B
Notes: 2, 5, 6 (by prior arrangement), 7, 10, 11

DOVER

Highland Farm Bed and Breakfast

148 County Farm Road, 03820
(603) 743-3399

All that you hope for in a B&B: homemade pastries and deliciously prepared entrees with the freshest, healthiest ingredients. Spacious antique-filled guest rooms offer comfortable beds with freshly-ironed linens, fluffy towels, and choice of twin, full, or queen beds. Views of rolling fields down to the Cocheco River and nature trails to view the flora and fauna. Our home offers easy access to the NH seacoast, Lake Winnipesaukee, the White Mountains, and the southern Maine coast. Nearby attractions include historic Portsmouth, Kittery outlets, University of NH in Durham, antique shops, whale-watch cruises, excellent restaurants featuring

year; 6 Pets welcome; 7 Children welcome; 8 Tennis nearby; 9 Swimming nearby; 10 Golf nearby;
11 Skiing nearby; 12 May be booked through travel agent

ocean-fresh seafood, and much more!

Hosts: Andy and Noreen Bowers
Rooms: 5 (1PB; 4SB) $60-78
Full Breakfast
Credit Cards: A, B
Notes: 2, 5, 7, 10

FREEDOM

Freedom House Bed and Breakfast

1 Maple Street, P.O. Box 478, 03836
(603) 539-4815

This Victorian home with six guest rooms is located 15 minutes from Conway. King Pine ski resort is five minutes away. Lake Ossipee and Loon Lake are great resort areas for enjoying an abundance of recreation. One church is located in the village; others are 15 minutes away. A smoke-free environment.

Hosts: Marjorie and Bob Daly
Rooms: 6 (SB) $35-50 + 8% M+R tax
Full Breakfast
Credit Cards: A, B
Notes: 2, 7, 8, 9, 10, 11

GREENFIELD

The Greenfield Inn

Box 400, Forest Road, 03047
(603) 597-6327

Bob Hope and his wife, Dolores, have visited twice because it is romance in Victorian splendor. Breakfast with crystal, china, and Mozart. In quiet valley surrounded by mountains and big veranda views. Only 90 minutes from Boston or 40 minutes from Manchester airports.

Hosts: Barbara and Vic Mangini
Rooms: 9 (7PB; 2SB) $49-99
Full Breakfast
Credit Cards: A, B
Notes: 2, 5, 7 (restrictions), 8, 9, 10, 11, 12

HAMPSTEAD

Stillmeadow Bed and Breakfast at Hampstead

P.O. Box 565, 545 Main Street, 03841
(603) 329-8381

Historic home built in 1850 with five chimneys, three staircases, hardwood floors, oriental rugs, and wood stoves. Set on rolling meadow adjacent to professional croquet courts. Single, doubles, and suites all with private bath. Families are welcome, with amenities such as fenced-in playyard and children's playroom. Easy commute to Manchester, New Hampshire, and Boston, Massachusetts. Complimentary refreshments, and the cookie jar is always full. Formal dining and living rooms, expanded Continental breakfast.

Hosts: Lori and Randy Offord
Rooms: 4 1/2 (4PB) $60-90
Expanded Continental
Credit Cards: C
Notes: 2, 5, 6 (with advance approval), 7, 8, 9, 10, 11, 12 (noncommissionable)

Stillmeadow

NOTES: Credit cards accepted: A Master Card; B Visa; C American Express; D Discover Card; E Diners Club; F Other; 2 Personal checks accepted; 3 Lunch available; 4 Dinner available; 5 Open all

HAMPTON

The Curtis Field House

735 Exeter Road, 03842
(603) 929-0082

A restored custom cape located on five
country acres on Route 27 just over the
Exeter Line which was established in 1638.
Seven miles from the Atlantic Ocean. Our
large rooms have A/C and are decorated
with antiques and many lovely reproductions crafted by a descendant of Darby
Field. A New England lobster dinner can
be ordered in advance. Limited smoking
area. Reservations required. AAA 3-
star. ABBA.

Hosts: Mary and Daniel Houston
Rooms: 3 (2PB; 1SB) $65 includes 8% tax
Full Breakfast
Credit Cards: A, B (to hold a room)
Notes: 2, 7 (limited), 8, 9, 10, 12

The Inn at Elmwood Corners

252 Winnacunnet Rd., 03842
(603) 929-0443; (800) 253-5691

A family-owned inn, the Elmwood was a
farmhouse built in 1870. A mile from the
ocean, filled with quilts and country decorations, this B&B offers comfortable surroundings and wonderful food served in
our dining porch. Inspected and liscensed
by the state, it's a mix of old-fashioned
charm and modern conveniences.

Hosts: John and Mary Hornberger
Rooms: 7 (2PB; 5SB) $50-85
Full Breakfast
Credit Cards: A, B
Notes: 2 (reservations only), 4, 5, 7, 8, 9, 10, 12

The Inn at Elmwood Corners

HOLDERNESS

The Inn on Golden Pond

Route 3, P. O. Box 680, 03245-0680
(603) 968-7269

An 1879 Colonial home is nestled on 50
wooded acres offering guests a traditional
New England setting where you can escape and enjoy warm hospitality and personal service of the resident hosts. Rooms
are individually decorated with braided
rugs and country curtains and bedspreads.
Hearty, home-cooked breakfast features
farm fresh eggs, muffins, homemade bread,
and Bonnie's most requested rhubarb jam.

Hosts: Bonnie and Bill Webb
Rooms: 9 (PB) $85-135
Full Breakfast
Credit Cards: A, B, C
Notes: 2, 5, 8, 9, 10, 11, 12

HOPKINTON

The Country Porch B&B

281 Moran Road, 03229
(603) 746-6391

Situated on 15 peaceful acres of lawn,
pasture, and forest, this B&B is a repro-

---

year; 6 Pets welcome; 7 Children welcome; 8 Tennis nearby; 9 Swimming nearby; 10 Golf nearby;
11 Skiing nearby; 12 May be booked through travel agent

duction of an 18th century Colonial. Sit on the wraparound porch and gaze out over the meadow, bask in the sun, and then cool off in the pool. The comfortably appointed rooms have either a colonial or an Amish theme. King-size or twin beds are available. Summer and winter activities are plentiful and close by and fine country dining is a short drive away. "Come and sit a spell."

Hosts: Tom and Wendy
Rooms: 2 (PB) $75 + 8% tax
Full Breakfast
Credit Cards: A, B
Notes: 2, 5, 9, 10, 11

Ellis River House

JACKSON

Ellis River House

Route 16, P. O. Box 656, 03846
(603) 383-9339; (800) 233-8309; (603) 383-4140 (FAX)

Sample true New England hospitality at this enchanting small hotel and country inn within a short stroll of the village. Eighteen comfortable king- and queen-size guest rooms, fireplaces, two person jacuzzis, scenic balconies, period antiques, air-conditioning, family and two room suites, sauna, heated outdoor pool, and indoor whirl pool. Enjoy a full breakfast with homemade breads or a delicious trout dinner.

Hosts: Barry and Barbara Lubao
Rooms: 18 (15PB; 3SB) $59-229
Full Country Breakfast
Credit Cards: A, B, C, D, E
Notes: 2,4, 5, 6 (limited), 7, 8, 10, 11, 12

JEFFERSON

Applebrook

Route 115A, 03583-0178
(603) 586-7713; (800) 545-6504

Taste our mid-summer raspberries while enjoying spectacular mountain views. Applebrook is a comfortable, casual bed and breakfast in a large Victorian farmhouse with a peaceful, rural setting. After a restful night's sleep, you will enjoy a hearty breakfast before venturing out for a day of hiking, fishing, antique hunting, golfing, swimming, or skiing. Near Santa's Village and Six-Gun City. Dormitory available for groups. Brochures available. Hot tub under the stars.

Hostess: Sandra J. Conley
Rooms: 12 + dormitory (3PB; 8SB) $40-60
Full Breakfast
Credit Cards: A, B, D
Notes: 2, 5, 6, 7, 8, 9, 10, 11

The Jefferson Inn

Route 2, 03583
(603) 586-7998; (800) 729-7908

This charming, 1896 Victorian near Mt. Washington has a 360-degree mountain view. Summer activities include hiking from our door, a swimming pond, six golf courses nearby, summer theater, and excellent cycling. In the winter, enjoy Bretton Woods, cross-country skiing, and skating across the street. Afternoon tea is served daily. Isolated family wing with suites including

---

NOTES: Credit cards accepted: A Master Card; B Visa; C American Express; D Discover Card; E Diners Club; F Other; 2 Personal checks accepted; 3 Lunch available; 4 Dinner available; 5 Open all

kitchenettes. Discounted rates in spring, and midweek discounts in the summer and fall.

Hosts: Greg Brown and Bertie Koelewijn
Rooms: 13 (PB) $52-78
Full Breakfast
Credit Cards: A, B, C, D, E
Notes: 2, 7, 8, 9, 10, 11, 12

MILFORD

The Ram in the Thicket
24 Maple St., 03066
(603) 654-6440

Country Victorian dining and lodging. Horses, sheep, a sweet bearded collie named Mandy who loves to play soccer, swimming pool, spa, and the best food *on earth*! We change the menu each month. Four-stars, Boston Globe, and Worchester Telegram (only two others in history), Conservative politician, Dr. Andrew Tempelman will quiz you on the name of the Inn, while Priscilla will cook you a meal that melts your heart!

Hosts: Dr. Andrew and Priscilla Tempelman
Rooms: 9 (3PB; 6SB) $60-75
Continental Breakfast
Credit Cards: C
Notes: 2, 4, 5, 6 ($10 fee), 7, 8, 9, 10, 11

NEW IPSWICH

The Inn at New Ipswich
Porter Hill Road, P. O. Box 208, 03071
(603) 878-3711

Relax awhile in a graceful 1790 Colonial amid stone walls and fruit tree. With cozy fireplaces, front-porch rockers, and large guest rooms furnished country-style, you'll feel right at home. Breakfasts are bountiful! Situated in New Hampshire's Monadnock Region, activities abound: hiking, band concerts, antique auctions, maplesugaring, apple-picking, unsurpassed autumn color, and cross-country and downhill skiing. No smoking. Children over eight welcome.

Hosts: Ginny and Steve Bankuti
Rooms: 6 (PB) $65
Full Breakfast
Credit Cards: A, B
Notes: 2, 5, 10, 11, 12

NEW LONDON

Pleasant Lake Inn
125 Pleasant Street, P. O. Box 1030, 03257
(603) 526-6271; (800) 626-4907

Our 1790 lakeside country inn is nestled on the shore of Pleasant Lake with Mt. Kearsarge as its backdrop. The panoramic location is only one of the many reasons to visit. All four seasons offer activities from our doorway: lake swimming, fishing, hiking, skiing, or just plain relaxing. Dinner is available. Call or write for a brochure.

Hosts: Margaret and Grant Rich
Rooms: 11 (PB) $75-95
Full Breakfast
Credit Cards: A, B
Notes: 2, 4, 5, 7 (over seven), 8, 9, 10, 11, 12

year; 6 Pets welcome; 7 Children welcome; 8 Tennis nearby; 9 Swimming nearby; 10 Golf nearby; 11 Skiing nearby; 12 May be booked through travel agent

NEWPORT

The Inn at Coit Mountain

523 North Main Street, 03773
(603) 863-3583; (800)-367-2364; (603) 863-7816
(FAX)

All four seasons provide nature's backdrop to this gracious, historic, Georgian home. Whether you prefer the greening spring, languid summer afternoons, colorful autumn foliage, or winter-white mornings, you will delight in a stay at the inn. Available for small retreats of ten to fifteen people.

Hosts: Dick and Judi Tatem
Rooms: 6 (3PB; 3SB) $85-140
Full Breakfast
Credit Cards: A, B, C
Notes: 2, 4 (by arrangement), 7,8, 9, 10, 11, 12

NORTH CONWAY

The 1785 Inn

3582 White Mtn Hwy, P.O. Box 1785,
03860-1785
(603) 356-9025; (800) 421-1785 (reservations for
U.S. and Canada); (603) 356-6081 (FAX)

The 1785 Inn is a relaxing place to vacation at any time of the year. The 1785 Inn is famous for its views and food. Located at The Scenic Vista, popularized by the White Mountain School of Art, its famous scene of Mt. Washington is virtually unchanged from when the inn was built over 200 years ago. The inn's homey atmosphere will make you feel right at home, and the food and service will make you eagerly await your return.

Hosts: Becky and Charlie Mallar
Rooms: 17 (12PB; 5SB) $59-159
Full Breakfast
Credit Cards: A, B, C, D, E
Notes: 2, 4, 5, 7, 8, 9, 10, 11, 12

The Buttonwood Inn

Mt. Surprise Road, P. O. Box 1817, 03860
(603) 356-2625; (800) 258-2625 outside New
Hampshire; (603) 356-3140 (FAX)

The Buttonwood is tucked away on Mt. Surprise in the heart of the White Mountains. It is secluded and quiet, yet only two miles from excellent restaurants and factory outlet shopping. Built in 1820, this New England-style Cape Cod has antique-furnished guest rooms with wide-plank floors, a large outdoor pool, hiking, and cross-country skiing from the door. Alpine skiing is one mile away. A hearty dinner is served weekends during the winter. Triple Diamond rating with AAA and Triple Crown ABBA rating.

Hosts: Peter and Claudia Needham
Rooms: 10 (4PB; 6SB) $60-120
Full Breakfast
Credit Cards: A, B, C, E
Notes: 2, 5, 7, 8, 9, 10, 11, 12

The Buttonwood Inn

NOTES: Credit cards accepted: A Master Card; B Visa; C American Express; D Discover Card; E Diners Club; F Other; 2 Personal checks accepted; 3 Lunch available; 4 Dinner available; 5 Open all

The Center Chimney— 1787

River Road, P.O. Box 1220, 03860-1220
(603)356-6788

Cozy, affordable cape with beautiful early fireplace in living room over 200 years old. The Center Chimney is located in a quiet wooded area just off the Saco River with swimming, canoeing, and fishing, but only a short walk to Main Street. North Conway Village with summer theatre, free cross-country skiing and ice skating, shops, restaurants, etc. Package plans available.

Host: Farley Ames Whitley
Rooms: 4 (SB) $44-55
Continental Breakfast
Credit Cards: None
Notes: 2, 5, 7, 8, 9, 10, 11

The Center Chimney—1787

Merrill Farm Resort

428 White Mountain Hwy., 03860
(603) 447-3866 (voice and FAX)

Cozy rooms in the main house. Efficiency cottages and spacious loft units. Some fireplaces. Cable TV and phones. Outdoor pool, canoes on the river, and conference facilities. Relaxed, informal setting. Tax free outlet shopping, winter and summer recreation area.

Hosts: Lee and Christine Gregory
Rooms: 60 (PB) $49-139
Continental Buffet Breakfast
Credit Cards: A, B, C, D, E
Notes: 5, 7, 8, 9, 10, 11, 12

Nereledge Inn

River Road, off Main St. (RT. 16), 03860
(603)356-2831

Enjoy the charm, hospitality, and relaxation of a small 1787 bed and breakfast inn overlooking Cathedral Ledge. Walk to river or village. Close to all activities. Comfortable, casual atmosphere. Rates include delicious breakfast with warm apple pie.

Hosts: Valerie and Dave Halpin
Rooms: 11 (6PB; 5SB) $59-89
Full Breakfast
Credit Cards: A, B, C
Notes: 2, 5, 7, 8, 9, 10, 11

The Victorian Harvest Inn

P.O. Box 1763, 28 Locust Lane, 03860
(immediately off 16/360 White Mountain hwy.)
(603)356-3548; (800) 642-0749; (603)356-8430
(FAX)

Non-smokers delight in your comfortably elegant B&B home at the edge of quaint North Conway Village. Explore unique shoppes, outlets, and the AMC trails. Our 1850s multi-gabled Victorian find comes with six large comfy rooms, all with mountain views. Start your romantic adventure with a bounteous dining experience and classic New England hospitality. Relax by the fireplace or snuggle with a literary treasure in our elegant library. Private baths, lovely in-ground pool, and full A/C add to your comfort. AAA three-diamond award. American Bed and Break-

---

year; 6 Pets welcome; 7 Children welcome; 8 Tennis nearby; 9 Swimming nearby; 10 Golf nearby; 11 Skiing nearby; 12 May be booked through travel agent

fast Association: rated "A" three-crowns. Cross-country skiing from the door, and 3-10 minutes to downhill skiing.

Hosts: Linda and Robert Dahlberg
Rooms: 6 (4PB; 2SB) $65-100
Full Breakfast
Credit Cards: A, B, C, D
Notes: 2, 5, 7(over 6), 8, 9, 10, 11, 12

The Victorian Harvest Inn

PLYMOUTH

Northway House

Rural Free Delivery 1, Box 71, 03264
(603) 536-2838

Located in the heart of New Hampshire in the beautiful Pemigewasset River Valley, the Northway House is near Newfound, Squam, and Winnepesaukee Lakes, as well as the ski areas of Waterville Valley, Loon, and Cannon. Hospitality-plus awaits the traveler in this charming Colonial house that is homey, comfortable, and reasonably priced.

Hosts: Micheline and Norman McWilliams
Rooms: 3 (SB) $30-45
Full Breakfast
Credit Cards: None
Notes: 2, 5, 6, 7, 9, 10, 11

RYE

Rock Ledge Manor Bed and Breakfast

1413 Ocean Boulevard, Route 1-A, 03870
(603) 431-1413

A gracious, traditional, seaside, manor home with an excellent location offers an ocean view from all rooms. It is central to all New Hampshire and southern Maine seacoast activities; six minutes to historic Portsmouth and Hampton; 20 minutes to the University of New Hampshire; 15 minutes to Exeter Academy. Reservations are advised.

Hosts: Norman and Janice Marineau
Rooms: 4 (2PB; 2SB) $60-85
Full Breakfast
Credit Cards: None
Notes: 2, 5, 7 (over 10), 8, 9, 10, 11

THORNTON

Amber Lights Inn Bed and Breakfast

Route 3, 03223
(603) 726-4077

Amber Lights Inn B&B is a beautifully restored, 1815 Colonial in the heart of the White Mountains in Thornton, NH, in a quiet country setting. We have five meticulously clean guest rooms, all appointed with luxurious queen-size beds, handmade quilts, and antiques. In the early evening, join in a conversation with the innkeepers over our nightly hors d'oeuvres and beverages. We are conveniently located between Loon Mountain and Waterville

NOTES: Credit cards accepted: A Master Card; B Visa; C American Express; D Discover Card; E Diners Club; F Other; 2 Personal checks accepted; 3 Lunch available; 4 Dinner available; 5 Open all

Valley, close to all White Mountain attractions. Ask about our murder mystery weekends.

Hosts: Paul Sears and Carola Warnsman
Rooms: 5 (1PB; 4SB) $45-60 (continental breakfast); $60-75 (full breakfast + hors d'oeuvres)
Full or Continental Breakfast
Credit Cards: A, B, C, D
Notes: 2, 5, 6, 7, 8, 9, 10, 11, 12

WARNER

Jacob's Ladder Bed and Breakfast

69 E. Main Street, 03278
(603) 456-3494

Situated in the quaint village of Warner, Jacob's Ladder is conveniently located between exits 8 and 9 off I-89. The early-1800s home is furnished predominantly with antiques, creating a tasteful country atmosphere. Cross-country ski and snowmobile trail on site with three downhill ski areas within 20 miles. Lakes, mountains,

covered bridges, arts and crafts, and more nearby. No smoking.

Hosts: Deb and Marlon Baese
Rooms: 4 (SB) $40
Full Breakfast
Credit Cards: D
Notes: 2, 5, 7, 8, 9, 10, 11

WOLFEBORO

The Tuc' Me Inn

118 N. Main St., PO Box 657, 03894
(603) 569-5702

Our 1850, Colonial, Federal is located within walking distance of the lake and the quaint village of Wolfeboro, "The oldest summer resort in America." Family antiques in country, Victorian style. High tea, upon request, in our Victorian garden room. Relax in our music room, parlor, screened-in porches, or our cozy reading room.

Hosts: Ernie, Terry, Tina Foultz and Idabel Evans
Rooms: 7 (3PB; 4SB) $59-75
Full Breakfast
Credit Cards: A, B
Notes: 2, 5, 7, 8, 9, 10, 11, 12

The Tuc' Me Inn

year; 6 Pets welcome; 7 Children welcome; 8 Tennis nearby; 9 Swimming nearby; 10 Golf nearby; 11 Skiing nearby; 12 May be booked through travel agent

New Jersey

Amanda's Bed and Breakfast Reservation Service

21 S. Woodland Ave., East Brunswick, 08816
(908) 249-4944; (908) 246-1961 (FAX)

Listing approximately 55 inns, in and about **New Jersey, Pennsylvannia,** and **New York.** Andover, Stewartsville, Stockton, Lambertville, Alloway, Cape May, Spring Lake, Princeton, and many more New Jersey towns. In PA: Washington's Crossing, Milford, Manheim, Kempton, Emmaus, Chalfont, Kennett Square, Delaware Water Gap, and the Poconos. Master Card and Visa accepted. Children over 12 welcome. Orie Barr, coordinator.

ANDOVER

Crossed Keys Bed and Breakfast

289 Pequest Rd., 07821
(201) 786-6661; (201) 786-7627 (FAX)

Crossed Keys is located on 12 beautifully landscaped acres with pond, stream, and reflecting pools. Decorated with fine antiques, reproduction furnishings, and elegant linens in an 1800 setting that is beautifully updated. Artist studio features pool table, shuffleboard, and comfortable sofas for reading. We feature a stone guest house with a two person jacuzzi—a touch of France. Full country breakfast served with beautiful crystal china and silver in a 1700 dining room. We are near Waterloo village, Delaware National recreation park, Great Gorge ski area, home of New Jersey Redbirds, hiking, and more!

Hosts: Pat Toyc and Peter Belder
Rooms: 5 (3PB; 2SB) $90-135
Full Breakfast
Credit Cards: A, B, C
Notes: 5, 9, 10, 11, 12

AVON-BY-THE-SEA

The Avon Manor Inn

109 Sylvania Avenue, 07717-1338
(908) 774-0110

The Avon Manor Inn is a gracious turn-of-the-century home (circa 1907) built in the Colonial Revival style. Enjoy breakfast in our sunny dining room, ocean breezes on our full wraparound veranda, and the charm of this small seaside town. Eight air conditioned bedrooms and only one block to beach and boardwalk. The large living room has a cozy fireplace for winter nights. Rediscover romance at this

---

NOTES: Credit cards accepted: A Master Card; B Visa; C American Express; D Discover Card; E Diners Club; F Other; 2 Personal checks accepted; 3 Lunch available; 4 Dinner available; 5 Open all

charming seaside inn.

Hosts: Kathleen and Jim Curley
Rooms: 8 (6PB; 2SB) $70-110
Full and Continental Breakfast
Credit Cards: A, B, C
Notes: 5, 7, 8, 9, 10, 12

Cashelmara Inn

22 Lakeside Avenue, 07717
(908) 776-8727; (800) 821-2976

A tastefully restored turn-of-the-century inn rests on the bank of a swan lake and the Atlantic Ocean. This desirable setting offers a unique opportunity to smell the fresh salt air, to feel the ocean breeze, and to hear the sounds of the surf and the sea gulls from the privacy of your seaside room. Hearty breakfasts are a tradition at the Cashelmara Inn.

Hosts: Mary E. Wiernasz and Martin Mulligan
Rooms: 13 (PB) $65-165
Full Breakfast
Credit Cards: A, B, C, D
Notes: 2, 5, 7, 8, 9, 10

CAPE MAY

The Albert Stevens Inn

127 Myrtle Avenue, 08204
(609) 884-4717; (800) 890-CATS

Built in 1898 by Dr. Albert G. Stevens as a wedding gift for his bride, Bessie, the inn is just a ten-minute walk to the beach and two blocks from Victorian shopping. The guest rooms are furnished with antiques, and have private baths and air conditioning. A 102-degree, six-person jacuzzi is privately scheduled for guests' comfort. Home of the original Cat's Garden Tea and Tour, the Inn is known for its comfort,

privacy, and gourmet breakfasts. Resident pet cats. Dinner is served from January to April.

Hosts: Curt and Diane Rangen
Rooms: 8 (PB) $85-165
Full Breakfast
Credit Cards: A, B, C, D
Notes: 2, 4, 8, 9, 10, 12

Captain Mey's Inn

817 Washington Street, 08204
(609) 884-1355

The Inn is an 1890 Colonial Revival Victorian named after the Dutch explorer, Captain Cornelius Mey. The Dutch heritage is evident from the Persian rugs on the tabletops to the Delft Blue china collection. The wraparound veranda is furnished with wicker furniture, hanging ferns, and Victorian wind curtains. A full breakfast is served by candlelight with classical music in the formal dining room; in the summer breakfast is served on the veranda.

Hosts: George and Kathleen Blinn
Rooms: 9 (6PB; 3SB) $75-225
Full Breakfast
Credit Cards: A, B, C
Notes: 5, 7 (over 8), 8, 9, 10, 12 (off season and midweek only)

Captain Mey's Inn

year; 6 Pets welcome; 7 Children welcome; 8 Tennis nearby; 9 Swimming nearby; 10 Golf nearby; 11 Skiing nearby; 12 May be booked through travel agent

Duke of Windsor Inn

817 Washington Street, 08204
(609) 884-1355

This grand 1890 Victorian home offers gracious, relaxing accommodations furnished with period antiques, high-backed beds, and marble-topped tables and dressers. Two octagon rooms in our 40-foot turret are particularly fun and romantic. The dining room has five chandeliers and an elaborate plaster ceiling. We are within walking distance of the beach, historical attractions, tennis, and shopping.

The Inn on the Ocean

Hosts: Bruce and Fran Prichard
Rooms: 9 (8PB; 1SB) $65-165
Full Breakfast
Credit Cards: A, B (for deposit only)
Open February to December.
Notes: 2, 8, 9, 10

The Inn of Cape May

601 Beach Dr., 08204
(609) 884-3500; (800) 884-0669

Cape May boasts of being the oldest seaside resort in the United States and one of the grandest oceanfront hotels in "The Inn of Cape May" which dates back to 1894. It offers the charm of Victorian Cape May in a full service historical hotel, including two restaurants with complimentary breakfast, pool, kiddie pool, and antique gift shop. The rooms are quiet and comfortable and are of many sizes, shapes, and offerings in keeping with the Victorian era.

Rooms: 123 (100PB; 23SB) $50-210
Full Breakfast
Credit Cards: A, B, C, D, E
Notes: 3, 4, 6, 7, 8, 9, 10, 12

The Inn on the Ocean

25 Ocean Street, 08204
(800) 304-4477

An intimate, elegant, Victorian inn. Fanciful Second Empire style with an exuberant personality. Beautifully restored. King and queen beds. Private baths. Fireplaces. Fully air-conditioned. Full breakfast. Wicker-filled ocean view porches. Billiard room. Open all seasons. Free on-site parking. Guest says, "A magical place!," "Second visit as lovely as first!," and "Compliments to the chef!"

Hosts: Jack and Katha Davis
Rooms: 5 (PB) $95-165 (by season)
Full Breakfast
Credit Cards: A, B, C, E
Notes: 2, 5, 8, 9, 10, 12

The Mason Cottage

625 Columbia Avenue, 08204
(609) 8844-3358; (800) 716-2766 (reservations)

Built in 1871 for a wealthy Philadelphia businessman, the inn is in the French Empire style. The Mason family purchased the house in 1945 and started welcoming guests in 1946. The curved wood-shingle mansard roof was built by the local ship-

---

NOTES: Credit cards accepted: A Master Card; B Visa; C American Express; D Discover Card; E Diners Club; F Other; 2 Personal checks accepted; 3 Lunch available; 4 Dinner available; 5 Open all

yard carpenters, and restored original furniture remains in the house. The house endured the 1878 Cape May fire and several hurricanes. Honeymoon packages and gift certificates available.

Hosts: Joan and Dave Mason
Rooms: 5 + 4 suites (PB) $95-165;
Suites $145-265
Full Gourmet Breakfast
Closed January
Credit Cards: A, B
Notes: 2, 7 (over 11), 8, 9, 10, 12

The Queen Victoria

102 Ocean Street, 08204
(609) 884-8702

The Queen Victoria includes three 1800s homes that have been restored and furnished with antiques. There are two parlors, one with fireplace and one with TV and games. Two dining rooms serve a hearty country breakfast and afternoon tea. Special services include free bicycles, beach showers, and towels, and turned-down beds with a special chocolate on your pillow. All rooms are air conditioned, and have private baths—many with whirlpool tubs.

Hosts: Dane and Joan Wells
Rooms: 23 (PB) $90-275
Full Breakfast
Credit Cards: A, B
Notes: 2, 5, 7, 8, 9, 10

Windward House

24 Jackson Street, 08204
(609) 884-3368

An elegant, Edwardian seaside inn has an entry room and staircase that are perhaps the prettiest in town. Spacious, antique-filled guest rooms have queen beds and air conditioners. With three sun-and-shade porches, cozy parlor fireplace, and Christmas finery, the inn is located in the historic district, one-half block from the beach and shopping mall. Rates include homemade breakfast, beach passes, parking, and bicycles. Midweek discounts September to June; off-season weekend packages.

Hosts: Owen and Sandy Miller
Rooms: 8 (PB) $80-150
Full Breakfast
Credit Cards: A, B (deposit only)
Notes: 2, 5, 7 (over 12), 8, 9, 10

The Wooden Rabbit Inn

The Wooden Rabbit Inn

609 Hughes Street, 08204
(609) 884-7293

Charming country inn in heart of Cape May, surrounded by Victorian cottages. Cool, shady street, the prettiest in Cape May. Two blocks to beautiful, sandy beaches, one block to shops and fine restaurants. Guest rooms are air conditioned, have private baths, TV, and comfortably sleep two-four. Decor is country, with relaxed family atmosphere. Delicious breakfasts and af-

year; 6 Pets welcome; 7 Children welcome; 8 Tennis nearby; 9 Swimming nearby; 10 Golf nearby; 11 Skiing nearby; 12 May be booked through travel agent

ternoon tea time. Two pet cats to fill your laps. Open year round.

Hosts: Greg and Debby Burow
Rooms: 3 (PB) $155-175
Breakfast
Credit Cards: A, B, D
Notes: 2, 5, 7, 8, 9, 10, 12

EDGEWATER PARK/BEVERLY

Historic Whitebriar, Home of John Fitch, Steam Ship Inventory 1787

1029 Cooper Street, Beverly, NJ 08010
(609) 871-3859

Historic Whitebriar is a German Salt Box Style home that has been added on to many times since it was the home of John Fitch, Steam Ship Inventory 1787. The latest addition is an English Conservatory, built in Beverly, England, from a 200-year-old design and shipped to Beverly, New Jersey, just a few years ago. The Conservatory is on the east side of the house, and breakfast is served here overlooking the season pool and spa. Whitebriar is a living history farm with animals to be tended, and guests are welcome to collect the eggs, brush the ponies, and pick the raspberries. Located just 30 minutes from historic Philadelphia, three hours from Washington, and one and one-half hours from The Big Apple, just off interstates.

Hosts: Carole and Bill Moore and their twin daughters Carrie and Lizzie
Rooms: 2 + apartments (SB) $50-85
Full Breakfast
Credit Cards: None
Notes: 2, 5, 6, 7 (additional charge), 9

FRENCHTOWN

Hunterdon House

12 Bridge Street, 08825
(908) 996-3632; (800) 382-0375 (outside NJ)
(908) 996-2921 (FAX)

Built in 1864, Hunterdon House is a true Victorian mansion notable for its distinctive Italianate style. We are one block from the Delaware River which offers sports enthusiasts fishing, boating, tubing, canoeing. A biking/hiking trail follows the river also. We are deep in antiquing territory just minutes from Bucks Co., PA. Fine restaurants are plentiful. For modern tastes, there is a wealth of local artists and craftsmen in the many specialty shops on Bridge Street.

Hosts: Gene Refalvy
Rooms: 7 (PB) $90-145
Full Breakfast
Credit Cards: A, B, C
Notes: 2, 5, 12

OCEAN CITY

Barna Gate B&B Inn

637 Wesley Avenue, 08226
(609) 291-9366

Enjoy the small, intimate accommodations of our 1895 seashore Victorian. The cozy rooms are decorated in country style with quilts on the antique beds and paddle fans to keep you cool. All rooms are named for flowers. Guests use our common area or front porch under burgundy awnings with white wicker rockers. Near Cape May, Atlantic City, county zoo, and antique shops. We've got everything—beach, boardwalk, and ocean. Hospitality is our

---

NOTES: Credit cards accepted: A Master Card; B Visa; C American Express; D Discover Card; E Diners Club; F Other; 2 Personal checks accepted; 3 Lunch available; 4 Dinner available; 5 Open all

specialty. Open year-round.

Hosts: Frank and Lois Barna
Rooms: 5 (1PB; 2SB) $65-75
Full Breakfast; Continental in summer
Credit Cards: A, B
Notes: 2, 5, 7, 8, 9, 10

DeLancey Manor

869 DeLancey Place, 08226
(609) 398-9831

A turn-of-the-century summer house just
100 yards to a great beach and our 2.45
mile boardwalk. Summer fun for families
and friends at "America's greatest family
resort." Two breezy porches with ocean
view. Walk to restaurants, boardwalk fun,
and the Tabernacle with its renowned
speakers. Located in a residential neighborhood in a dry town. Larger family
rooms available. Breakfast optional for a
small charge. Advance reservations recommended.

Hosts: Stewart and Pam Heisler
Rooms: 7 (3PB; 4SB) $40-70
Expanded Continental Breakfast
Credit Cards: None
Notes: 2, 7, 8, 9, 10

New Brighton Inn

519 Fifth Street, 08226
(609) 399-2829

This charming 1880 Queen Anne Victorian has been magnificently restored to its
original beauty. All rooms and common
areas (living room, library, sun porch) are
elegantly and comfortably furnished with
antiques. The front veranda is furnished
with rockers and a large swing. Rates
include beach tags and use of bicycles.

Hosts: Daniel and Donna Hand
Rooms: 6 (PB) $75-90
Full Breakfast
Credit Cards: A, B, C, D
Notes: 2, 5, 8, 9, 10

The Cordova

OCEAN GROVE

The Cordova

26 Webb Avenue, 07756
(908) 774-3084 in season; (212) 751-9577 winter

Ocean Grove was founded as a religious
retreat center at the turn of the century.
This flavor has lasted in the quiet, peaceful
atmosphere. Constant religious programs
for the family are arranged in the 7,000-seat
Great Auditorium. The Cordova rooms
are uniquely charming and Victorian.
Friendliness, hospitality, cleanliness, and
quiet one block from the magnificent white
sand beach and boardwalk. The porches
have a splendid ocean view. Midweek
specials; also, seven nights for the price of
five. Saturday night refreshments. The
Cordova was selected by *New Jersey
Magazine* as ". . .one of the seven best
places to stay on the Jersey shore." Also
featured in the travel guide, *O'New

Jersey, in 1992.

Hostess: Doris Chernik
Rooms: 16 + 2 cottages (4PB; 14SB) $40-70
Cottages: 2 (PB) $95-105 (weekly rates available)
Continental Breakfast
Credit Cards: None
Notes: 2, 7, 8, 9 (ocean), 12

PRINCETON

Bed and Breakfast of Princeton

P.O. Box 571, 08542
(609) 924-3189; (609) 921-6271(FAX)
Internet: 71035.757@compuserve.com
Compuserve: 71035,757

BBOP offers "homestay" accommodations in several local homes and two "self catering" apartments. Some accommodations are within walking distance of the town center while others are minutes away by automobile or public transportation. Some homes are non-smoking. Rates begin at $40 single and $50 double occupancy. Princeton is the site of many business, research, and academic institutions. Located midway between New York and Philadelphia it offers a variety of recreational, historical, cultural, and sightseeing opportunities. Director: John W. Hurley. Rooms: Aprox. 30 rooms in 15 homes. Rate range $50-65. Continental Breakfast

SPRING LAKE

The Hewitt Wellington Hotel

200 Monmouth Avenue, 07762
(908) 974-1212; (908) 974-2338 (FAX)

"Spring Lake's landmark in luxury." AAA

four-diamond award winner. Twelve beautifully appointed single rooms and 17 two-room suites on the lake overlooking the ocean have private balconies, wraparound porches, air-conditioning, ceiling fans, private marble baths, remote cable TVs, and phones. Heated pool and free beach passes. Refined dining in our intimate restaurant. Free brochure.

Rooms: 29 (PB) $70-210
Continental Breakfast
Credit Cards: A, B, C
Notes: 3, 4, 7, 8, 10

Sea Crest by the Sea

19 Tuttle Ave., 07762
(201) 449-9031; (800) 803-9031

Your romantic fantasy escape. A Spring Lake Bed & Breakfast Inn just for the two of you. Lovingly restored, 1885 Queen Anne Victorian for ladies and gentlemen on seaside holiday. Ocean views, open fireplaces, luxurious linens, feather beds, antique-filled rooms, sumptuous breakfast and afternoon tea. A Gourmet Magazine "top choice." John and Carol welcome you with old-fashioned hospitality to an atmosphere that will soothe your weary body and soul.

Hosts: John and Carol Kirby
Rooms: 11, 1 suite (PB) $92-239
Full Breakfast
Credit Cards: A, B, C
Notes: 2, 5, 8, 9, 10

Sea Crest by the Sea

New Mexico

ALBUQUERQUE

Enchanted Vista B&B
10700 Del Rey NE, 87122
(505) 823-1301

A southwest villa on a one-acre estate, totally fenced for privacy with parking in rear by private entrance to all suites. Spacious suites with decks and verandas that offer spectacular views. Continental breakfast served at your convenience in your suite. Suites include micro-kitchens, perfect for extended stays. Just 20 minutes from airport and 45 minutes to Sante Fe. Just minutes from ski slopes, and only five minutes from the "tram."

Hosts: Tillie and Al Gonzales
Rooms: 2 (PB) $62-74
Continental Breakfast
Credit Cards: None
Notes: 2, 5, 7, 8, 9, 10, 11, 12

ARTESIA

Heritage Inn
209 W. Main, 88210
(505) 748-2552; (505) 746-3407 (FAX)

New country/Victorian atmosphere will take you back in time and warm your heart and soul. Spacious rooms with private baths, room phones, color TV, continental breakfast, computer modem hookups for business travelers, outside patio and deck for relaxation. Very secure second floor, downtown location convenient to excellent restaurants. Smoke free. No pets.

Hosts: James and Wanda Maupin
Rooms: 8 (PB) $55
Continental Breakfast
Credit Cards: A, B, C, D
Notes: 2, 5

ESPAÑOLA

Casa Del Rio
PO Box 92, 87532
(505) 753-2035

Casa Del Rio is a micro-mini southwestern ranch with Arabian horses, fine wool sheep, and authentic adobe construction. Set against a magnificent cliff, locally known as Los Palacios, at the base of which runs the Chama River. It is furnished with hand-carved, traditional, Spanish Colonial furniture and crafts. A coffee or tea tray is delivered to each room as a wake-up. Gold Medallion certified and a three-diamond rating.

Hosts: Eileen and Mel Vigil
Rooms: 2 (PB) $85-105
Full Breakfast
Credit Cards: None
Notes: 2, 5, 6 (horses), 7(inquire), 9, 11, 12

---

year; 6 Pets welcome; 7 Children welcome; 8 Tennis nearby; 9 Swimming nearby; 10 Golf nearby; 11 Skiing nearby; 12 May be booked through travel agent

NOGAL

Monjeau Shadows

H.C. 67-Box 87, 88341
[near Bonita Lake, Hwy. 37 (3 mile marker)]
(505) 336-4191

Four-level Victorian farmhouse located on 10 acres of beautiful, landscaped grounds. Picnic area, nature trails. King and queen beds. Furnished with antiques. Just minutes from Lincoln National Forest and White Mountain Wilderness. Cross-country skiing, fishing, horseback riding. For fun or just relaxing. Enjoy the year-round comfort of Monjeau Shadows.

Hosts: J.R. and Kay Newton
Rooms: 6 (4PB; 2SB) $65-75
Full Breakfast
Credit Cards: A, B
Notes: 2, 5, 7, 9, 10, 11

Paz de Nogal

P.O. Box 93, 88341
(505) 354-2826

1870s restored adobe ranch on seven acres in the Sacramento Mountains, surrounded by Lincoln National Forest and White Mountain Wilderness. Endless hiking and horse trails. Tennis court on premises. Tranquil courtyard for dining. Short drive to Ski Apache (Sierra Blanca 12,300 feet), historic Lincoln, and Ruidoso. Horseback riding available. Day excursions to old mining towns where you can pan for gold.

Hostess: Jane Ketchman
Rooms: 4 (2PB; 2SB) $70-100
Full Breakfast
Credit Cards: None
Notes: 2, 4, 5, 6, 7, 8, 10, 11

SANTA FE

Alexander's Inn

529 E. Palace Ave., 87501
(505) 986-1431

For a cozy stay in Santa Fe, nestle into a bed and breakfast featuring the best of American country charm: Alexander's Inn. Quiet and romantic yet just minutes from the Plaza and Canyon Road, Alexander's Inn offers you a world of warmth and hospitality. Come share the Sante Fe experience with us.

Hostess: Carolyn Lee
Rooms: 7 (5PB; 2SB) $85-150 (off season rates available)
Full Breakfast
Credit Cards: A, B
Notes: 2, 5, 7 (6 and older), 8, 9, 10, 11, 12

TAOS

Orinda Bed and Breakfast

P.O. Box 4451, 87571
(800) 847-1837

A 50-year-old adobe home, dramatic pastoral setting on two acres. View of Taos Mountains, surrounded by elm and cottonwood trees. Decorated southwestern design. Original art presented in rooms and common areas. Kiva fireplaces in suites. Quiet, on private road, but only 15-minute walk to galleries, plaza, and restaurants.

Hosts: Cary and George Pratt
Rooms: 3 (PB) $70-90
Full Breakfast
Credit Cards: A, B
Notes: 2, 5, 7, 8, 9, 10, 11, 12

NOTES: Credit cards accepted: A Master Card; B Visa; C American Express; D Discover Card; E Diners Club; F Other; 2 Personal checks accepted; 3 Lunch available; 4 Dinner available; 5 Open all

New York

American Country Collection of Bed and Breakfasts and Country Inns Reservation Service

4 Greenwood Lane, Delmar, NY 12054-1606
(518) 439-7001 information and reservations;
(518) 439-4301 (FAX)

This reservation service provides reservations for eastern **New York**, western **Massachusetts**, all of **Vermont**, and **St. Thomas, U.S.V.I.** Just one call does it all. Relax and unwind at any of our 115 immaculate, personally-inspected bed and breakfasts and country inns. Many include fireplace, jacuzzi, and/or Modified American Plan. We cater to the budget-minded, yet also offer luxurious accommodations in older Colonial homes and inns. Urban, suburban, and rural locations available. $35-180. Arthur R. Copeland, coordinator.

ALBION

Friendship Manor

349 South Main Street, 14411
(716) 589-7973

This historic house, dating back to 1880, is surrounded by lovely roses, an herb garden, and lots of shade trees. A swimming pool and tennis court are provided for your pleasure. The intimate interior is an artful blend of Victorian-style furnishings with antiques throughout. Enjoy a breakfast of muffins, breads, fruit, juice, coffee, or tea in the formal dining room served buffet style for your convenience. Friendship Manor is central to Niagara Falls, Buffalo, or Rochester. For traveling through or just a getaway.

Hosts: John and Marilyn Baker
Rooms: 4 (2PB; 2SB) $55+tax
Continental Breakfast
Credit Cards: None
Notes: 2, 5, 7, 8, 9, 10, 12

BAINBRIDGE

Berry Hill Farm Bed and Breakfast

RD 1, Box 128, 13733
(607) 967-8745 (voice or FAX)

This restored 1820s farmhouse on a hilltop is surrounded by extensive herb and perennial gardens and 180 acres where you can hike, swim, bird-watch, skate, cross-country ski, or sit on the wraparound porch and watch the natural parade. Our rooms are furnished with comfortable antiques. A ten-minute drive takes you to restaurants, golf, tennis, auctions, and antique centers. You can also buy plants, dried flowers, and wreaths grown and handcrafted on the farm to take home with you. Cooperstown and most local colleges are only 45 minutes away.

Hosts: Jean Fowler and Cecilio Rios
Rooms: 4 (SB) $60-70
Full Breakfast
Credit Cards: A, B, C
Notes: 2, 5, 7, 8, 9, 10, 11, 12

BOLTON LANDING

Hilltop Cottage Bed and Breakfast

P.O. Box 186, Lakeshore Drive, 12814
(518) 644-2492

A clean, comfortable, renovated farmhouse is near Lake George in the beautiful eastern Adirondack Mountains. Walk to beaches, restaurants, and marinas. Enjoy a quiet, home atmosphere with hearty breakfasts. In the summer, this is a busy resort area. Autumn offers fall foliage, hiking, skiing. There is a wood-burning stove for use in winter. A brochure is available.

Hosts: Anita and Charlie Richards
Rooms: 4 (2PB; 2SB) $50-70
Full Breakfast
Credit Cards: A, B
Notes: 2, 5

BURDETT

The Red House Country Inn

4586 Picnic Area Road, 14818-9716
(607) 546-8566

The inn is located in the beautiful

13,000-acre Finger Lakes National Forest with 28 miles of maintained hiking and cross-country ski trails. Six award-winning wineries are within ten minutes from the completely restored 1840s farmstead on five acres of groomed lawns and flower gardens. Enjoy beautifully appointed rooms, country breakfasts, in-ground pool, fully equipped kitchen. Twelve minutes north of Watkins Glen, 20 minutes from Ithaca, 30 minutes from Corning.

Hostesses: Joan Martin and Sandy Schmanke
Rooms: 5 (SB) $60-85
Full Breakfast
Credit Cards: A, B, C, D
Notes: 2, 5, 9, 10, 11, 12

CAMILLUS

The Re Family Bed and Breakfast

4166 Split Rock Rd., 13031
(315) 468-2039

100-year-old early American farmhouse featuring lodge-style den, country kitchen, side deck utilized for fair weather breakfasts, 40' pool, lawns, 2 guest rooms with queen-size brass beds and orthopedic mattresses, pedestal sink in each room. Next to garden-style bathroom with walk-in tile shower, vanity with double sinks, and full-mirrored back wall. Also one room with full bed and captain's bed for two singles or for children. Stress-free environment close to Syracuse.

Hosts: Joseph and Terry Re
Rooms: 3 (SB) $55-75
Full or Continental Breakfast
Credit Cards: None
Notes: 2, 5, 7, 8, 9, 10, 11, 12

NOTES: Credit cards accepted: A Master Card; B Visa; C American Express; D Discover Card; E Diners Club; F Other; 2 Personal checks accepted; 3 Lunch available; 4 Dinner available; 5 Open all

CAMPBELL HALL

Point of View Bed and Breakfast

RR 2, Box 766H, Ridge Rd., 10916
(914) 294-6259; (800) 294-6259

Enjoy peace and tranquility in a country setting with spectacular views of rolling hills and farmland. Modern conveniences with back-home comfort. One hour from New York City, 20 minutes from Stewart Airport, and three miles from the quaint, historic village of Goshen. Spacious rooms, private baths, and guest sitting room.

Hosts: Rev. Bill Frankle and Elaine Frankle
Rooms: 2 (PB) $55-65
Full Breakfast
Credit Cards: A, B
Notes: 2, 5, 10, 11

The Edge of Thyme

CANDOR

The Edge of Thyme, A Bed and Breakfast

6 Main St., PO Box 48, 13743
(607) 659-5155

Featured in Historic Inns of the Northeast.

Located in this quiet rural village is a large, gracious Georgian home, leaded glass windowed porch, marble fireplaces, period sitting rooms, gardens, and pergola. Epicurean breakfast served in genteel manner. Central to Cornell, Ithaca College, Corning, Elmira, Watkins Glen, and wineries. Gift Shoppe; High Tea by appointment.

Hosts: Eva Musgrave and Frank Musgrave
Rooms: 4 (2PB; 2SB) $65-75
Full Breakfast
Credit Cards: A, B
Notes: 2, 5, 7 (well-behaved), 8, 9, 10, 11 (cross-country), 12

CANTON

White Pillars Bed and Breakfast

PO Box 185, 13617
(315) 386-2353; (800) 261-6292

Experience classic antiquity and modern luxury in this beautifully restored 1850s homestead set on 165 acres of rolling meadows. Guest rooms include whirlpool tub, marble floor, cable TV/VCR, air-conditioning, and expansive windows. Use the facilities at the hosts' cottage on Trout Lake, 20 minutes away, and enjoy swimming, canoeing, sailing, fishing, and hot tubbing. Expect to feel pampered, valued, and appreciaged by the hosts who love to share their home with others.

Hosts: Donna and John Clark
Rooms: 5 (2PB; 3SB) $45-65
Full Breakfast
Credit Cards: C
Notes: 2, 5, 7, 8, 9, 10, 11, 12

---

year; 6 Pets welcome; 7 Children welcome; 8 Tennis nearby; 9 Swimming nearby; 10 Golf nearby; 11 Skiing nearby; 12 May be booked through travel agent

White Pillars B&B

CLARENCE

Asa Ransom House

10529 Main Street, 14031
(716) 759-2315; (716) 759-2791 (FAX)

Warmth, comfort, and hospitality are our main attractions. Nine guest rooms have antique and period furnishings, seven of these have fireplaces. Many rooms have a porch or balcony. We also have a library, gift shop, and herb garden on a two-acre lot in the village. The original building housing the library, gift shop and tap room dates back to 1853, built by Asa Ransom who received the land from the Holland Lace Company in 1799.

Hosts: Bob and Judy Lenz
Rooms: 4 (PB) $85-145
Full Breakfast
Credit Cards: A, B, D
Closed Fridays and January
Notes: 2, 4, 7, 8, 9, 10

Asa Ransom House

COOPERSTOWN

Berrywick II

Rd. 2, Box 486, 13326
(607) 547-2052

Located six miles from Cooperstown. Home of the Baseball Hall of Fame, the Farmer's Museum, and the New York State Historical Association—Fenimore House and the Glimmerglass Opera House. All beautifully situated around nine mile long Otsego Lake. Berrywick II is a renovated 19th century farmhouse with separate entrance for guests to converted, two-bedroom apartment. Queen, double, and twin-bedded rooms with kitchen/sitting room and bath perfectly suitable for families with well-behaved children. Sorry, no pets or smoking.

Hosts: Helen and Jack Weber
Rooms: 3 (1SB) $75
Continental or Full Breakfast
Credit Cards: None
Notes: 2, 5, 7, 9, 10

CORNING

1865 White Birch Bed and Breakfast

69 East First Street, 14830
(607) 962-6355

The White Birch, Victorian in structure but decorated in country, has been refurbished to show off its winding staircase, hardwood floors, and wall window in the dining room that overlooks the backyard. We are located in a residential area two blocks from restored historic Market Street and six blocks from the Corning Museum of Glass. A warm fire during the colder months welcomes guests in the common room where TV and great conversation are available. A full gourmet breakfast is served each morning.

Hosts: Kathy and Joe Donahue
Rooms: 4 (2PB; 2SB) $60-80
Full Gourmet Breakfast
Credit Cards: A, B, C
Notes: 2, 5, 7, 8, 9, 10, 11

Delevan House

188 Delevan Avenue, 14830
(607) 962-2347

This Southern Colonial house sits on a hill overlooking Corning. It is charming, graceful, and warm in quiet surroundings. Delicious breakfast. Check-in time 3 PM, check-out time 10:30 AM. Breakfast served from 8:00-9:00 AM. Free transportation to airport.

Hostess: Mary De Pumpo
Rooms: 3 (1PB; 2SB) $55-85
Full Breakfast
Credit Cards: None
Notes: 2, 5, 7 (over 10), 10, 11, 12

CORNWALL

Cromwell Manor Inn

Angola Road, 12518
(914) 534-7136

Built in 1820 Cromwell Manor Inn is a fully-restored, romantic, country estate. Set on seven landscaped acres overlooking a 4000-acre, mountain, forest preserve. The 6000 sq. ft. manor is fully furnished with period antiques and fine furnishings. Enjoy a full breakfast served on the veranda or in our country breakfast

room, at your own private table. 1764 restored cottage is also available for larger groups; sleeps eight. We are located 55 minutes north of New York City and 5 miles from historic West Point.

Hosts: Dale and Barbara Ohara
Rooms: 13 (12PB; 1SB) $120-150;
Suites: $220-250
Full-Served Breakfast
Credit Cards: A, B
Notes: 2, 5, 7, 8, 9, 10, 11, 12

CROTON ON HUDSON

Alexander Hamilton House

49 Van Wyck St., 10520
(914) 271-6737; (914) 271-3927 (FAX)

The Alexander Hamilton House, circa 1889, is a sprawling Victorian home situated on a cliff overlooking the Hudson. Grounds include a mini-orchard and in-ground pool. The home has many period antiques and collections and offers a queen bedded suite with fireplaced sitting room, two large rooms with queen beds (one with an additional daybed), and a bridal chamber with king bed, jacuzzi, entertainment center, pink marble fireplace, and lots of skylights. The master suite, with queen bed, fireplace, picture windows, stained glass, full entertainment center, jacuzzi, skylight, and winding river views was finished last year. A one bedroom apartment with double bed, living room with kitchen on one wall, private bath, and separate entrance is also available for longer stays. Nearby attractions include West Point, the Sleepy Hollow Restorations, Lyndhurst, Boscobel, the Rockefeller mansion, hiking, biking, and sailing. New

---

year; 6 Pets welcome; 7 Children welcome; 8 Tennis nearby; 9 Swimming nearby; 10 Golf nearby; 11 Skiing nearby; 12 May be booked through travel agent

York City under an hour away by train or car. No smoking or pets. All rooms have AC, private bath, color cable TV, and phone. Off-street parking. Weekly and monthly rates available on request. Credit card guarantee required. Seven day cancellation policy.

Hostess: Barbara Notarius
Rooms: 7 (PB) $95-250
Full Breakfast
Credit Cards: A, B, C, D
Notes: 2, 5, 7, 9, 10, 12

DOLGEVILLE

Adrianna Bed and Breakfast

44 Stewart Street, 13329
(315) 429-3249; (800) 335-4233

Rural, Little Falls area near I-90 exit 29A. Cozy residence blending antique and contemporary furnishings. Convenient to Saratoga, Cooperstown, historic sites, and snowmobile, cross-country and hiking trails. Four guest rooms, two with private bath, full breakfast. Smoking restricted. Air conditioning.

Hostess: Adrianna Naizby
Rooms: 4 (2PB; 2SB) $46.50-55+tax
Full Breakfast
Credit Cards: A, B
Notes: 2, 5, 6 (well-behaved), 7 (over 5), 10, 11, 12

EAST HAMPTON

Mill House Inn

33 North Main Street, 11937
(516) 324-9766

This 1790 Colonial is located in "America's

most beautiful village." Enjoy lemonade while overlooking the old Hook windmill, or take a restful nap in our backyard hammock. In the off-season, enjoy tea or cider by the fireplace or a brisk walk to the ocean beach. Antiquing, golf, tennis, Long Island wineries, threatre, and whale watching are nearby.

Hosts: Dan and Katherine Hartnett
Rooms: 8 (6PB; 2SB) $115-180
Sumptuous Extended Continental Breakfast
Credit Cards: A, B, C
Notes: 2, 5, 7; (over 11), 8, 9, 10

EDINBURG

Rock Ridge Orchard Bed and Breakfast

224 South Shore Road, 12134
(518) 883-8318

Experience a relaxing, comfortable stay at this country lake house on the Sacandaga Lake, located in the southern Adirondacks. Swimming, fishing, boating, hiking, hunting, and skiing out your door. Saratoga Springs only 30 minutes away. Family fun, you'll enjoy a delightful breakfast and afternoon tea in the sun porch or dining room with views of the lake, mountains, and orchard. Opening June of 1995. Country comfort with a personal touch.

Hosts: Kim and Ginny Turner
Rooms: 3 (SB) $45-55 (seasonal rates)
Full Breakfast
Credit Cards: None
Notes: 2, 5, 7, 9, 11

FAIR HAVEN

Frost Haven Resort, Inc.

14380 West Bay Road, Box 241, 13064
(315) 947-5331

Fosterdale Heights House

Located on Little Sodus Bay on the southern shores of Lake Ontario, the inn is surrounded with views of the waterfront and spacious, well-kept grounds. A full breakfast is served from 5:00 to 9:00 AM to accommodate fishermen to those on vacation. The area offers spectacular trout and salmon fishing, lots of peace and quiet, and a variety of sightseeing opportunities. A free brochure is available upon request.

Hosts: Brad and Chris Frost
Rooms: 4 (SB) $66 + tax
Full Breakfast
Credit Cards: A, B, C
Notes: 2, 5, 7, 8, 9, 10, 11 (cross-country), 12

FOSTERDALE

Fosterdale Heights House

205 Mueller Road, 12726
(914) 482-3369

This historic, 1840, European-style, country estate in the Catskill Mountains is less than two hours from New York City. It is gentle and quiet, with a bountiful breakfast. Enjoy the mountain view overlooking the pond, acres of Christmas trees (cut your own in season), and natural forest. Informal evenings of chamber music and parlor games break out frequently.

Host: Roy Singer
Rooms: 11 (5PB; 6SB) $58-117
Full Breakfast
Credit Cards: A, B
Notes: 4, 5, 8, 9, 10, 11

FULTON

Battle Island Inn

RR 1, Box 176, 13069
(315) 593-3699

Battle Island Inn is a pre-Civil War farm estate that has been restored and furnished with period antiques. The inn is across the road from a golf course that also provides cross-country skiing. Guest rooms are elegantly furnished with imposing high-back beds, TVs, phones, and private baths. Breakfast is always special in the 1840s dining room.

Hosts: Joyce and Richard Rice
Rooms: 5 (PB) $60-85
Full Breakfast
Credit Cards: A, B, C, D
Notes: 2, 5, 7, 10, 11

GOWANDA

The TEEPEE

14396 Four Mile Level Rd., Rt. 438, 14070-9796
(716) 532-2168

The TEEPEE is operated by full-blooded, Seneca Indians on the Cattaraugus Indian Reservation. Max is of the Turtle Clan and Phyllis is of the Wolf Clan. Tours of the reservation are available and also tours of

---

year; 6 Pets welcome; 7 Children welcome; 8 Tennis nearby; 9 Swimming nearby; 10 Golf nearby; 11 Skiing nearby; 12 May be booked through travel agent

the nearby Amish community. Good base when visiting Niagara Falls.

Hosts: Max and Pyllis Lay
Rooms: 4 (SB) $45
Full Breakfast
Credit Cards: None
Notes: 2, 5, 7, 8, 9, 10, 11

HAMBURG

Sharon's Lake House Bed and Breakfast

4862 Lakeshore Rd., 14075
(716) 627-7561

Built on the shore of Lake Erie, both rooms and sitting room offer a magnificent view of Buffalo city skyline and the Canadian shore only fifteen minutes west of the city. Rooms are new and beautifully decorated with waterfront view. Hot tub room with widow's watch overlooking the lake is one of the amenities. All prepared food is gourmet quality style.

Hostess: Sharon DiMaria
Rooms: 2 (1PB; 1SB) $55-110 per night (2 night minimum)
Full Gourmet Breakfast
Credit Cards: None
Notes: 2, 3, 4, 5, 7 (by reservation only), 9, 10, 11

HAMMONDSPORT

Gone with the Wind B&B on Keuka Lake

453 West Lake Road, Branchport, 14418
(607) 868-4603

The name paints the picture of this 1887 stone Victorian on 14 acres on a slight rise

that is adorned by an inviting gazebo overlooking a quiet lake cove. Feel the magic of total relaxation and peace of mind in the solarium hot tub, nature trails, three fireplaces, delectable breakfasts, private beach, and dock. One hour south of Rochester in the Finger Lakes area of New York.

Hosts: Linda and Robert Lewis
Rooms: 6; $70 queen-125 king (only one king-size)
Full Breakfast
Credit Cards: None
Notes: 2, 5, 8, 9, 10, 11

Gone with the Wind on Keuka Lake

HAMPTON BAYS

House on the Water

Box 106, 11946-3108
(516) 728-3560

Quiet waterfront residence in Hampton Bays surrounded by two acres of garden on Shinnecock Bay. A pleasant neighborhood on a peninsula, good for jogging and walking. Two miles to ocean beaches. Seven miles to Southampton. Kitchen facilities, bicycles, boats, lounges, and umbrellas. A full breakfast from 8:00 AM to 12:00 PM is served on the terrace overlooking the water. Watch the boats and swans go by. Adults only. No pets. Rooms have water view, private baths and entrances. German, French, and Spanish spoken.

Hostess: Mrs. UTE
Rooms: 3 (2PB; 1SB)) $75-95 (less off-season, mid-week, and specials)
Full Breakfast (8 AM to 12PM)
Credit Cards: None
Notes: 2, 8, 9, 10, 12 (10%)

HOBART

Breezy Acres Farm Bed and Breakfast

R.D. 1, Box 191, 13788
(607) 538-9338

You'll feel right at home in our circa 1830s rambling farmhouse. Remodeled with our guests' comfort in mind, each of our three rooms is individually decorated and has its own full bath. Relax on the huge leather sofa in the TV room or in front of the living room fireplace. Take a soak in our spa or hike through our 300 wooded acres. Wake up to a delightful breakfast—all homemade. Friendly, country hospitality.

Hosts: Joyce and David Barber
Rooms: 3 (PB) $50-60
Full Homemade Breakfast
Credit Cards: A, B, C
Notes: 2, 5, 7 (some restrictions), 8, 9, 10, 11

ITHACA

A Slice of Home

178 N. Main St., Spencer, 14883
(607) 589-6073

Newly remodeled 150-year-old farmhouse with 4 bedrooms and two baths. Country cooking with hearty weekend breakfasts and continental weekday breakfasts. Acre-

age to ski, hike, fish. 20 minutes to Ithaca, Elmira and Watkins Glen. No smoking, outside pets.

Hostess: Beatrice Brownell
Rooms: 4 (1PB; 2SB) $35-75
Both Full and Continental Breakfasts
Credit Cards: None
Notes: 2, 5, 7 (over 12), 12

Log Country Inn Bed and Breakfast of Ithaca

P.O. Box 581, 14851
(607) 589-4771; (800) 274-4771; (607) 589-6151 (FAX)

Rustic charm of a log house at the edge of 7,000 acres of state forest; 11 miles south from Ithaca, off 96B. Modern accommodations provided in the spirit of international hospitality. Home atmosphere. Sauna and afternoon tea. Full Eastern European breakfast. Convenient to Cornell, Ithaca College, Corning Glass Center, Watkins Glen, wineries, and antique stores. Open year round.

Hostess: Wanda Grunberg
Rooms: 3 (1PB; 2SB) $45-65
Full Breakfast
Credit Cards: A, B
Notes: 2, 5, 6, 7, 10, 11

Breezy Acres Farm

year; 6 Pets welcome; 7 Children welcome; 8 Tennis nearby; 9 Swimming nearby; 10 Golf nearby; 11 Skiing nearby; 12 May be booked through travel agent

LAKE PLACID

Highland House Inn

3 Highland Place, 12946
(518) 523-2377; (518) 523-1863 (FAX)

The Highland House Inn is centrally located in a lovely residential setting just above Main Street in the village of Lake Placid. Seven tastefully decorated rooms are available, along with a darling, fully efficient, country cottage. A full breakfast is served with blueberry pancakes, a renowned specialty served in our year-round garden dining room. New additions include outdoor hot tub spa, ceiling fans, and televisions in all rooms.

Hosts: Teddy and Cathy Blazer
Rooms: 7 plus cottage (PB) $55-100
Full Breakfast
Credit Cards: A, B
Notes: 2, 5, 7, 8, 9, 10, 11, 12

LANSING

The Federal House

175 Ludlowville Road, 14882
(607) 533-7362; (800) 533-7362; (607) 533-7899 (FAX)

A gracious circa 1815 Inn featuring spacious rooms, exquisitely furnished with antiques and handcarved mantels in the parlor and Seward Suite. The Inn is in the heart of the Finger Lakes, just 15 minutes from Cornell and Ithaca colleges, downtown, wineries, state parks, and less than two miles from Cayuga Lake. The land-

scaped grounds with gardens and gazebo bordering the Salmon Creek and falls, a wonderful, relaxing fishing and biking area. AAA approved.

Hostess: Diane Carroll
Rooms: 3 (PB) $65-130
Full Breakfast
Credit Cards: A, B, C, D
Notes: 2, 5, 8, 9, 10, 11, 12

LIMA

The Fonda House Bed and Breakfast

1612 Rochester St. (15A), 14485
(716) 582-1040

National Register-listed Italianate Village home circa 1853 situated on 2-acre, wooded lot. All rooms tastefully decorated with antiques. Be pampered in the Victorian style. Within walking distance to village services and Elim Bible Institute. Beautiful drive to Finger Lakes, Letchworth State Park, and Niagara Falls. Breakfast of homemade goodies.

Hostess: Millie Fonda
Rooms: 3 (1PB; 2SB) $50-70
Full Breakfast
Credit Cards: None
Notes: 2, 5, 7, 8, 9, 10, 11, 12

LONG EDDY

The Rolling Marble Guest House

P.O. Box 33, 12760
(914) 887-6016

Stay right on the beautiful Delaware River

NOTES: Credit cards accepted: A Master Card; B Visa; C American Express; D Discover Card; E Diners Club; F Other; 2 Personal checks accepted; 3 Lunch available; 4 Dinner available; 5 Open all

in this charming three-story Victorian with colorful details and wraparound porches. 106-years-old and recently restored, the house is an elegant reminder of Long Eddy's historic past. Small and secluded, you will find this is a marvelous place to hole up and do nothing, enjoy the river and property, or explore the possibilities of many nearby activities. Casual comfort and a bountiful breakfast buffet are part of the magical atmosphere created by the innkeepers.

Hosts: Karen Gibbons and Peter Reich
Rooms: 4 (SB) $70
Full Breakfast
Credit Cards: A, B
Notes: 2, 7, 8, 9, 10, 11

MAYVILLE

The Village Inn Bed and Breakfast

111 S. Erie St. (Rt. 394), 14757
(716) 753-3583

Turn-of-the-century Victorian home located near the shores of Lakes Chautauqua and Erie, three miles from Chautauqua Institution and less than 30-minute drive from Peek'n Peak and Cockaigne ski centers. We offer comfort in both single and double rooms in a home furnished with many antiques and trimmed in woodwork crafted by European artisians. In the morning enjoy a breakfast of homemade waffles, nut kuchen, in-season fruit, coffee, and juice in our sunny breakfast room.

Host: Dean R. Honby
Rooms: 3 (SB) $50-55
Full Breakfast
Credit Cards: C
Notes: 2, 5, 6, 7, 8, 9, 10, 11,12

MUMFORD—ROCHESTER

The Genesee Country Inn

948 George Street, 14511-0340
(716) 538-2500; (716) 538-4565 (FAX)

Let us share our magic, quiet, and hospitality. Storybook stone mill, c. 1833, chosen by *Country Inns Magazine* among Top Ten Inns USA 1992. Nine country-elegant guest rooms, seven secluded, wooded acres, and waterfalls. Gourmet breakfast, tea, fireplaces, canopy beds, balconies, and antiques. Flyfish; visit nearby Genessee Country museum, Rochester, Letchworth Park, and "Grand Canyon of the East;" or go birding, biking, or hiking. Take your coffee out to the falls and watch mink, blue heron, and ducks. AAA, Mobil, and FODORS. No smoking. Pets in residence.

Hostesses: Glenda Barcklow, proprietor, and Kim Rasmussen, innkeeper.
Rooms: 9 (PB) $85-130
Full Breakfast
Credit Cards: A, B, E
Notes: 2, 5, 8, 9, 10, 11

NIAGARA FALLS/YOUNGSTOWN

The Cameo Manor North

3881 Lower River Road, Youngstown 14174
(716) 745-3034

Located just seven miles north of Niagara Falls, our English manor house is the perfect spot for that quiet getaway you have

year; 6 Pets welcome; 7 Children welcome; 8 Tennis nearby; 9 Swimming nearby; 10 Golf nearby; 11 Skiing nearby; 12 May be booked through travel agent

been dreaming about. Situated on three secluded acres, the manor offers a great room with fireplaces, solarium, library, and an outdoor terrace for your enjoyment. Our beautifully appointed guest rooms include suites with private sun rooms, cable TV. A breakfast buffet is served daily.

Hosts: Greg and Carolyn Fisher
Rooms: 5 (3PB; 2SB) $65-130
Full Breakfast
Credit Cards: A, B, D
Notes: 5, 7, 8, 9, 10, 11,12

OLCOTT BEACH

Bit-O-Country Guest Rooms

6053 East Lake Road, PO Box 147, 14126-0147
(716) 778-8161

We have a lovely, 200-year-old, updated, one and a half-story, private home located on beautiful Lake Ontario and bordered on two sides by lovely Krull Park. Our guests are invited to share our home for reading, relaxation, conversation, or TV viewing at their leisure. We have a large screened, electrified, and carpeted gazebo that we encourage guests to use. Our policy is to make you comfortable. We are a non-smoking establishment. We provide all info requested about the area.

Hosts: Judy and Howie Diez
Rooms: 2 with 3 single beds each (SB) $40 ($20, each person)
Continental Plus Breakfast
Credit Cards: F (travelers' checks and cash)
Notes: 2 (reservations only), 5, 7 (if carefully supervised by parents), 8, 9, 10

OLEAN

The White House

505 West Henley Street, 14760
(716) 373-0505

The entrance way of this 145-year-old Victorian home greets visitors with its name spelled in the green and white tile. The home's deep hues of green and maroon are very relaxing with white lace curtains everywhere to add to the Victorian ambience and keep the rooms filled with natural light. All the rooms are furnished with period antique or replica antique furniture. The 7,000 sq. ft. house includes on the first floor: a living room, TV room, garden room, dining room, kitchen, wash room, and a bedroom with a full bath; on the second floor: six bedrooms and three full baths; the third floor, when completed, will include three bedrooms with private baths and a large recreation room. Our hopes and dreams will be fulfilled when all the work is completed and guests from all over the world come and enjoy The White House as a comfy Victorian retreat.

Hostesses: Pam Wienk and Pat Blue
Rooms: 6 (4PB; 2SB) $65-95
Full Breakfast
Credit Cards: A, B
Notes: 2, 5, 7, 8, 9, 10, 11, 12

OLIVEREA

Slide Mountain Forest House

805 Oliverea Rd, 12410
(914) 254-5365

Nestled in the Catskill Mountains State Park, our inn offers the flavor and charm of

---

NOTES: Credit cards accepted: A Master Card; B Visa; C American Express; D Discover Card; E Diners Club; F Other; 2 Personal checks accepted; 3 Lunch available; 4 Dinner available; 5 Open all

the old country. Come and enjoy our beautiful country setting, superb lodging, fine dining, and chalet rentals. Family-run for over 60 years, we strive to give you a pleasant and enjoyable stay. German and continental cuisine, lounge, pool, tennis, hiking, fishing, antiquing, and more available for your pleasure.

Hosts: Ralph and Ursula Combe
Rooms: 19 (17PB; 2SB) $50-70
Full Breakfast
Credit Cards: A, B, D
Notes: 2, 3, 4, 5 (chalets only), 7, 8, 9, 10, 11

The Wagener Estate

PENN YAN

The Wagener Estate Bed and Breakfast

351 Elm Street, 14527
(315) 536-4591

Centrally situated in the Finger Lakes, this bed and breakfast is in an historic 1796 home furnished with antiques. Located on a hillside surrounded by four acres of lawn, apple trees, and stone walls, it is a five minute walk to the village. About an hour from Corning, Syracuse, and Rochester. Near wineries, restaurants, and festivals. Hospitality, country charm, comfort, and an elegant breakfast await.

Hosts: Norm and Evie Worth
Rooms: 5 (3PB; 2SB) $60-70
Full Breakfast
Credit Cards: A, B
Notes: 2, 5, 7 (over 6), 8, 9, 10, 11 (40 minute drive), 12

PINE BUSH

The Milton Bull House

1065 Rt. 302, 12566
(914) 361-4770

The Milton Bull House is located in the foothills of the Shawangunk Ridge and has stood for two hundred years. Two rooms are available: one with twin beds, the other with two double beds. A full bath is shared by the two rooms. Our home is large, airy, and furnished with antiques. Breakfast is served at our guests' convenience, catering to special dietary needs; fresh fruit and home-baked goods served. The house is surrounded by shady lawns and gardens. An in-ground swimming pool is available to our guests. We are conveniently located near major highways.

Hosts: Graham and Ellen Jamison
Rooms: 2 (1PB; 2SB) $59 includes $4 tax
Full Breakfast
Credit Cards: None
Notes: 2, 5, 8, 9, 10, 11

PINE HILL

Birchcreek Inn

Route 28, Box 583, 12465
(914) 254-5222; (914) 254-5812 (FAX)

A century-old estate on 23 wooded acres in the heart of the Catskill Forest Preserve. Beautifully decorated guest rooms, all with private bath. Vintage billiard room, guest library, enormous wraparound porch. Close to skiing, antiquing, golf, auctions, hiking, fly fishing. 35 minutes to Woodstock, 2-1/2 hours from New York City.

Hosts: Ron and Julie Odato
Rooms: 6 (PB) $50-150
Full Breakfast
Credit Cards: A, B, C
Notes: 2, 5, 6, 7, 8, 9, 10, 11, 12

POUGHKEEPSIE

Inn At The Falls

50 Red Oaks Mill Road, 12603
(914) 462-5770; (800) 344-1466

Inn At The Falls in Dutchess County combines the most luxurious elements of a modern hotel with the ambiance and personal attention of a country home. Complimentary European-style breakfast delivered to your room each morning. Twenty-two Hotel rooms and fourteen Suites all individually decorated for those who demand the finest in overnight accommodations.

Host: Arnold Sheer
Rooms: 36 (PB) $110-150
Continental Breakfast
Credit Cards: A, B, C, D, E
Notes: 5, 7, 8, 9, 10, 11, 12

Inn At The Falls

QUEENSBURY

Crislip's Bed and Breakfast

693 Ridge Road, Box 57, 12804
(518) 793-6869

Located in the Adirondack area just minutes from Saratoga Springs and Lake George, this landmark Federal home provides spacious accommodations complete with period antiques, four-poster beds, and down comforters. The country breakfast menu features buttermilk pancakes, scrambled eggs, and sausages. Your hosts invite you to relax on the porches and enjoy the mountain view of Vermont.

Hosts: Ned and Joyce Crislip
Rooms: 3 (PB) $55-75
Full Breakfast
Credit Cards: A, B, C
Notes: 2, 5, 7, 8, 9, 10, 11

RICHFIELD SPRINGS

Country Spread Bed and Breakfast

23 Prospect Street, P. O. Box 1863, 13439
(315) 858-1870

From our guest book. . . . "A refreshing night and fun conversation." Enjoy genuine hospitality in our 1893 country-decorated home. Located in the heart of central New York, we are close to the National Baseball Hall of Fame in Cooperstown, opera, antiquing, and four-season recreation. Delicious breakfasts (your choice) await. Member of local and national associations. Families welcome. Rated and approved by the American Bed and Breakfast Association.

Hosts: Karen and Bruce Watson
Rooms: 2 (PB) $45-65
Full Breakfast
Credit Cards: A, B
Notes: 2, 5, 7, 8, 9, 10, 11, 12

ROUND TOP

Tumblin' Falls House Bed and Breakfast

P.O. Box 281, 12473
(518) 622-3981 (voice and FAX)

Experience the magic of Tumblin' Falls House. Perched high on a cliff, overlooking beautiful Shinglekill Falls. An absolute paradise for bird-wathcers, hikers, skiers, bicycle enthusiasts, or maybe you would just like to lie in a hammock and listen! Fall asleep to the soothing sounds of gentle waters. Wake up to a wonderful country breakfast served on the front porch overlooking the falls.

Hosts: Hugh and Linda Curry
Rooms: 5 (1PB; 4SB) $65-125
Full Breakfast
Credit Cards: A, B
Notes: 2, 3, 4, 5, 6, 7, 9, 10, 11, 12

The Inn on Bacon Hill

SARATOGA SPRINGS

The Inn on Bacon Hill Bed and Breakfast

P.O. Box 1462, 12866
(518) 695-3693

Relax in the peacefulness of elegant living in this spacious, recently restored, 1862 Victorian just 12 minutes from historic Saratoga Springs and its racetracks. Four air-conditioned bedrooms overlook fertile farmland. A baby grand piano adorns the Victorian Parlor Suite. Enjoy our lovely gardens, extensive library, comfortable guest parlor, and many architectural features unique to the Inn, an inn where you come as strangers and leave as friends! Off season, a comprehensive innkeeping course is offered.

Hostess: Andrea Collins-Breslin
Rooms: 4 (2PB; 2SB) $65-85 (seasonal rates)
Full Breakfast
Credit Cards: A, B
Notes: 2, 5, 7 (over 12), 8, 9, 10, 11, 12

Six Sisters Bed and Breakfast

149 Union Ave., 12866
(518) 583-1173; (518) 587-2470 (FAX)

A uniquely styled 1880s Victorian beckons you with its relaxing veranda. Conveniently situated within walking distance of museums, city park, downtown specialty shops, antiques, and restaurants. Spacious rooms, each with private bath and luxurious bed, prepare you for a full home-cooked breakfast. Mineral bath and massage package

year; 6 Pets welcome; 7 Children welcome; 8 Tennis nearby; 9 Swimming nearby; 10 Golf nearby; 11 Skiing nearby; 12 May be booked through travel agent

available November-March.

Hosts: Kate Benton and Steve Ramirez
Rooms: 4 (PB) $60-125 (except racing season)
Full Breakfast
Credit Cards: A, B, C
Notes: 2, 5, 7 (over 10), 8, 9, 10, 11, 12

Six Sisters Bed and Breakfast

SHELTER ISLAND

The Bayberry Bed and Breakfast

36 South Menantic Road, P.O. Box 538,
11964-0538
(516) 749-3375

Experience an island accessible only by
ferry with a simple, peaceful, life-style and
a third of it is a nature conservancy. Activities include hiking, bird-watching, biking,
beaches, boating, fishing, winery tours,
and antiquing. Our home is in a setting
abounding with wildlife, furnished with
antiques, has exceptionally large king-size
bedroom and a twin bedroom, cozy living
room with piano and fireplace, hammocks,
and swimming pool.

Hosts: Suzanne and Richard Boland
Rooms: 2 (PB) $105-125 (seasonal rates
available)
Full Breakfast
Credit Cards: None
Notes: 2, 5, 7 (over 12), 8, 9, 10

SYRACUSE AREA— ELBRIDGE

Elaine's Bed and Breakfast Reservation Service

4987 Kingston Rd., Elbridge, 13060
(315) 689-2082

Presently listing B&Bs in **New York**
State in the following towns: Apulia,
Auburn, Baldwinsville, Clay, Cleveland
and Constantia on Oneida Lake, Con-
quest, DeWitt, Durhamville, Edmeston
(near Cooperstown), Elbridge,
Fayetteville, Geneva, Glen Haven,
Gorham, Groton, Homer, Jamesville,
Lafayette, Liverpool, Manlius, Marathon
(near Binghamton and Ithaca), Marcellus,
Ovid, Owasco Lake, Phoenix, Pompey,
Port Ontario, Pulaski, Rome, Saranac
Lake, Sheldrae-on-Cayuga, Skaneateles,
Syracuse, Tully, Vernon, Vesper, Water-
loo, and Watertown. Elaine Samuels,
Coordinator.

WARRENSBURG

Bent Finial Manor

194 Main St., 12885
(518) 623-3308

Spacious Victorian manor that preserves
the turn-of-the-century atmosphere with
its cherry staircase and stained glass windows. Five bed chambers, queen beds,
private baths, full candlelight breakfast
with homemade maple syrup, strawberry
jam amd apple cider. Enjoy coffee on our
porch, in front of a crackling fireplace or in

NOTES: Credit cards accepted: A Master Card; B Visa; C American Express; D Discover Card; E
Diners Club; F Other; 2 Personal checks accepted; 3 Lunch available; 4 Dinner available; 5 Open all

our conservatory. One mile to I-87, hiking, biking, riding, sleigh rides, skiing, swimming, boating and antiquing, too!

Hostess: Patricia Scully
Rooms: 5 (PB) $75-85
Full Breakfast
Credit Cards: None
Notes: 2, 3, 4, 5, 7 (limited), 8, 9, 10

White House Lodge

53 Main Street, 12885
(518) 623-3640

An 1847 Victorian home in the heart of the queen village of the Adirondacks, an antiquer's paradise. The home is furnished with many Victorian antiques which send you back in time. Five minutes to Lake George, Fort William Henry, and Great Escape. Walk to restaurants and shopping. Enjoy air-conditioned TV lounge for guests only. Wicker rockers and chairs on front porch. Window and casablanca fans.

Hosts: Jim and Ruth Gibson
Rooms: 3 (SB) $85
Continental Breakfast
Credit Cards: A, B
Notes: 5, 7 (over 8 years), 9, 10, 11

WATERVILLE

Bed and Breakfast of Waterville

211 White Street, 13480
(315) 841-8295

This lovely Victorian home in Waterville's

Historic Triangle District is near Hamilton College and Colgate University and many antique shops along U.S. Route 20. Cooperstown's museums and Glimmerglass Opera are a short distance away. Accommodations include a first floor room with private bath and two on the second floor with a shared bath. A delicious full breakfast is served.

Hosts: Stanley and Carol Sambora
Rooms: 3 (1PB; 2SB) $40-50
Full Breakfast
Credit Cards: A, B
Notes: 2, 5, 7, 8, 10, 12

WESTHAMPTON BEACH

1880 House

2 Seafield Lane, P. O. Box 648, 11978
(800) 346-3290

The Seafield House is a hidden, 100-year-old country retreat perfect for a romantic hideaway, a weekend of privacy, or just a change of pace from city life. Only 90 minutes from Manhattan, Seafield House is ideally situated on Westhampton Beach's exclusive Seafield Lane. The estate includes a swimming pool and tennis court and is a short, brisk walk to the ocean beach. The area offers outstanding restaurants, shops, and opportunities for antique hunting. Indoor tennis, Guerney's International Health Spa, and Montauk Point are nearby.

Hostess: Elsie Collins
Rooms: 3 suites (PB) $100-195
Full Breakfast
Credit Cards: A, B, C
Notes: 2, 5, 8, 9, 10, 12

---

year; 6 Pets welcome; 7 Children welcome; 8 Tennis nearby; 9 Swimming nearby; 10 Golf nearby; 11 Skiing nearby; 12 May be booked through travel agent

WINDSHAM

Country Suite Bed and Breakfast
P.O. Box 700, 12496
(518) 734-4075

Lovely 100-year-old farmhouse, furnished with family heirlooms and antiques, nestled in Catskill Mountains on 10.5 acres of land. Rennovated by current owners to accommodate guests seeking the quiet charm and ambiance of country life and relaxation. Open year round for those who need "to get away."

Hostesses: Sondra Clark and Lorraine Seidel
Rooms: 9 (3PB; 6SB) $55-75
Full Complimentary Breakfast
Credit Cards: C
Notes: 2, 5, 7 (well-behaved), 8, 9, 10, 11, 12

WINDSOR

Country Haven
66 Garrett Rd., 13865
(607) 655-1204

A restored 1800s farmhouse in a quiet country setting on 350 acres. A haven for today's weary traveler and a weekend hideaway where warm hospitality awaits you. Craft shops with 70 artisans. Six mile Volkssport Hiking Trail. Located 1 mile from Rt. 17 East, Exit 78, 12 miles east of Binghamton and 7 miles from Rt. 81.

Hostess: Rita Saunders
Rooms: 4 (1PB; 2SB) $45-55
Full Breakfast
Credit Cards: A, B, D
Notes: 2, 5, 7, 8, 9, 10

1880 House

NOTES: Credit cards accepted: A Master Card; B Visa; C American Express; D Discover Card; E Diners Club; F Other; 2 Personal checks accepted; 3 Lunch available; 4 Dinner available; 5 Open all

North Carolina

The Doctor's Inn

ASHEBORO

The Doctor's Inn

716 South Park St., 27203
(910) 625-4916 or (910) 625-4822

The Doctor's Inn is a home filled with antiques. It offers its guests the utmost in personal accommodations. Amenities include a gourmet breakfast served on fine china and silver, fresh flowers, terry-cloth robes and slippers, and ice cream parfaits. Nearby are over 60 potteries, and the North Carolina Zoo (five miles).

Hosts: Marion and Beth Griffin
Rooms: 2 (1PB; 1SB) $75-85
Full Breakfast
Credit Cards: None
Notes: 2, 5, 8, 9, 10

ASHEVILLE

Albemarle Inn

86 Edgemont Road, 28801-1544
(704) 255-0027

A distinguished Greek Revival mansion with exquisite carved oak staircase, balcony, paneling, and high ceilings. Beautiful residential area. On the National Register of Historic Places. Spacious, tastefully decorated, comfortable guest rooms with TV, telephones, air-conditioning, and private baths with clawfoot tubs and showers. Delicious full breakfast served in our dining room and sun porch. Unmatched hospitality.

Hosts: Kathy and Dick Hemes
Rooms: 11 (PB) $75-130
Full Breakfast
Credit Cards: A, B, D
Notes: 2, 5, 7 (over 13), 8, 9, 10, 12

Cairn Brae

217 Patton Mountain Road, 28804
(704) 292-9219

A mountain retreat on three secluded acres above Asheville features beautiful views, walking trails, and a large terrace overlooking Beaver Dam Valley. Homemade full breakfast. Quiet, away from traffic,

---

year; 6 Pets welcome; 7 Children welcome; 8 Tennis nearby; 9 Swimming nearby; 10 Golf nearby;
11 Skiing nearby; 12 May be booked through travel agent

only minutes from downtown.

Hosts: Edward and Millicent Adams
Rooms: 3 (PB) $80-95
Full Breakfast
Credit Cards: A, B
Open April-November
Notes: 2, 3, 7 (over 10), 8, 9, 10

Reed House

119 Dodge Street, 28803
(704) 274-1604

This comfortable Queen Anne Victorian with rocking chairs and swings on the porch has a rocking chair in every room. Breakfast features homemade muffins, rolls, and jams and is served on the porch. Listed on the National Register of Historic Places; near Biltmore Estate. Open May 1 through November 1.

Hostess: Marge Turcot
Rooms: 2 (SB) $50, 2BR Family Cottage $95
Suite: 1 (PB) $70
Continental Breakfast
Credit Cards: A, B
Open May 1 through November 1.
Notes: 2, 7, 8, 9, 10, 11

BREVARD

Carolina Maple Getaway

291 Maple Street, 28712
(704) 884-5813; (704) 884-4879 (FAX)

Hosts provide warm hospitality and a homemade breakfast of breads or muffins in this main street town getaway for a few days or a week. Two bedrooms, living room, fully equipped kitchen, bath, and dressing room are all private for guests' use. Private entrance and garden grounds on an acre estate. 15-30 minutes to the Blue Ridge

Mountain Parkway, 100 waterfalls, and Asheville's famous Biltmore House, and Asheville National Airport.

Hosts: Clyde and Linda Brooks
Rooms: 5 (PB) $55-75
Continental Breakfast
Credit Cards: None
Notes: 2, 5, 6 (to board at vet accommodations), 7, 8, 9, 10, 11

The Red House Inn

412 West Probart Street, 28712
(704) 884-9349

The Red House was built in 1851 and has served as a trading post, a railroad station, the county's first courthouse, and the first post office. It has been lovingly restored and is now open to the public. Charmingly furnished with turn-of-the-century antiques. Convenient to the Blue Ridge Parkway, Brevard Music Center, and Asheville's Biltmore Estate.

Hostess: Mary Lynne MacGillycuddy
Rooms: 6 (4PB; 2SB) + one cottage (PB) $45-69
Full Breakfast
Credit Cards: A, B, C
Closed January-March
Notes: 2, 7, 8, 9, 10, 12

Womble Inn

301 W. Main Street, 28712
(704) 884-4770

The Womble Inn invites you to relax in a welcoming, comfortable atmosphere. Each of the six guest rooms is especially furnished in antiques and decorated to make you feel cared for. All of the guest rooms have private baths and air conditioning. Your breakfast will be served to you on a silver tray or you may prefer to be seated in the dining room. The Inn is one-half mile from the exciting Brevard Music Center.

Hosts: Beth and Steve Womble
Rooms: 6 (PB) $48-58
Continental Breakfast Included (full available)
Credit Cards: A, B
Notes: 2, 3 (M-F), 5, 7, 8, 10

BRYSON CITY

Randolph House Country Inn

P.O. Box 816, 28713
(704) 488-3472

The inn is located 60 miles southwest of Asheville in a quaint mountain town at the gateway to the Great Smoky Mountain National Park. It overlooks the town and is close to white water activities, horseback riding, hiking, trout streams, Cherokee Indian Reservation, the Blue Ridge Parkway, Fontana Lake, and scenic trails and highways. Near depot and excursions on the Great Smoky Mountain railway. Listed on the National Register of Historic Places and recommended by *The New York Times*.

Hosts: Bill and Ruth Randolph Adams
Rooms: 6 (3 PB; 3 SB) $75-85
Full Breakfast
Credit Cards: A, B, C, D
Closed November-March
Notes: 2, 4, 8, 12

BURNSVILLE

NuWray Inn

Town Square, 28714
(704) 682-2329; (800) 368-9729

Historic country inn...since 1833. Nestled

in the Blue Ridge Mountains in a quaint town-square setting. Thirty miles northeast of Asheville. Close to Mt. Mitchell, Blue Ridge Parkway, Grandfather Mountain, antiques, golf, crafts, hiking, fishing, or just relaxing on the porch. Room rates include a hearty country breakfast and afternoon refreshments, with our nationally famous family-style dinners also available.

Hosts: Chris and Pam Strickland
Rooms: 26 (PB) $70-110
Full Breakfast
Credit Cards: A, B, C
Notes: 2, 4, 5, 7, 8, 9, 10, 11, 12

CANDLER

"Creek Side" Bed and Breakfast

R. 1, Box 576, 28715
(704) 667-9654 (voice and FAX)

"Creek Side" is a retreat that consists of 25 acres on beautiful Mt. Pisgah with easy access to the Blue Ridge Parkway, Asheville, Maggie Valley, and much, much more. If you are looking for the perfect place to spend a quiet night or a few days of fun and relaxation in a home filled with European and American antiques, then we would like to invite you to come and sit by the fire or rock on the porch with us.

Hostess: JC Sides
Rooms: 4 (SB) $50
Full Country Breakfast
Credit Cards: None
Notes: 2, 3, 4, 5, 7(WELL -behaved), 11

year; 6 Pets welcome; 7 Children welcome; 8 Tennis nearby; 9 Swimming nearby; 10 Golf nearby; 11 Skiing nearby; 12 May be booked through travel agent

CAPE CARTERET

Harborlight Guest House Bed and Breakfast

332 Live Oak Drive, 28584
(919) 393-6868; (800) 624-VIEW

The Harborlight is situated on a peninsula with water on three sides; thus, all suites offer panoramic vistas that are simply spectacular. All suites offer private entrances and private baths; luxury suites feature two-person jacuzzis, fireplaces, and in-room breakfast. The guest house is minutes from area beaches, secluded island excursions, and the outdoor drama "Worthy is the Lamb"—a passion play that depicts the life of Christ.

Hosts: Bobby and Anita Gill
Rooms: 7 (PB) $75-155
Full Breakfast
Credit Cards: A, B, C
Notes: 5, 8, 9, 10

CASHIERS

Millstone Inn

Highway 64, PO Box 949, 28717
(704) 743-2737

Selected by *Country Inns* magazine as one of the best 12 inns, it has breathtaking views of the Nantahala forest. The exposed beams are complemented by the carefully selected antiques and artwork. Enjoy a gourmet breakfast in our glass-enclosed dining room overlooking Whiteside mountain. Located at 3,500 ft., it's always cool and comfortable for a hike to the nearby Silver Slip Falls, or enjoy the nearby golf, tennis, restaurants, and antique shops.

Hosts: Paul and Patricia Collins
Rooms: 11 (PB) $87-128
Full Breakfast
Credit Cards: A, B, D
Notes: 2, 8, 9, 10, 11, 12

The Elizabeth Bed and Breakfast

CHARLOTTE

The Elizabeth Bed and Breakfast

2145 East 5th Street, 28204
(704) 358-1368

This 1927 lavender "lady" is located in historic Elizabeth, Charlotte's second oldest neighborhood. European country-style rooms are beautifully appointed with antiques, ceiling fans, decorator linens, and uniques collections. A guest cottage offers a private retreat in elegant southwestern style. All rooms have central air and private baths; some have TV and phones. Enjoy a generous continental breakfast, then relax in our garden courtyard, complete with charming gazebo, or stroll beneath giant oak trees to convenient restaurants and shopping. Nearby attractions include the Mint Museum of Art, Blumenthal Performing Arts Center, Discovery Place,

---

NOTES: Credit cards accepted: A Master Card; B Visa; C American Express; D Discover Card; E Diners Club; F Other; 2 Personal checks accepted; 3 Lunch available; 4 Dinner available; 5 Open all

and professional sporting events.

Hostess: Joan Mastny
Rooms: 4 (PB) $55-88
Generous Continental Breakfast
Credit Cards: A, B
Notes: 2, 5, 9, 12

The Homeplace B&B

5901 Sardis Road, 28270
(704) 365-1936

Restored 1902 country Victorian with wrap around porch and tin roof is nestled among two and one-half wooded acres. Secluded "cottage style" gardens with a gazebo, brick walkways, and a 1930s log barn further enhance this nostalgic oasis in southeast Charlotte. Experienced innkeepers offer four guest rooms, a full breakfast, and a Victorian Garden Room for small meetings and special occasions. Opened in 1984, the Homeplace is a "reflection of the true bed and breakfast."

Hosts: Peggy and Frank Dearien
Rooms: 4 (2PB; 2P½B -shared shower) $68-88
Full Breakfast
Credit Cards: A, B, C
Notes: 2, 5, 7 (over 10), 12 (10%)

The Homeplace

McElhinney House

10533 Fairway Ridge Road, 28277
(704) 846-0783

A two-story traditional home located in popular southeast Charlotte, 25 minutes from Charlotte-Douglas Airport. Close to fine restaurants, museums, Carowinds Park, and many golf courses. A lounge area with cable TV, a hot tub, laundry facilities, and barbecue are available. Families are welcome. A continental breakfast is served in the lounge or on the deck.

Hosts: Mary and Jim McElhinney
Rooms: 2 (PB) $55-65
Continental Breakfast
Credit Cards: A, B
Notes: 2, 5, 7, 8, 9, 10

The Morehead Inn

1122 E. Morehead St., 28204
(704) 376-3357; (704) 335-1110 (FAX)

A Southern estate endowed with quiet elegance. Spacious public areas with intimate fireplaces. Luxurious private rooms furnished with English and American antiques. Just minutes from uptown Charlotte in Historic Dilworth.

Rooms: 10 (PB) + 1 apartment with 2 bedrooms (SB) $75-110
Continental Plus Breakfast
Credit Cards: A, B, C, E
Notes: 2, 5, 7, 10, 12

CLINTON

The Shield House

216 Sampson Street, 28328
(910) 592-2634; (800) 462-9817 (reservations only) call for FAX number

Reminiscent of *Gone with the Wind* and listed on the National Register of Historic Places, the Shield House has many dramatic features, including soaring Corinthian

year; 6 Pets welcome; 7 Children welcome; 8 Tennis nearby; 9 Swimming nearby; 10 Golf nearby; 11 Skiing nearby; 12 May be booked through travel agent

columns, wrap around porches, coffer ceilings with beading, and a large foyer with enclosed columns outlining a grand central-flight staircase. The red-carpeted stairs twist up to a landing and then back to the front of the house. A large guest lounge is naturally lighted through glass doors that open only onto a balcony. Private phones, cable TV. Five Victorian street lights on one and a half acres.

Hosts: Anita Green and Juanita G. McLamb
Rooms: 6 + bungalow (PB) $50-100
Continental Plus Breakfast
Credit Cards: A, B, C, D, E
Notes: 2, 5, 7(prior arrangements), 8, 10, 12

CLYDE

Windsong: A Mountain Inn

120 Ferguson Ridge, 28721
(704) 627-6111; (704) 627-8080 (FAX)

A romantic, contemporary, log inn high in the breathtaking Smoky Mountains. Intimate rooms are large and bright with high-beamed ceilings, pine log walls, and Mexican tile floors. Fireplaces, tubs for two, separate showers, and private decks or patios. Billiards, swimming, tennis, hiking, and llama trekking. Also, a new deluxe, two-bedroom guest house, tub for two, and woodstove.

Hosts: Donna and Gale Livengood
Rooms: 5 + 1 guest house with 2 bedrooms (PB) $89-130
Full Breakfast (Continental in Guest House)
Credit Cards: A, B
Notes: 2, 5, 7 (over 8), 8, 9, 10, 11, 12 (10%)

DURHAM

Arrowhead Inn

106 Mason Road, 27712
(919) 477-8430 (voice and FAX)

The 1775 Colonial manor house is filled with antiques, quilts, samplers, and warmth. Located on four rural acres, Arrowhead features fireplaces, original architectural details, air conditioning, and homemade breakfasts. A two-room log cabin is also available. Easy access to restaurants, Duke University, University of North Carolina-Chapel Hill, Raleigh, and historic sites, including Duke Homestead Tobacco Museum, Bennett Place. Near I-85.

Hosts: Jerry, Barbara, and Cathy Ryan
Rooms: 8 (6PB; 2SB) $75-150
Full Breakfast
Credit Cards: A, B, C, E
Notes: 2, 5, 7, 8, 9, 10, 12

Captain's Quarters Inn

EDENTON

Captain's Quarters Inn

202 W. Queen Street, 27932
(919) 482-8945

The Inn is a 17-room, c.1907 home in the

Edenton historic district with a 65 ft. wrap-around front porch (swings and rockers). Eight charming bedrooms with modern, private baths (seven queen beds, one twin bedded room). We serve plenty of gourmet food, including welcome refreshments, continental breakfast and a full three-course breakfast, as well as gourmet dinner on weekends. Sailing offered spring, summer and fall; mystery weekends in fall, winter, and spring.

Hosts: Bill and Phyllis Pepper
Rooms: 8 (PB) $75-85
Continental AND Full Breakfast
Credit Cards: A, B
Notes: 2, 4 (inn guests only), 5, 7(over 7), 8, 9, 10

The Lords Proprietors' Inn

300 North Broad Street, 27932
(919) 482-3641; (919) 482-2432 (FAX)

The Lords Proprietors' Inn, full-service Village Inn in the heart of Historic Edenton has twenty spacious rooms furnished with antiques and exquisite reproductions made by a local cabinetmaker, and the finest dining in Eastern North Carolina. The inn offers guest an opportunity to enjoy this beautiful waterfront town in a truly wonderful way.

Hosts: Arch and Jane Edwards
Rooms: 20 (PB) $155-215 MAP(incudes dinner)
Full Breakfast and Dinner
Credit Cards: None
Notes: 2, 4, 5, 7(additional rate), 8, 9, 10, 12

MeadowHaven Bed and Breakfast

FRANKLIN

Lullwater Retreat

950 Old Highlands Road, 28734
(704) 524-6532

The 120-year-old farmhouse and cabins are located on a river and creek in a peaceful mountain cove. Hiking trails, river swimming, tubing, and other outdoor activities are on the premises. It serves as a retreat center for church groups and family reunions. Guests cook their own meals or visit nearby restaurants. Chapel, rocking chairs, wonderful views, indoor and outdoor games. Christian videos and reading materials are supplied.

Hosts: Robert and Virginia Smith
Rooms: 10 (5PB; 5SB) $39-50
Self-serve Breakfast
Credit Cards: None
Notes: 2, 7, 8, 9, 10, 11

GERMANTON

MeadowHaven Bed and Breakfast

NC Highway 8, PO Box 222, 27019-0222
(910) 593-3996; (910) 593-3138 (FAX)

A contemporary retreat on 25 acres along Sauratown Mountain. Convenient to Winston-Salem, Hanging Rock and Pilot Mountain State Parks, and the Dan River. Heated indoor pool, hot tub, game room, guest pantry, fishing pond, fireplaces, TV/VCR, and movies. "Luv Tubs" and sauna available. Hiking, canoeing, horseback riding, golf, winery, art gallery, fresco, and

year; 6 Pets welcome; 7 Children welcome; 8 Tennis nearby; 9 Swimming nearby; 10 Golf nearby; 11 Skiing nearby; 12 May be booked through travel agent

dining nearby. Plan a "Lovebirds' Retreat" to MeadowHaven!

Hosts: Sam and Darlene Fain
Rooms: 3 + 1 luxury cabin (PB) $60-125
Full Breakfast
Credit Cards: A, B, C
Notes: 2, 5, 8, 9, 10, 12

HAZELWOOD

Belle Meade Inn

804 Balsam Rdl, 28738
(704) 456-3234

Nestled in the mountains is this craftsman-style home built in 1908. The Inn features four bedrooms, each with private bath. Chestnut woodwork in the formal rooms and a large fieldstone fireplace works with antique and traditional furnishings to create an interesting and eye appealing blend. Golf, hiking, rafting, and the Biltmore House nearby. No smoking inside.

Hosts: Gloria and Al DiNofa
Rooms: 4 (PB) $55-60
Full Breakfast
Credit Cards: A, B, D
Notes: 2, 5, 7 (over 6), 8, 10, 11

HENDERSONVILLE

Claddagh Inn at Hendersonville

755 North Main Street, 28792
(704) 697-7778; (800) 225-4700 reservations

The Claddagh Inn at Hendersonville is a recently renovated, meticulously clean bed and breakfast that is eclectically furnished with antiques and a variety of collectibles. The inn is located two blocks from the main shopping promenade of beautiful, historic downtown Hendersonville. The friendly, homelike atmosphere is complemented by a safe and secure feeling guests experience while at this lovely inn. The Claddaugh Inn is listed on the National Register of Historic Places.

Hosts: Vicki and Dennis Pacilio
Rooms: 15 (PB) $69-99
Full Breakfast
Credit Cards: A, B, C, D, E
Notes: 2, 5, 7, 8, 9, 10, 12

Mountain Home B&B

10 Courtland Blvd., P.O. Box 234, Mountain Home, 28758
(704) 697-9090; (800) 397-0066

Between Asheville and Hendersonville, near airport. Antiques and Oriental-style rugs grace this English-style home. Large Tennessee pink marble porch and rocking chairs to relax the day or night away. Cable TV and telephones in all rooms. Guest kitchen and laundry. Some rooms with private entrance. Full candlelight breakfast. Convenient to Biltmore Estate (on their preferred lodging list), Chimney, Pisgah National Forest, Carl Sandburg Home, and much more. Wheelchair-accessible ramp to front and one room.

Hosts: Bob and Donna Marriott
Rooms: 7 (5PB; 2SB) $70-95
Full Breakfast
Credit Cards: A, B, C, D
Notes: 2, 5, 7, 8, 10, 11, 12

The Waverly Inn

783 N. Main St., 28792
(800) 537-8195 (reservations); (704) 693-9193 (guest calls); (704) 692-1010 (FAX)

Listed on the National Register, this is the oldest inn in Hendersonville. Recently

---

renovated, there is something for everyone including: claw foot tubs, king and queen canopy beds, a suite, telephones, rocking chairs, sitting rooms, and all rooms have private baths. Enjoy our complimentary soft drinks and fresh baked goods. Walk to exceptional restaurants, antique stores, shopping. Biltmore Estate, Blue Ridge Parkway, Connemara nearby. Full country breakfast included in rates. Rated as one of 1993s top 10 bed and breakfasts in the USA by *INNovations*.

Hosts: John and Diane Shiery, Darla Olmstead
Rooms: 15 (PB) $90-180
Full Breakfast
Credit Cards: A, B, C, D
Notes: 2, 5, 7, 8, 9, 10, 12

HERTFORD

Gingerbread Inn & Bakery

103 S. Church St., 27944
(919) 426-5809

This beautifully restored turn-of-the-century Victorian home is on the local historic tour and boasts a wraparound porch with paired columns. The comfortably furnished central air-conditioned rooms with cable TV are spacious with single, queen, or king size beds and plush carpeting. The aroma of freshly baked gingerbreads is someting you can't miss during your stay. When you enjoy your delicious full breakfast your hostess even offers a souvenir cookie for the ride home.

Hosts: Jenny and Hans Harnisch
Rooms: 3 (PB) $45 + tax
Full Breakfast
Credit Cards: A, B
Notes: 2, 5, 7 (over age 5), 10, 12

HIGHLANDS

Long House B&B

Highway 64 East, PO Box 2078, 28741
(704) 526-4394; (800) 833-0020

Long House B&B offers a comfortable retreat in the scenic mountains of western North Carolina. Guests enjoy the beauty and charm of the quaint town and scenic wonders of the Nentahala National Forest. This rustic mountain B&B offers all the comforts with country charm and warm hospitality. A hearty breakfast is served family-style and is one of the many highlights of everyone's visit!

Hosts: Lynn and Valerie Long
Rooms: 4 (PB) $55-85
Very Full Breakfast
Credit Cards: A, B
Notes: 2, 7, 8, 9, 10, 11

KILL DEVIL HILL

Cherokee Inn Bed and Breakfast

500 N. Virginia Dare Trail, 27948
(919) 441-6127; (800) 554-2764; (919) 441-1072 (FAX)

Our beach house, located at Nags Head Beach on the outer banks of North Carolina, is 600 feet from the ocean. Fine food, history, sports, and adventure galore. We welcome you for a restful, active, or romantic getaway. Enjoy the cypress walls, white ruffled curtains, and wraparound porch.

Hosts: Bob and Kaye Combs
Rooms: 6 (PB) $60-90
Continental Breakfast
Credit Cards: A, B, C
Notes: 2, 8, 9, 10, 12

---

year; 6 Pets welcome; 7 Children welcome; 8 Tennis nearby; 9 Swimming nearby; 10 Golf nearby; 11 Skiing nearby; 12 May be booked through travel agent

LAKE JUNALUSKA

Providence Lodge

207 Atkins Loop, 28745
(704) 456-6486, (704) 452-9588

Providence Lodge is located on the assembly grounds of the United Methodist Church and near the Great Smoky Mountain National Park, Biltmore Estate, and the Cherokee Indian Reservation. The lodge is old, rustic, clean, and comfortable. Meals are especially good—bountiful, delicious food served family style in our large dining room.

Hosts: Ben and Wilma Cato
Rooms: 16 (10PB; 6SB) $45-80
Full Breakfast
Credit Cards: None
Closed September 1-June 1
Notes: 2, 4, 7, 8, 9, 10

Sunset Inn

300 North Lakeshore Drive, 28745
(704) 456-6114; (800) 733-6114

A beautiful mountain inn with large porches, comfortable rooms, and a location that lends itself to sightseeing, area attractions, or rest. We take pride in maintaining our reputation for excellent food, and we try to make our guests feel pampered. Located on the assembly grounds of the United Methodist Church which schedules daily programs in summer.

Hosts: Arthur O'Neil and Melissa Sexton-O'Neil
Rooms: 14 (12 PB; 2 SB) $80
Full Breakfast and Dinner
Credit Cards: None
Notes: 2, 4, 7, 8, 9, 10, 11

Tranquil House Inn

MADISON

The Boxley Bed and Breakfast Inn

117 E. Hunter St., 27025
(800) 429-3516

The Greek, Federal-style plantation home, built in 1825, is located in the historic district of Madison. Boxwoods adorn the long front walk and the gardens in the rear. The porch connecting the main house to the dining room and kitchen is wonderful to sit and relax and enjoy the peacefulness and serenity of the 19th century setting. JoAnn and Monte want you to make yourself at home.

Hosts: JoAnn and Monte McIntosh
Rooms: 4 (PB) $60 + tax
Full Breakfast
Credit Cards: A, B
Notes: 2, 5, 8, 10

MANTEO

Tranquil House Inn

P.O. Box 2045, 27954
(800) 458-7069; (919) 473-1526 (FAX)

Located in a charming waterfront village only minutes from the fabled Outer Banks beaches, you are a million miles from the rat race. Have your complimentary conti-

---

NOTES: Credit cards accepted: A Master Card; B Visa; C American Express; D Discover Card; E Diners Club; F Other; 2 Personal checks accepted; 3 Lunch available; 4 Dinner available; 5 Open all

nental breakfast and coffee or evening wine on our breezy deck, or relax there after a day of touring the area's historic sites—The Lost Colony Outdoor Drama, Elizabethan Gardens, and *Elizabeth II* sailing Vessel. Enjoy dinner at our restaurant, 1587, where you will experience the ultimate in culinary vision and gracious hospitality. Complimentary bikes. Canoeing and kayaking available nearby.

Hosts: Don and Lauri Just
Rooms: 25 (PB) $79-159
Continental Breakfast
Credit Cards: A, B, C, D
Notes: 2 (advance deposits), 4, 5, 7, 8, 9, 10, 12

MARSHALL

Marshall House Bed and Breakfast

5 Hill Street, P.O. Box 865, 28753
(704) 649-9205; (800) 562-9258; (704) 649-2999 (FAX)

Built in 1903, the inn overlooks the peaceful town of Marshall and the waters of the French Broad River. This country inn listed on the National Historic Register is decorated with fancy chandeliers, antiques, and pictures. Four fireplaces, formal dining room, parlor, and upstairs TV/reading room. Storytelling about the house, the town, the people, and the history. Loving house pets, the toot of a choo-choo train, and good service make your visit a unique experience.

Hosts: Ruth and Jim Boylan
Rooms: 9 (2PB; 2SB) $38.50-70
Continental Plus Breakfast
Credit Cards: A, B, C, D, E
Notes: 3, 4, 5, 6, 7, 9, 10, 11, 12

MOORESVILLE

Spring Run B&B

24 Spring Run, 28115
(704) 664-6686

Enjoy an award-winning, three-course, gourmet breakfast at this bed and breakfast located on Lake Norman which hosts many fine lakeside eateries. Each guest room has a private bath, cable TV, and free movie channels. Amenities include exercise room with game table, gathering room with fireplace and jukebox, paddle boat, lake swimming, boat hook-up at pier, and fishing. Enjoy tennis and golf at the golf course across the street. We are 25 minutes north of Charlotte and 15 miles south of Statesville. Three-diamond rating from AAA. Perfect score of 100 for over three years from the B.O.H.

Hostess: Mary Farley
Rooms: 2 (PB) $89
Full Gourmet Breakfast
Credit Cards: A, B
Notes: 2, 5, 8, 9, 10, 12

NAGS HEAD

First Colony Inn ®

6720 South Virginia Dare Trail, 27959
(919) 441-2343; (800) 368-9390 reservations;
(919) 441-5340 (FAX)

Enjoy Southern hospitality in our completely renovated historic inn on the National Register with a boardwalk directly to our private ocean beach. We are the only historic bed and breakfast inn on North Carolina's Outer Banks. The Wright Brothers Memorial, lighthouses, Fort Raleigh (site of the first English colony in the

year; 6 Pets welcome; 7 Children welcome; 8 Tennis nearby; 9 Swimming nearby; 10 Golf nearby; 11 Skiing nearby; 12 May be booked through travel agent

New World) are nearby, or just rock on our two stories of wraparound verandas.

Hosts: The Lawrences
Rooms: 26 (PB) $75 winter - $225 summer
Continental Plus Buffet Breakfast
Credit Cards: A, B, D
Notes: 2 (30 days in advance), 5, 7, 8, 9 (on premises), 10, 12

NEW BERN

The Aerie

509 Pollock Street, 28562
(919) 636-5553; (800) 849-5553

Just one block from the Tryon Palace in the heart of the historic district, the Aerie offers the closest accommodations to all of New Bern's historic attractions. The Victorian inn is furnished with antiques and reproductions, yet each of the seven individually decorated guest rooms has a modern private bathroom, telephone, and color television. Complimentary beverages are offered throughout your stay, and generous breakfasts await you each morning in the dining room.

Hosts: Howard and Dee Smith
Rooms: 7 (PB) $79-89
Full Breakfast
Credit Cards: A, B, C
Notes: 2, 5, 8, 10, 12

Harmony House Inn

215 Pollock Street, 28560
(919) 636-3810; (800) 636-3113

Enjoy comfortable elegance in an unusually spacious Greek Revival inn built circa 1850 with final additions circa 1900. Guests enjoy a parlor, front porch with rocking chairs and swings, antiques and reproduc-

tions, plus a full breakfast in the dining room. All rooms have fully private, modern bathrooms. Located in the historic district near Tryon Palace, shops, and restaurants. No smoking!

Hosts: Ed and Sooki Kirkpatrick
Rooms: 9 (PB) $85
Full Breakfast
Credit Cards: A, B, C, D
Notes: 2, 5, 7, 8, 10, 12

The King's Arms Colonial Inn

212 Pollock St., 28260
(919) 638-4409; (800) 872-9306

Innkeepers Richard and Pat Gulley uphold the Southern hospitality with spacious rooms, private baths, comfortable decor, and afternoon treats. Enjoy breakfast of coffee, juice, home-baked breads, muffins, ham, biscuits, and fresh fruits served to your room with the morning paper. The King's Arms is located within walking distance of all major attractions in New Bern. Carriage rides available on weekends.

Hosts: Richard and Patricia Gulley
Rooms: 9 (PB) $85
Continental Plus Breakfast
Credit Cards: A, B, C
Notes: 2, 5, 7, 8, 9, 10, 12

ORIENTAL

The Tar Heel Inn

205 Church Street, P. O. Box 176, 28571
(919) 249-1078

The Tar Heel Inn is over 100 years old and has been restored to capture the atmosphere of an English country inn. Guest rooms have four-poster or canopy king and queen beds. Patios and bicycles are for guest use. Five churches are within walking distance. Tennis, fishing, and golf are nearby. This quiet fishing village is known as the sailing capital of the Carolinas. Sailing cruises can be arranged, and there are great restaurants. Smoking on porch and patios only. Three-diamond AAA rating.

Hosts: Shawna and Robert Hyde
Rooms: 8 (PB) $65-85
Full Breakfast
Credit Cards: A, B
Notes: 2, 7 (by arrangement), 8, 9, 10, 12

ROBBINSVILLE

Snowbird Mountain Lodge
275 Santeetlah Road, 28771
(704) 479-3433

We are a 21-room lodge on 97 acres of land in western North Carolina. It is built of chestnut logs and native stone, designed to harmonize with its mountain setting. From its spacious flagstone terrace you have a magnificent, everchanging, panoramic view of the Snowbird Mountain range. Canoe rental, hiking, horseback riding, and white water rafting nearby. Three meals included in the rate. Lunches packed. Three miles from Joyce Kilmer Virgin Forest.

Hosts: Bob and Connie Rhudy
Rooms: 21 (PB) $119-135 (FAP)
Full Breakfast (lunch and dinner included)
Credit Cards: A, B
Notes: 2, 3, 4, 9

SPARTA

Turby-Villa
East Whitehead Street, Star Route 1, Box 48, 28675
(910) 372-8490

At an altitude of 3,000 feet, this contemporary two-story home is the centerpiece of a 20-acre farm located two miles from town. The house is surrounded by an acre of trees and manicured lawn with a lovely view of the Blue Ridge Mountains. Breakfast is served either on the enclosed porch with white wicker furnishings or in the more formal dining room with Early American furnishings. Mrs. Mimi Turbiville takes justifiable pride in her attractive, well-maintained bed and breakfast.

Hostess: Maybelline "Mimi" Turbiville
Rooms: 3 (PB) $35 (single) -50 + tax
Full Breakfast
Credit Cards: None
Notes: 2, 5, 7, 8, 10

Aunt Mae's B&B

STATESVILLE

Aunt Mae's B&B
532 East Broad Street, 28677
(704) 873-9525

Aunt Mae's century-old home, filled with

---

year; 6 Pets welcome; 7 Children welcome; 8 Tennis nearby; 9 Swimming nearby; 10 Golf nearby; 11 Skiing nearby; 12 May be booked through travel agent

nostalgia, located just one mile off I-40/I-77 is convenient for the traveler or for an extended stay. Stroll to quaint shops and fine restaurants, retreat to our lower lawn and the serenity of nature in action, and browse through 90 years of collections. Special amenities for special occasions. Welcome to Aunt Mae's!

Hostess: Sue Rowland
Rooms: 3 (PB) $60
Full Breakfast
Credit Cards: A, B
Notes: 2, 5, 8, 9, 10, 12

Cedar Hill Farm B&B

778 Elmwood Rd, 28677
(704) 873-4332; (800) 484-8457, Ext. 1254

An 1840 farmhouse and private cottage on a 32-acre sheep farm in the rolling hills of North Carolina. Antique furnishings, air conditioning, cable TV, and phones in rooms. After your full country breakfast, swim, play badminton, or relax in a porch rocker or hammock. For a busier day, visit two lovely towns with historic districts, Old Salem, or two larger cities in a 45-mile radius. Convenient to restaurants, shopping, and three interstate highways.

Hosts: Brenda and Jim Vernon
Rooms: 2 (PB) $60-75
Full Breakfast
Credit Cards: A, B
Notes: 2, 5, 6 (limited), 7, 9, 10, 12

Madelyn's B&B

514 Carroll Street, 28677
(704) 872-3973; (704) 871-0713 (FAX)

Relax on one of the most peaceful streets in Statesville, the Crossroads of the Carolinas. When you arrive, fresh fruit, candy, and a plate of homemade cookies await.

Take a short walk down tree-lined streets, and shop and eat in historic downtown Statesville. Truly a charming home where John and Madelyn will greet you with a smile. A full gourmet breakfast is served.

Hosts: John and Madelyn Hill
Rooms: 3 (PB) $55-65
Full Gourmet Breakfast
Credit Cards: A, B
Notes: 2, 5, 8, 9, 10, 12

TRYON

Fox Trot Inn

P. O. Box 1561, 800 Lynn Rd. (Rt. #108), 28782
(704) 859-9706

This lovingly restored residence, circa 1915, is situated on six wooded acres within the city limits. It is convenient to everything, yet secluded with a quietly elegant atmosphere. Full gourmet breakfast, afternoon refreshments, heated swimming pool, fully furnished guest house with two bedrooms, kitchen, living room, deck with mountain views. Two guest rooms have sitting rooms.

Hosts: Betty Daugherty and Mimi Colby
Rooms: 4 (PB) $60-110
Guest House: $450 weekly
Full Breakfast
Credit Cards: None
Notes: 2, 7 (in guest house), 8, 9, 10

WARSAW

The Vintage Inn

748 NC 24 and 50, 28398
(910) 296-1831

The Squire's Vintage Inn is located in the heart of Duplin County, as is its companion

---

NOTES: Credit cards accepted: A Master Card; B Visa; C American Express; D Discover Card; E Diners Club; F Other; 2 Personal checks accepted; 3 Lunch available; 4 Dinner available; 5 Open all

restaurant, The Country Squire, noted for its delicious cuisine and good taste. The rural setting adds to the privacy, intimacy, and relaxation for an overall feeling of "getting away from it all." Located near historic Kenansville.

Rooms: 12 (PB) $56 + tax
Continental Breakfast
Credit Cards: A, B, C, E
Notes: 2, 3, 4, 5, 7, 10

Palmer House Bed and Breakfast

WAYNESVILLE

Palmer House Bed and Breakfast

108 Pigeon Street, 28786
(704) 456-7521

Built in the 1880s, the Palmer House is the last of Waynesville's once numerous 19th-century hotels. Located less than one block from Main Street, the Palmer House is also near the Blue Ridge Parkway, the Great Smoky Mountains, Cherokee, and Biltmore Estate. Guests are entitled to a 10% discount off any purchase at the Palmer House Bookshop on Main Street.

Hosts: Jeff Minick and Kris Gillet
Rooms: 7 (PB) $55-65
Full Breakfast
Credit Cards: A, B, C, D
Notes: 2, 5, 7, 10, 12

WEAVERVILLE

Dry Ridge Inn

26 Brown Street, 28787
(800) 839-3899

This casually elegant bed and breakfast is quietly removed 10 minutes north of Asheville's many attractions. Country-style antiques and contemporary art enhance this unique 1800s village farmhouse. A full breakfast is served with individual seating. Relax in our outdoor spa or with quality, spiritual reading after enjoying a day of mountain adventure.

Hosts: Paul and Mary Lou Gibson
Rooms: 7 (PB) $65-80
Full Breakfast
Credit Cards: A, B, C, D
Notes: 2, 5, 7, 10, 11, 12

Weaverville Feather Bed and Breakfast

3 Perrion Ave., 28787
(800) 789-7944; (704) 658-3905 (FAX)

Our "romantic Revival," mountaintop home was built at the turn of the century in a era when true comfort was the mark of excellence. Enjoy the awesome mountain view from every room. Majestic sunsets and fluffy featherbeds ensure the "ultimate"

year; 6 Pets welcome; 7 Children welcome; 8 Tennis nearby; 9 Swimming nearby; 10 Golf nearby; 11 Skiing nearby; 12 May be booked through travel agent

peaceful night's rest. Wake to crisp mountain air and a full mountian-size breakfast! Just seven miles north of Asheville and all its attractions.

Hostesses: Sharon Ballas and Shelley Burtt
Rooms: 5 (PB) $85-195
Full Breakfast
Credit Cards: A, B, C, D, E, F
Notes: 2, 5, 7, 10, 11, 12

Dry Ridge Inn

WILSON

Miss Betty's Bed and Breakfast Inn

600 West Nash Street, 27893-3045
(919) 243-4447; (800) 258-2058 reservations only

Selected as one of the **"best places to stay in the South,"** Miss Betty's is ideally located midway between Maine and Florida along the main North-South route, I-95. Comprised of three beautifully restored structures in the downtown historic section; the National Registered Davis-Whitehead-Harriss House (circa 1858) the adjacent Riley House (circa 1900), and Rosebud (circa 1942), the recapture of the elegance and style of days gone by, where quiet Victorian charm abounds in

an atmosphere of all modern-day conveniences. Guests can browse for antiques in the Inn or visit any of the numerous antique shops that have given Wilson the title "Antique Capital of North Carolina." A quiet eastern North Carolina town known for its famous barbecue. Wilson also has four beautiful golf courses and numerous tennis courts.

Hosts: Betty and Fred Spitz
Rooms: 10 including 3 king suits (PB) $60-75
Full Breakfast
Credit Cards: A, B, C, D, E
Notes: 2, 5, 8, 9, 10

WINSTON-SALEM

Lady Anne's Victorian Bed and Breakfast

612 Summit St., 27101
(919) 724-1074

Warm, Southern hospitality surrounds you in this 1890 Victorian home, listed on the National Register of Historic Places. An aura of romance touches each suite or room, all individually decorated with period antiques, treasures, and modern luxuries. Some rooms have two-person whirlpools, cable, HBO, stereo, telephone, coffee, refrigerator, private entrances, and balconies. An evening dessert and full breakfast are served. Lady Anne's is ideally located near downtown attractions, performances, restaurants, shops, and Old Salem Historic Village. Smoking only on the porch!

Hostess: Shelley Kirley
Rooms: 4 (PB) $55-150
Full Breakfast
Credit Cards: A, B, C
Notes: 5, 8, 9, 10, 12 (no commission)

NOTES: Credit cards accepted: A Master Card; B Visa; C American Express; D Discover Card; E Diners Club; F Other; 2 Personal checks accepted; 3 Lunch available; 4 Dinner available; 5 Open all

North Dakota

MCCLUSKY

Midstate Bed and Breakfast

Route 3, Box 28, 58463
(701) 363-2520 (voice and FAX)

In the center of North Dakota, this country home built in 1980 operates under the banner of "The beauty of the house is order, the blessing of the house is contentment, and the glory of the house is hospitality." The guest entrance opens the way to a complete and private lower level with your bedroom, bath, large TV lounge with fireplace, and kitchenette. Three upstairs bedrooms share a bath. Breakfast in your choice of locations: your room, formal dining room, the plant-filled atrium, or on the patio. Very easy to locate: mile marker 232 on ND200. In an area of great hunting of deer, waterfowl, and upland game. Our guests are allowed hunting privileges on over 4000 acres. Special rates and provisions for hunting parties. Air-conditioned. Children welcome.

Hosts: Allen and Grace Faul
Rooms: 4 (1PB; 3SB) $25-30
Full Breakfast
Credit Cards: None
Notes: 2, 3, 4, 5, 6, 7, 8, 9

REGENT

Prairie Vista

101 Rural Ave. SW, 58650
(701) 563-4542; (701) 563-4642 (FAX)

Ranch-style brick house is located on seven acres with many evergreens. There is an indoor, heated swimming pool with exercise equipment available. Not far from Theodore Roosevelt National Park and historic Medore.

Hostess: Marlys Prince
Rooms: 3 (SB) $50
Full Breakfast
Credit Cards: None
Notes: 2, 4, 5, 7 (over 7), 9, 10

NORTH DAKOTA

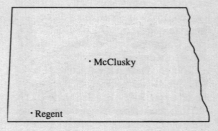

· McClusky

· Regent

---

year; 6 Pets welcome; 7 Children welcome; 8 Tennis nearby; 9 Swimming nearby; 10 Golf nearby; 11 Skiing nearby; 12 May be booked through travel agent

Ohio

ATHENS / ALBANY

The Albany House Bed and Breakfast

9 Clinton St., Albany, 45701
(614) 698-6311; (800) 600-4941

Enjoy today's comfort in yesterday's atmosphere at The Albany House. A 150-year-old house, renovated for a B&B in the village of Albany, seven miles west of Athens and Ohio University. Enjoy antiques, quilts, Oriental rugs, and family heirlooms, plus modern amenities of air-conditioning, indoor heated pool, fireplace, and guest living room with TV/VCR. Resident cat.

Hosts: Sarah and Ted Hutchins
Rooms: 4 (2PB; 2SB) $65-95
Continental Plus Breakfast
Credit Cards: None
Notes: 2, 5,, 7 (over age 8), 8, 9, 10 (indoor), 12

The Albany House Bed and Breakfast

BLUE ROCK

McNutt Farm II / Outdoorsman Lodge

6120 Cutler Lake Road, 43720
(614) 674-4555

Country bed and breakfast for overnight travelers in rustic quarters on a working farm in the quiet of the Blue Rock hill country. Only 11 miles from I-70, 35 miles from I-77, and 60 miles from I-71. B&B guests enjoy their own private kitchen, living room with fireplace or woodburner, private bath, porch with swing, and a beautiful view of forests and pastured livestock. Choose either the log cabin or the carriage house. For those who want more than an overnight stay, please ask about our log cabin by the week, or weekend. A cellar-house cabin is available, although it is somewhat primitive. Sleep to the sounds of the whippoorwills and tree frogs. Awake to the ever-crowing rooster, the wild turkey calling, and sometimes the bleating of a newborn fawn can be heard. We welcome you by reservation and deposit.

Hosts: Don R. and Patty L. McNutt
Rooms: 2 suites (PB) $40-100
Continental Breakfast
Credit Cards: A, B
Notes: 2 (deposit cash for balance), 5, 6 (prearranged), 7 (prearranged), 9, 10

NOTES: Credit cards accepted: A Master Card; B Visa; C American Express; D Discover Card; E Diners Club; F Other; 2 Personal checks accepted; 3 Lunch available; 4 Dinner available; 5 Open all

COLUMBUS

Harrison House Bed and Breakfast

313 West 5th Ave., 43201
(614) 421-2202; (800) 827-4203; (614) 421-2232
(FAX)

Built in 1890, this Queen Anne Victorian is listed on the National Register of Historic Placse. While retaining the gracious flavor of the past, it additionally affords all the comforts of the 20th century. Four newly-decorated bedrooms with private baths and gourmet breakfasts await you. Located within easy walking distance of The Ohio State University, or only minutes by car or public transportation from downtown Columbus and the airport.

Hosts: Maryanne and Dick Olson
Rooms: 4 (PB) $79-89
Full Breakfast
Credit Cards: A, B, C, D
Notes: 2, 5, 12

DAYTON

Candlewick Bed and Breakfast

4991 Bath Road, 45424
(513) 233-9297

This tranquil Dutch Colonial home sits atop a hill on five rolling acres. George, a retired engineer, and Nancy, a retired teacher, invite you to spend a peaceful night in comfortable rooms containing a blend of antiques and Colonial and country furnishings. Continental breakfast includes fresh fruit and juice, choice homemade pastries, and freshly brewed coffee.

Weather permitting, enjoy breakfast on the screened porch overlooking a large pond often visited by wild ducks and geese. Convenient to the Air Force Museum and major universities, Candlewick is a perfect retreat for either business or pleasure.

Hosts: Nancy and George Thompson
Rooms: 2 (SB) $50-55
Continental Plus Breakfast
Credit Cards: None
Notes: 2, 5

DEFIANCE

Sanctuary Ministeries

20277 Schick Rd., 43512
(419) 658-2069

Sanctuary Ministries is a quiet getaway in a Christian atmosphere. A two-story cedar-sided home with air-conditioning, a six-acre lake, a pond, and five acres of woods make for a peaceful getaway. This is a favorite fishing hole for many with row boat and canoe. Picnicking and bird-watching from porch swings add to the tranquil atmosphere.

Hosts: Emil and Barbara Schoch
Rooms: 2 (SB) $35-50
Full Breakfast
Credit Cards: None
Notes: 2, 5, 7, 9, 10

EAST FULTONHAM

Hill View Acres Bed and Breakfast

7320 Old Town Road, 43735
(614) 849-2728

Old World hospitality and comfort await

year; 6 Pets welcome; 7 Children welcome; 8 Tennis nearby; 9 Swimming nearby; 10 Golf nearby; 11 Skiing nearby; 12 May be booked through travel agent

each of our guests. During your visit, wander over the 21 acres, relax on the deck or patio, use the pool or year-round spa, or cuddle up by the fireplace in the cooler months. A hearty, country breakfast with homemade breads, jams, and jellies is served. We are located ten miles southwest of Zanesville.

Hosts: Jim and Dawn Graham
Rooms: 2 (SB) $37.30-42.60 (Prices include tax)
Full Breakfast weekends; Expanded Continental on weekdays.
Credit Cards: A, B
Notes: 2, 3, 4 (by arrangement), 5, 7, 9, 10

FRESNO

Valley View Inn

32327 SR 643 (2.5 miles from New Bedford),
43824
(216) 897-3232

The panoramic view from the back of the Inn is nothing short of breathtaking and is enhanced only by the changing seasons. Guests can enjoy the coziness of the fireplace in the living room or relax in the family room. A player piano, checkers, ping pong table, chess, or just comfortable Lazy Boy chair await you. No TVs to interrupt the serenity that abounds as one enjoys gazing at the surrounding fields and farms, woods and wildlife. The Inn is located between Roscoe Village and Sugarcreek and within minutes from all Amish shopping places. We're in the heart of Amish country.

Hosts: Dan and Nancy Lembke
Rooms: 10 (PB) $70-105
Full Breakfast (Continental on Sunday)
Credit Cards: A, B
Notes: 2, 5, 10

GAHANNA (COLUMBUS)

Shamrock Bed and Breakfast

5657 Sunbury Road, 43230-1147
(614) 337-9849

Located near interstate and airport. Handicapped accessible. All first floor. 1-1/4 acres of landscaped quiet: gardens, arbor, and patio. Inside find a fireplace, Flordia Room, firplace, large library and films, antiques, original art, and air-conditioning. Close to shopping, entertainment, Polaris Ampitheater, OSU, German Village, parks, gardens, and galleries.

Host: Tom McLaughlin
Rooms: 2 (PB) $45-55 (discount for 3 or more days)
Full Irish Breakfast with menu
Credit Cards: None
Notes: 2, 3, 5, 7, 8, 9, 10, 11

GENEVA-ON-THE-LAKE

Otto Court Bed and Breakfast

5653 Lake Road, 44041
(216) 466-8668

Otto Court Bed and Breakfast is a family-run business situated on two acres of lakefront property. There are eight cottages and a 19-room hotel overlooking Lake Erie. Besides a small game room, there is a horseshoe pit, a volleyball court, picnic tables, and beach with area for a bonfire. Within walking distance is the Geneva State Park and Marina. The Old Firehouse winery, Geneva-on-the-Lake Amusement Center, and the Jennie Munger

---

NOTES: Credit cards accepted: A Master Card; B Visa; C American Express; D Discover Card; E Diners Club; F Other; 2 Personal checks accepted; 3 Lunch available; 4 Dinner available; 5 Open all

Museum are nearby.

Hosts: Joyce Otto and Family
Rooms: 12 (8PB; 4SB) $46.50-50
Full Breakfast
Credit Cards: A, B, D, F
Notes: 2, 4, 5, 7, 9, 10, 11, 12

HAMILTON

Eaton Hill Bed and Breakfast

1951 Eaton Road, 45013
(513) 856-9552

Eaton Hill has a country feel although it is officially part of Hamilton. The white Colonial home is surrounded by fields, trees, and flower beds. Only ten miles from the Miami University campus and conveniently situated for parents, guests, and friends of the University and Butler County residents. Two double bedrooms with shared bath will provide you with a quiet night's rest amid antique furnishings. Children welcome ($10 each). A portable crib and highchair are available.

Hostess: Pauline K. Zink
Rooms: 2 (SB) $50 + 6% tax
Full Breakfast
Credit Cards: None
Notes: 2, 5, 6 (caged), 7, 8, 9, 10

LEXINGTON

The White Fence Inn

8842 Denman Road, 44904
(419) 884-2356; (800) 628-5793

The White Fence Inn is a beautiful country retreat situated among 73 acres. The

105-year-old farmhouse is decorated in a warm, country style. Common rooms include a large dining room with French doors, a parlor with fireplace and piano, a spacious sitting room with fireplace and TV. Breakfast is served indoors or outdoors. Guest rooms are decorated in individual themes—primitive, baskets and bottles, Victorian, Southwest, Amish, and country. One room has a fireplace and cathedral ceiling.

Hosts: Bill and Ellen Hiser
Rooms: 6 (4PB; 2SB) $51-95
Full Breakfast
Credit Cards: None
Notes: 2, 5, 6, 7, 8, 10, 11

The Bed and Breakfast at Willow Pond

MANSFIELD

The Bed and Breakfast at Willow Pond

3360 S. R. 545, 44903
(419) 522-4644 (voice or FAX); (800) 772-7809

This beautifully restored, three-story Federal-Adam-style farmhouse, built in 1866, overlooks the big valley of historic Weller Township, a stop on the underground railway to Canada. You'll find plenty to do here, thanks to attractions like Richland

---

year; 6 Pets welcome; 7 Children welcome; 8 Tennis nearby; 9 Swimming nearby; 10 Golf nearby; 11 Skiing nearby; 12 May be booked through travel agent

Carousel Park, Kingwood Center Gardens, Ashland University, Living Bible Museum, the mid-Ohio sports car course, and a flourishing Amish community. Willow Pond's rooms, furnished with antiques, include guest quarters, a formal parlor, a farm kitchen, a gathering room with its original cooking fireplace, and a screened porch. There is also a picnic house and pond with a duck in residence. Breakfasts feature homemade quick breads, fresh fruit, juice, cereal, and a hot entree.

Hosts: Bud and Marianna Henderson
Rooms: 4 (2PB; 2SB) $55-65
Full Breakfast
Credit Cards: None
Notes: 2, 5, 8, 9, 10, 11

MARION

Olde Towne Manor

245 St. James St., 43302
(614) 382-2402

Elegant stone home nestles on a beautiful acre of land on a quiet street in Marion's historic district. Enjoy a quiet setting in the gazebo or the soothing sauna, or relax reading one of the more than 1,000 books available in the library. A pool table is also available for your enjoyment. A leisurely stroll will take you to the home of President Warren G. Harding and the Harding Memorial. Awarded the 1990 Marion's Beautifications Most Attractive Building.

Hostess: Mary Louisa Rimbach
Rooms: 4 (PB) $55-65
Full Breakfast
Credit Cards: A, B, C
Notes: 2, 5, 8, 9, 10

MARTINS FERRY

Mulberry Inn Bed and Breakfast

53 North 4th Street, 43935
(614) 633-6058

Victorian frame home built in 1868 by Dr. Ong, the thirteen-room home was also used as his office. In 1911 Dr. Blackford bought the house and also used three rooms for his practice. The Probsts purchased the home in 1971. It became a bed and breakfast in 1987. The guest rooms are done in different periods. The Roosevelt Room (1930s) has a queen bed, Victorian, Country, and Lucinda Rooms have twin beds. All others have double beds. Guests have a beautiful parlor in which to relax and a private dining room. There is a wood-burning fireplace for cold winter nights in the parlor. Homemade quilts, up-down lights, pocket doors, antiques, 3 stairways. 5 minutes from Wheeling, WV, 15 minutes from Olgebay Park, famous for its Festival of Lights November thru February.

Hosts: Charles and Shirley Probst
Rooms: 4(2PB; 2SB) $45
Full Breakfast
Credit Cards: A, B, D
Notes: 2, 5, 7(over 5), 8, 9, 10, 11, 12

MILAN

Gastier Farm B&B

1902 Strecker Road, 44846
(419) 499-2985

The farm homestead has been in the family for over 100 years. Now the farmhouse is

---

NOTES: Credit cards accepted: A Master Card; B Visa; C American Express; D Discover Card; E Diners Club; F Other; 2 Personal checks accepted; 3 Lunch available; 4 Dinner available; 5 Open all

available for sharing with travelers. Located two miles west of the Ohio Turnpike exit 7 next to the Norfolk Southern Railroad between Toledo and Cleveland. No pets or smoking. Reservations required.

Hosts: Ted and Donna Gastier
Rooms: 3 (SB) $50
Continental Plus Breakfast
Credit Cards: A, B
Notes: 2, 5, 7, 8, 9, 10

Gastier Farm Bed and Breakfast

MILLERSBURG

Indiantree Farm Bed and Breakfast

5488 S.R. 515, 44654
(216) 893-2497

Peaceful lodging in guest house on picturesque hilltop farm in the heart of Amish country, a mile from Walnut Creek. Large front porch, farming with horses, hiking trails. Apartments, with kitchen and bath, for the price of a room. An oasis where time slows and the mood is conversation, not television.

Host: Larry Miller
Rooms: 3 (PB) $50-60
Continental Breakfast
Credit Cards: None
Notes: 2, 5, 11

OXFORD

The Duck Pond

6391 Morning Sun Rd., S.R. 732 N, 45056
(513) 523-8914

An 1863 farmhouse situated three miles north of Miami University and uptown Oxford, and two miles south of Hueston Woods State Park, which has an 18-hole golf course, nature trails, boating, swimming, and fishing. Antiquing is just 15 miles away. Come and enjoy the quaintness that only a bed and breakfast can offer. Be our guest and enjoy our famous Hawaiian French Toast. Reservations are required, so please call in advance. Cat in residence.

Hosts: Don and Toni Kohlstedt
Rooms: 4 (1PB; 3SB) $50-70 + $10 for extra person
Full Country Breakfast
Credit Cards: None
Notes: 2, 5, 7 (over 12), 8, 9, 10

PLAIN CITY

Yoder's Bed and Breakfast

8144 Cemetery Pike, 45064
(614) 873-4489

Located on a 107-acre farm northwest of Columbus. Big Darby Creek runs along the front yard. Excellent bird-watching and fishing in the creek. The house is air conditioned. Rooms have king- and queen-size beds. No smoking. We are within minutes of two Amish restaurants, gift shops, cheesehouse, chocolate house, Amish furniture store, bookstores, and antique shops. Only about 30 minutes

year; 6 Pets welcome; 7 Children welcome; 8 Tennis nearby; 9 Swimming nearby; 10 Golf nearby; 11 Skiing nearby; 12 May be booked through travel agent

from downtown Columbus.

Hosts: Loyd and Claribel Yoder
Rooms: 4 (1PB; 3SB) $55-65
Full Breakfast
Credit Cards: None
Notes: 2, 5, 9, 10

ST. CLAIRSVILLE

My Father's House

173 South Marietta St., 43950
(614) 695-5440

My Father's House Bed and Breakfast combines the old with the new in decor and hospitality. Antique and modern furnishings combine to create a quaint yet comfortable overnight travel experience. Guests enjoy air-conditioned queen-size bedrooms and private bathrooms. The living room features a romantic open fireplace, while the parlor affords guests the opportunity to relax and watch television. Located just one-half mile from I-70 at the S.R. 9 exit (#216) in St. Clairsville proper, our guests can enjoy a small town stay with the convenience of interstate travel. Fifteen minutes from Wheeling, West Virginia.

Hosts: Mark and Polly Loy
Rooms: 3 (PB) $50-55
Continental Plus Breakfast
Credit Cards: A, B
Notes: 2, 5, 7, 8, 9, 10

Mad River Railroad Bed and Breakfast

SANDUSKY

The 1890 Queen Anne Bed and Breakfast

714 Wayne Street, 44870
(419) 626-0391

Spacious accommodations with charm and elegance await guests at The 1890 Queen Anne B&B in downtown Sandusky. Built of native limestone, this 104-year-old Victorian home lends ambience and romance for guests. Three large air-conditioned rooms offer tranquil luxury for relaxation. Beauty abounds in the regal outdoors as viewed from a screened-in porch where continental plus breakfasts are enjoyed. Easy access abounds to beaches, Lake Erie Island boat trips, Cedar Point, shopping, and other recreational opportunities. Brochure available upon request.

Hosts: Bob and Joan Kromer
Rooms: 3 (2PB; 1SB) $70-80
Continental "Plus" Breakfast
Credit Cards: A, B, D
Notes: 2, 5, 8, 9, 10

TIFFIN

Mad River Railroad Bed and Breakfast

107 W. Perry Street, 44883
(419) 447-2222 or (419) 447-0665

Relax in the comfort of the Colonial Revival home built in the late 1890s. Three guest rooms are provided in this historically registered home, decorated with antiques and period furnishings. The house is situated beside the former site of the first railroad in the area which now has been

NOTES: Credit cards accepted: A Master Card; B Visa; C American Express; D Discover Card; E Diners Club; F Other; 2 Personal checks accepted; 3 Lunch available; 4 Dinner available; 5 Open all

transformed into a tree and flower adorned walk and bike path for your enjoyment. Cedar Point and Lake Erie attractions within one hour. Our home is open for your pleasure while you visit us.

Hosts: Bill and Nancy Cook
Rooms: 3 (2PB; 1SB) $55-65
Full Breakfast
Credit Cards: None
Notes: 2, 7

TIPP CITY

The Willow Tree Inn
1900 West State Route 571, 45371
(513) 667-2957

This restored, pre-Civil War (1830), Federal manor home has a pond and combination springhouse and smokehouse. The original 1830 barn is also on the premises. Four working fireplaces, porches on which to swing and relax, and TV and air conditioning in all rooms; all but one room are suites. Easily located off Exit 68W from N75, just minutes north of Dayton.

Hosts: Tom and Peggy Nordquist
Rooms: 4 (1PB; 3SB) $48-68
Full Breakfast
Credit Cards: A, B
Notes: 1, 7 (over 8), 8, 9, 10

TROY

Allen Villa Bed and Breakfast
434 S. Market Street, 45373
(513) 335-1181

Located 1.5 miles east of I-75 (exit 73) and 15 minutes north of Dayton Airport is this 1874 restored, true Victorian home.

Snack bar, central air-conditioning, in-room private bath, TV/VCR, telephone, and queen- and king-size beds. A pleasant walk to three fine, family restaurants in the historic district.

Hosts: Bob and June Smith
Rooms: 5+2 furnished kitchenettes (PB) $49-74
Full Breakfast
Credit Cards: A, B, C, D, F (travelers checks)
Notes: 2, 5, 8, 9, 10, 12 (no comm.)

URBANA

At Home in Urbana Bed and Breakfast
301 Scioto St., 43078
(800) 800-0970; (513) 652-4400 (FAX)

Restored 1842 home in historic district. Furnished in Victorian period pieces and family antiques. Two blocks away from downtown shops and restaurants. All rooms are air-conditoned and have private baths. Non-smoking guests only.

Hosts: Grant and Shirley Ingersoll
Rooms: 3 and 1 two-room suite (PB) $60-90
Full Breakfast
Credit Cards: A, B, C, D
Notes: 2, 5, 10, 11

WALNUT CREEK

Troyer's Country View Bed and Breakfast
P.O. Box 91, 4859 Olde Pump St., 44687
(216) 893-3284

In the heart of Amish Country this century year old home, newly remodeled into self-contained suites, each with private bath, country or Victorican blend decor, cable

TV (free Showtime and Disney channels), and air-conditioning. Price includes full breakfast stocked in your private kitchenette (with oak table and chairs in kitchen area). Couch or bentwood rockers in sitting area. Private deck entrances from beautiful viewing decks. Fenced animals to watch in summertime. New honeymoon and anniversary suite has heartshaped jacuzzi with waterfall spigot. This suite also has a microwave, plus all the above amenities. Comfortable Amishcrafted beds. AAA approved.

Hosts: Owen and Sue Troyer
Rooms: 4 (PB) $55-95
Full Self-Serve Breakfast
Credit Cards: A, B. D
Notes: 2(from Ohio), 5, 7(limited), 8, 9, 10

WAVERLY

Governor's Lodge

171 Gregg Road, 45690
(614) 947-2266

Governor's Lodge is a place like no other. Imagine a beautiful, shimmering lake and an iridescent sunset. A quiet calm in the friendly atmosphere of an eight-room bed and breakfast open all year and situated on a peninsula in Lake White. Every room has a magnificent view. An affiliate of Bristol Village Retirement Community, we offer a meeting room and group rates for gatherings using the whole lodge. Now approved by AAA.

Hosts: David and Jeannie James
Rooms: 8 + 1 cottage (PB) $44-68
Continental Plus Breakfast
Credit Cards: A, B
Notes: 2, 7, 9, 11

WOOSTER

Historic Overholt House Bed and Breakfast

1473 Beall Ave., 44691
(216) 263-6300; (800) 992-0643

Built in 1874, The Historic Overholt House, listed on the National Registry, is Stick Victorian elegance at its finest. Centrally located in Wooster adjacent to the College of Wooster Campus. Near Amish Country and the "Everything Rubbermaid" store. Homemade bread, cookies, and breakfast.

Hosts: Sandy Pohalski and Bobbie Walton
Rooms: 3 (PB) $60-70
Continental and Full Breakfast
Credit Cards: A, B, D
Notes: 2, 5, 8, 9, 10

Historic Overholt House Bed and Breakfast

NOTES: Credit cards accepted: A Master Card; B Visa; C American Express; D Discover Card; E Diners Club; F Other; 2 Personal checks accepted; 3 Lunch available; 4 Dinner available; 5 Open all

Oklahoma

ALINE

Heritage Manor
RR 3, Box 33, 73716
(405) 463-2563 or 463-2566

Heritage Manor is a country getaway on 80 acres that was settled in the 1893 Land Run in northwest Oklahoma. Two pre-statehood homes have been joined together and restored by innkeepers using Victorian theme. Beautiful sunrises, sunsets, and stargazing from rooftop deck and relaxing in the hot tub or reading a book from the 5000-volume library. Ostriches, donkeys, and Scotch Highland cattle roam a fenced area. Close to Salenite Crystal digging area and several other attractions.

Hosts: A.J. and Carolyn Rexroat
Rooms: 4 (3SB) $50+tax
Full Breakfast
Credit Cards: None
Notes: 2, 3 (by reservation), 4 (by reservation), 5, 6 (prearranged), 7, 9, 10 (30 miles)

EDMOND

The Arcadian Inn B&B
328 East First, 73034
(405) 348-6347; (800) 299-6347

With angels watching over you, you are ministered peace and relaxation. The Arcadian Inn is a step back in time to the era of Christian love, and hospitality, and family values. The historical home of Dr. Ruhl, the inn has five luxurious Victorian guest rooms with tubs, and fireplaces, canopy beds, and sunrooms. Sumptuous homemade breakfast served in the sunny dining room beneath cherub paintings. Perfect for romantic getaways, business travelers, or old-fashioned family gatherings. Jacuzzi and outdoor spa available.

Hostess: Martha and Gary Hall
Rooms: 5 (PB) $55-120
Full Breakfast
Credit Cards: A, B, C, D
Notes: 2, 4 (by reservation), 5, 8, 9, 10

The Arcadian Inn

year; 6 Pets welcome; 7 Children welcome; 8 Tennis nearby; 9 Swimming nearby; 10 Golf nearby; 11 Skiing nearby; 12 May be booked through travel agent

KEYES

Cattle Country Inn

HCR 1, Box 34, 73947
(405)543-6458

We are truly country located. If you like wide open spaces where you can see for miles and not be in hearing distance of any highway traffic, you are welcome to stay with us. Located in the panhandle between Guymon and Boise City, the Inn is a nice stopping place on the way to or from the Rockies. Come experience the hospitality and hearty cookin' served up by your host in ths beautiful, spacious, and very modern ranch-style home. Located 38 miles west of Guymon on Hwy. 64 then 4 miles south on dirt roads. Cimaron County, the last county west, has many points of interest, as well as plenty of good prairie dog and pheasant hunting.

Hosts: Lane and Karen Sparkman
Rooms: 6 (3SB) $45-65
Full Breakfast
Credit Cards: A, B, C
Notes: 2; 3, 4, 5, and 7 (all by reservation)

OKLAHOMA CITY

The Grandison Bed and Breakfast

1841 N.W. 15th, 73106
(405) 521-0011; (800) 240-INNS

This three-story country Victorian sits on a large double lot with beautifully landscaped gardens, trees taller than the house, and a gazebo. Built in 1912, the home has all the original brass and crystal chandeliers and stained glass windows. It is furnished with antiques from the turn-of-the-century throughout. There is a jacuzzi in the third-floor suite. Just 10 minutes from Myriad Gardens and Convention Center, State Fairgrounds, Remington Park Raceway, Oklahoma City Zoo, The National Cowboy Hall of Fame, and many wonderful restaurants and shopping facilities.

Hostess: Claudia Wright
Rooms: 5 (PB) $55-125
Full Breakfast
Credit Cards: A, B, C, D
Notes: 2, 3, 4, 5, 6 (by reservation), 7 (by reservation)

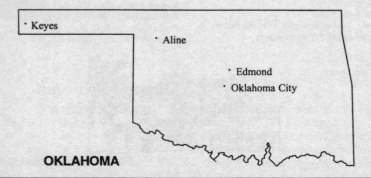

OKLAHOMA

NOTES: Credit cards accepted: A Master Card; B Visa; C American Express; D Discover Card; E Diners Club; F Other; 2 Personal checks accepted; 3 Lunch available; 4 Dinner available; 5 Open all

Oregon

ASHLAND

Cowslip's Belle B&B

159 N. Main St., 97520
(503) 488-2901; (800) 888-6819

Teddy bears and chocolate truffles, roses, antiques, cozy down comforters, and scrumptious breakfasts. Just three blocks to restaurants, shops, and theaters. Nestled in Ashland's historic district, this beautiful 1913 Craftsman bungalow and carriage house is featured in "Northwest Best Places," "The Best Places to Kiss in the Pacific Northwest," and "Weekends for Two in the Pacific Northwest—50 Romantic Getaways."

Hosts: Jon and Carmen Reinhardt
Rooms: 4 (PB) $75-115
Full Breakfast
Credit Cards: A, B
Notes: 2, 5, 8, 9, 10, 11, 12

The Redwing Bed and Breakfast

115 N. Main Street, 97520
(503) 482-1807

The Redwing, nestled in Ashland's charming historic district, is a 1911 craftsman-style home with its original lighting fixtures, beautiful wood, and comfortable decor. Each of our inviting guest rooms enjoys its

own distinctive intimacy, queen-size beds, and private bath. We are located one city block from the Shakespeare Festival, Lithia Park, restaurants, and gift shops. In addition, downhill and cross-country skiing, river rafting, and fishing are nearby. Full breakfasts are offered.

Hosts: Mike and Judi Cook
Rooms: 3 (PB) $70-95
Full Breakfast
Credit Cards: None
Notes: 2, 5, 10, 11

Columbia River Inn

ASTORIA

Columbia River Inn Bed and Breakfast

1681 Franklin Ave., 97103-3616
(503) 325-5044; (800) 953-5044

Columbia River Inn Bed and Breakfast is

---

year; 6 Pets welcome; 7 Children welcome; 8 Tennis nearby; 9 Swimming nearby; 10 Golf nearby; 11 Skiing nearby; 12 May be booked through travel agent

charming in every way. Built in 1870, this beautiful "Painted Lady" Victorian now has a gazebo for weddings and parties. Come see the unique gardens and "stairway to the stars." Many memories are discovered and the experience will last forever. My specialty is hospitality, "Home is where the heart is."

Hostess: Mrs. Karen N. Nelson
Rooms: 5 (PB) $70-85
Full Breakfast
Cerdit Cards: A, B
Notes: 2, 5, 7, 10

Grandview Bed and Breakfast

1574 Grand Ave., 97103
(503) 325-5555; (800) 488-3250

Antiques and white wicker furnishings grace this Victorian home, born in 1896. Ivy and alders grow profusely on west side, sheltering birds and birdhouses. Most rooms have bird cages for decoration. Some rooms overlook the Columbia River. Breakfast, served in the tower or bullet turret, may include smoked salmon, cream cheese, and bagels. Astoria was established in 1811. Fur trading, then salmon and logging gave this town its start.

Hostess: Charleen Maxwell
Rooms: 9 (6PB; 3SB) $39-92
Full Breakfast
Cerdit Cards: A, B, D
Notes: 5, 7 (over 6), 8, 9

Inn-Chanted Bed and Breakfast

707-8th St., 97103
(503) 325-5223

The historic Fulton House, built in 1883, is

beautifully decorated with silk brocade wallpaper, crystal chandeliers, and ornately painted medallions and columns. Guest rooms have magnificent views of the Columbia River, private baths, queen-size beds and TVs. Full gourmet breakfasts. Dolls and trains displayed. Within walking distance to historic buildings, town, and antique shops.

Hosts: Richard and Dixie Swart, owners.
Rooms: 3 (PB) $70-100
Full Breakfast
Cerdit Cards: A, B, C, D
Notes: 2, 5, 7, 8, 12

BROOKINES

Holmes Sea Cove

17350 Holmes Dr., 97415
(503) 469-3025

1965 coastal-style cedar home. Each of the three guest rooms boast a spectacular ocean view, private entrance, bath, refrigerator, and color TV. Walk to winding trail to gazebo, private park, or beach. Continental plus breakfast served in rooms. Open all year.

Hosts: Jack and Lorene Holmes
Rooms: 3 (PB) $80-95
Continental Plus Breakfast
Cerdit Cards: A, B
Notes: 2, 5, 7 (limited), 8, 9, 12

Holmes Sea Cove

CANNON BEACH

Tern Inn Bed and Breakfast

3663 South Hemlock, 97110
(503) 436-1528

A personal touch in an impersonal world. Home-baked goods and homemade jams and jellies are part of the complete, hot breakfast or brunch cooked from scratch and served in your room anytime between 8:30 and 11.30AM. We are located on the north coast of Oregon, in the arts resort of Cannon Beach. We offer light goose-down quilts for year-round comfort, private bath, and color TV. Choose between a fireplace or a sun room to warm your heart. Both rooms have an ocean view.

Hosts: Gunter-Chris and Enken Friedrichsen
Rooms: 2 (PB) $85-105
Full Breakfast
Cerdit Cards: None
Notes: 8, 10

CLOVERDALE

Sandlake Country Inn

8505 Galloway Road, 97112
(503) 965-6745

Sshhh. . . we're a secret hideaway on the awesome Oregon Coast, a private, peaceful place for making marriage memories. This 1894 shipwreck-timbered farmhouse on the Oregon Historic Registry is tucked into a bower of old roses. Hummingbirds, Mozart, cookies at midnight, marble fireplaces, whirlpools for two, bikes, honeymoon cottage, breakfast "en suite," vintage movies, "green" rooms, no smoking,

wheelchair accessible, closed-caption TV.

Hosts: Margo and Charles Underwood
Rooms: 4 (PB) $65-100
Full Breakfast
Credit Cards: A, B, D
Notes: 2, 3, 4, 5, 12

Sandlake Country Inn

CORVALLIS

Abed and Breakfast at Sparks' Hearth

2515 SW 45th Street, 97333
(503) 757-7321

Our country home of 22 years is on the Corvallis Country Club golf course in the midst of peace, quiet, and serenity. Three miles to downtown and OSU. Guest amenities include outdoor spa, luxurious robes, wraparound porch, large decks, spacious living room, and warm hospitality. King beds in king-size rooms. Sumptuous breakfasts feature a fruit compote, hot entree, and homemade pie. Coffee and soft drinks anytime—help yourself!

Hosts: Neoma and Herb Sparks
Rooms: 4 (SB) $60-80
Full Breakfast
Credit Cards: A, B, C, D
Notes: 2, 5, 7 (over 8), 8, 9, 10

---

year; 6 Pets welcome; 7 Children welcome; 8 Tennis nearby; 9 Swimming nearby; 10 Golf nearby; 11 Skiing nearby; 12 May be booked through travel agent

ELMIRA

McGillivray's Log Home Bed and Breakfast

88680 Evers Road, 97437
(503) 935-3564

Fourteen miles west of Eugene, on the way to the coast, you will find the best of yesterday and the comforts of today. King beds, air-conditioning, and quiet. Old-fashioned breakfasts are usually prepared on an antique, wood-burning cookstove. This built-from-scratch 1982 log home is near Fern Ridge Lake.

Hostess: Evelyn R. McGillivray
Rooms: 2 (PB) $50-70
Full Breakfast
Credit Cards: A, B
Notes: 2, 5

EUGENE

Camille's Bed and Breakfast

3277 Onyx Place, 97405
(503) 344-9576; (503) 484-3138 (FAX)

Camille's Bed and Breakfast is a 60s contemporary home in a quiet, woodsy neighborhood furnished with American country antiques. Rooms offer wonderfully comfortable queen beds, work space, and reading lamps. Guest sitting room with phone and TV. Fax available. Ample breakfast. Laundry facilities. Located just south of the University of Oregon, downtown is minutes away. Bus lines, bike paths, and park with major jogging trail nearby. Excellent restaurant within walking distance. One hour drive to Oregon coast.

Hosts: Bill and Camille Kievith
Rooms: 2 (1PB; 2SB) $55-70
Full Breakfast
Credit Cards: None
Notes: 2, 5, 8, 9, 10

The Campbell House, A City Inn

252 Pearl, 97401
(503) 343-1119; (800) 264-2519; (503) 343-2258 (FAX)

Splendor and romance in the tradition of a fine European Hotel. Each of the elegant rooms feature private bath, TV/VCR, telephone, and robes. Selected rooms feature four-poster bed, fireplace, jetted or clawfoot tub. Take pleasure from the Old World ambiance of the parlor and library with a fine selection of books and videos to choose from. Walking distance to restaurants, theaters, museums, and shops. Two blocks from nine miles of riverside bike paths and jogging trails.

Hostesses: Myra Plant and Sonja Cruthers
Rooms: 14 (PB) $80-225
Full Breakfast
Credit Cards: A, B, C
Notes: 5, 7, 10, 12

FOSSIL

Bowerman's Lightning B Ranch

Clarno Route, 97830
(503) 489-3367

An underground bunkhouse built into the mountainside combines pioneer styling with modern construction, including a fully-

---

NOTES: Credit cards accepted: A Master Card; B Visa; C American Express; D Discover Card; E Diners Club; F Other; 2 Personal checks accepted; 3 Lunch available; 4 Dinner available; 5 Open all

equipped kitchen. Midway between Antelope and Fossil and four miles south of Hwy. 218, you'll find the perfect spot to relax in peaceful solitude. You'll share our ranch and four miles of riverfront with us, our horses, some resident eagles, and a few deer, elk, antelopes, and coyotes. Hiking, horseback riding, fishing, self-guided fossil bed tours, and maybe a little ranch work are available.

Hosts: Jon and Candy Bowerman
Rooms: 2 (PB) $50
Full Breakfast
Credit Cards: None
Notes: 2, 3 + 5 (by prior arrangement), 5, 6 (including horses), 7

GRANTS PASS

Home Farm Bed and Breakfast

157 Savage Creek Rd., 97527
(503) 582-0980

Our 1944 farmhouse bed and breakfast with comfy, country decor invites you to make your stay with us—dozing in our country air, feasting on our hearty breakfasts, playing checkers, pitching horseshoes! There are two lovely guest rooms in the main house and two guest suites in the "bunkhouse"—one with a western motif (wheelchair accessible) and one with an Americana flavor. All rooms are furnished with queen or king beds, and all have private baths. River sports are available nearby.

Hosts: Bill and Cheri Murray
Rooms: 4 (PB) $50-70
Full Breakfast
Credit Cards: None
Notes: 2, 5, 7 (limited), 9, 10

Martha's Bed and Breakfast Inn

764 Northwest Fourth Street, 97526
(503) 476-4330; (800) 261-0167

Martha's Inn is "a home away from home." A Victorian farmhouse with a large, old-fashioned front porch, furnished with wicker antiques. Located in the historic district. Martha's Inn is five minutes from I-5. Ideal for overnight travelers from Seattle to San Francisco. Close to restaurants. One and one-half hours to Crater Lake or the Oregon coast. Private baths, queen beds, herb garden and English cutting garden. Healthy breakfasts are featured. TV, air conditioning. In the heart of the Rogue River Valley.

Hosts: Evelyn and Glenn Hawkins
Rooms: 3 (PB) $65-85
Full Breakfast
Credit Cards: A, B, D
Notes: 2, 5, 7, 10, 12

Martha's Bed and Breakfast

---

year; 6 Pets welcome; 7 Children welcome; 8 Tennis nearby; 9 Swimming nearby; 10 Golf nearby; 11 Skiing nearby; 12 May be booked through travel agent

HEREFORD

Fort Reading Bed and Breakfast

HCR 86, Box 140, 97837
(503) 446-3478 (voice or FAX)

A working cattle ranch located 40 miles southwest of Baker City, in the Burnt River Valley where history abounds. While you're with us, enjoy a stroll around the ranch, the comfort of your own two-bedroom cottage, and a ranch-style breakfast served in the ranchhouse breakfast room. Fishing and hunting in nearby streams and forests are just a few activities that can be enjoyed. No smoking.

Hosts: Daryl and Barbara Hawes
Rooms: 2 (SB) $40-75
Full Breakfast
Credit Cards: None
Notes: 2, 3, 4 (by arrangement), 6, 7

LAGRANDE

Stang Manor Inn

1612 Walnut, 97850
(503) 963-2400 (Voice and FAX)

The Inn is an impressive 1922 lumber baron's Georgian Colonial mansion. The spacious, 10,000-square-foot structure features extraordinary architectural detail, including a basement ballroom and stage. The Manor sits on spacious grounds with a rose garden and magnificent trees. Guest rooms have queen beds and private baths. One room has balcony overlooking the rose garden—the suite features a sitting room with fireplace. Full breakfast in the formal dining room sparkles with silver, crystal, and candles.

Hosts: Marjorie and Pat McClure
Rooms: 4 (PB) $70-90 (includes tax)
Full Breakfast
Credit Cards: A, B
Notes: 2, 5, 10, 11, 12

LINCOLN CITY

Brey House "OCEAN VIEW" Bed and Breakfast

3725 N.W. Keel, 97367
(503) 994-7123

The ocean awaits you just across the street. Enjoy whalewatching, stormwatching, or just beach-combing. We are conveniently located a short walking distance away from local restaurants and retail shops. Four beautiful rooms to choose from, all private baths, queen beds. Flannel sheets and electric blankets in all rooms. Enjoy Milt and Shirley's talked-about breakfast. Three-story, Cape Cod-style house.

Hosts: Milt and Shirley Brey
Rooms: 4 (PB) $65-85
Full Breakfast
Credit Cards: A, B, D
Notes: 2, 5, 9, 10, 12

MOUNT HOOD AREA

Falcon's Crest Inn

87287 Government Camp Loop Highway, P.O. Box 185, **Government Camp**, 97028
(503) 272-3403; (800) 624-7384; (503) 272-3454 (FAX)

Falcon's Crest Inn is a beautiful mountain

NOTES: Credit cards accepted: A Master Card; B Visa; C American Express; D Discover Card; E Diners Club; F Other; 2 Personal checks accepted; 3 Lunch available; 4 Dinner available; 5 Open all

lodge/chalet-style house, architecturally designed to fit into the quiet natural forest and majestic setting of the Cascades. Conveniently located at the intersection of Highway 26 and The Government Camp Loop Highway, it is within walking distance to Ski Bowl, a year-round playground featuring downhill skiing in the winter and the Alpine Slide in the summer! The Inn has five suites, all with private baths. Each guest room is individually decorated with interesting and unique collectibles and views of mountains and forest. Telephones are available for guest use in each suite. Smoking restricted.

Hosts: BJ and Melody Johnson
Rooms: 5 (PB) $85-169
Full Breakfast
Credit Cards: A, B, C, D
Notes: 2, 4, 5, 9, 10, 11, 12

NEWBERG

Secluded Bed and Breakfast
19719 NE Williamson Road, 97132
(503) 538-2635

This secluded, beautiful, country home on ten acres is an ideal retreat in a wooded setting for hiking, walking in the country, and observing wildlife. Located near Newberg behind the beautiful Red Hills of Dundee, it is convenient to George Fox College. McMinnville is a 20-minute drive, and the Oregon coast is one hour away. A delectable breakfast varies for your pleasure, tempting you with succulent fresh, farm fruit from the famous Willamette Valley of Oregon. The home has many antiques and collectibles and stained glass in each room.

Hosts: Del and Durell Belanger
Rooms: 2 (1PB; 1SB) $40-50
Full Gourmet Breakfast
Credit Cards: None
Notes: 2, 5, 7, 8, 9, 10, 11, 12

NEWPORT

Oar House Bed and Breakfast
520 SW Second Street, 97365
(503) 265-9571

A Lincoln County historic landmark built in 1900, renovated and expanded in 1993. Centrally located in the picturesque Nye Beach area. An enclosed cupola with widow's walk and 360° view of ocean, lighthouses, mountains, romantic sunsets, and winter storms. A nautical theme; elegantly and tastefully furnished guest living room with TV; and a sitting room with music system. A gracious breakfast in the dining room. Large sheltered deck. Off-street parking.

Hostess: Jan LeBrun
Rooms: 4 (PB) $80-120
Full Breakfast
Credit Cards: A, B
Notes: 2, 5, 8, 9, 10

year; 6 Pets welcome; 7 Children welcome; 8 Tennis nearby; 9 Swimming nearby; 10 Golf nearby; 11 Skiing nearby; 12 May be booked through travel agent

OTIS

Salmon River Bed and Breakfast

5622 Salmon River Hwy., 97368
(503) 994-2639; (for reservations or inquiry call
(800) PWMORSE—after reply dial BAB and
leave message)

Deep-woods setting along the Salmon
River 10 miles from Lincoln City and the
Oregon Coast. Nearby: beaches with
seal- and whale-watching possibilities,
Factory Outlet Mall, lake with paddle
bikes, water skiing, bike rentals, horseback riding, four golf courses, racquetball
club, excellent eating emporiums, lake,
river, and ocean fishing, biking trails, etc.
Breakfast served anytime up to 10:30AM
(9:30 AM on Sundays). Host is a retired
meteorologist; hostess retired Medical
Records Supervisor.

Hosts: Marvin and Pawnee Pegg
Rooms: 4 (2PB; 2SB) $45-60
Full Breakfast
Credit Cards: A, B, D
Notes: 2, 5 (except Thanksgiving and Christmas),
7, 8, 9, 10, 12

PORTLAND

John Palmer House

4314 N. Mississippi Ave., 97217
(503) 284-5893; (503) 284-7789 (FAX)

This Victorian inn is run by three generations of the same family, and you become
one of the family the moment you enter the
door. We are told we serve the best
breakfast in town. Close to the ocean and
the mountains. Make this your home away
from home whether on business or vacation.

Rooms: 7 (2PB; 6SB) $35-125
Full Breakfast
Credit Cards: A, B, C, D
Notes: 2, 5, 7 (by arrangement), 8, 9, 10, 11, 12
(with restrictions)

Pittock Acres Bed and Breakfast

103 NW Pittock Ave., 97210
(503) 226-1163

Charming, warm contemporary home located in scenic urban area only one and a
half miles from downtown Portland. Convenient to historic Pittock Mansion, restaurants, shops, transit, convention center,
zoo, and Japenese and rose gardens. Delightful breakfast and decorations. Air-
conditioned. No smoking. Resident dog.

Hosts: Linda and Richard Matson
Rooms: 3 (2PB; 1SB) $70-80
Full Breakfast
Credit Cards: A, B, C, D
Notes: 2, 5, 7 (over 13), 8, 10, 12

ROSEBURG

The Umpqua House

7338 Oak Hill Road, 97470
(503) 459-4700

Country home on six wooded acres.
Rooms with spectacular view of Umpqua
Valley, handmade quilts, private entrance,
deck, and lounging chairs. Local activities
include jogging, hiking, fishing, berry picking, wine tasting, tennis, golf, and wild life
preserve. Breakfasts include freshly

NOTES: Credit cards accepted: A Master Card; B Visa; C American Express; D Discover Card; E
Diners Club; F Other; 2 Personal checks accepted; 3 Lunch available; 4 Dinner available; 5 Open all

squeezed juices, seasonal fruits, home-baked breads, and muffins, as well as, the house specialty of the day.

Hosts: Allen and Rhoda Mozorosky
Rooms: 2 (SB) $50
Full Breakfast
Credit Cards: None
Notes: 2, 5, 6, 7, 8, 9, 10, 12

SEASIDE

10th Avenue Inn Bed and Breakfast

125 10th Avenue, 97138
(503) 738-0643 (voice and FAX); (800) 569-1114

Enjoy this 1908 ocean view home just steps from the beach and a short walk on the promenade to restaurants and shopping. Light, airy guest rooms are decorated in soft colors, sprinkled with antiques, and include TVs. Full breakfast. Please, no smoking or pets.

Hosts: Francie and Vern Starkey
Rooms: 4 (PB) $55-70 + 7% tax
Full Breakfast
Credit Cards: A, B
Notes: 2, 5, 7 (over 9), 8, 9, 10

SISTERS

Conklin's Guest House

69013 Camp Polk Road, 97759
(503) 549-0123

Conklin's Guest House is surrounded by a sprawling meadow with a panoramic backdrop of snow-capped peaks. Rich in history, the near-century-old homesite gives evidence that early settlers chose the most beautiful sites first! Modern conveniences and attention to detail ensure a comfortable and restful stay. The house offers guests a truly peaceful environment within walking distance of the bustling shops and restaurants of Sisters. Guests are welcome to use the barbecue, swimming pool, laundry facilities, and to otherwise *be at home!* The ponds are stocked with trout for catch and release fishing. The Sisters area has something for everyone from rafting and rock climbing to dining and shopping and much more, all the time!

Hosts: Marie and Frank Conklin
Rooms: 5 (2PB; 3SB) $70-110
Full Breakfast
Credit Cards: None
Notes: 2, 5, 8, 9, 10, 11

10th Avenue Inn Bed and Breakfast

---

year; 6 Pets welcome; 7 Children welcome; 8 Tennis nearby; 9 Swimming nearby; 10 Golf nearby; 11 Skiing nearby; 12 May be booked through travel agent

STAYTON

Gardener House Bed and Breakfast

633 N. 3rd Avenue, 97383
(503) 769-6331

Well house suite! This extraordinary suite has coordinated decor, a separate entrance, kitchen, dining room, large bathroom, sitting room, queen size bed, telephone, CATV, and VCR. The Madonna room is in the main house and has much the same as the Well Suite. The dining room is on the same floor in a glassed-in porch. A bright room on any day.

Host: Richard Jungwirth
Rooms: 2 (PB) $55-65
Full Breakfast
Credit Cards: A, B, C, D, E
Notes: 2, 4, 5, 6, 7, 8, 9, 10

Horncroft

42156 Kingston-Lyons Dr., 97383
(503) 769-6287

This private home in a quiet, rural area southeast of Stayton, is 12 miles east of Salem, the center of the Willamette Valley, a rich and scenic agricultrual area. Mt. Jefferson Wilderness Area is one hour east; ocean beaches are one and one-half hours west.

Hosts: Dr. and Mrs. K. H. Horn
Rooms: 3 (1PB; 2SB) $35-45
Full Breakfast
Credit Cards: None
Closed Holidays
Notes: 2, 8, 9, 10, 11

YACHATS

Serenity Bed and Breakfast

5985 Yachats River Road, 97498
(503) 547-3813

Wholesome retreat nestled in the lush Yachats Valley. Gentle place to relax after countryside, forest, and tide pool exploration or bird-watching. Minutes from Cape Perpetua, Sea Lion Caves, and the Oregon Coast Aquarium. Elegant European comfort with private two-person jacuzzi tubs. Centrally located between Newport and Florence, Yachats is the gem of the Oregon Coast. German cooking at its best.

Hosts: Sam and Baerbel Morgan
Rooms: 4 (PB) $69-145
Full German Breakfast
Credit Cards: A, B
Notes: 2, 5, 8, 9, 10

NOTES: Credit cards accepted: A Master Card; B Visa; C American Express; D Discover Card; E Diners Club; F Other; 2 Personal checks accepted; 3 Lunch available; 4 Dinner available; 5 Open all

Pennsylvania

ADAMSTOWN

Adamstown Inn

62 West Main Street, 19501-0938
(717) 484-0800; (800) 594-4808

Experience simple elegance in a Victorian home resplendent with leaded-glass windows and door, magnificent chestnut woodwork, and Oriental rugs. All four guest rooms are decorated with family heirlooms, handmade quilts, lace curtains, fresh flowers, and many distinctive touches. Accommodations range from antique to king beds. Two rooms have jacuzzis for two. The inn is located in a small town brimming with antique dealers and only minutes from Reading and Lancaster.

Hosts: Tom and Wanda Berman
Rooms: 4 (PB) $65-95
Expanded Continental Breakfast
Credit Cards: A, B
Notes: 2, 5, 8, 9, 10, 12

AIRVILLE

Spring House

Muddy Creek Forks, 17302
(717) 927-6906

Built in 1798 of warm fieldstone, Spring House is a fine example of colonial architecture with original stenciling. Overlooking a river valley. Now on the National Registry of Historic Places, the house has welcomed guests from around the world who seek a historic setting, tranquility, and access to Amish country and Gettysburg with scenic railroad soon to be open to the public. Regional breakfast specialties and Amish cheeses welcome the traveler.

Hosts: Ray Constance Hearne and
Michael Schuster
Rooms: 5 (3 PB; 2 SB) $50-85
Full Breakfast
Credit Cards: None
Notes: 2, 5, 7, 8, 9, 10, 12

ANNVILLE

Swatara Creek Inn

Box 692, R.D. 2, 17003
(717) 865-3259

1860s Victorian mansion situated on four acres in the peaceful country. All rooms have private baths, canopied queen-size beds, air-conditioning, and include a full breakfast. Sitting room, dining room, and gift shop on the first floor. Wheelchair accessible. Close to Hershey, Mt. Hope Winery, Mt. Gretna, Reading outlets, and Lancaster Amish area. Close to a lot of historical sites: Cornwall Mines, Ephrata

year; 6 Pets welcome; 7 Children welcome; 8 Tennis nearby; 9 Swimming nearby; 10 Golf nearby;
11 Skiing nearby; 12 May be booked through travel agent

Cloisters, Gettysburg, etc. No smoking in house.

Hosts: Dick and Jeanette Hess
Rooms: 10 (PB) $50-75
Full Breakfast
Credit Cards: A, B, C, D, E
Notes: 2, 5, 7 (well behaved), 8, 9, 10, 12

ATGLEN

Glen Run Valley View Mennonite Farm

Rural Delivery 1, Box 69, 19310
(215) 593-5656

This is a beautiful cozy farm owned by two likable people who go out of their way to make their guests at home. Hannah's farm breakfasts are enormous, and what guests say about their visits here indicate that it is a very special place. Two guest rooms, one which has a double bed, one with a twin bed. Share bath. In the heart of Pennsylvania Dutch country. Near craft and antique shops.

Hosts: Harold and Hanna Stoltzfus
Rooms: 3 (1PB; 2SB) $45-50
Full Breakfast
Credit Cards: None
Notes: 2, 5, 6, 7, 10

BEDFORD

Conifer Ridge Farm

R. D. 2, Box 202A, Clearville, 15535
(814) 784-3342

Conifer Ridge Farm has 126 acres of woodland, pasture, Christmas trees, and crops. There is a one-acre pond with a pier for swimming, fishing, and boating. The home's rustic exterior opens to a spacious

contemporary design. You'll feel its country character in the old barn beams and brick walls that collect the sun's warmth for solar heat. Near Bedford Village and Raystown Dam.

Hosts: Dan and Myrtle Haldeman
Rooms: 2 + cabin for 4 people (PB) $55
Cabin: $30
Full Breakfast
Credit Cards: None
Notes: 2, 4, 5, 7, 9, 10, 11

BIGLERVILLE

Mulberry Farm B&B

616 Flohrs Church Rd., 17307
(717) 334-5827

Mulberry Farm B&B is seven miles west of Gettysburg offering peace, solitude, rest, and romance. An 1819 brick farm house. Beautiful gardens and wonderful walks are part of the experience. Four-poster, queen-size beds adorn the Colonial atmosphere of the guest rooms. A living room with two fireplaces enhances the atmosphere provided.

Hosts: Mimi and Jim Agard
Rooms: 5 (PB) $100-125
Full Breakfast
Credit Cards: None
Notes: 2, 5, 7, 8, 9, 10, 11

BIRD-IN-HAND

The Village Inn of Bird-in-Hand

Box 253, 2695 Old Phila. Pike, 17505
(717) 293-8369; (717) 768-1511 (FAX)

Listed on the National Historic Register, our Inn is located on Route 340, five miles

NOTES: Credit cards accepted: A Master Card; B Visa; C American Express; D Discover Card; E Diners Club; F Other; 2 Personal checks accepted; 3 Lunch available; 4 Dinner available; 5 Open all

east of Lancaster in the heart of the Pennsylvania Dutch Country. Each room features its own private bath and includes a continental plus breakfast, free use of indoor and outdoor pools and tennis courts located within walking distance, and a complimentary two-hour tour of the surrounding Amish farmlands. Reservations suggested. Package available.

Hosts: Richmond and Jania Young
Rooms: 11 (PB) $75-149
Continental Breakfast
Credit Cards: A, B, C, D
Notes: 2, 5, 8, 9

Brookview Manor

CANADENSIS

Brookview Manor

Route 447, R.R. #1, Box 365, 18325
(717) 595-2451

Situated on four picturesque acres, the Inn offers the traveler an ideal retreat from workaday world. Enjoy the simple pleasures of hiking trails or a cozy porch glider on a spacious wraparound porch. Each room offers a panoramic view of the forest, mountains and stream, and all have private baths. Breakfast is served in our cheery dining room and includes fruits, juices, fresh muffins, and a hearty main entree.

Hosts: Nancie and Lee Cabana
Rooms: 6 (PB) $70-145
Full Breakfast
Credit Cards: A, B, C, D, E
Notes: 2, 5, 7 (over 12), 8, 9, 10, 11, 12

Dreamy Acres

Route 447 and Seese Hill Road, 18325-0007
(717) 595-7115

Esther and Bill Pickett started Dreamy Acres as a bed and breakfast inn in 1959, doing bed and breakfast before it was in style. Situated on three acres with a stream and a pond, Dreamy Acres is in the heart of the Pocono Mountains vacationland, close to stores, churches, gift shops, and recreational facilities. Guest rooms have air conditioning, color cable TV, and some have VCRs.

Hosts: Esther and Bill Pickett
Rooms: 6 (4PB; 2SB) $36-50
Expanded Continental Breakfast, Continental breakfast served May 1 through October 31.
Credit Cards: None
Notes: 2, 5, 8, 9, 10, 11

The Overlook Inn

Dutch Hill Road, Box 680, 18325
(717) 595-7519

A 19th-century inn in the tradition of European inns where the traveler is greeted by a warm and friendly atmosphere. All rooms have private baths and are furnished with antiques. Excellent cuisine— enjoy romantic dining in informal elegance. Open year-round—An Inn for all Seasons!

Hosts: Peter Wawra and Hannele, innkeeper
Rooms: 20 (PB) $70-95; MAP rates $150-190
Full Breakfast
Credit Cards: A, B, C
Notes: 2, 4, 5, 7, 8, 9 (outdoor), 10, 11, 12

CANTON

M-mm Good Bed and Breakfast

R.D. 1, Box 71, 17724
(717) 673-8153

Located along Route 414, three miles from Canton in a quiet country setting in the center of the Endless Mountains. Clean, comfortable rooms. Enjoy hiking, fishing, or picnicing under the maple trees in the large lawn.

Hosts: Melvin and Irene Good
Rooms: 3 (SB) $23.50
Full Breakfast
Credit Cards: None
Notes: 2, 5, 7

CARLISLE

Line Limousin Farmhouse

2070 Ritner Highway, 17013
(717) 243-1281

Relax and unwind in an 1864 brick and stone farmhouse on 100 acres, two miles off I-81, Exit 12. French Limousin cattle are raised here. Enjoy antiques, including a player piano, the use of a golf driving range. Join us for worship at our historic First Presbyterian Church. One suite and two rooms with king/twin extra-long beds. Smoking is not permitted.

Hosts: Bob and Joan Line
Rooms: 3 (2PB; 1SB) $53.00-68.90
Full Breakfast
Credit Cards: None
Notes: 2, 5, 7, 10

Pheasant Field Bed and Breakfast

Pheasant Field Bed and Breakfast

105 Hickorytown Road, 17013
(717) 258-0717 (voice and FAX)

Stay in a homey, old, brick farmhouse in quiet surroundings. Wake up to a full, cooked breakfast including homemade bread or muffins. We have four air-conditioned guest rooms; two with private bath. There is a tennis court on the grounds and overnight horse boarding is available. "Come Home to the Country." AAA—three-star rating.

Hosts: Dee Fegan and Chuck DeMarco
Rooms: 4 (2PB; 2SB) $65-95
Full Breakfast
Credit Cards: A, B, C
Notes: 2, 5, 7 (over 8), 8 (on-site), 9, 10, 11, 12

CHAMBERSBURG

Falling Spring Inn

1838 Falling Spring Road, 17201
(717) 267-3654; (717) 267-2584 (FAX)

Enjoy country living only two miles from I-81, Exit 6 and Route 30, on a working farm with animals and Falling Spring, a nationally renowned, freshwater trout stream. A large pond, lawns, meadows, ducks, and birds all make a pleasant stay. Historic Gettysburg is only 25 miles away.

NOTES: Credit cards accepted: A Master Card; B Visa; C American Express; D Discover Card; E Diners Club; F Other; 2 Personal checks accepted; 3 Lunch available; 4 Dinner available; 5 Open all

Relax in our air-conditioned rooms with queen beds.

Hosts: Adin and Janet Frey
Rooms: 5 (PB) $49-69
Full Breakfast
Credit Cards: A, B
Notes: 2, 5, 7, 8, 9, 10, 11, 12

CHRISTIANA

The Georgetown

1222 Georgetown Road, 17509
(717) 786-4570

Once a miller's home, the original structure was converted to a bed and breakfast for the enjoyment of guests in a relaxing home away from home. Entrance to the house is by a brick walkway. The herb garden on the left lets guests smell the lavender and mint that are just two of the herbs used to garnish morning breakfasts. There is a choice of three bedrooms decorated with antiques and collectibles. Lancaster County Amish, a unique group of people who travel in horsedrawn carriages, pass in front of The Georgetown. Visit the local Strasburg Train Museum.

Hostess: Doris W. Woerth
Rooms: 3 (1PB; 2SB) $40
Full Breakfast
Credit Cards: None
Notes: 2, 5, 9, 10

Victorian Loft

CLEARFIELD

Victorian Loft

216 S. Front St., 16830
(814) 765-4805; (800) 464-1268 (reservations only); (814) 765-9596 (FAX)

Elegant 1894 Victorian home on the river in historic district. Amenities include: memorable breakfast featuring home-baked goods, air conditioned rooms with skylights, private kitchen and dining, guest entertainment center, family movies, and whirlpool bath. Sewing studio featured in *Threads* Magazine—weaving and spinning demonstrations. Hosts are Bible college graduates. Perfect stop on I-80—just three miles off exit 19 in West Central Pennsylvania. Also completely equipped three-bedroom cabin on eight wooded acres nestled in State Forest available for one party only.

Hosts: Tim and Peggy Durant
Rooms: 5 (2PB; 3SB) $45-90
Full Breakfast
Credit Cards: A, B, C
Rooms: 2, 5, 6, 7, 8, 9, 11, 12

COLUMBIA

The Columbian

360 Chestnut Street, 17512
(717) 684-5869; (800) 422-5869

A restored turn-of-the-century Colonial Revival mansion, featuring an ornate stained glass window and magnificent tiered staircase. Decorated with antiques in Victorian or country style, large, air-conditioned rooms offer queen-size beds, private baths, and cable TV. Breakfast here consists of a hearty buffet offering a variety of fresh fruit, hot main dishes, and homemade

year; 6 Pets welcome; 7 Children welcome; 8 Tennis nearby; 9 Swimming nearby; 10 Golf nearby; 11 Skiing nearby; 12 May be booked through travel agent

breads. Guests may relax on the wrap-around porch or in the sitting room which has a fireplace.

Hosts: Becky and Chris Will
Rooms: 6 (SB) $70-85
Full Breakfast
Credit Cards: A, B
Notes: 2, 5, 7, 8, 9, 10,11

CRESCO

LaAnna Guest House
R. R. 2, Box 1051, 18326
(717) 676-4225

The 111-year-old Victorian is furnished with Victorian and Empire antiques and has spacious rooms, quiet surroundings, and a trout pond. Walk to waterfalls, mountain views, and wildlife.

Hostesses: Julie Wilson and Kay Swingle
Rooms: 3 (SB) $25-30
Continental Breakfast
Credit Cards: None
Notes: 2, 5, 7, 8, 9, 10,11

DUSHORE

Heritage Guest House and Antique Shop
R. R. 2, Box 2078, 18614
(717) 928-7354

Our home is located in a small town in the Endless Mountains of PA. Our house dates to the early 1800s, so we do have those squeaky floors. We offer you simplicity, serenity, fresh mountain air, and congenial people with good food and flexible schedules. The antiques in the house, as well as, in the shop are all for sale. We are only a short distance from cross-coun-

try skiing, snowmobiling, canoeing/rafting, swimming, hiking, biking, fishing, hunting, and two large state parks. Smoking limited.

Hostes: Bill and Gertrude Wilson
Rooms: 5 (2PB; 3SB) $27.50-60
Full Breakfast
Credit Cards: A, B
Notes: 2, 7, 8, 9, 10,12

EAGLES MERE

Shady Lane B&B
Allegheny Ave., P.O. Box 314, 17731
(717) 525-3394

Surrounded by tall trees on a mountaintop with a mesmerizing view of the Endless mountains. A five-minute walk to swimming, boating, canoeing, and fishing on the gorgeous mile-long, springfed lake (with groomed path around the perimeter). Minutes' walk to craft and gift shops in small village. All in a Victorian "town that time forgot," a resort town since the late 1800s, with summer theater and winter cross-country skiing, ice skating, and famous toboggan slide.

Hosts: Pat and Dennis Dougherty
Rooms: 7 (PB) $75
Full Breakfast
Credit Cards: None
Notes: 2, 5, 8, 9, 10, 11, 12

ELIZABETHTOWN

West Ridge Guest House
1285 West Ridge Road, 17022
(717) 367-7783

Tucked midway between Harrisburg and Lancaster, this European manor can be found four miles off Route 283 at Rheems-Elizabethtown exit. Nine guest rooms with private baths, phones, and TV. Some rooms have fireplaces and whirlpool tubs. Two are two-room suites. An exercise room with hot tub and large great room is in an adjacent guest house. You may relax on one of the decks or gazebo and enjoy the restful view and quiet country setting. Twenty to 40 minutes to local attractions, including Hershey Park, Lancaster County Amish community, outlet shopping malls, Masonic homes, and Harrisburg, the state capital.

Hostess: Alice P. Heisey
Rooms: 9 (PB) $60-100
Full Breakfast
Credit Cards: A, B, C, D
Notes: 2, 5, 7, 8, 12

EMLENTON

Whippletree Inn and Farm
R. D. 3, Box 285, 16373
(412) 867-9543

The inn is a restored, turn-of-the-century home on a cattle farm. The house, barns, and 100 acres of pasture sit on a hill above the Allegheny River. A pleasant trail leads down to the river. Guests are welcome to use the one-half-mile racetrack for horses and carriages. Hiking, biking, cross-country skiing, canoeing, hunting, and fishing are nearby. Emlenton offers antique and craft shopping in the restored Old Mill.

Hosts: Warren and Joey Simmons
Rooms: 4 (2PB; 2SB) $45-50
Full Breakfast
Credit Cards: None
Notes: 2, 5, 7, 8, 9, 10

EPHRATA

Historic Smithton Inn
900 West Main Street 17522
(717) 733-6094; (717) 733-3333 (FAX)

Smithton Inn originated prior to the Revolutionary War. The inn is a romantic and picturesque place located in Lancaster County. Its big, square rooms are bright and sunny. Each room has its own working fireplace, and can be candlelighted during evening hours. There is a sitting area in each room with comfortable leather upholstered chairs, reading lamps and a writing desk. Most beds have canopies, soft goose down pillows and bright, handmade Pennsylvannia Dutch quilts. Feather beds are available upon request. Smithton's Dahlia Gardens feature a striking display of blossoms that are grown from tubers that were all winners in American Dahlia Society competitions. Mannerly children and pets are welcome, but please make prior arrangements. Smoking is prohibited. Reservations are prepaid.

Hostess: Dorthy Graybill
Rooms: 8 (PB) $65-135 suites $140-170
Full Breakfast
Credit Cards: A, B, C
Notes: 2, 5, 6 (by prior arrangement) 7, 8, 9, 10, 12

The Inns at Doneckers
318-324 North State and 301 West Main, 17522
(717) 738-9502; (717) 738-9554 (FAX)

Relax in country elegance in historic Lancaster County. Four inns of 40 distinctive rooms, decorated in fine antiques, some fireplace/jacuzzi suites. A few steps

---

year; 6 Pets welcome; 7 Children welcome; 8 Tennis nearby; 9 Swimming nearby; 10 Golf nearby; 11 Skiing nearby; 12 May be booked through travel agent

from The Doneckers Community of exceptional fashion store for the family and home, award-winning gourmet restaurant; art, craft, and quilt galleries and artists' studios; farmer's market. Minutes from antique and collectible markets. Special begin-the-week getaway Sunday thru Thursday. "An oasis of sophistication in Pennsylvania Dutch country"—*Country Inns Magazine.*

Hostess: Jan Grobengieser
Rooms: 40 (38PB; 2SB) $59-175
Continental Breakfast
Credit Cards: A, B, C, D, E
Notes: 2, 3, 4, 5, 7, 8, 9, 10

FRANKLIN

Quo Vadis Bed and Breakfast "Whither Goest Thou?"

1501 Liberty St., 16323
(814) 432-4208; (800) 360-6598

A stately home, accented with terra cotta tile, Quo Vadis is an 1867, eclectic, Queen Anne house. It is located in an historic district listed on the National Register with a walking tour. The high- ceilinged, spacious rooms, parquet floors, detailed woodworking, moldings, and friezes are from a time of caring craftsmanship and Victorian elegance. The furniture is mahogany, rosewood, oak, walnut, and wicker and has been acquired by the same family for four generations. The quilts, embroidery, and lacework are the handiwork of two beloved ladies. Restaurants, museums, antiques, Barrow-Civic Theatre, DeBonce Antique Music World, bicycle paths, train trip, fishing, Allegheny River Valley are all nearby to enjoy. Smoking allowed only on the porch.

Hosts: Kristal and Stanton Bowmer-Vath
Rooms: 6 (PB) $60-70
Full Breakfast
Credit Cards: A, B, C
Notes: 2, 5, 7 (10 and over), 8, 9, 10, 11, 12

Quo Vadis Bed and Breakfast

GAP

Ben Mar Farm Bed and Breakfast

5721 Old Phila. Pike, 17527
(717) 768-3309

Come stay with us on our working dairy farm. We are located in the heart of famous "Amish Country." Experience quiet country life while staying in the large, beautifully decorated rooms of our 200-year-old farmhouse. Our efficiency apartment is a favorite including a full kitchen, queen and double bed with private bath. Enjoy a fresh continental breakfast brought to your room. Air conditioned.

Hosts: Herb and Melanie Benner
Rooms: 3 (PB) $38-48
Continental Breakfast
Credit Cards: None
Notes: 2, 5, 7

NOTES: Credit cards accepted: A Master Card; B Visa; C American Express; D Discover Card; E Diners Club; F Other; 2 Personal checks accepted; 3 Lunch available; 4 Dinner available; 5 Open all

GETTYSBURG—SEE ALSO HANOVER

The Brafferton Inn
44 York Street, 17325
(717) 337-3423

In 1786, an elegant fieldstone house was constructed and the village of Gettysburg was born. Now the Brafferton Inn, this National Registry Home has been fully restored, including a private bath for each of the ten guest rooms. The enlivening humor of the new innkeepers, Sam and Jane Back, as well as their family portraits, antiques, and china, seem designed for this very place. The inn is located in the center of historic Gettysburg, within the encircling battlefields.

Hosts: Jane and Sam Back
Rooms: 10 (10PB) $75-120
Full Breakfast
Credit Cards: A, B
Notes: 2, 5, 7 (over 7), 8, 9, 10, 11, 12

Keystone Inn
231 Hanover Street, 17325
(717) 337-3888

The Keystone Inn is a large, brick, Victorian home built in 1913. The high-ceilinged rooms are decorated with lace and flowers, and a handsome chestnut staircase rises to the third floor. The guest rooms are bright, cheerful, and air conditioned. Each has a reading nook and writing desk. Choose your own breakfast from our full breakfast menu. One suite available.

Hosts: Wilmer and Doris Martin
Rooms: 4 + suite (3PB; 2SB) $59-100
Full Breakfast
Credit Cards: A, B
Notes: 2, 5, 7, 8, 9, 10, 11

GREENSBURG

Huntland Farm Bed and Breakfast
R. D. 9, Box 21, 15601
(412) 834-8483

Nestled in the foothills of the Allegheny Mountains, the 100-acre Huntland Farm is three miles northeast of Greensburg. The house, built in 1848 and listed in *Historic Places in Western PA*, is furnished with antiques. A large living room, as well as porches and gardens are available for guests' use. Four, large, corner bedrooms make it comfortable for up to eight people. Nearby are many scenic and historical places, walking trails, hot air ballooning, restaurants, and shops.

Hosts: Robert and Elizabeth Weidlein
Rooms: 4 (SB) $70
Full Breakfast
Credit Cards: C
Notes: 2, 5, 7 (over 12), 10, 12

GORDONVILLE

Colonial Ridge Bed and Breakfast
3840B Ridge Rd., 17529
(717) 768-7567; (800) 777-7274

Nestled among Amish farms, Colonial Ridge B&B is your home away from home. This peaceful setting offers picturesque views of Amish farmers working their fields as they have for centuries. Colonial Ridge can accommodate you with single and double beds, private or shared baths. Our master suite includes a queen-size bed,

---

year; 6 Pets welcome; 7 Children welcome; 8 Tennis nearby; 9 Swimming nearby; 10 Golf nearby; 11 Skiing nearby; 12 May be booked through travel agent

private jacuzzi, sun room with daybed, TV and VCR. The Stoltzfus family has had its roots in Lancaster County for generations. We would be happy to assist you in your exploration of the area.

Host: Mr. Lee Stoltzfus
Rooms: 3 (1PB; 2SB) $45-65
Continental Breakfast
Credit Cards: None
Notes: 2, 5, 7, 8, 12

Old Leacock Road Bed and Breakfast

244 Old Leacock Rd., 17529
(717) 768-3824

Welcome to Lancaster County. A complimentary rumble seat ride in our 1929 Model "A" Ford awaits all our guests. You will experience the lush Lancaster County farmland and travel through a covered bridge. Arrangements for dinner with an Amish family are available. Our rooms are furnished in period antiques. We are close to all attractions and shopping, yet surrounded by the serene Amish farms.

Hosts: Richard and Sandee Hughes
Rooms: 3 (1PB; 2SB) $50-65
Full Breakfast
Credit Cards: None
Notes: 2, 5, 6, 7, 10

HANOVER

Beechmont Inn

315 Broadway, 17331
(717) 632-3012; (800) 553-7009

An elegant, 1834 Federal Period inn with

seven guest rooms, all private baths, fireplaces, air conditioning, afternoon refreshments, and gourmet breakfast. One large suite has a private whirlpool tub, canopy bed, and fireplaces. Gettysburg Battlefield, Lake Marburg, golf, and great antiquing nearby. Convenient location for visits to Hershey, York, or Lancaster. Weekend and golf packages and romantic honeymoon or anniversary packages offered. Picnic baskets available. Great area for biking and hiking. AAA and Mobil approved.

Hosts: William and Susan Day
Rooms: 7 (PB) $80-135
Full Breakfast
Credit Cards: A, B, C
Notes: 2, 5, 8, 9, 10 (packages available)

HERSHEY

Hershey Bed and Breakfast Reservation Service

P.O. Box 208, 17033-0208
(717) 533-2928

Renee invites you to experience the country living in **south central PA**, where the atmosphere of friendliness awaits you with easy access to many recreation facilities. Whatever your wishes, be it the town that chocolate made famous or a country farm/inn or a private home, you will feel most welcome. Approximately 40 rooms available. Many have private baths and serve a full breakfast. Major credit cards accepted. Call Renee Deutel, coordinator, for more information.

Pinehurst Bed and Breakfast

50 Northeast Dr., 17033
(717) 533-2603; (717) 534-2639 (FAX)

Spacious brick home surrounded by lawns and countryside. There is a warm, welcoming, many-windowed living room, or for outdoor relaxing, a large porch with an old-fashioned porch swing. All this within walking distance of all Hershey attractions: Hershey Museum, Rose Gardens, Hersheypark, and Chocolate World. Less than one hour's drive to Gettysburg and Lancaster County. Each room welcomes you with a queen-size bed and a Hershey Kiss on each pillow.

Hosts: Roger and Phyllis Ingold
Rooms: 15 (2PB; 12SB) $45-69
Complete Breakfast
Credit Cards: A, B
Notes: 2, 5, 7, 8, 9, 10, 12

HESSTON

Aunt Susie's Country Vacations

Rural Delivery 1, Box 225, 16647
(814) 658-3638

Experience country living in a warm, friendly atmosphere with antiques and oil paintings. Nearby attractions include 28-mile-long Raystown Lake, historic houses, and a restored general store.

Hosts: John and Susan
Rooms: 8 (2PB; 6SB) $50-55
Expanded Continental Breakfast
Credit Cards: None
Notes: 2, 5, 7, 8, 9, 10, 11, 12

INTERCOURSE

Carriage Corner Bed and Breakfast

3705 E. Newport Road, P.O. Box 371, 17534-0371
(717) 768-3059

"A comfortable bed, a hearty breakfast, a charming village, and friendly hosts" has been used to describe our B&B. We have four comfortable rooms, two with private baths and two with a shared bath. Our bed and breakfast offers a relaxing country atmosphere with hand-crafted touches of folk-art and country. Rooms are air-conditioned. We are centered in the heart of beautiful farms and a culture which draws many to nearby villages of Intercourse, Bird-in-Hand, and Paradise. Amish dinners arranged. There is much to learn from these calm and gentle people.

Hosts: Gordon and Gwen Schuit
Rooms: 4 (2PB; 2SB) $55-65
Full Breakfast
Credit Cards: A, B
Notes: 2, 5, 7, 12

JIM THORPE

The Inn at Jim Thorpe

24 Broadway, 18229
(717) 325-2599; (717) 325-9145 (FAX)

The Inn rests in a unique and picturesque setting in the heart of historic Jim Thorpe. Our elegant, restored guestrooms are complete with private baths, remote-controlled, color TVs and air-conditioning. While in town, take historic walking tours, shop in over 50 quaint shops and galleries, go mountain biking on the northeast's best trails, or raft the turbulent Lehigh River. It's all right outside our door!

Host: David Drury
Rooms: 22 (PB) $65-100
Continental Breakfast
Credit Cards: A, B, C, D, E
Notes: 3, 4, 5, 7, 9, 11, 12

KENNETT SQUARE

Meadow Spring Farm Bed and Breakfast
201 East Street Road, Rt. 926, 19348
(610) 444-3903

1836 farmhouse on a 150-acre working farm. Guests can participate in gathering eggs for breakfast. The house is filled with family antiques, quilts, and a doll collection including Santa and cows. The hosts will prepare a full country breakfast before the guests start touring the area, swimming in the pool, or just walking the farm. Minutes from Longwood, Brandywine River Museum, and Winterthur.

Hosts: Anne Hicks and Debbie Hicks Axelrod
Rooms: 7 (4PB; 3SB) $55-100
Full Breakfast
Credit Cards: None
Notes: 2, 5, 7, 8, 9, 10

KINZERS

Sycamore Haven Farm
35 South Kinzer Road, 17535
(717) 442-4901

We have approximately 40 milking cows and many young cattle and cats for children to enjoy. Our farmhouse has three guest rooms, all with double beds and one single. We also have cots and a playpen. Located

15 miles east of Lancaster on Route 30.

Hosts: Charles and Janet Groff
Rooms: 3 (SB) $30-40
Continental Breakfast
Credit Cards: None
Notes: 2, 5, 6, 7, 8, 9, 10

LAMPETER—SEE LANCASTER COUNTY

LANCASTER

Australian Walkabout Inn
837 Village Road, 17537
(717) 464-0707; (717) 464-2678 (FAX)

This 1925, brick, Mennonite farmhouse features large wraparound porches, balconies, English gardens, and antique furnishings. The inn takes its name from the Australian word which means to go out and discover new places. Australian-born host Richard will help you explore the Amish country surrounding the home. An elegant, full breakfast is served by candlelight. The honeymoon and anniversary rooms/suites are beautiful. AAA—three-diamonds.

Hosts: Richard and Margaret Mason
Rooms: 5 (PB) $79; suites $129-149
Suites: 1 (PB) $179 for five adults
Full Breakfast
Credit Cards: A, B, C
Notes: 2, 3, 4, 5, 7, 8, 9, 10, 12

Flowers and Thyme B&B
238 Strasburg Pike, 17602
(717) 393-1460

Charming brick, Colonial home in a country setting amid flowers, herbs, and perennials. Oak, brass, or Shaker poster

---

NOTES: Credit cards accepted: A Master Card; B Visa; C American Express; D Discover Card; E Diners Club; F Other; 2 Personal checks accepted; 3 Lunch available; 4 Dinner available; 5 Open all

beds, country decor, cable TV, ceiling fans, one room with jacuzzi, and air-conditioned for your comfort. Warm hospitality and marvelous breakfasts await you. Dinner with Amish family available. Located in the heart of the Pennsyvania Dutch country; five minutes from the PA Dutch Visitors Bureau, one mile from Millstream Village Outlet, and two miles from Rockvale Square outlets.

Hosts: Don and Ruth Harnish
Rooms: 3 (2PB; 1SB) $50-85
Full Breakfast
Credit Cards: None
Notes: 2, 5, 7 (over 12 or by special arrangement), 8, 9, 10

The King's Cottage, A Bed and Breakfast Inn

1049 East King St., 17602
(717) 397-1017; (800) 747-8717; (717) 397-3447 (FAX)

Traditionally-styled elegance, modern comfort, and warm hospitality in Amish country. King and queen beds, private baths, gourmet breakfasts, and personal service create a gracious friendly atmosphere at this award-winning Spanish-style mansion. Relax by the fire and enjoy afternoon tea in the library while chatting with innkeepers about directions to restaurants and attractions. Special Amish dinners or personal tours arranged. No pets, please. Near farmers' markets, Gettysburg, and Hershey. On National Register, AAA, and Mobil listed EXCELLENT!

Hosts: Karen and Jim Owens
Rooms: 8 (PB) $80-125
Full Breakfast
Credit Cards: A, B, D
Notes: 2, 5, 8, 9, 10, 12

Lincoln Haus Inn

1687 Lincoln Highway East, 17602
(717) 392-9412

Lincoln Haus Inn is the only inn in Lancaster County with a distinctive hip roof. It is furnished with antiques and rugs on gleaming, hardwood floors, and it has natural oak woodwork. I am a member of the Old Order Amish Church, serving family-style breakfast with a homey atmosphere. Convenient location, close to Amish farmlands, malls, historic Lancaster; five minutes from Route 30 and Pennsylvania Dutch Visitors' Bureau.

Hostess: Mary K. Zook
Rooms: 6 (PB) $45-65
Apartment: 2 (PB)
Full Breakfast
Credit Cards: None
Notes: 2, 4, 5, 7, 8, 9, 10, 12

Meadowview Guest House

2169 New Holland Pike, 17601
(717) 299-4017

Large contemporary home located in the heart of the Pennsylvannia Dutch Amish area. Three guest rooms and kitchen on the second floor. There is a stove, refrigerator, sink, and dishes. A breakfast tray is put in the kitchen in the morning for our guests. Close to many historical sites, farmers and antique markets, excellent restaurants, and many attractions to help guests enjoy the beautiful county. Personalized maps are provided.

Hosts: Edward and Sheila Christie
Rooms: 3 (1PB; 2SB) $30-45
Continental Breakfast
Credit Cards: None
Notes: 2 (for deposit), 5, 7 (over 6), 8, 9, 10

year; 6 Pets welcome; 7 Children welcome; 8 Tennis nearby; 9 Swimming nearby; 10 Golf nearby; 11 Skiing nearby; 12 May be booked through travel agent

Witmer's Tavern—Historic 1725 Inn

New Life Homestead Bed and Breakfast

1400 East King Street (Route 462), 17602-3240
(717) 396-8928

In the heart of the Amish area is a stately, brick Victorian close to all attractions, markets, farms, and outlets. Each room is decorated with family heirlooms and antiques. Full breakfast and evening refreshments are served. Tours and meals are arranged with local families. Worship with us in our Mennonite church. Private baths and air-conditioning.

Hosts: Carol and Bill Giersch
Rooms: (PB) $40-70
Full Breakfast
Credit Cards: None
Notes: 2, 5, 7, 8, 9, 10, 12

O'Flaherty's Dingeldein House

1105 East King Street, 17602
(717) 293-1723; (800) 779-7765; (717) 293-1947 (FAX)

Enjoy genuine warmth and hospitality in the friendly atmosphere of our home. Our Dutch Colonial home is traditionally ap-

pointed for your comfort, two fireplaces in the fall and winter and A/C when needed to provide a restful, relaxing stay in beautiful Lancaster County. Conveniently located near downtown Lancaster attractions and just a short, scenic ride to the Amish farmland, outlet shopping, and antique area. Amish dining arranged. Personalized maps prepared. Our breakfast gurantees you won't go away hungry.

Hosts: Jack and Sue Flatley
Rooms: 4 (2PB; 2SB) $60-70
Full Breakfast
Credit Cards: A, B, D
Notes: 2, 5, 7, 8, 10, 12

Witmer's Tavern— Historic 1725 Inn

2014 Old Philadelphia Pike, 17602
(717) 299-5305

This three-story, all stone inn, originally built in 1725 and later added to, rest just off the nation's first turnpike. It is the sole, still functioning survivor of some 62 pre-Revolutionary War inns and is listed on the local, state, and national registers of historic places and landmarks. Restored to the original, simple pioneer state, each romantic room has its own working fireplace, antique quilts, and fresh flowers. Pandora's antique and quilt shop is in the east end. Add your names to the guest list that includes John Adams, Marquis de Lafayette, and others. Villages of Bird-in-Hand and Intercourse are just beyond.

Hosts: Brant Harung and family
Rooms: 7 (2PB; 5SB) $60-100
Continental Breakfast
Credit Cards: None
Notes: 2, 5, 7, 8, 9, 10, 11, 12

NOTES: Credit cards accepted: A Master Card; B Visa; C American Express; D Discover Card; E Diners Club; F Other; 2 Personal checks accepted; 3 Lunch available; 4 Dinner available; 5 Open all

Pennsylvania Dutch Country
Lancaster County

**LANCASTER COUNTY (SEE
ALSO—ATGLEN, BIRD-IN-HAND,
CHRISTIANA, ELIZABETHTOWN, EPHRATA,
GAP, GORDONVILLE, INTERCOURSE,
KINZERS, LANCASTER, LITITZ, MANHEIM,
MARIETTA, MOUNT JOY, PARADISE, PEACH
BOTTOM, AND QUARRYVILLE)**

Bed and Breakfast— The Manor

830 Village Rd., Box 416, **Lampeter**, 17537
(717) 464-9564

This cozy farmhouse is minutes away from Lancaster's historical sites and attractions. Guests delight in Mary Lou's homemade breakfasts featuring Eggs Mornay, crepes, stratas, fruit cobblers, and homemade breads and jams. A swim in the pool and a nap under a shade tree is the perfect way to cap your day of touring. Dinner, an overnight stay, and a buggy ride with an Old Order Amish family can be arranged. Amish waitresses. Children welcome.

Hosts: Mary Lou Paolini and Jackie Curtis
Rooms: 6 (4PB; 2SB) $79-99
Gourmet Buffet-syle Breakfast
Credit Cards: A, B
Notes: 2, 3, 4, 5, 7, 8, 9 (on premises), 10

The Decoy B&B

958 Eisenberger Road, **Strasburg**, 17579
(717) 687-8585; (800) 726-2287; (717) 687-8585
(FAX)

This former Amish home is set in farmland with spectacular views and an informal atmosphere. Craft shops and attractions are nearby, and bicycle tours can be arranged. Two cats in residence.

Hosts: Debby and Hap Joy
Rooms: 5 (PB) $42.40-63.60 (taxes included)
Full Breakfast
Credit Cards: None
Notes: 2, 5, 7, 8, 10

Homestead Lodging

184 East Brook Road, Route 896, **Smoketown**, 17576
(717) 393-6927

Welcome to Homestead Lodging in the heart of the Pennsylvannia Dutch Amish farmlands. Listen to the clippity-clop of horse and buggies go by or stroll down the lane to the scenic farmlands around us. Within walking distance of restaurants and minutes from farmers' markets; quilt, antique, and craft shops; museums; and auctions. Tours available. Family-operated B&B with clean, country rooms each with private bath, TV/radio, refrigerator, AC/heat. Microwave oven available.

Hosts: Robert and Lori Kepiro
Rooms: 4 (PB) $33-56
Continental Breakfast
Credit Cards: A, B
Notes: 2 (deposit only), 5, 7, 8, 9, 10, 11

Old Road Guest Home

2501 Old Phila. Pike, **Smoketown**, 17576
(717) 393-8182

Old Road Guest Home is nestled in the rolling farmlands in the heart of PA Dutch country. Comfortable air conditioned

year; 6 Pets welcome; 7 Children welcome; 8 Tennis nearby; 9 Swimming nearby; 10 Golf nearby; 11 Skiing nearby; 12 May be booked through travel agent

rooms with TV. Ground floor rooms available. Spacious shaded lawn to enjoy picnics. Easy parking. Private and shared baths. Near fine restaurants. Alcoholic beverages and indoor smoking prohibited.

Hostess: Marian Buckwalter
Rooms: 6 (3PB; 3SB) $28-35
No Breakfast
Credit Cards: None
Notes: 2, 5, 7, 9, 10

LANDENBERG

Cornerstone Inn Bed and Breakfast

Rd. 1, Box 155, 19350
(610) 274-2143; (610) 274-0734 (FAX)

Cornerstone dates back to 1704, the time when early records document a land grant from William Penn of England to William Penn's son in Philadelphia. The original house was built in the early 1700s, with additions constructed at three later times. Then, in 1820, Cornerstone was completed as the proud, gracious structure that will soon welcome you. Each bedroom's quaint decor is surrounded by a sense of timeless romance. Bringing together the unhurried pace of the past and the conveniences of today. For long-term guests, Cornerstone's renovated barn is the home of two furnished guest apartments. Come to your home in the country. Call today for reservations or information. It's a place with a long history of pampered guests.

Hosts: Linda and Marty Mulligan
Rooms: 7 (PB) $85-150
Full Breakfast
Credit Cards: A, B, D
Notes: 2, 5, 7, 8, 9, 10, 12

LEWISBURG

The Inn On Fiddler's Tract

RD #2, Box 573A, 17837
(717) 523-7197

Experience the picturesque charm, enchanting rooms, warmth, and congeniality of this 1787, lovingly restored estate situated on 33 acres in the beautiful Susquehanna Valley. Relax in our large library with an extensive book collection or visit historic Victorian Lewisburg, home of Bucknell University. We look forward to having you enjoy the many pleasures of the Inn. ABBA—3½ crowns.

Hosts: Jodi and Sherri Hosterman
Rooms: 5 (PB); $75-95
Breakfast
Credit Cards: A, B
Notes: 2, 5, 8, 9, 10

The Inn On Fiddler's Tract

LITITZ

The Alden House Bed and Breakfast

62 East Main Street, 17543
(717) 627-3363; (800) 584-0753

This 1850 brick Victorian house is located

in the center of the town's historic district within walking distance to fine shops, boutiques, and dining. The Inn consists of six rooms, three of which are two-room suites, ideal for families. All rooms, including the suites, have private baths. In the morning there is a choice of a full breakfast being served by candlelight in our dining room, or dining outside on one of the porches.

Hostess: Fletcher and Joy Coleman
Rooms: 6 (PB) $75-100
Full Breakfast
Credit Cards: A, B, C
Notes: 2, 5, 7 (over 6), 8, 9, 10

Swiss Woods Bed and Breakfast

500 Blantz Road, 17543
(717) 627-3358; (800) 594-8018; 717-627-3483 (FAX)

A visit to Swiss Woods is reminiscent of a trip to one of Switzerland's quaint, charming guest houses. Located in beautiful Lancaster County, this inn was designed with comfort in mind. Breakfast is a memorable experience of inn specialties. The gardens are a unique variety of flowering perennials and annuals. A massive sandstone fireplace dominates the sunny common room. Rooms feature natural woodwork and queen beds with down comforters, some with jacuzzis, patios, and balconies. Enjoy our spectacular view and special touches. German spoken.

Hosts: Debrah and Werner Mosimann
Rooms: 7 (PB) $75-130
Full Breakfast
Credit Cards: A, B
Notes: 2, 9, 12

MALVERN

The Great Valley House of Valley Forge

110 Swedesford Road, R.D. 3, 19355
(610) 644-6759; (610) 644-7019 (FAX)

"Did George Washington sleep here?" is the most often asked question at this 300-year-old stone farmhouse dating back to 1690. The house retains original fireplaces, random-width wood floors, and hand-forged nails. Each of the guest rooms are hand-stenciled, decorated with antiques, and accented with handmade quilts. The surrounding four acres contain an old smokehouse, a cold storage keep, and ancient trees, as well as a modern diversion: a large swimming pool.

Hostess: Pattye Benson
Rooms: 3 (2PB; 2SB) $75-85
Full Breakfast
Credit Cards: None
Notes: 2, 5, 7, 8, 9, 11, 12

MANHEIM

Herr Farmhouse

2256 Huber Drive, 17545
(717) 653-9852

Historic, circa 1750, stone farmhouse nestled on 11.5 acres of scenic farmland. The Inn has been fully restored and retains all original trim, flooring, and doors. Of the six working fireplaces, two are located in guest rooms. Take a step into yesteryear amidst the Colonial furnishings. Breakfast served in country kitchen with walk-in fireplace. Amish dining, family suite, and

---

year; 6 Pets welcome; 7 Children welcome; 8 Tennis nearby; 9 Swimming nearby; 10 Golf nearby; 11 Skiing nearby; 12 May be booked through travel agent

indoor bicycle storage available. Nine miles west of Lancaster outside of Mount Joy. Excellent dining nearby.

Host: Barry Herr
Rooms: 4 (2PB; 2SB) $75-90; suite for 14 people $100
Expanded Continental Breakfast
Credit Cards: A, B
Notes: 2, 5, 8, 9, 10

The Inn at Mt. Hope

2232 E. Mt. Hope Rd., 17545-0155
(717) 664-4708; (800) 664-4708; (717) 270-2688 (FAX)

An 1850s stone home with high ceilings and magnificent pine floors. The Inn sits on four and one-half acres of woodland and grass bordered by a stream. Convenient to all Lancaster County attractions as well as Hershey and adjacent to the Mt. Hope Winery and Pennsylvania Renaissance Faire. Ideal setting for a small couples retreat or getaway. Screened porch and family/TV room are available for relaxation.

Rooms: 5 (2PB; 3SB) $50-115
Full Breakfast
Credit Cards: A, B
Notes: 2, 5, 7, 9, 10

Penn's Valley Farm and Inn

6182 Metzler Rd., 17545
(717) 898-7386

A country decor guest house is situated next to the farmhouse breezeway. Guest house is a completely private facility accommodating 2 to 7 people. Breakfast is optional in the farmhouse dining room.

One newly refurbished room for two people is also available in the farmhouse. Farm is located on 64 acres of farmland, twenty minutes from tourist attractions.

Host: Melvin and Gladys Metzler
Rooms: 1 (SB) + 1 guesthouse (PB) $50-65
Full Breakfast (served if desired)
Credit Cards: A, B, C
Notes: 2, 5, 7, 10

Wenger's Bed and Breakfast

571 Hosslen Road, 17545
(717) 665-3862

Relax and enjoy your stay in the quiet countryside of Lancaster County. Our ranch-style house is within walking distance of our son's 100-acre dairy farm. The spacious rooms will accommodate families. You can get a guided tour through the Amish farmland. Hershey, the chocolate town, Pennsylvania's state capital at Harrisburg, and the Gettysburg Battlefield are all within one hour's drive.

Hosts: Arthur and Mary K. Wenger
Rooms: 2 (PB) $40-45
Full Breakfast
Credit Cards: None
Notes: 2, 5, 7

MARIETTA

The River Inn
258 West Front Street, 17547
(717) 426-2290; (717) 426-2966 (FAX)

Situated in the National Historic District of
Marietta, the River Inn offers a convenient
location for Lancaster, York, Gettysburg,
and Hershey attractions. The 200-year-
old home boasts crown moldings, handmade lighting, six working fireplaces, a
"tavern" area on screened porch for breakfast, a four-square, and herb gardens.
Bikes and Susquehanna river fishing are
available to guests. Gourmet and family
restaurants are within walking distance.
Marietta and this home have been featured
in *Colonial Homes* magazine.

Hosts: Joyce and Bob Heiserman
Rooms: 3 (PB) $60-70
Full Breakfast
Credit Cards: A, B, D, E
Notes: 2, 5, 7 (over 9), 10, 12

MIDDLEBURY CENTER

Wood's Rustic Inn Bed and Breakfast
Little Marsh R. R. 2, Box 98A, 16935
(717) 376-3331

We are located in a small village near the
Pennsylvannia Grand Canyon. Quiet and
peaceful with lovely flowers and a patio to
enjoy nature. We own 300 acres at this
location on which we raise beef cattle and
Belgian horses. Our inn is very clean,
modern, and on a main road. Each room

is beautifully decorated and has a TV. An
ideal vacation for the whole family. Great
for taking long walks, riding bikes, sitting
along the creek, which runs in front of the
house, fishing, and enjoying wild life, especially the deer. We also make our own
maple syrup in the spring.

Hosts: Waldo and Olive Wood
Rooms: 4 at inn + 2 at hosts' house next door
(PB) $39-44
Full Breakfast
Credit Cards: None
Notes: 2 (and travelers' checks), 7, 8, 9, 10

MILFORD

Cliff Park Inn and Golf Course
RR 4, Box 7200, 18337
(717) 296-6491; (800) 225-6535; (717) 296-3982
(FAX)

Historic country inn on secluded 600-acre
estate. Spacious rooms with private bath,
telephone, and climate control. Victorian-
style furnishings. Fireplaces. Golf at the
door on one of America's oldest golf
courses (1913). Hike or cross-country
ski on seven miles of marked trails. Golf
and ski equipment rentals. Golf school.
Full service restaurant rated 3-stars by
Mobil Guide. MAP or B&B plans available. Specialists in business conferences
and country weddings.

Host: Harry W. Buchanan III
Rooms: 18 (PB) $90-155
Full Breakfast
Credit Cards: A, B, C, D, E
Notes: 2, 3, 4, 5, 7, 8, 9, 10, 11, 12

---

year; 6 Pets welcome; 7 Children welcome; 8 Tennis nearby; 9 Swimming nearby; 10 Golf nearby;
11 Skiing nearby; 12 May be booked through travel agent

Green Acres Farm Bedand Breakfast

MONTOURSVILLE

The Carriage House at Stonegate

R. R. 1, Box 11A, 17754
(717) 433-4340; (717) 433-4653 (FAX)

The Carriage House at Stonegate is the original carriage house for one of the oldest farms in the beautiful Loyalsock Valley. It offers 1,400 square feet of space on two levels and is totally self-contained and separate from the main house. It is located within easy access to I-80, I-180, and U.S. 15 and on the edge of extensive forests offering a wide range of outdoor activities in all seasons.

Hosts: Harold and Dena Mesaris
Rooms: 2 (SB) $50
Continental Breakfast
Credit Cards: None
Notes: 2, 5, 6, 7, 8, 9, 10, 11

MOUNT JOY

Cedar Hill Farm

305 Longenecker Road, 17552
(717) 653-4655

This 1817 stone farmhouse overlooks a peaceful stream and was the birthplace of the host. Stroll the acreage or relax on the wicker rockers on the large front porch. Enjoy the singing of the birds and serene countryside. A winding staircase leads to the comfortable rooms, each with a private bath and centrally air conditioned. A room for honeymooners offers a private balcony. Breakfast is served daily by a walk-in fireplace. Located midway between the Lancaster and Hershey areas where farmers' markets, antique shops, and good restaurants abound. Gift certificates for anniversary or holiday giving. Open all seasons.

Hosts: Russel and Gladys Swarr
Rooms: 5 (PB) $65-70
Continental Plus Breakfast
Credit Cards: A, B, C, D
Notes: 2, 5, 7, 8, 10

Green Acres Farm Bed and Breakfast

1382 Pinkerton Road, 17552
(717) 653-4028; 717-653-2840 (FAX)

Our 1830 farmhouse is furnished with antiques and offers a peaceful haven for your getaway. The rooster, chickens, wild turkey, Pigmy goats, lots of kittens, pony,

NOTES: Credit cards accepted: A Master Card; B Visa; C American Express; D Discover Card; E Diners Club; F Other; 2 Personal checks accepted; 3 Lunch available; 4 Dinner available; 5 Open all

and 1,000 hogs give a real farm atmosphere on this 160-acre grain farm. Children love the pony cart rides and the 8 x 10 playhouse, and everyone enjoys the trampoline and swings. We offer tour information in the Amish country.

Hosts: Wayne and Yvonne Miller
Rooms: 7 (PB) $55
Full Breakfast
Credit Cards: A, B
Notes: 2, 5, 6, 7, 8, 9, 10

MUNCY

The Bodine House
307 South Main Street, 17756
(717) 546-8949

The Bodine House, featured in the December 1991 issue of *Colonial Homes* magazine, is located on tree-lined Main Street in the historic district. Built in 1805, the house has been authentically restored and is listed on the National Register of Historic Places. Most of the furnishings are antiques. The center of Muncy, with its shops, restaurants, library, and churches, is a short walk down the street. No smoking.

Hosts: David and Marie Louise Smith
Rooms: 4 (PB) $55-70
Full Breakfast
Credit Cards: A, B, C
Notes: 2, 5, 7 (over 6), 8, 9, 10, 11, 12

NEW ALBANY

Waltman's B&B
RD 1, Box 87, 18833
(717) 363-2295

Retired farm couple will welcome you to

their century-old home in a beautiful country setting. Enjoy bird-watching from inviting porches in summer and cozy fireplace in winter. Homemade jams, muffins, and maple syrup. Hunters and fishermen welcome. No smoking or alcohol.

Hosts: Ivan and Mae Waltman
Rooms: 3 (SB) $39.20
Continental Breakfast
Credit Cards: None
Notes: 2, 5, 7

The Inn at Olde New Berlin

NEW BERLIN

The Inn at Olde New Berlin
321 Market Street, 17855-0390
(717) 966-0321

"A luxurious base for indulging in a clutch of quiet pleasures" is *The Philadelphia Inquirer's* most apt decription for this elegantly appointed Victorian inn. The superb dining opportunities at Gabiel's Restaurant (on-site) coupled with the antique-filled lodging accommodations provide romance and ambience. An upscale experience in a rural setting. Guests relay that they depart feeling nurtured, relaxed,

---

year; 6 Pets welcome; 7 Children welcome; 8 Tennis nearby; 9 Swimming nearby; 10 Golf nearby; 11 Skiing nearby; 12 May be booked through travel agent

yet most of all inspired. Gifts, herb garden, A/C, AAA approved.

Hosts: Nancy and John Showers
Rooms: 6 (PB) $75-85
Full Breakfast
Credit Cards: A, B
Notes: 2, 3, 4, 5, 7, 8, 9, 10

NEW WILMINGTON

Behm's Bed and Breakfast

166 Waugh Ave., 16142
(800) 932-3315

Located but one block from Westminster College campus, Behm's 100-year-old B&B is comfortably furnished with family, primitive, and collected antiques. Located within walking distance of shops and restaurants, Behm's is surrounded by rural Old Order Amish whose "clip-clopping" buggy horses can be heard and seen in every direction.

Hosts: Bob and Nancy Behm
Rooms: 5 (1PB; 4SB) $50
Full, Healthy Breakfast
Credit Cards: A, B
Notes: 2, 5, 7, 8, 9, 10

NEWVILLE

Nature's Nook Farm

740 Shed Rd., 17241
(717) 776-5619

Nature's Nook Farm is located in a quiet, peaceful setting along the Blue Mountains. Warm Mennonite hospitality and clean, comfortable lodging await you. Enjoy freshly brewed garden tea in season. Homemade cinnamon rolls, muffins or coffee cake a specialty. Stroll along the

flower gardens, close to Colonel Denning State Park with hiking trails, fishing, and swimming. Two hours to Lancaster, one hour to Harrisburg, one and a half hours to Gettysburg and Hershey. Wheelchair accessible.

Hosts: Don and Lois Leatherman
Rooms: 1 (PB) $45
Continental Breakfast
Credit Cards: None
Notes: 2, 5, 7, 8, 9, 10

NORTH EAST

Vineyard Bed and Breakfast

10757 Sidehill Road, 16428
(814) 725-5307

Your hosts would like to welcome you to the "Heart of Grape Country" on the shores of Lake Erie where you are surrounded by vineyards and orchards. Our turn-of-the-century farmhouse is quiet and peaceful with rooms furnished with queen- or king-size beds and tastefully decorated to complement our name.

Hosts: Clyde and Judy Burnham
Rooms: 4 (2PB; 2SB) $55
Full Breakfast
Credit Cards: A, B
Notes: 2, 5, 7, 9, 10, 11

NORTH WALES

Joseph Ambler Inn

1005 Horsham Rd., 19454
(215) 362-7500; (215) 361-5924 (FAX)

The Joseph Ambler Inn is a historical Colonial estate featuring exceptional

---

NOTES: Credit cards accepted: A Master Card; B Visa; C American Express; D Discover Card; E Diners Club; F Other; 2 Personal checks accepted; 3 Lunch available; 4 Dinner available; 5 Open all

evening dining. Beautifully appointed guest rooms are furnished with antiques and reproductions, all with private baths. Full, country breakfast is included. The Inn offers exclusive facilities for banquets, meetings, and private parties. Set on 13 acres of lawns and gardens, it is perfect for small wedding receptions and rehearsal dinners. Please call for a tour or reservations.

Hosts: Steve and Terry Kratz
Rooms: 28 (PB) $95-140
Full Breakfast
Credit Cards: A, B, C, D, E
Notes: 2, 4, 5, 7, 8, 9, 10, 12

ORRTANNA

Hickory Bridge Farm

96 Hickory Bridge Rd., 17353
(717) 642-5261

Only eight miles west of historical Gettysburg. Unique country dining and B&B. Cozy cottages with woodstoves and private baths located in secluded wooded settings along a stream. Full, farm breakfast served at the farmhouse which was built in the late 1700s. Country dining offered on Fridays, Saturdays, and Sundays in a 130-year-old barn decorated with many antiques. Family owned and operated for over 15 years.

Hosts: Dr. and Nancy Jean Hammett
Rooms: 7 (6PB; 1SB) $79-89
Full Breakfast
Credit Cards: A, B
Notes: 2, 4 (on weedends)5, 7, 8, 9, 10, 11

OXFORD

Log House Bed and Breakfast

15225 Limestone Road, 19363
(610) 932-9257

Clean, quiet, comfortable, Chester County log home. Away from city and traffic noises. Midway between Lancaster (Amish country), Philadelphia, and Wilmington. Air-conditioned rooms, private baths. Private baths. Family room available. No smoking. Surrounded by Brandywine Valley activities: gardens, museums, art galleries, etc. Open year round.

Hosts: Ephraim and Arlene Hershey
Rooms: 4 (3PB; 1SB) $50
Full Breakfast served by candlelight
Credit Cards: None
Notes: 2, 5, 7, 8, 9, 10, 11

PARADISE

Maple Lane Farm Bed and Breakfast

505 Paradise Lane, 17562
(717) 687-7479

This 200-acre family owned dairy farm is situated in the heart of Amish Country with nearby quilt and craft shops, museums, farmers' markets, antique shops, outlets, and auctions. The large front porch overlooks spacious lawn, green meadows, and rolling hills with no busy highways. Pleasantly furnished rooms have quilts, crafts, canopy, and poster beds, TV, and air-conditioning. Victorian parlor for guest use. Breakfast served daily. Featured in

year; 6 Pets welcome; 7 Children welcome; 8 Tennis nearby; 9 Swimming nearby; 10 Golf nearby; 11 Skiing nearby; 12 May be booked through travel agent

several national magazines.

Hosts: Ed and Marion Rohrer
Rooms: 4 (2PB; 2SB) $45-58
Continental Plus Breakfast
Credit Cards: None
Notes: 2, 5, 7, 8, 9, 10, 12

PEACH BOTTOM

Inn - Between

177 Riverview Road, 17563
(717) 548-2141

Our century-old farmhouse sits in the roling hills of Lancaster County. From the enclosed second floor porch you can look out over the beautiful countryside. We offer a peaceful, comfortable stay after a day of sight-seeing or shopping, or a quiet getaway for a weekend. A full breakfast is provided including specially prepared dishes along with homemade breads and pastries.

Hosts: Bob and Miriam Dempsey
Rooms: 3 (1PB; 2SB) $50-60
Full Breakfast
Credit Cards: None
Notes: 2, 5, 7, 10

Pleasant Grove Farm

368 Pilottown Road, 17563
(717) 548-3100

Located in beautiful, historic Lancaster County, this 160-acre dairy farm has been a family-run operation for 110 years, earning the title of Century Farm by the Pennsylvania Department of Agriculture. As a working farm, it provides guests the opportunity to experience daily life in a rural setting. Built in 1814, 1818, and 1820, the

house once served as a country store and post office. Full country breakfast served by candlelight.

Hosts: Charles and Labertha Tindall
Rooms: 4 (SB) $45-60
Full Breakfast
Credit Cards: None
Notes: 2, 5, 7, 9

Inn - Between

PHILADELPHIA

Association of Bed and Breakfasts in Philadelphia, Valley Forge, and Brandywine

P.O. Box 562, Valley Forge, 19481
(610) 783-7838; (800) 344-0123; (610) 783-7783 (FAX)

There is a B&B for you!—whether business, vacation, getaways, or relocating. Also serving Bucks and Lancaster Counties. Over 500 rooms available in historic city/coutry inn, town houses, unhosted estate cottages, apartments. Request a free brochure, family plan, jacuzzi, fireplace, pool, or descriptive directory ($3). Special services include gift certificates, dinner reservations, wedding/special occasions/photography at unique B&Bs, personal attention, and gracious hospitality. Featured in *Philadephia Magazine*.

NOTES: Credit cards accepted: A Master Card; B Visa; C American Express; D Discover Card; E Diners Club; F Other; 2 Personal checks accepted; 3 Lunch available; 4 Dinner available; 5 Open all

Rates rage from $35 to $135. Major credit cards accepted. Carolyn Williams, coordinator.

PITTSBURGH

Country Road Bed and Breakfast

Moody Rd., Box 265, Clinton, 15026
(412) 899-2528

A peaceful, quiet, farm setting just five miles from Gr. Pittsburgh Airport with pick-up service available, and twenty minutes from downtown. A restored 100-year-old farmhouse with trout pond, in-ground pool, screened-in front porch. Recently a cottage, once a springhouse, and 200-year-old log cabin were restored and made available to guests. Golf course within walking distance, and air tours available in vintage, Piper restored aircraft.

Hosts: Jan and David Cornell
Rooms: 5 (4PB; 1SB) $55-100
Full Breakfast
Credit Cards: A, B
Notes: 2, 5, 7, 9, 10

POCONO MOUNTAINS (SEE ALSO—CANADENSIS AND CRESCO)

Eagle Rock Lodge B&B

Box 265 River Road, **Shawnee on Delaware**, 18356
(717) 421-2139

This century-old, seven-room inn is located on 10½ Delaware River acres adjacent to the scenic Delaware Water Gap National Recreation Area and the Pocono Mountains. Breakfast is served on an 80 ft. screened porch overlooking the river. Enjoy a step back in time to a more relaxed bygone era.

Hosts: Jane and Jim Cox
Rooms: 8 (1PB; 6SB) $60-95
Full Breakfast
Credit Cards: C
Notes: 2, 5, 7, 8, 9, 10, 11, 12

Eagle Rock Lodge Bed and Breakfast

POINT PLEASANT (NEW HOPE)

Tattersall Inn

Cafferty and River Road, Box 569, 18950
(215) 297-8233

This 18th-century, plastered, fieldstone home with its broad porches and manicured lawns resembles the unhurried atmosphere of a bygone era. Enjoy the richly wainscoted entry hall, formal dining room with marble fireplace, and a collection of vintage phonographs. Step back in time when you enter the Colonial common room with beamed ceiling and walk-in fireplace. The spacious, antique-furnished guest rooms are a joy. Air conditioned. Private baths.

Hosts: Gerry and Herb Moss
Rooms: 6 (PB) $70-109
Continental Breakfast
Credit Cards: A, B, C, D
Notes: 2, 5, 7, 8, 9, 12

year; 6 Pets welcome; 7 Children welcome; 8 Tennis nearby; 9 Swimming nearby; 10 Golf nearby; 11 Skiing nearby; 12 May be booked through travel agent

Tattersall Inn

QUARRYVILLE

Runnymede Farm Guest House Bed and Breakfast

1030 Robert Fulton Highway, 17566
(717) 786-3625

Enjoy our comfortable farmhouse in southern Lancaster County. The rooms are clean and air conditioned, and the lounge has a TV. Close to tourist attractions, but not in the mainstream. Country breakfast is optional.

Hosts: Herbert and Sara Hess
Rooms: 3 (SB) $35-40
Full Breakfast
Credit Cards: None
Notes: 2, 5, 7, 8, 9, 10

SAINT THOMAS

Heavenly Sent B&B

7886 LWW, 17252
(717) 369-5882; (717) 369-3996 (FAX)

Come to Heavenly Sent B&B and enjoy a memorable experience. Gorgeous views of the mountains and orchards; delicious, healthy breakfast by candlelight; herbal walkways and gardens; relaxation treatments; meticulously decorated rooms. Whirlpools, private baths. Near state parks, White Tail, antiquing, and golf. Open to individuals, married couples, and families. For reservations call the above number.

Hosts: Dr. Gregg and Karen Brady
Rooms: 2 (PB) $80-120
Choice of Continental or Full Breakfast
Credit Cards: A, B
Notes: 2, 3 & 4 (for additional charge), 5, 7 (limited), 9, 10, 11, 12 (restricted)

SCOTTDALE

Pine Wood Acres Bed and Breakfast

Rural Route 1, Box 634, 15683-9567
(412) 887-5404

A country home surrounded by four acres of woods, wildflowers, and herb and flower gardens. Ten miles from the Pennsylvania Turnpike and I-70, New Stanton exits; 22 miles from Frank Lloyd Wright's Fallingwater. Full breakfasts and warm hospitality are yours to enjoy at Pine Wood Acres. Hosts are members of the Mennonite Church.

Hosts: Ruth and James Horsch
Rooms: 3 (SB) $58.30 (SB)-79.50 (PB)
Full Breakfast
Credit Cards: None
Notes: 2, 5, 6, 7, 8, 9, 10, 11, 12

SHIPPENSBURG

Field and Pine Bed and Breakfast

2155 Ritner Highway, 17257
(717) 776-7179

Surrounded by stately pine trees, Field

NOTES: Credit cards accepted: A Master Card; B Visa; C American Express; D Discover Card; E Diners Club; F Other; 2 Personal checks accepted; 3 Lunch available; 4 Dinner available; 5 Open all

and Pine is a family-owned bed and breakfast with the charm of an early American stone house on an 80-acre gentleman's farm. Built in 1790, the house has seven working fireplaces, original wide-pine floors, and stenciled walls. Bedrooms are furnished with antiques, quilts, and comforters. A gourmet breakfast is served in the formal dining room. Three miles from I-81 between Carlisle and Shippensburg.

Hosts: Mary Ellen and Allan Williams
Rooms: 3 (1PB; 2SB) $65-75
Full Breakfast
Credit Cards: A, B
Notes: 2, 5, 8, 9, 10, 12

Wilmar Manor Bed and Breakfast

303 West King Street, 17257
(717) 532-3784

A beautiful Victorian mansion built in the heart of Shippensburg in 1898. You can stroll down Main Street of our historic village or enjoy the serenity of our spacious landscaped gardens. The air-conditioned guest rooms are comfortably furnished with antiques. Your choice of private or shared baths at reasonable rates. Enjoy a delicious breakfast served in our formal Vidtorian dining room.

Hosts: Marise and Wilton Banks
Rooms: 7 (2PB; 5SB) $48-60
Full Breakfast
Credit Cards: None
Notes: 2, 5, 7, 8, 9, 10, 11, 12

SMOKETOWN—SEE LANCASTER COUNTY

SOMERSET

H.B.'s Cottage

231 West Church Street, 15501
(814) 443-1204; (814) 443-4313 (FAX)

H.B.'s Cottage, an exclusive and elegant B&B located within the Borough of Somerset, is a stone and frame 1920s cottage with an oversize fireplace in the living room. It is furnished in the traditional manner with accent pieces from overseas travels by innkeepers—a retired Naval Officer and his wife—and collectible Teddy bears from the hostess' extensive collection. The guest room is warmly and romantically decorated and has a private porch. Downhill and cross-country skiing, mountain biking, and tennis are specialties of the hosts. Located close to Seven Springs Mountain Resort, Falling Water Hidden Valley Resort, biking and hiking trails, and white water sports. Advance reservations are suggested.

Hosts: Hank and Phyllis Vogt
Rooms: 1 (PB) $65
Fulll Breakfast (Tea served 3-5PM)
Credit Cards: A, B
Notes: 2, 6 (limited), 8, 9, 10, 11

H.B.'s Cottage

year; 6 Pets welcome; 7 Children welcome; 8 Tennis nearby; 9 Swimming nearby; 10 Golf nearby; 11 Skiing nearby; 12 May be booked through travel agent

SPRUCE CREEK

The Dells' B&B at Cedar Hill Farm

HC-01, Box 26, Rte 45 east, 16683
(814) 632-8319

This early 1800s farmhouse is located in Huntingdon County on an active livestock farm. Individual and family activities are available at Old Bedford Village, Horse Shoe Curve, Bland's Park, Raystown Lake, Lincoln and Indian Caverns, and Penn State University. Member Pennsylvania Farm Vacation Association. Fishing and hunting available on private and state game lands during stated seasons; proper licenses required.

Hostess: Sharon M. Dell
Rooms: 4 (SB) $35-50
Full Breakfast
Credit Cards: A, B
Notes: 2, 5, 7, 11

STAHLSTOWN

Thorn's Cottage Bed and Breakfast

R.D. #1, Box 254, 15687
(412) 593-6429

Located in the natural, cultural, and historic Ligonier Valley area of Pennsylvania's scenic Laurel Mountains, PA turnpike eight miles away, fifty miles east of Pittsburgh, the secluded three-room cottage offers guests a homey, woodland privacy. In addition, the hosts offer one bedroom, shared bath in their cozy, arts-and-crafts bungalow. Porches and herb garden complement the European, country-in-spired ambience. Breakfast includes homebaked muffins and scones to complement country, gourmet-style dishes.

Hosts: Larry and Beth Thorn
Rooms: 1 cottage (PB); 1 room (SB) $40-55
Full Breakfast
Credit Cards: None
Notes: 2, 5, 7, 9, 10, 11

STARRUCCA

Nethercott Inn B&B

P.O. Box 26, 18462
(717) 727-2211

This lovely, 1893 Victorian home is nestled in a small village in the Endless Mountains and furnished in antiques. All rooms have queen size beds and private baths. A full breakfast is included. Located three and one-half hours from New York City and Philadelphia, and eight hours from Toronto, Canada.

Hosts: Ned and Ginny Nethercott
Rooms: 5 (PB) $65
Full Breakfast
Credit Cards: A, B, C, D
Notes: 2, 5, 7, 10, 11, 12 (10%)

STRASBURG—SEE LANCASTER COUNTY

THOMPSON

Farmhouse Bed and Breakfast

Campsite Road, RR 2, Box 57, 18465
(717) 727-3061

An 1864 farmstead that raises sheep and other farm animals. Enjoy the quiet of our

---

NOTES: Credit cards accepted: A Master Card; B Visa; C American Express; D Discover Card; E Diners Club; F Other; 2 Personal checks accepted; 3 Lunch available; 4 Dinner available; 5 Open all

country home. Secluded getaway decorated in period pieces and painteds with antique woodstove and glass enclosed sunporch. Full country breakfast included. Delectable pasta dishes prepared by your Italian hostess upon advance request. Also private loft for groups up to eight.

Hosts: Marion and Harold Hartnett
Rooms: 4 (1PB; 3SB) $55-65
Full Breakfast
Credit Cards: None
Notes: 2, 4, 5, 7, 11

Jefferson Inn

Route 171, Rural Delivery 2, Box 36, 18465
(717) 727-2625; (800) JEFFINN

Built in 1871, the inn offers reasonably priced accommodations and a full-service restaurant. Situated in the rolling hills of northeast Pennsylvania, there are thousands of acres available nearby for fishing, boating, and some of the best deer and turkey hunting around. Other seasonal activities include skiing, snowmobiling, horseback riding, and golf. Good, Gospel-preaching churches are nearby.

Hosts: Douglas and Marge Stark
Rooms: 6 (3PB; 3SB) $30-50
Continental Breakfast (full available for extra fee)
Credit Cards: A, B
Notes: 2, 3, 4, 5, 6, 7, 8, 9, 10, 11, 12

THORNTON

Pace One Restaurant and Country Inn

P.O. Box 108, 19373
(610) 459-3702; (610) 558-0825 (FAX)

Pace One is a beautifully renovated 1740s

stone barn. We have six overnight rooms, all with private baths and queen-size beds. Pac One is known for its restaurant. The seventy-five seat restaurant and bar is very relaxed and rustic. The menu is country imaginative and has an offering of fresh seafood, steaks, fowl, and lamb. All deserts are homemade. Private rooms are also available for meetings and dining. Reservations for the Inn rooms are taken Monday thru Friday, 9 AM to 5 PM by the sales office.

Proprietor: Ted Pace
Rooms: 6 (PB)
Continental Plus Breakfast
Credit Cards: A, B, C, E
Notes: 2, 3, 4, 5, 7, 8, 10, 12

THREE SPRINGS

Aughwick House Bed and Breakfast

Box 977, R.D. 1, 17264
(814) 447-3027

Come visit us! We are located at the end of a country road along the beautiful Aughwick Creek; it is a fine, safe stream well suited for family fun. Quiet and peaceful, built with a Gothic style, the wood frame house is a feast for the eyes. Rambling and numerous porches for your enjoyment. Inside is done in 1890s fashion. Enjoy our breakfast, we dare you to find better eating. Not just a stop, we are a vacation!

Hosts: Billy and Caroline Wible
Rooms: 9 (SB) $25-30 per person per night
Full Breakfast Only
Credit Cards: None
Notes: 2, 3, 5, 7, 9

year; 6 Pets welcome; 7 Children welcome; 8 Tennis nearby; 9 Swimming nearby; 10 Golf nearby; 11 Skiing nearby; 12 May be booked through travel agent

WELLSBORO

Kaltenbach's Bed and Breakfast

R. D. 6, Box 106A, Stony Fork Road, 16901
(717) 724-4954; (800) 722-4954

This sprawling, country home with room for 32 guests offers visitors comfortable lodging, home-style breakfasts, and warm hospitality. Set on a 72-acre farm, Kaltenbach's provides ample opportunity for walks through meadows, pastures, and forests, picnicing, and watching the sheep, pigs, rabbits, and wildlife. All-you-can-eat country-style breakfasts are served. Honeymoon suites have tubs for two. Hunting and golf packages are available. Pennsylvania Grand Canyon. ABBA 2 crown award-winner.

Host: Lee Kaltenbach
Rooms: 11 (9PB; 2SB) $60-125
Full Breakfast
Credit Cards: A, B
Notes: 2, 3, 4, 5, 7, 8, 9, 10, 11

WILKES-BARRE

Ponda-Rowland Bed and Breakfast Inn and Farm Vacations

Rural Route 1, Box 348, Dallas, 18612
(717) 639-3245; (800) 854-3286; (717) 639-5531 (FAX)

The farmhouse, circa 1850, features a large stone fireplace, beamed ceilings, fireplaces in rooms, and museum-quality country antiques. On this large, scenic farm in the Endless Mountain region of Pennsylvania, guests can see and touch pigs, goats, sheep, cows, rabbits, and a horse. They also can enjoy 34 acres of a private wildlife refuge, including six ponds, walking and skiing trails, canoeing, swimming, and ice skating. Nearby are horseback riding, air tours, state parks, trout fishing, hunting, restaurants, county fairs, downhill skiing.

Hosts: Jeanette and Cliff Rowland
Rooms: 5 (PB) $55-85
Full Breakfast
Credit Cards: A, B, C, D
Notes: 2, 5, 7, 9, 10, 11, 12

Kaltenbach's Bed and Breakfast

YORK

The Smyser-Bair House

30 South Beaver Street, 17401
(717) 854-3411

A magnificent Italianate town house in the historic district. Rich in history and architectural details with crystal chandeliers and stained glass windows. Enjoy our antiques, warm hospitality, and player piano. Near Lancaster, Gettysburg, and Baltimore. Walk to farmer's markets. Convenient parking.

Hosts: The King Family
Rooms: 4 (1PB; 3SB) $60-80
Full Breakfast
Credit Cards: A, B
Notes: 2, 5, 7, 10, 12

NOTES: Credit cards accepted: A Master Card; B Visa; C American Express; D Discover Card; E Diners Club; F Other; 2 Personal checks accepted; 3 Lunch available; 4 Dinner available; 5 Open all

Rhode Island

BLOCK ISLAND

The Barrington Inn
P.O. Box 397, (Corner of Beach & Ocean Aves),
02807-0397
(401) 466-5510; (401) 466-5170 (FAX)

Known for its warmth and hospitality, The Barrington Inn is an 1886 farmhouse situated on a knoll overlooking the New Harbor area of Block Island. There are six individually decorated guest rooms with private baths, and two housekeeping apartments. A light breakfast is served each morning by the hosts. Amenities include two guests' sitting rooms (one with TV), guests' refrigerator, ceiling fans, comfortable beds, front porch, back deck, afternoon beverages. No smoking.

Rooms: 6 (PB) $45-145
Continental Plus Breakfast
Credit Cards: A, B
Notes: 2, 7 (over 12), 9

The Continental
Box 575, 02807
(401) 466-5136

One of the island's smallest inns, beautifully situated overlooking Continental Pond, which is surrounded by willow trees and home to ducks and geese. A tranquil country setting. The country style is cozy and inviting, with a large deck overlooking the pond, providing guests with a place to relax and enjoy the special view. In the historic district at the very top of the hill and within easy walking distance from the ferry, beach, and town.

Hostess: Lila Clerk
Rooms: 2 (SB) $65-115 (seasonal)
Full Breakfast
Credit Cards: None
Notes: 2, 5, 8, 9

Hotel Manisses
1 Spring Street, 02807
(401) 466-2421; (401) 466-2858 (FAX)

Restored Victorian hotel with authentic turn-of-the-century furnishings and today's comforts. All rooms with private bath and telephone; some have jacuzzis. Fine dining in our dining room overlooking the fountains and gardens. After-dinner drinks and flaming coffees served in upstairs parlor.

Hosts: Justin and Joan Abrams; Steve and Rita Draper
Rooms: 17 (PB) $100-350
Full Breakfast
Credit Cards: A, B, C
Notes: 2, 4, 5, 7 (over 10), 8, 9, 10, 12

The Rose Farm Inn
Roslyn - Box E, 02807
(401) 466-2034 or 2021; (401) 466-2053 (FAX)

Experience the romance of the Victorian

year; 6 Pets welcome; 7 Children welcome; 8 Tennis nearby; 9 Swimming nearby; 10 Golf nearby; 11 Skiing nearby; 12 May be booked through travel agent

era. Treat yourself to a romantic room beautifully furnished with antiques and king- or queen-size bed. Enjoy the peaceful tranquility of the farm from shaded decks cooled by gentle breezes. Gaze at the ocean from your window or share a whirl- pool bath for two. Awaken to a light buffet breakfast served in our charming porch dining room with an ocean view.

Hostess: Judith B. Rose
Rooms: 19 (17PB; 2SB)) $90-175
Continental Plus Breakfast
Credit Cards: A, B, C, D
Open April to Nov.
Notes: 2, 7 (over 11), 8, 9

The Sheffield House

Box C-Z High Street, 02807
(401) 466-2494; (401) 466-5067 (FAX)

Lovely Victorian set amid gardens in the historic district—five minute walk to ferry dock, shops, restaurants, and beaches. Porch with rocking chairs adds to the tranquil ambiance. Buffet breakfast and afternoon tea in the day room. Special off season prices.

Hosts: Steve and Claire McQueeny
Rooms: 7 (5PB; 2SB) $50-150
Expansive Continental Breakfast
Credit Cards: A, B, C
Notes: 2, 5, 8, 9, 12

CHARLESTON

Willows

P.O. Box 1260, 5310 Route 1, 02813
(401) 364-7727; (401) 364-0576 (FAX)

Visit this 15-acre estate beside a salt water pond with boating, outdoor pool, and tennis court. Enjoy quiet, relaxing sur- roundings—very well maintained. All rooms have air-conditioning and telephone.

Hosts: Scott and Loren Duhamel
Rooms: 10 (PB) $50-120
Full Breakfast
Credit Cards: A, B
Notes: 4, 8, 9, 10

The Sheffield House

Ye Ole General Stanton Inn

P.O. Box 1263, 02813
(401) 364-0100

Deeply rooted in fascinating American history, The General Stanton Inn, circa 1667, combines a unique atmosphere with present-day convenience. The Inn's rooms are a warm departure from the average, while the kitchen is run to the highest standards of the culinary art. Close to some of the country's most beautiful and uncrowded beaches, the world's largest casino, Newport, antique shops, and Mystic Seaport.

Hosts: The Winegars
Rooms: 15 (PB)
Full Breakfast in summer, Continental in winter
Credit Cards: A, B, D
Notes: 3, 4, 5, 7, 8, 9, 10, 11

NOTES: Credit cards accepted: A Master Card; B Visa; C American Express; D Discover Card; E Diners Club; F Other; 2 Personal checks accepted; 3 Lunch available; 4 Dinner available; 5 Open all

Ye Ole General Stanton Inn

KINGSTON

Hedgerow B&B

1747 Mooresfield Road, P.O. Box 1586, 02881
(401) 783-2671; (800) 486-4587

A lovely Colonial built in 1933 on two and one-quarter acres with tennis courts and formal gardens. Conveniently located 15 miles from Newport, 30 miles south of Providence, and next to the University of Rhode Island. The ferry to Block Island, beaches, and Mystic and Connecticut's seaport are within easy reach. Call for price information.

Hosts: Ann and Jim Ross
Rooms: 4 (SB-2 rooms share 1 bath) $60 + 7% tax
Full Breakfast
Credit Cards: D
Notes: 2, 5, 7, 8, 9, 10

MIDDLETOWN

Finnegan's Inn at Shadow Lawn

120 Miantonomi Ave., 02842
(401) 849-1298; (800) 828-0000; (401) 849-1306 (FAX)

Finnegan's Inn is one of Newport County's

finest B&B inns, set on two acres of beautifully landscapted lawns and gardens. This 1850s Vicotorian mansion, with its crystal chandeliers and stained-glass windows, has eight large bedrooms each with private bath, TV, refrigerator, and air-conditioning. Five rooms also have attached kitchens. Come and enjoy a bottle of complimentary wine.

Hosts: Randy and Selma Fabricant
Rooms: 8 (PB)
Breakfast
Credit Cards: A, B
Notes: 5, 7 (over 12), 8, 9, 10, 12

Lindsey's Guest House

6 James St., 02842
(401) 846-9386

Walk to beaches and restaurants. Five minutes to Newport's famous mansions, Ocean Drive, Cliff Walk, boat and bus tours, and bird sanctuary. Quiet residential neighborhood with off-street parking. Large yard and deck with hostess available for information about events and discounts. Split-level, owner-occupied home with expanded continental breakfast. One room is wheelchair accessible for 28-inch wheelchair.

Hostess: Anne Lindsey
Rooms: 3 (1PB; 2SB) $45-85
Continental Plus Breakfast
Credit Cards: A, B
Notes: 2, 5, 7, 8, 9, 10, 12

NEWPORT

Cliffside Inn

2 Seaview Avenue, 02840
(800) 845-1811; (401) 848-5850 (FAX)

Nestled upon a quiet neighborhood street

year; 6 Pets welcome; 7 Children welcome; 8 Tennis nearby; 9 Swimming nearby; 10 Golf nearby; 11 Skiing nearby; 12 May be booked through travel agent

just steps away from the historic Cliff Walk, the Cliffside Inn displays the grandure of a Victorian manor with the warmth and comfort of a home. A full breakfast, consisting of homemade muffins, granola, fresh fruit, and a hot entree, such as eggs benidect or whipped cream topped french toast, is served each morning in the spacious parlor. In the evening between 5-7PM appetizers are also served. There are twelve quest rooms, each uniquely decorated in period Victorian antiques blended with luxurious Laura Ashley linens and drapes. Each room contains a telephone and private bath, some with working fireplaces and jacuzzis, or steambaths. Smoking is permitted on the large front veranda, furnished with wicker furniture and covered with floral cushions. All rooms are air-conditioned.

Host: Stephen Nicolas
Rooms: 13 (PB) $135-325
Full Hot Gourmet Breakfast
Credit Cards: A, B, C, D
Notes: 2, 5, 7 (14 and over), 8, 9, 10, 12

John Easton House

23 Catherine Street, 02840
(401) 849-6246 (Voice and FAX)

This gracious Victorian inn is listed on the National Historic Register and is situated in the heart of Newport. Each room is spacious, elegantly furnished, and has a sparkling private bathroom, air conditioning, and color television. Some rooms have kitchenettes, and some have working fireplaces for that autumn or off-season chill. Our off-season rates are lower, too. Excellent location within walking distance to the beach and waterfront boutiques.

Ample off-street parking. All rooms are non-smoking. Weekly and monthly rates.

Hosts: Ted and Carmen Gloria Critz
Rooms: 7 (PB) $65-125
Continental Breakfast
Credit Cards: A, B, D
Notes: 5, 7, 8, 9, 10, 12

Spring Street Inn

353 Spring Street, 02840
(401) 847-4767

Spring Street Inn is a charming restored Victorian home, circa 1858. We have seven double guestrooms and private baths, a harbor-view apartment for two to four people, and a comfortable guest sitting room with CATV. We serve a home-cooked, full breakfast and have off-street parking. The Inn is within walking distance to all Newport's highlights, only one block from the harbor.

Hosts: Parvin and Damian Latimore
Rooms: 8 (6PB; 2SB) $45-140
Full Breakfast
Credit Cards: A, B
Notes: 2, 5, 7, 8, 9, 12

PROVIDENCE

The Old Court Bed and Breakfast

144 Benefit Street, 02903
(401) 751-2002; (401) 272-6566 (FAX)

The Old Court is filled with antique furniture, chandeliers, and memorabilia from the nineteenth century, with each room designed to reflect period tastes. All rooms have private baths, and the antique, Victo-

NOTES: Credit cards accepted: A Master Card; B Visa; C American Express; D Discover Card; E Diners Club; F Other; 2 Personal checks accepted; 3 Lunch available; 4 Dinner available; 5 Open all

rian beds are comfortable and spacious. Just a three-minute walk from the center of downtown Providence, near Brown University and Rhode Island School of Design.

Hostess: Gail and Paul Koehler
Rooms: 11(PB) $95-160
Continental Breakfast
Credit Cards: A, B, C, D
Notes: 8

State House Inn

43 Jewett Street, 02908
(401) 785-1235; (401) 351-4201 (FAX)

A country inn usually means peace and quiet, friendly hosts, comfort and simplicity, with beautiful furnishings. The State House Inn has all of these qualifications, but just happens to be located in the city of Providence. Our inn has fireplaces, hardwood floors, Shaker or Colonial furnishings, canopy beds, and modern conveniences such as FAX, TV, and phone. Located near downtown and local colleges and universities.

Hosts: Frank and Monica Hopton
Rooms: 10 (PB) $59-99
Full Breakfast
Credit Cards: A, B, C
Notes: 2 (with CC for ID), 5, 7, 12

State House Inn

WAKEFIELD

Larchwood Inn

521 Main St., 02879
(401) 783-5454; (401) 783-1800 (FAX)

Watching over the main street of this quaint New England town for over 160 years, this grand old house, surrounded by lawns and shaded by stately trees, dispenses hospitality and good food and spirits from early morning to late at night. Historic Newport, picturesque Mystic Seaport, salty Block Island, and Foxwoods Casino are a short ride away.

Hosts: Francis and Diann Browning
Rooms: 19 (12PB; 7SB) $30-90
Full Breakfast
Credit Cards: A, B, C, D, E
Notes: 2, 3, 4, 5, 6, 7, 8, 9, 10, 11, 12

WESTERLY

Woody Hill Bed and Breakfast

149 South Woody Hill Road, 02891
(401) 322-0452

This Colonial reproduction is set on a hilltop overlooking 20 acres of informal gardens, woods, and fields. Antiques, wide-board floors, handmade quilts, and fireplaces create an early American atmosphere. A full breakfast and use of secluded 40 ft. in-ground pool are included. Close to Newport, Block Island, Mystic, and Casino.

Hostess: Ellen L. Madison, Ph. D.
Rooms: 4 (3PB; 2SB) $60-105
Full Breakfast
Credit Cards: None
Notes: 2, 5, 7, 8, 9, 10, 12

year; 6 Pets welcome; 7 Children welcome; 8 Tennis nearby; 9 Swimming nearby; 10 Golf nearby; 11 Skiing nearby; 12 May be booked through travel agent

WYOMING

The Cookie Jar Bed and Breakfast

64 Kingstown Road (Rte. 138 off I-95), 02898
(401) 539-2680; (800) 767-4262

The heart of our home, the living room, was built in 1732 as a blacksmith's shop.

Later, the forge was removed and a large granite fireplace was built by an American Indian stonemason. The original wood ceiling, hand-hewn beams, and granite walls remain today. The property was called the Perry Plantation, and, yes, they had two slaves who lived above the blacksmith's shop. We offer friendly, home-style living in a comfortable, country setting. On Route 138 just off I-95.

Hosts: Dick and Madelein Sohl
Rooms: 3 (1PB; 2SB) $60-65
Full Breakfast
Credit Cards: None
Notes: 2, 5, 7, 8, 9, 10, 12

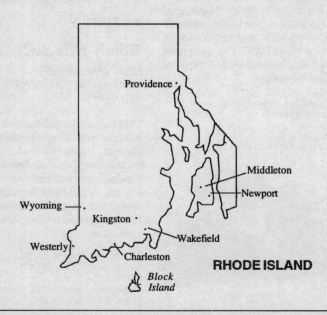

Providence •

Middleton

Newport

Wyoming —— •

Kingston •

Wakefield

Westerly •

Charleston

RHODE ISLAND

Block
Island

South Carolina

BEAUFORT

TwoSuns Inn B&B

1705 Bay Street, 29902
(803) 522-1122 (Voice and FAX); (800) 532-4244

Southern charm in Historic Beaufort (*Prince of Tides* film site) and informal ambience in a three-story, 1917, grand home right on the bay await TwoSun's guests. Visit our quaint downtown, enjoy a carriage ride through our historic waterfront community, and relax in our newly restored home, complete with Carrol's weavings, collectibles, period decor, wheelchair accessibility and business amenities.

Hosts: Carrol and Ron Kay
Rooms: 5 (PB) $89-109
Full Breakfast
Credit Cards: A, B, C
Notes: 2, 5, 8, 9, 10, 12

Two Suns Inn Bed and Breakfast

BENNETTSVILLE

The Breeden House Inn and Carriage House

404 East Main Street, 29512
(803) 479-3665; (803) 479-1040

Built in 1886, the romantic Southern mansion is situated on two acres in Bennetsville's historic district. Beautiful decor and comfortable surroundings will capture your interest and inspire your imagination. A haven for antique lovers. Listed on the National Register of Historic Places. The Inn is located 25 minutes from I-95—a great halfway point between Florida and New York. Our porches and grounds... truly a Southern tradition can be enjoyed at both guest houses. Swings, rockers, wicker, cast iron, adirondacks, and even ceiling fans await to lay a part in helping you unwind. Curl up with a book under the old magnolia tree... Sun by the pool—there's a comfy spot for everyone. Come...we have some peace, quiet, and comfort for you. No smoking. Owned and operated by a Christian family.

Hosts: Wesley and Bonnie Park
Rooms: 7 (PB) $65
Full Breakfast
Credit Cards: A, B, D
Notes: 2, 5, 7, 9, 10, 12

---

year; 6 Pets welcome; 7 Children welcome; 8 Tennis nearby; 9 Swimming nearby; 10 Golf nearby; 11 Skiing nearby; 12 May be booked through travel agent

CHARLESTON

1837 Bed and Breakfast

126 Wentworth Street, 29401
(803) 723-7166

Enjoy accommodations in a wealthy cotton planter's home and brick carriage house centrally located in Charleston's historic district. Canopied, poster, rice beds. Walk to boat tours, the old market, antique shops, restaurants, and main attractions. Near the Omni and College of Charleston. Full gourmet breakfast is served in the formal dining room and includes sausage pie, Eggs Benedict, ham omelets, and home-baked breads. The 1837 Tea Room serves afternoon tea to our guests and the public. Off-street parking.

Hosts: Sherri and Richard Dunn
Rooms: 8 (PB) $59-99
Full Breakfast
Credit Cards: A, B, C
Notes: 2, 5, 8, 9, 10

Ashley Inn Bed and Breakfast

201 Ashley Avenue, 29403
(803) 723-1848; (803) 723-9080 (FAX)

Stay in a stately, historic, circa 1835 home. So warm and hospitable, the Ashley Inn offers seven intimate bedrooms featuring canopy beds, private baths, fireplace, and air conditioning. Delicious breakfasts are served on a grand columned piazza overlooking a beautiful Charleston garden, or in the formal dining room. Relax with tea and cookies after touring nearby historic sites or enjoying the complimentary touring bicycles. Simple elegance in a warm, friendly home noted for true Southern hospitality.

Hosts: Sally and Bud Allen
Rooms: 7 (PB) $69-125
Full Breakfast
Credit Cards: A, B, C, D
Notes: 2, 5, 7 (over 12), 8, 9, 10, 12

The Belvedere

40 Rutledge Avenue, 29401
(803) 722-0973

A late 1800s Colonial mansion in the downtown historic district on Colonial Lake has an 1800 Georgian interior with mantels and woodwork. Three large bedrooms have antiques, Oriental rugs, and family collections. Easy access to everything in the area.

Hosts: David Spell and Rick Zender
Rooms: 3 (PB) $110
Continental Plus Breakfast
Credit Cards: None
Closed December 1-February 15
Notes: 2, 7 (over 8), 8, 9, 10

Country Victorian Bed and Breakfast

105 Tradd Street, 29401-2422
(803) 577-0682

Come relive the charm of the past. Relax in a rocker on the piazza of this historic home and watch the carriages go by. Walk to antique shops, churches, restaurants, art galleries, museums, and all historic points of interest. The house, built in 1820, is located in the historic district south of Broad. Rooms have private entrances and contain antique iron and brass beds, old quilts, antique oak and wicker furniture, and braided rugs over heart-of-pine floors.

NOTES: Credit cards accepted: A Master Card; B Visa; C American Express; D Discover Card; E Diners Club; F Other; 2 Personal checks accepted; 3 Lunch available; 4 Dinner available; 5 Open all

Homemade cookies will be waiting. Many extras!

Hostess: Diane Deardurff Weed
Rooms: 2 (PB) $65-90
Expanded Continental Breakfast
Credit Cards: None
Notes: 2, 5, 7, 8, 9, 10, 12

King George IV Inn and Guests

32 George Street, 29401
(803) 723-9339

A 200-year-old, circa 1790, Charleston Historic House located in the heart of historic district. The inn is Federal style with three levels of Charleston side porches. All rooms have decorative fireplaces, 10-12 foot ceilings, wide-planked hardwood floors, old furnishings, and antiques. Private baths, parking, AC, TVs. One-minute walk to historic King Street, five-minute walk to historic market. A step back in time!

Hosts: Lynn, Sara, BJ, and Mike
Rooms: 8 (PB) $65-130
Continental Breakfast
Credit Cards: A, B
Notes: 2, 5, 6 (by arrangement), 7, 8, 9, 10, 12

The Kitchen House, Circa 1732

126 Tradd Street, 29401
(803) 577-6362

Nestled in the heart of the historic district, the Kitchen House is a completely restored, 18th-century, kitchen dwelling. Southern hospitality, absolute privacy, cozy fireplaces, antiques, patio, and colonial herb garden await you. The refrigerator and pantry are stocked for breakfast. The pre-Revolutionary War house was featured in *Colonial Homes* magazine and written up in the *New York Times*.

Hostess: Lois Evans
Rooms: 3 (PB) $95-175
Full Breakfast
Credit Cards: A, B
Notes: 2, 5, 7, 8, 9, 10, 12

Rutledge Victorian Inn and Guest House

114 Rutledge Avenue, 29401
(803) 722-7551

Welcome to the past! This century-old Victorian house in Charleston's downtown historic district is quaint but elegant, with large, decorative porches, columns, and antique gingerbread. The authentic Old Charleston house has decorative fireplaces, hardwood floors, 12-foot ceilings, 10-foot doors and windows, old furnishings, and antiques. Modern amenities include air conditioning, TV, private or shared baths, ice machine, and refrigerator. Walking distance to all historic attractions. Homemade goodies served in continental breakfast.

Hosts: Sara, BJ, Lynn, and Mike
Rooms: 11 (7PB; 4SB) $45-130
Continental Breakfast
Credit Cards: A, B
Notes: 2, 5, 6 (some), 7, 8, 9, 10, 12

Richland Street Bed and Breakfast

COLUMBIA

Richland Street Bed and Breakfast

1425 Richland Street, 29201
(803) 779-7001; (800) 779-7011

Richland Street Bed and Breakfast is a Victorian home located in the heart of Columbia's Historic District in walking distance of tour homes, restaurants, and downtown shopping. Inside you are greeted with a large gathering area, seven oversize guest rooms with private baths, and loads of hospitality. Each room has its own personality, decorated with period antiques. The Bridal Suite with whirlpool tub is especially inviting. You will enjoy the front porches with gazebo and rockers. Special attention given to each guest includes a deluxe continental breakfast served in classic Victorian style.

Host: Naomi S. Perryman
Rooms: 7 (PB) $79-120
Deluxe Continental Breakfast
Credit Cards: A, B, C
Notes: 2 (in advance), 5, 10

GEORGETOWN

Ashfield Manor

3030 S. Island Rd., 29440
(803) 546-0464; (800) 483-5002

This Christian home offers southern hospitality in the style of a real southern plantation. Ashfield Manor offers an elegant country setting. All rooms are oversized and redecorated with period furnishings; private entrance and color TV. Continental breakfast is served in your room, the parlor, or on the 57-foot screened porch.

Georgetown is quaint and historic with many attractions.

Hosts: Dave and Carol Ashenfelder
Rooms: 4 (SB) $45-65
Continental Breakfast
Credit Cards: A, B, C, D, E
Notes: 2, 5, 7, 8, 9, 10, 12

The Shaw House

613 Cypress Court, 29440
(803) 546-9663

A spacious two-story Colonial home in a natural setting—a beautiful view overlooking miles of marshland—perfect for bird watchers. Within walking distance to downtown and great restaurants on the waterfront. Rooms are large with many antiques and private baths. Breakfast is served at our guests' convenience. Also included are nighttime chocolates on each pillow, turn backs, and some loving extras—guest always leave with a little gift like prayers, recipes, and/or jellies. AAA, Moblie, and ABBA approved.

Hosts: Mary and Joe Shaw
Rooms: 3 (PB) $50-60
Full Breakfast
Credit Cards: None
Notes: 2, 5, 7, 8, 9, 10

the Shaw House

"Shipwright's" Bed and Breakfast

609 Cypress Ct., 29440
(803) 527-4475

Three thousand plus square feet of beautiful, quiet, clean home is yours to use when you stay. It's nautically attired and tastefully laced with family heirlooms. Guests say they feel like they just stayed at their best friend's home. The bedrooms and baths are beautiful and very comfortable. You'll never get "Grandma Eicker's Pancakes" anywhere else (the inn is famous for them). There's a great story behind the pancakes! The view from the large porch is breathtaking. Five minutes from Ocean Beach.

Hostess: Lea Wright
Rooms: 2 (1PB; 1SB) $50
Full Breakfast
Credit Cards: None
Notes: 2, 5, 7, 8, 9, 10

GREENWOOD

Inn on the Square

104 Court Street, 29646
(803) 223-4488; (803) 223-7067 (FAX)

Each of the 48 rooms at the Inn is spacious and filled with lovely antique reproductions including rice-carved or pencil post beds with genuine Bates spreads, writing desks, armoires, all in solid mahogany. The Inn is convenient to shopping and has a quiet atmosphere of privacy and service. A small inn with lots of big city services!

Rooms: 48 (PB) call for 1995 rates
Full Breakfast (Continental on the weekend)
Credit Cards: A, B, C, D, E
Notes: 2, 3, 4, 5, 7, 8, 9, 10, 12

HONEA PATH

"Sugarfoot Castle"

211 S. Main St., 29654
(803) 369-6565

Enormous trees umbrella this 19th-century, brick, Victorian home. Fresh flowers grace the 14-inch thick walled rooms furnished with family heirlooms. Enjoy the living room's interesting collections or the library's comfy chairs, TV, VCR, books, fireplace, desk, and game table. Upon arising, guests find coffee and juice outside their doors, followed by breakfast of hot breads, cereal, fresh fruit, and beverages served by candlelight in the dining room. Rock away the world's cares on a screened porch overlooking peaceful grounds. AAA approved.

Hosts: Gale and Cecil Evans
Rooms: 3 (SB) $48-51
Heavy Continental Breakfast
Credit Cards: A, B
Notes: 2, 5, 8, 9, 10

Wade-Beckham House

year; 6 Pets welcome; 7 Children welcome; 8 Tennis nearby; 9 Swimming nearby; 10 Golf nearby; 11 Skiing nearby; 12 May be booked through travel agent

LANCASTER

Wade-Beckham House

3385 Great Falls Highway, 29720
(803) 285-1105

A circa 1832 plantation house listed on the National Register of Historic Places. Rural setting offering the Rose Room, the Summer House Room, the Wade Hampton Room. Antique and craft stores on premises. Peaceful homey environment.

Hosts: Bill and Jan Duke
Rooms: 3 (SB) $60
Full Breakfast
Credit Cards: None
Notes: 2, 8, 10

MCCLELLANVILLE

Laurel Hill Plantation

8913 North Highway 17, P. O. Box 190, 29458
(803) 887-3708

A nature lover's delight! Laurel Hill faces the Atlantic Ocean. Wraparound porches provide spectacular views of creeks and marshes. The reconstructed house is furnished with antiques that reflect the Low Country lifestyle. A perfect blend of yesterday's nostalgia and today's comfort in a setting of unparalleled coastal vistas. Located on Highway 17, 30 miles north of Charleston, 25 miles south of Georgetown and 60 miles south of Myrtle Beach.

Hosts: Jackie and Lee Morrison
Rooms: 4 (PB) $65-85
Full Breakfast
Credit Cards: A, B
Notes: 2, 5, 7 (restricted), 9, 10, 12

Serendipity, an Inn

MYRTLE BEACH

Serendipity, an Inn

407 North 71st Avenue, 29577
(803) 449-5268

An award-winning, mission-style inn is just 300 yards from the ocean beach and has a heated pool and Jacuzzi. All rooms have air conditioning, color TV, private baths, and refrigerators. Secluded patio, Ping-Pong, and shuffleboard. Over 70 golf courses nearby, as well as fishing, tennis, restaurants, theaters, and shopping. Ninety miles to historic Charleston. Near all country music theaters.

Hosts: Terry and Sheila Johnson
Rooms: 14 (PB) $52-92
Hearty Continental Breakfast
Credit Cards: A, B, C, D
Notes: 7, 8, 9, 10, 12

Laurel Hill Plantation

NOTES: Credit cards accepted: A Master Card; B Visa; C American Express; D Discover Card; E Diners Club; F Other; 2 Personal checks accepted; 3 Lunch available; 4 Dinner available; 5 Open all

ROCK HILL

East Main Guest House
600 E. Main St., 29730
(803) 366-1161

After extensive renovations, the upstairs contains three professionally decorated guest rooms with private baths, TV, and sitting room. The honeymoon suite features a canopy bed, fireplace, and whirlpool bath. A gourmet continental breakfast is served in the gracious dining room, and weather permitting under the patio garden percola. We are located 20 minutes from downtown Charlotte, NC.

Hosts: Jerry and Melba Peterson
Rooms: 3(PB) $59-79
Expanded Continental Breakfast
Credit Cards: A, B, C
Notes: 2, 5, 8, 9, 10, 11, 12

SUMTER

The Bed and Breakfast of Sumter
6 Park Avenue, 29150
(803) 773-2903; (803) 775-6943 (FAX)

Charming 1896 home facing lush park in the historic district. Large front porch with swing and rocking chairs. Gracious guest rooms with antiques, fireplaces and all private baths. Formal Victorian parlor and TV sitting area. HBO, FAX. Gourmet breakfast including fruit, entree, and home-baked breads. Antiques, Swan Lake, and 15 golf courses closeby.

Hosts: Jess and Suzanne Begley
Rooms: 5 (PB) $60-65
Full Breakfast
Credit Cards: A, B
Notes: 2, 5, 8, 10, 12

East Main Guest House

year; 6 Pets welcome; 7 Children welcome; 8 Tennis nearby; 9 Swimming nearby; 10 Golf nearby; 11 Skiing nearby; 12 May be booked through travel agent

South Dakota

ALEXANDRIA

Leonard and Marie Bettmeng Home
R.R. 2 Box 123, 57311
(605) 239-4671

We have a comfortable home with a covered deck that overlooks a lake just four miles off I-90 or 15 miles east of Mitchell which has the world's only Corn Palace. St. Mary of Mercy Church in Alexandria, four miles from us, has a Mid-America Fatima Family Shrine. The third weekend in each June a spiritual Congress is conducted with national and international speakers and special liturgical services. Registration or information obtained through Fatima Family Apostolate, PO 55, Redfield, SD 57469. The gas grill is available to guests, as are paddleboats.

Hosts: Leonard and Marie
Rooms: 2 (SB)
Full or Continental Breakfast
Credit Cards: None
Notes: 2, 5, 6 (if chained), 7, 9

CANOVA

Skoglund Farm
Route 1, Box 45, 57321
(605) 247-3445

Skoglund Farm brings back memories of Grandpa and Grandma's home. It is furnished with antiques and collectibles. A full, home-cooked evening meal and breakfast are served. You can sightsee in the surrounding area, visit Little House on the Prairie Village, hike, or just relax. Several country churches are located nearby.

Hosts: Alden and Delores
Rooms: 5 (SB) $30 each adult; $20 each teen; $15 each child; children 5 and under free
Full Breakfast
Credit Cards: None
Notes: 2, 3, 4 (included), 5, 6, 7, 8, 9, 10, 12

CHAMBERLAIN

Riverview Ridge
HC69, Box 82A, 57325
(605) 734-6084

Contemporary home built on a bluff overlooking a scenic bend in the Missouri River. King and gueen beds, full breakfast, and secluded country peace and quiet.

NOTES: Credit cards accepted: A Master Card; B Visa; C American Express; D Discover Card; E Diners Club; F Other; 2 Personal checks accepted; 3 Lunch available; 4 Dinner available; 5 Open all

Three and one half miles north of downtown Chamberlain on highway 50. Enjoy outdoor recreation; visit museums, Indian reservations, and casinos; or just relax and make our home your home.

Hosts: Frank and Alta Cable
Rooms: 3 (1PB; 2SB) $45-55
Full Breakfast
Credit Cards: None
Notes: 2, 5, 7, 9, 10

CUSTER

Custer Mansion Bed and Breakfast

35 Centennial Drive, 57730
(605) 673-3333

Historic 1891, Victorian Gothic home listed on the National Register of Historic Places features a blend of Victorian elegance and country charm with Western hospitality. Clean, quiet accommodations and delicious home-cooked breakfast. Central to all Black Hills attractions such as Mt. Rushmore, Crazy Horse Memorial, and many others. Recommended by *Bon Appetit*, AAA, and *Mobil Travel Guide*.

Hosts: Mill and Carole Seaman
Rooms: 6 (2PB; 4SB) $42.50-72.50
Full Breakfast
Credit Cards: None
Notes: 2, 5, 7, 8, 9 , 10, 11

The Rose Garden Bed and Breakfast

Rt. 1, Box 108A, 57730
(605) 673-2714

The Rose Garden is one mile south of Custer, the mother city of the Black Hills.

Our suites are furnished with quaint, nostalgic atmosphere including clawfoot tubs, mirrored canopy beds, hot tub, and fresh fruit. Full, home-cooked, candlelight breakfasts served in our gracious dining room. Short drives to Mt. Rushmore, Crazy Horse, Custer State Park, and Wind Cave National Park. Beautiful scenery, including rock formations, beckon you!

Hosts: Ted and Charlene Hartman
Rooms: 6 (PB) $55-95
Full Breakfast
Credit Cards: A, B
Notes: 2, 5, 8, 9 , 10, 11

The "B and J" Bed and Breakfast

HOT SPRINGS

The "B and J" Bed and Breakfast

HCR 52, Box 101-B, 57747
(605) 745-4243

Nestled in the Southern Black Hills, this charming, historic 1880 log cabin, decorated in local antiques, provides guests with a unique pioneer setting. The cabin is 450 sq. ft. and sleeps two to four. Enjoy the relaxed mountain surroundings while listening to the bubble of the famous Fall River that never freezes. Early morning, in

year; 6 Pets welcome; 7 Children welcome; 8 Tennis nearby; 9 Swimming nearby; 10 Golf nearby; 11 Skiing nearby; 12 May be booked through travel agent

the surrounding meadows, deer and wild turkey may be seen. True western hospitality and a good home-cooked breakfast are always available in Jeananne's kitchen. The "B and J" is located one mile south of Hot Springs on US 385/18. In Hot Springs, swim at the historic Evans Plunge where the water is alwasy 87 degrees, visit the world's largest deposit of mammoth bones, and golf at the most beautiful course in the Black Hills.

Hosts: Bill and Jeananne Wintz
Rooms: 1 cabin (PB) $75-100
Full Breakfast
Credit Cards: None
Notes: 2, 7, 8, 9, 10, 11

Hotel Alex Johnson

RAPID CITY

Abend Haus Cottage and Audrie's Cranbury Corner Bed and Breakfast

23029 Thunderhead Falls Rd., 57702
(605) 342-7788

The ultimate in charm and Old World hospitality, our country home and five-acre estate is surrounded by thousands of acres of national forest in a secluded, Black Hills setting. Each quiet, comfortable suite and cottage has private entrance, hot tub, patio, cable TV, and refrigerator. Free trout fishing, hiking, biking available on property.

Hosts: Hank and Audry Kuhnhauser
Rooms: 6 (PB) $85
Full Breakfast
Credit Cards: None
Notes: 2, 5, 8, 9, 10, 11

Hotel Alex Johnson

523 6th Street, 57701
(605) 342-1210; (800) 888-2539

Visit the Hotel Alex Johnson and stay at a historic landmark. 141 newly restored guest rooms. Old World charm combined with award-winning hospitality, this legend offers a piece of Old West history in the heart of downtown Rapid City. Listed on the National Registry of Historic Places.

Rooms: 141 (PB) $58-88
Full Breakfast in Restaurant Setting.
Credit Cards: A, B, C, D, E
Notes: 2, 3, 4, 5, 7, 8, 10, 12

SENECA

Rainbow Lodge

HC 78, Box 81, 57473
(605) 436-6795

Spend a quiet, relaxing day or evening by the lake on the prairie. Beautiful landscap-

---

NOTES: Credit cards accepted: A Master Card; B Visa; C American Express; D Discover Card; E Diners Club; F Other; 2 Personal checks accepted; 3 Lunch available; 4 Dinner available; 5 Open all

ing and trees, meditation areas, and chapel. You will enjoy country charm and hospitality on this oasis on the prairie; handicapped accessible; great getaway for couples; four miles off Highway 212. Reservations required.

Hosts: Ralph and Ann Wheeler
Rooms: 3 (SB) $30-45
Full Breakfast
Credit Cards: None
Notes: 2, 4, 5

YANKTON

Mulberry Inn
512 Mulberry Street, 57078
(605) 665-7116

The beautiful Mulberry Inn offers the ultimate in comfort and charm in a traditional setting. Built in 1873, the inn features parquet floors, six guest rooms furnished with antiques, two parlors with marble fireplaces, and a large porch. Minutes from the Lewis and Clark Lake and within walking distance of the Missouri River, fine restaurants, and downtown. The inn is listed on the National Register of Historic Places.

Hostess: Millie Cameron
Rooms: 6 (2PB; 4SB) $35-51 May-September; $32-45 October-April
Continental Breakfast (Full breakfast available with extra charge)
Credit Cards: A, B, C
Notes: 2, 5, 7, 8, 9, 10

Mulberry Inn

year; 6 Pets welcome; 7 Children welcome; 8 Tennis nearby; 9 Swimming nearby; 10 Golf nearby; 11 Skiing nearby; 12 May be booked through travel agent

Tennessee

CHATTANOOGA

Alford House
5515 Alford Hill Dr., Rt. 4, 37419
(615) 821-7625: (800) 817-7625

Family owned and operated in a Christian atmosphere—within ten minutes to all local attractions and the Tenessee Aquarium. A three-story brick home built in 1940 yet filled with Victorian charm: a collection of beautiful glass baskets displayed for your viewing plus antiques, many of which are for sale. Coffee is served early and, by request, breakfast is served in the gazebo where you can enjoy the mountain view. Ask about off-season rates and local discounts.

Hostess: Rhoda Alford
Rooms: 4 (2PB; 2SB) $60-85
Expanded Continental Breakfast
Credit Cards: B
Notes: 2, 5, 7(limited), 8, 9, 10, 11, 12

CHRISTIANA

Cedar Thicket Bed and Breakfast
3552 Rock Springs Rd., Christiana, 37037
(615) 893-4015

Built on its original foundation dating back to the Civil War, this Victorian farmhouse was reconstructed in 1895 and is in the ownership of the sixth generation. The two-story home, complete with many of the original furnishings, is located on a 180- acre farm which is listed as a Century Farm. Area attractions include Stones River Battlefield, Nashville, and Opryland. Also available during the summer months is a quaint guest house with kitchen and bathroom, a great place for those who prefer a more private atmosphere.

Hosts: Gilbert and Ginny Gordon
Rooms: 2 (PB) $50-60
Full Breakfast
Credit Cards: None
Notes: 2, 5, 7

DANDRIDGE

Mill Dale Farm Bed and Breakfast
140 Mill Dale Road, 37725
(615) 397-3470; (800) 767-3471

Nineteenth-century farmhouse located in Tennessee's second oldest town. Floating staircase leads to three guest rooms, all with private baths. Nearby is fishing, boating, swimming, tennis, golf, the Great Smoky Mountains, Gatlinburg, and Pi-

---

NOTES: Credit cards accepted: A Master Card; B Visa; C American Express; D Discover Card; E Diners Club; F Other; 2 Personal checks accepted; 3 Lunch available; 4 Dinner available; 5 Open all

geon Forge. Delicious country breakfast.

Hostess: Mrs. T. Hood (Lucy C.) Franklin
Rooms: 3 (PB) $65+tax
Full Breakfast
Credit Cards: None
Notes: 2, 5, 7, 8, 9, 10, 11

Sugar Fork Bed and Breakfast

743 Garrett Road, 37725
(615) 397-7327; (800) 487-5634

Guests will appreciate the tranquil setting of Sugar Fork, a short distance to the Great Smoky Mountains. Situated on Douglas Lake, the B&B has private access and floating dock. Enjoy warm-weather water sports and fishing year-round. Fireplace in common room, guest kitchenette, wraparound deck, swings, and park bench by the lake. A hearty breakfast is served family-style in the dining room or, weather permitting, on the deck. No smoking in guest rooms.

Hosts: Mary and Sam Price
Rooms: 3 (2PB; 2SB) $55 (SB)-65 (PB)+tax
Full Breakfast
Credit Cards: A. B
Notes: 2, 5, 7, 8, 9, 10, 11

Sugar Fork Bed and Breakfast

Butcher House in the Mountains

GATLINBURG

Butcher House in the Mountains

1520 Garrett Lane, 37738
(615) 436-9457 (voice and FAX)

Nestled 2800 ft. above the main entrance to the Smokies, Butcher House in the Mountains offers mountian seclusion as well as convenience. The Swiss-like cedar and stone chalet enjoys one of the most beautiful views in the state. Antiques are tastefully placed throughout the house and a guest kitchen is available for coffee and lavish desert. European gourmet brunch served. AAA rated 3-diamond. ABBA rated excellent.

Hosts: Hugh and Gloria Butcher
Rooms: 5 (PB) $79-109
Full European Gourmet Breakfast
Credit Cards: A, B, C
Notes: 2, 5, 8, 9, 10, 11, 12

Olde English Tudor Inn

135 W. Holly Ridge Road, 37738
(615) 436-7760; (800) 541-3798

The Olde English Tudor Inn Bed and Breakfast is set on a hillside overlooking

year; 6 Pets welcome; 7 Children welcome; 8 Tennis nearby; 9 Swimming nearby; 10 Golf nearby; 11 Skiing nearby; 12 May be booked through travel agent

the beautiful mountian resort of Gatlinburg. It is ideally located within a few minutes walk to downtown and a few minutes drive to The Great Smoky Mountain National Park. The Inn has seven spacious guest rooms with their own modern bath and cable TV(HBO). Each guest is made to feel at home in the large community room, furnished with TV/VCR and freestanding wood-burning stove. Call toll free for a brochure.

Hosts: Larry, Kathy, and Willie Schuh
Rooms: 7 (PB) $69-99
Full Breakfast
Credit Cards: A, B
Notes: 2, 5, 7, 8, 9, 10, 11, 12

JACKSON

Highland Place Bed and Breakfast

519 N. Highland Ave., 38301
(901) 427-1422

A stately home of distinct charm, offering comfortable accommodations and soutern hospitality. Highland Place B&B is West Tennessee's 1995 Designers Showplace. Each room, hall, staircase, and even hidden away nooks has been designed and decorated by the outstanding designers of West TN. Experience the pleasure of sharing the surroundings of one of the state's finest homes. Circa 1911, the Inn was totally renovated in early 1995 and reopens in April of 1995.

Hosts: Glenn and Janice Wall
Rooms: 3 (2PB; 1SB)) $65-85
Full Breakfast
Credit Cards: A, B
Notes: 2, 5, 10, 12

KNOXVILLE

Nessly House B&B

9809 Crestline Drive, 37922
(615) 675-5934

A comfortable stone farmhouse shaded by a 250-year-old tree, dogwoods, and gardens. We are near the New Pellisippi Parkway making it convenient to the Great Smokey Mountians, Gatlinburg, Pigeon Forge, The University of Tennessee events, and the Knoxville airport. Our guest rooms have queen-size beds. Cookies and tea or coffee will be served when you arrive.

Hostess: Peggy Nessly
Rooms: 2 (PB) $65
Full Breakfast
Credit Cards: None
Notes: 2, 4 (by reservation), 5, 8, 9, 10

KODAK

Grandma's House

734 Pollard Road, P.O. Box 445, 37764
(615) 933-3512; (800) 676-3512; (615) 933-0748 (FAX)

Colonial-style home on three acres at the base of the Great Smoky Mountains. Only two miles off I-40 at the 407 exit. Owners live on premises and are both native East Tennesseans. Country decor with handmade quilts and crafts. Farm-style "loosen your belt" breakfast begins when guests gather around the big oak table and Hilda says the blessing.

Hosts: Charlie and Hilda Hickman
Rooms: 3 (PB) $65
Full Breakfast
Credit Cards: A, B
Notes: 2, 5, 10, 11, 12

NOTES: Credit cards accepted: A Master Card; B Visa; C American Express; D Discover Card; E Diners Club; F Other; 2 Personal checks accepted; 3 Lunch available; 4 Dinner available; 5 Open all

LIMESTONE

Snapp Inn B&B

1990 Davy Crockett Pk. Rd., 37681
(615) 257-2482

Gracious c. 1815 Federal style home, furnished with antiques. Come to the country for a relaxing weekend getaway. Enjoy the peaceful mountain view or play a game of pool. Located close to Davy Crockett Birthplace State Park. A 15-minute drive to historic Jonesborough or Greenville.

Hosts: Dan and Ruth Dorgan
Rooms: 3 (PB) $50
Full Breakfast
Credit Cards: None
Notes: 2, 5, 6, 7 (1 only), 8, 9, 10, 12

LYNCHBURG

Lynchburg Bed and Breakfast

Mechanic Street, PO Box 34, 37352
(615) 759-7158

A 19th century home located within walking distance to the Jack Daniels Distillery, the oldest registered distillery in the USA. One of the oldest homes in Moore County, also the home of the first Moore County Sherriff. Begin your day with our special continental breakfast served at your convenience, then relax with a view from our shady front porch.

Hostess: Virginia Tipps
Rooms: 3 (PB) $50-60
Continental Breakfast
Credit Cards: A, B
Notes: 5, 7, 8, 9

MEMPHIS

Lowenstein-Long House

217 N. Walden/1084 Poplar, 38105
(901) 527-7174

This huge house is one of the few surviving great mansions in Memphis. This 75 foot tall, five-story mansion was built with 10 bedrooms and has 9½ baths. The home was built to reflect the wealth and status of one of Memphis's most prominent families and features mahogany woodwork and gilded Italian plaster.

Hosts: Col. Charles and Margaret Long
Rooms: 4 (4PB: 3SB)) $30-75
Full Breakfast
Credit Cards: None
Notes: 2, 5

Lynchburg Bed and Breakfast

MONTEAGLE

Adams Edgeworth Inn

Monteagle Sunday School Assembly, 37356
(615) 924-4000; (615) 924-3236 (FAX)

Circa 1896, Adams Edgeworth Inn has provided fine lodging for almost 100 years and is still the region's leader in elegance and quality. Recently refurbished in English Manor decor, the inn is a showcase for fine antiques, important original paintings and sculptures, and a prize-winning rose garden. Stroll through the 96-acre Victorian Village which surrounds the inn, or drive 6 miles to the Gothic campus of Sewanee, University of the South. Cultural activities are year round; 150 miles of hiking trails, scenic vistas, waterfalls. Tennis, swimming, golf, riding nearby. Five-course fine dining by candlelight every night. "One of the best inns I've ever visited anywhere..." (Sara Pitzer, *Recommended Country Inns* in *Country Inns Magazine*).

Hosts: Wendy and David Adams
Rooms: 12 (PB) $65-115; 1 suite $150
Full Breakfast
Credit Cards: A, B, C
Notes: 2, 4, 5, 7, 8, 9, 10, 12

MURFREESBORO

Cedar Thicket Bed and Breakfast

3552 Rock Springs Rd., Christiana, 37037
(615) 893-4015

Built on its original foundation dating back to the Civil War, this Victorian farmhouse was reconstructed in 1895 and is in the ownership of the sixth generation. The two-story home, complete with many of the original furnishings, is located on a 180-acre farm which is listed as a Century Farm. Area attractions include Stones River Battlefield, Nashville, and Opryland. Also available during the summer months is a quaint guest house with kitchen and bathroom, a great place for those who

prefer a more private atmosphere.

Hosts: Gilbert and Ginny Gordon
Rooms: 2 (PB) $50-60
Full Breakfast
Credit Cards: None
Notes: 2, 5, 7

Clardy's Guest House

435 East Main Street, 37130
(615) 893-6030

This large Victorian home was built in 1898 and is located in Murfreesboro's historic district. You will marvel at the ornate woodwork, beautiful fireplaces, and magnificent stained glass overlooking the staircase. The house is filled with antiques, as are local shops and malls. The hosts will help you with dining, shopping, and touring plans.

Hosts: Robert and Barbara Deaton
Rooms: 3 (2PB; 1SB) $35-50
Continental Breakfast
Credit Cards: None
Notes: 2, 5, 8, 9, 10

NATCHEZ TRACE—SEE NATCHEZ TRACE, MISSISSIPPI

PIKEVILLE

Fall Creek Falls Bed and Breakfast Inn

Rt. 3 Box 298B, 37367
(615) 881-5494; (615) 881-5040 (FAX)

New country manor home located on 40 acres of rolling hills one mile from the nationally acclaimed Fall Creek Falls State

Resort Park. Rooms have lovely Victorian or country furnishings. ABBA three-crown rating. AAA three-diamond rating. Featured in August 1994 Tennesse Magazine. Information about touring, dining, and shopping given by host who is a native to the area. Beautiful rooms and reasonable rates.

Hosts: Rita and Doug Pruett
Rooms: 8 (6PB; 2SB) $59.75-89.75
Full Breakfast
Credit Cards: A, B
Notes: 2, 3 (boxed by reservation), 7 (over 7 and well-behaved), 8, 9, 10, 12

PIGEON FORGE

Day Dreams Country Inn

2720 Colonial Drive, 37863
(615) 428-0370

Delight in the true country charm of this antique-filled, secluded two-story log home with its six uniquely decorated guest rooms. Enjoy an evening by our cozy fireplace, relax on the front porch to the soothing sound of Mill Creek, or take a stroll around our three wooded acres. Treat your tastebuds to our bountiful country breakfast each morning. Within walking distance of Parkway. Perfect for family reunions and retreats. From Parkway, take 321 S., go one block, turn left on Florence Dr., go three blocks, and turn right on Colonial Dr.

Hosts: Bob and Joyce Guerrera
Rooms: 6 (PB) $79-99
Full Breakfast
Credit Cards: A, B
Notes: 2, 3 (special arrangement), 4 (special arrangement), 5, 7, 8, 9, 10, 11, 12

Hilton's Bluff Bed and Breakfast Inn

2654 Valley Heights Dr., 37863
(615) 428-9765; (800) 441-4188, (Ext. 8)

Truly elegant country living. Secluded hilltop setting only 1/2 mile from heart of Pigeon Forge. Minutes from outlet shopping, Dollywood, and Smoky Mountain National Park. The honeymoon, executive, and deluxe rooms, all with private baths, five with two-person jacuzzis, king beds, and waterbeds. Tastefully decorated in romantic mingling of the old and new. Private balconies, covered decks with rockers and checkerboard tables. Den with mountain-stone fireplace, game room/conference room. Southern gourmet breakfast. Group rates for corporate seminars and church groups.

Hosts: Jack and Norma Hilton
Rooms: 10 (PB) $79-109
Full Breakfast
Credit Cards: A, B, C
Notes: 2, 3&4 (to groups reserving entire inn), 5, 7 (by arrangement), 8, 9, 10, 11, 12 (certain restrictions apply)

ROGERSVILLE

Hale Springs Inn

Town Square, 37857
(615) 272-5171

Tennessee's oldest operational inn built in 1824 and recently restored to its former glory. Air-conditioned and central heat. Most rooms have workable fireplaces. Private, modern bathrooms, antique furniture, and poster beds. Dine fireside in candlelit dining room. Presidents Andrew

Jackson, James Polk, and Andrew Johnson stayed here. Easy one-hour drive to historic sites and mountian resorts.

Hosts: Ed Pace and Capt. and Mrs. Carl Netherland-Brown
Rooms: 9 (PB) $35-60
Continental Breakfast
Credit Cards: A, B
Notes: 4, 5, 8, 10, 11, 12

RUGBY

Newbury House Bed and Breakfast

P.O. Box 8, Hwy 52, 37733
(615) 628-2441

Restored 1880 Newbury House bedrooms are furnished with Victorian antiques, guest parlor, front veranda, complimentary tea and coffee. Pioneer and Percy cottages sleep from one to ten; kitchen facilities. Historic Rugby is listed on the National Register of Historic Places. Daily guided tours include: School House Visitor Centre; Thomas Hughes Library 1882,

Kingstone Lisle (the founder's home), 1884, and the Christ Church Episcopal, 1887, with original hanging lamps and 1849 rosewood organ still played for Sunday services.

Rooms: 5 + 2 cottages (3PB; 2SB) $58-68
Full Breakfast
Credit Cards: A, B
Notes: 2, 3, 4, 5, 7 (at cottages), 9, 10

SEVIERVILLE

Blue Mountain Mist Country Inn

1811 Pullen Rd., 37862
(615) 428-2335; (800) 497-2335; (615) 453-1720 (FAX)

Experience the silent beauty of mountain scenery while rocking on the big wraparound porch of this Victorian-style farmhouse. Common rooms filled with antiques lead to twelve individually decorated guest rooms. Enjoy many special touches such as old-fashioned claw foot tubs, high antique headboards, quilts, and jacuzzis. Nestled in

Von-Bryan Inn

NOTES: Credit cards accepted: A Master Card; B Visa; C American Express; D Discover Card; E Diners Club; F Other; 2 Personal checks accepted; 3 Lunch available; 4 Dinner available; 5 Open all

the woods behind the inn are five country cottages designed for romantic getaways. The Great Smoky Mountains National Park and Gatlinburg are only twenty minutes away.

Hosts: Norman and Sarah Ball
Rooms: 12 and 5 cottages (PB) $79-125
Full Breakfast
Credit Cards: A, B
Notes: 2, 5, 7, 8, 9, 10, 11, 12

Von-Bryan Inn

2402 Hatcher Mountain Rd., 37862
(615)453-9832; (800)633-1459; (615)428-8634 (FAX)

A mountaintop log inn with an unsurpassed panoramic view of the Great Smoky Mountians. Greet the sunrise with singing birds and the aroma of breakfast. Swim, hike, rock, rest, read, and relax the day away, then watch the sunset just before the whipporwills begin their nightly calls. Swimming pool, hot tub, steam shower, whirlpool tubs, library, complimentary dessert, refreshments, and breakfast. Three bedroom, log chalet is great for families.

Hosts: The Vaughn Family: D.J., JoAnn, David, and Patrick.
Rooms: 6 + 3 bedroom chalet (PB) $80-125
Full Breakfast
Credit Cards: A, B, C, D
Notes: 2, 5, 7, 9 (on-site), 10, 11, 12 (10% com.)

TOWNSEND

Richmont Inn

220 Winterberry Lane, 37882
(615)448-6751; (615)448-6480 (FAX)

Situated on "the peaceful side of the Smokies," this Appalachian barn is beau-tifully furnished with eighteenth-century English antiques and French paintings. Breathtaking mountain views, graciously appointed rooms with sitting areas, woodburning fireplaces, spa tubs for two, and balconies. French and Swiss cuisine are served at breakfast with flavored coffees and gourmet desserts by candlelight in the evenings. Featured in *Country Inns* B&B magazine as "a sweet rendezuous" and received *Gourmet Magazine's* grand prize award for one of its desserts. The Smoky Mountains, art/craft shops, outlet shopping, and historic Cades Cove are all nearby.

Hosts: Susan and Jim Hind
Rooms: 10 (PB) $85-115
Full Breakfast
Credit Cards: None
Notes: 2, 5, 9, 10, 12

WAVERLY

The Nolan House Inn

Route 4, Hwy. 13 N., 37185
(615)296-9063 or (615)296-2511

The Nolan House is a 12-room Victorian house built in 1870; restored and placed on the National Historical Register in 1986. It has five B&B rooms furnished Victorian, many porches, cisterns, cellars, and a family graveyard dating back to early 1880s. It is located seven miles from Loretta Lynn's dude ranch. 20 miles from Kentucky Lake resort.

Hostess: LaVerne Turner
Rooms: 5 (3PB; 2SB) $35
Continental Breakfast (full on Saturdays)
Credit Cards: None
Notes: 2, 5, 7, 9, 12

year; 6 Pets welcome; 7 Children welcome; 8 Tennis nearby; 9 Swimming nearby; 10 Golf nearby; 11 Skiing nearby; 12 May be booked through travel agent

Texas

ALTO

Lincrest Lodge
Alto/Rusk Texas, P.O. Box 799, 75925
(409) 858-2223; (409) 858-2232 (FAX)

A charming, spacious, newly built, country mansion set on the side of a hill with a 16-acre park located in the green hills and forests of central east Texas and a 35-mile view. Featuring fine food and hospitality including romantic gourmet dinners—the perfect country retreat. Twenty miles west of Nacogdochos, the oldest town in Texas.

Hosts: Chet and Charlie Woj
Rooms: 6 (2PB; 4SB) $75
Full Breakfast
Credit Cards: A, B, C
Notes: 2, 4, 5

BIG SANDY

Annie's Bed and Breakfast Country Inn and Guest House
P.O. Box 928, Hwy. 155 North, 75755
(903) 636-4355; (903) 636-4744 (FAX)

Come capture a special moment in time at Annie's B&B, a special place to savor the charm of bygone days...back to a time when a stay away from home was an experience worth remembering. This elegant Victorian country inn offers gracious accommodations with all the romance and charm of the turn of the century. Come enjoy our old-fashioned hospitality and let us turn back the hands of time...just for you. Each room is individually decorated with cozy quilts, soft floral wallpapers, antqiue furnishings, elegant appointments, and a small old-fashioned refrigerator. Some rooms feature balcomies, many have private baths, and three even have lofts.

Hosts: Clifton and Kathy Shaw
Rooms: 13 (8PB; 3SB) $50-115
Full Breakfast Sun.-Fri.; Continental Breakfast Sat.
Credit Cards: A, B, C, D
Notes: 2, 3, 4, 5, 8, 10

BULVERDE

Homestead Bed and Breakfast
1324 Bulverde Road, 78163
(210) 980-2571

A private cottage facility located in the heart of a 300-acre working ranch where cattle, deer, jack rabbits, turkey, and foxes still roam. 30 minutes from historic Boerne,

---

NOTES: Credit cards accepted: A Master Card; B Visa; C American Express; D Discover Card; E Diners Club; F Other; 2 Personal checks accepted; 3 Lunch available; 4 Dinner available; 5 Open all

New Braunfels, and downtown San Antonio Riverwalk and other major attractions plus Sea World and Fiesta Texas. Homestead sits on the original homestead founded by the Krause-Bremer families. It houses many of their original antique furnishings. The interior features a beaded board ceiling in the kitchen and dining room, two bedrooms, and living room and bath. Breakfast fixings are in the fridge; fresh breads baked each morning.

Hosts: James and MaryJane Jahnsen
Rooms: 2 in private cottage (PB) $75
Continental Breakfast fixing in refrigerator.
Credit Cards: None
Notes: 2, 5, 7, 8, 9, 10

CANYON

Hudspeth House Bed and Breakfast Inn

1905 4th Ave., 79015-4023
(806) 655-9800

This historic inn is only 12 miles from Palo Duro Canyon, home of the famous "Texas" musical drama. Built to board teachers and students at West Texas A&M University (Normal College 1909) it was converted to a B&B in 1987. The house is over 8,000 sq. ft. with 35 rooms, 7 fireplaces, 107 doors, 17 closets, 84 windows, and even a one-chair chapel with stained glass window!

Hosts: Mark and Mary Clark
Rooms: 9 (5PB; 4SB) $55-85
Full Breakfast
Credit Cards: A, B, C, D
Notes: 2, 5, 9, 10, 12

COLUMBUS

Raumonda

1100 Bowie, P.O. Box 112, 78934
(409) 732-2190 or (409) 732-5135; (409) 732-8730 (FAX attn Buddy Rau)

In this Victorian home, built in 1887, you will be greeted with warmth and hospitality reminiscent of the Old South. Three fireplaces with white marble mantles, original, grained, painted woodwork, and Victorian bronze hardware make this one of the most outstanding houses in Texas. We also manage the Gant Guest House.

Host: R.F. "Buddy" Rau
Rooms: 3 (PB) $80
Enhanced Continental Breakfast
Credit Cards: None
Notes: 2, 5, 8, 9, 10, 12

The Victorian Bed and Breakfast

The Victorian Bed and Breakfast

1336 Milam Street (PO Box 325), 78934
(409) 732-2125; (409) 732-5212 (FAX)

This beautiful two-story, newly restored, Victorian home dates from 1883. It features gingerbread, porches, 14-foot ceilings, and wainscoting. Included on 1993 tour of homes. Tree-lined streets of town sit on site of old Indian village. General Sam Houston camped here. Today Columbus boasts large number of historic markers and an 1886 opera house with productions. Tennis, golf, canoeing, bicycling area, antique shows, auctions, and more. Complimentary guided tour. Houston one hour away.

Hostess: Carolyn Youens Hastedt
Rooms: 3 (1PB; 2SB)) $65-80 + tax
Continental Breakfast
Credit Cards: None
Notes: 2, 5, 8, 9, 10

CROSBYTON

Smith House B&B Inn

306 West Aspen, 79322
(806) 675-2718; (806) 675-2619 (FAX)

The Inn was built in 1921 by J. Frank Smith, a cowboy from the nearby Two Buckle Ranch. The original oak furniture and iron beds highlight the early West Texas charm. The Inn has a large dining room, a separate meeting room, a parlor for entertaining. Guests can enjoy a rocking chair on the large front porch. Available for groups, retreats, or dinners.

Hosts: Terry and Sandy Cash
Rooms: 12 (8PB; 4SB) $50-85
Full Breakfast
Credit Cards: A, B
Notes: 2, 5, 7, 8, 9, 12

DENTON

The Redbud Inn

815 N. Locust Street, 76201
(817) 565-6414; (817) 565-6515 (FAX)

Step back into a time of gracious hospital-

ity when entering Denton's first and only B&B. Experience a cozy warmth and loving pride in this home which was built around 1910 and indulge yourself when waking to the aroma of freshly baked bread and steaming coffee. Two of our five rooms are suites with cable TV and VCR. All the baths have clawfoot tubs and showers. Weekly rates for stays of five days or more. Near two universities, antique shopping, and outlet malls. Beautiful Victorian porch and garden gazebo for relaxing.

Hosts: John and Donna Morris
Rooms: 5 (PB) $49-75
Full Breakfast
Credit Cards: A, B, D
Notes: 2, 5, 7, 9, 10, 12

ENNIS

Raphael House

500 W. Ennis Avenue, 75119
(214) 875-1555; (214) 875-0308 (FAX)

This elegant, 1906 Neoclassic Revival mansion is on the National Register and for the last four years was voted one of the top B&B's in the USA. The 19-room mansion is a showcase of quality antiques, rich wall coverings, and luxurious fabrics. Amenities include large baths with antique clawfoot tubs, down comforters and pillows, imported toiletries, afternoon refreshments and turn down service. Swedish massage, honeymoon packages, and corporate deals available. Very romantic!

Hosts: Brian and Danna Cody Wolf
Rooms: 6 (PB) $60-100
Full Breakfast; Continental Plus midweek
Credit Cards: A, B, C, E, F
Notes: 2, 5, 8, 9, 10

NOTES: Credit cards accepted: A Master Card; B Visa; C American Express; D Discover Card; E Diners Club; F Other; 2 Personal checks accepted; 3 Lunch available; 4 Dinner available; 5 Open all

FREDERICKSBURG

The Austin Street Retreat
408 W. Austin, 78624
(210) 997-5612 (for reservations)

Hear the church bells ring from the lush rock terraces. Sophisticated decor in this historic home. Originally a log and rock settlers cabin, this luxurios villa now offers five suites. Each has private bath with whirlpool tubs, private outdoor terrace space in luscious surroundings. Four suites have fireplaces. Four suites are one-bedroom with king-size beds and one suite has two bedrooms with queen-size beds.

Rooms: 5 (PB) $95-100
Continental Breakfast
Credit Cards: A, B, D
Notes: 2, 5, 7, 8, 9, 10, 12

Longhill Home
231 W. Main St., 78624
(210) 997-5612 (for reservations)

Located six miles east of Fredericksburg on a hill overlooking the Perdenales Valley. Full kitchen stocked with coffe, tea, hot chocolate, and juices. King-size bed upstairs; trundle bed downstairs (house sleeps four). Bath has tub/shower. House is of country decor located on 30 acres. You are free to roam the area and share it with the cattle that graze here. Central heat/air plus ceiling fans. No firearms or smoking.

Hosts: Danny and MaryBeth Richardson (out-of-town)
Rooms: whole house, sleeps 4 (1PB) $75
Breakfast not provided.
Credit Cards: A, B, D
Notes: 2, 5, 7, 12

Magnolia House
101 East Hackberry, 78624
(210) 997-0306

Circa 1925; restored 1991. Enjoy Southern hospitality in a grand and gracious manner. Outside, lovely magnolias and a bubbling fish pond and waterfall set a soothing mood. Inside, beautiful living room, and formal dining room provide areas for guests to mingle. Four romantic rooms and two suites have been thoughtfully planned. A Southern-style breakfast completes a memorable experience.

Hosts: Joyce and Patrick Kennard
Rooms: 4 (2PB; 2SB) $80-110
Suites: 2 (PB)
Full Breakfast
Credit Cards: None
Notes: 2, 5, 8, 9, 10

Schmidt Barn
Route 2, Box 112A3, 78624
(210) 997-5612 — Ask for Schmidt Barn

The Schmidt Barn is located one and one-half miles outside historic Fredericksburg. This 1860s limestone structure has been turned into a charming guest house with loft bedroom, living room, bath, and kitchen. The hosts live next door. German-style breakfast is left in the guest house for you. The house has been featured in *Country Living* and *Travel and Leisure* and is decorated with antiques.

Hosts: Dr. Charles and Loretta Schmidt
Guest House: 1 (PB) $75-105
Continental Breakfast Plus
Credit Cards: A, B, D
Notes: 2, 5, 6, 7, 8, 9, 10, 12

year; 6 Pets welcome; 7 Children welcome; 8 Tennis nearby; 9 Swimming nearby; 10 Golf nearby; 11 Skiing nearby; 12 May be booked through travel agent

GALVESTON

Coppersmith Inn Bed and Breakfast

1914 Ave. M, 77550
(409) 763-7004

Beautiful Victorian home (1887) with gingerbread trim and turret bay windows. Half mile from beach and Strand Historical District. Refreshments upon arrival. Delicious breakfast. Welcoming, luxurious atmosphere.

Hostess: Lisa Hering
Rooms: $85-135
Full Breakfast
Credit Cards: A, B, C
Notes: 2, 5, 7 (over 5), 9, 12

Madame Dyer's Bed and Breakfast

1720 Postoffice Street, 77550
(409) 765-5692

A unique way to enjoy Galveston's growing popularity and experience a traditional Victorian B&B with a personal touch. From the moment you enter this carefully restored 1889 home you will be entranced by period details such as wraparound porches, high airy ceilings, wooden floors, and lace curtains. Each room is furnished with delightful antiques that bring back memories of days gone by. Awaken to a coffee tray outside your door and an abundant homemade breakfast served in the dining room.

Hostess: Linda Welle
Rooms: 3 (1PB; 2SB)
Continental Breakfast
Credit Cards: A, B
Notes: 2, 5, 9, 10, 12

Coppersmith Inn Bed and Breakfast

GEORGE WEST

Country Estates Bed and Breakfast

Rt. 1, Box 285, 78022
(512) 566-2335

You'll enjoy a peaceful, relaxing atmosphere when you pass through the gate on this 850-acre South Texas, family-owned, cattle ranch. Ranch tours, birds and wildlife, or roaming and hiking at leisure. Fish in stock tanks for bass and catfish. Country home furnished with antiques and collectibles, mesquite-burning fireplaces, three guest rooms: Wicker and Old Lace, Quilt, and Cactus. Large porches, swimming pool, game room with pool table. Full ranch breakfast with homemade jams and jellies. Other meals optional with homegrown vegetables and fruit in season. Texas mesquite BBQ, picnics. Golf, fishing, and antiques nearby. Located between San Antonio and Corpus Christi. Dinner and luncheon parties and hunting packages available. Warm Christian atmosphere. No smoking.

Hosts: Fred and Evelyn
Rooms: 3 (1PB; 2SB) $75-85
Full Breakfast
Credit Cards: None
Notes: 2, 3, 4, 5, 7 (by arrangement), 9, 10, 12

NOTES: Credit cards accepted: A Master Card; B Visa; C American Express; D Discover Card; E Diners Club; F Other; 2 Personal checks accepted; 3 Lunch available; 4 Dinner available; 5 Open all

GRANBURY

Dabney House Bed and Breakfast

106 South Jones, 76048
(817) 579-1260; (817) 579-0426 (FAX—
attention: Dabney House)

Craftsman-style one-story home built in 1907 by local banker. Furnished with antiques, hardwood floors, and original woodwork. Long-term business rates available per request, and romance dinner by reservation only. We offer custom special occasion baskets in room upon arrival by advance order only. Book whole house for family occasions, staff retreats, or Bible retreats at discount rate.

Hosts: John and Gwen Hurley
Rooms: 4 (PB) $60-105
Full Breakfast
Credit Cards: A, B, C
Notes: 2, 5, 8, 9, 10, 12

HOUSTON

Sara's Bed and Breakfast Inn

941 Heights Blvd., 77008
(713) 868-3533; (713) 868-1160 (FAX)

This Queen Anne Victorian with its turret and widow's walk is located in Houston Heights, a neighborhood of historic homes, many of which are on the National Historic Register. Each bedroom is uniquely furnished, having either single, double, queen, or king-size beds. The Balcony Suite consists of two bedrooms, two baths, kitchen, living area, and balcony. Breakfast is served in the beautiful garden room in the Inn. The sights and sounds of downtown Houston are five miles away.

Hosts: Donna and Tillman Arledge
Rooms: 14 (12PB; 2SB) $55-95
Continental Plus Breakfast
Credit Cards: A, B, C, D, E, F
Notes: 2, 5, 7, 8, 9, 10, 12

HUNT

River Bend Bed and Breakfast

Rt. 1, Box 114
(210) 238-4681 (voice and FAX); (800) 472-3933

"A peaceful and relaxing retreat," nestled in the Hill Country along the beautiful Guadalupe River. Wake to the smell of freshly brewed coffee, feast on a gourmet breakfast buffet, and relax in a quaint, Victorian room filled with antique furnishings, wrought iron beds, lace curtains, and clawfooted tubs. Outside the river offers summer refreshment or winter tranquility. Hike, fish, tube, and canoe. River Bend is only a short drive to antiquing, art galleries, museums, and many wonderful restaurants.

Hostess: Becky Key
Owners: Conrad and Terri Pyle
Rooms: 15 (PB) $85-145
Full Breakfast
Credit Cards: A, B, C, D
Notes: 2, 5, 7, 8, 9, 10, 12

The Whistler Bed and Breakfast Inn

year; 6 Pets welcome; 7 Children welcome; 8 Tennis nearby; 9 Swimming nearby; 10 Golf nearby; 11 Skiing nearby; 12 May be booked through travel agent

HUNTSVILLE

The Whistler B&B Inn

906 Avenue M, 77340
(409) 295-2834

Genuine Victorian elegance. Lawns shaded with huge oak and cypress trees. A beautiful (c. 1959) two-story home with five guest rooms and four private baths. All guest rooms have antique double beds with the exception of one upstairs, which has twin beds. Formal reception room, music room, old-fashioned parlor, dining room, and spacious kitchen/family room. The house has been in the family for four generations.

Hostess: Mary T. Clegg
Rooms: 5 (4PB; 12SB) $90-115
Full Breakfast in formal setting.
Credit Cards: None
Notes: 2, 5

JEFFERSON

McKay House Bed and Breakfast Inn

306 East Delta, 75657
(903) 665-7322; (214) 348-1929

Jefferson is a town where one can relax, rather than get tired. The McKay House, an 1851 Greek Revival cottage, features a pillared front porch and many fireplaces, offering genuine hospitality in a Christian atmosphere. Heart-of-pine floors, 14-foot ceilings, and documented wallpapers complement antique furnishings. Guests enjoy a full "gentleman's" breakfast. Victorian nightshirts and gowns await pampered guests in each bed chamber.

Hosts: Alma Ann and Joseph Parker
Rooms: 4 + 3 suites (PB) $75-145
Full Sit-down Breakfast
Credit Cards: A, B
Notes: 2, 5, 10, 12

Pride House

409 Broadway, 75657
(903) 665-2675; (800) 894-3526

Breathtaking East Texas landmark Victorian mansion in historic former steamboat port. Myth America lives in this town of 2,200, on the banks of the Cypress, along brick streets, behind picket fences in antique houses. Pride House has luscious interiors, luxurious amenities, and legendary breakfasts! We have ten rooms with private baths, big beds, spacious rooms, and just about everything anybody's asked for over the past fourteen years!

Hostesses: Carol and Lois
Rooms: 10 (PB) $65-100
Full Breakfast
Credit Cards: A, B, D
Notes: 2, 5, 7, 10, 12

LEANDER

Trail's End Bed and Breakfast

12223 Trail's End Rd. #7, 78641
(512) 267-2901; (800) 850-2901

Trail's End Bed and Breakfast has an elegant Main House with two guest rooms upstairs. The private Guest House is in the woods in a wooded country setting on six acres within easy driving distance from Lake Travis, Austin, and other quaint Hill Country towns. The many romantic porches, decks, patios, and gazebo with

---

NOTES: Credit cards accepted: A Master Card; B Visa; C American Express; D Discover Card; E Diners Club; F Other; 2 Personal checks accepted; 3 Lunch available; 4 Dinner available; 5 Open all

garden areas provide lots of inviting out-door spaces. The two fireplaces, lots of seating areas in both houses provide ro-mantic and cozy togetherness inside. You may also shop in the B&B store in the Main House. We provide business people a comfortable lodging alternative, a great place to have that getaway and work or play. We look forward to serving you and hope you'll try our B&B. I know you will not be disappointed.

Hosts: JoAnn and Tom Patty
Rooms: 4 (2PB; 2SB) $65-95
Full Breakfast
Credit Cards: A, B, C
Notes: 2, 4, 5, 7, 9, 12 (10%)

Trail's End

LEDBETTER

Ledbetter Bed and Breakfast

P.O. Box 212, 78946
(409) 249-3066

Ledbetter B&B, established in 1988, is a collection of mulitgeneration, family, 1800-1900s homes within walking distance of 1870s remaining downtown businesses.

Full country breakfast buffet can serve up to 70 guests daily. Hayrides, walks, horse and buggy rides, games, Christmas lights, chuch wagon or romantic dinners, indoor heated swimming pool, VCR, TV, and phone on advance request. Each unit accommodates approximately four people. Only non-alcholic beverages are allowed outside private quarters. Only outdoor smoking is allowed.

Hosts: Chris and Jay Jervis
Rooms: 16-22 depending on grouping (17PB; 8SB) $70-100
Full Country Buffet Breakfast
Credit Cards: A, B
Notes: 2, 3, 4, 5, 7, 8, 9, 10, 12

NACOGDOCHES

Pine Creek Lodge

Rt. 3, Box 1238, 75964
(409) 560-6282

On a beautiful tree covered hill overlook-ing a springfed creek sits Pine Creek Lodge. Built on a 140-acre property with lots of lawns, rose gardens, and a multitude of flowers, deep in the East Texas woods yet only ten miles from historic Nacogdoches. Our rustic lodge features king-size beds in tastefully decorated rooms with phone, TV/VCR, lots of decks, swimming pool, spa, fishing, biking, and much more. We have become the destination for many city dwellers.

Hosts: The Pitts Family
Rooms: 3 (PB) $65
Full Breakfast
Credit Cards: A, B, C
Notes: 2, 4, 5, 7, 10

year; 6 Pets welcome; 7 Children welcome; 8 Tennis nearby; 9 Swimming nearby; 10 Golf nearby; 11 Skiing nearby; 12 May be booked through travel agent

NEW BRAUNFELS

Antik Haus Bed and Breakfast

118 S. Union Avenue, 78130
(210) 625-6666

Step back in time with a visit to a wonderful, two-story, restored Victorian home complete with a gazebo, strombella, and hot-water spa. We are located next to Landa Park where you can enjoy a two-hour tube ride on the Comal River, a bicycle built-for-two ride through the park, or walk to the Schlitterbahn Water Park. A full gourmet breakfast is served.

Hosts: Donna and Jim Irwin
Rooms: 4 (1PB; 3SB) $35-85
Full Breakfast
Credit Cards: None
Notes: 2, 5, 7 (over 12), 8, 9, 10

Aunt Nora's Bed and Breakfast

120 Naked Indian Trail (at Canyon Lake), 78132
(210) 905-3989

In the Texas hill country, minutes from New Braunfels, Guadalupe River at Canyon Lake is a country house with a touch of Victorian, nestled on a hillside. Breathe fresh country air from the front porch swing, enjoy patio hot tub and hand built queen beds. Tastefully decorated rooms and cottages all in a delightful hill country setting.

Hosts: Alton and Iralee Haley
Rooms: 3 (PB) $85-150
Full Breakfast
Credit Cards: None
Notes: 2, 5, 8, 9, 10

Historic Kuebler-Waldrip Haus

1620 Hueco Springs Loop Rd., 78132-3001
(210) 625-8372 (Voice and FAX); (800) 299-8372

Relax and enjoy informal Texas hospitality and the "best breakfast in Texas" in a restored German hand-hewn limestone, home (1847) and school (1863) on 43 hill country acres. Located five minutes from river recreation, Historic Gruene, bicycling, restaurants, shops, museums, golf, tennis, and stables. Enjoy wildlife, pets (deer, bloodhound, and cats), cozy fireplace, vintage history and school books, or play table games, volleyball, or croquet. Eight large rooms with private baths (1 for disabled and 2 whirlpools), kitchen, and laundry. Sleeps 14-25 people. Plan family or romantic vacations, reunions, weddings and receptions, and small conferences. Smoking outside only, please.

Hosts: Maggy K. Waldrip and son, Darrel Waldrip
Rooms: 8 (PB) $85-200
Full Candlelight Breakfast
Credit Cards: A, B, C, D
Notes: 2, 5, 6 (conditionally), 7, 8, 9, 10, 11 (water), 12 (Sun.-Thurs.)

The Rose Garden

195 South Academy, 78130
(210) 629-3296

Come to our Rose Garden with designer bedrooms, fluffy towels, scented soaps, and potpourri-filled rooms. Our half-century old home is only one block from downtown. Enjoy a movie, browse our antique shops, or stroll along the Comal Springs—all within walking distance. We offer two guest rooms. The Royal Rose Room has a four-poster rice-queen bed with a crystal chandelier and country French decor. The Country Rose Room has a Victorian-style, iron-and-brass queen bed with pine walls also done in country French. A full gourmet breakfast is served in the formal dining room.

Hostess: Dawn Mann
Rooms: 2 (1PB; 1SB) $65-95
Full Breakfast
Credit Cards: None
Notes: 2, 5, 8, 9, 10, 12

Hotel Garza Bed and Breakfast

POST

Hotel Garza Bed and Breakfast
302 E. Main, 79356
(806) 495-3962

This restored 1915 hotel projects friendliness and the history of this "Main Street City" where cereal magnate C. W. Post settled in 1907 to create his "Utopia." Guest can enjoy live theatre, colorful shops, museums, and the monthly event of Old Mill Trade Days. The guest rooms boast original furniture. From the comfy library you can look down on a quaint lobby and the dining area where a hearty breakfast is served.

Hosts: Jim and Janice Plummer
Rooms: 10 (6PB; 4SB) $40-65
Full Breakfast
Credit Cards: A, B
Notes: 2, 3, 4, 5, 7, 10

SALADO

The Rose Mansion and The Inn at Salado
P.O. Box 500, 76571
(817) 947-8200

Two inns nestled in a small community within a few blocks of each other. The Rose Mansion, a Greek Revival-style mansion (1870), and four complimentary cottages are located on four acres of landscaping surrounded by white picket fence. Shaded seating areas and swings are located across the grounds. The Inn at Salado, located in the heart of the historic district, has been renovated to its original 1872 splendor. The Inn offers nine rooms, most with fireplaces, antiques, porches, and two brick terraces. On the Inn's grounds is located Allen Hall (1901). Originally a country chapel, the hall is now available for business and pleasure gatherings. Both B&Bs are listed on state and national historic registers.

Rose Mansion Hostess: Lori Long
The Inn Hostess: Gabrielle Oborski
Rooms: 20 (PB) $90-120
Full Breakfast
Credit Cards: A, B, C, D
Notes: 2, 4 (for groups of 75+), 5, 7 (well-behaved), 8, 9, 10

---

year; 6 Pets welcome; 7 Children welcome; 8 Tennis nearby; 9 Swimming nearby; 10 Golf nearby; 11 Skiing nearby; 12 May be booked through travel agent

SAN ANTONIO

Beckman Inn and Carriage House

222 E. Guenther Street, 78204
(210) 229-1449

A wonderful Victorian house (1886) located in the King William historic district, across the street from the start of the Riverwalk. Beautifully landscaped, it will take you on a leisurely stroll to the Alamo, downtown shops, and restaurants. You can also take the trolley which stops at the corner and within minutes you're there in style. The beautiful wrap-around porch welcomes you to the main house and warm, gracious Victorian hospitality. The large guest rooms feature antique, ornately carved, Victorian, queen-size beds, private baths, and ceiling fans. Gourmet breakfast, with breakfast dessert, is served in the dining room with china, crystal, and silver.

Hosts: Betty Jo and Don Schwartz
Rooms: 5 (PB) $80-130
Full Breakfast
Credit Cards: A, B, C, E
Notes: 2, 5, 7 (over 12), 10, 12

Beauregard House B&B

215 Beauregard, 78204
(210) 222-1198

Charming two-story Victorian home (1910) in the historic King William neighborhood. The home has hardwood floors throughout and rooms are filled with furnishings appropriate to the era. Central air and heat. Each room is designed for your comfort and has a private bath. One room offers a fireplace. One block from convenient downtown trolley connecting you to the Alamo, Alamodome, Convention Center Arena, Market Square, and more. Also only one block from the famous River Walk. Spacious off-street, lighted parking. No smoking indoors.

Hostess: Ann Trabal
Rooms: 3-4 (PB) $80-95
Full Breakfast
Credit Cards: A, B
Notes: 2, 5, 12

Beauregard House Bed and Breakfast

The Belle of Monte Vista

505 Belknap Place, 78212
(210) 732-4006 (voice and FAX)

J. Riely Gordon designed this 1890 Queen Anne Victorian home located conveniently in this famous Monte Vista historic district, one mile from downtown San Antonio. The house has eight fireplaces, stained glass windows, hand-carved oak interior, and Victorian furnishings. Near zoo, churches, river walk, El Mercardo, arts, and universities. Transportation to and from airport, bus, and train station upon request. Easy access from all major highways.

Hosts: Jim Davis and Joan and David Bell
Rooms: 8 (SB) $60+tax
Full Breakfast
Credit Cards: None
Notes: 2, 5, 7, 8, 10

North Brackenridge House Bed and Breakfast

230 Madison, 78204
(210) 271-3442; (800) 221-1412

A Greek Revival home (1903) set in the King William historic district with four two-story white Corinthian columns and first and second floor verandas. The original pine floor, double-hung windows, and high ceilings are enhanced by antique furnishings, many of them family heirlooms. All guest rooms have private baths and entrances, phones, and mini-refrigerators. A bridal suite decorated in all white is available. Breakfast is served in the guest dining room on the second floor. Located only six blocks from downtown, two blocks from the Riverwalk, and one block from the ten cent trolley and the San Antonio Mission Trail. Convenient walking to four delightful restaurants.

Hostess: Frances Bochat; Owner: Carolyn Cole
Rooms: 5 (PB) $90-115
Full Breakfast
Credit Cards: A, B, C, D
Notes: 2, 5, 12

Riverwalk Inn

329 Old Guilbeau Road, 78204
(210) 212-8300; (800) 254-4440; (210) 229-9442 (FAX)

The Riverwalk Inn is comprised of five two-story log homes, circa 1840, which have been restored on the San Antonio Riverwalk. Tastefully decorated in period antiques giving a feeling of "country elegance." Amenties include fireplace, refrigerator, private baths, phones, balconies, 80 ft. porch, conference room, ex-

panded continental breakfast

Innkeeper: Johnny Halpenny; Proprietors: Jan and Tracy Hammer
Rooms: 11 (PB) $89-145
Continental Breakfast
Credit Cards: A, B, C, D
Notes: 2, 5, 12

Sherwood Train Depot Bed and Breakfast

SILSBEE

Sherwood Train Depot Bed and Breakfast

134 Sherwood Trail, 77656
(409) 385-0188

A beautiful wooded setting of a two-story cypress home in the midst of beech and oak trees. Within the home, a unique design of knottie cypress wood. Fireplaced living room which at the ceiling begins a "G" scale "LGB" train system that runs on a cypress ceiling-hung rail system that is 130 ft. long running throughout the downstairs and even spiraling to the upstairs. You have to see to see this unusual track layout to believe it. Both suites feature king bed, private bath, TV/VCR and cable, phone, and one suite even has a two person hot tub. Guests can also enjoy exercise equipment, walking trails, bird-

year; 6 Pets welcome; 7 Children welcome; 8 Tennis nearby; 9 Swimming nearby; 10 Golf nearby; 11 Skiing nearby; 12 May be booked through travel agent

watching, and much more.

Hostess: Jerry Allen
Rooms: 2 (PB) $60-75
Continental and Full Breakfast
Credit Cards: None
Notes: 2, 3, 4, 5, 7, 9, 10

SPRING

McLachlan Farm Bed and Breakfast

P.O. Box 538 (24907 Hardy Rd.), 77383
(713) 350-2400; (800) 382-3988

The Mclachlan family homestead, built in 1911, was restored and enlarged in 1989 by the great-grandaughter and her husband of the original McLachlan family who settled the land in 1862. Set back among 35 acres of towering sycamore and pecan trees, neatly mowed grounds, and winding forest trails. It is a quiet oasis that returns guests to a time when life was simpler. Visitors may swing on the porches, walk in the woods, or visit Old Town Spring (one mile south) where there are more than 100 shops to enjoy.

Hosts: Jim and Joycelyn Clairmonte
Rooms: 4 (2PB; 2SB) $75-85
Full Country Breakfast
Credit Cards: None
Notes: 2, 5, 10, 12

TEXARKANA

Mansion on Main Bed and Breakfast Inn

802 Main, 75501
(903) 792-1835

"Twice as Nice," the motto of Texarkana,

USA (Texas and Arkansas), is standard practice at Mansion on Main. The 1895 Neoclassic Colonial mansion, surrounded by 14 tall columns, was recently restored by the owners of McKay House, the popular bed and breakfast in nearby Jefferson. Six bed chambers vary from the Governor's Suite to the Butler's Garret. Guests enjoy Southern hospitality, period furnishings, fireplaces, and a gentleman's breakfast. Thirty miles away is the town of Hope, birthplace of President Clinton.

Hosts: Kay and Jack Roberts
Rooms: 4 and 2 suites (PB) $55-110 (corp. rates available)
Full Sit-Down Breakfast
Credit Cards: A, B
Notes: 2, 5, 10, 12

WIMBERLY

Southwind Bed and Breakfast

Rt. 2 Box 15, 78676
(512) 847-5277; (800) 508-5277

Southwind, a prayerful place, sets on 25 secluded acres of hills and trees. Two long porches are provided with rocking chairs to enjoy the fresh air, wildlife, and sunsets. Star gazing is especially grand from the hot tub. A guest living room with fireplace and kitchen and dining room priveleges complement the three spacious, private guest rooms. A full, tasty breakfast with coffee or tea served on the porch is a wonderful way to start the day at Southwind.

Hostess: Carrie Watson
Rooms: 3 (PB) $70-80
Full Breakfast
Credit Cards: A, B, D
Notes: 2, 5, 8, 9, 10, 12

NOTES: Credit cards accepted: A Master Card; B Visa; C American Express; D Discover Card; E Diners Club; F Other; 2 Personal checks accepted; 3 Lunch available; 4 Dinner available; 5 Open all

WINNSBORO

Thee Hubbell House

307 West Elm, 75494
(903) 342-5629; (800) 227-0639; (903) 342-6627
(FAX)

Thee Hubbell House

We spell "Thee" that way on purpose!
This is not only the old English spelling but
represents our religious heritage as well.
We have twelve rooms all with private
baths, two acres of landscaped grounds,
four historical homes all restored and furnished in antiques. Spa House by reservation and romantic candlelight dinners also
by reservation. Seven golf courses, ten
lakes, and over one hundred antique/craft
shops in the area.

Hosts: Dan and Laurel Hubbell
Rooms: 12 (PB) $75-175
Full Breakfast (Continental Breakfast available)
Credit Cards: A, B, C, D, E
Notes: 2, 4, 5, 7 (family cottage only), 8, 9, 10, 12

Utah

DUCK CREEK VILLAGE

Meadow View Lodge

P.O. Box 1331, 84762
(801) 682-2495; (801) 682-2075 (FAX)

A unique mountain inn located within beautiful Dixie National Forest. Our common area boasts a large circular fireplace where we serve homemade goodies during our evening "social hour." Rooms of knotty pine have a warm country feel. Within minutes of Bryce Canyon and Zion National Parks and Cedar Breaks National Monument. Paradise for fishermen, mountain bikers, hikers, snowmobilers, and skiers! Let us spoil you with gourmet, delicious, homey, comfort and warm hospitality.

Hosts: Craig and Kimberly Simmerman
Rooms: 9 (PB) $50-60
Full Country Breakfast
Credit Cards: A, B
Notes: 5, 7, 8, 9, 11, 12

MOUNTAIN GREEN

Hubbard House Bed and Breakfast Inn

5648 W. Old Highway Rd., 84050
(801) 876-2020 (voice and FAX)

Hubbard House, built in the 1920s, has the warmth and charm of days gone by with hardwood floors and stained glass windows. It has an awesome view of God's magestic mountians. Three ski resorts within the area, also fishing, boating, golfing, hiking, and hunting. Piano in dining room. Come and enjoy homemade goodies, laughter, and good old hospitality at Hubbard House. One mile east from Exit 92 off I-84.

Hosts: Donald and Gloria Hubbard
Rooms: 3 (1PB; 2SB) $55-75
Full Country Breakfast
Credit Cards: A, B
Notes: 5, 7, 8, 9, 10, 11

Aunt Annie's Inn

ST. GEORGE

Aunt Annie's Inn

139 N. 100 West, 84770
(801) 673-5504; (800) 257-5504 (in Utah only)

Built in 1891 for an early cattleman, the

NOTES: Credit cards accepted: A Master Card; B Visa; C American Express; D Discover Card; E Diners Club; F Other; 2 Personal checks accepted; 3 Lunch available; 4 Dinner available; 5 Open all year; 6 Pets

home has been carefully renovated, restored, and decorated with a variety of fine American antiques. Located in the heart of the historic district, the Inn is within walking distance of Brigham Young's winter home, Pioneer Museum, many convenient stores, fine restaurants, gift shops, and much more. A recent guest said, "Your hospitality was the best—you made us feel like friends, as well as guests."

Hosts: Bob and Claudia Tribe
Rooms: 4 (PB) $45-60
Full Breakfast
Credit Cards: A, B, C
Notes: 2, 5, 7, 8, 9, 10, 11, 12

Greene Gate Village

76 W. Tabernacle St., 84770
(801) 628-6999; (800) 350-6999; (801) 628-6989 (FAX)

Behind the green gates, nine beautifully restored homes provide modern comfort in pioneer elegance. Our guests love the nostalgic charm of the Bentley House with elegant Victorian decor—and the quaint Tolley House, where eleven children were born and raised. The Grainery sleeps three in rooms where early settlers loaded supplies for their trek to California. The Orson Pratt Home, built by another early Mormon leader, is on the National Regis-

ter of Historic Places. Green Hedge, with one of the village's two bridal suites, was originally built in another part of town but was moved to Green Gate Village in 1991. Family reunions or other large groups (up to 22) may share the comfort and charm of the Greenehouse, built in 1872. The Greenehouse has all the modern conveniences of a full kitchen, swimming pool, and tennis court.

Hosts: John, Sheri and Barbara Greene
Rooms: 17 (PB) $45-110
Full Breakfast
Credit Cards: A, B, C
Notes: 2, 4, 5, 7, 8, 9, 10, 11, 12

Seven Wives Inn

217 N. 100 West, 84770
(801) 628-3737; (800) 600-3737

The Inn consists of two adjacent pioneer adobe homes with massive handgrained moldings framing windows and doors. Bedrooms are furnished with period antiques and handmade quilts. Some rooms have fireplaces; two have a whirlpool tub. Swimming pool on premises.

Hosts: Donna and Jay Curtis; Alison and Jon Bowcutt
Rooms: 12 (PB) $50-75, suites $100-110
Full Breakfast
Credit Cards: A, B, C, D, E
Notes: 2, 5, 7, 8, 9, 10, 12

Saltair Bed and Breakfast

welcome; 7 Children welcome; 8 Tennis nearby; 9 Swimming nearby; 10 Golf nearby; 11 Skiing nearby; 12 May be booked through travel agent

SALT LAKE CITY

Saltair Bed and Breakfast

164 South 900 E., 84102
(801) 533-8184; (801) 733-8184; (801) 328-2060
(FAX)

Antiques and charm complement queen-size brass beds, Amish quilts, and period lamps. A full breakfast featuring House juice and wake-up favorites such as pumpkin/walnut waffles and Saltair muffins greet each guest. Hospitality offered by innkeepers Jan and Nancy includes snacks, use of elegant parlor, dining room, TV room, and phone room. Close to the University of Utah, historic downtown, skiing, and canyons.

Host: Jan Bartlett; Hostess: Nancy Saxton
Rooms: 7 (4PB; 3SB) $55-139
Full Breakfast
Credit Cards: A, B, C, E
Notes: 2, 5, 7, 8, 9, 10, 11, 12

SANDY

Mountain Hollow Bed and Breakfast Inn

10209 S. Dimple Dell Road, 84092
(801) 942-3428

Nestled at the base of Little Cottonwood Canyon just minutes from world class skiing and 18 miles from downtown Salt Lake City. Wooded country estate with streams, waterfall, and outdoor hot tub. Beautiful cathedral ceilings in lounge, gameroom, video library, and breakfast buffet.

Hosts: Doug and Kathy Larson
Rooms: 10 (2PB; 8SB) $65-150
Extended Continental Breakfast
Credit Cards: A, B, C, D
Notes: 2, 5, 7 (over 5), 8, 9, 10, 11, 12

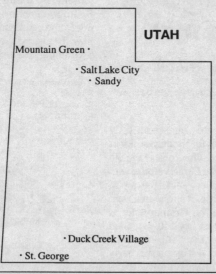

UTAH

Mountain Green ·

· Salt Lake City
· Sandy

· Duck Creek Village
· St. George

Vermont

American Country Collection of Bed and Breakfasts and Country Inns Reservation Service

4 Greenwood Lane, Delmar, NY 12054-1606
(518) 439-7001 information and reservations;
(518) 439-4301 (FAX)

This reservation service provides reservations for eastern **New York**, western **Massachusetts**, all of **Vermont**, and **St. Thomas, U.S.V.I.** Just one call does it all. Relax and unwind at any of our 115 immaculate, personally-inspected bed and breakfasts and country inns. Many include fireplace, Jacuzzi, and/or Modified American Plan. We cater to the budget-minded, yet also offer luxurious accommodations in older Colonial homes and inns. Urban, suburban, and rural locations available. $35-180. Arthur R. Copeland, coordinator.

ALBURG

Thomas Mott Homestead Bed and Breakfast

Blue Rock Road on Lake Champlain
Route 2, Box 149-B, 05440
(802) 796-3736 (voice and FAX); (800) 348-0843
(Canada and USA ext. VT)

Formerly an importer and distributor of fine wines, your host also enjoys gourmet cooking. His completely restored farmhouse has a guest living room with TV and fireplace overlooking the lake; game room with bumper pool and darts; quilt decor. Full view of Mt. Mansfield and Jay Peak. One hour to Montreal/Burlington; one and one-half hours to Lake Placid, New York, and Stowe. Lake activities winter and summer. Amenities include Ben and Jerry's ice cream, lawn games, and horseshoes. Prodigy accessable.

Host: Patrick J. Schallert, Sr., M.A., B.A.
Rooms: 5 (PB) $55-70
Full Breakfast
Credit Cards: A, B, D
Notes: 2, 3, 4 (gourmet dinners w/advance notice), 5, 7 (over 6), 8, 9, 10, 11, 12

ARLINGTON

The Arlington Inn

Historic Rt. 7A, PO Box 369, 05250
(802) 375-6532

A stately Greek Revival mansion set on lushly landscaped lawns. Elegantly appointed rooms filled with antiques and amenities. All rooms have private baths, air-conditioning and include breakfast. Located between Bennington and Manchester. Antique shops, boutiques, museums, skiing, hiking, biking, canoeing, fly fishing, golf, and many other outdoor activities are nearby. Tennis on our private court. Outstanding cuisine is served by romantic candlelight in our fireplaced, award winning dining room with superb service. A non-smoking inn. AAA—3 diamonds. Mobil—3 stars.

Hosts: Mark and Deborah Gagnon
Rooms: 13 (PB) $65-155
Full Breakfast
Credit Cards: A, B, C, D, E
Notes: 2 (deposits only), 4, 5, 7, 8 (on-site), 9, 10, 11, 12

The Arlington Inn

Hill Farm Inn

R. R. 2, Box 2015, 05250
(802) 375-2269; (800) 882-2545

Hill Farm is one of Vermont's original farmsteads granted from King George III in 1775. It has been an inn since 1905 and still retains the character of an old farm vacation inn on 60 beautiful acres between the Taconic and Green Mountains with a mile frontage on the Battenkill River. We offer hearty home cooking, charming rooms, and hiking, biking, canoeing, and relaxing with spectacular views.

Hosts: Regan and John Chichester
Rooms: 13 (8PB; 5SB) $70-120
Full Hot Country Breakfast
Credit Cards: A, B, C, D
Notes: 2, 4, 5, 6 (limited), 7, 8, 9, 10, 11, 12

Shenandoah Farm

Battenkill Rd., 05250
(802) 375-6372

Experience New England in this lovingly restored 1820 Colonial overlooking the Battenkill River. Wonderful "Americana" year-round. Full "farm-fresh" breakfast is served daily and is included.

Host: Woody Masterson
Rooms: 5 (1PB; 4SB) $60-75
Full Breakfast
Credit Cards: A, B
Notes: 2, 5, 8, 10, 11, 12

BELLOWS FALLS

Blue Haven Bed and Breakfast

227 Westminister Road, 05101
(802) 463-9008; (800) 228-9008; (802) 463-1454 (FAX)

Explore Vermont's beauty from our 1830 restored schoolhouse. Experience canopy beds, hand-painted touches, and a big country kitchen where hearth-baked Vermont breakfasts are served. Have tea time treats at the antique glass laden sideboard, or in the ruddy pine common room. Expect a peaceful and pleasant time here. Christian fellowship available. Open to one and all in God's love. Please come!

Hostess: Helene Champagne
Rooms: 6 (4PB; 2SB) $45-75
Full Breakfast (weekends); Continental Breakfast (weekdays)
Credit Cards: A, B, C
Notes: 2, 5, 7, 8, 9, 10, 11, 12

NOTES: Credit cards accepted: A Master Card; B Visa; C American Express; D Discover Card; E Diners Club; F Other; 2 Personal checks accepted; 3 Lunch available; 4 Dinner available; 5 Open all

CHESTER

Henry Farm Inn

P. O. Box 646, Green Mountain Turnpike, 05143
(802) 875-2674; (800) 723-8213

The Henry Farm Inn supplies the beauty of Vermont with old-time simplicity. Nestled on fifty acres of rolling hills and meadows, assuring peace and quiet. Spacious rooms, private baths, country sitting areas, and a sunny dinning room all guarantee a feeling of home. Come and visit for a day or more!

Hosts: The Bowmans
Rooms: 7 (PB) $50-90
Full Breakfast
Credit Cards: A, B, C
Notes: 2, 5, 7, 8, 9, 10, 11, 12

The Hugging Bear Inn and Shoppe

Main Street, 05143
(802) 875-2412; (800) 325-0519

Teddy bears peek out the windows and are tucked in all the corners of this beautiful Victorian house built in 1850. If you love teddy bears, you'll love the Hugging Bear. There are six guest rooms with private shower baths and a teddy bear in every bed. Full breakfast and afternoon snack are served.

Hosts: Georgette, Paul, and Diane Thomas
Rooms: 6 (PB) $55-90
Full Breakfast
Credit Cards: A, B, C, D
Notes: 2, 5, 7, 8, 9, 10, 11

Inn Victoria

On the Green, 05143
(800) 732-4288; (802) 875-4323 (FAX)

Circa 1850s B&B furnished in period antiques with private baths that feature jacuzzis and soaking bubble tubs. Our seven charming rooms and suites include a gourmet breakfast and afternoon tea, Victorian, of course. Fireplace. Look for our purple shutters. "The most romantic inn in southern Vermont," says *The Green Moutain Guide.* Take home a unique teapot from the shop next door.

Hosts: KC and Tom Lanagan
Rooms: 7 (PB) $65-150 (depending on season)
Full Breakfast
Credit Cards: A, B
Notes: 2, 4, 5, 8, 9, 10, 11. 12

CUTTINGSVILLE

Buckmaster Inn

Lincoln Hill Road, Rural Route 1, Box 118, Shrewsbury, 05738
(802) 492-3485

The Buckmaster Inn (1801) was an early stagecoach stop in Shrewsbury. Standing on a knoll overlooking a picturesque barn scene and rolling hills, it is situated in the Green Mountains. A center hall, grand staircase, and wide-pine floors grace the home, which is decorated with family antiques and crewel handiwork done by your hostess. Extremely large, airy rooms, wood-burning stove, four fireplaces, two large porches.

Hosts: Sam and Grace Husselman
Rooms: 3 (2PB; 1SB) $55-65 (private bath) + tax
Full Breakfast
Credit Cards: None
Notes: 5, 7, 8, 9, 10, 11

year; 6 Pets welcome; 7 Children welcome; 8 Tennis nearby; 9 Swimming nearby; 10 Golf nearby; 11 Skiing nearby; 12 May be booked through travel agent

Maple Crest Farm

Box 120 Lincoln Hill Rd., 05738
(802) 492-3367

This 27-room 1808 farmhouse has been preserved for five generations and is located in the heart of the Green Mountains in Shrewsbury. It has been a bed and breakfast for 23 years. Ten miles north of Ludlow and ten miles south of Rutland, an area that offers much to visitors. Pico, Killington, and Okemo are nearby for downhill skiing. Cross-country skiing and hiking are offered on the premises.

Hosts: William, Donna and Russell Smith
Rooms: 4 (SB) $25-35 per person
Full Breakfast
Credit Cards: None
Notes: 2, 5, 7, 8, 9, 10, 11, 12

DANBY

Quail's Nest Bed and Breakfast

P.O. Box 221, Main St., 05739
(802) 293-5099 (Voice and FAX)

Nestled in a quiet mountain village, our inn offers the guest friendly conversation around the fireplace, rooms filled with cozy quilts and antiques, and a hearty, home-cooked breakfast in the morning. Hiking, skiing, swimming, and outlet shopping are all very close by as well as our local craft and antique shops. Our guests are all treated as part of the family, which is what makes a real difference.

Hosts: Gregory and Nancy Diaz
Rooms: 6 (4PB; 2SB) $60-85
Full Breakfast
Credit Cards: A, B
Notes: 2, 5, 7, 8, 9, 10, 11

Silas Griffith Inn

South Main Street, R. R. 1, Box 66F, 05739
(802) 293-5567

Built by Vermont's first millionaire, this Victorian inn was built in 1891 in the heart of the Green Mountains, with spectacular mountain views. It features 17 delightful, antique-furnished rooms and a fireplace in the living and dining room. Hiking, skiing, antiquing nearby. Come and enjoy our elegant meals and New England hospitality.

Hosts: Paul and Lois Dansereau
Rooms: 17 (11PB; 6SB) $69-86
Full Breakfast
Credit Cards: A, B, C
Notes: 2, 4, 5, 7, 9, 10, 11, 12

DERBY LINE

Derby Village Inn

46 Main St., 05830
(802) 873-3604

Enjoy this charming, old, Victorian mansion situated in the quiet village of Derby Line, within walking distance of the Canadian border and the world's only international library and opera house. The nearby countryside offers year-round recreation—downhill and cross-country skiing, water sports, cycling, fishing, hiking, golf, snowmobiling, sleigh rides, antiquing, and most of all peace and tranquility. We are a non-smoking facility.

Hosts: Tom and Phyllis Moreau
Rooms: 5 (PB) $55-65
Full Breakfast
Credit Cards: A, B, D
Notes: 2, 5, 7, 8, 9, 10, 11

NOTES: Credit cards accepted: A Master Card; B Visa; C American Express; D Discover Card; E Diners Club; F Other; 2 Personal checks accepted; 3 Lunch available; 4 Dinner available; 5 Open all

ENOSBURG FALLS

Berkson Farms

RR1, Box 850, 05450
(802) 933-2522; (802) 933-8331 (FAX)

Relax in our 150-year-old farmhouse on a working dairy farm. Located on 600 acres of meadowland surrounded by a variety of animals, nature, and warm hospitality. Picnic, hike, bike in the warmer months; cross-country ski and sled in the winter. Enjoy our hearty home-style meals using our maple syrup and farm-fresh dairy products. Close to Canada and major ski areas. Children and pets welcome. Reservations suggested.

Hosts: Susan and Terry Spoonire
Rooms: 4 (1PB; 3SB) $55-65
Full Breakfast
Credit Cards: None
Notes: 2, 3, 4, 5, 6, 7, 9, 10, 11

FAIR HAVEN

Maplewood Inn

Route 22A South, 05743
(802) 265-8039; (800) 253-7729 (outside VT)

Exquisite 1843 Greek Revival on the Vermont Register of Historic Places and a romantic, antique-filled haven! Keeping room with fireplace, gathering room with books and games, parlor with complimentary cordials. Elegant rooms and suites are air conditioned, have fireplaces, color cable TVs, radios, and in-room phone available. Near everything! Bikes, canoes, and antique shop on site. Lakes Region. Pet boarding arranged. A true four-season experience! Guidebook, Mobil—3 stars,

and AAA—3 diamonds—recommended.

Hosts: Doug and Cindy Baird
Rooms: 5 (PB) $70-105
Continental Plus Breakfast
Credit Cards: A, B, C, D, E, F
Notes: 2, 5, 7 (over 5), 8, 9, 10, 11, 12

FAIRLEE

Silver Maple Lodge and Cottages

R. R. 1, Box 8, 05045
(802) 333-4326; (800) 666-1946

A historic bed and breakfast country inn is located in a four-season recreational area. Enjoy canoeing, fishing, golf, tennis, and skiing within a few miles of the lodge. Visit nearby flea markets and country auctions. Choose a newly renovated room in our antique farmhouse or a handsome, pine-paneled cottage room. Three cottages with working fireplaces. Many fine restaurants are nearby. Darmouth College is 17 miles away. Also offered are hot air balloon packages, inn-to-inn bicycling, canoeing, and walking tours. Brochure available.

Hosts: Scott and Sharon Wright
Rooms: 16 (14PB; 2SB) $49-72
Continental Breakfast
Credit Cards: A, B, C, D
Notes: 2, 5, 7, 8, 9, 10, 11, 12

The Peak Chalet

year; 6 Pets welcome; 7 Children welcome; 8 Tennis nearby; 9 Swimming nearby; 10 Golf nearby;
11 Skiing nearby; 12 May be booked through travel agent

KILLINGTON

The Peak Chalet
P.O. Box 511, South View Path, 05751
(802) 422-4278

The Peak Chalet is a four room B&B located within the beautiful Green Mountains. The exterior is authentically European alpine. The interior is furnished with a fine country inn flavor and reflects high quality with attention to detail. We offer panoramic mountian views with a cozy stone fireplace to unwind by. All rooms have queen-size beds and private baths. Centrally located within Killington Ski Resort, this is a truly relaxing experience.

Hosts: Gregory and Diane Becker
Rooms: 4 (PB) $50-110
Continental Breakfast
Credit Cards: A, B, C, E
Notes: 3, 4, 5, 7 (over 12), 8, 9, 10, 11, 12

LOWER WATERFORD

Rabbit Hill Inn
Pucker Street and Route 18, 05848
(802) 748-5168; (800) 76-BUNNY;
(802) 748-8342 (FAX)

Full of whimsical and charming surprises, this Federal-period inn, established in 1795, has been lavished with love and attention. Many guest rooms have fireplaces and canopied beds. Chamber music, candlelit gourmet dining, and turn-down service make this an enchanting and romantic hideaway in a tiny, restored village overlooking the mountains. Award-winning, nationally acclaimed inn. Our service is inspired by Philippians 2:7.

Hosts: John and Maureen Magee
Rooms: 18 (PB) $89-199
Full Breakfast
Credit Cards: A, B
Closed first two weeks of November and all of April
Notes: 2, 4, 8, 9, 10, 11, 12

LUDLOW

The Combes Family Inn
RFD #1, Box 275, 05149
(802) 228-8799; (800) 822-8799

Bring your family home to ours here in Vermont at The Combes Family Inn. The Inn, a century-old farmhouse, located on a country back road offers a quiet respite from the hustle and bustle of today's lifestyle! Relax and socialize (BYOB) in our Vermont Barnboard "Keeping Room" furnished with turn-of-the-century oak. Sample Bill's country breakfasts and Ruth's delicious home-cooking. Our lush Green Mountains invite you to join us for a relaxing, casual vacation. Eleven, cozy, country-inspired guest rooms—all with private baths.

Hosts: Ruth and Bill Combes
Rooms: 11 (PB) $68-90
Full Breakfast
Credit Cards: A, B, C, D
Closed April 15 through May 15
Notes: 2, 4, 6, 7, 8, 9, 10, 11, 12

MANCHESTER VILLAGE

The Battenkill Inn
P.O. Box 948, 05254
(802) 362-4213; (800) 441-1628

Enjoy afternoon croquet on sweeping lawns with mountain views, or savor evening

---

NOTES: Credit cards accepted: A Master Card; B Visa; C American Express; D Discover Card; E Diners Club; F Other; 2 Personal checks accepted; 3 Lunch available; 4 Dinner available; 5 Open all

hors d'oeuvres by a marble mantled fire. The Battenkill Inn offers warm hospitality in the dramatic elegance of an 1840 Italianate Victorian setting. Convenient to skiing, hiking, biking, fishing, canoeing, outlet shopping, and some of the finest dining in New England. Sumptuous breakfasts included. Some fireplaced rooms, all with private baths and air-conditioning.

Hosts: Ramsay and MaryJo Gourd
Rooms: 10 (PB) $75-160
Very Full Breakfast
Credit Cards: A, B, C
Notes: 3 (boxed), 5, 7 (well attended), 9, 10, 11, 12

MIDDLEBURY

Middlebury Inn

14 Courthouse Square, 05753
(802) 388-4961; (800) 842-4666

This 1827, historic, 75-room landmark overlooks the village green in a picturesque New England college town. Discover Middlebury, Vermont—the splendor of its historic district—Vermont State Craft Center, Middlebury College, boutique shopping, and four season recreation. Elegantly restored rooms, private bath, telephone, color TV, and air-conditioning (in season). The inn offers breakfast, lunch, dinner, seasonal porch dining, afternoon tea, and Sunday brunch. Recommended by AAA and a Member of Historic Hotels of America.

Hosts: Jane and Frank Emanuel, Innkeepers
Rooms: 75 (PB) $90-180
Full and Continental Breakfast (not included in rate but can be added)
Credit Cards: A, B, C, E
Notes: 3, 4, 5, 6 (limited), 7, 8, 9, 10, 11, 12

The Battenkill Inn

MONTGOMERY CENTER

The Inn on Trout River

P.O. Box 76, The Main Street, 05471
(802) 326-4391; (800) 338-7049 (US + Canada)

A "Currier and Ives" style village setting is where you'll find our 100-year-old country Victorian inn featuring private baths, queen-size beds, down comforters, an feather pillows. Our restaurant is one of the finest in the area serving sumptuous sustenance with superior service. Fireplaces, large living room/library, and gameroom all add to your comfort and pleasure. We are AAA—3-diamond Historic Country Inn.

Hosts: Michael and Lee Forman
Rooms: 10 (PB) $86-132
Full Menu Breakfast
Credit Cards: A, B, D
Notes: 2 (advance deposit only), 4, 5, 7, 8, 9, 10, 11, 12

MORETOWN

Camel's Hump View

Rt. 100B, Box 720, 05660
(802) 496-3614

Camel's Hump View is a unique old-style country inn dating to 1831, with the Mad

year; 6 Pets welcome; 7 Children welcome; 8 Tennis nearby; 9 Swimming nearby; 10 Golf nearby; 11 Skiing nearby; 12 May be booked through travel agent

River to the east and Camel's Hump Mountain to the west. Warm up by the glowing fire in the winter, or enjoy cattle grazing in the fields during the summer. The inn can accommodate 16 guest and serves hearty country meals from the gardens. Skiing, golf, fishing, horseback riding, and hiking are all available. No smoking.

Hosts: Jerry and Wilma Maynard
Rooms: 8 (1PB; 7SB) $50-60
Full Breakfast
Credit Cards: F
Notes: 2, 4, 5, 7, 8, 9, 10, 11

NORTH TROY

The 1893 House Bed and Breakfast

30A Highland Ave., Rt. 105, 05859
(802) 988-9614

Come visit us in our 1893 Victorian home in North Troy, Vermont, a quaint valley town surrounded by beautiful mountains. We are eight miles from Jay Peak, and one and one-half hours from Montreal. Lots of hiking trails, biking routes, skiing, antiquing, or just relaxing in the quiet country.

Hosts: Rick and Pat Shover
Rooms: 3 (1PB; 2SB) $50
Full Breakfast
Credit Cards: None
Notes: 2, 5, 7, 8, 9, 10, 11

ORLEANS

Valley House Inn

4 Memorial Square
(802) 754-6665; (800) 545-9711

One quarter mile off I-91, Exit 26. An

1800s country inn in the center of the Northeast Kingdom's lakes region. Easy access to scenic hiking, biking, hunting, and lake and river fishing. Cocktail lounge on premises. The grand lobby with pressed metal ceiling and walls, with half-moon front desk make you feel like you are stepping back to the turn of the century. Staying at a nice Vermont country inn doesn't have to be expensive.

Hosts: David and Louise Bolduc
Rooms: 22 (20PB; 2SB) $35-70
Breakfast not included (restaurant on premises)
Credit Cards: A, B, C, D
Notes: 2, 3, 4, 5, 7, 8, 9, 10, 11,12

PERKINSVILLE

The Inn at Weathersfield

Rt. 106, P.O. Box 165, 05151
(802) 263-9217; (800) 477-4828 for reservations;
(802) 263-9219 (FAX)

Congeniality and caring make this "Colonial Sampler" a special place. Nestled in the lap of Vermont history on 21 scenic acres with swimming pond, hiking trails, and horsedrawn sleigh/carriage rides. There are 12 individually decorated guest rooms and suites, all with private bath, many with canopy beds and working fireplaces. Afternoon Colonial tea, 5-course dinner, and buffet breakfast served daily. A tavern, extensive wine cellar, and duo-grand pianists during dining hours round out the ultimate inn experience.

Hosts: Mary Louise and Ron Thorburn
Rooms: 12 (PB) $175-190 w/3 meals
Full Breakfast; 5-course dinner; high tea
Credit Cards: A, B, C, D, E, F (Carte Blanche)
Notes: 2, 4 (included), 5, 7 (w/ prior arrangements), 8, 9, 10, 11, 12

NOTES: Credit cards accepted: A Master Card; B Visa; C American Express; D Discover Card; E Diners Club; F Other; 2 Personal checks accepted; 3 Lunch available; 4 Dinner available; 5 Open all

Swiss Farm Lodge

PITTSFIELD

Swiss Farm Lodge

P.O. Box 630, Rt. 100, 05762
(802) 746-8341; (800) 245-5126

Working Hereford beef farm. Enjoy the casual, family-type atmosphere in our living room with fireplace and TV or in the game room. Home-cooked meals and baking served family style. Our own maple syrup, jams, and jellies. Walk-in cooler available for guests' use. Cross-country trails on site. B&B available all year. M.A.P. November to April only. Mountain bike trails close by. Owned and operated by the same family for 50 years. Lower rates for children in same room as parents.

Hosts: Mark and Sandy Begin
Rooms: 17 (14PB; 3SB) $40-50
Full Breakfast
Credit Cards: A, B
Notes: 2, 5, 7, 8, 9, 10, 11

Liberty Hill Farm

ROCHESTER

Liberty Hill Farm

R.R. 1, Box 158, Liberty Hill Rd., 05060
(802) 767-3926

Working dairy farm nestled between the White River and the Green Mountain National Forest. Hearty family-style breakfasts and dinners included. Plenty of recreational activities yearround, or visit the barn and help with chores. Children always welcome.

Hosts: Bob and Beth Kennett
Rooms: 7 (SB) $100 (MAP)
Full Breakfast and Dinner
Credit Cards: None
Notes: 2, 4, 5, 7, 8, 9, 10, 11, 12

RUTLAND

The Inn at Rutland

70 N. Main St. (Rt.7), 05701
(802) 773-0575; (800) 808-0575

Beautifully restored 1890s Victorian mansion with ten large, comfortable rooms all with private baths, remote color cable TV, and phones. Some rooms have A/C. Gourmet continental breakfast included. Large front porch with beautiful views of mountians and valleys. Close to all central Vermont attractions. Common rooms with fireplaces, TV/VCR, and games. Carriage house for ski and bike storage. 10 minutes to Pico and Killington ski areas. Call our toll-free number.

Hosts: Bob and Tanya Liberman
Rooms: 10 (PB) $85-140
Continental Breakfast Plus
Credit Cards: A, B
Notes: 2, 5, 7 (over 8), 8, 9, 10, 11, 12

year; 6 Pets welcome; 7 Children welcome; 8 Tennis nearby; 9 Swimming nearby; 10 Golf nearby; 11 Skiing nearby; 12 May be booked through travel agent

The Inn at Rutland

STOWE

Brass Lantern Inn

717 Maple Street, 05672
(802) 253-2229; (800) 729-2980; (802) 253-7425
(FAX)

This traditional, Vermont, bed and breakfast, country inn in the heart of Stowe is an award-winning restoration of an 1810 farmhouse and carriage barn overlooking Mt. Mansfield, Vermont's most prominent mountain. The inn features period antiques, quilts, and planked floors. The entire inn is air conditioned. Most rooms have views, and some have fireplaces and some have whirlpools. Special packages include honeymoon, skiing, golf, sleigh and surrey rides, and more. No smoking.

Host: Andy Aldrich
Rooms: 9 (PB) $70-150
Full Breakfast
Credit Cards: A, B, C
Notes: 2, 5, 8, 9, 10, 11, 12

The Siebeness Inn

3681 Mountain Rd., 05672
(802) 253-8942; (800) 426-9001; (802) 253-9232
(FAX)

A warm welcome awaits you at our charm-ing country inn nestled in the foothills of Mt. Mansfield. Romantic rooms have country antiques, private baths, air conditioning. Awake to the aroma of freshly baked muffins, which accompany your hearty New England breakfast. Relax in our outdoor hot tub in winter, or our pool with mountain views in summer. Fireplace in lounge. Bike, walk, or cross-country ski from inn on recreation path. Honeymoon, golf, and ski packages.

Hosts: Sue and Nils Anderson
Rooms: 11 (PB) $60-100
Full Breakfast
Credit Cards: A, B, C, D, E
Notes: 2, 4 (winter), 5, 7, 8, 9, 10, 11, 12

Ski Inn

Route 108, 05672
(802) 253-4050

Back in the forties Larry and Harriet Heyer, the only original owners left in Stowe, designed their ski lodge along New England architectural lines. The result, a lovely white Vermont country inn with fieldstone fireplace on a sloping hillside in a setting of green hemlocks and fur trees. In appearance a traditionally old New England inn, but comfortably modern. Located back from the highway among the evergreens, this is a quiet restful place to relax and sleep soundly. Flat hiking road, trout stream, and cookout on 28 acres of woodlands.

Hostess: Harriet Heyer
Rooms: 10 (5PB; 5SB) $40-55
Continental Breakfast
Credit Cards: C
Notes: 2, 4 (winter), 5, 6 (advance notice), 7, 8, 9, 10, 11

NOTES: Credit cards accepted: A Master Card; B Visa; C American Express; D Discover Card; E Diners Club; F Other; 2 Personal checks accepted; 3 Lunch available; 4 Dinner available; 5 Open all

Timberhölm Inn
452 Cottage Club Road, 05672
(802) 253-7603; (800) 753-7603; (802) 253-8559
(FAX)

This delightful country inn in a quiet, secluded, wooded setting has a wonderful view of Worchester Mountains. We serve afternoon tea and refreshments in the summer and après ski soup in the winter. We have ten individually decorated rooms with quilts and antiques. Two are two-bedroom suites ideal for families. There is a very large common room with an oversized fieldstone fireplace. Large outdoor deck and hot tub. Game room, shuffleboard, cable TV/VCR, refrigerator, and microwave. No smoking.

Hosts: Pete and Louise Hunter
Rooms: 10 (PB) $50-110
Full Country Breakfast
Credit Cards: A, B
Notes: 2, 5, 7, 8, 9, 10, 11, 12

Timberhölm Inn

VERGENNES

Strong House Inn
82 West Main St., 05491
(802) 887-3337

Comfortable and elegant lodging in an 1834 Federal home. Listed on the Register of Historic Places. Perfectly located in the heart of the Lake Champlain Valley with fine views of the Green Mountains and Adirondack ranges. The area offers some of the finest cycling in Vermont. Nearby is a lake, hiking, golf, skiing, and Shelburne Museum. The Inn offers 7 rooms, 2 suites, private baths, and working fireplaces. A full country breakfast is included.

Hosts: Mary and Hugh Bargiel
Rooms: 7 (5PB; 2SB) $65-140
Full Breakfast
Credit Cards: A, B, C
Notes: 2, 4, 5, 7, 8, 9, 10, 11, 12

WAITSFIELD

Mountain View Inn
R. F. D. Box 69, Route 17, 05673
(802) 496-2426

The Mountain View Inn is an old farmhouse, circa 1826, that was made into a lodge in 1948 to accommodate skiers at nearby Mad River Glen. Today it is a country inn with seven rooms. Meals are served family style around the antique harvest table where good fellowship prevails. Sip mulled cider around a crackling fire in our living room when the weather turns chilly.

Hosts: Fred and Suzy Spencer
Rooms: 7 (PB) $35-65 per person
Full Breakfast
Credit Cards: None
Notes: 2, 4, 5, 7, 8, 9, 10, 11, 12

Newtons' 1824 House Inn
Route 100, Box 159, 05673
(802) 496-7555; (800) 426-NEWTON
(802) 496-7558 (FAX)

Enjoy relaxed elegance in one of seven beautiful guest rooms at this quintessential

year; 6 Pets welcome; 7 Children welcome; 8 Tennis nearby; 9 Swimming nearby; 10 Golf nearby; 11 Skiing nearby; 12 May be booked through travel agent

farmhouse on 52 acres. The inn features antiques, original art, fireplaces, and classical music. Breakfast by the fire includes such whimsical gourmet delights as soufflés, crepes, blueberry buttermilk pancakes, and freshly squeezed orange juice. Cross-country skiing and private river swimming hole are nearby. Featured in *Glamour* and *Vermont Life*. National Historic Register. AAA three-diamond and Mobile three-star rated.

Hosts: Nick and Joyce Newton
Rooms: 7 (PB) $85-125
Full Breakfast
Credit Cards: A, B, D
Notes: 2, 5, 8, 9, 10, 11, 12

WARREN

Beaver Pond Farm Inn

Golf Course Road, RD Box 306, 05674
(802) 583-2861

Beaver Pond Farm Inn, a small, gracious country inn near the Sugarbush ski area, is located 100 yards from the first tee of the Sugarbush Golf Course, transformed into 40 kilometers of cross-country ski trails in the winter. *Bed & Breakfast in New England* calls it "The best of the best." Rooms have down comforters and beautiful views. Hearty breakfasts are served, and snacks are enjoyed by the fireplace. Continental dinners are offered three times a week during the winter. Hiking, biking, soaring, and fishing nearby. Ski and golf packages are available.

Hosts: Bob and Betty Hansen
Rooms: 6 (4PB; 2SB) $72-96
Full Breakfast
Credit Cards: A, B, C
Notes: 2, 4 (3 times a week), 7 (over 7), 8, 9, 10, 11, 12

The Sugartree, A Country Inn

Sugarbush Access Rd. R.R. 1 Box 38, 05674
(802) 583-3211; (800) 666-8907

Old-fashioned comfort and hospitality await you at the Sugartree. Rooms with brass, canopy, or antique beds; one fireplaced suite. The parlor is a gathering place for games and conversation. In winter, unwind with a hot chocolate by the fire. In summer, enjoy a cool lemonade in the gazebo. Awaken to a scrumptious breakfast of homemade muffins, fruit crisps, chocolate chip pancakes, and bananas. Situated in the mountains. Ideal for hiking, biking, and skiing.

Hosts: Kathy and Frank Partsch
Rooms: 9 (PB) $74-135
Full Breakfast
Credit Cards: A, B, C, D
Notes: 2, 5, 8, 9, 10, 11, 12

WATERBURY/STOWE

Grünberg Haus Bed and Breakfast

Route 100 S., R. R. 2, Box 1595-CB, 05676-9621
(802) 244-7726; Reservations (800) 800-7760

Our romantic Austrian inn rests on a quiet hillside in Vermont's Green Mountains, perfect for trips to Stowe, Montpelier, Waterbury, and Burlington. Choose guestrooms with wonderful views from carved wood balconies, secluded cabins hidden along wooded trails, or a spectacular carriage house with sky windows, balconies, and modern kitchen. Relax by the fire or jacuzzi, ski expertly-groomed trails, gather fresh eggs, or catch innkeeper Chris playing the grand piano during your memo-

NOTES: Credit cards accepted: A Master Card; B Visa; C American Express; D Discover Card; E Diners Club; F Other; 2 Personal checks accepted; 3 Lunch available; 4 Dinner available; 5 Open all

rablebreakfast. Explore Vermont.

Hosts: Christopher Sellers and Mark Frohman
Rooms: 14 (10PB; 5SB) $55-140
Full Musical Breakfast
Credit Cards: A, B, C, D, F
Notes: 2, 4 (for 10 or more), 5, 7, 8, 9, 10, 11, 12

Inn at Blush Hill

Blush Hill Road, R. R. 1, Box 1266, 05676
(802) 244-7529; (800) 736-7522; (802) 244-7314
(FAX)

This Cape Cod bed and breakfast, circa 1790, sits on five acres with spectacular mountain views. The inn has a large common room, library, antiques, and four fireplaces, one in a guest room. Enjoy a breakfast of Vermont products at a ten-foot farmhand's table in front of a bay window overlooking the Worcester Mountains. Afternoon refreshments are served. We are adjacent to Ben and Jerry's ice cream factory, and skiing at Stowe and Sugarbush are only minutes away.

Hosts: Gary and Pamela Gosselin
Rooms: 6 (4 PB; 2 SB) $55-125 seasonal
Full Breakfast
Credit Cards: A, B, C, D
Notes: 2, 5, 7, 8, 9, 10, 11, 12

WESTON

The Colonial House

287 Route 100, Box CBB, 05161-5402
(802) 824-6286; (800) 639-5033; (802) 824-3934
(FAX)

Family oriented with old-fashioned hospitality, a comfortable inn and motel. "Vermont's Favorite Breakfast" with dinners to match. Conveniently located on Route 100 outside Weston, with summer theater, shops, museums, and 7 minutes

from Weston Priory. Three downhill ski areas and 400 km of cross-country within 20 minutes. The place to stay while visiting southern Vermont. 2-Star Mobil Travel Guide. 2 Diamond AAA.

Hosts: John and Betty Nunnikhoven
Rooms: 15 (9PB; 6SB) $50-84
Full Breakfast
Credit Cards: A, B, D
Notes: 2, 4, 5, 7, 8, 9, 10, 11

The Inn at Weston

P.O. Box 56 (Rt. 100), 05161
(802) 824-6789

A full service country inn nestled in a picture book Vermont village in the heart of the Green Mountains. Enjoy gourmet dining in an award winning dining room, recently featured in *Gourmet Magazine*. A pleasant walk to lovely shops, galleries, and the Weston Playhouse, the oldest professional summer theater in Vermont. The Weston Priory, a Benedictine monastery, is just north of the village. Walking trails abound. Winter brings excellent alpine and nordic skiing.

Rooms: 19 (12PB; 7SB) $66-112
Full Breakfast
Credit Cards: A, B, C, D
Notes: 2, 4, 5, 8, 9, 10, 11

The Wilder Homestead Inn

25 Lawrence Hill Road, 05161
(802) 824-8172

Built in 1827 with Rumford fireplaces and original Moses Eaton stenciling, the inn has been carefully restored by us and has quiet surroundings and antique furnishings. Walk to village shops, museums, summer the-

year; 6 Pets welcome; 7 Children welcome; 8 Tennis nearby; 9 Swimming nearby; 10 Golf nearby; 11 Skiing nearby; 12 May be booked through travel agent

ater. Nearby are Weston Priory, fine restaurants, skiing. Weston is a village that takes you back in time. Craft Shoppe on premises. No smoking.

Hostess: Margaret M. Varner
Rooms: 7 (5PB; 2SB) $60-100
Full Breakfast
Credit Cards: A, B (deposit only)
Notes: 2, 7 (over 6), 8, 9, 10, 11

WILLISTON

Partridge Hill
287 Route 100, Box CBB, 05161-5402
(802) 824-6286; (800) 639-5033; (802) 824-3934 (FAX)

On top of a hill with a great view to the east of the Vermont Green Mountains, Partridge Hill is ideal for a summer visit with Shelburne museum nearby. The colors surrounding the grounds are ablaze in the fall. We have four rooms for different combination of guests but we only take two different families at a time. No smoking.

Hosts: Roger and Sally Bryant
Rooms: 4 (SB) $65-75
Full Breakfast
Credit Cards: None
Notes: 2, 5, 7

WILMINGTON

Shearer Hill Farm Bed and Breakfast
P.O. Box 1453, 05363
(802) 464-3253; (800) 437-3104

Pristine farm setting on country road, large rooms (king, queen, twin), private baths, delicious Vermont breakfast. Cross-coun-try trails on property. Near downhill skiing, shopping, swimming, fishing, horseback riding. Only 210 miles from New York, 120 miles from Boston, 90 miles from Hartford, and 70 from Albany.

Hosts: Bill and Patti Pusey
Rooms: 4 (PB) $70-80
Full Breakfast
Credit Cards: A, B, C
Notes: 2 (prefered), 5, 8, 9, 10, 11, 12

WOODSTOCK

Canterbury House B&B
43 Pleasant St., 05091
(802) 457-3077

115-year-old Victorian town house just a stroll to the village green and fine dining. The Inn is beautifully decorated with era antiques and is for the discriminating traveler. The Inn has won awards from *Yankee* magazine and the American B&B Assocation, and it is recommended as the best value in town by *Glamour* magazine. Each room is decorated to a different theme.

Hosts: Celeste and Fred Holden
Rooms: 8 (PB) $85-140
Full Gourmet Breakfast
Credit Cards: A, B, C
Notes: 2, 5, 7 (over 7), 8, 9, 10, 11, 12

Canterbury House Bed and Breakfast

NOTES: Credit cards accepted: A Master Card; B Visa; C American Express; D Discover Card; E Diners Club; F Other; 2 Personal checks accepted; 3 Lunch available; 4 Dinner available; 5 Open all

Virginia

ALEXANDRIA

Morrison House

116 South Alfred Street, 22314
(703) 838-8000; (703) 684-6283 (FAX)

Built in the style of an 18th-century manor house, award-winning Morrison House offers 45 elegantly appointed guest rooms, each different from the others, including three suites. All guest rooms are enhanced by fine Federal-period reproductions including mahogany four-poster beds, brass chandeliers, decorative fireplaces, and Italian marble baths. 24-hour butler, concierge, and room services, indoor valet parking, specialized laundry and valet services including shoeshine, newspaper delivery to each room, nightly turndown with chocolates, and health club privileges. Afternoon tea served daily from 3-5 PM in the parlor. Centrally lcoated in Old Town, Alexandria, Morrison House is a stroll from historic landmarks, quaint boutiques, and international dining. Downtown Washington, DC, is less than 10 minutes away, National Airport is only three miles, and the metro is an easy 10 minute walk.

Hosts: Mr. and Mrs. Robert E. Morrison
Rooms: 45 (PB) $205-295
Complimentary Coffee and Tea in the Parlor.
Credit Cards: A, B, C, E, F (Carte Blanche)
Notes: 2, 3, 4, 5, 7, 8, 9, 10, 12

Princely Bed and Breakfast Ltd.

819 Prince st., 22314
(703) 683-2159 (Mon.-Fri. 10-6)

Historic (1770-1896) homes in heart of Old Town Alexandria, within very short walk to all fine restaurants, shops, and historic sites. Many of the houses are furnished with museum quality antiques and have enchanting gardens. Hosts are long-time residents with a broad knowledge of all facets of cultural, historical, and educational activities in the Washington, DC area. Public transporation to DC is fast (20 minutes) and frequent on the metro. 25 available rooms. Rates range $75-100 + tax. E. J. Mansmann, president.

CHINCOTEAGUE (ALSO NEW CHURCH)

The Garden and the Sea Inn

Virginia Eastern Shore, Route 710, P. O. Box 275,
New Church, 23415
(804) 824-0672

This elegant, European-style country inn with French-style gourmet restaurant is near Chincoteague and Assateague Islands. Five large, luxurious guest rooms,

welcome; 7 Children welcome; 8 Tennis nearby; 9 Swimming nearby; 10 Golf nearby; 11 Skiing nearby; 12 May be booked through travel agent

beautifully designed; spacious private baths; Victorian detail; stained glass; Oriental rugs; antiques; bay windows; library; and patio. Beautiful beach and wildlife refuge are nearby; afternoon tea; romantic escape package; and chamber music dinner-concerts. Mobil three-star and AAA three-diamond rated and American B&B Association three-crown ratings. Extended stay discounts available. Open April 1 through November 1.

Hosts: Jack Betz and Victoria Olian
Rooms: 5 (PB) $85-135
Expanded Continental Breakfast
Credit Cards: A, B, C, D, E
Notes: 2, 4, 7, 8, 9, 10, 12

Watson House Bed and Breakfast

Watson House Bed and Breakfast

4240 Main Street, 23336
(804) 336-1564; (800) 336-6787

The Watson House has been tastefully restored with Victorian charm. Nestled in the heart of Chincoteague, the house is within walking distance of shops and restaurants. Each guest room includes antiques, private bath, and air-conditioning. A full, hearty breakfast and afternoon tea are served in the dining room or on the veranda. Enjoy free use of bicycles to tour the Chincoteague National Wildlife Refuge and Beach. AAA—3-diamonds.

Hosts: Tom and Jacque Derrickson and David and Anne Snead
Rooms: 6 (PB) $65-105
Full Breakfast plus Afternoon Tea
Credit Cards: A, B
Notes: 2, 7 (over 9), 8, 9, 10

CULPEPER

Fountain Hall

609 South East Street, 22701
(800) 29-VISIT; (703) 825-7716 (FAX)

Fountain Hall is a charming 1859 Colonial Revival bed and breakfast. All of our rooms are tastefully restored and most are furnished with antiques. Three guest rooms have private porches overlooking the grounds. Fireplaces can be found in the common rooms along with books, local literature, board games, music, and TV/VCR. Fountain Hall is within walking distance to Historic Downtown Culpeper and Amtrak. Charlottesville and Dulles airports are nearby.

Hosts: Steve, Kathi and Leah-Marie Walker
Rooms: 5 (PB) $65-115
Expanded Continental Breakfast
Credit Cards: A, B, C, D, E, F
Notes: 2, 5, 7, 8, 9, 10

FREDRICKSBURG

Kenmore Inn

1200 Princess Anne St., 22401
(703) 371-7622; (800) 437-7622; (703) 371-5480 (FAX) Area code changes to 540 July 1995.

Lovely and romantic Colonial inn built in late 1700s with 12 guest rooms, four with working fireplaces, all with private bath,

NOTES: Credit cards accepted: A Master Card; B Visa; C American Express; D Discover Card; E Diners Club; F Other; 2 Personal checks accepted; 3 Lunch available; 4 Dinner available; 5 Open all year; 6 Pets

phone, and complimentary sherry. Candle-light dining features local Virginia cuisine and wines. Within walking distance of attractions, museums, Rappahannock River, Amtrak, and shopping. Garden available for outdoor dining and small conference room.

Hostess: Alice Bannan
Rooms: 12 (PB), $95-150
Continental Plus Breakfast
Credit Cards: A, B, C, E
Notes: 2, 3, 4, 5, 7, 8, 9, 10, 12

La Vista Plantation

4420 Guinea Station Rd., 22408
(540) 898-8444; (540) 898-1041 (FAX)
Area code remains 703 until July 1995.

This Classical revival-style manor house, circa 1838, is situated on ten quiet, country acres and is surrounded by farm fields and mature trees. Stocked pond, six fireplaces, antiques, rich Civil War past, radio, phone, TV, and bicycles. Fresh eggs and homemade jams are served for breakfast; air conditioned; close to historic attractions. Choose from fromal room or complete apartment.

Hosts: Edward and Michele Schiesser
Rooms: 1 + 1 large apartment (PB), $85
Full Breakfast
Credit Cards: A, B
Notes: 2, 5, 7, 9, 10, 12

HARRISONBURG

Kingsway Bed and Breakfast

3581 Singers Glen Road, 22801
(703) 867-9696

Enjoy the warm hospitality of your hosts who make your comfort their priority. This private home is in a quiet rural area with a view of the mountains in the beautiful Shenandoah Valley. Carpentry and home-making skills, many house plants and outdoor flowers, a large lawn, and the in ground pool help to make your stay restful and refreshing. Just four and one-half miles from downtown; nearby is Skyline Drive, caverns, historic sites, antique shops, and flea markets.

Hosts: Chester and Verna Leaman
Rooms: 2 (PB) $50-55
Expanded Continental Breakfast
Credit Cards: None
Notes: 2, 5, 6, 7, 9, 10, 12

LEESBURG

The Norris House Inn

108 Loudoun St. SW, 22075
(703) 777-1806; (800) 644-1806; (703) 771-8051 (FAX)

Elegant accommodations in the heart of Leesburg's historic district. Six guest rooms, all furnished with antiques and three wood-burning fireplaces. Full country breakfast served by candlelight. Convenient in-town location with several fine restaurants within easy walking distance. Just an hour's drive from Washington, DC in Virginia's Hunt Country, rich in Colonial

welcome; 7 Children welcome; 8 Tennis nearby; 9 Swimming nearby; 10 Golf nearby; 11 Skiing nearby; 12 May be booked through travel agent

and Civil War history, antiquing, and quaint villages. Perfect for romantic getaways, small meetings, and weddings. Open daily by reservation. Stone House Tea Room located on the Inn's right.

Hosts: Pam and Don McMurray
Rooms: 6 (SB) $75-140
Full Breakfast
Credit Cards: A, B, C, D, E
Notes: 2, 5, 7 (over 12), 8, 10, 12

LURAY

Shenandoah River Roost

Route 3, Box 566, 22835
(703) 743-3467

Sit on the front porch of this two-story log home and enjoy beautiful views of the mountains and the Shenandoah River. Located three miles west of Luray Caverns, and ten miles west of Skyline Drive and Shenandoah National Park. Swimming, tubing, canoeing, and golf are all nearby. No smoking.

Hosts: Rubin and Gerry McNab
Rooms: 2 (SB) $65+tax
Full Breakfast
Credit Cards: None
Closed November 1-May 1
Notes: 2, 8, 9, 10

MIDDLEBURG

Middleburg Inn and Guest Suites

105 West Washington Street, 22117
(703) 687-3115; (800) 432-6125; (703) 687-4109 (FAX)

In the heart of Hunt Country, elegantly

furnished suites for short or long term stays. Our one and two bedroom suites are beautifully appointed with antiques and accessories in the 18th century style. Centrally air-conditioned, the suites feature canopy beds, private baths, color TVs, direct dial phones, fresh cut flowers, and cotton bath robes. The spacious living room in our largest suite has a wood-burning, stone fireplace.

Rooms: 5 suites (PB) $130-195
Continental Breakfast at Red Fox (1 bock up)
Credit Cards: A, B
Notes: 2, 7

MT. JACKSON

The Widow Kip's Country Inn

335 Orchard Drive (State Rd. 698), 22842
(703) 477-2400

A stately 1830 Colonial on seven rural acres in the Shenandoah Valley overlooking the mountains. Friendly rooms filled with family photographs, bric-a-brac, and antiques. Each bedroom has a working fireplace; canopy, sleigh, or Lincoln bed. Two cozy cottages are also available. Pool on the premises. Nearby battlefields and caverns to explore, canoeing, hiking, or downhill skiing. Bicycles, picnics, and grill available.

Hostess: Betty Luse
Rooms: 5 +2 courtyard cottages (PB) $65-85
Full Breakfast
Credit Cards: A, B
Notes: 2, 5, 6+7 (in cottages), 8, 9 , 10, 11, 12

NOTES: Credit cards accepted: A Master Card; B Visa; C American Express; D Discover Card; E Diners Club; F Other; 2 Personal checks accepted; 3 Lunch available; 4 Dinner available; 5 Open all year; 6 Pets

NATURAL BRIDGE

Burger's Country Inn

Route 2, Box 564, 24578
(703) 291-2464

This historic inn is furnished in antiques and country collectibles. The rambling farmhouse with wraparound porch and large columns is on ten wooded acres. Four guest rooms and three baths are available. Enjoy croquet in summer and relax by the fire in winter. Special continental breakfast is included. Visit the Natural Bridge and historic Lexington. Beautiful Blue Ridge Parkway nearby. Call or write for brochure/reservations.

Host: Frances B. Burger
Rooms: 4 (2PB; 2SB) $45-50
Expanded Continental Breakfast
Credit Cards: None
Notes: 2, 5, 6, 7, 9, 10, 12

NOKESVILLE

Shiloh Bed and Breakfast

13520 Carriage Ford Road, 22123
(703) 594-2235

Shiloh B&B is a Georgian home built in 1987 on 153 acres overlooking a five-acre bass lake. Amid acres of evergreen forests with many trails for walking and a black walnut grooves with three hammocks, our guests find all they could ask for in desired solitude. Civil War battlefields, tennis, farmers' markets, golf courses, and well known bike trips are available within easy commute. Two beautifully decorated suites with private entrances, baths, and kitchenettes with patio hot tub exceed guest expectations in every way.

Hosts: Alan and Carolee Fisiker
Rooms: 2 (PB) $95-120
Full Breakfast
Credit Cards: A, B
Notes: 2, 5, 7 (over 12), 8, 9, 10

Shiloh Bed and Breakfast

ONANCOCK

The Spinning Wheel Bed and Breakfast

31 North Street, 23417
(804) 787-7311

This 1890s Folk Victorian home, in the historic waterfront town of Onancock on Virginia's Eastern Shore, has antiques and spinning wheels throughout. All guest rooms have queen beds, private baths, and air-conditioning. Guests can visit Kerr Place (1799 museum), cruise to Tangier Island from Onancock Wharf, and walk to restaurants. Bicycles, tennis, and golf are available. Chincoteague/Assateaque Island beach close by. A calm Eastern Shore getaway from D.C., Maryland, Virginia, Delaware, and New Jersey on the Chesapeake Bay, five miles from the Atlantic.

Hosts: David and Karen Tweedie
Rooms: 5 (PB) $85-95
Full Breakfast
Credit Cards: A, B
Notes: 2, 8, 9, 10, 12

PROVIDENCE FORGE

Jasmine Plantation Bed and Breakfast

4500 N. Courthouse Road, 23140
(804) 966-9836

Restored 1750s farmhouse convenient to Williamsburg, Richmond, and the James River Plantations. Genuine hospitality, a historical setting, and rooms decorated in various period antiques await the visitor. Settled prior to 1683, guests are invited to walk the 47 acres and use their imagination as to what events have occurred here during its 300-year history. Located only 2.4 miles from I-64, the Inn offers both convenience and seclusion to their guests. Fine dining located nearby.

Hosts: Joyce and Howard Vogt
Rooms: 6 (4PB; 2SB) $70-95
Full Breakfast
Credit Cards: A, B
Notes: 2, 5, 7 (over 12), 10, 12

RICHMOND

The William Catlin House

2304 East Broad Street, 23223
(804) 780-3746

Richmond's first and oldest bed and breakfast features antique, canopy poster beds, and working fireplaces. A delicious full breakfast is served in the elegant dining room. Built in 1845, this richly appointed home is in the Church Hill historic district and was featured in *Colonial Homes* and *Southern Living* magazines. Directly across from St. John's Church, where Patrick Henry gave his famous Liberty or

Death speech. Just two minutes from I-95 and Route 64.

Hosts: Robert and Josie Martin
Rooms: 5 (3 PB; 2 SB) $89.50 (price includes all taxes)
Full Breakfast
Credit Cards: A, B, D
Notes: 2, 5, 7 (over 12), 10, 12

Jasmine Plantation Bed and Breakfast

SMITH MOUNTAIN LAKE

The Manor at Taylor's Store

Route 1, Box 533, 24184
(703) 721-3951; (800) 248-6267; (703) 721-5243 (FAX)

This historic 120-acre estate with an elegant manor house provides romantic accommodations in guest suites with fireplaces, antiques, canopied beds, private porches, and use of hot tub, billiards, exercise room, guest kitchen, and many other amenities. A separate three-bedroom, two-bath cottage is ideal for a family. Enjoy six private, springfed ponds for swimming, canoeing, fishing, and hiking. Full heart-healthy, gourmet breakfast is served in the dining room with panoramic views of the countryside.

Hosts: Lee and Mary Lynn Tucker
Rooms: 6 (4 PB; 2 SB) $80-125
Full Breakfast
Credit Cards: A, B
Notes: 2, 3, 5, 7, 8, 9, 10, 11, 12

SMITHFIELD

Isle of Wight Inn

1607 S. Church Street, 23430
(804) 357-3176

Luxurious Colonial B&B inn located in a delightful historic river port town. Several suites with fireplaces and jacuzzis. Antique shop featuring tallcase clocks and period furniture. More than 60 old homes in town dating from 1750. Just 30 minutes and a short ferry ride to Williamsburg and Jamestown; less than an hour from James River plantations, Norfold, Hampton, and Virginia Beach.

Hosts: The Harts and the Earls
Rooms: 9 (PB) $49-99
Full Breakfast
Credit Cards: A, B, C, D
Notes: 2, 5, 7, 8, 9, 10, 12

STANLEY

Jordan Hollow Farm Inn

Rt. 2, Box 375, 22851
(703) 778-2285; (703) 778-1759 (FAX)

A 200-year-old Colonial farm restored into a full service country inn. There are 150 acres with five miles of walking trails, horseback riding, swimming, and a game room. A fully equipped meeting room can accommodate groups. AAA, Mobile,

IIA, and ABBA approved. Featured in *Country Magazine, Southern Living, Condé Nost,* and more.

Hosts: Jetze and Marley Beers
Rooms: 21 (PB) $140-180
Full Breakfast (and dinner)
Credit Cards: A, B, D, E
Notes: 2, 3, 4, 5, 6 (horses only), 7, 8, 9, 10, 11, 12

The Manor at Taylor's Store

STAUNTON

Ashton Country Home

1205 Middlebrook Avenue, 24401
(703) 885-7819; (800) 296-7819

Ashton is a delightful blend of town and country. This 1860 Greek Revival home is located on 24 acres, yet one mile from the center of Staunton. There are four air-conditioned, comfortable, and attractive bedrooms, each with a private bath. A graduate of the New York Restaurant School, innkeeper Sheila Kennedy greets guests each morning with a hearty breakfast of eggs, bacon, homefries, muffins, fruit, juice, and coffee. Innkeeper Stanley

Polanski often provides the music of Gershwin and Porter on the grand piano.

Hosts: Sheila Kennedy and Stanley Polanski
Rooms: 4 (PB) $75-90
Full Breakfast
Credit Cards: None
Notes: 2, 5, 8, 9, 10, 11

Frederick House

28 N. New Street
(800) 334-5575

An historic town house hotel in the European tradition, Frederick House is located downtown in the oldest city in the Shenandoah Valley. It is convenient to shops and restaurants; across the street from Mary Baldwin College; two blocks from Woodrow Wilson's birthplace. All rooms are furnished with TV, phone, air-conditioning, private bath, and private entrance.

Hosts: Joe and Evy Harman
Rooms: 14 (PB) $65-95
Full Breakfast
Credit Cards: A, B, C, D, E
Notes: 2, 3, 4, 5, 7, 8, 9, 10, 11, 12

Thornrose House at Gypsy Hill

531 Thornrose Avenue, 24401
(703) 885-7026

Outside, this turn-of-the-century Georgian residence has a wraparound veranda, Greek colonnades, and lovely gardens. Inside, a fireplace and grand piano create a formal but comfortable atmosphere. Five attractive bedrooms with private baths are on the second floor. Your hosts offer afternoon tea, refreshments, and conver-

sation. Adjacent to a 300-acre park that is great for walking, with tennis, golf, and ponds. Other nearby attractions include the Blue Ridge National Park, natural chimneys, Skyline Drive, Woodrow Wilson's birthplace, and the Museum of American Frontier Culture.

Hosts: Suzanne and Otis Huston
Rooms: 5 (PB) $55-75
Full Breakfast
Credit Cards: None
Notes: 2, 5, 7 (over 6), 8, 9, 10

Frederick House

STRASBURG

Hotel Strasburg

201 Holliday Street, 22657
(703) 465-9191; (800) 348-8327; (703) 465-4788 (FAX)

Step back in time with a stylish Victorian dining experience at the Hotel Strasburg. Spend the night in one of our finely appointed rooms or one of nine jacuzzi suites, rich with period antiques and a decor that will leave you amid the romanticism of the 1890s.

Hosts: Gary and Carol Rutherford
Rooms: 29 (PB) $69-149
Continental Breakfast
Credit Cards: A, B, C, E
Notes: 2, 3, 4, 5, 6 (call first), 7, 8, 9, 10, 11, 12

NOTES: Credit cards accepted: A Master Card; B Visa; C American Express; D Discover Card; E Diners Club; F Other; 2 Personal checks accepted; 3 Lunch available; 4 Dinner available; 5 Open all year; 6 Pets

Sunset Inn

TANGIER ISLAND

Sunset Inn

Box 156, 23440
(804) 891-2535

Enjoy accommodations one-half block from the beach with a view of the bay. Deck, air conditioning, bike riding, and nice restaurants.

Hosts: Grace and Jim Brown
Rooms: 9 (8PB; 1SB) $50-$60
Continental Breakfast
Credit Cards: None
Notes: 2, 5, 7, 9

VIRGINIA BEACH

Barclay Cottage B&B

400 16th St., 23451
(804) 422-1956

Casual sophistication in a warm, historic, inn-like atmosphere. Designed in turn-of-the-century style, the Barclay Cottage is two blocks from the beach in the heart of the Virginia Beach recreational area. The inn is completely restored with antique furniture to bring the feeling of yesterday with the comfort of today. Formerly the home of Lillian S. Barclay, the inn has been

a guest home for many years. We have kept the historic ambience of the old inn while modernizing it significantly to meet today's needs. We look forward to welcoming you to the Barclay Cottage where the theme is "We go where our dream lead us."

Hosts: Peter and Claire
Rooms: 6 (3PB; 3SB) $65-80
Full Breakfast
Credit Cards: A, B, C, D
Notes: 8, 9, 10, 12

Barclay Cottage Bed and Breakfast

WARM SPRINGS

Three Hills Inn

P.O. Box 9, 24484
(703) 839-5381; (703) 839-5199 (FAX)

A premier B&B inn in the heart of Bath County, Virginia. Enjoy a casually elegant retreat in a beautifully restored historic manor. Spectacular mountain views, acres of woods and trails—serenity at its best! Elegant suites available, some with kitchens and fireplaces. Fitness center with excercise equipment and outdoor hot tub on premises. Four miles from the historic Homestead Resort. Your hosts have missionary backgrounds and speak fluent Spanish. From a romantic getaway to an executive retreat (meeting/conference fa-

welcome; 7 Children welcome; 8 Tennis nearby; 9 Swimming nearby; 10 Golf nearby; 11 Skiing nearby; 12 May be booked through travel agent

cility), the Inn is the perfect choice for the discriminating traveler.

Hosts: Doug and Charlene Fike and Dan and Joy Adams
Rooms: 18 (PB) $47-145
Full Gourmet Breakfast (Afternoon tea weekends)
Credit Cards: A, B, F
Notes: 2, 5, 6, 7, 8, 9, 10, 11, 12

WASHINGTON

Caledonia Farm—1812

Route 1, Box 2080, Flint Hill, 22627
(703) 675-3693; (800) BNB-1812 (for reservations)

Enjoy ultimate hospitality, comfort, scenery, and recreation adjacent to Virginia's Shenandoah National Park. This romantic getaway to history and nature includes outstanding full breakfasts, fireplaces, air-conditioning, hayrides, bicycles, lawn games, VCR, and piano. World's finest dining, caves, Skyline Drive, battlefields, stables, antiquing, hiking, and climbing are all nearby. Washington, D.C., is 68 miles away; Washington, Virginia, just four miles. A Virginia historic landmark, the farm is listed on the National Register of Historic Places. AAA three-diamond rated.

Host: Phil Irwin
Rooms: 2 and 1 suite (1 PB; 2 SB) $80-140
Full Breakfast
Credit Cards: A, B, D
Notes: 2, 5, 7 (over 12), 8, 9, 10, 11, 12

WAYNESBORO

The Iris Inn

191 Chinquapin Dr., 22980
(703) 943-1991

The charm and grace of Southern living in a totally modern facility, nestled in a wooded tract on the western slope of the Blue Ridge, overlooking the historic Shenandoah Valley—that's what awaits you at the Iris Inn in Waynesboro. It's ideal for a weekend retreat, a refreshing change for the business traveler, and a tranquil spot for the tourist to spend a night or a week. Guest rooms are spacious, comfortably furnished, and delightfully decorated in nature and wildlife motifs. Each room has private bath and individual temperature control.

Hosts: Wayne and Iris Karl
Rooms: 7 (PB) $80-100
Full Breakfast
Credit Cards: A, B
Notes: 2, 5, 8, 9, 10

WILLIAMSBURG

Applewood Colonial B&B

605 Richmond Road, 23185
(804) 229-0205; (800) 899-2753

The owner's unique apple collection is evidenced throughout this restored colonial home. Four elegant guest rooms (one suite with fireplace) are conveniently located four short blocks from Colonial Williamsburg and very close to the College of William and Mary campus. Antiques complement the romantic atmosphere. The dining room has a beautiful built-in corner cupboard and a crystal chandelier above the pedestal table where homemade breakfast is served. Afternoon tea. No smoking.

Host: Fred Strout
Rooms: 4 (PB) $70-120
Continental Deluxe Breakfast
Credit Cards: A, B
Notes: 2, 5, 7, 8, 10, 12

NOTES: Credit cards accepted: A MasterCard; B Visa; C American Express; D Discover Card; E Diners Club; F Other; 2 Personal checks accepted; 3 Lunch available; 4 Dinner available; 5 Open all year; 6 Pets

The Cedars

616 Jamestown Rd., 23185
(804) 229-3591; (800) 296-3591

Across the street from the College of William and Mary and a 10-minute walk to Colonial Williamsburg, The Cedars offers traditional Colonial elegance, comfort, and hospitality. The three-story brick Georgian is the oldest and largest B&B in Williamsburg. Scrumptuous, full breakfasts are served by candlelight from a hand-hewn huntboard on the tavern porch. In the evening, the porch serves as a meeting place for cards, chess, or other diversions. On cool evenings, the fireplace in the sitting room invites relaxation and conversation. Each guest room has a unique personality. Four-poster and canopy beds abound. Off street parking.

Hosts: Carol, Jim, and Brona Malecha
Rooms: 8 + cottage (PB) $95-130
Full Breakfast
Credit Cards: A, B
Notes: 2, 5, 7, 10, 12

Fox Grape

701 Monumental Avenue, 23185
(804) 229-6914; (800) 292-3699

Genteel accommodations just five blocks north of Virginia's restored colonial capital. Furnishings include canopied beds, antiques, counted cross stitch, a duck decoy collection, and a cup-plate collection. Points of interest include Colonial Williamsburg, Carters Grove Plantation, Jamestown, Yorktown, and the College of William and Mary.

Hosts: Pat and Bob Orendorff
Rooms: 4 (PB) $70-78
Continental Breakfast
Credit Cards: A, B, D
Notes: 2, 5, 7, 8, 9, 10, 12

Hite's Bed and Breakfast

704 Monumental Avenue, 23185
(804) 229-4814

An attractive Cape Cod B & B just a seven-minute walk to Colonial Williamsburg. Large rooms cleverly furnished with antiques and collectibles. Each room has TV, phone, radio, coffeemaker, robes, and private baths. You will especially like the suite with its large sitting room and old-fashioned bathroom with clawfoot tub. In the parlor for your enjoyment is an antique pump organ and hand-crank Victrola. You can swing in the back yard and enjoy the squirrels, birds, and goldfish pond.

Hosts: Faye and James Hite
Rooms: 2 (PB) $65-75
Continental Plus Breakfast
Credit Cards: None
Notes: 2, 5, 7

Newport House B&B

710 South Henry Street, 23185-4113
(804) 229-1775

A reproduction of an important 1756 home, Newport House has museum-standard period furnishings, including canopy beds. A five-minute walk to the historic area. Full breakfast with Colonial recipes; Colonial dancing in the ballroom every Tuesday evening (beginners welcome). The host is a historian/author (including a book on Christ) and former museum director. The hostess is a gardener, beekeeper, 18th-century seamstress, and former nurse. A pet rabbit entertains at breakfast. No smoking.

Hosts: John and Cathy Millar
Rooms: 2 (PB) $105-130
Full Breakfast
Credit Cards: None
Notes: 2, 5, 7, 10, 12

welcome; 7 Children welcome; 8 Tennis nearby; 9 Swimming nearby; 10 Golf nearby; 11 Skiing nearby; 12 May be booked through travel agent

The Travel Tree Bed and Breakfast Reservation Service

P.O. Box 838, 23187
(800) 989-1571

Searching for Bed & Breakfast lodgings in a small inn or private homestay becomes a one-step process when you make your reservations through The Travel Tree, Williamsburg's B&B Reservation Service. We offer a select variety of accommodations, with rates ranging from $75-125, double occupancy. Office hours are from 6PM to 9PM, Monday through Thursday. Please send your SASE for a brochure. Gift certificates available.

Williamsburg Sampler Bed and Breakfast

922 Jamestown Road, 23185
(804) 253-0398; (800) 722-1169

This 18th century plantation-style three-story brick Colonial was awarded AAA Three Diamond Award. Located in the heart of Williamsburg and within walking distance to historic Colonial Williamsburg. Richly furnished bedrooms with private baths and king- or queen-size beds. Collection of antiques, pewter, and samplers are displayed throughout the house. A "Skip Lunch" breakfast is served. Internationally recognized as a favorite spot for a romantic honeymoon and for the special care to guests. The inn was featured on CBS This Morning on July 7, 1994. AAA three-diamond award gets the inn featured

in *AAA Hostmark* magazine.

Hosts: Helen and Ike Sisanc
Rooms: 4 (PB) $85-90
Full Breakfast
Credit Cards: A, B, C
Notes: 2, 5, 8, 9, 10, 12

WOODSTOCK

Azalea House Bed and Breakfast

551 South Main Street, 22664
(703) 459-3500

A large Victorian house built in 1892 featuring family antiques and stenciled ceilings. It was used as a parsonage initially, serving a church three blocks away for about 70 years. Located in the historic Shenendoah Valley, it is close to Skyline Drive and the mountains. Many Civil War sites are within short driving distance. Nearby activities include antiquing, hiking, and horseback riding.

Hosts: Price and Margaret McDonald
Rooms: 3 (PB) $45-70
Full Breakfast
Credit Cards: A, B, C
Notes: 2, 7 (over 5), 9, 10, 11

Williamsburg Sampler Bed and Breakfast

NOTES: Credit cards accepted: A MasterCard; B Visa; C American Express; D Discover Card; E Diners Club; F Other; 2 Personal checks accepted; 3 Lunch available; 4 Dinner available; 5 Open all year; 6 Pets

Washington

ANACORTES

Albatross Bed and Breakfast

5708 Kingsway West, 98221
(360) 293-0677; (800) 484-9597 (for reservations only)

Our 1927 Cape Cod-style home offers king and queen beds and private baths in all guest rooms. The quiet, relaxing living room, patio, and deck areas view waterfront, islands, and mountains. You can walk to Washington Park, Skyline marina, fine dining, and inspirational beaches. We also offer sightseeing cruises aboard a 46-foot sailboat and have 2-speed cross bikes available. We are close to the State Ferry Boat terminal for access to the San Juan Islands and Victoria, B.C. We are also close to over 25 churches.

Hosts: Ken and Barbie
Rooms: 4 (PB) $75-85
Full Breakfast
Credit Cards: A, B
Notes: 2, 5, 7, 8, 9, 10, 11, 12

Hasty Pudding House

1312-8th St., 98221
(360) 293-5773

You will enjoy your visit to this 1913 craftsman house. The decor is Victorian and attention has been paid to restoring the original charm of this inviting, friendly place to stay. You have four beautiful rooms to choose from with comfortable beds for a good rest.

Hosts: Mikel and Melinda
Rooms: 4 (2PB; 2SB) $65-105
Full Breakfast
Credit Cards: A, B, C, D
Notes: 2, 5, 7, 8, 9, 10, 11, 12

Sunset Beach Bed and Breakfast

100 Sunset Beach, 98221
(360) 293-5428; (800) 359-3448

On exciting Rosario Straits. Relax and enjoy the view of seven major islands from our decks, stroll on the beach, or walk in the beautiful Washington Park, adjacent to our private gardens. Also enjoy boating, hiking, and fishing. Private entry, bathrooms, and TV. Full breakfast. Five minutes to San Juan Ferries, fine restaurants, marina, and convenience store nearby. Sunsets are outstanding! No smoking.

Hosts: Joann and Hal Harker
Rooms: 3 (1PB; 2SB) $59-79
Full Breakfast
Credit Cards: A, B
Notes: 2, 5, 7 (over 6), 9, 10, 11, 12

welcome; 7 Children welcome; 8 Tennis nearby; 9 Swimming nearby; 10 Golf nearby; 11 Skiing nearby; 12 May be booked through travel agent

ANDERSON ISLAND

The Inn at Burg's Landing

8808 Villa Beach Road, 98303
(206) 884-9185

Catch the ferry from Steilacoom to stay at this contemporary log homestead built in 1987. It offers spectacular views of Mt. Rainier, Puget Sound, and the Cascade Mountains and is located south of Tacoma off I-5. Choose from three guest rooms, including the master bedroom with queen-size "log" bed with skylight above and private whirlpool bath. The inn has a private beach. Collect seashells and agates, swim on two freshwater lakes nearby, enjoy a game of tennis or golf. Tour the island by bicycle or on foot and watch for sailboats and deer. Hot tub. Full breakfast. Families welcome. No smoking.

Hosts: Ken and Annie Burg
Rooms: 3 (2PB; 1SB) $65-90
Full Breakfast
Credit Cards: A, B
Notes: 2, 5, 7, 8, 9, 10, 11

ASHFORD

Mountain Meadows Inn Bed and Breakfast

28912 S.R. 706 E, 98304
(206) 569-2788

Built in 1910, as a mill superintendent's house, Mountain Meadows Inn Bed and Breakfast has made a graceful transition to quiet country elegance. An era of Northwest logging passed by and was seen in vivid detail from the vantage point of spring

board and misery whip. Old growth stumps scattered around the house and pond still wear spring board notches as witness to a time when trees, men, and the stories of both were tall. The innkeeper says guests tell him its the best B&B they have ever stayed in. Model railroad museum.

Host: Chad Darrah
Rooms: 5 (PB) $55-95
Full Breakfast
Credit Cards: A, B
Notes: 2, 5, 7 (10 + over), 9, 10, 11, 12

BELLEVUE

Petersen Bed and Breakfast

10228 Southeast Eighth Street, 98004
(206) 454-9334

We offer two rooms five minutes from Bellevue Square with wonderful shopping and one-half block from the bus line to Seattle. Rooms have down comforters, and we have a hot tub on the deck. Children are welcome. No smoking.

Hosts: Eunice and Carl Petersen
Rooms: 2 (SB) $50-55
Full Breakfast
Credit Cards: None
Notes: 2, 5, 7

BELLINGHAM

Bed and Breakfast Service

P.O. Box 5025, Bellingham, 98226
(206) 733-8642

We are a reservation service with host homes **all over the United States**

NOTES: Credit cards accepted: A Master Card; B Visa; C American Express; D Discover Card; E Diners Club; F Other; 2 Personal checks accepted; 3 Lunch available; 4 Dinner available; 5 Open all year; 6 Pets

incuding Hawaii. Call and let us set up your next stay at a bed and breakfast. Our rates are reasonable in the European tradition. Coordinators are Dolores and George Herrmann.

Circle F Bed and Breakfast

2399 Mt. Baker Highway, 98226
(206) 733-2509; (206) 734-3816 (FAX)

Circle F Bed and Breakfast is a home away from home for all of our guests. The Victorian-style ranch house was built in 1892 and is located on 330 acres of pasture and woodlands. We are a working farm, and you can enjoy hiking trails and visits with the farm animals. A hearty breakfast is served by a friendly farm family who enjoys the company of all visitors.

Host: Guy J. Foster
Rooms: 4 (1 PB; 3 SB) $45-60
Full Breakfast
Credit Cards: None
Notes: 2, 5, 7

BOW

Benson Farmstead B&B

1009 Avon-Allen Rd., 98232
(206) 757-0578

Located just minutes from the Skagit Valley, tulip fields, the historical town of LaConner, and ferries to the San Juan Islands, the Benson Farmstead is a beautiful restored farmhouse. The Bensons are a friendly couple who serve homemade desserts in the evening and a wonderful breakfast. They have filled their home with charming antiques, old quilts, and curios

from their Scandinavian heritage. The extensive yard features an English Garden and a large playground.

Hosts: Jerry and Sharon Benson
Rooms: 4 (2PB; 2SB) $65-75
Full Breakfast
Credit Cards: A, B
Notes: 2, 5 (weekends only Sept.-March), 7, 8, 9, 10, 11

CAMANO ISLAND

Willcox House Bed and Breakfast

1462 Larkspur Lane, 98292
(206) 629-4746

This island retreat, a short drive from Seattle, is designed for relaxing! Enjoy the panoramic view of the Cascade Mountains. Named for the owner's great aunt, early 1900s illustrator, Jesse Willcox Smith, and decorated with her works. It's a step back in time to a less stressful pace. Leisurely, country breakfast of Willcox House blended coffee, assorted omelettes, Swedish pancakes, muffins, and fresh fruits in season, with sun streaming into a cozy breakfast room.

Hostess: Esther Harmon
Rooms: 4 (PB) $65
Full Breakfast
Credit Cards: A, B
Notes: 2, 5, 8, 9, 10, 11

CASHMERE

Cashmere Country Inn

5801 Pioneer Dr., 98815
(509) 782-4212; (800) 782-4212

This delightful 1907 farmhouse with five

bedrooms welcomes guest with charm and hospitality. Every effort has been made to make each stay memorable. Among many outstanding features, the food is superb—prepared skillfully and presented beautifully. There is a pool and hot tub, and a large fireplace in the living room. Looking for that extra-special inn that defines a B&B? You'll be pleased to discover Cashmere Country Inn.

Hosts: Patti and Dale Swanson
Rooms: 5 (PB) $75-80
Huge, Full Breakfast
Credit Cards: A, B, C
Notes: 2, 4, 5, 8, 9 (on-site), 10, 11, 12

CLE ELUM, SOUTH

The Moore House Country Bed and Breakfast

P.O. Box 629, 526 Marie Avenue, 98943
(509) 674-5939; (800) 2-2-TWAIN (WA or Canada only)

Relive the grand era of railroading at this former Chicago, Milwaukee, St. Paul, and Pacific Crewman's Hotel. Now restored as a unique tearoom inn filled with railroad memorabilia and artifacts. Our rooms range from economical to exquisite. We also offer two genuine cabooses as guest rooms. Located adjacent to Iron Horse State Park, a non-motorized recreational trail. Located five miles from historic Roslyn, a.k.a Cicely, Alaska, in the CBS television series *Northern Exposure.*

Hosts: Eric and Cindy Sherwood
Rooms: 12 (6PB; 6SB) $45-115 +7.5% tax
Full Breakfast
Credit Cards: A, B, C
Notes: 2, 5, 7, 10, 11, 12

Cooney Mansion

COSMOPOLIS

Cooney Mansion

1705 Fifth Street, Box 54, 98537
(206) 533-0602

This 1908 National Historic Register home, situated in wooded seclusion, was built by Neil Cooney, owner of one of the largest sawmills of the time. It captures the adventure of the Northwest. Share the lumber baron's history and many of his original "craftsman" style antiques. Enjoy 18 holes of golf (in backyard) or a leisurely walk around Mill Creek Park. Relax in the sauna and jacuzzi, curl up with one of the many books from the library, or watch TV in the ballroom.

Hosts: Judi and Jim Lohr
Rooms: 9 (5PB; 3SB) $49-115
Full Breakfast
Credit Cards: A, B, D, E
Notes: 2, 5, 8, 10

DARRINGTON

Sauk River Farm Bed and Breakfast

32629 State Route 530 NE, 98241
(206) 436-1794

The wild and scenic Sauk River runs through

this farm nestled in a valley of the North Cascades. All-season recreational opportunities await you. Wildlife abounds year round. The Native American Loft Room is a collector's delight; The Victorian Room offers pastoral privacy. Hallmarks of the farm are its views of rugged mountains, intimate atmosphere, comfortable accommodations, and solitude for those seeking relaxation. Step back in time and sample Darrington hospitality with its Bluegrass music and crafters. No smoking.

Hosts: Leo and Sharon Mehler
Rooms: 2 (SB) $40-60
Full Breakfast
Credit Cards: None
Notes: 2, 5, 11

DEER HARBOR—ORCAS ISLAND

Palmer's Chart House

P.O. Box 51, 98243
(206) 376-4231

The first B&B on Orcas Island (since 1975) with a magnificent water view. The 33-foot private yacht "Amante" is available for a minimal fee with skipper Don. Low-key, private, personal attenion makes this B&B unique and attractive. Well traveled hosts speak Spanish.

Hosts: Don and Mayjean Palmer
Rooms: 2 (PB) $60 + tax
Full Breakfast
Credit Cards: None
Notes: 2, 5, 7 (over 12), 8, 10, 11, 12

EASTSOUND

Turtleback Farm Inn

Route 1, Box 650, 98245
(206) 376-4914

Turtleback Farm Inn, built in the late 1800s, is noted for its detail perfect restoration, elegantly comfortable and spotless rooms, and award-winning breakfasts. The Inn, centrally located in the Crow Valley and six miles from the ferry landing, overlooks 80 acres of forest and farmland in the shadow of Turtleback Mountain. Orcas Island, considered by most to be the loveliest of the San Juan Islands that dot Puget Sound, is a haven for anyone who enjoys spectacular scenery, varied outdoor activities, unique shopping, and superb food.

Rooms: 7 (PB) $70-155
Full Breakfast
Credit Cards: A, B
Notes: 2, 5, 8, 9, 10, 12

ELLENSBURG

Murphy's Country Bed and Breakfast

2830 Thorp Hwy. S., 98926
(509) 925-7986

Two large guest rooms in a lovely 1915 country home with a sweeping view of the valley. Full breakfast. Close to fly fishing and golfing.

Hostess: Doris Callahan-Murphy
Rooms: 2 (S1.5B) $60
Full Breakfast
Credit Cards: A, B, C
Notes: 2, 5, 10

---

welcome; 7 Children welcome; 8 Tennis nearby; 9 Swimming nearby; 10 Golf nearby; 11 Skiing nearby; 12 May be booked through travel agent

FERNDALE

Slater Heritage House Bed and Breakfast

1371 W. Axton Rd., 98248
(206) 384-4273; (800) 815-4273; (206) 384-4273
(FAX)

The home is an old Victorian house that has been completely restored to its original beauty and charm. It features four guest rooms with antiques. Queen-size beds and private baths. It is located less that a mile from I-5 and 12 miles from the Canadian Border. It is close to golfing, hiking, skiing, and water. It is five miles from Bellis Fair, the largest shopping mall in the Pacific Northwest. Rates include full breakfast. Step back a century, slow down a bit, and breathe an atmosphere of forgotten elegance.

Hosts: The Armitage Family
Rooms: 4 (PB) $60-85
Full Breakfast
Credit Cards: A, B
Notes: 2, 5, 7, 8, 9, 10, 11

FRIDAY HARBOR

Tucker House B&B with Cottages

260 B Street, 98250
(206) 378-2783; (800) 742-8210; (206) 378-6437
(FAX)

A Victorian home (c. 1898) with two upstairs bedrooms, queen beds, and shared bath. Three separate cottages with queen beds, private bath, woodstoves, kitchenettes, TV, outside hot tub, and off-street parking. A full, gourmet breakfast with homemade cinnamon bread. Property abounds in flowers, stately trees, and is surrounded by a white picket fence. Two blocks from the ferry landing, and two blocks to the heart of picturesque Friday Harbor. Gift certificates available.

Hosts: Skip and Annette Metzger
Rooms: 5 (3PB; 2SB) $75-125
Full Gourmet Breakfast
Credit Cards: A, B, C, D
Notes: 2, 5, 6, 7, 8, 9, 10, 12

GRAPEVIEW

Llewop Retreat

Box 97, 98546
(206) 275-2287

Bed and breakfast is provided in the large contemporary home on a wooded knoll that overlooks Case Inlet and Stretch Island. Many windows, skylights, and decks allow a feeling of oneness with the incredible beauty of the environment. Guests are welcome to explore the property, play pickleball, or unwind in the whirlpool spa. No pets. Families welcome. Smoking on outside decks only; TV; extra beds; excellent golf course and restaurants just four miles away. Clergy discount.

Host: Kris Powell
Rooms: 3 (PB) $78-98
Full Breakfast
Credit Cards: None
Notes: 2, 5, 7, 9, 10, 12

LANGLEY—WHIDBEY ISLAND

Log Castle B&B

3273 East Saratoga Road, 98260
(360) 221-5483

A log house on a private, secluded beach

NOTES: Credit cards accepted: A Master Card; B Visa; C American Express; D Discover Card; E Diners Club; F Other; 2 Personal checks accepted; 3 Lunch available; 4 Dinner available; 5 Open all year; 6 Pets

features turret bedrooms, wood-burning stoves, porch swings, and panoramic views of the beach and mountains. Relax before a large stone fireplace or listen to the call of gulls as you watch for bald eagles and sea lions.

Hosts: Senator Jack and Norma Metcalf
Rooms: 4 (PB) $80-105
Full Breakfast
Credit Cards: A, B
Notes: 2, 8

LEAVENWORTH

All Seasons River Inn Bed and Breakfast
8751 Icicle Rd., 98826
(509) 548-1425; (800) 254-0555

Riverfront guest rooms, magnificent Cascade views and warm hospitality are but a few reasons why All Seasons River Inn was selected as one of the 50 most romantic getaways in the Pacific Northwest, and it is why a stay here will call you back again and again. Built as a bed and breakfast, all guest rooms are very spacious with antique decor, river-view deck, and private bath; some with jacuzzi tub and/or fireplace. Full gourmet breakfast, adults only. No smoking on premises.

Hosts: Kathy and Jeff Falconer
Rooms: 6 (PB) $85-125
Full Breakfast
Credit Cards: A, B
Notes: 2, 5, 8, 9, 10, 11, 12 (with exceptions)

Enzian Motor Inn
590 Hwy. 2, 98826
(509) 548-5269 (voice and FAX)

On the Cascades' eastern slopes is a

Bavarian village called Leavenworth. In the center of this valley is the Enzian Motor Inn. Like the flavor it represents, the Inn is adorned with a delicate alpine beauty. Its handcrafted woodwork and imported furnishings are unequaled. Enjoy year-round recreation, then soak in our steaming hot pool. Your breakfast buffet the next morning is on us.

Hosts: The Johnsons
Rooms: 104 (PB) $86-165
Full Buffet Breakfast
Credit Cards: A, B, C, D, E
Notes: 5, 7, 9 (on-site), 10, 11, 12

Run of the River
9308 E. Leavenworth Rd. P.O. Box 285, 98826
(509) 548-7171; (800) 288-6491; (509) 548-7547 (FAX)

Imagine the quintessential Northwest log bed and breakfast inn. Spacious rooms feature private baths, hand-hewn log beds, and fluffy down comforters. Or, celebrate in a suite with your own heartwarming wood stove, jetted jacuzzi surrounded by river rock, and a bird's eye loft to laze about with a favorite book. From your room's log porch swing, drink in the Icicle River, surrounding bird refuge and the Cascade peaks, appropriately named the Enchantments. To explore the Icicle Valley, get off the beaten path with hiking, biking, and driving guides written just for you by the innkeepers, avid bikers and hikers. Take a spin on complimentary mountain bikes. A hearty breakfast sets the day in motion.

Hosts: Monty and Karen Turner
Rooms: 6 (PB) $90-140
Full Breakfast
Credit Cards: A, B, C, D
Notes: 2, 5, 8, 9, 10, 11, 12

welcome; 7 Children welcome; 8 Tennis nearby; 9 Swimming nearby; 10 Golf nearby; 11 Skiing nearby; 12 May be booked through travel agent

LOPEZ ISLAND

Aleck Bay Inn

Aleck Bay Road, Route 1, Box 1920, 98261
(206) 468-3535; (206) 468-3533 (FAX)

The Inn has seven acres bounded by the beaches and offshore islands situated at the south end of Lopez Island. Enjoy a sun deck with hot tub overlooking the strait of San Juan De Fuca. Full breakfast is served in the solarium beside the bay. All rooms have private bath, queen bed, decorated by Victorian canopies, floral linens, etc. Two with jacuzzi tub. You may enjoy the TV/VCR, table tennis, billiards, piano, violin, all kinds of games. Bike rental is available.

Hosts: May and David Mendes
Rooms: 4 (PB) $79-139
Full Breakfast
Credit Cards: A, B, C
Notes: 2, 5, 9, 10, 12

MacKaye Harbor Inn

Route 1, Box 1940, 98261
(206) 468-2253; (206) 468-9555 (FAX)

This Victorian beachfront bed and breakfast in the San Juan Islands is an ideal getaway, full of warmth and nostalgia. There is a sandy beach and extensive grounds on a tree-lined harbor. Wildlife frequent the area. Kayak and bicycle rentals. Quiet, excellent location for small groups or couples. The kitchen is available for guest use. No smoking.

Hosts: Robin and Mike Bergstrom
Rooms: 5 (2PB; 3SB) $69-145
Full Breakfast
Credit Cards: A, B
Notes: 2, 5, 8, 10, 12

LYNDEN

Century House B&B

401 So. B.C. Avenue, 98264
(206) 354-2439; (206) 354-6910 (FAX)

Located on 35 acres at the edge of town, Century House is a 107-year-old Victorian home. You'll find this completely restored home a quiet retreat with spacious gardens and lawns for your enjoyment. The quaint Dutch village of Lynden is within an easy walk boasting the best museums in the area and gift shops galore . . .but sorry; the town is closed on Sundays. Take day trips to the Cascade Mountains and Mount Baker, the sea, Seattle, Vancouver, or Victoria, British Columbia.

Hosts: Jan and Ken Stremler
Rooms: 4 (2PB; 2SB) $60-85
Full Breakfast
Credit Cards: A, B
Notes: 2, 5, 7, 8, 9, 10, 11

MONTESANO

Sylvan House

P.O. Box 416 (417 Wilder Hill), 98563
(206) 241-3453

A country hideaway that is only a ten-minute hike to Lake Sylvia State Park, hunting, fishing, and swimming. The three story, 1970 family home has been used as a B&B for six years. High on a hilltop with a sweeping view of the valley below. Gourmet food. Charter member of Washington State Bed and Breakfast Guild. In Washington's State magazine *Destination Washington*. Four rooms; two queen, one twin, three baths. Wedding room with canopied bed, view window, and private bath in room. No smoking. High decks.

NOTES: Credit cards accepted: A Master Card; B Visa; C American Express; D Discover Card; E Diners Club; F Other; 2 Personal checks accepted; 3 Lunch available; 4 Dinner available; 5 Open all year; 6 Pets

Limited to older children. No pets. In several cookbooks and B&B books on the West Coast. Advanced reservations required.

Hosts: Mike and Jo Anne Murphy
Rooms: 4 (2PB; 2SB) $55-65
Full Breakfast
Credit Cards: None
Notes: 2, 5, 7 (over 14), 8, 9, 11, 12

OAK HARBOR

North Island Bed and Breakfast

1589 N. West Beach Rd., 98277
(206) 675-7080

A newly contructed Whidbey Island home located on the waterfront. Each guest room has been designed specially with private bath, king-size bed, individual heating, fireplace, and beautiful furnishings for our guests' complete comfort and privacy. From your private deck or patio you'll enjoy a view of the Olympic Mountains and San Juan Islands. A separate entrance and private parking are provided. All Whidbey Island's wonderful attractions are close by.

Hosts: Jim and Mary Vern Loomis
Rooms: 2 (PB) $80-90
Continental Breakfast
Credit Cards: A, B, C, D
Notes: 2, 5, 10

Harbinger Inn

OLGA

Buck Bay Farm

Star Route Box 45, 98279
(206) 376-2908

Buck Bay Farm is located on beautiful Orcas in the San Juan Islands of Washington State. Orcas is an idyllic vacation destination with lots of outdoor fun: hiking, bicycling, boating or kayaking, whale watching, golf, fishing, and much more. The B&B is a farmhouse recently rebuilt by the owner. A warm welcome and hearty, home-style breakfast await you.

Hosts: Rick and Janet Bronkey
Rooms: 4 (PB) $80-110
Full Breakfast
Credit Cards: A, B
Notes: 2, 5, 7 (by arrangement), 10

OLYMPIA

Harbinger Inn

1136 East Bay Drive, 98506
(206) 754-0389

Built in 1910, the house is of finely detailed grey, ashler block construction with white pillars and wide balconies—all completely restored. Distinctive features of the grounds have also been kept as the mysterious street-to-basement tunnel and the hillside waterfall fed by an artesian well. Throughout the Inn, turn-of-the-century furniture has been used in keeping with the original wall stencils and oak pocket doors of the first floor. Guests will find a warm, informal atmosphere at the Harbinger. In addition to its spectacular view of the nearby Capitol, the location makes not only boat-

welcome; 7 Children welcome; 8 Tennis nearby; 9 Swimming nearby; 10 Golf nearby; 11 Skiing nearby; 12 May be booked through travel agent

ing, bicycling, and jogging readily available but also downtown shopping and fine dining.

Hosts: Terrell and Marisa Williams
Rooms: 4 (1PB; 3SB) $60-90
Continental Breakfast
Credit Cards: A, B, C
Notes: 2, 5, 6, 7 (over 12), 9, 10, 12

Puget View Guesthouse
7924-61st Ave. NE, 98516
(360) 459-1676

Puget sound at your doorstep. Classic waterfront guest cottage suite with a post-card view is a romantic hideaway or family camp. The cottage sleeps four and includes a microwave, barbeque, and mini-refrigerator. Elegant breakfast is served to your cottage door. Your hosts know the area well and are excellent sources of information on what to see and do on nearby islands, in the Capitol, at Mount Rainer in Seattle, and on the Olympic Peninsula. "Pleasing our guests since 1984."

Hosts: Dick and Barbara Yunker
Rooms: 1 cottage (PB) $79 off-season
Continental Plus Breakfast
Credit Cards: A, B
Notes: 2, 5, 6, 7, 9, 12

PORT TOWNSEND

Chanticleer Inn
1208 Franklin St., 98368
(206) 385-6239; (800) 858-9421

Welcome to Port Townsend, Victorian seaport on the majestic Olympic Peninsula, gateway to the spectacular San Juan Islands, and beautiful Victoria/Vancouver,

BC. The innkeepers invite you to join them in their restored 1876 Victorian home located high above the water. Enjoy fine, crisp linen, fluffy duvets, and a creative breakfast beside a crackling fire garnished by the sounds of live, classical harp music.

Hosts: Susan and David Ross
Rooms: 5 (3PB; 2SB) $60-100
Full Breakfast
Credit Cards: A, B
Notes: 2, 5, 7 (limited), 12

The English Inn
718 "F" St., 98368
(206) 385-5302 (voice and FAX)

The English Inn was built in 1885 in the Italianate style. It is one of the more gracious Victorian mansions in Port Townsend. It has five large, sunny bedrooms, three of which have views of the Olympic Mountains. Beautiful scenery, hiking, antiquing, and only two hours from Seattle. A lovely garden, hot tub, and lots of comfort, but best of all, fresh scones for breakfast!

Hostess: Juliette Swenson
Rooms: 5 (PB) $65-95
Full Breakfast
Credit Cards: A, B
Notes: 2, 8, 10, 12

Heritage House

Heritage House

305 Pierce St., 98368-8131
(206) 385-6800

Heritage House, a stately Italianate built c. 1870, has the largest collection of antiques in Port Townsend. The house is listed on the National Register of Historic Places. Heritage House sits on a bluff providing guests with a commanding view of the bay and the snowcapped Olympic Mountains. Breakfast is a delight—Crystal and Royal Albert "Old Country Rose" china grace the ornate dining table. Visit us and relive times gone by.

Hosts: Kathy, Gary, and Shanon Hambley
Rooms: 6 (4PB; 2SB) $60-110
Full Breakfast
Credit Cards: A, B, C
Notes: 2, 5, 7, 8, 9, 10, 12

Lizzie's Victorian Bed and Breakfast

731 Pierce St., 98368
(206) 385-4168; (800) 700-4168; (206) 385-9467 (FAX)

Elegant, yet invitingly comfortable, Victorian mansion in a quiet, historic district. Two parlors, with fireplaces and pianos, enveloped with quiet music, and the ever-present coffee and tea. Breakfast in the sunny kitchen around 11-foot oak table is a special treat and the "Lizzie" replica doghouse may itself be worth the whole trip. Walking distance to theaters, restaurants, shopping, and beaches. Quite simply, the finest!

Hosts: Bill and Patti Wickline
Rooms: 8 (5PB; 3SB) $58-105
Full Breakfast
Credit Cards: A, B, D
Notes: 2, 5, 8, 10

Holly Hedge House

RENTON

Holly Hedge House

908 Grant Avenue South, 98055
(206) 226-2555

Experience the ultimate in pampering and privacy in this meticulously restored 1900 scenic hilltop retreat. This unique lodging facility reserves the entire house for **one couple** at a time to indulge in the beauty and affordable luxury. Landscaped grounds; wood deck with hot tub; swimming pool; stocked gourmet kitchen; whirlpool bath tub; CD, video, and reading libraries; fireplace; glassed-in veranda. Ten minutes from Sea Tac International Airport; 20 minutes from Seattle; 5 minutes from Lake Washington. A vacation, honeymoon, or corporate travel getaway that will long be remembered! Ask about the "Spirit Package."

Hosts: Lynn and Marian Thrasher
Rooms: 1 (PB) $110
Full Breakfast
Credit Cards: A, B
Notes: 2, 5, 8, 9, 10, 11

welcome; 7 Children welcome; 8 Tennis nearby; 9 Swimming nearby; 10 Golf nearby; 11 Skiing nearby; 12 May be booked through travel agent

Chambered Nutilus Bed and Breakfast Inn

SEATTLE

Chambered Nautilus Bed and Breakfast Inn

5005-22nd Avenue Northeast, 98105
(206) 522-2536

A gracious 1915 Georgian Colonial that is nestled on a hill and furnished with a mixture of American and English antiques and fine reproductions. A touch of Mozart, Persian rugs, a grand piano, two fireplaces, four lovely porches, and national award-winning breakfasts help assure your special comfort. Excellent access to Seattle's theaters, restaurants, public transportation, shopping, bike and jogging trails, churches, Husky Stadium, and the University of Washington campus.

Hosts: Bill and Bunny Hagemeyer
Rooms: 6 (4 PB; 2 SB) $79.50 - 105.50
Full Breakfast
Credit Cards: A, B, C, E, F
Notes: 2, 5, 8, 9, 10, 11, 12

Chelsea Station Bed and Breakfast

4915 Linden Avenue North, 98103
(206) 547-6077 (voice and FAX)

Chelsea Station consistently provides the peaceful surroundings travelers enjoy. Lace curtains, ample breakfasts, and comfy king beds share warm feelings of "Grandma's time." The nearby Seattle Rose Garden contributes beauty to the human spirit. With a cup of tea in the afternoon, Chelsea Station is a perfect place for relaxation and renewal. No smoking.

Hosts: Dick and Mary Lou Jones
Rooms: 6 (PB) $69-109
Full Breakfast
Credit Cards: A, B, C, D, E
Notes: 2, 5, 8, 9, 10, 12

The Shafer-Baillie Mansion Guest House

907 14th Avenue East, 98112
(206) 322-4654; (206) 329-4654 (FAX)

Antiques of yesteryear; a quiet and enjoyable atmosphere; formal living room and fireplace with comfortable seating for our guests; full library with TV and VCR; formal dining room seats 50; billiard room with copper fireplace; spacious grounds and garden for summer parties and weddings; port cochere and gazebos on north and south lawns with tables and seating; great food in your price range; casual buffet or gourmet sumptuous fare. With your event in mind, we will help you plan your occasion, whether it's a breakfast, luncheon, or meeting all day with both. There are telephones in every room.

Host: Erv Olssen—owner/proprietor
Rooms: 13 (10PB; 3SB) $65-115
Continental Breakfast
Credit Cards: C, D
Notes: 2, 5, 6 (on request), 8, 9, 10, 11, 12

NOTES: Credit cards accepted: A MasterCard; B Visa; C American Express; D Discover Card; E Diners Club; F Other; 2 Personal checks accepted; 3 Lunch available; 4 Dinner available; 5 Open all year; 6 Pets

SEAVIEW

Gumm's Bed and Breakfast Inn

P.O. Box 447 (Hwy. 101 and 33 Ave.), 98644
(206) 642-8887

This fine old house was built in 1911 and features a large living room with a great stone fireplace. Four inviting guest rooms are all uniquely decorated with special thoughts to guests' comfort. Full breakfast. Children welcome. Outdoor hot tub. TV. Non-smoking. A wonderful sun porch offers a warm spot for casual conversation or reading for a relaxing day.

Hostess: Mickey Slack
Rooms: 4 (2 PB; 2 SB) $65-85
Full Breakfast
Credit Cards: A, B
Notes: 2, 5, 7, 8, 10, 12

SEQUIM

Greywolf Inn

395 Keeler Road, 98382
(206) 683-5889

Nestled in a crescent of towering evergreens, this Northwest country estate overlooking the Dungeness Valley is the ideal starting point for year round light adventure on the Olympic peninsula...hiking, fishing, biking, boating, bird-watching, sightseeing, and golf. Enjoy Greywolf's sunny decks, Japanese-style hot tub, and meandering five-acre woodswalk, or curl up by the fire with a good book. Then, retire to one of the inn's cozy comfortable theme rooms. It is the perfect ending to an exciting day.

Hosts: Peggy and Bill Melang
Rooms: 6 (PB) $68-110
Full Breakfast
Credit Cards: A, B, C
Notes: 2, 3, 5, 7 (over 12), 8, 9, 10, 11, 12

Margie's Inn on the Bay

120 Forest Road, 98382
(360) 683-7011

Sequim's only waterfront bed and breakfast. A contemporary ranch-style home with 180 feet on the water. Five well-appointed bedrooms with private baths. A large sitting room with VCR and movies. Two Persian cats and a talking parrot. Close to the marina, fishing, Dungeness National Wildlife Refuge and Spit, Olympic Game Farm, hiking and biking, Hurricane Ridge, gift shops, and much more. Great restaurants in the area. AAA inspected.

Hosts: Margie and Don Vorhies
Rooms: 5 (PB) $69-125
Full Breakfast
Credit Cards: A, B
Notes: 2, 7 (over 12), 8, 9, 10, 11, 12

SILVERDALE

Seabreeze Beach Cottage on Hood Canal

16609 Olympic View Road, NW, 98383
(360) 692-4648

Challenged by lapping waves at high tide, this private retreat will awaken your five senses with the smell of salty air, a taste of fresh oyster and clams, views of the Olympic Mountains, and the exhilaration of sun, surf, and sand. Free brochure. Hot at the

welcome; 7 Children welcome; 8 Tennis nearby; 9 Swimming nearby; 10 Golf nearby; 11 Skiing nearby; 12 May be booked through travel agent

water's edge.

Host: Dennis Fulton
Rooms: 2 (PB) $119-149
Continental Breakfast
Credit Cards: A, B
Notes: 2, 5, 6, 7, 9, 10, 12

SNOHOMISH

Victorian Rose

124 Avenue D, 98290
(206) 568-7673

A Victorian/Queen Ann home located two blocks from downtown Snohomish, the antique capital of Washington. Rooms are decorated with Victorian furnishings and have queen beds. Enjoy sports—bike rides, hot air balloons, and parachuting—or just sit on the huge deck and watch it all happen above your head. We even have vintage clothing in the Herron Room for you to try on and have your picture taken. We enjoy people and would love to have you share our home.

Hosts: Dave and Sheri Kelnhofer
Rooms: 2 (PB) $65-75
Full Breakfast
Credit Cards: None (but soon)
Notes: 2, 5, 7 (over 13), 8, 9, 10

SPOKANE

Marianna Stoltz House Bed and Breakfast

E. 427 Indiana Avenue, 99207
(509) 483-4316

Our 1908 historic home is situated five minutes from downtown. Furnished with

antiques, old quilts, and Oriental rugs. We offer a wraparound veranda, sitting room, and parlor which provide relaxation and privacy. Enjoy king, queen or single beds with private or shared baths, air-conditioning and TV. A tantalizing, unique, and hearty breakfast is prepared each morning. Close to shopping, opera house, convention center, Centennial Trail, riverfront park, and bus.

Hosts: Jim and Phyllis Maguire
Rooms: 4 (2PB; 2SB) $60-69+tax
Full Breakfast
Credit Cards: A, B, C, D, E
Notes: 2, 5, 7 (over 10), 8, 9, 10, 11, 12

WHITE SALMON

Llama Ranch Bed and Breakfast

1980 Highway 141, 98672
(509) 395-2786; (800) 800-LAMA

Hospitality plus unforgettable delight. Jerry and Rebeka share their love of llamas on free llama walks through the woods with each guest walking a "llovable" llama. There are stunning views of both Mt. Adams and Mt. Hood. The ranch is located between the Mt. Adams wilderness area and the Columbia Gorge national scenic area with many varied activities close by. Picturesque views and photographic memories abound along with the serenity, dignity, and beauty of llamas.

Hosts: Jerry and Rebeka Stone
Rooms: 7 (2 PB; 5 SB) $55-75
Full Breakfast
Credit Cards: A, B, D
Notes: 2, 5, 6, 7, 10, 11, 12

NOTES: Credit cards accepted: A Master Card; B Visa; C American Express; D Discover Card; E Diners Club; F Other; 2 Personal checks accepted; 3 Lunch available; 4 Dinner available; 5 Open all year; 6 Pets

West Virginia

BERKELEY SPRINGS

The Country Inn

207 S. Washington Street, 25411
(304) 258-2210; (800) 822-6630 (Reservations);
(304) 258-3986 (FAX)

Just over the mountain. . .less than 100 miles from Balto. Enjoy the warmth and service of a unique and charming country inn. 70 distinctive rooms, creative cuisine, and light specialties. Relax in our full service spa, art gallery, and serene gardens. Many irresistible packages available. Call for reservations.

Hosts: Mr. and Mrs. Jack Barker
Rooms: 70 (57PB; 13SB) $35-80
Full Breakfast
Credit Cards: A, B, C, D, E
Notes: 2, 3, 4, 5, 7, 8, 9, 10, 11, 12

HUTTONSVILLE

Hutton House

P.O. Box 88, Routes 250/219, 26273
(304) 335-6701

Meticulously restored and decorated, this Queen Anne Victorian on the National Register of Historic Places is conveniently located near Elkins, Cass Railroad, and Snowshoe Ski Resort. It has a wrap-around porch and deck for relaxing and enjoying the view, TV, game room, lawn for games, and a friendly kitchen. Breakfast and afternoon refreshments are served at your leisure; other meals are available with prior reservation or good luck! Come see us!

Hosts: Loretta Murray and Dean Ahren
Rooms: 6 (PB) $60-70
Full Breakfast
Credit Cards: A, B
Notes: 2, 5, 7, 8, 10, 11, 12

General Lewis Inn

LEWISBURG

General Lewis Inn

301 E. Washington St., 24901-1425
(304) 645-2600 (voice and FAX)

Come rock in a chair on the veranda of the General Lewis Inn. See passengers alight from a horsedrawn carriage. On chilly

---

days dream by the fireplace, solve one of the puzzles, or play a fascinating game. Don't miss Memory Lane's display of ancient tools for home and farm. Antiques furnish every room, including comfortable canopy, spool, and poster beds. The dining room in the 1834 wing features Southern cooking. Nestled in beautiful Greenbrier Valley, the Inn offers nearby walking tours. Check out the Lewisburg historical district and browse the antique shops. Outdoor recreational activities abound throughout the Valley.

Hosts: Mary Noel and Jim Morgan
Rooms: 25 (PB) $66-86
Full Breakfast
Credit Cards: A, B, C
Notes: 2, 3, 4, 5, 6, 7, 8, 9, 10, 11, 12

VALLEY CHAPEL (WESTON)

Ingeberg Acres
Millstone Rd., P.O. Box 199, 26446
(304) 269-2834

A unique experience can be yours at this scenic 450-acre horse and cattle farm. Ingeberg Acres is located in the heart of West Virginia seven miles from Weston, overlooking its own private valley. Hiking, swimming, hunting, and fishing or just relaxing can be the orders of the day. Observe or participate in numerous farm activities.

Hosts: Inge and John Mann
Rooms: 3 (SB) $59
Full Breakfast
Credit Cards: None
Notes: 2, 5, 7, 9, 10

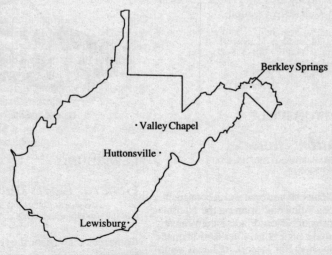

· Valley Chapel

Berkley Springs

Huttonsville ·

Lewisburg ·

WEST VIRGINIA

Wisconsin

ALBANY

Albany Guest House
405 South Mill St., 53502
(608) 862-3636

An experience in tranquility, just 30 miles south of the capital dome in Madison. Enjoy king and queen beds in air-conditioned rooms in a restored 1908 home. Relax on the wide, flower-filled front porch or light the fireplace in the master bedroom. Canoe, tube, or fish the Sugar River; bike, hike, or cross-country ski the Sugar River Trail. Visit nearby New Glarus, America's Little Switzerland, or Monroe, The Swiss Cheese Capital.

Hosts: Bob and Sally Braem
Rooms: 4 (PB) $50-68
Full Breakfast
Credit Cards: None
Notes: 2, 5, 7, 9, 10, 11

Oak Hill Manor
401 E. Main Street, 53502
(608) 862-1400

A 1908 brick manor house on the Sugar River Bicycle Trail. Spacious sunny corner rooms are air-conditioned and all have queen-size beds. Choose a room with a fireplace, a porch, or a canopy bed. Stroll the acre of gardens or sit by the fire in the

guest parlor. Gourmet fireside breakfast served daily. Hike, bike, canoe, golf, and cross country ski. Bicycles available at no charge. No smoking.

Hosts: Lee and Mary DeWolf
Rooms: 4 (PB) $55-60
Full Breakfast
Credit Cards: A, B
Notes: 2, 5, 8, 10, 11, 12

Sugar River Inn
304 South Mill St., 53502
(608) 862-1248

Our turn-of-the-century inn, with many original features, has the charm of yesteryear, and Christian fellowship. We are located in a quiet village in southern Wisconsin along the Sugar River. We have spacious lawn, canoeing, and fishing in the back yard. We are minutes away from the bike trail. Comfortable and light airy rooms await you, queen-size beds, fine linens, afternoon refreshments, and wake up coffee. We are near New Glarus, House on the Rock, Little Norway, and the state capital in Madison. Cash or check. Children allowed by arrangement.

Hosts: Jack and Ruth Lindberg
Rooms: 4 (1PB; 3SB) $45-55
Full Breakfast
Credit Cards: None
Notes: 2, 5, 7 (by arrangement), 10

---

year; 6 Pets welcome; 7 Children welcome; 8 Tennis nearby; 9 Swimming nearby; 10 Golf nearby; 11 Skiing nearby; 12 May be booked through travel agent

ALGOMA

Amberwood Inn

N7136 Hwy. 42, 54201
(414) 487-3471

Luxury Lake Michigan beachfront accommodations. Located on two and one-half private acres with 300 feet of beach. Each suite is large, romantic, and very private. Private baths, whirlpool tubs, hot tub, sauna, and private decks open to water. Awaken to sunrise over water; sleep to the sound of the waves. Ten minutes to Door County.

Rooms: 5 (PB) $65-85
Full Breakfast
Credit Cards: A, B
Notes: 2, 7, 9, 10

BAILEYS HARBOR (DOORS COUNTY)

Loving's Guest Home

7445 Hwy. 57, 54202
(414) 839-2049

Located in beautiful Door County, Wisconsin on Kangaroo Lake (½ mile from Lake Michigan). Comfortable family home surrounded by gardens on large lot invites relaxing. Quiet setting, yet close to all Door Peninsula activities. Adults only. Non-smoking in house.

Hosts: George and Margaret Loving
Rooms: 3 (each w/ 1 double bed) (SB) $45
Full Continental Breakfast
Credit Cards: None
Notes: 2, 5, 8, 9, 10, 11

Pine Haven Bed and Breakfast

BARABOO

Pine Haven Bed and Breakfast

E13083 Hwy. 33, 53913
(608) 356-3489

Our home is located in a scenic valley with small private lake and Baraboo Bluffs in the background. The guest rooms are distinctly different with wicker furniture and antiques, queen and twin beds. Take a walk in this peaceful country setting. Area activities include Devil's Lake State Park, Circus World Museum, Wisconsin Dells, and ski resorts.

Hosts: Lyle and Marge Getschman
Rooms: 4 (PB) $65-75
Full Breakfast
Credit Cards: A, B
Notes: 2, 5, 7 (over 5), 9, 10, 11

The Victorian Rose

423 Third Ave., 53913
(608) 356-7828

Nostalgic retreat. A place for all seasons. Spend tranquil moments with memories to treasure. Nestled in the heart of historical Baraboo. Centrally located to all area attractions. Enjoy the splendor of the Victorian era by resting on the wraparound

NOTES: Credit cards accepted: A Master Card; B Visa; C American Express; D Discover Card; E Diners Club; F Other; 2 Personal checks accepted; 3 Lunch available; 4 Dinner available; 5 Open all

front porch or relaxing in two formal parlors with beautiful cherub fireplace and TV/VCR. Romantic guestrooms, candlelight breakfast, and Christian hospitality.

Hosts: Robert and Carolyn Stearns
Rooms: 3 (PB) $65-80
Full Breakfast
Credit Cards: None
Notes: 2, 5, 8, 9, 10, 11, 12

BAYFIELD

Pinehurst Inn at Pikes Creek

Route 1 Box 222, 54814
(715) 779-3676

The Inn is an 1885 Gothic Victorian with beautiful stone work and woodcrafting. Located on Pikes Creek, across the road from Lake Superior. A peaceful country setting offering Victorian flower garden, reflective pool, and rock garden. All rooms appointed in antiques, quilts, and collectables. Renowned for our gourmet breakfast.

Host: Morris Lewis
Rooms: 6 (PB) $55-69
Full Breakfast
Credit Cards: A, B
Notes: 2, 5, 6, 7, 9, 10, 11

Abendruh Bed and Breakfast Swisstyle

BELLEVILLE

Abendruh Bed and Breakfast Swisstyle

7019 Gehin Road, 53508-9752
(608) 424-3808

Experience B&B Swisstyle. This highly acclaimed Wisconsin B&B offers true Swiss charm and hospitality. The serenity of this peaceful retreat is one of many treasures that keeps guests coming back. Spacious guestrooms adorned with beautiful family heirlooms. Sitting room with high cathedral ceiling and cozy fireplace. An Abendruh breakfast is a perfect way to start a new day or end a peaceful stay.

Hostess: Mathilde Jaggi
Rooms: 2 (PB) $60-65 + tax
Full Breakfast
Credit Cards: A, B
Notes: 2, 5, 8, 9, 10, 11, 12

BROWNTOWN

Honeywind Farm

W. 8247 County P, 53522
(608) 325-5215

Honeywind Farm is a B&B blended into a beautiful southwest Wisconsin dairy farm. We emphasize family farm vacations. On our 300 acres is a fishing stream, 20 acres of woods, natural wetlands, plus corn and hay fields, all contributing to an abundance of wildlife and numerous ways to enjoy your time. Our chldren will welcome yours. Depending on the season, you may have opportunity to help with varous farm activities and/or take home a sampling of

year; 6 Pets welcome; 7 Children welcome; 8 Tennis nearby; 9 Swimming nearby; 10 Golf nearby; 11 Skiing nearby; 12 May be booked through travel agent

farm products.

Hosts: Ryan and Claudia Wilson and Family
Rooms: 2 (PB) $65-85
Full Breakfast
Credit Cards: None
Notes: 2, 5, 7

CEDARBURG

The Stagecoach Inn Bed and Breakfast

W61 N 520 Washington, 53012
(414) 375-0208

The Stagecoach Inn is a historic, restored 1853 stone building of Greek Revival style and an 1847 restored frame house annex. Its 12 cozy and comfortable rooms feature stencilled walls, central air-conditioning, and private baths. Situated in the heart of historic Cedarburg within walking distance to shops and restaurants, the Inn also features an on-premises pub with a 100-year-old bar and a chocolate shop.

Hosts: Liz and Brook Brown
Rooms: 12 (PB) $65-110
Continental Plus Breakfast
Credit Cards: A, B, C, D, E
Notes: 2, 5, 7 (over 12), 8, 9, 10, 11, 12

The Washington House Inn

W62 N 573 Washington Avenue, 53012
(414) 375-3550; (800) 554-4717; (414) 375-9422 (FAX)

Built in 1884 and listed on the National Register of Historic Places, 34 guest rooms feature antiques, down comforters, whirlpool baths, fireplaces, and cable TV. Located in the heart of the Cedarburg historic district, within walking distance of area antique shops, fine dining, and historic Cedar Creek settlement.

Hostess: Wendy Porterfield
Rooms: 34 (PB) $59-159
Embellished Continental Breakfast
Credit Cards: A, B, C, D, E
Notes: 2, 5, 7, 8, 9, 10, 11

CHETEK

Trails End Bed and Breakfast

641 Ten Mile Lake Drive, 54728
(715) 924-2641

Peace and tranquility await you in this modern spacious log lodge, situated on our private island. The 4,000-square-foot, three-level log home houses antiques of every sort, with stories behind most every unique feature of the home from an 1887 jail door to a 300 pound, seven-foot wagon wheel and a huge stone fireplace. Each guest's bedroom—the Romantic, Indian, and Western Rooms—are decorated with antiques of yesteryear.

Hosts: Richard and Bonnie Flood
Rooms: 3 (1PB; 2SB) $80-95
Full Breakfast
Credit Cards: A
Notes: 5, 9, 10

CRANDON

Courthouse Square B&B

210 E. Polk Street, 54520
(715) 478-2549

Guests frequently comment about the peace and tranquility of the setting. Flower

---

NOTES: Credit cards accepted: A Master Card; B Visa; C American Express; D Discover Card; E Diners Club; F Other; 2 Personal checks accepted; 3 Lunch available; 4 Dinner available; 5 Open all

and herb gardens, birds and squirrels are enjoyed at the many benches placed throughout the gardens or stroll down the hill to the lake through the forget-me-nots and view wildlife. *The Rhinelander Daily News* wrote, "Traditional hospitality is emphasized at Courthouse Square B&B, and it's evident from the moment you enter this delightful home where tranquility and peace abounds. You will no doubt smell something delicious baking in Bess's kitchen as gourmet cooking is one of her specialties."

Hosts: Les and Bess Aho
Rooms: 3 (1PB; 2SB) $50-60
Full Gourmet Candlelit Breakfast
Credit Cards: None
Notes: 2, 5, 7 (ask about 12+), 8, 9, 10, 11

EAGLE RIVER

Brennan Manor—Old World Bed and Breakfast

1079 Everett Rd., 54521
(715) 479-7353

This castle in the forest evokes images of King Arthur with its suit of armor, arched windows, hand-hewn wood work, and a 30-foot stone fireplace. You'll stay in one of four antique-decorated rooms (private baths) that opens onto a balcony overlooking the Great Rooms. There, wintertime guests gather to sip hot chocolate and munch popcorn after cross-country skiing in the Nicolet National Forest or snowmobiling on 500 miles of trails. Situated on the largest freshwater chain of lakes in the world, the inn's frontage includes boathouse and piers for warm weather fun. A three-bedroom guest house

is also available. No smoking.

Hosts: Connie and Bob Lawton
Rooms: 4 (PB) $69-89
Full Breakfast
Credit Cards: A, B
Notes: 2, 5, 8, 9, 10, 11, 12

The Inn at Pinewood

P.O. Box 549, 1800 Silver Forest Lane, 54521
(715) 479-4114

Northwoods elegance at its finest. Warmest hospitality awaits you the minute you arrive at this delightful 21 room bed and breakfast. Eight romantic guest rooms, all with king-size beds, private baths, and balconies. Many with double whirlpool baths and fireplaces. Summers: swim, hike, fish, play tennis. Winters: ski, snowmobile, then relax by the fire in the huge stone fireplace. Reserve the entire inn for conferences and retreats. Scrumptious full breakfasts. Gift certificates available.

Hosts: Edward and Nona Soroosh
Rooms: 8 (PB) $65-95
Full Breakfast
Credit Cards: A, B
Notes: 2, 5, 7, 8, 9, 10, 11, 12

EAU CLAIRE

Otter Creek Inn

2536 Hwy. 12, 54701
(715) 832-2945

Pamper yourself with breakfast in bed amid the antiques of yesteryear in this spacious 6,000 square foot, three-story inn. Discover amenities of today tucked amidst the country Victorian decor as every guest room contains a double whirl-

year; 6 Pets welcome; 7 Children welcome; 8 Tennis nearby; 9 Swimming nearby; 10 Golf nearby; 11 Skiing nearby; 12 May be booked through travel agent

pool, private bath, phone, AC, and cabe
TV. Explore the creek or snuggle up inside
near the fire to watch the wildlife saunter
by. All this country charm is located less
than one mile from numerous restaurants
and shops.

Hosts: Randy and Shelley Hansen
Rooms: 5 (PB) $59-129
Expanded Continental Breakfast
Credit Cards: A, B, C, D
Notes: 2, 5, 8, 9, 10, 11

Otter Creek Inn

EDGERTON

The Olde Parsonage Bed and Breakfast

120 Swift Street, 53534
(608) 884-6490

Retreat to this well preserved parsonage
of 1906 graced with herring bone floors,
leaded glass windows, and original oak
woodwork. Relax in the parlor with cozy
conversation or play euchre in the reading
room before retiring to your own room.
Located two miles off I-90 in Edgerton,
the boyhood home of Sterling North. Visit
antique and specialty shops or Tobacco
City Museum. Enjoy golf, tennis, or water
sports at Lake Koshkonong, three miles
east of Edgerton.

Hostess: Connie Frank
Rooms: 4 (SB) $45-75
Hearty Continental Breakfast
Credit Cards: None
Notes: 2, 5, 8, 9, 10

EPHRAIM (DOOR COUNTY)

Hillside Hotel of Ephraim

9980 Water Street (Hwy. 42), 54211-0071
(414) 854-2417; (800) 423-7023

Authentic, restored country-Victorian inn
featuring full specialty breakfasts and afternoon teas, feather beds, original antiques, gorgeous harbor view, 100-foot
veranda overlooking the beach, individually decorated guest rooms, clawfoot tubs
with showers, and brass fixtures. We have
eleven years experience and *love* what we
do!

Hosts: David and Karen McNeil
Rooms: 11 + 2 cottages (11SB) $79-115
Full Breakfast and Afternoon Tea
Credit Cards: A, B, D
Notes: 2, 5, 7, 8, 9, 10, 11

FORT ATKINSON

The Lamp Post Inn

408 South Main, 53538
(414) 563-6561

We welcome you to the charm of our 115-
year-old Victorian home filled with beautiful antiques. Five grammophones for your
listening pleaure. For the modern, one of
our baths features a large jacuzzi. We are
located 7 blocks from the famous Fireside
Playhouse. You come a stranger, but

---

leave here a friend. No smoking.

Hosts: Debbie and Mike Rusch
Rooms: 3 (2PB; 1SB) $60-90
Full Breakfast
Credit Cards: None
Notes: 2, 5, 7, 8, 9, 10, 11

HARTFORD

Jordan House Bed and Breakfast

81 S. Main Street, 53027
(414) 673-5643

Warm and comfortable Victorian home furnished with period antiques. 40 miles from Milwaukee. Near majestic Holy Hill Shrine, Horicon Wildlife Refuge, and Pike Lake State Park. Walk to the state's largest antique auto museum, antique malls, and downtown shops. Call or write for brochure.

Hosts: Kathy Buchanan and Art Jones
Rooms: 4 (1PB; 3SB) $55-65
Full Breakfast
Credit Cards: A, B
Notes: 2, 5, 7, 8, 9, 10, 11

Jordan House Bed and Breakfast

HAZEL GREEN

DeWinters of Hazel Green

2225 Main St. PO Box 384, 53811
(608) 854-2768

DeWinters of Hazel Green, housed in a Federal and Greek Revival style brick building, is the family home of the Simison Family since 1846. The birthplace of your host, Don, son of the original owner. DeWinters has been refurbished over the past ten years: furnished with family heirlooms and made into a very comfortable home. Enjoy a quiet, historic, lead mining town ten minutes from Galena, IL and Dubuque, IA. Come prepared to eat a full home-cooked breakfast.

Hosts: Don and Cari Simison
Rooms: 3 (1PB; 2SB) $45-75
Full Breakfast
Credit Cards: None
Notes: 2, 5, 7 (well behaved), 8, 9, 10, 11, 12

Wisconsin House Stage Coach Inn

2105 E. Main St., 53811-0071
(608) 854-2233

Built as a stage coach inn in 1846, the Inn now offers six rooms and two suites for your comfort. Join us for an evening's rest. Dine and be refreshed in the parlor where General Grant spent many an evening with his friend Jefferson Crawford. Most conveniently located for all the attractions of the Tri-State Area. Galena, Illinois, is ten minutes away, Dubuque, Iowa, 15 miles,

year; 6 Pets welcome; 7 Children welcome; 8 Tennis nearby; 9 Swimming nearby; 10 Golf nearby;
11 Skiing nearby; 12 May be booked through travel agent

and Platteville is 20 miles away.

Hosts: Ken and Pat Disch
Rooms: 8 (6PB; 2SB) $55-100
Full Breakfast
Credit Cards: A, B
Notes: 2, 4, 5, 8, 9, 10, 11, 12

IOLA

Taylor House Bed and Breakfast

210 E. Iola St., P.O. Box 101, 54945
(715) 445-2204

Turn-of-the-century Victorian home. Four antique-furnished rooms; one with fireplace. Parlor with fireplace. Queen-size beds. No smoking. Air-conditioned. Paved country roads are ideal for biking. Twenty minutes from the Waupaca Chain O' Lakes area. We offer a glimpse of the lifestyle of the 1800s with all the conveniences of the modern age. Call or write for a free brochure.

Hosts: Crystal and Richard Anderson
Rooms: 4 (2PB; 2SB) $46-55
Full Breakfast
Credit Cards: None
Notes: 2, 5, 7, 9, 10, 11

LA FARGE

Trillium

Rt. 2, Box 121, 54639
(608) 625-4492

A fully furnished private cottage on our diversified farm. Cottage has complete bath, full kitchen, porch with swing, and a stone fireplace in the living room. The cottage has two double beds plus a crib

and high chair. Located in Southwestern Wisconsin, offering a wide variety of seasonal recreational opportunities.

Hostess: Roasanne Boyett
Rooms: One private cottage (PB) $65-75
Full Breakfast
Credit Cards: None
Notes: 2, 5, 7, 8, 9, 10, 11

LAKE DELTON

The Swallow's Nest Bed and Breakfast

141 Sarrington, P.O. Box 418, 53940
(608) 254-6900

The unique decor is English in taste with period collectibles. New home with cathedral windows and ceiling. Offers seclusion among the trees and bird's-eye view of the lake. Relax in the library or by the fireplace. Fine restaurants nearby. Close to Wisconsin Dells, Devils Head, two state parks, and Circus World Museum. Full breakfast, four rooms, and four private baths. No pets and no smoking. Gift certificates available.

Hosts: Rod and Mary Ann Stemo
Rooms: 4 (PB) $60-70
Full Breakfast
Credit Cards: A, B
Notes: 2, 5, 8, 9, 10, 11

LIVINGSTON

Oak Hill Farm

9850 Hwy. 80, 53554
(608) 943-6006

A comfortable country home with a warm hospitable atmosphere that is enhanced

---

NOTES: Credit cards accepted: A Master Card; B Visa; C American Express; D Discover Card; E Diners Club; F Other; 2 Personal checks accepted; 3 Lunch available; 4 Dinner available; 5 Open all

with fireplaces, porches, and facilities for picnics, bird-watching and hiking. In the area you will find state parks, museums, and lakes.

Hosts: Elizabeth Johnson and Victor Johnson
Suites: 4 (1PB; 3SB) $42
Continental Breakfast
Credit Cards: None
Notes: 2, 6, 7, 8, 9, 10, 11, 12

Victorian Treasure Inn

LODI

Victorian Treasure Bed and Breakfast Inn

115 Prairie Street, 53555
(800) 859-5199; (608) 592-4352 (FAX)

Experience timeless ambience, thoughtful amenities, and caring innkeepers at a classic bed and breakfast inn. Timeless ambience. . .1897 Queen Anne architecture, wraparound front porch, stained and leaded glass, pocket doors, gas and electric chandeliers, and more. Thoughtful amenities... turn-down service, cotton terry robes, glycerine soaps, down pillows and comforters, dual control electric blankets. Caring innkeepers. . .educated and experienced in hotel and restaurant management, gourmet cooks, fussy about details, and genuinely interested in exceeding guest's expectations. Located in the scenic Lake Wisconsin recreational area, between Madison and Wisconsin Dells. Call toll-free for a brochure, and to learn more about this exceptional inn.

Hosts: Todd and Kimberly Seidl
Rooms: 4 (PB) $65-110
Full Breakfast
Credit Cards: A, B
Notes: 2, 5, 8, 9, 10, 11

MADISON

Annie's Bed and Breakfast

2117 Sheridan Drive, 53704
(608) 244-2224; (608) 242-9611 (FAX)

When you want the world to go away, come to Annie's, the quiet inn on Warner Park with the beautiful view. Luxury accommodations at reasonable rates. Close to the lake and park, it is also convenient to downtown and the University of Wisconsin campus. There are unusual amenities in this charming setting, including a romantic gazebo surrounded by butterfly gardens, a shaded terrace, and pond. Two beautiful two-bedroom suites. Double jacuzzi. Full air conditioning. Winter cross-country skiing, too!

Hosts: Anne and Larry Stuart
Suites: 2-2 room suites (PB) $84-94
Full Breakfast
Credit Cards: A, B, C
Notes: 2, 5, 7 (over 12), 8, 9, 10, 11

MEQUON

Port Zedler Motel

10036 North Port Washington Road, 53092
(414) 241-5850

AAA approved; air-conditioned; conve-

year; 6 Pets welcome; 7 Children welcome; 8 Tennis nearby; 9 Swimming nearby; 10 Golf nearby; 11 Skiing nearby; 12 May be booked through travel agent

nient to downtown and excellent restaurants (12 minutes from downtown Milwaukee); free cable, color TV (HBO and Showtime); touch tone in-room phones; free ample parking; free ice; children under 12 stay free; senior/AARP/AAA discounts; in-room refrigerator and microwave oven on request, if available; German is spoken. I-43 northbound one-half mile NW of exit 83; I-43 southbound exit 28A, 1 block east and one and one-half mile north on Port Washington Rd. (Hwy. W)

Hostess: Sheila
Rooms: 16 (PB) $34.95-49.95
Continental Breakfast
Credit Cards: A, B, C, D
Notes: 5, 6, 7, 8, 9, 10, 11, 12

PLAIN

Bettinger House B&B

855 Wachter Ave., 53577
(608) 546-2951 (voice and FAX)

Hostess's grandparents' 1904 Victorian farmhouse. Grandma was a midwife and delivered 300 babies in this house. Choose from six spacious bedrooms that blend the old with the new, each named after noteworthy persons of Plain. Central air-conditioning. Start your day with on of the old-fashioned, full-course breakfasts we are famous for. Near "House on the Rock," Frank Loyd Wright's original Taliesin, American Players Theatre, White Mound Park, and much more.

Hosts: Jim and Marie Neider
Rooms: 5 (2PB; 3SB) $45-55
Full Breakfast
Credit Cards: A, B
Notes: 2, 5, 7 (inquire first), 8, 9, 10, 11, 12

PORT WASHINGTON

The Inn at Old Twelve Hundred

806 West Grand Avenue, 53074
(414) 284-6883

Beautifully restored and decorated Queen Anne. Original Master Suite features fireplace, private porch, and king-size bed. Two rooms offer oversize whirlpools, fireplaces, and sitting room or private porch. Spacious yard, gazebo, croquet, tandem bicycles available. Port Washington is a quaint village on Lake Michigan. Minutes to Cedarburg, Harrison Beach, State Park, and Kohler. Air-conditioned. Restricted smoking.

Hostesses: Stephanie and Ellie Bresette
Rooms: 5 (PB) $65-145
Continental Breakfast
Credit Cards: A, B, C
Notes: 2, 5

Breese Waye Bed and Breakfast

PORTAGE

Breese Waye Bed and Breakfast

816 MacFarlane Road, 53901
(608) 742-5281

Standing on the manicured lawn with the

Lamb's Inn Farm Bed and Breakfast

house towering behind, you can almost hear the clop, clop, clop of the horses and the commotion of the water traffic on the nearby historical canal. You can take yourself back in time even before you step into our stately Victorian house which was home to one of the founding fathers of Portage, Llywellyn Breese. The interiour is as warm and inviting as the exterior is imposing. Come share history with us.

Hosts: Keith and Gretchen Sprecher
Rooms: 4 (PB) $50-70
Full Breakfast
Credit Cards: None
Notes: 2, 5, 6, 7, 8, 9, 10, 11

RICHLAND CENTER

Lamb's Inn Farm Bed and Breakfast

Route 2 Box 144, 53581
(608) 585-4301

Relax on our 180-acre farm, located in a scenic valley surrounded by spectacular

hills. Beautifully renovated farmhouse, furnished with country antiques...porch for watching deer and other wildlife... cozy library for rainy days. Our new cottage has a spiral stair to the loft and a deck to relax on. Large homemade breakfasts served at the B&B with homemade breads, egg dishes, and often old-fashioned bread pudding. Our hope is that your stay will be a memorable and relaxing time for you.

Hosts: Dick and Donna Messerschmidt
Rooms: 4 (PB) $70-105
Full Breakfast
Credit Cards: A, B
Notes: 2, 5, 7(restricted), 8, 9, 10, 11

SPARTA

The Franklin Victorian Bed and Breakfast

220 East Franklin Street, 54656
(608) 269-3894; (800) 845-8767

This turn-of-the-century home welcomes

year; 6 Pets welcome; 7 Children welcome; 8 Tennis nearby; 9 Swimming nearby; 10 Golf nearby; 11 Skiing nearby; 12 May be booked through travel agent

you to bygone elegance with small-town quiet and comfort. The four spacious bedrooms provide a perfect setting for ultimate relaxation. Full home-cooked breakfast is served before starting your day of hiking, biking, skiing, canoeing, antiquing, or exploring this beautiful area.

Hosts: Lloyd and Jane Larson
Rooms: 4 (2 PB; 2 SB) $60-80
Full Breakfast
Credit Cards: A, B
Notes: 2, 5, 7 (over 10), 8, 9, 10, 11

Dreams of Yesteryear

STEVENS POINT

Dreams of Yesteryear Bed and Breakfast
1100 Brawley Street, 54481
(715) 341-4525; (715) 344-3047 (FAX)

Featured in *Victorian Homes Magazine* and listed on the National Register of Historic Places. Your hosts are from Stevens Point and enjoy talking about the restoration of their turn-of-the-century home which has been in the same family for three generations. All rooms are furnished in antiques. Guests enjoy use of parlors, porches, and gardens. Two blocks from the historic downtown, antique and specialty shops, picturesque Green Circle Trails, the university, and more. Dreams of Yesteryear is truly "a Victorian dream come true."

Hosts: Bonnie and Bill Maher
Rooms: 5 (2PB; 2SB) $55-95
Full Breakfast
Credit Cards: A, B, C, D
Notes: 2, 5, 7 (over 12 or with approval), 8, 9, 10, 11, 12

Victorian Swan on Water
1716 Water Street, 54481
(715) 345-0595

A happy memory never wears out. Create those happy memories with this restored 1889 home. Unique woodwork and antiques with air-conditioned comfort as its main ingredient. A Secret room, a Roman bath, restful gardens, whirlpool, and refreshments by the fireplace—A respite for your soul. Complete those memories with a delicious full breakfast and a river walk.

Hostess: Joan Ouellette
Rooms: 4 (PB) $50-120
Full Breakfast
Credit Cards: A, B, C, D
Notes: 2, 5, 10, 11, 12

STURGEON BAY

Hearthside Inn
2136 Taube Rd., 54235
(414) 746-2136

This remodeled 1800s farmhouse has a pleasant blend of contemporary and antique furnishings. Lake Michigan can be seen in the distance. The old barn still stands nearby. Within easy driving distance are fantastic state parks, beaches for swimming in summer, or skiing in the winter. Lighthouses, U.S. Coast Guard Station, lake cruises, airport, ship building, and weekend festivals. The rooms are charming, three with queen beds. The upper east wing room has three twin beds. Customers may use TVs, VCRs, living and sun rooms, plus group meeting rooms.

Hosts: Don and Lu Keussendorf
Rooms: 4 (PB) $35-65
Full Home-cooked Breakfast
Credit Cards: A, B
Notes: 2, 5, 7, 8, 9, 10, 11

TWO RIVERS

Red Forest Bed and Breakfast

1421-25th Street, 54241
(414) 793-1794

We invite you to step back in time to 1907 and enjoy our gracious three-story shingle style home. Highlighted with stained glass windows, heirloom antiques, and cozy fireplace. Four beautifully appointed guest rooms await your arrival. Stroll along our sugar sand beaches or downtown antiquing. The Red Forest is located on Wisconsin's East Coast, minutes from Manitowoc, Wisconsin's port city of Lake Michigan Carferry. Also located midway from Chicago and the Door County Pennisula.

Hosts: Alan and Kay Rodewald
Rooms: 4 (2PB; 2SB) $60-75
Full Breakfast
Credit Cards: A, B, C
Notes: 2, 5, 7 (older), 8, 9 (beach), 10, 11, 12
(10% comm.)

WISCONSIN DELLS

Historic Bennett House Bed and Breakfast

825 Oak Street, 53965
(608) 254-2500

The 1863 home of an honored pioneer photographer is listed on the National Register of Historic Places. We'll pamper you with elegant lace, crystal, antiques, romantic bedrooms, and luscious fireside breakfast. The private suite has a parlor, Eastlake bedroom, and shower bath. The English room has a walnut and lace canopy bed. And the garden room has a brass bed. Walk to river tours, antiques, and crafts. Minutes to hiking, biking, canoeing, four golf courses, five ski areas, five state parks, greyhound racing, bird-watching, and Indian culture. Bennett, Rockwell, circus, and railroad museums are also near by. Gift certificates are available.

Hosts: Gail and Rich Obermeyer
Rooms: 3 (1 PB; 2 SB) $70-90
Full Breakfast
Credit Cards: None
Notes: 2, 5, 8, 9, 10, 11, 12

Red Forest Bed and Breakfast

Wyoming

BIG HORN

Spahn's Big Horn Mountain B&B

Box 579, 82833
(307) 674-8150

Towering log home and secluded guest cabins on the mountainside in whispering pines. Borders one million acres of public forest with deer and moose. Gracious mountain breakfast served on the deck with binoculars to enjoy the 100-mile view. Owner is former Yellowstone ranger. Ten minutes from I-90 near Sheridan.

Hosts: Ron and Bobbie Spahn
Rooms: 4 (PB) $65-100
Full Breakfast
Credit Cards: A, B
Notes: 2, 3, 4, 6, 7

CHEYENNE

The Storyteller Pueblo Bed and Breakfast

5201 Ogden Road, 82009
(307) 634-7036

Native American art from over 30 tribes— pottery, beadwork, baskets, and rugs. Contemporary home of country and primitive antiques. Down home hospitality on a quiet street. Convenient to shopping and major restaurants. Breakfast with all the amenities. Fireplaces and family rooms for your enjoyment. Reservations recommended. Special rates during the last ten days of every July.

Hosts: Howard and Peggy Hutchings
Rooms: 3 (1PB; 2SB) $40-55
Full Breakfast
Credit Cards: None
Notes: 2, 5, 7 (by arrangement), 8, 9, 10, 11, 12

CODY

The Lockhart Bed and Breakfast Inn

109 W. Yellowstone Ave., 82414
(307) 587-6074; (800) 377-7255; (307) 587-8644 (FAX)

Historic home of famous Cody authoress, Caroline Lockhart. Circa 1890, refurbished in 1985 and again in 1884 offering antiques, parlor, dining area, wood-burning stove, piano, games, direct dial phones, and cable TV. Complimentary coffee, teas, brandy, spiced cider, and hot cocoa. AAA rated.

Hostess: Cindy Baldwin
Rooms: 7 (PB) $55-82
Full Breakfast
Credit Cards: A, B, E
Notes: 2 (preferred), 5, 7, 8, 9, 10, 11, 12

ENCAMPMENT

Platt's Rustic Mountain Lodge
Star Route 49, 82325
(307) 327-5539

A peaceful mountain view, located on a working ranch with wholesome country atmosphere and lots of western hospitality. Horseback riding, pack trips, cattle drives, youth programs, photograhic safaris, wilderness fishing, hiking, and rock hounding. Fully guided tours available to ranch recreational activities and scenic mountain areas. Enjoy the flora and fauna, historic trails, and old mining camps, plus snowmobiling, ice fishing, and cross-country skiing in the winter. Groups and families welcome. A terrific atmosphere for workshops. Lodge and cabin rentals available. Reservation only. Private fishing cabin rentals available May through September.

Hosts: Mayvon and Ron Platt
Rooms: 3 (SB) $55
Full Breakfast
Credit Cards: None
Closed Thanksgiving and Christmas
Notes: 5, 6, 7, 11

The Lockhart
Bed and Breakfast Inn

JACKSON

H.C. Richards Bed and Breakfast
PO Box 2606, 83001
(307) 733-6704; (307) 733-0930 (FAX)

Your hostess, a fourth-generation Jackson native has converted her grandparents home into a B&B for your enjoyment. The 6600 sq. ft. home was designed by her grandfather and every detail was attended to. Three large guest rooms are on the main floor of the home, all decorated in an English manner and beckon you to a bygone era. Within walking distance to many museums, art galleries, restaurants, theatres, and shops, the town square (1½ blocks), a lovely park behind the B&B, and skiing (6 blocks). The gateway to Grand Teton and Yellowstone National Parks.

Hostess: Jackie Williams
Rooms: 3 (PB) $90
Full Breakfast
Credit Cards: A, B
Notes: 2, 5, 6, 7 (over 9), 8, 9, 10, 11, 12

year; 6 Pets welcome; 7 Children welcome; 8 Tennis nearby; 9 Swimming nearby; 10 Golf nearby; 11 Skiing nearby; 12 May be booked through travel agent

PINEDALE

Pole Creek Bed and Breakfast

Box 278, 82941
(307) 367-4433

Relive the charm of the Old West in a rustic log home overlooking a peaceful meadow and the spectacular Wind River Mountains. Pole Creek Ranch features horseback riding, wagon and seigh rides, and a hot tub. Fishing, backpacking, white-water rafting, snowmobiling, skiing, and historic museums are all close by. Long-term family stays are welcome.

Hosts: Dexter and Carole Smith
Rooms: 3 (SB) $50
Full Breakfast
Credit Cards: None
Notes: 2, 3, 4, 5, 6, 7, 10, 11

WILSON

Teton View Bed and Breakfast

2136 Coyote Loop, PO Box 652, 83014
(307) 733-7954

Rooms have mountain views. The lounge eating area where homemade pasteries, fresh fruit, and coffee are served, connects to a private upper deck with fantastic mountian and ski resort views. Private entrance. Convenient to Yellowstone and Grand Teton National Parks. Approx. four miles from the ski area.

Hosts: John and Joanna Engelhart
Rooms: 3 (1PB; 2SB) $60-90
Full Breakfast
Credit Cards: A, B
Closed April and Nov.
Notes: 2, 4, 7, 8, 9, 10, 11, 12

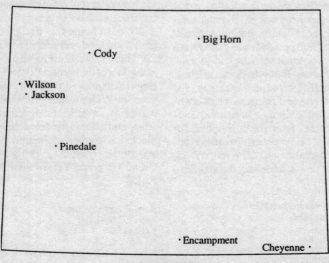

WYOMING

NOTES: Credit cards accepted: A Master Card; B Visa; C American Express; D Discover Card; E Diners Club; F Other; 2 Personal checks accepted; 3 Lunch available; 4 Dinner available; 5 Open all

Alberta

Cougar Creek Inn

CANMORE

Cougar Creek Inn
P.O. Box 1162, T0L 0M0
(403)678-4751

Quiet, rustic, cedar chalet with mountain views in every direction. Grounds border on Cougar Creek and are surrounded by rugged mountain scenery which invites all types of outdoor activity. Hostess has strong love for the mountains and can assist with plans for local hiking, skiing, canoeing, mountain biking, backpacking, etc., as well as scenic drives. The bed and breakfast has a private entrance with sitting area, fireplace, games, TV, sauna and numerous reading materials for guests' use. Breakfasts are hearty and wholesome with many home-baked items.

Hostess: Mrs. Patricia Doucette
Rooms: 4 (SB) $55-60 (Canadian)
Full Breakfast
Credit Cards: None
Notes: 2, 3, 5, 7, 8, 9, 10, 11

NANTON

Timber Ridge Homestead
Box 94, T0L 1R0
(403) 646-2480 (winter); (403) 646-5683 (summer)

Timber Ridge Homestead is a rustic establishment in beautiful foothills ranching country about 70 miles SW of Calgary. We have good, quiet horses to help you see the abundant wild flowers, wild life and wonderful views of the Rockies. Good plain cooking if you want it. To get here, go to Nanton, 50 miles south of Calgary, drive West on highway 533 for 4 miles, turn south and follow winding road into hills for twelve miles and the gate is on the right.

Hostess: Bridget Jones
Rooms: 3 (SB) $25 per person
Full Breakfast
Credit Cards: None
Notes: 2, 3, 4, 7

welcome; 7 Children welcome; 8 Tennis nearby; 9 Swimming nearby; 10 Golf nearby; 11 Skiing nearby; 12 May be booked through travel agent

British Columbia

CLINTON

Kelly Lake Ranch B&B

Box 547, V0K 1K0
(604) 459-2313

Historic Kelly Lake Ranch B&B—Ranch house and three log cabins on original Cariboo Gold Rush Trail. Breakfst in sun room overlooking gardens, corrals, and Kelly Lake. Other meals on request. Horses and boats. Art studio/gallery. Eleven miles west of Clinton on paved Kelly Lake Road. German spoken.

Hostess: Mrs. Karin (P.T.L) Lange
Rooms: 5 (SB) $50-60 for cabin
Full Breakfast
Credit Cards: None
Notes: 2 (and travelers' checks), 4, 5, 9, 11, 12

DUNCAN

Fairburn Farm Country Manor

3310 Jackson Rd., RR#7, V9L 4W4
(604) 746-4637 (voice or FAX)

Secluded 130 acre farm thirty miles north of Victoria. Victorian manor house. Organic fruit and vegetables, grind wheat for flour, and churn golden butter from brown swiss cows. Bedrooms with queen or twin beds and private bathrooms. Library,

sitting room, and terrace. Trails, mountain stream, fields, virgin timber, reforestation, working sheepdogs, antique sawmill, and barns. Approved by Fodor Canada's *Great Country Inns and Sanctuaries.*

Hosts: Darrel and Anthea Archer
Rooms: 6 (PB) $80-110 (US equivalent)
Full Breakfast
Credit Cards: A
Notes: 2, 7, 8, 9, 10, 12

Fairburn Farm Country Manor

FORT STEELE

Wild Horse Farm Bed and Breakfast

Box 7, V0B 1N0
(604) 426-6000

Step back into a time of leisure and luxury

NOTES: Credit cards accepted: A Master Card; B Visa; C American Express; D Discover Card; E Diners Club; F Other; 2 Personal checks accepted; 3 Lunch available; 4 Dinner available; 5 Open all year; 6 Pets

at Wild Horse Farm, a secluded, historic, park-like 80-acre estate in the Canadian Rocky Mountains adjoining Fort Steele Historic Town. The log covered home was built by the New York Astors in the early 1900's with spacious high ceilinged rooms, five fieldstone fireplaces, and antique furnishings. Screened verandas invite you to relax in a setting which reflects generations of tradition and comfort. Awaken to hot tea or coffee brought to your room. Enjoy a leisurely gourmet breakfast later in the dining room.

Hosts: Bob and Orma Termuende
Rooms: 5 (2PB; 3SB) $58-93
Full Breakfast
Credit Cards: None
Notes: 5, 7 (by arrangement), 8, 9, 10, 11, 12 (10%)

MILL BAY/VANCOUVER ISLAND

Pine Lodge Farm Bed and Breakfast

3191 Mutter Road, V0R 2P0
(604) 743-4083; (604) 743-7134 (FAX)

Our beautiful antique-filled lodge is located 25 miles north of Victoria. It is situated on a 30-acre farm overlooking ocean and islands. Arbutus trees, walking trails, farm animals, and wild deer add to the idyllic setting. Each room has en suite baths and shower. Full farm breakfast. No smoking.

Hosts: Cliff and Barb Clarke
Rooms: 7 (PB) $75-85
Cottage: 1 (PB) $110-160
Full Breakfast
Credit Cards: A, B
Notes: 2, 5, 10, 12

NAKUSP

"Country" Bed and Breakfast

1012 Hwy. 6 East, V0G 1P0
(604) 265-4448

"Country" B&B boast private entrance to three guest rooms which include shared bathroom, sitting room with cable TV/VCR, library, and phone. B&B can accommodate up to eight people. Pets welcome and outdoor paddocks available for those travelling with horses. Located five km from downtown Nakusp and close to the Hot Springs, golf, hiking, biking and riding trails, skiing, marina, beach, and fishing. Closed Friday nights.

Hosts: John and Elena Walker
Rooms: 3 (SB) $45
Full Breakfast
Credit Cards: None
Notes: 2, 5, 6 (+ horses), 7, 8, 9, 10, 11

Country Hills Bed and Breakfast

RR 1., S10, C17, (108 Henke Road), V0G 1R0
(604) 265-3004

Country Hills is located in the exquisite setting of Arrow Lakes Vacation Country in central British Columbia. It backs onto a nine hole golf course with driving range and is within an hour drive of three other nine hole courses. Nearby trails offer walking in summer and cross-country skiing in winter. Nakusp Hot Springs is only a 30 minute drive away through gorgeous mountain scenery. Fishing, swimming, water skiing, and marina are all available on Upper Arrow Lake in Nakusp. A full

---

welcome; 7 Children welcome; 8 Tennis nearby; 9 Swimming nearby; 10 Golf nearby; 11 Skiing nearby; 12 May be booked through travel agent

country breakfast is served daily.

Hostesses: Anne Lang and Audrey Shandro
Rooms: 3 (SB)
Full Breakfast
Credit Cards: None
Notes: 2, 5, 6, 7, 8, 9, 10, 11, 12

NANOOSE BAY

The Lookout at Schooner Cove

3381 Dolphin Drive, V0R 2R0
(604) 468-9796 (voice and FAX)

Situated midway between Victoria and Tofino on Vancouver island our West Coast contemporary home is in a natural woodsy setting with a wraparound deck affording a 180° view of Georia Strait with its many islands and a backdrop of coastal mountains of the mainland. Relax and enjoy a hearty breakfast while watching

for orca whales, majestic eagles, sea lions, sail boats, and Alaskan cruise ships. Picturesque Schooner Cove Marina and famous Fairwinds golf course are at our doorstep. Fishing charters available.

Hosts: Marj and Herb Wilkie
Rooms: 4 (2PB; 2SB) $55-80 Canadian
Self-contained Suite: $450 weekly
Full Breakfast
Credit Cards: None
Notes: 2, 8, 9, 10, 11, 12

ORTH DELTA

Sunshine Hills Bed and Breakfast

11200 Bond Blvd., V4E 1M7
(604) 596-6496; (604) 596-2560 (FAX)

Private entrance. Two cozy bedrooms with TV, shared bathroom, and a beautiful gardens. Close to U.S. Border, airport, and ferries (20 minutes). Kitchenette. We are originally Dutch, very European. Breakfast includes fresh fruit, orange juice, and much more. Your host knows the city very well and can be of help to all the guests.

Hosts: Putzi and Wim Honing
Rooms: 2 (SB) $50
Full Breakfast
Credit Cards: None
Notes: 7, 8, 10

UCLUELET

B&B at Burley's

Box 550, 1078 Helen Road, V0R 3A0
(604) 726-4444

A waterfront home on a small "drive to" island at the harbor mouth. Watch the ducks and birds play, heron, and kingfisher work, and eagles soar. In the harbor, trollers, draggers, and seiners attract the gulls. Loggers work in the distant hills. There is a view from every window, a large livingroom, fireplace, books, and recreation room with pool table.

Hosts: Ron Burley and Micheline Burley
Rooms: 6 (SB) $45-65
Continental Breakfast
Credit Cards: A, B
Notes: 8, 9, 10

VANCOUVER

AAA Bed and Breakfasts

658 East 29 Avenue, V5V 2R9
(604) 872-0938; (604) 877-7786 (FAX)

Affordable, comfortable accommodation in quiet neighborhood. Ten minutes from downtown and walking distance to Queen Elizabeth Park.

Hosts: Catherine and Robert
Rooms: 6 (3PB; 3SB) $45-89
Full Breakfast
Credit Cards: A, B
Notes: 5, 7, 8, 10, 11, 12

Beautiful B&B

428 West 40 Avenue, V5Y 2R4
(604) 327-1102 (voice and FAX)

Gorgeous colonial home furnished with antiques, fresh flowers, and views from bedrooms. Great central location five minutes to Downtown. Walking distance to tennis, golf, Queen Elizabeth Park, Van Dusen Gardens, swimming, the X, three cinemas, and a major shopping center. Friendly helpful host, quiet street, comfortable beds, and a generous breakfast

served in a formal dining room. Luxurious suite with pink, marble fireplace, large balcony, views (north and south), double sinks, and extra large tub.

Hosts: Corinne and Ian Sanderson
Rooms: 5 (1PB; 4SB) $70-150 (Canadian)
Full Breakfast
Credit Cards: None
Notes: 7 (over 14), 8, 9, 10, 11, 12

Green Gables Bed and Breakfast

Green Gables Bed and Breakfast

628 Union Street, V6A 2B9
(604) 253-6230

Receive a warm welcome and friendly hospitality at Green Gables. Recently renovated, this 1898 heritage home is only one block from public transport or a ten-minute walk to downtown. Our twin rooms are bright and comfortable and guests are encouraged to feel at home in the living and dining areas, as well as, the back sundeck overlooking the colorful garden. Over a delicious full breakfast

welcome; 7 Children welcome; 8 Tennis nearby; 9 Swimming nearby; 10 Golf nearby; 11 Skiing nearby; 12 May be booked through travel agent

plans are made for the day and your well-traveled hosts are glad to help with tourist info. Smoking outside. We are looking forward to your visit.

Hosts: Carl and Mariko Shepherd
Rooms: 7 (SB) $40-59
Full Breakfast
Credit Cards: None
Notes: 5, 7, 8, 11

VERNON

Citylights Bed and Breakfast

R.R. #8, S-9, C-9, V1T 8L6
(604) 542-5086 (voice and FAX)

New home on ten acres with panoramic view of the Okanagan Valley and city. Enjoy our friendly relaxed atmosphere in our lovely country setting. We serve a healthy European-style breakfast. Each room has its own private bath. Separate entrance. Laundry facilities available. Please, no smoking or pets. Adult oriented. German speaking; *wir sprechen deutsch.*

Hosts: Frank and Lotte Meissner
Rooms: 3 (PB) $65-85
Full European-style Breakfast
Credit Cards: B
Notes: 2, 3, 4, 5, 9, 10, 11, 12

VICTORIA

AA—Accommodations West B&B Service

660 Jones Terrace, V8Z 2L7
(604) 479-1986; (604) 479-9999 (FAX)

No reservation fee. Over seventy choice locations. Inspected and approved. Ocean view, farm tranquility, cozy cottage, city convenience, historic heritage! Assistance with itineraries includes **Victoria, Vancouver Island,** and some **adjacent islands.** For competent, caring service, call Doreen. C.P. 7 days. Open 7AM-10PM Monday thru Saturday and 2PM-9PM on Sundays.

All Seasons Bed and Breakfast Agency Inc.

PO Box 5511 Station B, V8R 6S4
(604) 655-7173

All the best B&B of **Victoria, Vancouver Island,** and the **Gulf Islands.** Specializing in waterfront and garden homes and inns. There's an accommodation style for everyone. When you want to get away from it all, trips are much more enjoyable with a bit of advance planning. You know where you'll be welcome at night, so you can travel for the sheer fun of it. Listing approx. 40 B&Bs. Visa, MasterCard, and personal checks accepted. Kate Catterill, coordinator.

Battery Street Guest House

670 Battery Street, V8V 1E5
(604) 385-4632

Newly renovated guesthouse, built in 1898 with four bright comfortable rooms, two with bathrooms. Centrally located within walking distance to Downtown, Beacon Hill Park, and Victoria's scenic Marine Drive only one block away. A full hearty

---

NOTES: Credit cards accepted: A Master Card; B Visa; C American Express; D Discover Card; E Diners Club; F Other; 2 Personal checks accepted; 3 Lunch available; 4 Dinner available; 5 Open all year; 6 Pets

breakfast served by a Dutch hostess. No smoking.

Hostess: Pamela Verduyn
Rooms: 4 (2 PB; 2 SB) $65-85 (US)
Full Breakfast
Credit Cards: None
Notes: 2

Dashwood Seaside Manor

1 Cook Street, V8V 3W6
(604) 385-5517

Enjoy the comfort and privacy of your own elegant suite in one of Victoria's traditional Tudor mansions. Gaze out your window at the ocean and America's Olympic Mountains. If you're an early riser, you may see seals, killer whales, or sea otters frollicking offshore. Watch an eagle cruise by. Help yourself to breakfast from your private, well-stocked kitchen. You're minutes away from the attractions of town. Stroll there through beautiful Beacon Hill Park.

Host: Derek Dashwood
Rooms: 14 (PB) $65-240
Self-catered, Full Breakfast
Credit Cards: A, B, C
Notes: 2, 5, 6 (small), 7, 8, 10, 12

Graham's Cedar House

Graham's Cedar House Bed and Breakfast

1825 Lands End Road, Sidney, V8L 5J2
(604) 655-3699; (604) 655-1422 (FAX)

Modern air-conditioned chalet home nestled in a six-acre wooded country estate where tall Douglas firs sprinkle sunlight over lush fern beds. Stretch out in spacious, beautifully appointed one or two bedroom suites with king/queen beds and private patio deck entrances overlooking natural strolling gardens featuring statuary, fountains, and benches. Explore our forest, walk to beach, marinas, or British-stlye "Pub." Breakfast served at your convenience. Close to Victoria, Butchart Gardens, and USA/Canadian ferries.

Hosts: Dennis and Kay Graham
Rooms: 2 suites (PB) $75-125 (Canadian funds)
Full Breakfast
Credit Cards: A, B
Notes: 5, 7 (over 10), 8, 9, 10, 12

Gregory's Guest House

5373 Pat Bay Hwy. (Route 17), V8Y 1S9
(604) 658-8404; (604) 658-4604 (FAX)

Early 1900s farmstead overlooking Elk Lake features farm animals, gardens, and country setting. Only ten minutes from downtown. Bountiful complimentary breakfast served in the cozy parlor with fireplace and antique furnishings. Convenient to ferries, airport, and Buchart Gardens.

Hosts: Elizabeth and Paul Gregory
Rooms: 4 (2 PB; 2 SB) $65-75
Full Breakfast
Credit Cards: A
Notes: 2, 7, 8, 9, 10, 12

Oak Bay Guesthouse

1052 Newport Avenue, V8S 5E3
(604) 598-3812

Built from designs by famous architect Samuel McLure. This classy, 1912 inn, established since 1922, has your comfort at heart. Set in beautiful gardens in the prime peaceful location of Oak Bay, only one block from the water and minutes from Downtown. Ten rooms with private bathrooms, antiques; sitting room with Inglenook fireplace; sunroom with Library and TV. Home-cooked breakfast. Golf, shopping, and city bus at door.

Hosts: Pam and Dave Vandy
Rooms: 10 (PB) $79-165 (Canadian)
Full Breakfast
Credit Cards: A, B
Notes: 8, 9, 10, 12

Peggy's Cove Bed and Breakfast

279 Coal Point Lane, R.R. #1, Sidney, V8L 3R9
(604) 656-5656; (604) 655-3118 (FAX)

Spoil yourself! Come join me in my beautiful home bordered by spectacular ocean views on all sides. Imagine a gourmet breakfast on the sundeck, watching sea lions at play, eagles soaring, and if you are lucky a family of killer whales may appear. Enjoy fishing at your doorstep, a stroll on the beach, and, in the evening, canoe into the sunset then spend a romantic moment in the **"hot tub under the stars."** Victoria's world famous Butchart Gardens, BC and Anacortes Ferries are only minutes away. Many consider Peggy's Cove a honeymoon paradise.

Hostess: Peggy Waibel
Rooms: 3 (1PB; 2SB) $100 + (US)
Full Gourmet Breakfast
Credit Cards: None
Notes: 2, 5, 6, 7, 8, 9, 10, 12

Peggy's Cove Bed and Breakfast

Prior House Bed and Breakfast Inn

620 St. Charles Street, V8S 3N7
(604) 592-8847; (604) 592-8223 (FAX)

Formerly a private residence of the English Crown, this grand B&B inn has all the amenities of the finest European inn. Featuring rooms with fireplaces, marble jacuzzi tubs, ocean and mountain views, sumptuous breakfasts, and afternoon tea. Special private suites available for families. Rated as "Outstanding" by *Northwest Best Places* and AAA—3-diamond.

Hostess: Candis C. Cooperrider
Rooms: 7 (PB) $73-190 (US)
Full Breakfast
Credit Cards: A, B
Notes: 5, 7 , 8, 10

NOTES: Credit cards accepted: A Master Card; B Visa; C American Express; D Discover Card; E Diners Club; F Other; 2 Personal checks accepted; 3 Lunch available; 4 Dinner available; 5 Open all year; 6 Pets

Sonia's Bed and Breakfast by the Sea

175 Bushby St., V8S 1B5
(604) 385-2700; (800) 667-4489; (604) 744-3763 (FAX)

Sonia has queen- and king-size beds, private bathrooms with a big, hot breakfast. The new suite looks out over the Straits of Juan de Fuca. A lovely walk to the Inner Harbour—Empress Hotel. Close to everything—shopping, good restaurants, Beacon Hill Park, and bus at door. No smoking. Adults only.

Hosts: Sonia and Brian McMillan
Rooms: 3 + 1 suite (PB) $55-150 (US)
Full Hot Breakfast
Credit Cards: None
Notes: 2, 8, 9, 10, 12 (no commission)

Top O'Triangle Mountain

3442 Karger Terr, V9C 3K5
(604) 478-7853; (604) 478-2245 (FAX)

Our home, built of solid cedar construction, boasts a spectacular view of Victoria, the Juan de Fuca Strait, and the Olympia Mountains in Washington. We are a relaxed household with few rules, lots of hospitality, and clean, comfortable rooms. A hearty breakfast is different each morning.

Hosts: Pat and Henry Hansen
Rooms: 3 (PB) $65-85 Canadian
Full Home-cooked Breakfast (different each morning)
Credit Cards: A, B
Notes: 5, 8, 9, 10, 12

Wellington Bed and Breakfast

66 Wellington Avenue, V8V 4H5
(604) 383-5976; (604) 385-0477 (FAX)

You're in for a treat of the finest Victorian hospitality in this 1912, fully restored, Edwardian B&B. Inge is an interior designer and each room is specially designed with private baths, queen or king bed, walk-in closet, duvets, lace, and some fireplaces. A guest living room offers books and relaxation. Only ½ block from ocean and bus. A 20-minute walk will take you to downtown through the park. Only minutes from shops, restaurants, and sites. A full, delicious breakfast is served in the dining room.

Hosts: Inge and Sue Ranzinger
Rooms: 4 (PB) $65-90 Can. or $50-70 US
Full Breakfast
Credit Cards: A
Notes: 2, 5, 7 (over 12), 8, 9, 10, 12

Top O'Triangle Mountain

WEST VANCOUVER

Beachside Bed and Breakfast

4208 Evergreen Avenue, V7V 1H1
(604) 922-7773; (800) 563-3311; (604) 926-8073 (FAX)

Guests are welcomed to this beautiful waterfront home with a basket of fruit and fresh flowers. Situated on a quiet cul-de-sac in an exclusive area of the city, the house, with Spanish architecture accented by antique stained glass windows, affords a panoramic view of Vancouver's busy harbor. There are private baths, a patio leading to the beach, and a large jacuzzi at the seashore, where you can watch seals swim by daily. Near sailing, fishing, hiking, golf, downhill skiing, and antique shopping.

Hosts: Gordon and Joan Gibbs
Rooms: 3 (PB) $73-130 (US) $100-180 (Canada)
Full Breakfast
Credit Cards: A, B
Notes: 2, 5, 8, 10, 11, 12, 13

WHISTLER

Golden Dreams Bed and Breakfast

6412 Easy Street, V0N 1B6
(604) 932-2667; (800) 668-7055; (604) 932-7055 (FAX)

Uniquely decorated Victorian, Oriental and Aztec theme rooms feature sherry decanter, cozy duvets. Relax in the luxurious private jacuzzi and awake to a nutritious vegetarian breakfast including homemade jams and fresh herbs served in the country kitchen. A short walk to the valley trail to village activities and restaurants.

Hostess: Ann Spence
Rooms: 3 (1PB; 2SB) $65-95
Full Breakfast
Credit Cards: A, B
Notes: 2, 5. 7, 8, 9, 10, 11

NOTES: Credit cards accepted: A Master Card; B Visa; C American Express; D Discover Card; E Diners Club; F Other; 2 Personal checks accepted; 3 Lunch available; 4 Dinner available; 5 Open all year; 6 Pets

New Brunswick

FREDERICTON

Appelot B&B

R.R. 4 (Located on Hwy. 105), E3B 4X5
(506) 444-8083

Attractive farmhouse overlooking the St. John River. Three bedrooms with a view in a restful country atmosphere. Full homemade breakfast served on the spacious sunporch. Orchards and woodlands with walking trails, "a bird-watcher's delight." Board games, TV, VCR, books, and piano inside; picnic table, gas BBQ, and lawn swing outside. Area attractions include several golf courses, Mactaquac Park, Kings Landing Historical Village, museums in Fredericton, the Beaverbrook Art Gallery, and the Provincial Archives.

Hostess: Elsie Myshrall
Rooms: 3 (1PB; 2SB) $55
Full Breakfast
Credit Cards: None
Open May 1 through October 31
Notes: 2, 9, 10, 12

Appelot Bed and Breakfast

Carriage House Inn

230 University Avenue, E3B 4H7
(506) 452-9924; (506) 458-0799 (FAX)

The Carriage House may be Fredericton's Heritage Inn, but it offers modern convenience: off-street parking, wake-up calls, a library, and FAX service. The location is perfect, just a few paces from Fredericton's Green along the St. John River at the edge of the historic preservation area. Within strolling distance are the Christ Church Cathedral, art galleries, the Legislative Assembly Building, restaurants, and craft shops. Three-star propery.

Hosts: Joan, Nathan, and Frank Gorham
Rooms: 10 (5PB; 5SB) $55-80
Full Breakfast
Credit Cards: A, B
Notes: 2, 5, 7, 8, 9, 10, 11, 12

Carriage House Inn

welcome; 7 Children welcome; 8 Tennis nearby; 9 Swimming nearby; 10 Golf nearby; 11 Skiing nearby; 12 May be booked through travel agent

Nova Scotia

Amherst Shore Country Inn

AMHERST

Amherst Shore Country Inn

RR 2 Amherst (Highway 366), B4H 3X9
(902) 661-4800; (800) 661-ASCI

Escape to the quiet natural beauty of Nova Scotia's Northumberland Strait. This renovated century-old farmhouse offers comfortable rooms, suites, cottages, and country style gourmet meals. Enjoy a walk on our 600-foot long private beach before having dinner served at 7:30PM (with reservation) each night. Curried potato soup, sole stuffed with crab, chicken with brandied cream sauce, and meringue torte with almond butter are representative of what dinner is like each night. Open May 1 to October 13, 1994.

Hostess: Donna Laceby
Rooms: 8 (PB) $99-119
Full Breakfast (additional fee)
Credit Cards: A, B
Notes: 4 (by reservation), 9, 10, 12

Victoria Garden

196 Victoria St. East, B4H 1Y9
(902) 667-2278; (902) 667-6161 (FAX)

Situated on the famous Sunrise Trail in downtown Amherst is an elegant, circa 1903, Victorian home on a tree-lined street in the midst of heritage properties. Each room is tastefully decorated and has antique furniture. For the guests enjoyment we also have fireplaces, piano, organ, TV, VCR, and barbecue. Full breakfast—house specialty Nova Scotia blueberry pancakes with Nova Scotia maple syrup. Pleased to cater to special diets with prior notice. Tea and sweets served in the evening. Smoking is limited to the out of doors. Rated 3½ stars by the Tourism Industry of Nova Scotia Canada Select.

Hosts: Carl and Bea Brander
Rooms: 3 (1PB; 2SB) $45-55
Full Breakfast
Credit Cards: None
Notes: 8, 9, 10, 11, 12

NOTES: Credit cards accepted: A Master Card; B Visa; C American Express; D Discover Card; E Diners Club; F Other; 2 Personal checks accepted; 3 Lunch available; 4 Dinner available; 5 Open all year; 6 Pets

Blomidon Inn

WOLFVILLE

Blomidon Inn

P.O. Box 839, 127 Main St., B0P 1X0
(902) 542-2291; (902) 542-7461 (FAX)

Escape to Nova Scotia's Annapolis Val-

ley and visit our beautifully restored 19th century sea-captain's mansion for a relaxed lunch or dinner. We offer Christmas parties, corporate gatherings, and other memorable times. Or, perhaps a getaway in one of our 26 guest rooms (all with ensuite baths), many with four-poster beds. Either way, you'll find yourself transported back to the style and relaxation of the Victorian era, without sacrificing the modern amenities. Come be our guest.

Hosts: Jim and Donna Laceby
Rooms: 26 (PB) $79-129 Canadian
Continental Buffet Breakfast
Credit Cards: A, B
Notes: 3, 4, 5 (except Christmas), 7 (limited), 8, 10, 11, 12

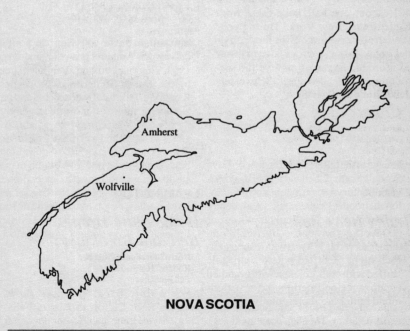

Amherst

Wolfville

NOVA SCOTIA

welcome; 7 Children welcome; 8 Tennis nearby; 9 Swimming nearby; 10 Golf nearby; 11 Skiing nearby; 12 May be booked through travel agent

Ontario

CARDINAL

Roduner Farm
R.R. 1, K0E 1E0
(613) 657-4830

Enjoy true country hospitality at our 300-acre active dairy farm. We are located just three miles north of Cardinal, one and one-half miles north of Trans Canada Route 401, about one-half hour drive from Ogdensburg, New York. During your stay here observe some of the farm activities, relax on our spacious lawn or in our comfortable home, or explore the surroundings. We also speak Schweizerdeutsch and a little French.

Hosts: Walter and Margareta Roduner
Rooms: 2 (1PB; 1SB) $32-40
Full Breakfast
Credit Cards: None
Notes: 2, 4 (by arrangement), 5, 6, 7, 8, 9, 10, 11

ELMIRA

Teddy Bear Bed and Breakfast
Wyndham Hall, RR 1, N3B 2Z1
(519) 669-2379; (519) 669-3271 (FAX)

Hospitality abounds in our gracious countryside converted 1907 schoolhouse, minutes from Elmira. The elegance and charm of our home is enhanced by antiques and Canadian and Old Order Mennonite handmade quilts and hooked rugs. Beautifully decorated bedrooms. Lounge; complimentary refeshments; and full country-style breakfasts. "Truly a magical heritage and cultural hideaway in horse and buggy country." Close to Elora, Kitchener-Waterloo, St. Jacob's, and Stratford.

Hosts: Gerrie and Vivian Smith
Rooms: 3 (PB) $65 (Canadian)
Full Breakfast
Credit Cards: A, B
Notes: 2, 5, 10, 11, 12

Teddy Bear Bed and Breakfast

LEAMINGTON

Home Suite Home Bed and Breakfast
115 Erie Street South, N8H 3B5
(519) 326-7169

Near Point Pelee National Park. Enroute from Detroit to Niagra Falls. Home Suite Home features 2 honeymoon

---

NOTES: Credit cards accepted: A Master Card; B Visa; C American Express; D Discover Card; E Diners Club; F Other; 2 Personal checks accepted; 3 Lunch available; 4 Dinner available; 5 Open all year; 6 Pets

suites, 2 additional rooms, and large inground pool. Large, traditional home decorated Victorian Country. Four and one-half baths, plush carpet, and fine linen. In house central air, hearty, full, country breakfast. Area attractions include dinner theaters, cycling and canoeing, tropical gardens, and trips to Pelee Island. Log-burning fireplace for cool winter evenings. No smoking. No pets. Agatha is coordinator for Point Pelee Bed and Breakfast Association.

Hosts: Harry and Agatha Tiessen
Rooms: 5 (PB) $40-65
Full Breakfast
Credit Cards: None
Notes: 2, 5, 9, 10

Camelot Country Inn

MADOC

Camelot Country Inn

R.R. 5, K0K 2K0
(613) 473-0441

Relax in the quiet, country setting of our 1853 brick and stone home. It is surrounded by plantings of red and white pine on 25 acres of land in the heart of Hastings County. Original woodwork and oak floors have been lovingly preserved. There are three guest rooms available, two doubles and one twin. The full breakfast may be

chosen by guests from the country breakfast or one of two gourmet breakfasts.

Hostess: Marian Foster
Rooms: 3 (SB) $45
Full Breakfast
Credit Cards: None
Notes: 2, 4 (by arrangement), 5, 7, 9, 10, 11

NIAGARA FALLS

Gretna Green Bed and Breakfast

5077 River Rd., L2E 3G7
(905) 357-2081

A warm welcome awaits you in this Scots-Canadian home overlooking the Niagara River Gorge. All rooms are air-conditioned and have their own TV. Included in the rate is a full breakfast with home-made scones and muffins. We also pick up at the train or bus stations. Many people have called this a "home away from home."

Hosts: Stan and Marg Gardiner
Rooms: 4 (PB) $45 (Oct-April), $55 (May-Sept.) (Canadian funds)
Full Breakfast
Credit Cards: None
Notes: 5, 7, 8, 10

NOTTAWA (NEAR COLLINGWOOD)

Pretty River Valley Farm Inn

R.R. #1, L0M 1P0
(705) 445-7598 (voice and FAX)

Cozy, quiet country inn in scenic Blue Mountains overlooking Pretty River Valley Wilderness Park. Distinctive pine fur-

welcome; 7 Children welcome; 8 Tennis nearby; 9 Swimming nearby; 10 Golf nearby; 11 Skiing nearby; 12 May be booked through travel agent

nished studios and suites with in-room fireplaces and ensuite baths. Suites also have in-room whirlpools for two. Spa; AC. Close to Collingwood, beaches, golfing, fishing, hiking (Bruce Trail), bicycle paths, antique shops, and restaurants. Complimentary tea served on arrival. No smoking.

Hosts: Steve and Diane Szelestowski
Rooms: 8 (6 studios + 2 suites) (PB) $65-100
Full Breakfast
Credit Cards: A, B
Notes: 5, 7 (well behaved), 8, 9, 10, 11, 12

Auberge McGEE'S Inn

OTTAWA

Auberge McGEE'S Inn

185 Daly Avenue, K1N 6E8
(613) 237-6089; (613) 237-6021 (FAX)
Note: Phone and fax numbers in our exchange area may change in the new year. Please check number(s) with Directory Enquiries if encountering difficulty.

A 14-room, smoke-free, historic Victorian inn celebrating 10+ great years of award-winning hospitality! Centrally located downtown on a quiet avenue withing walking distance of excellent restaurants, museums, Parliament, canal, and University of Ottawa. Rooms with cable TV, phone, jacuzzi ensuites. Kitchenette facili-

ties for longer stays. Recommended by AAA. Full breakfast served in Art Deco dining room. All denominations welcome.

Hostesses: Anne Schutte and Mary Unger
Rooms: 14 (10 PB; 4 SB) $58-150 (Canadian)
Full Breakfast
Credit Cards: A, B
Notes: 5, 7, 8, 9, 10, 11

Australis Guest House

35 Marlborough Avenue, K1N 8E6
(613) 235-8461

We are the oldest, established, and still operating bed and breakfast in the Ottawa area. Located on a quiet, tree-lined street one block from the Rideau River, with its ducks and swans, and Strathcona Park. We are a 20-minute walk from the parliament buildings. This period house boasts leaded-glass windows, fireplaces, oak floors, and unique eight-foot-high stained-glass windows overlooking the hall. Hearty, home-cooked breakfasts with home-baked breads and pastries. Winner of the Ottawa Hospitality Award for April 1989. Recommended by *Newsweek*, January 1990, and featured in the *Ottawa Sun* newspaper, January 1992 for our Australian bread. Baby sitting is available.

Hosts: Carol and Brian Waters
Rooms: 3 (1 PB; 2 SB) $49-65 (Canadian)
Full Breakfast
Credit Cards: None
Notes: 2, 5, 7, 8

STRATFORD

Burnside Guest Home

139 William Street, N5A 4X9
(519) 271-7076; (519) 393-5239 (FAX)

Burnside is a turn-of-the-century home on

the north shore of Lake Victoria, the site of the first Stratford logging mill. The home features many family heirlooms and antiques and is centrally air-conditioned. Our rooms have been redecorated with light and cheery colors. Relax in the gardens overlooking the Avon River on handcrafted furniture amid the rose, herb, herbaceous, and annual flower gardens. Within walking distance of Shakespearean theaters. Stratford is the home of a world renowned Shakespearean festival from early-May to mid-November. Also enjoy farmers' market, Mennonite country, art and craft shops, outstanding architecture, and the outdoor Art in the Park.

Host: Lester J. Wilker
Rooms: 4 (SB) $50-65 Canadian; (student rates available)
Full Breakfast
Credit Cards: A
Notes: 2, 5, 7, 8, 9, 10, 11

Burken Guest House

TORONTO

Burken Guest House

322 Palmerston Blvd., M6G 2N6
(416) 920-7842; (416) 960-9529 (FAX)

Lovely, non-smoking home located in Downtown close to all attractions. Eight guest rooms furnished with antiques, washbasin, telephone, and ceiling fans. Continental breakfast served on deck in summer. TV-lounge, parking, and maid-service.

Hosts: Burke and Ken
Rooms: 8 (SB) $60-65 (Canadian)
Continental Breakfast
Credit Cards: A, B
Notes: 5, 12

Toronto Bed and Breakfast Inc.

Box 269, 253 College St., M5T 1R5
(416) 588-8800; (416) 596-1118; (416) 977-2601 (FAX)

Let us simplify your travel plans throughout **Metro Toronto, Ottowa, Kingston, and Niagara Falls!** Now in its 16th year, Toronto's oldest and original bed and breakfast registry is serving the entire area. Our reservation service of quality inspected B&B homes provides a high level of safety, comfort, cleanliness, and hospitality. Advance reservation recommended; free brochure on request. Traveler's checks, Visa, MC, AE, DC.

Prince Edward Island

MURRAY RIVER

Bayberry Cliff Inn

R. R. 4, Little Sands, C0A 1W0
(902) 962-3395

Located on the edge of a 40-foot cliff are two uniquely redecorated post-and-beam barns, antiques, and marine art. Seven rooms have double beds, three with extra sleeping lofts. One room has two single beds. Two rooms, including the honeymoon suite, have private bath. Seals, occasional whale sightings, restaurants, swimming, innertubing, and craft shops are all nearby.

Hosts: Don and Nancy Perkins
Rooms: 8 (2PB; 6SB) $45-75
Full Breakfast
Credit Cards: A, B
Notes: 2, 9, 10, 12

O'LEARY

Smallman's Bed and Breakfast

Knutsford, Rural Route 1, C0B 1V0
(902) 859-3469 or (902) 859-2664 (please call AM or after 6 PM)

We have a split-level house with a garage on the west end and brick gate posts. We have a horse racetrack behind the house where some guests like to go for a walk. There are churches, stores, craft shops, tennis, golf, and museums. Lovely beaches for relaxing, walking, and watching the sun on the waters. We live in a quiet, country area on Route 142 off Hwy. 2 or Hwy. 14. Come into O'Leary and go four miles west. Travelers checks accepted. Three-star rating.

Hostess: Eileen Smallman
Rooms: 4 (SB) $25-40
Full or Continental Breakfast
Credit Cards: None
Notes: 3, 4, 5, 6 (on leash), 7, 8, 9, 10, 11, 12

NOTES: Credit cards accepted: A Master Card; B Visa; C American Express; D Discover Card; E Diners Club; F Other; 2 Personal checks accepted; 3 Lunch available; 4 Dinner available; 5 Open all year; 6 Pets

Quebec

DESCHAMBAULT

Auberge Du Roy

106-rue St-Laurent, GOA ISO
(418)286-6958

Between Montreal and Quebec, the town of Deschambault invites you to discover its historic past by staying at our Victorian inn. Our antiques will make you feel serenity and romance near our fireplace. Our guests can also relax with the murmuring waterfall and the St. Lawrence breezes. We hope to see your smile soon.

Hosts: Francine Bouthat, Gilles LaBerge
Rooms: 8 (4 PB; 4 SB) $59-74
Full Breakfast
Credit Cards: B
Notes: 4, 5, 7, 8, 9, 10

Auberge Du Roy

MONTRÉAL

Armor Inn

151 Sherbrooke Est, H2X 1C7
(514)285-0140; (514)284-1126(FAX)

The Armor Inn is a small hotel with a typical European character. In the heart of Montreal, it offers a warm family atmosphere and is ideally situated close to Métro, Saint Denis, and Prince Arthur streets. It is a 15-minute walk to Old Montreal, the Palais of Congress, and numerous underground shopping centers.

Host: Annick Morvan
Rooms: 15 (7 PB; 8 SB) $38-55
Continental Breakfast
Credit Cards: A, B
Notes: 5, 7, 12

Auberge de la Fontaine

1301 Rachel St., East, H2J 2K1
(514)597-0166; (800)597-0597; (514)597-0496 (FAX)

The Auberge de la Fontaine is a nice stone house, newly renovated, where the 21 rooms, in a warm and modern decor, are of unique style in Montréal. Comfortable, friendly atmosphere and attentive, personal service are greatly appreciated by our corporate and leisure travelers. Each room is tastefully decorated. The suites with whirlpool baths, as well as the luxuri-

welcome; 7 Children welcome; 8 Tennis nearby; 9 Swimming nearby; 10 Golf nearby; 11 Skiing nearby; 12 May be booked through travel agent

ous rooms, have brick walls and exclusive fabrics. It will settle you in an elegant and quiet environment. Duvet and decorative pillows will ensure you a cozy comfort. Breakfast is a given at the Auberge. A delicious variety of breakfast foods are set out each morning and you have access to the kitchen for snacks. There are no parking fees. We want our guests to feel comfortable and be entirely satisfied with their stay.

Hostesses: Céline Bourdeau and Jean Lamothe
Rooms: 21 (PB) $99-175 (canadian)
Generous Continental Buffet Breakfast
Credit Cards: A, B, C, E, F
Notes: 5, 7, 8, 9, 12

Auberge de la Fontaine

Hotel Casa Bella Inc.

264 Sherbrooke West, H2X 1X9
(514) 849-2777; (514) 849-3650 (FAX)

The same owner has operated this charming hotel for 21 years. The 100-year-old European-style house has been renovated and is located Downtown, near "La Place Des Arts," U.S. Consulate, Metro, bus, and within walking distance of Old Montreal, Prince Arthur Street, and shop-

ping center. Rooms are comfortable for a low price. Parking is available.

Hostess: Louise Rannou
Rooms: 20 (14 PB; 6 SB) $45-80
Continental Breakfast
Credit Cards: A, B, E
Notes: 5, 7

Le Jardin d'Antoine

2024-rue St-Denis, H2X SK7
(514) 843-4506; (514) 281-1491 (FAX)

Located in the heart of French Montréal in the midst of the Latin Quarter, an area known for its boutiques, restaurants, and terraces. All rooms are fully renovated and have private bathrooms. Some have a double whirlpool. 15-minute drive from Sorval Airport. One block from a main subway station; 15-minute walk to Old Montréal.

Hosts: Antoine and Francine Giardina
Rooms: 20 (PB) $59-130
Full Breakfast
Credit Cards: A, B, C
Notes: 5

Manoir Sherbrooke

157 Sherbrooke Est, H2X 1C7
(514) 845-0915; (516) 284-1126 (FAX)

The Manoir Sherbrooke is a small hotel with a European character offering a family atmosphere. It is convenient to Métro and Saint Denis and Prince Arthur streets. It is within walking distance of Old Montreal, the Palais of Congress, and numerous shopping centers.

Host: Annick Legall
Rooms: 22 (14 PB; 8 SB) $42-70
Continental Breakfast
Credit Cards: A, B
Notes: 5, 7, 12

NOTES: Credit cards accepted: A Master Card; B Visa; C American Express; D Discover Card; E Diners Club; F Other; 2 Personal checks accepted; 3 Lunch available; 4 Dinner available; 5 Open all year; 6 Pets

Bay View Farm

NEW CARLISLE WEST

Bay View Farm

337 Main Highway, Route 132, Box 21, G0C 1Z0
(418) 752-2725 or (418) 752-6718

On the coastline of Quebec's picturesque
Gaspé Peninsula, guests are welcomed
into our comfortable home located on
Route 132, Main Highway. Enjoy fresh
sea air from our wrap-around veranda,
walk, or swim at the beach. Visit natural
and historic sites. Country breakfast, fresh
farm, garden and orchard produce, home
baking, and genuine Gaspesian hospitality.
Light dinners by reservation. Craft, quilting, and folk music workshops. August
Folk Festival. Also a small cottage for
$350 per week. English and French spo-
ken.

Hostess: Helen Sawyer
Rooms: 5 (SB) $35
Full Breakfast
Credit Cards: None
Notes: 3, 4, 5, 7, 8, 9, 10, 11

QUÉBEC

Au Petit Hôtel des Ursulines Enr. (Au Petit Hotel)

3, Ruelle des Ursulines, G1R 3Y6
(418) 694-0965; (418) 692-4320 (FAX)

True to its name, the Au Petit Hotel provides the ideal mix between the intimacy of
a family operated bed and breakfast and a
full service hotel. Located near the St.
Louis gate in the small Ursulines street
within the old city of Quebec, the Au Petit
Hotel opens its doors to you, offering the
kind of lodging which effectively combines
a quiet surrounding within the warm and
hospitable atmosphere of the Old City.

Hosts: The Tims Family
Rooms: 16 (PB) $55-85 (Canadian)
Continental Breakfast
Credit Cards: A, B, C, E
Notes: 2 (for deposit only), 5, 7

Au Petit Hotel

welcome; 7 Children welcome; 8 Tennis nearby; 9 Swimming nearby; 10 Golf nearby; 11 Skiing nearby; 12
May be booked through travel agent

Hayden's Wexford House

450 Rue Champlain, G1K 4J3
(418) 524-0525; (418) 648-8995 (FAX)

Ancestral home built in the beginning of the 18th century, at the heart of our heritage and located in the Old Quebec, and very near the main points of interest. In the summer, relax in the flower garden and in the winter, by the fireside. Enjoy breakfast in a warm decor and relaxed atmosphere.

Host: Michelle Paquet Riviere
Rooms: 3 (SB) $62
Full Breakfast
Credit Cards: B
Notes: 5, 7, 9, 10, 11

Manoir des Remparts

3½ Rue des Remparts, G1R 3R4
(418) 692-2056; (418) 692-1125 (FAX)

Located minutes from the train/bus terminal and the famed Chateau Frontenac, with some rooms overlooking the majestic Saint Lawrence River. The Manior des Remparts boasts having one of the most coveted locations available in the old city of Québec. Newly renovated, it is able to offer its guests a vast choice of rooms ranging from a budget room with shared washrooms, to an all inclusive room with private terrace.

Hostess: Sitheary Ngor
Rooms: 36 (22PB; 14SB) $35-75
Continental Breakfast
Credit Cards: A, B, C
Notes: 5, 7, 11, 12

Tim House (La maison Tim)

84 Rue St-Lous, G1R 3Z5
(418) 694-0776 or (418) 694-0104; (418) 692-4320 (FAX)

Built in 1900 on what is now one of Québec City's main streets, Tim House offers its guests the luxury and charm of its Victorian architecture, complemented by the convenience of its very central location. Breakfast is served daily between 8 and 10 AM in the beautiful dining room located on the second floor. Free parking available. All rooms are non-smoking.

Host: Supheauy Tim
Rooms: 3 (1PB; 2SB) $44-75 Can. (includes tax)
Continental Breakfast
Credit Cards: A, B, C
Notes: 5, 7, 11

NOTES: Credit cards accepted: A MasterCard; B Visa; C American Express; D Discover Card; E Diners Club; F Other; 2 Personal checks accepted; 3 Lunch available; 4 Dinner available; 5 Open all year; 6 Pets

Puerto Rico

CABO ROJO

Parador Perichi's

HC-01, Box 16310, Carr 102, Joyuda, 00623
(809) 851-3131; (809) 851-0560 (FAX)

Parador Perichi's Hotel in Joyuda, Cabo Rojo, site of Puerto Rico's resorts on the West. Excellence has distinguished Perichi's in its 12 years of hospitality and service. Our 30 air-conditioned rooms are covered with wall to wall carpeting, private baths and balconies, color TV, and telephone. Perichi's award-winning restaurant features the finest foods—not to be missed. After sunset meet friends in our cozy lounge. Live music on weekends at the pool area. Comfortable banquet room for 300 persons, those who like to combine business with pleasure and much more.

Rooms: 30 (PB) call for rates
Full Breakfast
Credit Cards: A, B, C, D, E
Notes: 3, 4, 5, 7, 8, 9, 10, 11, 12

MARICAO

Parador La Hacienda Juanita

P.O. Box 777, Road 105, KM 23-5, 00606
(809) 838-2550; (809) 838-2551 (FAX)

1830. This hacienda-style building once served as the main lodge for a coffee plantation. Twenty-four acres, 1,600 feet above sea level in the cool tropical mountains of a Puerto Rican rain forest. Bird watchers' paradise.

Hosts: Radamés and Abraham Rivera
Rooms: 21 (PB) $65
Continental Breakfast
Credit Cards: A, B, C
Notes: 2, 3, 4, 5, 7, 8, 9, 12

SAN JUAN

El Canario Inn

1317 Ashford Avenue-Condado, 00907
(809) 722-5058; (800) 533-2649 (for reservations);
(809) 722-8590 (FAX)

San Juan's most historic and unique B&B inn. All 25 guest rooms are air-conditioned with private baths, cable TV, and telephone, and come with complimentary continental breakfast. Our tropical patios and sundeck provide a friendly and informal atmosphere. Centrally located near beach, casinos, restaurants, boutiques, and public transportation.

Hosts: Jude and Keith Olson
Rooms: 25 (PB) $65-90
Continental Breakfast
Credit Cards: A, B, C, D, E
Notes: 5, 7, 8, 9, 12

welcome; 7 Children welcome; 8 Tennis nearby; 9 Swimming nearby; 10 Golf nearby; 11 Skiing nearby; 12 May be booked through travel agent

Tres Palmas Guest House

2212 Park Boulevard, 00913
(809) 727-4617

Remodeled in 1990, all rooms include air-conditioners, ceiling fans, CATV with remote control, AM/FM clock radio, small decorative refrigerators, and continental breakfast. Oceanfront, beautiful sandy beach; daily maid service; newspapers; magazines; games; oceanview sun deck; fresh beach towels; and chairs. Tourist information available. Centrally located ten minutes from the airport and Old San Juan.

Host: Elving Torres
Rooms: 9 plus 3 apartments (11 PB; 1 SB)
$50-90; $45-60 off-season
Continental Breakfast
Credit Cards: A, B, C
Notes: 3, 4, 5, 7, 9

El Canario Inn

NOTES: Credit cards accepted: A Master Card; B Visa; C American Express; D Discover Card; E Diners Club; F Other; 2 Personal checks accepted; 3 Lunch available; 4 Dinner available; 5 Open all year; 6 Pets

Virgin Islands

ST. CROIX

Pink Fancy Inn

27 Prince Street, Chrishensted, 00820
(809) 773-8460; (800) 524-2045;
(809) 773-6448 (FAX)

A small, unique historic inn located a block and a half away from the center of Christiansted. From our inn, there are 20 restaurants, duty-free shopping, and historic sites. All our rooms are on a courtyard with a tropical garden, a pool, hammocks, and gazebo. Our rooms all consist of kitchenettes, CA TV, telephone, fridge, air-conditioning and ceiling fans. And to top it off, we have a twenty-four hour honor and continental breakfast.

Hostess: Dixie Ann Tang-innkeeper
Rooms: 12 (PB) $90
Expanded Continental Breakfast
Credit Cards: A, B, C
Notes: 5, 7, 8, 9, 10, 12

ST. THOMAS

Heritage Manor Guest House

P.O. Box 90, 00804
(809) 774-3003; (800) 828-0757; (809) 776-9585
(FAX)

Restored 19th Century mansion located in the downtown historic district of Charlotte Amalie. Conveniently located just a five-minute walk to all duty-free shops, restaurants, and ferries. A home away from home with a splash pool built around on old Danish oven, courtyard with TV and telephone. All rooms have air-conditioning, refrigerators, and fans.

Hostess: Susan Murphy
Rooms: 8 (4PB; 4SB) winter $70-130; summer $50-95
Continental Breakfast Dec. 1-Apr. 30
Credit Cards: A, B, C
Notes: 5, 7 (over 9), 8, 9, 10, 12

---

welcome; 7 Children welcome; 8 Tennis nearby; 9 Swimming nearby; 10 Golf nearby; 11 Skiing nearby; 12 May be booked through travel agent

Mafolie Hotel

P.O. Box 1506, 00804
(809) 774-2790; (800) 225-7035; (809) 774-4091
(FAX)

World famous view. 10 minutes from everything! "It's the best value on St. Thomas!" Free continental breakfast and transport to Magen's Bay (save $26 a day). Family owned and operated for 23 years. Recent renovation. 800 feet above the town and harbor (Location used in movies and commercials). All rooms have private bath, cable TV, and air-conditioning. The Frigate restaurant is recommended by the *New York Times*. Freshwater pool.

Hosts: Tony and Lyn Eden
Rooms: 23 (PB) $75 summer -97 winter
Large Continental Breakfast
Credit Cards: A, B, C
Notes: 3, 4, 5, 7, 8, 9 (on-site), 10, 12

Villa Elaine

44 Water Island, 00802
(809) 774-0290; (809) 776-0890 (FAX)

Lovely ocean front apartment: fully furnished, kitchen, livingroom, dining room, two bedrooms, two baths, and veranda. Swim and snorkel from own private beach. Hike around 500-acre water island in an hour. Beautiful, peaceful, and secure retreat. 10-minute ferry ride to St. Thomas. Minimum stay of three days.

Hostess: Elaine Grissom
Rooms: 1-2 bedroom apartment (PB) $100-165
Continental Breakfast
Credit Cards: None
Notes: 2, 5, 8, 9, 10 (St. Thomas)

NOTES: Credit cards accepted: A Master Card; B Visa; C American Express; D Discover Card; E Diners Club; F Other; 2 Personal checks accepted; 3 Lunch available; 4 Dinner available; 5 Open all year; 6 Pets

The Christian Bed and Breakfast Directory

P.O. Box 719
Uhrichsville, OH 44683

INN EVALUATION FORM

Please copy and complete this form for each stay and mail to the address above. Since 1990 we have maintained files that include thousands of evaluations from inngoers. We value your comments. These help us to keep abreast of the hundreds of new inns that open each year and to follow the changes in established inns.

Name of inn: _____

City and State: _____

Date of stay: _____

Length of stay: _____

Please use the following rating scales for the next items.
A: Outstanding. B: Good. C: Average. D: Fair. F: Poor.

Attitude of innkeepers: _____ Attitude of helpers: _____

Food Service: _____ Handling of Reservations: _____

Cleanliness: _____ Privacy: _____

Beds: _____ Bathrooms: _____

Parking: _____ Worth of price: _____

Comments on the above: _____
_____
_____
_____
_____

What did you especially like? _____
_____
_____
_____

Suggestions for improvements: _____
_____
_____
_____

1995-96

Christian Bed & Breakfast Directory

Listing Reservation Form

*You will receive a complimentary copy of the
Directory upon publication.*

PLEASE TYPE OR PRINT CLEARLY, answering all questions. Return with your check, money order, or credit card information for the **$25.00 fee** to *The Christian Bed & Breakfast Directory,* P.O. Box 719, 1810 Barbour Drive, Uhrichsville, OH 44683 or to FAX (614) 922-5948. **All materials must be in by August 25, 1995, to be included in the 1996-1997 edition.**

NAME OF INN _____

ADDRESS _____

CITY_____ STATE_____ ZIP_____

TELEPHONE _____ FAX _____

__Enclosed is my check or money order for $25.00 United States Dollars.

__Charge $25.00 to my credit card: Visa__MC__American Express__Discover

Credit Card Number_____ Exp. Date _____

Signature _____

PLEASE ATTACH A DESCRIPTION OF YOUR BED AND BREAKFAST OF 50 TO 70 WORDS.

Host(s)/Hostess _____

Number of guest rooms _____

Number with private baths_____ Number with shared baths _____

Rate range for two people sharing one room (lowest to highest) _____

Full or continental breakfast? _____

Circle those that apply:

1. Credit Cards
   A. MasterCard
   B. Visa
   C. American Express
   D. Discover Card
   E. Diners Club
   F. Other
2. Personal checks accepted
3. Lunch available
4. Dinner available
5. Open all year
6. Pets welcome
7. Children welcome
8. Tennis nearby
9. Swimming nearby
10. Golf nearby
11. Skiing nearby
12. May be booked by a travel agent